LDAP PROGRAMMING WITH JAVA™

LDAP PROGRAMMING WITH JAVA™

ROB WELTMAN and TONY DAHBURA

ADDISON–WESLEY

Boston • San Francisco • New York • Toronto • Montreal
London • Munich • Paris • Madrid
Capetown • Sydney • Tokyo • Singapore • Mexico City

The publisher offers discounts on this book when ordered in quantity for special sales. For more information, please contact:

Pearson Education Corporate Sales Division
One Lake Street
Upper Saddle River, NJ 07458
(800) 382-3419
corpsales@pearsontechgroup.com

Visit AW on the Web: www.awl.com/cseng/

Library of Congress Cataloging-in-Publication Data

Weltman, Rob, 1953–
LDAP programming with Java™ / Rob Weltman, Tony Dahbura.
p. cm.
ISBN 0-201-65758-9
1. Java (Computer program language). 2. Computer network protocols. I. Dahbura, Tony. II. Title.
QA76.73.J38 W47 2000
005.2'762—dc21 99–054510

Text printed on recycled and acid-free paper.

ISBN 0201657589

3 4 5 6 7 8 CR 03 02 01 00

3rd Printing November 2000

Contents

Preface

After a maturation phase in the early and mid-1990s, Lightweight Directory Access Protocol (LDAP) exploded into the mainstream of enterprise and Internet software environments. Just a few years ago, only researchers and a few brave souls doing pilot projects concerned themselves with the new protocol for sharing and accessing directory information. Today, one of the requirements of any major enterprise-level or Internet-oriented application is to be able to use an existing shared resource for user information, authentication, and authorization, and nowadays that resource in a great many cases is an LDAP directory.

Why LDAP and Java?

The impetus for *LDAP Programming with Java* was the mushrooming need for accurate, concise, and complete information on how to access this new key element of enterprise and Internet programming—LDAP. Programmers around the world have found innovative ways to use Directory SDK for Java to solve their LDAP access problems, and sometimes they have shared their questions and experiences on the newsgroups for LDAP, but there has been no authoritative guide.

This book is dedicated to the programmers and system administrators who are faced with LDAP-enabling their applications, tools, and systems.

There are various programming language interfaces to LDAP: C, Perl, Microsoft's ADSI. Java and LDAP are a particularly good fit, with all the options available today for deploying Java on servers—Java servlets, Java Server Pages (JSP), Enterprise JavaBeans (EJB), and server-side JavaScript—and in clients as Java applications, applets, or client-side JavaScript. The Netscape Navigator Web browser includes Directory SDK for Java, making it easy to deploy Web-based client applications that use LDAP to authenticate or to retrieve and store data.

In this book we've provided a very large number of examples for every aspect of programming with Directory SDK for Java, from simple code snippets to more than two dozen complete components and applications. You may be able to use some of them as starting points for your own projects.

We do not discuss directory deployment scenarios or how to configure an LDAP server. Such topics are explored in detail in other books and in documentation provided by vendors of LDAP servers.

To Get the Most Out of This Book

We're assuming that readers of this book are somewhat familiar with programming in Java, so we will not introduce or explain standard Java constructs. There are many excellent books on Java programming in general, and on Java client-server programming in particular. However, we will start at ground zero when it comes to directories and LDAP.

How the Book Is Organized

Introduction to LDAP

Chapter 1 presents the role of directories in software systems today and describes how applications can benefit from using them, as well as presenting cases in which directories are not as good a fit as relational databases.

Chapter 2 introduces the LDAP protocol against this background and presents the LDAP naming and information models that together define how data is stored and accessed in a directory.

After acquainting you with the basic LDAP concepts and terminology, in **Chapter 3** we will look at how Directory SDK for Java can help a Java program, servlet, or applet gain access to an LDAP server. After installing the SDK, we will try a few simple searches with the SDK's command-line search tool to become familiar with how a client typically interacts with an LDAP server.

Getting Started

In **Chapter 4** we will install an LDAP server for use in the remainder of the book. If you already have a directory installed that is compatible with version 3 of the LDAP protocol (LDAPv3), you need only add to the directory the sample database file that is provided on the CD-ROM that accompanies the book. The examples in the book do not generally assume any particular vendor's directory product; exceptions are indicated clearly.

With the SDK installed and a directory available, **Chapter 5** dives into how to retrieve data from an LDAP server. Searching is the predominant LDAP operation in most programs, and we will cover all parameters that affect the results to be returned, as well as how to obtain optimal performance.

Chapter 6 explores the add, modify, delete, and rename operations for updating data in a directory, along with how to use groups.

Authentication is touched on briefly in Chapter 6 because most directories are configured not to allow anonymous clients to update any data. **Chapter 7**, however, covers the topic thoroughly. Besides covering simple authentication with a distinguished name (DN) and password, it introduces authentication with Secure Sockets Layer (SSL) and Simple Authentication and Security Layer (SASL), and it explains how access control is configured and updated in Netscape Directory Server.

Down and Dirty

Chapter 8 discusses the special considerations for LDAP client code that is intended to run as an applet in a browser. The steps required to digitally sign an applet for use with Microsoft Internet Explorer, Netscape Navigator, and the Sun Java Plug-in Software are presented in detail.

In **Chapter 9** we investigate how to access the SDK from JavaScript in a browser.

Chapter 10 demonstrates how to encapsulate LDAP functionality in a JavaBean and provides full source for a directory tree browser JavaBean and a table JavaBean for listing the results of a search operation.

In **Chapter 11** we take a detailed look at how an application can store configuration and preferences in a directory.

In a directory, data is stored as a tree. **Chapter 12** illustrates how directory data can model relationships other than the physical tree relationships. A JavaBean is developed to extract reporting relationships from LDAP data and present the results as an organizational chart. Another JavaBean presents the contents of a directory entry. The chapter concludes by hooking up into simple applications the graphical JavaBeans that have been developed up to that point in the book.

Chapter 13 develops a complete server-side application: a corporate online "phone book." The application is a Java servlet that makes selected personal directory information, such as phone numbers and photographs, available to any user with a browser.

In **Chapter 14** we summarize and discuss all the options and constraints that may be selected by an application for searching and other operations.

Beyond the Basics

Chapter 15 discusses various aspects of the SDK and of LDAP programming in general that are not discussed as often as the other topics in this book, such as

LDAP URLs, the use of multiple threads and multiple connections, and performance tips.

Advanced topics, such as schema management, LDAP controls, and the asynchronous operation methods, are presented in **Chapter 16**.

The **appendices** contain important reference material for the SDK and for LDAP in general.

If You're in a Hurry

In general, the book contains a logical progression of information and examples, each chapter building on previous ones.

If you are familiar with the use of directories and with LDAP concepts, you may choose to skip over the first two chapters. If you already have an LDAP server available and the SDK is installed, you can go directly to Chapter 5.

If you are not interested in writing applets or JavaScript applications that use LDAP, you can safely skip over Chapters 8 and 9. Similarly, if you do not need to know how to write a Java servlet that uses LDAP, you may choose to skip over Chapter 13.

The Companion CD-ROM

The CD-ROM includes reference documentation and source code for Directory SDK for Java, as well as for all the examples and programs mentioned in the book. The SDK and examples are also provided as precompiled class and JAR files so that you can run any program directly, without compiling or copying to a local hard disk. The full text of the book is also included, to allow you to view the contents in a browser and to search for any word.

Acknowledgments

Susan Walton, then of Netscape Publishing, helped us understand what is involved in writing and publishing a book. Netscape/AOL generously agreed to let us share with you the experience we gained in using the SDK in Netscape products during the past two years. Karen Gettman and Mary Hart at Addison-Wesley took on the project enthusiastically and helped make a book out of our scribbling. Stephanie Hiebert's diligent copyediting gave consistency to the formatting and prose of the book and made it easier to read in the process.

The book would not have been as complete and technically accurate without the contributions of many reviewers, including Megan Alexander, Jim Sermersheim, Gabor Liptak, Vasanthan S. Dasan, Bob Kitzberger, Atma Sutjianto, Mark Wilcox, Luke Howard, and Ellen Stokes.

We would also like to thank the many adopters of LDAP with whom we have had the good fortune of interacting. Their inquiries and need for information have helped form the content of this book and many of the programming examples.

Rob would have succumbed to a combination of exhaustion, dehydration, and starvation within the first few weeks of working on this book without the constant attention and support of loving wife Helena.

Tony thanks his parents, Anton and Bonnie, for supporting his very early love of computers at a time when no one knew what this "thing" could do. His wife, Tracy, made Tony's contributions possible by assuming all the responsibilities of the household, including two young children, and providing her support during the authoring of the book.

PART I

INTRODUCTION

CHAPTER 1

What Can You Find in a Directory?

In many ways, developing software applications has become orders of magnitude more demanding in the past 15 years, especially when the target environment is a desktop computer. In 1985, applications were generally small, had a single purpose, had a command-line interface, and typically did not interact with each other. In the PC environment, sneakernet was the dominant means of distributing programs and program output: you copied the data to a floppy and carried it over to another PC if the data was needed there.

Today millions of computers are connected to each other. Companies have internal networks that permanently connect company computers with each other and that periodically connect computers with servers all over the world. Programs can be downloaded and data shared instantly between users at opposite ends of the earth.

Today users have different expectations for applications. Users expect applications to interoperate; they expect different applications to share inputs, outputs, and to some extent, configuration information. For example, users expect applications to "remember" configuration information and preferences, no matter where the applications are used. When you read e-mail, browse the Web, and use other applications, you want the same preferences set, regardless of whether you are at home or at work.

Users expect different applications to share login information. They don't want to remember a dozen passwords, and they don't want to log into another application every few seconds. Many companies deploy large numbers of Web-based applications for internal use on company intranets or for customers on the Internet, and it would not be acceptable to require the user to identify herself every time she jumped between Web pages and Web-based applications.

Although there are greater demands on applications today, there are also much greater possibilities. If applications are integrated, they can simplify work for a user. Users don't need to enter redundant information or make the same changes to preferences for different applications.

But how can different applications share information about users? How can applications keep track of user-specific settings in a common location, regardless of which computer the user is using? One possible solution is a directory that stores user information.

What Is a Directory?

A directory is a service that allows you to search a structured repository of information. Although that may sound like a database (a directory generally does contain or interact with a database internally), a directory is defined by how users interact with it: through its protocol and its application program interface (API). Most directories offer a hierarchical rather than a relational view of the data. Figure 1-1 gives one example of how information about a person is stored in a directory. As this example shows, all attributes of a particular person are stored as a single object, and in this case all objects that represent people are grouped under a single location in the hierarchy. The structure of the tree defines the basic relationships between objects. Attributes have standardized names, such as `cn` for "common name" and `sn` for "surname."

Figure 1-2 shows how information about people typically is stored in a relational database. In this example, user information is stored in one table, and organizational unit information in another. A third table contains organizational information. A column in the user table maps users to organizations. To retrieve all information for a particular person, a query does a join on these tables.

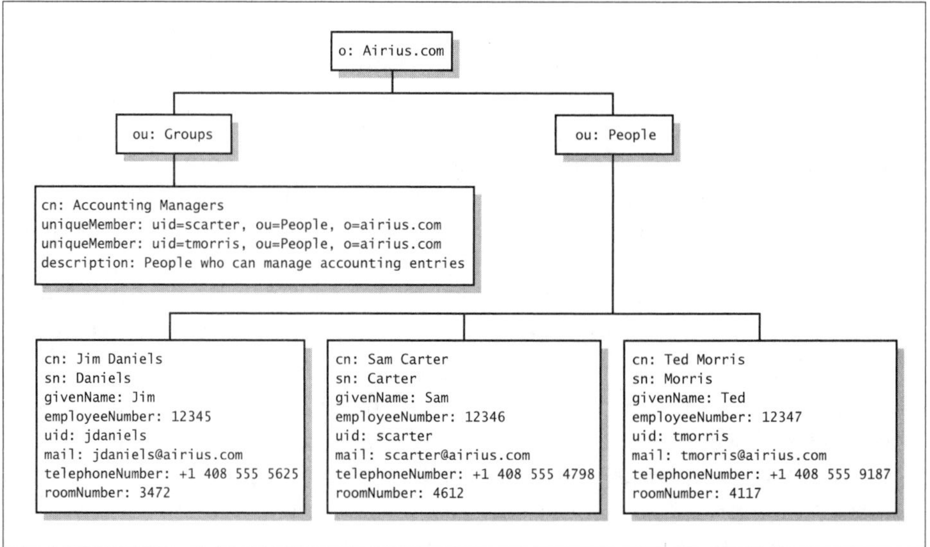

FIGURE 1-1. *How data is organized in a directory.*

User table

ID	EMP. NR.	FULL NAME	LAST	FIRST	**uid**	PHONE	E-MAIL	**ou**
1	12345	Jim Daniels	Daniels	Jim	jdaniels	+1 408 555 5625	jdaniels@Airius.com	1
2	12346	Sam Carter	Carter	Sam	scarter	+1 408 555 4798	scarter@Airius.com	1
3	12347	Ted Morris	Morris	Ted	tmorris	+1 408 555 9187	tmorris@Airius.com	1

Organizational Unit table

ID	NAME	ORGANIZATION
1	People	1
2	Groups	1
3	Accounting	2

Organization table

ID	NAME
1	Airius.com
2	acme.com

FIGURE 1-2. *How data is organized in a relational database.*

In addition, directories tend to be used in a context in which data is retrieved more frequently than it is updated. In general, directories are not designed to store very large objects, but they are designed to store very large numbers of objects.

The following list identifies some of the main differences between a directory and a relational database:

- Directories are generally intended for environments in which one or more clients are doing many times more read or search operations than write operations. As a consequence, relational databases tend to perform better than directories when data is being updated more frequently.
- Directories usually do not support the advanced relational queries (with table joins) of a relational database. For example, a directory can efficiently tell you all the employees of a company whose manager is Jim Johnson, and it can tell you all the managers who are located in Savannah, but it cannot easily tell you all the employees whose managers are located in Savannah.

- Directories do not support transactional integrity across multiple operations. There is no way to ensure that several operations either all succeed or all fail.
- On the other hand, directories have better and more flexible support for substring searches and for searches for approximate matches.
- Whereas directories ship with preconfigured schemas (which are often standardized among vendors) that are sufficient or require few enhancements to support applications, relational databases generally require schemas to be defined before anything else can be done. The schema defines which attributes may be used in the directory and which attributes are required or allowed in a particular entry.
- Directories tend to be more often and widely replicated (for performance and for redundancy) than relational databases.
- Directory protocols (such as Lightweight Directory Access Protocol, or LDAP) are better suited for wide-area network use, such as on the Internet or on large corporate networks.
- Directories are usually much simpler to configure, tune, and manage than industrial-quality relational databases, and they are much less expensive. Both the cost of acquisition and the cost of ownership are therefore considerably lower.

What's That Phone Number?

One of the first major uses for general-purpose directories was to replace the company phone book. These listings of employees and their phone numbers are frequently reprinted but chronically out-of-date. Maintaining a useful printed listing is a nontrivial task in a large company, where people frequently come and go, change locations, and change job titles. The manual labor involved in compiling the listing, printing copies, and distributing the list to hundreds or thousands of employees is considerable. In fact, by the time the listing is available, it may already be out-of-date!

Now let's see how this setup might be replaced with an online directory. We assume that all employees have access to a computer that is on a company network.

First we'll install a directory and add all the current employee names and phone numbers. Most directories come with some kind of client software that allows users to search, view, and update directory information. Once all employees have a copy of that software, they can use the directory to look up any phone number instantly. If the directory is configured to allow users to update their own information, a user can correct typos or provide new information without the assistance of any Information Systems or Human Resources personnel.

When an employee is hired, Human Resources adds the information about the employee to the directory, and all employees in the company instantly have that information at their fingertips. Similarly, when an employee leaves or changes location, a simple change to the directory can make the updated information available everywhere.

Beyond this basic model, a directory could be integrated with the direct sources of user information. For example, the phone branch exchange (PBX) is the most current and the most authoritative source of telephone number information in a company. If an employee does not have a phone number registered in the PBX, that employee cannot be contacted by phone. A mechanism could be introduced to synchronize employee names and phone numbers between the PBX and the directory. A synchronization service to handle this task could be a simple offline script or program that runs frequently or infrequently, collecting changes in the PBX and propagating them to the directory, or it could be a more tightly coupled process that immediately passes on any change. At this point, the directory is self-maintained (as far as employee names and phone numbers go): no one needs to update the directory manually to keep the listings up-to-date.

Directory Clients for an Online Phone Book

Netscape Directory Server is an example of a **Lightweight Directory Access Protocol (LDAP)** directory service. Using Netscape Directory Server, you can set up your own directory of employee phone numbers. Chapter 4 explains how to download, install, and configure this server.

Netscape Directory Server provides two simple but useful types of clients: a set of command-line tools and a Web-based interface to the directory. Netscape also provides two SDKs for building your own directory clients: one for Java and one for C/C++/Visual Basic.

The set of command-line tools includes `ldapsearch`, a tool for searching the directory. If you've installed Netscape Directory Server, these tools are located in the `shared/bin` directory under the installation root directory.

The following example is a command for searching the directory for information on an employee named Ted Morris.

```
ldapsearch -h directory.acme.com -b "o=Airius.com" "cn=Ted Morris"
telephoneNumber
```

The example is set up to work against the `Airius.com` sample directory on a machine named `directory.acme.com`. We'll take a closer look at the syntax for this command in Chapter 5.

You can use this command-line tool as a building block for your own simpler, user-friendly scripts. The cn portion of the syntax shown here identifies the first and last name of the employee you want to find. You can write a shell script (UNIX) or batch file (Windows) to allow users to enter all or part of an employee's name. For example,

```
phone.bat (Windows)
ldapsearch -h directory.acme.com -b "o=Airius.com" "cn=*%1*"
telephoneNumber

phone.sh (UNIX)
ldapsearch -h directory.acme.com -b "o=Airius.com" "cn=*$1*"
telephoneNumber
```

In these scripts, the first argument is passed to the `ldapsearch` command-line tool as the name of the employee to find. You can then type

```
phone Morris
```

and get back

```
dn: uid=tmorris, ou=People, o=Airius.com
telephoneNumber: +1 408 555 9187
```

The other client application provided is a Web-based interface to the directory. The interface is called an LDAP gateway (a gateway to LDAP directory services) and is a collection of Common Gateway Interface (CGI) programs and HTML templates installed on a Web server. Since this is a Web-based interface, you do not need to install or configure any additional client software on the employees' computers. Employees just need to point a Web browser to the right URL.

Netscape Directory Server includes two sets of templates for the gateway: one for end users and one for administrators. Directory Express consists of a set of templates to allow end users to search for employee information. Directory Server Gateway, the other set of templates, is intended for more general-purpose directory searches and updates—for example, by administrators. You can get to both gateways by pointing your browser to the URL of the administration server for the directory server—in other words, `http://<directory_server>:<admin_server_port>` (for example, `http://directory.acme.com:17200`). Figure 1-3 illustrates the administration server home page. The gateways may also be installed on any Web server.

In Directory Express (Figure 1-4) and Directory Server Gateway, many parameters are already defined in a template and do not need to be specified for each search, including the host name and port number of the directory server, the directory entry

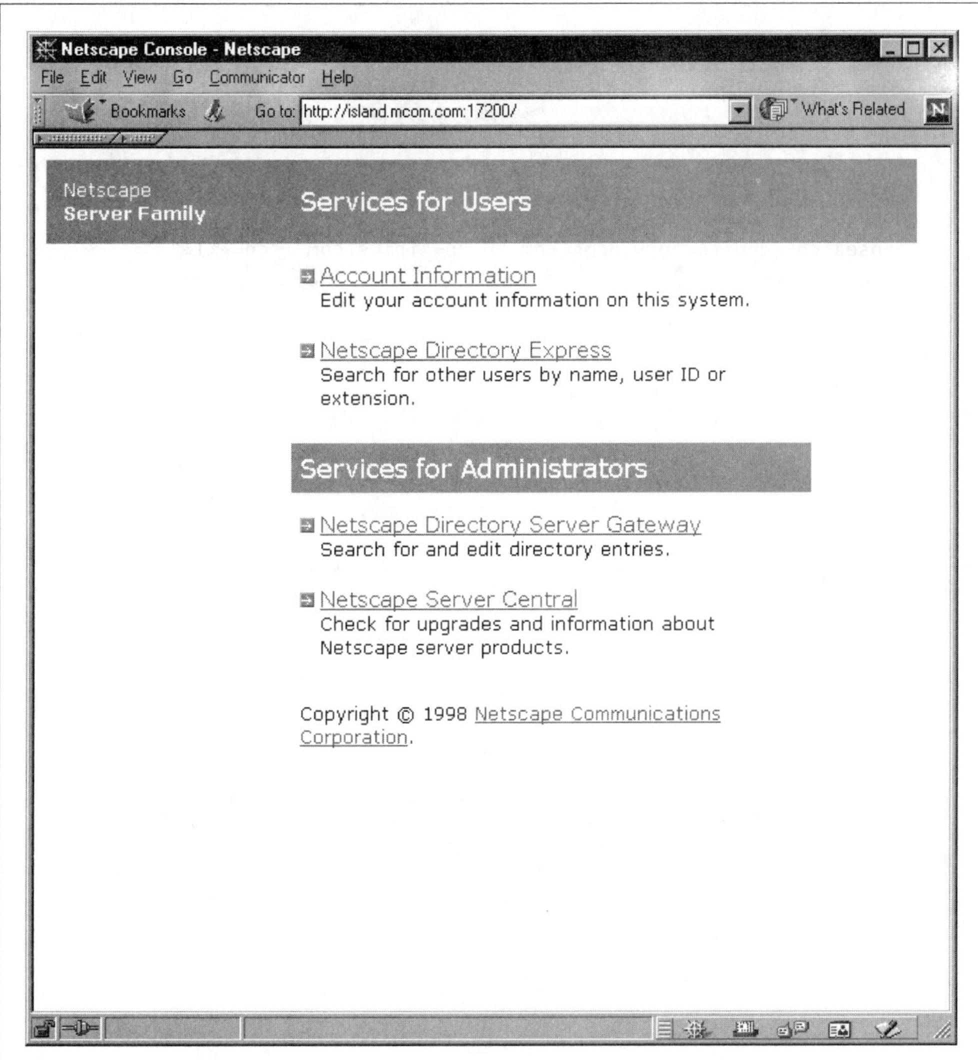

FIGURE 1-3. *Netscape Administration Server home page.*

from which to search (the starting point of the search), and the search scope (which is always subtree scope). You just enter part of a name to search for. These parameters are described in more detail in Chapter 5.

You can also update some of the information with Directory Express, as Figure 1-5 shows.

Directory Server Gateway (Figure 1-6) offers a more complete view of the information.

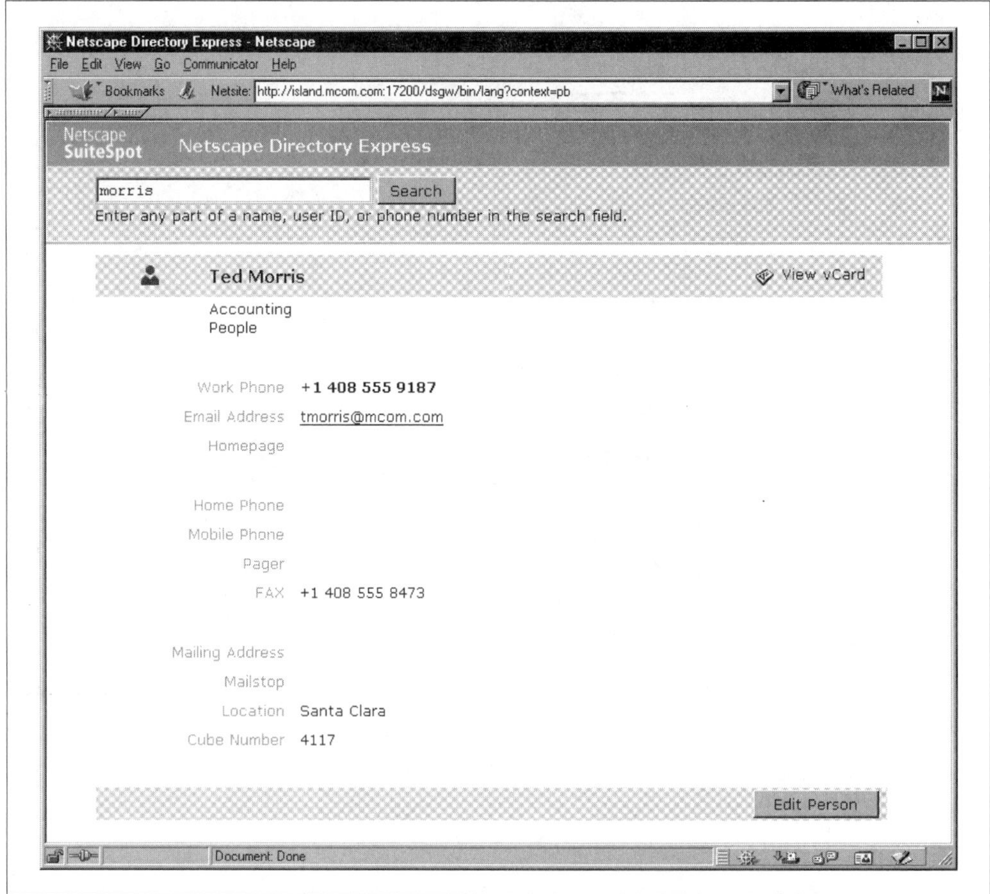

FIGURE 1-4. *Directory Express search page.*

Though relatively simple, these are applications that many companies find useful out of the box. If these applications do not meet your needs, you can purchase commercial software for more sophisticated access, or you can write your own client software. This book will explain how to use Directory SDK for Java to write your own directory clients.

Is He Really Who He Says He Is?

Another very common use for directories is authentication.

Suppose you wrote a Web application for betting on college basketball scores. This application is intended to be used (officially, of course) as a company team-building

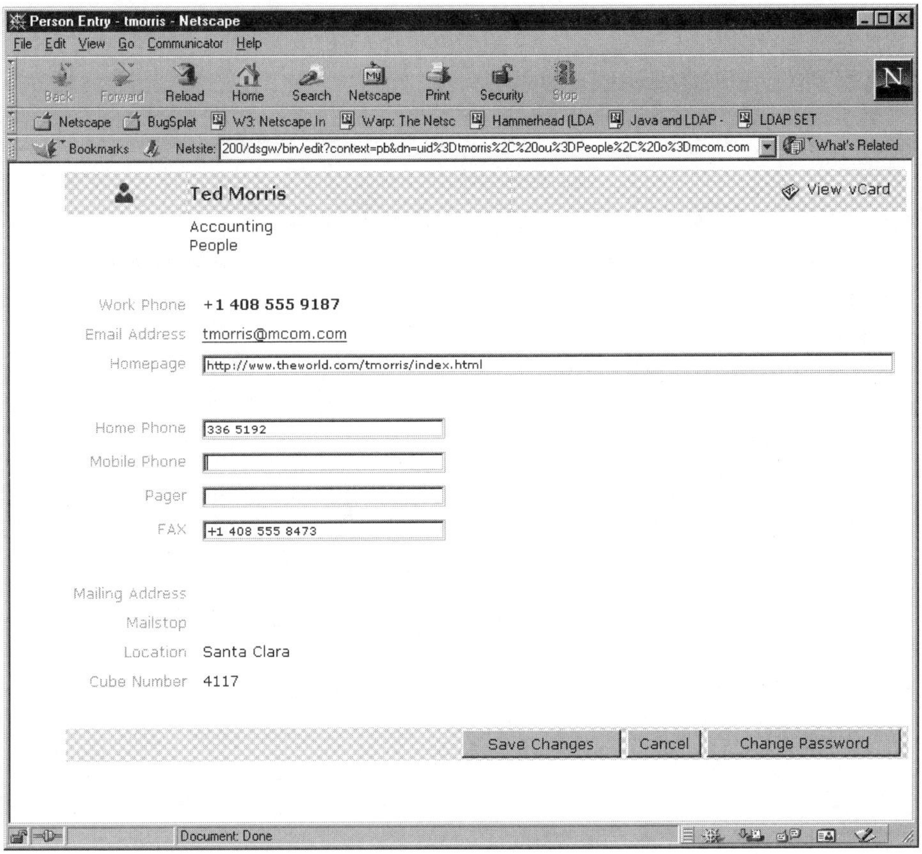

FIGURE 1-5. *Directory Express update page.*

exercise. To ensure that each player is responsible for his or her bets (and is not making bets for someone else), you set up a small database of users and passwords. When the user directs a browser to the betting home page, the user is prompted to enter a user name and password.

At first, this system works just fine. But the idea becomes quite popular, and a colleague, Jim, decides to publish another Web application on his own Web server. This application takes bets on the number of irate customer phone calls that will be received by the Customer Support Department during the coming week. Jim sets up his own database, and all players must register a new user name and password. The players must be sure to use the right user names and passwords for this application when they enter the application's home page.

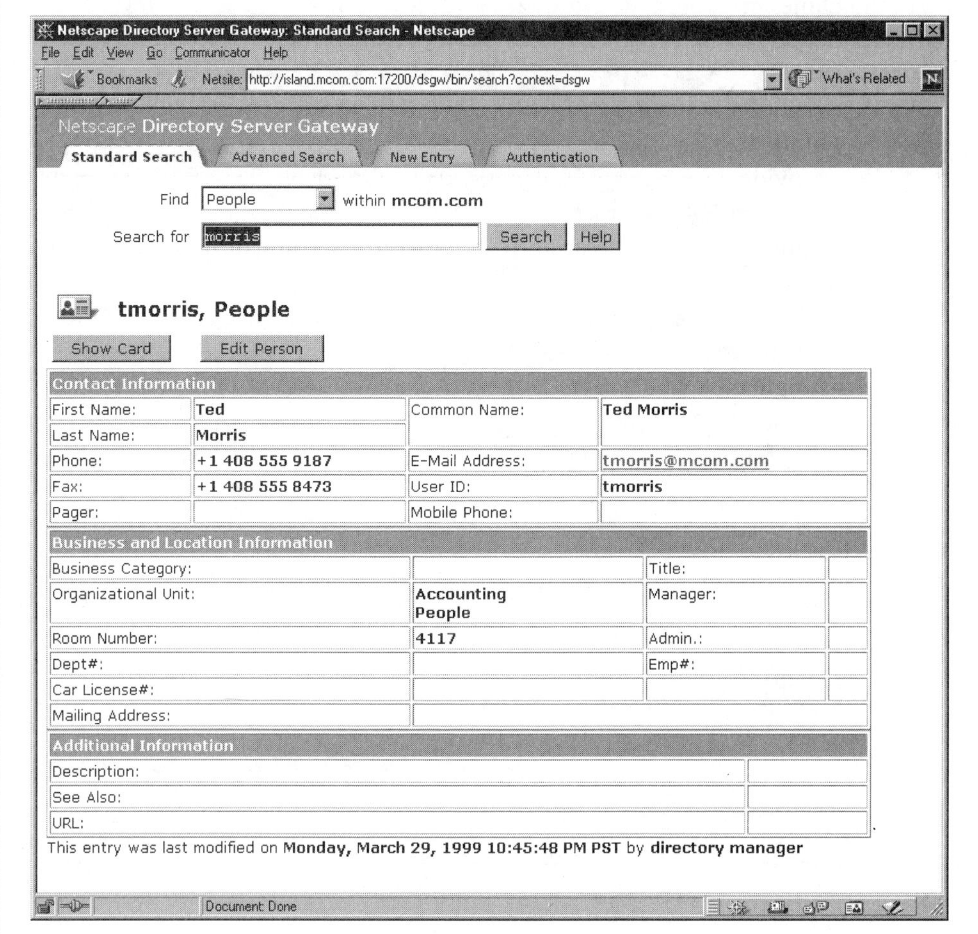

FIGURE 1-6. *Directory Server Gateway search page.*

In the meantime, the mail server that distributes e-mail to all employees has its own database of users and passwords, and the company Web application for ordering office supplies has another database.

At this point, things are getting messy: there are four different databases with different user names and passwords. Employees need to memorize all these names and passwords, and they need to remember when to use which password for which application. Beyond this simple example, some companies deploy dozens or even hundreds of Web applications in which it is important to make sure users are who they say they are and to keep track of who the current user is. These applications may be running on Web servers on dozens or hundreds of different machines. Users may even have to log into machines on extranets and the Internet. As more applications and computers come into the picture, it becomes even more essential to centralize and simplify user authentication.

Directories are excellent at supplying the required functionality. With a directory service, you simply connect to the central directory from any machine and any application. You provide a user name and password to authenticate, and you receive an instantaneous response.

As an example of authenticating to the directory, you can use the `ldapsearch` command-line tool. It is unlikely you will have a program that just authenticates to a directory and does nothing else, but you can use `ldapsearch` to demonstrate authentication. After connecting to the directory server, `ldapsearch` attempts to authenticate using the **distinguished name** (DN) and password you've provided. Distinguished names identify users in the directory, as will be explained in more detail in Chapter 2. If authentication fails, `ldapsearch` reports the error and does not search the directory. For example,

```
ldapsearch -D "uid=tmorris, ou=People, o=Airius.com" -w "irrefutable"
    -b "" -s base "objectclass=*" dn
dn:
```

The authentication was successful, so `ldapsearch` went on to read the contents of the "" (root) entry and print out its DN (which is "").

```
ldapsearch -D "uid=tmorris, ou=People, o=Airius.com" -w
    "wrongpassword" -b "" -s base "objectclass=*" dn
ldap_bind: No such object
```

Now the authentication failed, so `ldapsearch` printed a message indicating a failure to "bind" (authenticating in LDAP is called binding) and did not do a search.

A real authentication application would interpret the results and report them in a more user-friendly way. This example just demonstrates how easy it is to validate credentials using a directory.

A common scenario for using a directory service is to set up a central directory for authentication. In this scenario, the directory is used to store user names and passwords for many different Web applications, as well as other services not based on the Web (such as a mail server). You can run new Web applications on any Web server on the network and still leverage the user information in the directory.

There are even large-scale applications in which the *only* purpose of the directory is to provide user authentication.

An extension of this use is single sign-on. In a single sign-on solution, a user needs to enter a password only once. After entering the password, the user is not prompted for a password again, even when starting a new application.

Directories are considered central to the success of a public-key authentication and encryption solution; there is no other realistic way to publish or manage a large number of certificates. For example, suppose you want to use another user's public key to encrypt an e-mail message to that user. With a directory, client e-mail software can automatically look up the public-key certificate of the e-mail recipient and use the key to encrypt a message. If certificates need to be revoked or replaced, you can just execute those operations in the directory.

Working Together

Why should the employee information in the directory be limited to phone numbers, user names, and passwords? A natural extension of the phone book and authentication engine concepts is to use the directory as a central access point for application information (such as user preferences), as opposed to just the information that users want to see.

Consider a situation in which a new employee arrives at a large company. The employee fills out various forms with all her name, address, and other information, and a member of the Human Resources (HR) Department types the information into the HR database.

One of the forms that the new employee filled out goes to the Information Systems (IS) Department. Someone in IS reads the form and extracts information to create a UNIX computer account for the new employee. The user's full name is recorded, a user name is assigned, and a temporary password is put in place.

Since the company has a mix of computer types on its network, the form is sent along to the Windows specialist in IS, who then creates a Windows account on an NT server for the new employee. If all goes well, the same full name, user name, and password are assigned as for the UNIX account.

Another form goes to the postmaster in IS to set up an e-mail account. Again, the hope is that the same full name, username, and password will be assigned, and that no typos will be made.

Finally, a form goes to the Webmaster for the intranet, who types in the same information to provide the employee with access to the online benefits enrollment program.

In this scenario there is a lot of duplicated data entry, and there is plenty of room for mistakes. If the employee decides to change her name, the changes need to be made in each of the databases (with the possibility in each case that typos will be introduced). If an employee resigns, records must be purged and accounts deleted in all these data stores. How can the problem of duplicate work be solved?

It's the directory to the rescue! For political and other reasons, Human Resources may not want to move all employee information from its minicomputer relational database into a directory. Some of the information, for instance, is not rele-

Netscape's implementation of the single sign-on solution uses **digital certificates**. In this solution, digital certificates that identify each user are stored in the user's entry in the directory. Digital certificates are discussed in detail in Chapters 7 and 8.

The user's client software (in this example, Netscape Communicator) keeps a local database of the private keys for the user. These keys have corresponding public keys and digital certificates that "certify" that the public-private key pairs belong to the user. This local database is password protected. When the user first attempts to access any server that requires certificate-based authentication, Communicator prompts the user for the password to access the private-key database. Communicator does this only once per session, even if the user needs to authenticate to other servers.

Communicator uses the private key to sign a piece of data as proof of the user's identity. Communicator sends the signed data and the user's certificate to the server. The server can look up the user's entry in the directory and can verify that the certificate presented by the client is identical to the certificate in the directory.

In this solution, the user needs to enter a password only once. During subsequent requests for authentication, Netscape Communicator sends signed data and the user's certificate without prompting the user for a password. Applications that require authentication can use the directory to look up the user's certificate and verify the user's identity.

For more information on Netscape's single sign-on solution, see the Single Sign-On Deployment Guide at Netscape's DevEdge Web site: `http://developer.netscape.com/docs/manuals/security/SSO/index.htm`.

vant to other departments or applications (for example, salary history, vacations, benefit allocations). But there is a core of clearly shareable data, including the employee's name, social security number, address, department, manager, main file server, home phone number, user name, password, and so on. "Shareable" does not necessarily mean editable or even viewable by anyone; a fine-grained access control may determine what information is available to each potential application or user.

But how is the information made shareable through the directory? The problem can be divided into two parts: getting the information into the directory, and allowing applications to retrieve information from the directory (once the information is there).

Since Human Resources maintains a sizable database of personnel information in its own system, you need to set up a synchronization mechanism to update the directory with relevant changes made in the HR database. These types of mechanisms have been implemented as ad hoc tools (using Perl scripts and C programs) by IS departments in many companies. Typically, these programs check the HR database for changes on a periodic basis. The programs dump recent changes into a text file, process the file to produce a format suitable for import to a directory, and then import the results into the directory. Some full-scale metadirectory products are designed for this purpose as well.

Once employee information is in the directory, however, how does this information get to the UNIX user database (NIS or NIS+, for example), the NT server, the mail server, and the Web-based benefits enrollment program?

In the case of the mail server and the benefits enrollment program, we're in luck. Recent versions of mail servers and Web servers can be configured so that they get their information from a directory.

For the UNIX user database and the NT server, another synchronization mechanism is required. Some directories already include these mechanisms, and many IS departments write their own solutions. And here, too, a commercial metadirectory can provide the required functionality.

Computers, Printers, Toasters . . .

There is no intrinsic limit to the type of data you can store in a directory. So far, we've discussed only information about people. But you may want to store information about shared resources on a network, such as file servers or printers. Then developers could write applications to search for appropriate resources and take action based on the properties of the resources. For example, you can write a utility to search for a particular printer on the company network. You might want to find the closest printer to your department that does dye sublimation full-color glossies. Once the application finds the directory entry for the printer, the application can read the printer properties from the directory and dispatch an appropriately configured print job.

Configuration information for applications can also be stored in a directory. A rapidly increasing number of people access their e-mail from more than one place—from home, from work, or while on the road. Traditionally, e-mail programs have stored configuration information (such as the mail server name, the user name, the password, and mailbox names) either in a file or in the Windows registry. Some configuration information (for example, indexes of mailbox contents) is updated automatically and silently by programs whenever they run.

Keeping the configuration in synch among multiple computers is difficult or impossible. This is even more true of Web browser bookmarks. Recent versions of e-mail and browser programs (for example, Netscape Communicator) offer a solution to this problem: an option to store all this configuration in a directory on the Internet. No matter what computer you use, no matter where you connect from, no matter whether the computer is running Linux or Windows or Mac OS, the program will always get its configuration from the same place—a central directory.

Even programs can be stored in a directory. Remember that directories are generally not designed to handle very large objects, but small Java classes should not be a problem. The opportunities for creating radically dynamic applications are mind-blowing. Customizable applications that assemble themselves and configure their language, user interface, and component set on the fly from classes stored in the directory to match the needs of a particular user? Not unrealistic at all. Jini—the framework for Java object lookup and collaboration—and directories make very good partners. What better catalog for Jini object lookups than a directory?

Jini allows Java objects to locate each other and exploit each other's services over a network. When a Jini-enabled device is connected to a network, it looks for a catalog service and registers itself. If a Jini-enabled object needs a particular service, it can find a catalog service and enumerate the objects that are registered to find one that suits its purposes. The object may also register for notification when new objects are registered in the catalog. If it finds an appropriate catalog entry, the object can then download and run the object that the catalog entry represents (or a stub interface).

For example, a word-processing application might need to list available printers when the user selects the print menu option. The application can then present a list of printer objects found in a nearby (in the network sense) catalog. The user selects a printer and the application downloads the printer object and runs it. There is no need to contact the printer vendor or the operating system vendor to obtain an up-to-date driver for the printer because the "driver"—the printer Java object—comes with the printer itself and is always the right one for that particular printer. Read more about Jini at `http://www.sun.com/jini/`.

CHAPTER 2

The Lingua Franca of Directories Is LDAP

LDAP is not the first protocol to provide directory services over a network. This chapter will briefly outline the predecessors to LDAP, as well as other technologies that provide similar services today. The chapter will also introduce some basic concepts in LDAP, including the information and naming models. Finally, the chapter will summarize the state of LDAP today and the software development kits for LDAP that are currently available.

A Brief History of Electronic Directories

I Heard It through the Grapevine

The first widely distributed directory service for sharing user account information among many networked computers was the Xerox Clearinghouse. The Clearinghouse was based on research done around the distributed computing system called Grapevine at Xerox's Palo Alto Research Center in the early 1980s. The Grapevine provided message delivery, resource location, authentication, and access control services in a network of networks (an internet). When completed, it extended across both coasts of the United States and to Canada and England. More than 1,500 computers participated in the more than 50 local networks that were linked by Grapevine. The Grapevine Registration Database was the precursor to the Clearinghouse.

Registration Database contained about fifteen hundred individuals and five hundred groups. The total message traffic was about twenty-five hundred messages per day. The five computers that hosted Registration Database and Message Server each had 128K of memory and 5MB of disk storage.

The Clearinghouse allowed a user with a Xerox Network Systems (XNS) account to log into the network from any Xerox workstation anyplace in the world. No matter which workstation was used, users always saw their personal desktops. This idea was revolutionary at the time; in some ways, the rest of the networking world is just beginning to catch up with this radical concept.

In recent years, the World Wide Web and the general availability of thin clients (Web browsers) has made a subset of this portable desktop functionality accessible to the general public. From any workstation, users can check their e-mail messages (using Web-based e-mail), access their bookmarks and personal preferences for Web browsers (with location-independent browsers), and view the latest news and information tailored for their particular interests (through the personalized Web pages offered by many portal sites).

Although it was a pioneer in directory services, the Clearinghouse remained a proprietary invention with a proprietary protocol, and as a result it was never adopted outside of Xerox-supplied networks.

Directories for the Internet

The introduction of the Internet, along with the availability of a powerful operating system with university access to source code—UNIX—gave rise to numerous projects, each of which resulted in a limited, special-purpose form of networked directory service.

One of these services was the Domain Name System (DNS), which translates a "plain English" computer name, such as `myserver.acme.com`, into an IP address, such as "207.200.75.200." When you work with a software application, you may find it easier to remember computers by their names. The software applications, however, need to use the IP addresses in order to find a route through the network to the computer.

For example, it's much easier to remember a Web site by the name `www.netscape.com` than by the IP address "205.188.247.5." But the Web browser needs the IP address to find and connect to the Web site. When you type `www.netscape.com` in your browser's location text field, the browser makes a system call, which uses the DNS protocol to contact a DNS server and ask for the corresponding IP address. If the server doesn't have the address, it can look up the name of a server that does have the address and can contact that server to get the address. The DNS can be considered one of the earliest wide-area directory services (DNS has been available since 1984), although it has a very limited and specialized functionality.

Other early Internet directory services with limited functionality include whois (a database of domain name registrations) and PH (user information lookup servers). These services are still available today.

Directories for a Single Network: Proprietary Solutions

NIS and NIS+

Sun Microsystems developed the Network Information System (NIS), later extended under the name NIS+ to allow hierarchical naming schemes and to share within a network the mappings between host names and IP addresses (like DNS), as well as user account information. Although NIS and NIS+ could be used for more than this, these are the most common uses. Nowadays NIS is ubiquitous on UNIX systems, and it allows a user to log into a network from any machine that shares the same NIS user database. However, although NIS and NIS+ will continue to be supported on UNIX systems, the current trend is to use LDAP to provide these directory functions.

NDS

In 1993, Novell replaced its limited user and network database—the Bindery—with a sophisticated, scalable, and hierarchical service capable of managing arbitrary information: Novell Directory Services (NDS). Although NDS initially was available only with the NetWare operating system, Novell has aggressively licensed the source code to various UNIX vendors, attempting to make it a de facto standard.

The information and naming models of NDS are very close to those of X.500 (which we'll discuss shortly), but the access protocol is proprietary. In 1997, Novell made available an LDAP gateway to allow LDAP clients to access NDS.

However, the same Internet standards pressure that has pushed Novell to provide native TCP/IP support in its products (instead of its proprietary network protocol IPX) has also influenced Novell's directory strategy. Currently, Novell is rewriting NDS to be a native LDAP server, with extensions to support Novell-specific features.

Active Directory

Before Windows 2000, Microsoft provided only a very simple, flat user information system for networks, based on domains (not to be confused with a DNS domain). The system is not scalable and requires complicated "trust relationships" between domains to span a large company. The system is to be replaced with the advent of Windows 2000 by a modern, LDAP-based directory: Active Directory. Although intended primarily for management of Microsoft networks, Active Directory should be usable for general-purpose services, assuming that full access is provided to LDAP clients.

X.500: The "Heavyweight" Directory Service

The rapid expansion of distributed systems and telecommunications networks spurred the quest for a standardized, wide-area directory service. The International Telecommunication Union (ITU, formerly the CCITT) joined forces with the International Organization for Standardization (ISO) to develop a series of specifications for a directory service that could provide telephone numbers and e-mail addresses and manage information about network objects. This service was intended to be vastly scalable and extensible.

In 1988, the first standards document for this service was produced. The standard was called X.500. In 1990, this standard was published under the name "ISO

9594, Data Communications Network Directory, Recommendations X.500-X.521." In spite of this new name, the name X.500 stuck. Today the standard comprises many documents (in the X.5 series) and is still in development.

A free implementation of X.500 (called Quipu) was developed at the University College of London. Today there are a few commercial implementations, including versions from ISOCOR, Datacraft, and Control Data.

The authors of the X.500 specifications were careful to design a protocol that would handle any directory needs, both in the present and in the future. Some of this work has resulted in a naming model that was adopted by both NDS and LDAP, and an information model that has been maintained in LDAP. Later in this chapter we will look at both of these models in more detail.

From Humble Beginnings

Early Goals of LDAP

Developing client applications to communicate with an X.500 server turned out to be very complex. The number of options and variants to protocol operations, along with the need to run on an OSI (Open System Interconnection) protocol stack (as opposed to the ubiquitous TCP/IP of the Internet), stood in the way of widespread adoption. Since most clients run in a TCP/IP network environment and need only a very small subset of these options, work began on a lightweight client access protocol. The work was successful: all current commercial X.500 servers now come with an LDAP gateway (Figure 2-1), a program that translates between the lightweight, TCP/IP-based client protocol and the native X.500 protocol of the server.

Early Work on LDAP

In 1993 the work on providing lightweight client access to X.500 servers resulted in the publication of RFC 1487, " X.500 Lightweight Access." Version 1 of the protocol

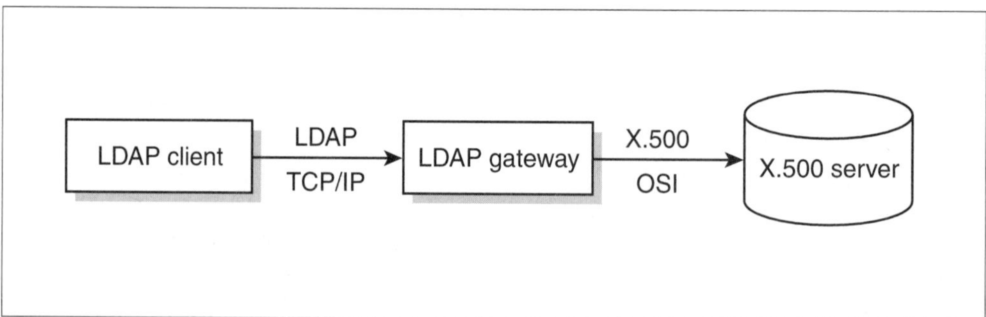

FIGURE 2-1. *LDAP as a gateway to X.500.*

didn't take off, but version 2 did. In 1995, LDAPv2 was defined in RFC 1777, "Lightweight Directory Access Protocol." Most of the early implementations of LDAP client libraries and gateways trace their lineage to freely available software from the University of Michigan. In many of these implementations, a client would use an LDAP client library to talk to an LDAP gateway, which would translate the protocol requests and pass them on to an X.500 server.

LDAP Simplifications of X.500

We've already mentioned that LDAP uses TCP/IP (although it could be made to run on other network protocols) and does not require OSI.

The encoding of requests and responses also was significantly simplified. X.500 allows the data stream of requests and responses to be encoded in many different ways, all of which are variants of the Basic Encoding Rules (BER) specification of Abstract Syntax Notation One (ASN.1). Although ASN.1 is a very powerful and expressive syntax, it requires the client to be capable of interpreting the data types in many different encodings. In LDAP, only a small subset of BER is used and required, and most data types are transmitted as strings. As a result, LDAP clients do not need to handle the multitude of other encodings and data types required by X.500.

The authors of LDAP defined an API for accessing the protocol and assembled an SDK for applications developers. X.500 lacked a standard client API, which forced client application developers to write most of the code for using the protocol.

Initially the LDAP specifications omitted definitions for data replication, referrals (situations in which a server without the requested information can redirect a client to another server that has the information), access control, chaining (situations in which a server without the requested information contacts another server on behalf of a client), and many other standard X.500 features. Some of these features have been added to the LDAP specifications in version 3 or are currently under discussion as proposed additions. Other features have been implemented in software from the University of Michigan or from other vendors but have not been standardized.

Another critical difference between X.500 and LDAP is in the understanding of how directories can be combined to form a single globally searchable service. The X.500 developers envisioned a partition of all directory space in the world on a country basis. At the root of the tree in each directory is a null entry that cannot be searched and that has no user attributes. It represents a virtual shared root of all directories. Under the null node, the directory contains one or more country nodes. Under the country nodes, there are organization nodes, which correspond to companies.

Each company node can contain any structure appropriate to the company. Typically this structure consists of a tree of organizational unit nodes, each corresponding to departments or divisions of the company. If a request for company information is directed to a particular X.500 server, the server can quickly determine that the requested information is in a different country tree. The X.500 server can pass the request on to a server for that country, which can then pass it on to a server that holds information for the company requested.

In reality, it is not feasible to build a global, top-down network of directories in this way, both for practical and for political reasons. It is not even practical to use country nodes at the top of the tree of a company directory, since many companies have operations in more than one country.

LDAP imposes no such restrictions. With LDAP, you can build directories from the bottom up to meet the actual needs of an organization. You can then make the different organizations appear as a single unified organization by setting up referrals between the directories.

LDAP as a Complete System

By the time the second LDAP RFC was out in 1995, almost all access to X.500 servers went through the intermediary of LDAP gateways, rather than directly from native X.500 clients. The question then was: If all the clients want is the subset of X.500 represented by LDAP, why even build servers to implement X.500?

Many of the developers of the LDAP protocol now turned their attention to the prospect of a "lightweight" server. They discovered that a native LDAP directory server could be designed and implemented at a much lower cost than an X.500 server could. In addition, an LDAP server eliminated the need for gateways and translators. By the end of 1995, the first native LDAP directory server was made available for free (including the source code) by the University of Michigan.

The main developers who created this server brought their work to Netscape Communications, which released a commercial version of the directory server at the end of 1996. This server was derived from the University of Michigan source code.

Interest in and deployment of LDAP began to snowball. Although this activity was beneficial for the protocol, the newfound attention began to identify important omissions in the specifications and functionality of LDAP. Work began in the international LDAP community to specify a new version of the protocol: LDAPv3. The new version would fill the previous gaps in the protocol, add important functionality, and provide mechanisms to extend the functionality further without changing the protocol or the existing API. RFC 2251 is the document that contains the new proposed standard. Appendix A includes a list of current and proposed LDAP standards documents.

Future Directions for LDAP

The following are the main areas in which extensions to LDAP are being discussed within the Internet Engineering Task Force (IETF):

- *Authentication and privacy.* The only standardized authentication means in LDAP as of mid-1999 is simple authentication, which requires the client to pass a distinguished name (DN) and a password to the server in cleartext. Discussion is under way on another mandatory authentication method that makes use of a digest, eliminating the need to pass cleartext passwords over a network. Most current LDAP servers support use of the Secure Sockets Layer (SSL) for encrypting a session, typically through use of a dedicated port to ensure secure connections. SSL support will be standardized in the form of Transport Layer Security (TLS).
- *Replication.* Although most, if not all, current LDAP servers can replicate data to other servers from the same vendor, there is no standard yet for replicating data between servers from different vendors. The LDUP (LDAP Duplication and Update Protocol) working group in the IETF is defining the protocols and requirements for replication between any compliant servers.
- *Access control syntax and semantics.* The LDAP specifications do not define how access control is expressed in a directory, or how access control can be communicated to another server when data is replicated. The LDAPEXT (LDAP Extensions) working group in the IETF is preparing standards that allow a server to express its access control specifications in a portable way.
- *Dynamic attributes.* Most directories contain data that does not change as frequently as clients access it. There is a proposal to support short-lived data that is automatically removed if the sponsor disappears. Such a system could be useful for maintaining dynamic status information about applications or users.
- *Transactions.* Directories are now often being used in ways more like the ways in which traditional relational databases are used—as a kind of a lightweight Internet database. Most traditional databases use transactions to control updates to the database. Updates that are interdependent can be grouped into transactions. If one of the updates does not complete successfully, that transaction can be rolled back, restoring the data to its previous state. There has been some interest in providing a similar feature for directories, making it possible to ensure that a number of directory operations either all complete successfully or all fail. LDAP guarantees only that all changes specified within a single operation are treated as a transaction.
- *Various controls to provide additional functionality:*
  - *Server-side sorting.* This control requests that the server return the results of a search sorted by one or more attributes.

- *Virtual List View (VLV).* The results of a search may be more than a client can manage at one time—thousands or even millions of entries. VLV lets a client request an arbitrary slice out of the results (for example, to allow the client to page through the results).
- *Proxied authorization.* Server applications may need to do LDAP operations on behalf of (using the identity of) many different clients, perhaps connecting with a browser to a Web server. This control allows authorization credentials to be passed along with any LDAP request.
- *Duplicate Entry Representation.* By using the control with an LDAP search, a client requests that the server return separate entries for each value held in the specified attributes. For instance, if a specified attribute of an entry holds multiple values, the search operation will return multiple instances of that entry, each instance holding a separate single value of that attribute.

The LDAP Information and Naming Models: How Directories Are Organized

The LDAP Information Model

LDAP inherits its information and naming models from X.500, and we have already hinted at the contents of those models.

In LDAP, data is stored as entries. An **entry** has a **distinguished name** (DN) to identify it uniquely within the directory, as well as one or more **attributes** that describe the entry. Each attribute may have one or more values. Examples of attributes for an entry describing a person include `cn` (the first and last name, or common name, of the person), `mail` (the person's e-mail address), and `telephoneNumber` (the person's phone number).

Each entry must have at least the attribute **`objectclass`**, which defines the type of the entry. An object class defines what attributes are required to constitute an entry and what additional attributes are allowed to be part of the entry. For example, the `organization` object class defines a type of entry that represents an organization. Required attributes of the `organization` object class include `o` (the name of the organization) and `objectclass`. Allowed attributes include `street` (the street address of the organization) and `telephoneNumber` (the phone number of the organization). Appendix D contains a list of commonly used object classes and attributes.

Attribute names are case-insensitive, so `objectClass` can be used interchangeably with `objectclass` or `ObjectClass`.

An entry usually has more than one value for the `objectclass` attribute. Object classes are derived from other object classes. The base for all object classes is `top`. For example, the `organization` object class is derived from the `top` object class. In the `organization` object class, the `objectclass` attribute has two values: `top` and `organization`.

For object classes that are not directly derived from `top`, all ancestors, rather than just the most recently derived one, typically are specified as values when an entry is created. For example, the popular `inetOrgPerson` object class (used to define entries for people) is derived from `organizationalPerson`, which is derived from `person`, which is derived from `top`. When you create an entry of type `inetOrgPerson`, you specify all four of these values for the `objectclass` attribute.

If an entry has more than one `objectclass` value, the entry must contain the union of all required attributes, and it may contain the union of all allowed values. For `inetOrgPerson`, for example, the union of the values listed in Figure 2-2 apply. Each object class (and each attribute) has a unique object identifier (`OID`).

The definitions of attribute types and object classes together make up the **schema** of the directory. The example shown in Figure 2-2 uses the format of the schema configuration files in Netscape Directory Server. Most LDAP servers derived from the University of Michigan source code use a similar format. The server reads the schema configuration files when it starts up, and it will generally not allow a client to create an entry that violates the rules of the schema.

```
objectclass top
        oid 2.5.6.0
        requires
                  objectClass
        allows
                  aci

objectclass person
        oid 2.5.6.6
        superior top
        requires
                 sn,
                 cn
        allows
                 description,
                 seeAlso,
                 telephoneNumber,
                 userPassword
```

FIGURE 2-2. *The* `inetOrgPerson` *attributes.*

(continued)

```
objectclass organizationalPerson
        oid 2.5.6.7
        superior person
        allows
                destinationIndicator,
                facsimileTelephoneNumber,
                internationaliSDNNumber,
                l,
                ou,
                physicalDeliveryOfficeName,
                postOfficeBox,
                postalAddress,
                postalCode,
                preferredDeliveryMethod,
                registeredAddress,
                st,
                street,
                teletexTerminalIdentifier,
                telexNumber,
                title,
                x121Address

objectclass inetOrgPerson
    oid 2.16.840.1.113730.3.2.2
    superior organizationalPerson
      allows
                audio,
                businessCategory,
                carLicense,
                departmentNumber,
                displayName,
                employeeType,
                employeeNumber,
                givenName,
                homePhone,
                homePostalAddress,
                initials,
                jpegPhoto,
                labeledURI,
                manager,
                mobile,
```

FIGURE 2-2. *(continued)*

```
          pager,
          photo,
          preferredLanguage,
          mail,
          roomNumber,
          secretary,
          uid,
          x500uniqueIdentifier,
          userCertificate,
          userSMimeCertificate,
          userPKCS12
```

FIGURE 2-2. *(continued)*

Attributes are also defined in schema configuration files. Table 2-1 shows a few definitions of attributes.

The attribute `cn` represents the common name, and it is usually used to store the full name of a person. The attribute `sn` represents the surname, and `ou` represents the organizational unit.

The syntax type `cis` ("case-insensitive string") is the most common attribute syntax. The syntax does not necessarily tell how the attribute is stored in the directory, but simply how its values will be compared when searching.

A typical entry for an `inetOrgPerson` object might look like that shown in Figure 2-3.

Note that this entry has four values for `objectclass` and two for `ou`, but one for each of the other attributes present. Although the entry contains values for all three of the attributes required by its object classes (`objectclass`, `cn`, and `sn`), it contains only a fraction of the optional attributes allowed by them.

TABLE 2-1. *Attribute definitions.*

ATTRIBUTE	OID	SYNTAX
objectClass	2.5.4.0	cis
cn	2.5.4.3	cis
sn	2.5.4.4	cis
ou	2.5.4.11	cis

```
dn: uid=scarter, ou=People, o=airius.com
cn: Sam Carter
sn: Carter
givenName: Sam
objectclass: top
objectclass: person
objectclass: organizationalPerson
objectclass: inetOrgPerson
ou: Accounting
ou: People
l: Sunnyvale
uid: scarter
mail: scarter@Airius.com
telephoneNumber: +1 408 555 4798
facsimileTelephoneNumber: +1 408 555 9751
roomNumber: 4612
userPassword: sprain
```

FIGURE 2-3. *An* `inetOrgPerson` *entry.*

The LDAP Naming Model

Entries in LDAP, just as in X.500, are organized into a tree. At the top are one or more root nodes, called suffixes or naming contexts. Under each root node may be a subtree of additional nodes. Figure 2-4 illustrates a tree with three root nodes.

Each child of a particular node is distinguished from all siblings by its relative distinguished name (RDN). The RDN consists of the name of one of the attributes of

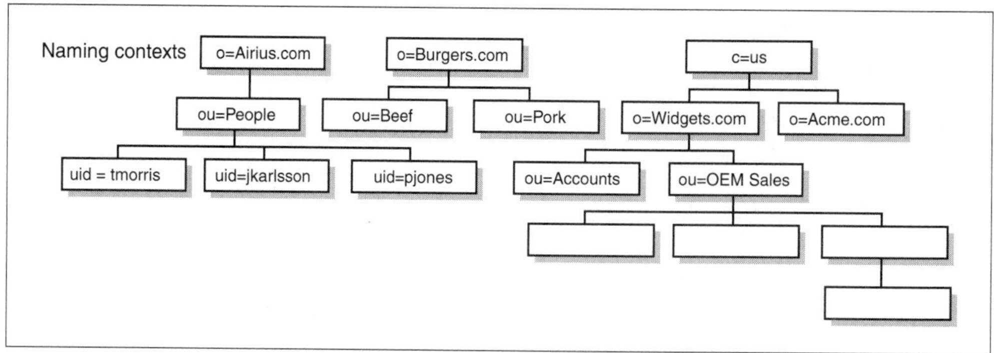

FIGURE 2-4. *Directory tree with multiple naming contexts.*

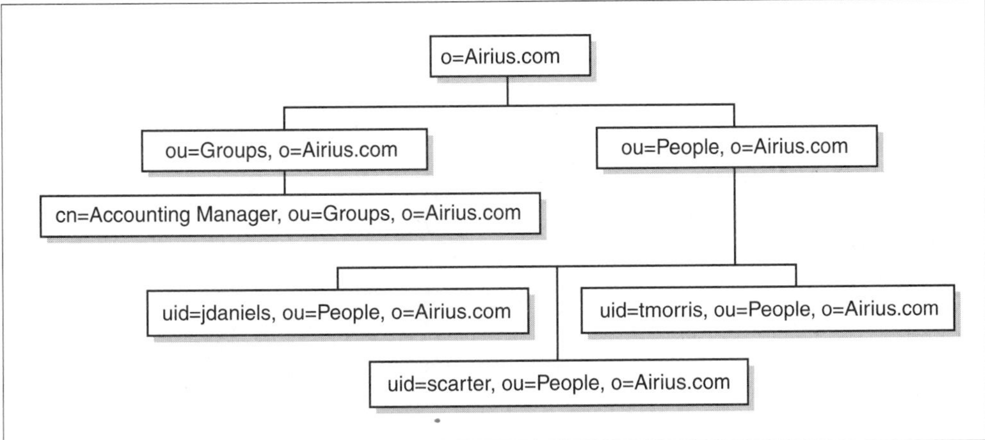

FIGURE 2-5. *A simple LDAP tree, showing only DNs.*

the entry, followed by the equal sign (=), followed by one of the values of the attribute (for example, `uid=tmorris` or `o=Airius.com`).

You can compose the DN (distinguished name) of the entry by taking the RDN and walking up the tree to a root node, adding a comma and the RDN of each parent found to the end (for example, `uid=tmorris, ou=People, o=Airius.com`). Conversely, you can take a DN and break it apart at the commas to produce the RDNs of the entry and all its parents.

Note that attribute names are case-insensitive, and that space between a comma and the following RDN, as well as space surrounding the equal sign, is ignored.

Figure 2-5 illustrates a directory tree and the DNs of entries in the tree. The DN of the entry `uid=tmorris, ou=People, o=Airius.com` is made up of the RDNs of the entries above it in the tree (`ou=People` and `o=Airius.com`).

LDAP Spoken Here

LDAP-aware software has mushroomed in the past two years, fueled by the explosion of electronic commerce on the Internet and by the maturing of commercial LDAP server products. LDAP is key to providing secure and controlled access to data shared on the Internet, and it is the natural hub for the storage and management of public certificates.

Stand-alone LDAP servers can be obtained from Netscape, the University of Michigan, the OpenLDAP Project (which is carrying forward the University of Michigan source code), IBM, Oracle, and Innosoft.

Several major operating systems include or will soon include an LDAP server: Solaris 8, the next version of HP-UX, Windows 2000, and NetWare 5.

Routers from the major vendors will use LDAP and will be manageable through LDAP, through the standards being developed for Directory Enabled Networking (DEN) and the Desktop Management Task Force (DMTF).

Browser and e-mail applications are increasingly able to look up users and e-mail addresses using LDAP. The latest versions of Netscape Communicator, Microsoft Internet Explorer, and Eudora from Qualcomm are all LDAP enabled. Whole new application areas are emerging, with work flow and personnel information management centering around an LDAP server to automate and streamline many Human Resources activities, such as provisioning and benefits administration, allowing a tremendous degree of (safe) employee self-administration and freeing the HR staff from much of the tedium and the company from much of the expense.

Many Roads to Rome

Directory SDK for C

The first SDK to provide client access to LDAP was developed for the C language at the University of Michigan. The API of this C SDK was formalized in RFC 1823. Netscape extended the C API to support all features of LDAPv3 and made the source code publicly available through Mozilla.org in 1998. The following is an example of a program written with the C SDK. The program performs a simple search for all people with the surname Jensen:

```
#include "ldap.h"

int main( int argc, char **argv ) {
    LDAP            *ld;
    LDAPMessage     *result, *e;
    BerElement      *ber;
    char            *a, *dn;
    char            **vals;
    int             i;

    /* get a handle to an LDAP connection */
    if ( (ld = ldap_init("localhost", 389 )) == NULL ) {
        perror("ldap_init" );
        return( 1 );
    }
    /* search for all entries with surname of Jensen */
    if ( ldap_search_s( ld, "o=Airius.com", LDAP_SCOPE_SUBTREE,
        "sn=jensen", NULL, 0, &result ) != LDAP_SUCCESS ) {
```

```
            ldap_perror( ld, "ldap_search_s" );
            return( 1 );
        }
        /* for each entry print out name + all attrs and values */
        for ( e = ldap_first_entry( ld, result ); e != NULL;
            e = ldap_next_entry( ld, e ) ) {
            if ( (dn = ldap_get_dn( ld, e )) != NULL ) {
                printf("dn: %s\n", dn );
                ldap_memfree( dn );
            }
            for ( a = ldap_first_attribute( ld, e, &ber );
                a != NULL; a = ldap_next_attribute( ld, e, ber ) ) {
                    if ((vals = ldap_get_values( ld, e, a)) != NULL ) {
                        for ( i = 0; vals[i] != NULL; i++ ) {
                            printf("%s: %s\n", a, vals[i] );
                        }
                        ldap_value_free( vals );
                }
                ldap_memfree( a );
            }
            if ( ber != NULL ) {
                ber_free( ber, 0 );
            }
            printf("\n" );
        }
        ldap_msgfree( result );
        ldap_unbind( ld );
        return( 0 );
    }
```

Directory SDK for Java

In early 1997, Netscape released an SDK entirely in Java. An Internet Draft was published at the same time, and in 1998 the source code was made available through Mozilla.org. This book is about using the Java SDK. We will go into the Java SDK in great detail shortly, but here we give a code example as a quick reference point. This program performs the same search as the preceding C progam.

```
import netscape.ldap.*;
import java.util.*;

public class Search {
    public static void main( String[] args ) {
        LDAPConnection ld = null;
```

```
int status = -1;
try {
     ld = new LDAPConnection();
     /* Connect to server */
     String MY_HOST = "localhost";
     int MY_PORT = 389;
     ld.connect( MY_HOST, MY_PORT );

     /* search for all entries with surname of Jensen */
     String MY_FILTER = "sn=Jensen";
     String MY_SEARCHBASE = "o=Airius.com";
     LDAPSearchResults res = ld.search( MY_SEARCHBASE,
                                LDAPConnection.SCOPE_SUB,
                                MY_FILTER,
                                null,
                                false );

     /* Loop on results until finished */
     while ( res.hasMoreElements() ) {
           /* Next directory entry */
           LDAPEntry findEntry = (LDAPEntry)res.nextElement();
           System.out.println( findEntry.getDN() );
           /* Get the attributes of the entry */
           LDAPAttributeSet findAttrs =
                   findEntry.getAttributeSet();
           Enumeration enumAttrs = findAttrs.getAttributes();
           System.out.println( "\tAttributes: " );
           /* Loop on attributes */
           while ( enumAttrs.hasMoreElements() ) {
                   LDAPAttribute anAttr =
                          (LDAPAttribute)enumAttrs.
                            nextElement();
                   String attrName = anAttr.getName();
                   System.out.println( "\t\t" + attrName );
                   /* Loop on values for this attribute */
                   Enumeration enumVals =
                          anAttr.getStringValues();
                   if (enumVals != null) {
                          while ( enumVals.hasMore Elements() ) {
                              String aVal =
                              ( String )enumVals.
                                nextElement();
                              System.out.println(
                                "\t\t\t" +
```

```
                                                                  aVal );
                                          }
                                   }
                            }
                     }
                     status = 0;
                } catch( LDAPException e ) {
                       System.out.println( "Error: " + e.toString() );
                }

                /* Done, so disconnect */
                if ( (ld != null) && ld.isConnected() ) {
                     try {
                           ld.disconnect();
                     } catch ( LDAPException e ) {
                           System.out.println( "Error: " + e.toString() );
                     }
                }
                System.exit(status);
          }
}
```

Java Naming and Directory Interface

Sun Microsystems, in collaboration with IBM, Novell, Netscape, and others, has developed a generic API for interaction with various types of naming contexts, including LDAP, NDS, and NIS. Support for each protocol is supplied by a service provider. Using the Java Naming and Directory Interface (JNDI), the previous example of a simple search program would look like this:

```
import java.util.Properties;
import java.util.Enumeration;
import java.naming.*;
import java.naming.directory.*;

class Search {
    public static void main(String[] args) {

        /* Specify host and port to use for directory service */
        Properties env = new Properties();
        String MY_HOST = "localhost";
        int MY_PORT = 389;
        String MY_FILTER = "sn=Jensen";
        String MY_SEARCHBASE = "o=Airius.com";
        env.put("jndi.service.host", MY_HOST);
```

```
        env.put("jndi.service.port", MY_PORT);
        try {
            /* get a handle to an Initial DSContext */
            DSContext ctx = new InitialDSContext(env);
            /* specify search constraints to search subtree */
            SearchConstraints constraints = new SearchConstraints();
            constraints.setSearchScope(SearchConstraints.SUBTREE_SCOPE);
            /* search for all entries with surname of Jensen */
            SearchEnumeration results
                = ctx.search(MY_SEARCHBASE, MY_FILTER, constraints);
            /* for each entry print out name + all attrs and values */
            while (results != null && results.hasMoreElements()) {
                SearchResult si = results.next();
                /* print its name */
                System.out.println("name: " + si.getName());
                AttributeSet attrs = si.getAttributes();
                if (attrs == null) {
                    System.out.println("No attributes");
                } else {
                    /* print each attribute */
                    for (AttributeEnumeration ae = attrs.getAttributes();
                         ae.hasMoreElements();) {
                        Attribute attr = ae.next();
                        String attrId = attr.getAttributeId();
                        /* print each value */
                        for (Enumeration vals = attr.getValues();
                            vals.hasMoreElements();
                            System.out.println(attrId + ": " +
                            vals.nextElement()));
                    }
                }
            }
        } catch (NamingException e) {
            System.err.println("Search example failed");
            e.printStackTrace();
        }
    }
}
```

CHAPTER 3

May We Introduce—Directory SDK for Java

The success of any directory architecture depends on the availability of APIs to access its services. LDAP has won wide acceptance by the Internet community and by many companies to a large extent because of the ease of access provided by the client SDKs.

What Directory SDK for Java Can Do for You

Directory SDK for Java provides the following functionality:

- Freedom from protocol handling
- The use of standard Java objects for returning and processing data
- Utility classes for handling LDAP-specific entities
- Full access to all LDAP services
- Flexible authentication models
- The ability to run code anywhere once it is written
- Multilayered functionality
- A platform for directory-enabled applications

Freedom from Protocol Handling

The key benefit the SDK provides is freeing your program from low-level protocol handling. The SDK handles all the data encoding that is necessary for communicating with an LDAP service from your client code to the server. The SDK provides simple

Java-based methods to handle connecting, searching, and modifying, including creating, adding, and deleting, LDAP data. The classes and associated methods are intuitive to use and require only small subsets to accomplish major LDAP communications tasks. These features allow you to focus on the task at hand without having to code socket-level client-server LDAP communications.

The Use of Standard Java Objects for Returning and Processing Data

The SDK utilizes standard Java data types for interaction with application code. Search results are returned as Java `Strings` and/or byte arrays. For instance, to indicate to the `LDAPConnection.search` method which attributes to return, a simple array is passed, such as `{"cn", "mail", "sn"}`. Data is prepared for insertion into the directory using the same data types. Using standard data types lets you use all of Java's built-in type support and makes it easy to use the SDK from existing Java code or from JavaScript, as we will see in later chapters.

Utility Classes for Handling LDAP-Specific Entities

Certain data entities that are specific to LDAP, such as a DN or LDAP URL, can be built or parsed automatically by methods in the SDK. The `LDAPDN.explodeDN` method takes a DN and returns a Java array of `Strings` of each component within the DN. For example:

```
String theDN="uid=tonyl, ou=People, o=Netscape, c=US";
String[] parsedDN = LDAPDN.explodeDN(theDN,false);
// parsedDN now has the value {"uid=tonyl", "ou=People",
                               "o=Netscape", "c=us"}
```

The boolean second parameter indicates whether to include the attribute names (`uid`, `ou`, etc.) or not.

There are also utility methods to parse LDAP URLs. LDAP URLs have the syntax `ldap://hostname:port/basedn?attributes?scope?filter`. They are fully described in RFC 2255, and they are discussed in detail in Chapter 5. The utility methods allow you to extract the host, port, attributes, and so on. An LDAP URL can also be passed directly to the `LDAPConnection.search` method, simplifying the representation of searches.

Full Access to All LDAP Services

The LDAP SDK provides communications and data handling to any LDAP-compliant directory service, although some directories might provide only a subset of the LDAP services.

You can use the SDK to make alterations to the schema, query the structure of the directory, or add new attributes to records. As an application or service programmer, you can interact with an LDAP directory at the level needed for your development project. The LDAP directory with which you are communicating does not even need to be your own; it can be a directory anywhere on the network or the Internet. Chapter 4 will take you step by step through the installation of your own LDAP server for use in programming and applying the examples in this book.

Flexible Authentication Models

The SDK provides authentication models that range from anonymous binds to using the **Secure Sockets Layer** (SSL). You can authenticate to an LDAP directory with a distinguished name (DN) and password, as well as digital certificates. Other authentication models are supported through the **Simple Authentication and Security Layer** (SASL).

Write Once, Run Anywhere

The promise of the Java environment is that code can be developed on one machine and run on any other machine. As organizations begin to work more closely with their external partners, interaction between dissimilar platforms becomes essential. Roaming users and Internet users by their nature use different platforms. Build the code to be portable and take advantage of future computing architectures.

Multilayered Functionality

Directory SDK for Java may appear overwhelming at first because of its large number of classes and methods, but a simple search operation requires the use of just three methods of the central class `LDAPConnection`. We will cover the use and calling of these methods in Chapter 5.

A Platform for Directory-Enabled Applications

The directory is fast becoming an essential part of new corporate applications because it provides a fast and consistent organizational, departmental, or individual view of all entities that form the company. For new Internet applications, LDAP's streamlined, efficient access to remote or distributed data sources makes it a strategic component. There is a whole new wave of application development in the area of **directory-enabled applications**.

A directory-enabled application allows an organization and its programming staff to minimize application-specific data stores. Every application-specific store requires maintenance, and at some point all these stores will contain redundant data. For example, a building-access code system needs to know who valid employees are. The Human Resources Department also needs this information. If both systems share a common LDAP directory, as the workforce changes both of these systems are immediately aware of who are valid employees.

Directory-enabled applications make use of directories to handle the authentication of users and the location of resources. To take advantage of these services, the application developer needs to make the directory an integral part of the application. The SDK provides this connection for the application developer.

An application developer can be someone writing Web server scripts, a Java servlet programmer, an Internet client application developer, an applet writer, or a developer who wants simply to add access to directory information to a Java application. In each case, the SDK is the key to unlocking and using the potential of the directory.

The powerful access control model of modern LDAP directories makes it possible to share data across divisions in a controlled and safe manner. If Division A is writing an application, it can allow appropriate people from Division B access while retaining control of the individuals' records. Different individuals, organizations, or services can be limited to different views of the same data. Removing an entry will immediately result in a new consistent view for all clients.

The directory is now a single source for all information companywide. The same directory can host data for your business and trading partners as well. The application developer can now concentrate on building the applications, while the directory, through the SDK, provides a "black box" of valid credential information, as well as any application-specific data.

What Else Can the SDK Do for Me?

Let's examine some specific examples in which the SDK in conjunction with an LDAP directory can benefit a project.

Dynamic Organizational Chart

One resource that any organization can benefit from having online is up-to-date organizational charts. In any medium-sized to large organization it is difficult to keep organizational charts up to date. Reorganizations, promotions, new hires, terminations—it seems as if the charts are never representative of the actual entities. The charts in most cases also require a significant amount of work: gathering data and preparing drawings or documents. Leveraging the personnel information stored in a directory, an up-to-date organizational chart can be created and presented on the fly.

The directory and SDK provide a great resource for empowering this kind of application, with the application running locally as a Java applet or remotely as a servlet. The directory contains an optional attribute for an `inetOrgPerson` called `manager` that stores a full DN to the corresponding LDAP record that represents that individual's manager. Using this information, an organizational chart application can traverse the directory tree and locate direct reports to an individual. Some simple pseudocode to do this would be as follows:

```
Search for all person entries lacking a manager
Divide them into groups based on their organizational units
Create an organizational tree, divided horizontally into groups
For each group {
       explore the reporting structure by calling getReports for
           each person in the group
}

display tree based on structure found

getReports(String inDN) {
       Search records in directory with manager attribute = inDN
       for each record found, call getReports, passing the DN of the
           record
       get the "common name" and "title" attributes of each record
           and add them as a child to inDN in the organizational tree
}
```

The data would need to be displayed in an attractive graphical user interface (GUI), but the basic algorithm for collecting the data is to call the `getReports` method recursively to build the organizational chart. In addition, the multithreading capabilities of Java allow this application to start each recursive search as a different thread. Output from such a program might look like what is presented in Figure 3-1.

Chapter 12 will present a Java program that dynamically draws an organizational chart based on organizational information in a directory.

Directory-Linking Tool

The goal of a directory-linking tool is to provide a way to join disparate data sources, bringing them together inside the LDAP directory. Most organizations have different systems that still use older or proprietary directories or databases. The LDAP directory can be the unifying source to feed these systems or to take information from them. The combination of Directory SDK and other Java packages enables this

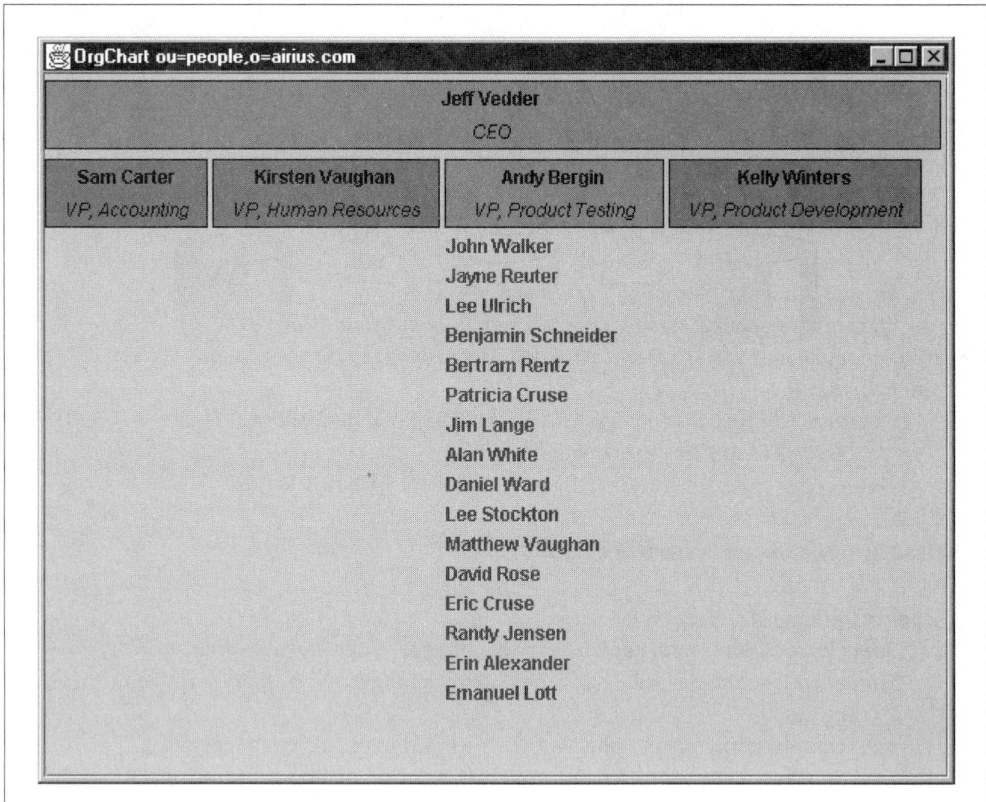

FIGURE 3-1. *Sample organizational chart.*

exchange of information by providing access to relational database sources through JDBC (Java Database Connectivity), or through a device driver accessible from Java. Pseudocode to perform this task would be as follows:

```
read record from source system, extracting needed fields
search for corresponding entry in the directory
if data or record does not match or exist {
      add or replace with new information
}
repeat sequence
```

Figure 3-2 illustrates a directory as the central hub for linking company data.

Within the Sun-Netscape Alliance, for example, many different systems are linked together via the LDAP server, which functions as the corporate directory.

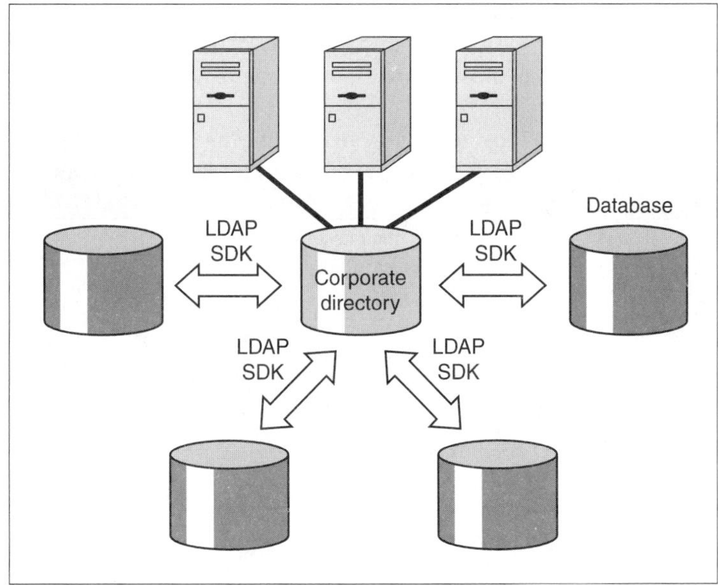

FIGURE 3-2. *Linking data repositories via the LDAP SDK.*

Access control has been defined for various parts of the directory tree, for different administrative groups, and for individual attributes and entries to allow only certain groups to view or change the data.

One such example is the employee photo for building-access badges. Privileged information is available only to security personnel. Other information, such as phone number and e-mail address, can be read by anyone but modified only by the user who corresponds to the entry or by an administrator. Through the use of a single assigned user ID and password, maintained in the LDAP system, controlled access is gained to all systems within the company. Many of these different systems are linked together through background processes to keep the data consistent. When a user changes her password or home phone number, for example, it is recognized companywide through the directory.

Access Control for Existing or New Applications

In the past, application developers were always faced with decisions on how to control access to their code, and often they ended up building access control into their application code. As a result, many of these applications required each user to be entered into a table or file. With LDAP, applications or processes can validate against the directory. Some simple pseudocode to handle this function is as follows:

```
obtain user ID and password
search for the entry with the specified user ID
if found, authenticate using the DN of the entry and the supplied
    password
if authentication failed, user is not authorized
check if user is allowed access to the application entry by
    attempting to read it
if allowed, continue the operation
```

Encapsulating this functionality into a JavaBean, class library, or EJB (Enterprise JavaBean) on the network that communicates with the directory to handle authentication information can make this a one-line check for the Java developer. The SDK code to authenticate against the directory is very short (shown here as a snippet, with error handling omitted for brevity):

```
LDAPConnection ldap_conn = new LDAPConnection();
try {
       ldap_conn.connect( HOSTNAME,PORT);
       String[] attrs = { ldap_conn.NO_ATTRS };
       LDAPSearchResults res =
                 ldap_conn.search( BASE,
                                   ldap_conn.SCOPE_SUB,
                                   "uid=" + uid,
                                   attrs,
                                   false);
       // Need the DN for authentication
       String dn = res.next().getDN();
       // Attempt validation
       ldap_conn.authenticate( dn, pwd );
       // User authenticated
} catch (LDAPException e) {
// User not validated
}
if ( ( ld != null ) && ld.isConnected() ) {
           try {
               ld.disconnect();
           } catch ( LDAPException e ) {
               System.out.println( e.toString() );
           }
}
```

Installation and Setup of the SDK

Staying Current

The SDK and SDK source code included on the CD-ROM are version 4.0 of Directory SDK for Java. To obtain the latest version of this software, visit the Netscape developer site at `http://developer.netscape.com/tech/directory/downloads.html`. You will be presented with a choice to download the software. If the version on the Web site is newer than 4.0, download the latest Directory SDK for Java. The complete source code to the SDK is also available at `http://www.mozilla.org/directory/`. Directory SDK for Java works with Java Development Kit (JDK) 1.1 or higher. The GUI examples in this book require JDK 1.2 or higher because they use Swing 1.1.

Installing the SDK

After downloading and expanding the compressed file in a location of your choice, you will have a series of subdirectories. To make it easier to follow the examples in the book, we recommend installing the files in the following location:

```
c:\netscape\ldapjava (Windows)
/usr/opt/netscape/ldapjava (UNIX)
```

The directory that contains `ldapjava` will be referred to in the text as `<LDAPSDKHOME>`. For example, `<LDAPSDKHOME>/doc` refers to the `doc` directory of the SDK. Figure 3-3 illustrates the directory structure of the SDK installation.

`<LDAPSDKHOME>/doc` contains the entire documentation set for the SDK in HTML format. To use the documentation, point your browser at the index.html file.

`<LDAPSDKHOME>/examples` contains many code samples, including code that calls the SDK from JavaScript and code that uses LDAP JavaBeans.

`<LDAPSDKHOME>/tools` contains command-line tools source code that implements the functionality of the platform-native command-line tools included with Netscape Directory Server.

`<LDAPSDKHOME>/beans` contains LDAP JavaBean class files.

`<LDAPSDKHOME>/packages` contains two JAR files that contain the classes of the SDK. Make sure you also have a Java compiler (javac) in your `PATH`. The compiler must be version 1.1 or later (1.2 or later for the GUI examples).

The next step is to set up your Java `CLASSPATH` environment variable to include the two JAR files in the `<LDAPSDKHOME>/packages` directory. These files are `ldapjdk.jar` and `ldapfilt.jar`. The `CLASSPATH` settings shown in the examples that follow should be applied so that they take effect for all windows opened (defined in your `.cshrc` or `autoexec.bat` files, or in `Control Panel/System/Environment`).

In UNIX with csh or tcsh, use the following command:

FIGURE 3-3. *SDK installation folders.*

```
setenv CLASSPATH <LDAPSDKHOME>/packages/ldapjdk.jar:<LDAPSDKHOME>/
    packages/ldapfilt.jar:$CLASSPATH
```

In Windows use

```
set CLASSPATH=<LDAPSDKHOME>/packages/ldapjdk.jar;<LDAPSDKHOME>/
    packages/ldapfilt.jar;%CLASSPATH%
```

After modifying the `CLASSPATH`, go to the directory `tools/java` and compile `LDAPSearch.java` to verify the development environment, as outlined here:

1. Open a command window on your system and switch to the directory `<LDAPSDKHOME>/tools`.

2. Compile the `LDAPSearch.java` file by issuing the following command:

```
javac LDAPSearch.java
```

If the compilation succeeds, the CLASSPATH is set up correctly and you can begin to use the SDK in the programming examples in this book. If you receive the following error:

```
LDAPSearch.java:4: Package netscape.ldap not found in import
```

there is a problem with your CLASSPATH.

If you are on the Internet and wish to search a publicly available directory (we will walk through installing your own directory server in Chapter 4), you can now exercise the class you just compiled with the following command:

```
java LDAPSearch -h memberdir.netscape.com -b
    "ou=member_directory,o=netcenter.com" "cn=tony d*" cn mail
```

This command executes a search against the Netcenter LDAP directory (one of the largest such directories on the Net, with many millions of entries). You will get results of the following form:

```
dn: uid=5473266:PCMv1, ou=member_directory, o=netcenter.com
cn: Tony Diaz
mail: admin@akfast.net

dn: uid=5793767:PCMv1, ou=member_directory, o=netcenter.com
cn: Tony DelNero
mail: tdelnero@binghamt.gannett.com

dn: uid=4132849:AIMv1, ou=member_directory, o=netcenter.com
cn: Tony Davis
mail: tony.davis@unisys.com

dn: uid=6053852:SWDv1, ou=member_directory, o=netcenter.com
cn: Tony Duffy
mail: tony.duffy@cableol.co.uk
```

You will probably get more hits than are shown here. In fact, you will probably receive a message like this:

```
netscape.ldap.LDAPException: error result (4); Sizelimit exceeded
```

This message indicates that you have exceeded the limit the server has been configured to return, or that the server would return more entries than you have requested. The default maximum number of results requested by the SDK is 1,000, but many public LDAP servers are configured to return no more than 100 (or even less). You can tell LDAPSearch and the SDK to request only 50 results by including "-z 50" in the command line:

```
java LDAPSearch -h memberdir.netscape.com -b
    "ou=member_directory,o=netcenter.com" -z 50 "cn=tony d*" cn mail
```

Let's examine what we requested and the result set returned. First the request:

```
java LDAPSearch -h memberdir.netscape.com -b
    "ou=member_directory,o=netcenter.com" "cn=tony d*" cn mail
```

The parameter -h specifies the host name we are searching. The option -b indicates the base in the directory from which to start the search. We have requested all entries that have a common name starting with "tony d." Note that common-name attribute values are case-insensitive, so the same results would be returned for "Tony D" or "ToNy D," for example. For all the entries that match these parameters we want the common name, which corresponds to the cn attribute, and the e-mail address, which corresponds to the mail attribute, returned.

Note that the result set does not contain the data in sorted order. The server can be asked to sort the data before returning it, or the SDK can do the sorting. We will cover sorting in more detail in Chapter 5. The server basically returned all values that matched our search in whatever order it found them.

Conclusion

If you develop applications, work in Information Systems, or handle processes that involve interacting with people, you can take advantage of Directory SDK for Java. The SDK provides access to the corporate directory that contains the most up-to-date people, network, or systems information. As a developer, you now have the software and an overview of the strategy to design and connect systems to share a common source for authoritative user and authentication information.

In this chapter we have examined some common applications that can be empowered through the SDK, as well as installation of the SDK. Chapter 4 will guide you through installing your own directory server, and then we will introduce detailed programming examples.

PART II

GETTING STARTED

CHAPTER 4

Setting Up Your Own Directory

Now that you're familiar with LDAP and the features available in Directory SDK for Java, you're ready to start writing your own LDAP applications. To develop and run your own LDAP applications, you will need access to an LDAP directory. Although you can use public directories on the Internet, it is useful to set up your own directory. You can use an evaluation copy of Netscape Directory Server, included on the CD-ROM that comes with this book, to test your LDAP applications. Other LDAP servers that comply with LDAP version 3 will also work with the code and examples in this book, and much of the code will work also with servers that support only LDAP version 2, but some of the more advanced sections may not work with other servers.

In this chapter you will install Netscape Directory Server. You will set up your own test directory and use the available tools to view the directory contents.

Downloading and Installing Netscape Directory Server

Netscape Directory Server is a robust, scalable LDAP server designed to manage an enterprise-wide or Internet-wide directory of users and resources. You can download an evaluation copy of Netscape Directory Server under Netscape's Test Drive program, or install the copy included on the CD-ROM for use with this book.

Before You Download and Install the Software

Before you install any of the software, check its system requirements.

- To determine the system requirements for Netscape Directory Server, see the Directory Server documentation page at `http://home.netscape.com/eng/server/directory/`. In the release notes, you can find a link to the installation requirements.

- To determine the system requirements for Netscape's Directory SDK for Java, see the Netscape Directory Developer Central Web page at `http://developer.netscape.com/tech/directory/`.

Downloading Netscape Directory Server

To download an evaluation copy of Netscape Directory Server, go to Netscape's product download page at `http://home.netscape.com/download/index.html`. Follow the links that point to the Directory Server download page.

You should also download a copy of the Directory Server product documentation from `http://home.netscape.com/eng/server/directory/`. The documentation is available in PDF format (which you can read in Adobe Acrobat Reader) and as HTML files.

Installing Netscape Directory Server

Before you install Netscape Directory Server, read the release notes and the *Netscape Directory Server Installation Guide*.

Since you will be installing the sample directory database, you can use the Express Installation option. When you use this option, many of the configuration options are already set for you.

Unzip the setup files from the CD-ROM , or the ones that you have downloaded, and run the setup program. Figures 4-1 through 4-6 illustrate the installation for the Windows NT version. When prompted by the setup program, you need to specify the following information:

- What you want to install. You will be given the option of installing Netscape Servers or Netscape Console (see Figure 4-1). Select Netscape Servers.
- The type of installation. You will be given the options of Express, Typical, or Custom (see Figure 4-2). Select Express.
- The location where you want to install the server (see Figure 4-3).
- The server components that you want to install (see Figure 4-4). Install Netscape Server Products Core Components (required for any Netscape server), Netscape Directory Suite, and Administration Services. You do not need to install Netscape Directory Server Synch Service.
- (UNIX only) The user and group that you want the server to run as.
- The ID and password for the Configuration Directory Server Administrator (see Figure 4-5). You will use this ID and password to log into Netscape

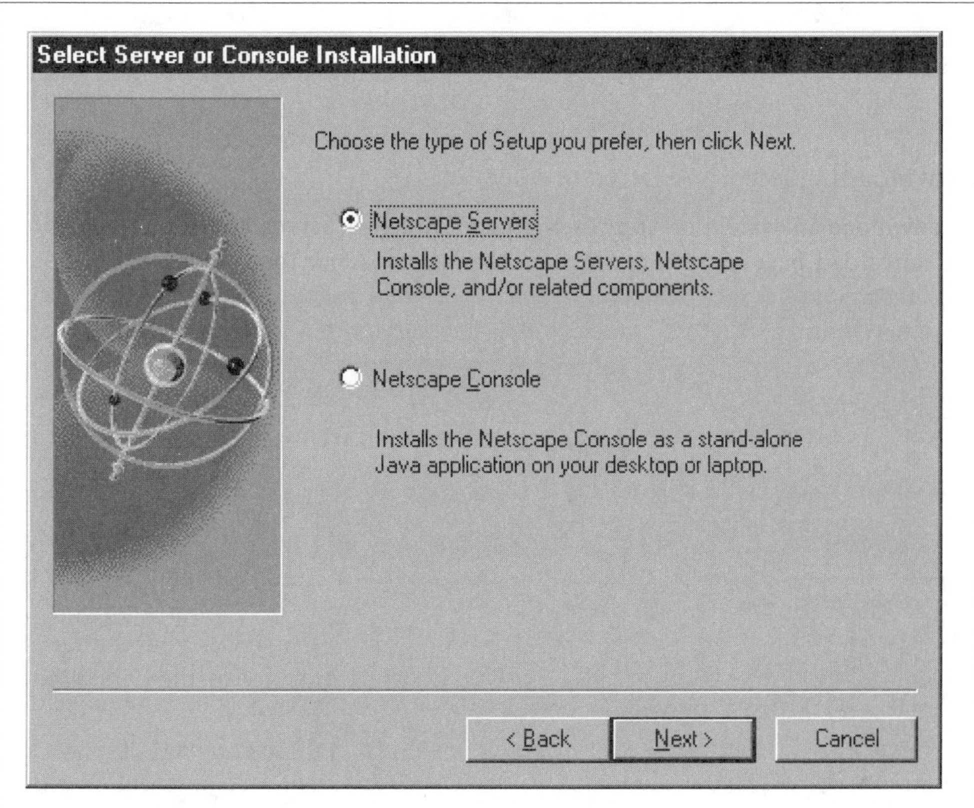

FIGURE 4-1. *Select server or console.*

Console (the administration GUI for Netscape servers). From Netscape Console, you can modify the Directory Server configuration settings. For example, you can use "admin" as the ID.

- The distinguished name (DN) and password of the Directory Manager (see Figure 4-6). This information identifies a user in the directory who has access and privileges to manage the directory. For example, the Directory Manager can add new users to the directory and modify existing users.

Keep track of the DN and password of the Directory Manager. You will need to use these when you use LDAP clients to add or modify data in the sample directory. You will also need this information to import the sample database into the Directory Server.

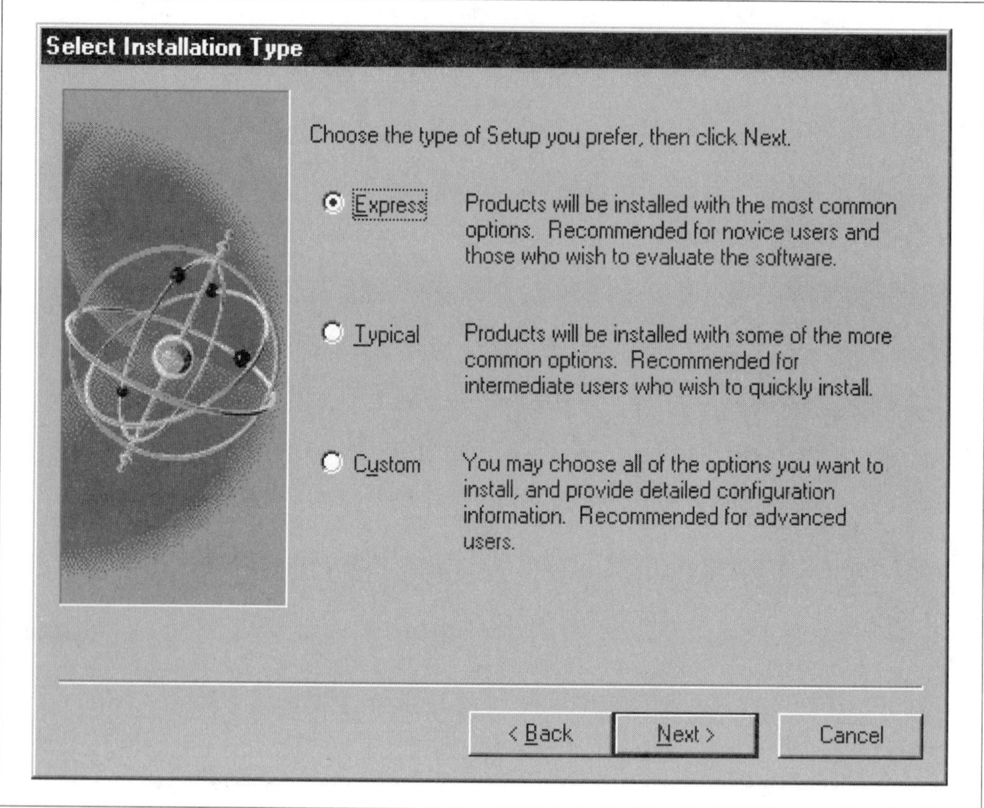

FIGURE 4-2. *Select installation type.*

The following are examples of DNs that you may want to assign to the Directory Manager:

- `cn=Directory Manager`
- `cn=root`
- `uid=ldapadmin`

Do not use `uid=admin`, because an administrative user entry with the user ID "admin" is created automatically during installation. The Directory Manager identity should be distinct from any user entries.

At the end of installation, you will be prompted to keep or delete the installation cache. You can delete this cache; it is used primarily to replay an installation with no user interaction.

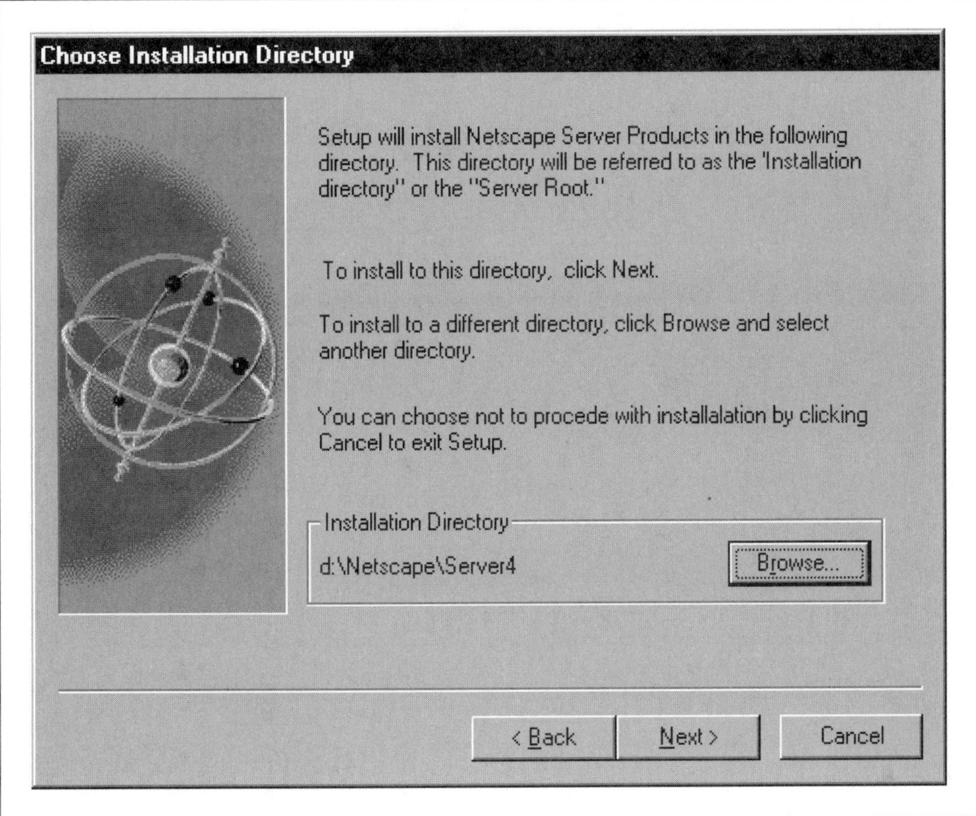

FIGURE 4-3. *Choose installation directory.*

After you finish the Express Installation, you can set up the sample database provided on the CD-ROM that accompanies this book.

Setting Up the Sample Database

The CD-ROM includes a sample database for a company. It will be used throughout this book, so you need to import this database into your directory. The sample database uses the naming context (the top of the directory tree) `o=Airius.com`. There is no standard way to create a naming context in a directory. If you installed Netscape Directory Server and chose Express Installation, the naming context has already been created. With Novell Directory Services version 8, you must use NWAdmin or one of the other administrative tools to create the naming context before you can import the database. Other servers require other procedures.

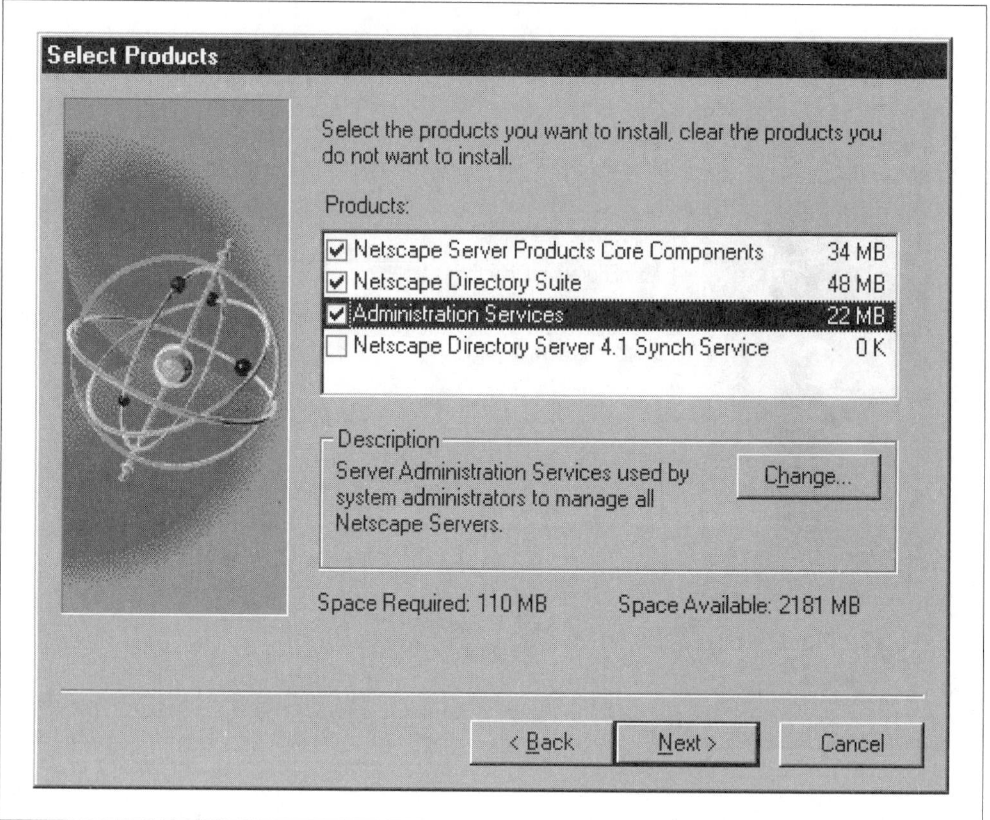

FIGURE 4-4. *Select products.*

To import the data, you can use the `LDAPModify` command-line tool in the SDK:

```
java LDAPModify -c -a -D "cn=Directory Manager" -w <password> -f
    <CDROM>/ldif/airiusplus.ldif
```

Replace `cn=Directory Manager` with the DN of a privileged user if you do not have an administrative user with that DN. Replace `<password>` with the password for the user, and `<CDROM>` with the location of the CD-ROM. The specified options tell the command to add all entries in the file `airiusplus.ldif`, to continue if it encounters an error (for example, if an entry already exists in the directory), to use the specified authentication DN and password, and to import data from the `airiusplus.ldif` file.

Figure 4-7 illustrates part of the hierarchy of the sample directory. Entries representing users are located under the `ou=People, o=airius.com` entry. Entries representing groups are located under the `ou=Groups, o=airius.com` entry.

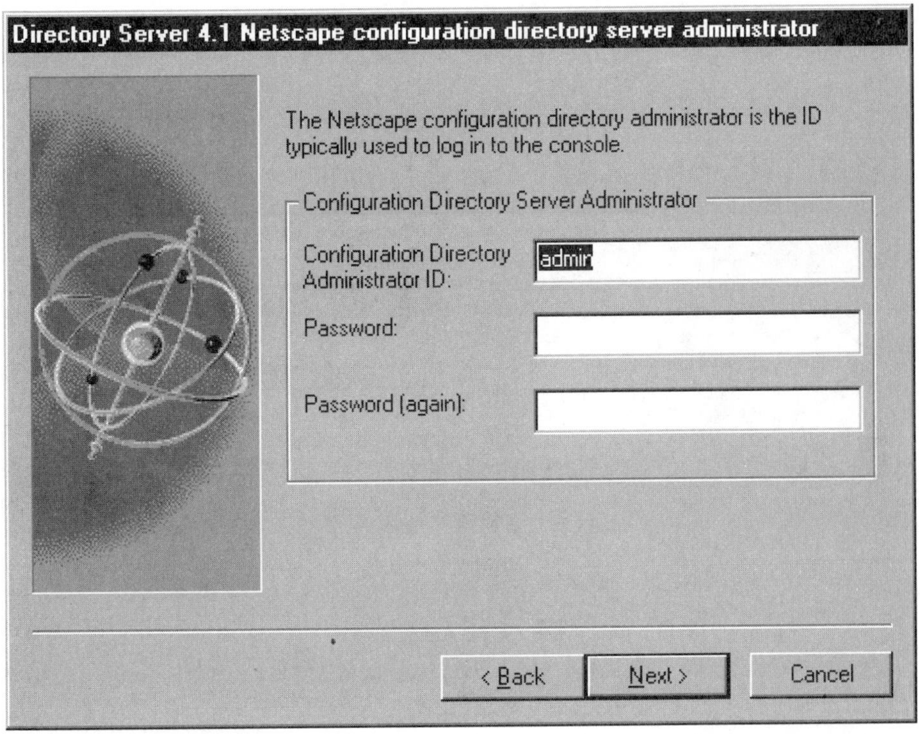

FIGURE 4-5. *Select Administrator ID and password.*

Using the Command-Line Tools with Your New Directory

Now that you have set up your own directory, you may want to view and modify its contents.

Directory SDK for Java includes the source code for several command-line tools that you can use to work with data in the directory. In Chapter 3 you compiled one of these tools. In the previous section we used `LDAPModify` to import the sample database. Now you can use these tools against the sample directory that you have set up.

Finding Entries with `LDAPSearch`

You can use the `LDAPSearch` tool to view entries in the sample directory. Here we provide some sample commands. The syntax for this tool (as well as the criteria required for performing searches) will be discussed in Chapter 5.

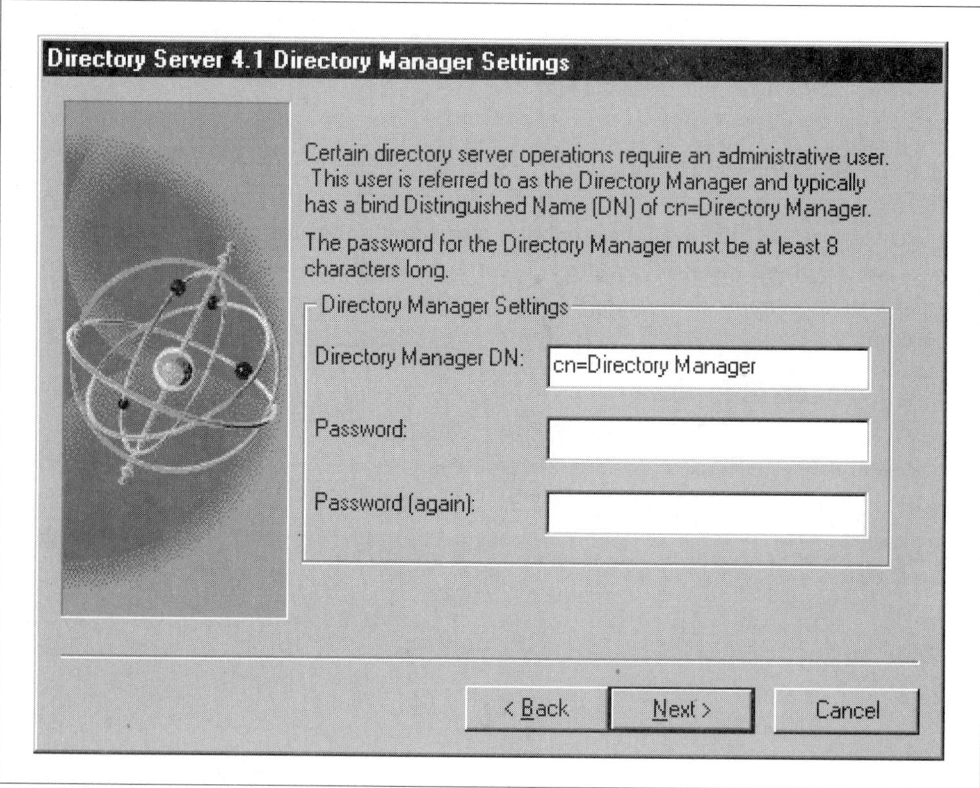

FIGURE 4-6. *Select Directory Manager ID and password.*

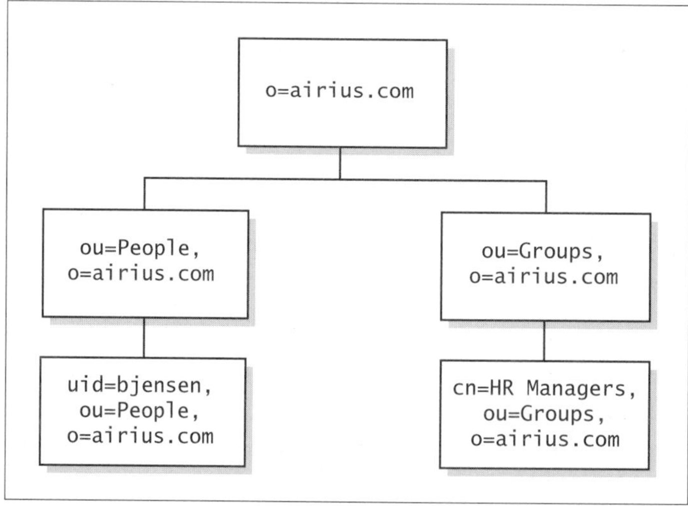

FIGURE 4-7. *Structure of the Airius database.*

Use the following command to find Barbara Jensen's entry in the directory:

```
java LDAPSearch -b "o=airius.com" "uid=bjensen"
```

> These examples assume that your directory is running on the same machine as Directory SDK for Java. The examples also assume that the server is running on port 389. If these assumptions are not correct, use the -h <hostname> option to specify the host name or IP address of the directory server, and use the -p <port number> option to specify the directory server port.

Use the following command to find any entry with the last name Jensen in Airius.com:

```
java LDAPSearch -b "o=airius.com" "sn=jensen"
```

Use the following command to display the e-mail addresses and telephone numbers of any entry with the last name Jensen in Airius.com:

```
java LDAPSearch -b "o=airius.com" "sn=jensen" mail telephoneNumber
```

Use the following command to find all entries at one level under the `o=airius.com` entry:

```
java LDAPSearch -b "o=airius.com" -s one "objectclass=*"
```

Use the following command to find all entries under the `ou=People, o=airius.com` entry:

```
java LDAPSearch -b "ou=People, o=airius.com" "objectclass=*"
```

Adding Entries to the Directory

To add an entry to the directory, you can use the `LDAPModify` command-line tool. Use the following syntax:

```
java LDAPModify -a [options]
```

The `-a` option indicates that you want to add entries to the directory. Some of the basic options you may want to specify include the following:

- **-h <hostname>.** Use this option to specify the host name or the IP address of Directory Server. If you have a directory server running on the same machine as Directory SDK for Java, you do not need to specify this option. By default, `LDAPModify` uses "localhost" as the host name.
- **-p <port number>.** Use this option to specify the port number of directory server. If your directory server is running on port 389 (the default port for LDAP), you do not need to specify this option. By default, `LDAPModify` uses 389 as the port number.
- **-D <bind DN>.** Use this option to specify the distinguished name of the user that you want to authenticate as. The sample `Airius.com` directory is set up to restrict most users from adding entries to it. One of the few users with permission to add an entry is the Directory Manager (whose DN and password you selected when you installed Directory Server). To add entries, you need to specify the `-D <bind DN>` option to authenticate as the Directory Manager.
- **-w <password>.** Use this option to specify the password of the user that you want to authenticate as. For example, when authenticating as the Directory Manager, use the `-w` option to specify the password for the Directory Manager.
- **-f <ldif_file>.** Use this option to specify the name of the file containing the entries you want to add. If you do not use this option, `LDAPModify` expects you to enter the entries directly at the command line. When you specify the entries to be added, you must use the LDAP Data Interchange Format (LDIF). LDIF is described in more detail in the next section.

You can also specify the `-H` option to get more information on the other options.

The next sections explain the LDIF file format and the types of entries you can add. The last section of the chapter provides examples of using `LDAPModify` to add entries.

Understanding LDIF: How to Describe a Directory Entry

The **LDAP Data Interchange Format** (LDIF) is a format for defining directory entries in text format. When you imported the sample database into the directory server, the sample data was in LDIF format. Before you can add your own entries to the sample database, you need to understand how to use the LDIF format to define the new entries.

An LDIF entry specifies the following information:

- **The distinguished name (DN) that identifies the entry.** The DN of an entry identifies its location in the directory. No two entries can have the same DN in a directory. For example, the DN `uid=bjensen, ou=People, o=Airius.com` identifies an entry for the user with the user name "bjensen." This entry is under the organizational unit `People` in the directory for the organization `Airius.com`.
- **The object classes that apply to the entry.** An object class defines the required and allowed attributes of an entry. For example, the object class for organization requires the attribute `o`, which identifies the organization (`o=Airius.com`). This object class also allows the attribute `telephoneNumber`, which represents the main telephone number of the organization. Object classes are described in more detail in the next section.
- **The attributes and corresponding values of the entry.** Attributes and their values specify information about an entry. For example, an entry describing a person named Barbara Jensen has the attributes `cn=Barbara Jensen` (`cn` identifies the common name of the person) and `sn=Jensen` (`sn` identifies the surname, or last name, of the person).

LDIF entries for adding data to a directory have the following format:

```
dn: <distinguished name>
objectClass: <object class>
objectClass: <object class>
...
<attribute type>[;optional subtype]: <attribute value>
<attribute type>[;optional subtype]: <attribute value>
...
```

> Unlike many other command-line tools, LDAPModify does not display usage information if you run the command without any options. LDAPModify expects you to enter data through standard input if you don't use the `-f <ldif_file>` option, so the tool will simply wait for you to enter LDIF data. If you want to see a list of the available options, you must specify the `-H`.

The following example is an LDIF entry for a user named Barbara Jensen:

```
dn: uid=bjensen, ou=People, o=airius.com
objectclass: top
objectclass: person
objectclass: organizationalPerson
objectclass: inetOrgPerson
cn: Barbara Jensen
cn: Babs Jensen
sn: Jensen
givenName: Barbara
ou: Product Development
ou: People
l: Cupertino
uid: bjensen
mail: bjensen@airius.com
telephoneNumber: +1 408 555 1862
facsimileTelephoneNumber: +1 408 555 1992
roomNumber: 0209
userPassword: hifalutin
```

This LDIF entry specifies the following information:

- Barbara Jensen's distinguished name is `uid=bjensen, ou=People, o=airius.com`.
- The entry for Barbara Jensen has four object classes: `top`, `person`, `organizationalPerson`, and `inetOrgPerson`.
- Some of the attributes for Barbara Jensen's entry include her first and last name, her e-mail address, and her telephone number.

You can break up any line into multiple lines if the line is long and you want the text to wrap around to the next line. Simply add a space at the beginning of each continued line. For example, suppose you want to break up the following lines into multiple lines:

```
cn: Barbara Jensen
cn: Babs Jensen
```

Add a space at the start of each line that continues the attribute definition:

```
cn: Barb
 ara Jen
```

```
 sen
cn: Babs Jen
 sen
```

If you want to see more examples of LDIF entries, use a text editor to open the `airiusplus.ldif` file (the file you imported into your directory earlier).

Object Classes: Determining What Information Makes Up an Entry

Object classes determine which attributes are required and which attributes are allowed in an entry. They effectively define a particular kind of entry. The following object classes are used for most of the entries in the sample directory:

- **`inetOrgPerson`.** This object class defines the type of entry that describes a person. The required attributes of entries with this object class are `cn`, which specifies the first and last name of the person (the common name), and `sn`, which specifies the last name of the person (the surname). When you add a new person to the directory, you must specify the `cn` and `sn` attributes in the LDIF entry for that person. Examples of allowed attributes for this object class include `mail` (the person's e-mail address) and `telephoneNumber` (the person's phone number). If an attribute is allowed, you can specify that attribute in the LDIF entry for that person.
- **`organizationalUnit`.** This object class defines the type of entry that describes an organizational unit. The only required attribute for this object class is `ou`, which specifies the name of the organizational unit. When you add an organizational unit to the directory, you must specify the `ou` attribute in the LDIF entry.
- **`organization`.** This object class defines the type of entry that describes an organization. The required attribute for this object class is `o`, which specifies the name of the organization. When you add an organization to the directory, you must specify the `o` attribute in the LDIF entry.

Object classes are defined in the schema of the directory. You can obtain a voluminous listing of all object classes and attributes with the `LDAPSchema.main` method, one of the classes in the SDK:

```
java netscape.ldap.LDAPSchema localhost 389
```

Replace `localhost` with the host name or IP address of your directory, and `389` with its port number.

If you have installed Netscape Directory Server, you can see a list of all object classes in the directory by using Directory Server Console:

1. Click on the Configuration tab. A two-pane window will be displayed: the left pane lists items that you can configure (including the database), and the right pane lists configuration options for the selected item.
2. Expand the Database item in the left pane, and select the Schema folder. In the right pane, a list of object classes for this directory is displayed under the Object Classes tab.
3. Select an object class from the list to display the required and allowed attributes for that class.

Appendix D lists the most commonly used LDAP object classes and attributes.

Choosing a Distinguished Name: Where Do You Want to Add the Entry?

One of the most important steps in creating a new entry is selecting the distinguished name for the entry. The DN identifies the entry and determines where the entry exists in the directory hierarchy.

In the sample database, most entries for people are located under the `ou=People, o=airius.com` entry. The DNs for these entries end with `ou=People, o=airius.com` (for example, `uid=bjensen, ou=People, o=airius.com`). If you are adding entries for people and want to add these entries under `ou=People, o=airius.com`, be sure that the DN for the entry ends with `ou=People, o=airius.com`.

If you want to add entries under your own organizational unit entry, you must add the organizational unit entry first. The directory does not create new parent entries automatically.

For example, suppose you want to add an entry with the distinguished name `uid=me, ou=My Group, o=airius.com`. You must first add the entry for `ou=My Group, o=airius.com`. Otherwise the server will report an error indicating that the entry `ou=My Group, o=airius.com` does not exist.

In addition, note that commas are used as delimiters in a DN. If you want to use a comma within a value (for example, `ou=Subsidiary, Ltd`), you must escape each comma with a backslash (for example, `ou=Subsidiary \, Ltd`).

Examples of Defining and Adding Entries

Now that you are familiar with the LDIF syntax, object classes, and distinguished names, you can create an LDIF file with new entries and use `LDAPModify` to add those entries to the directory.

Use a text editor to create a new LDIF file. When defining an LDIF entry, specify any required attributes for that entry. As you include attributes in an entry, be sure that those attributes are allowed for that type of entry.

If you are adding entries about people, use entries that have the object class `inetOrgPerson` if your directory server supports it. Netscape Directory Server and Novell Directory Services version 8 support the `inetOrgPerson` object class, and Microsoft Active Directory has a similar object class (`user`). These LDIF entries must include the following information:

```
dn: <distinguished name>
objectClass: top
objectClass: person
objectClass: organizationalPerson
objectClass: inetOrgPerson
cn: <first name and last name>
sn: <surname>
[any other allowed attributes that you want to specify]
...
```

For example, the following LDIF entry describes a person named Ulf Jensen:

```
dn: uid=ujensen, ou=People, o=airius.com
objectClass: top
objectClass: person
objectClass: organizationalPerson
objectClass: inetOrgPerson
cn: Ulf Jensen
sn: Jensen
uid: ujensen
mail: ujensen@airius.com
telephoneNumber: +1 408 555 1212
...
```

If you are adding entries for organizational units, you need to use entries that have the object class `organizationalUnit`. These LDIF entries must include the following information:

```
dn: <distinguished name>
objectClass: top
objectClass: organizationalUnit
ou: <name of the unit>
 [any other allowed attributes that you want to specify]
...
```

For example, the following LDIF entry describes an organizational unit named Quality Control:

```
dn: ou=Quality Control, o=airius.com
objectClass: top
objectClass: organizationalUnit
ou: Quality Control
...
```

Save the LDIF file and run `LDAPModify` to add the entries. For example, if the new entries are defined in a file named `entries.ldif` and if your Directory Manager has the DN `cn=Directory Manager` and the password "23skidoo," you can use the following command:

```
java LDAPModify -a -D "cn=Directory Manager" -w 23skidoo -f
    entries.ldif
```

Note that this example assumes you are running the directory on the same machine as Directory SDK for Java, as well as on port 389. If these assumptions are not correct, use the `-h <hostname>` option to specify the host name of the directory, and use the `-p <port number>` option to specify the Directory Server port number.

Conclusion

You have now installed a directory that you can search and update as you explore LDAP and Directory SDK for Java, and you've tried out a couple of the command-line tools included with the SDK to display and modify the directory contents. Chapter 5 will dive into Java programming for directories, introducing the support provided by the SDK for searching for information.

CHAPTER 5

Searching with the SDK

As you may recall from Chapter 1, the major feature of an LDAP directory is its ability to return search results on queries rapidly. The SDK provides many flexible methods for obtaining and handling search results from the directory. We will focus in this chapter on building queries using the SDK to retrieve the information we need.

The result set from a search can easily be parsed to return the entry's name and all or a subset of its attributes and values. In our discussion of searches, we will take an example-based approach. Most of the examples here can be run directly from the command-line interface with the `java` command. It is assumed that you have installed or have access to a directory server and have loaded the sample database from the LDIF file that is supplied on the CD-ROM that accompanies this book.

Our First Search

Before you can search an LDAP directory, you need certain information:

- **Host name** of the machine where the directory is installed
- **Port** number of the directory server
- **Base DN** of the directory tree managed by the server
- **Scope** of the search
- Search **filter**
- **Attributes** to request
- Optionally, **search preferences**

Host Name

The host name directs the search to the machine where the directory resides. This parameter is mandatory and is usually of the form `machinename.domain`—for example, `dirhost.acme.com`. If you are at the console on the machine that is running the LDAP server, you can use the host name "localhost" for your test server. You can specify the IP address of the host instead if you wish—for example, `127.0.0.1` for "localhost."

Port

The port is the TCP port of the machine (indicated by the host name) where the directory server is listening for LDAP connections. The standard port for LDAP is port 389 for non-SSL connections. You can use the constant `LDAPConnection.DEFAULT_PORT` for port 389. For SSL-based connections the default port is 636. This is not to say that you cannot have an LDAP server listening on any port you desire, but if you wish to communicate and make your services available to the widest audience, stick to the standard port numbers.

Base DN

The base distinguished name (DN) indicates where in the LDAP directory you wish to begin the search. An LDAP directory is arranged in tree fashion, with a root and various branches off this root. Figure 5-1 depicts a typical architecture. The base DN is used to indicate at which node the search should originate. For example, we could indicate a base of `o=airius.com` for a search that starts at the top and proceeds downward. If instead we specified a base DN of `ou=customers, o=airius.com`, then any entries above this tree level would not be eligible for searching. It is important to specify the base DN correctly to ensure that you receive the anticipated results.

Scope

Scope is the starting point of a search and the depth from the base DN to which the search should occur. There are three options (values) for the scope:

1. **`BASE`**, represented by the constant `LDAPConnection.SCOPE_BASE`, is used to indicate searching only the entry at the base DN, resulting in only that entry being returned (if it also meets the search filter criteria). Figure 5-2 depicts the scope of a base-level search.

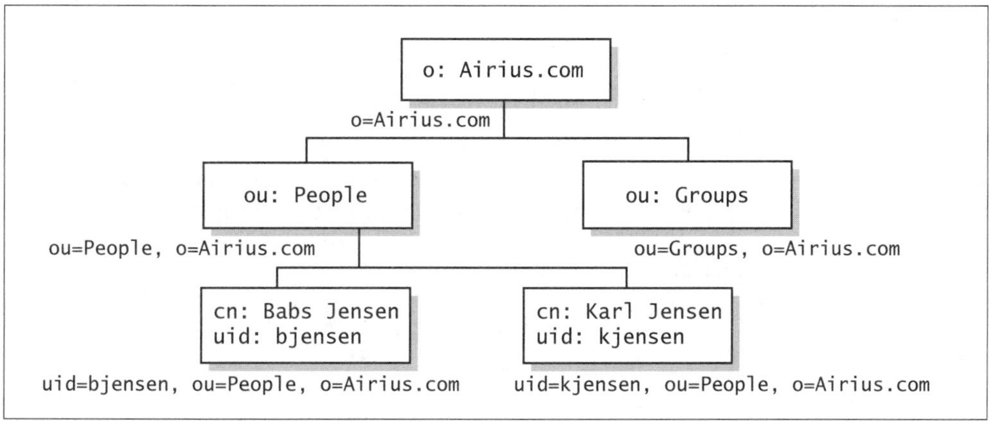

FIGURE 5-1. *Typical directory architecture.*

2. **ONE**, represented by the constant `LDAPConnection.SCOPE_ONE`, is used to indicate searching all entries one level under the base DN—but **not** including the base DN. Figure 5-3 depicts the scope of a one level search.

3. **SUBTREE**, represented by the constant `LDAPConnection.SCOPE_SUB`, is used to indicate searching of all entries at all levels under and *including* the specified base DN. Figure 5-4 depicts the scope of a subtree search.

The base DN and scope parameters can dramatically affect the number of records returned from a query. It is important to understand what is involved in using these arguments.

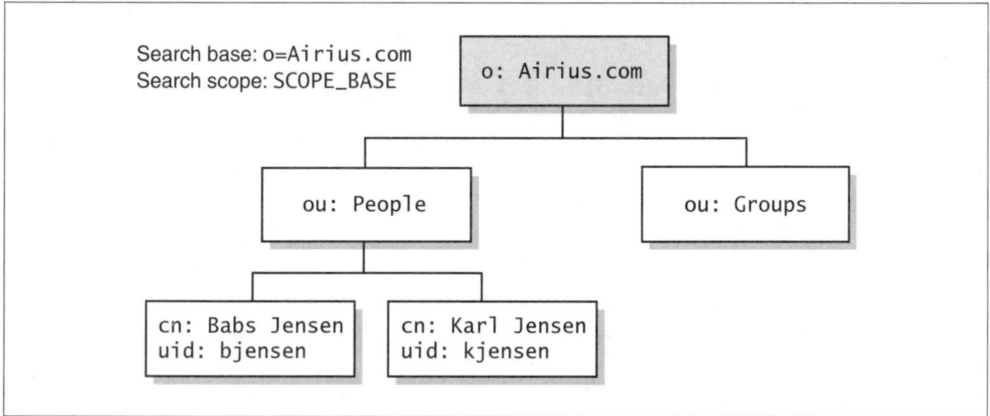

FIGURE 5-2. *Scope* BASE *search.*

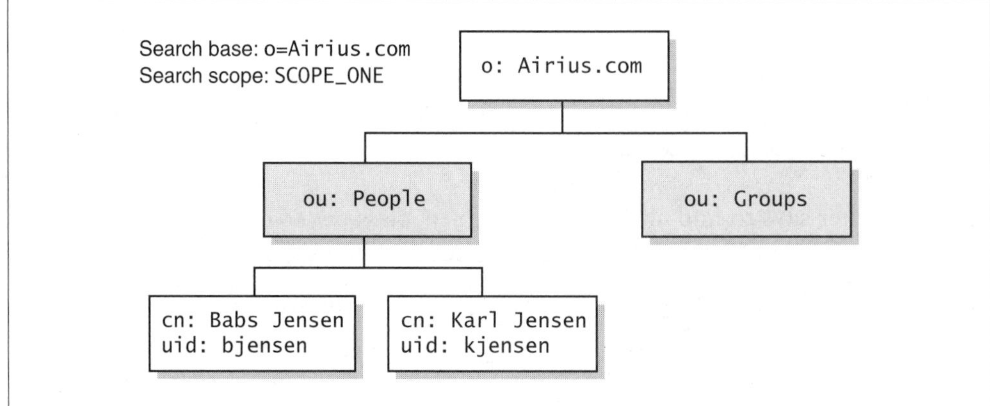

FIGURE 5-3. *Scope* ONE *search.*

Filter

The search filter is the query string. It is used to filter the entries in the directory and produce the desired set of matching records. Filters are built using parentheses and combinations of the symbols &, |, and !, which represent AND, OR, and NOT, respectively. If you wanted to locate all people with "tony" at the beginning of their names, the following filter would do the trick:

```
(&(objectclass=person)(cn=tony*))
```

This expression represents a search for all entries with an object class of type `person` in which the common name begins with "tony." Like most other LDAP attri-

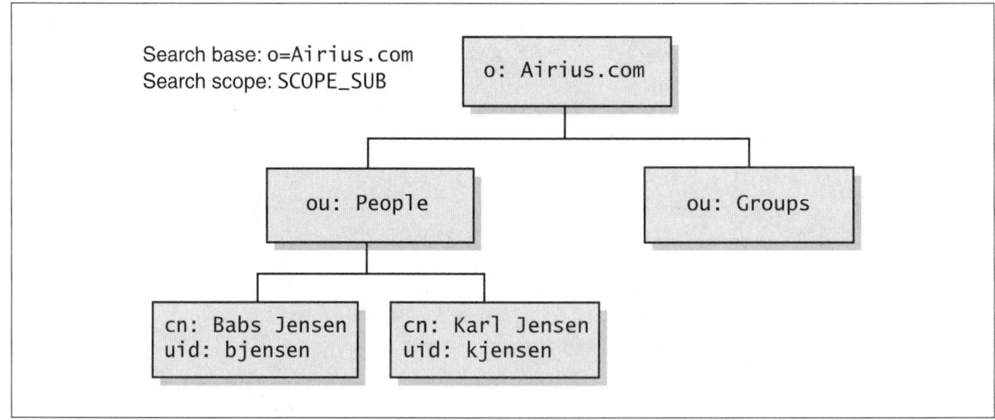

FIGURE 5-4. *Scope* SUBTREE *search.*

butes, the `cn` attribute has case-insensitive syntax, so replacing `tony*` with `Tony*` or `TONY*` would yield the same results.

Search filters can be nested to any level:

```
(&(objectclass=person)(|(cn=sam carter) (cn=tony*)))
```

This filter says to find all entries with object class `person` in which the common name is Sam Carter or begins with "tony." Complex filters can be built using the operators and corresponding parentheses. A logical operator should appear before the parenthesis enclosing the group of compares it affects. You can specify the order for operators by nesting parentheses.

Table 5-1 lists all the operators for a search filter. These options can be combined using parentheses, as shown in the examples already given. Wild cards can also be used for filters—for example, `(cn=tony*)`.

Attributes

Among the attributes of an LDAP entry for a person are `cn`, `sn`, and `givenName`. In the LDIF record for Babs Jensen that follows, the attribute names are marked in bold.

TABLE 5-1. *Search filter operators.*

OPERATOR	MEANING
|	OR
&	AND
!	NOT
=	Entry attribute equals value (e.g., `cn=John Doe`)
>=	Entry attribute is greater than or equal to value (e.g., `cn>=John Doe`, which would find Tom Doe among other entries)
<=	Entry attribute is less than or equal to value
=*	All entries that have a value for the attribute (e.g., `cn=*` for all entries with a `cn` value)
~=	Entries that approximately match the value—a soundex match for values that "sound like" the value (e.g., `cn~=olson` to match Olson, Olsson, and Oleson)

Each entry can contain numerous attributes—the specific ones determined by the object classes of the entry. Some attributes are optional for a particular object class, and some are required, as discussed in Chapter 2.

```
dn: uid=bjensen, ou=People, o=airius.com
cn: Babs Jensen
sn: Jensen
givenName: Barbara
objectclass: top
objectclass: person
l: Cupertino
uid: bjensen
mail: bjensen@airius.com
telephoneNumber: +1 408 555 1862
roomNumber: 0209
userPassword: hifalutin
```

The search attributes in a search request represent the values to return for records matching the filter, starting at the base DN and progressing through the scope level desired. You should request only attributes that you need. Requesting all attributes for a large result set can significantly increase processing time and memory usage. Note that specifying `null` for the attributes field of the `search` or `read` methods of `LDAPConnection` means to return *all* the attributes associated with each entry. If you wish to retrieve no attributes for an entry, use the constant `LDAPConnection.NO_ATTRS` for the attributes parameter.

LDAP attributes are either user attributes or operational attributes. **User attributes** appear in the directory only if they have been explicitly added to it, by the addition or modification of entries. **Operational attributes** are created by the server itself. Examples of operational attributes are `createTimeStamp` (the time when the entry was created) and `numSubordinates` (the number of direct children of the node). If you specify `null` for attributes in a search, operational attributes are not returned. Each operational attribute to be returned must be specified explicitly in the list of attributes. If you wish to receive operational attributes in addition to all user attributes, use the constant `LDAPConnection.ALL_USER_ATTRS` as one of the attributes—for example:

```
String[] attrs1 = { LDAPConnection.ALL_USER_ATTRS, "createTimeStamp",
                    "numSubordinates"};
String[] attrs2 = { "cn", "objectclass", "createTimeStamp",
                    "numSubordinates"};
```

The `String` array `attrs1` indicates to return all user attributes for this entry, as well as the two operational attributes `createTimeStamp` and `numSubordinates`. The

`String` array `attrs2` is used to return the two user attributes `cn` and `objectclass`, as well as the two operational attributes `createTimeStamp` and `numSubordinates`.

If you want to do client-side sorting of your result sets, you must include the attributes by which you are sorting as attributes to be returned by the server. If you are doing server-side sorting (which we will cover in Chapter 16), including these attributes is not necessary. Note that attribute names are always case-insensitive, so `{ "objectclass" }` is treated the same as "`{ "ObjectClass" }`" when specifying attributes to return. Also, you should not count on the server using the same case for names of attributes it returns.

Search Preferences

You may set certain preferences for a search. These preferences include the amount of time you wish to allow the server to spend on your search, the maximum number of records you will accept, and whether the search should wait (block) until all data is received or should return records as they are available. Search preferences are specified using the `LDAPSearchConstraints` class. Commonly used methods of `LDAPSearchConstraints` include the following:

- **`setBatchSize`** specifies how results are returned during a search. A value of zero indicates to wait until all results are in before returning them; a value of one means to return each result as it becomes available. The second option is useful if you want to populate a list and not make the user wait until everything is back before showing some data. On the other hand, if no data is to be processed until all results have arrived, it is more efficient to specify zero.
- **`setHopLimit`** specifies how many times a returned referral should be followed in finding a real entry. A referral is returned when a server does not contain the data being requested; instead it returns to the caller information on where the data resides. It is said to "refer" the caller to another source for the information.
- **`setMaxResults`** specifies the maximum number of results that should be returned from a search. For no limit on the number of results (unlimited returns), use a value of zero. Note that if this number is higher than the maximum number the server has been configured to return, you will get only the server's maximum, and an exception will be thrown indicating that the server size limit was exceeded.
- **`setReferrals`** specifies whether or not the SDK should follow referrals automatically.

- **`setServerTimeLimit`** specifies the maximum number of seconds for the server to spend on delivering search results.

All options for searching and other LDAP operations are covered in more detail in Chapter 14.

The following examples demonstrate setting these options:

```
// Get the preferences associated with this connection
LDAPSearchConstraints cons = ld.getSearchConstraints();
cons.setBatchSize( 1 );
cons.setHopLimit ( 5 );
cons.setMaxResults( 0 );
cons.setReferrals( true );
cons.setServerTimeLimit( 5 );
```

Our First Search Program

The following program is a command line-based Java search program. It assumes that the `airius.com` sample database was loaded as described in Chapter 4. The program provides a framework to try out different search filters. Let's look at the code for `FilterSearch.java`:

```
import netscape.ldap.*;
import java.util.*;

/**
 * Simple search program to experiment with filters
 */
public class FilterSearch {

    /**
     * Do a subtree search using a specified filter
     *
     * @parm args host, port, authDN, password, baseDN, filter
     */
    public static void main( String[] args ) {

        if ( args.length != 6 ) {
            System.out.println( "Usage: java FilterSearch " +
                                "<host> <port> " +
                                "<authdn> <password> " +
                                "<baseDN> <filter>" );
            System.out.println( "Example:" );
            System.out.println( "   java FilterSearch " +
```

```
                                  "localhost 389 " +
                                  "\"\" \"\" " +
                                  "\"o=airius.com\" " +
                                  "\"(|(cn=sam*)(cn=b*))\"" );
            System.exit(1);
        }
```

The code declares some needed values, including the host name of the machine and the port on which the LDAP server is listening.

The next section of code sets up our search constraints. The only value we set is to block on one result at a time. This setting will cause our program to get one value and allow us to display it while the next value is being retrieved from the server.

```
        String host = args[0];
        int port = Integer.parseInt( args[1] );
        String authid = args[2];
        String authpw = args[3];
        String base = args[4];
        String filter = args[5];
        String[] ATTRS = {"cn","mail","telephoneNumber"};

        int status = -1;
        LDAPConnection ld = new LDAPConnection();
        try {
            // Connect to server and authenticate
            ld.connect( host, port, authid, authpw );
```

The `getSearchConstraints` method returns a copy of the preferences in the connection. In addition, this program allows connecting with a user DN and password. An LDAPv3 server will assume an anonymous authentication if no user DN and password are specified. If communicating with an LDAPv2 server, you must authenticate, even if binding anonymously (for an anonymous bind, use empty strings for the user DN and password). We will cover authentication in detail in Chapter 6.

The program takes as input a search filter and does a `search` with a scope of `LDAPConnection.SCOPE_SUB`. Recall that `SCOPE_SUB` indicates searching all entries at all levels under and including the specified base DN. We specify the base DN as the top of our tree (`o=airius.com`).

```
            System.out.println( "Search filter=" + filter );
            LDAPSearchResults res = ld.search( base,
                                               ld.SCOPE_SUB,
                                               filter,
```

```
                                          ATTRS,
                                          false );

            // Loop on results until complete
            while ( res.hasMoreElements() ) {
                try {
                    // Next directory entry
                    LDAPEntry entry = res.next();
```

Once the search request is issued, we retrieve each eligible record and send it to `prettyPrint` for display on the console, as the following code shows. For now, we will ignore any referrals returned by the server. Referrals are discussed in detail in Chapter 16. If any errors result in an exception (`netscape.ldap.LDAPException`), we just print the error and continue to process any remaining results. All classes in the SDK have a `toString` method, which provides useful information about the state of each object.

```
                    prettyPrint( entry, ATTRS );
                    status = 0;
                } catch ( LDAPReferralException e ) {
                    // Ignore referrals
                    continue;
                } catch ( LDAPException e ) {
                    System.out.println( e.toString() );
                    continue;
                }
            }

        } catch( LDAPException e ) {
          System.out.println( e.toString() );
        }
```

The following block disconnects us from the LDAP server.

```
        // Done, so disconnect
        if ( (ld != null) && ld.isConnected() ) {
            try {
                ld.disconnect();
            } catch ( LDAPException e ) {
                System.out.println( e.toString() );
            }
        }

        System.exit( status );
    }
```

The method `prettyPrint` takes a returned entry and the array of the attributes we requested and pulls the values from the search result:

```
    /**
     * Print names and values of attributes in an entry
     *
     * @param entry entry containing attributes
     * @param attrs array of attribute names to display
     */
    public static void prettyPrint( LDAPEntry entry,
                                    String[] attrs ) {
       System.out.println( "DN: " + entry.getDN() );

        // Use array to pick attributes. We could have
        // enumerated them all using LDAPEntry.getAttributes
        // but this gives us control of the display order.
        for ( int i = 0; i < attrs.length; i++ ) {
            LDAPAttribute attr =
                entry.getAttribute( attrs[i] );
            if ( attr == null ) {
                System.out.println( attrs[i] +
                                    " not present" );
                continue;
            }
            Enumeration enumVals = attr.getStringValues();
            // Enumerate on values for this attribute
            boolean hasVals = false;
            while ( (enumVals != null) &&
                    enumVals.hasMoreElements() ) {
                String val = (String)enumVals.nextElement();
                System.out.println( attrs[i] + ": " + val );
                hasVals = true;
            }
            if ( !hasVals ) {
                System.out.println( attrs[i] +
                                   " has no values" );
            }
        }
        System.out.println("----------");
    }
}
```

The value or values for each attribute are obtained with `getStringValues`, which returns an `Enumeration`. Most LDAP attributes are strings, but some are binary. Examples of binary attributes are `userCertificate;binary` and `jpegPhoto`.

It is up to you, the programmer, to specify if you want the values delivered to you as strings or as binaries. The alternative interface is `getBinaryValues`. There is no way to query the directory to determine whether it is appropriate to call `getStringValues` or `getBinaryValues` on an attribute. As a programmer you must have some understanding of the data type represented in a particular attribute. For standard LDAP attributes the data type is typically a known format that is the same in all applications.

Data from the directory is always returned in binary or UTF8 format, not in any other character set (such as latin-1 or shift-jis). Strings are represented internally in UTF8 format, a form of Unicode, which allows representation of all the world's languages. When you call `getBinaryValues`, the SDK gives you the values exactly as they are stored in the directory. If you call `getStringValues`, the SDK attempts to convert the values into Java `String` objects, which are in UCS2 (another Unicode format), before returning them. If the data cannot be converted, which might be the case with the value of a `jpegPhoto` attribute, for example, then `getStringValues` returns `null`.

Using Search Filters

You should type in the code or load it from the CD-ROM and compile, using the following command:

```
javac FilterSearch.java
```

Let's execute some searches and see what different filters return:

```
java FilterSearch localhost 389 "" "" "o=airius.com" "(cn=sam carter)"
java FilterSearch localhost 389 "" "" "o=airius.com" "(cn=Sam Carter)"
```

These two commands will return the same single record, demonstrating that case does not matter in a search for the common name (which is defined in the LDAP server as a case-insensitive attribute):

```
dn: uid=scarter, ou=People, o=airius.com
cn: Sam Carter
mail: scarter@airius.com
telephoneNumber: +1 408 555 4798
```

Now let's try a more complex search filter. The following request will return a series of results. You will get all members whose names begin with "sam," "tony," or the letter *J*.

```
java FilterSearch localhost 389 "" "" "o=airius.com"
    "(|(cn=sam*)(cn=tony*)(cn=j*))"
```

The next search uses the telephone number field.

```
java FilterSearch localhost 389 "" "" "o=airius.com"
    "(telephoneNumber=650-9*)"
java FilterSearch localhost 389 "" "" "o=airius.com"
    "(telephoneNumber=6509*)"
```

One complication that arises with telephone numbers in many contexts is that some people store them as (XXX) XXX-XXXX, others use the syntax XXX-XXX-XXXX, and some may just store the digits (XXXXXXXXXX). It would be cumbersome if anyone doing a search had to know how each person had entered the telephone number. LDAP defines a special telephone number syntax for the `telephoneNumber` attribute. To enter a phone number to be searched, you can use any of the three formats described here, and the LDAP server strips the expression down to just the numbers before performing the comparison. The LDAP standard document RFC 2252 specifies many different syntaxes for attributes beyond the one most commonly used: case-insensitive string.

The following search is interesting:

```
java FilterSearch localhost 389 "" "" "o=airius.com" "(cn~=brian)"
```

This search uses the "sounds like" operator (see Table 5-1). The following results will be displayed:

```
Search filter=(cn~=brian)
DN: uid=bplante, ou=People, o=airius.com
cn: Brian Plante
mail: bplante@airius.com
telephoneNumber: +1 408 555 3550
----------
DN: uid=jbrown, ou=People, o=airius.com
cn: Judy Brown
mail: jbrown@airius.com
telephoneNumber: +1 408 555 6885
----------
```

The results indicate that "Brown" sounds close to "Brian" according to the syntax rules of the server, and of course Brian was found as well.

Any attribute that is in the directory and is not protected with access control from searches by an anonymous user is eligible to be searched against, as shown here:

```
java FilterSearch localhost 389 "" "" "o=airius.com" "(&(
    (objectclass=person) (cn=t*) (|(telephoneNumber=>650*) (mail=*))))"
```

This search expression indicates that we want all records in which (1) the entry includes the object class `person`, (2) the first name begins with the letter *T*, and (3) the area code of the telephone number is greater than or equal to 650 or the entry has a `mail` attribute. Note the syntax for mail: =*. This syntax indicates that we want every entry that contains a value for this attribute. The asterisk is a presence indicator when used in isolation on the right-hand side of a filter expression.

Handling Results

A significant aspect of working with LDAP searches is processing the results after issuing the query. The results from the search are returned as an `LDAPSearchResults` object, which implements `Enumeration`. Note that once you iterate over the result set, it is not available anymore. If you must do multiple passes over the result set, then you must save the values in a store that is internal to your program.

There are two methods for iteration: `nextElement` and `next`. The `nextElement` method returns `Object`, which could be `LDAPEntry`, `LDAPReferralException`, or `LDAPException`. You are responsible for detecting the type of result (using `instanceof`) and taking appropriate action. The `next` method returns `LDAPEntry` and may throw an `LDAPReferralException` or an `LDAPException`. We recommend using `next` in most cases.

When the `next` method of `LDAPSearchResults` is called, there are three possible consequences. The first is that an entry is returned as an `LDAPEntry` object. The second possibility is that you will be passed a referral (search reference) exception. This might happen if there is a referral configured in the directory tree you are searching and you have not set up the SDK to follow referrals automatically. The third possibility is that you will receive an `LDAPException`, which might happen if, for example, the entry specified as the base DN does not exist.

If referrals are followed automatically and if the referral hop limit has not been exceeded, the LDAP Java classes follow the referral and retrieve the entry for you and you will never get a referral exception, even when the classes are creating a new connection to the referred-to server in order to retrieve the entry for you. The default setting in the SDK is to *not* follow referrals automatically, so you might encounter one if you used the FilterSearch code above. You can indicate that you want automatic referral handling with the following code:

```
ld = new LDAPConnection();
ld.getSearchConstraints().setReferrals( true );
```

Referrals are discussed in detail in Chapter 16.

The `next` method of `LDAPSearchResults` returns an `LDAPEntry` object. The `LDAPEntry` class contains the following four methods:

1. **`getDN`** returns the full distinguished name of the entry as a `String` (for example, `uid=scarter, ou=People, o=airius.com`).
2. **`getAttribute( String name )`** takes a `String` argument of the attribute name that we are interested in retrieving and returns an object that represents this attribute. The return type is `LDAPAttribute`. An optional argument that identifies a language subtype can also be specified. Language subtypes (part of the LDAP RFC 2596) can be used to store different values for a single attribute in an environment where clients specify the language in which they want to view directory contents. Such attributes include a semicolon and the language subtype when they are added to the directory. For example:

   ```
   givenName;lang-en: John
   givenName;lang-fr: Jean
   givenName;lang-sp: Juan
   ```

   If all three values were present in an entry, you could retrieve the third one with the following code:

   ```
   LDAPEntry.getAttribute( "givenName", "lang-sp" );
   ```

   If the specified attribute does not exist in the entry, `null` is returned.

3. **`getAttributeSet`** returns an `LDAPAttributeSet` object that represents all the attributes in this entry. You can then call the `getAttributes` method of the `LDAPAttributeSet` to obtain an `Enumeration` on all the attributes in the entry:

   ```
   LDAPAttributeSet attrs = theEntry.getAttributeSet();
   Enumeration enum_attrs = attrs.getAttributes();  //allows iterating
                                                    //each one
   ```

4. **`toString`** returns the entire entry, including all the attributes retrieved, as a `String`. This method is useful for debugging and is called by the compiler when a conversion to `String` is implied. For example,

```
System.out.println( "This is what was returned: " + theEntry );
```

Once we have the attributes that are present in the entry, we can obtain the values for these attributes. The `LDAPAttribute` class has many methods for dealing with the attribute and its values. The methods most commonly used are the following:

- **`getStringValues`** returns an `Enumeration` of the values for a particular attribute as `Strings`. Remember that in LDAP, many attributes may have more than one value.
- **`getName`** returns the name of the attribute (for example, `mail` or `cn`).

If we examine the `prettyPrint` method, we can see the calls needed to extract the attribute values from an entry:

```
public static void prettyPrint( LDAPEntry entry,
                                String[] attrs ) {
```

The following line displays the DN of an entry, which we get by using the `getDN` method of `LDAPEntry`.

```
System.out.println("DN: "+theEntry.getDN() );
```

Knowing the DN of an entry is very important to an application developer, because it provides a method to obtain the entry uniquely if we should need to retrieve it again.

To specify the attributes to be extracted from the entry, the next block of code uses the `attrs` array, which contains `{"cn","telephoneNumber","mail"}`.

```
// Use array to pick attributes. We could have
// enumerated them all using LDAPEntry.getAttributes,
// but this gives us control of the display order.
for ( int i = 0; i < attrs.length; i++ ) {
    LDAPAttribute attr =
        entry.getAttribute( attrs[i] );
    if ( attr == null ) {
        System.out.println( attrs[i] +
                            " not present" );
        continue;
    }
```

Note that we check if any attribute is `null` for an entry. The value `null` indicates that the attribute is not present in this entry. Any attribute that is not mandatory for an entry may be omitted and will then not be returned during a search. Another popular programming method for handling attributes is just to enumerate over the values for the entry. We will examine a version of `prettyPrint` a bit later that will use this method.

After reaching this point, we know the entry has the attribute, but we do not know if the attribute has a value. Formally, LDAP does not allow attributes with no values, but it does allow attributes with a `null` value. Many attributes in an LDAP directory can have multiple values. For example, the `telephoneNumber` attribute could contain one or more telephone numbers. The following block of code gets the attribute values and handles multivalue situations by calling `LDAPAttribute.getStringValues`, which returns an `Enumeration` of the values:

```
Enumeration enumVals = attr.getStringValues();
// Enumerate on values for this attribute
boolean hasVals = false;
while ( (enumVals != null) &&
        enumVals.hasMoreElements() ) {
    String val = (String)enumVals.nextElement();
    System.out.println( attrs[i] + ": " + val );
    hasVals = true;
}
if ( !hasVals ) {
    System.out.println( attrs[i] +
                        " has no values" );
}
```

Finally, we mark the end of the output for this record:

```
        }
        System.out.println("----------");
    }
}
```

Attributes in Detail

One of the three following conditions will be true for an attribute in an entry: the attribute is present but has no value (actually a `null` value), the attribute is not present, or the attribute is present and has one or more values:

1. *Attribute present in entry with no value.* The following abbreviated LDIF record shows that this entry has the `telephoneNumber` attribute, but that the attribute has no value.

```
dn: uid=andy1, ou=People, o=airius.com
ou: People
cn: Andy Jones
...
telephoneNumber:
```

This is a valid condition, and when `prettyPrint` executes, it does not print the attribute in the listing. Code that detects this condition sets the boolean flag `hasVals` inside the enumeration loop:

```
while ( enumVals.hasMoreElements() ) {
    ...
    hasVals = true;
```

The output from `prettyPrint` is as follows:

```
Search filter=(uid=andy*)
DN: uid=andy1, ou=People, o=airius.com
cn: Andy James
mail: andy1@airius.com
telephoneNumber HAS NO VALUES
```

2. *Attribute not present.* As indicated by the following LDIF record, if the attribute is not mandatory for any of the object classes of the entry, then it may or may not be present.

```
dn: uid=andy2, ou=People, o=airius.com
ou: People
objectclass: top
objectclass: person
objectclass: organizationalPerson
objectclass: inetOrgPerson
cn: Andy James
```

The corresponding code in `prettyPrint` that handles this situation is as follows:

```
if (attr == null) {
    System.out.println(ATTRS[i] + " NOT PRESENT");
    continue;
}
```

Keep in mind that just because you requested a particular attribute does not mean that every entry will contain the attribute. If we had used the enumerated set returned by `getAttributes`, the `telephoneNumber` attribute would not have been in the enumeration. If using the enumeration, your program would need to track which attributes were returned for each entry. Otherwise, use the `getAttribute` method to retrieve a specific attribute; if `null` is returned, then the attribute is not present for this particular entry.

The output from `prettyPrint` is as follows:

```
DN: uid=andy2, ou=People, o=airius.com
cn: Andy Jones
mail: andy2@airius.com
telephoneNumber NOT PRESENT
```

3. *Attribute present and has one or more values.* This condition is the most common for most searches. The following LDIF record has multiple values for the `telephoneNumber` attribute. Often programmers are interested in only one value, but they must be prepared for the occurrence of multiple values.

```
dn: uid=andy3, ou=People, o=airius.com
ou: People
...
cn: Andy Stevens
telephoneNumber: 650-555-1212
telephoneNumber: 650-555-1213
```

The output from `prettyPrint` is as follows:

```
DN: uid=andy3, ou=People, o=airius.com
cn: Andy Stevens
mail: andy3@airius.com
telephoneNumber: 650-555-1212
telephoneNumber: 650-555-1213
```

I Want Only One Record and I Have the DN

The DN uniquely identifies a single entry in the directory. In some situations you have the DN (for example, because you saved it or because information is provided to allow you to build it), and you want to retrieve the single record corresponding to the DN. The `read` method of the `LDAPConnection` class provides this functionality. Although not as flexible as issuing a full search, this method provides the benefit of retrieving the single uniquely identified record with few parameters required. Within the SDK the method is just a search with the scope set to SCOPE_BASE and the filter to objectclass=*.

The following code is a modification of FilterSearch that takes a DN as argument instead of a search base and filter.

```
public class EntryRead {

    /**
     * Read an entry from the directory and display the contents
     *
     * @param args host, port, authDN, password, dn
     */
    public static void main( String[] args ) {

        if ( args.length != 5 ) {
            System.out.println( "Usage: java EntryRead " +
                                "<host> <port> " +
                                "<authdn> <password> " +
                                "<dn>" );
            System.out.println( "Example:" );
            System.out.println( "    java EntryRead " +
                            "localhost 389 " +
                            "\"\" \"\" " +
                            "\"uid=scarter, ou=People, " +
                                "o=airius.com\"" );
            System.exit(1);
        }

        String host = args[0];
        int port = Integer.parseInt( args[1] );
        String authid = args[2];
        String authpw = args[3];
        String base = args[4];
        String[] ATTRS = { "cn","mail","telephoneNumber" };

        int status = -1;
        LDAPConnection ld = new LDAPConnection();
        try {
            // Connect to server and authenticate
            ld.connect( host, port, authid, authpw );

            LDAPEntry entry = ld.read( base, ATTRS );
            prettyPrint( entry, ATTRS );
```

```
                status = 0;
            } catch ( LDAPReferralException e ) {
                // Ignore referrals
            } catch ( LDAPException e ) {
                System.out.println( e.toString() );
            }

            // Done, so disconnect
            if ( (ld != null) && ld.isConnected() ) {
             try {
                    ld.disconnect();
                } catch ( LDAPException e ) {
                    System.out.println( e.toString() );
                }
            }
            System.exit( status );
        }
    }
```

The method `prettyPrint` here is the same as in `FilterSearch`.

Executing the program with the following command:

```
java EntryRead localhost 389 "" "" "uid=scarter, ou=People, o=airius.com"
```

will result in the following output:

```
DN: uid=scarter, ou=People, o=airius.com
cn: Sam Carter
mail: scarter@airius.com
telephoneNumber: +1 408 555 4798
```

Searching and Comparing

The LDAP SDK allows you to compare a value in memory to the value of an attribute of an entry without actually retrieving the entry. This is called a **`compare`** operation. In many ways a `compare` can be simulated using a `search` by setting the scope of the `search` to `SCOPE_BASE` and providing a search filter with which the value can be compared; if an entry is returned, the `compare` operation was successful. A `compare`, however, may improve performance because the return data from the LDAP server is a small packet that says either that the value is the same or that it is different.

Let's examine a small piece of code to compare a specific record and see if the `l` attribute (the LDAP attribute for location) has the value `Santa Clara`. The following code is abbreviated to show simply how to call the `compare` method of `LDAPConnection`.

```
String ENTRYDN = "uid=scarter, ou=People, o=Airius.com";
LDAPAttribute attr = new LDAPAttribute( "l","Santa Clara" );
try {
    LDAPConnection ld = new LDAPConnection();
    ld.connect(HOST, PORT); //connect to server
    boolean ok = ld.compare( ENTRYDN, attr );
    if (ok) {
        System.out.println("Values matched!");
    } else {
        System.out.println("No Match!");
    }
} catch (LDAPException e) {
    System.out.println( "Error: " + e.toString() );
}
```

The `compare` method takes a DN, an `LDAPAttribute` object representing the attribute you wish to compare and the value to compare, and an optional `LDAPSearchConstraints` object. The method returns `true` if the entry has the attribute and specified value and `false` if the entry does not have the value or the attribute. An exception is thrown if the entry does not exist.

More on Filters

In the previous sections we spent a great deal of time on filters and the syntax to build them. Although filters are incredibly powerful, the power is magnified tenfold if we can build them dynamically (at run time) using templates. Take the case of providing a user with a text field in which to type some search data. How can we form a search using this data? The user might type in a phone number, or she might type in "tony." We should choose a search filter that includes `sn` in one case but `telephoneNumber` in the other case. It would also be wasteful to use a search of the form `(|(cn=searchstring)(telephoneNumber=searchstring))`, since the server is comparing against extra fields that are not needed and it might return unwanted results.

A filter configuration file allows building rules that can present the filter based on input at run time. The filter configuration file has the following format:

Tag					
	pattern	delimiters	filter1-1	description	(optional scope)
			filter1-n	description	(optional scope)
	pattern2	delimiters	filter2-1	description	(optional scope)

As an example, let's look at a filter configuration file we will be using:

"search"

"="	" "	"%v"	"arbitrary"
"^[0-9][0-9-]*$"	" "	"(telephoneNumber=*%v*)"	"phone number"
"@"	" "	"(mail=%v)"	"email address"
		"(mail=%v*)"	"start of email"
"^.[. _].*"	". _"	"(cn=%v1* %v2-)"	"first initial"
".*[. _].$"	". _"	"(cn=%v1-*)"	"last initial"
"[. _]"	". _"	"(|(sn=%v1-)(cn=%v1-))"	"exact"
		"(|(sn~=%v1-)(cn~=%v1-))"	"approximate"
"*"	"."	"(|(cn=%v1)(sn=%v1)(uid=%v1))"	"exact"
		"(|(cn~=%v1)(sn~=%v1))"	"approximate"

The tag is used to identify a block of patterns, allowing the mixing of multiple patterns in a single filter configuration file. The filter configuration file shown here has only one tag, named `search`. The patterns are regular expressions that are applied to the search string entered by the user. The first pattern—"="—indicates that if the search string entered by the user contains "=" anywhere, then the designated filter, in this case `%v`, should be applied.

Filters are built using the text entered by the user and static text from the configuration file. The filter `%v` indicates a variable substitution. By itself, `%v` means the whole string entered by the user. If we used the template `(mail=%v)` and the user entered "tony@abc.com," a filter string of `(mail=tony@abc.com)` would be built.

The filter `%v` has a series of different modifiers. Assume for the examples shown in Table 5-2 that the search string is "this is a test." Words are determined and split on the basis of the characters entered in the second column of the configuration file—the delimiter column.

Returning to our configuration file example, if the user enters a string of the form "cn=tony" (in the pattern "="), then the first rule will be used: return a filter consisting of the whole string entered by the user. This pattern allows advanced users to directly build their own filters at run time. The next pattern—`^[0-9][0-9-]*$`—is used to detect if a phone number has been entered. The character ^ indicates to start at

TABLE 5-2. *"This is a test" search.*

SYNTAX	ENTITY REPRESENTED	SAMPLE	RESULT
`%v`	Whole value entered	`%v`	`"this is a test"`
`%vN`	Word N	`%v2`	`"is"`
`%vN-`	Word N and all words following	`%v2-`	`"is a test"`
`%vN-M`	Words N through M	`%v3-4`	`"a test"`
`%v$`	Last word	`%v$`	`"test"`

the beginning and use the filter if the search string contains one or more digits: if the user types one or more digits, then return the filter `(telephoneNumber=*digits*)`.

The following Java command-line program will allow you to try out filters and `search` commands. The program presents all the filters that match a search string and builds a filter expression that can be issued to an LDAP search.

```
import netscape.ldap.*;
import netscape.ldap.util.*;
import java.util.*;

// Class to experiment with filter configuration files
public class CreateFilter {

    public static void main( String[] args ) {

        if ( args.length != 2 ) {
            System.out.println( "Usage: java CreateFilter " +
                                "<filterfile> <search " +
                                "expression> ");
            System.out.println( "Example:" );
            System.out.println( "    java CreateFilter " +
                                "tryfilt.conf \"*peter*\"" );
            System.exit( 1 );
        }

        LDAPFilterDescriptor filterDesc = null;
        LDAPFilterList filtlist = null;
        String srchfilter = "";
        int numfilts = 0;
```

```
        try {
            // Read a filter configuration file
            filterDesc = new LDAPFilterDescriptor( args[0] );
        } catch (Exception e) {
            System.out.println( "Cannot load file: " +
                                args[0] );
            System.exit(0);
        }

        try {
            // Construct filters from the parsed configuration
            // file and the search expression from the command
            // line
            filtlist =
                filterDesc.getFilters( "search", args[1] );
            numfilts = filtlist.numFilters();
            if ( numfilts > 1 ) {
                srchfilter += "(|";
            }
            // Iterate through constructed expressions
            while ( filtlist.hasMoreElements() ) {
                LDAPFilter fline = filtlist.next();
                String fstr = fline.getFilter();
                System.out.println( "Filter = " + fstr );
                // Concatenate the individual matches
                srchfilter += fstr;
            }
            if ( numfilts > 1 ) {
                srchfilter += ")";
            }
        } catch ( Exception e ) {
            System.out.println( "Filter error: " +
                                e.toString() );
        }
        System.out.println( "Search filter = " +
                            srchfilter );
    }
}
```

Some sample runs and corresponding output follow:

```
java CreateFilter tryfilt.conf 213
filter=(telephoneNumber=*213*)
search string=(|(telephoneNumber=*213*))
```

The above response indicates that a number was detected and that the filter for `telephoneNumber` was built. The value typed by the user—213—was inserted into a search string. Note that the program builds a search string by prepending it with "(|" and appending it with ")". The search string is built in this way to handle the case in which multiple filters may be returned, as in the next example:

```
java CreateFilter tryfilt.conf tony
filter=(|(cn=tony)(sn=tony)(uid=tony))
filter=(|(cn~=tony)(sn~=tony))
search string=(|(|(cn=tony)(sn=tony)(uid=tony))(|(cn~=tony)
(sn~=tony)))
```

Let's focus on the code used to handle the input and return these filters. Before anything can occur with a filter configuration, an `LDAPFilterDescriptor` object needs to be created. The constructor for an `LDAPFilterDescriptor` can take a file name, a `StringBuffer` containing the filter configuration information, or a URL to the filter file (allowing the file to exist anywhere on the Web).

The following instruction will read the file.

```
LDAPFilterDescriptor filtdesc = new LDAPFilterDescriptor("filename");
```

The next step is to call the `getFilters` method, passing in your search string and the tag for the section to use as an example:

```
LDAPFilterList filtlist = filltdesc.getFilters("tag","search string");
```

This method will return an enumerated list that can be iterated over to retrieve each filter and other information.

The following code fragment shows how to enumerate the filters.

```
while (filtlist.hasMoreElements()) {
    LDAPFilter fline = filtlist.next();
    System.out.println("description:"+ fline.getDescription());
    System.out.println("filter="+ fline.getFilter());
}
```

The primary information we need to retrieve is the filter, which is obtained with the `getFilter` method.

There are many advantages to using filter configuration files. They eliminate the need to predefine searches in the code, and they provide flexibility at run time for dynamically tailoring a query based on information provided by a user. The CD-ROM for this book contains a graphical Java application, a screen shot of which is shown in Figure 5-5. The application takes a search string entered by a user and issues a query against the directory. The results are displayed in a scrollable text box. The code demonstrates use of a filter configuration file, the searching functions of the LDAP SDK, and some AWT (Abstract Windows Toolkit) user interface code as well. The code is presented here for review, and it will be extended in the next section in our discussion of client-side sorting.

```
import java.lang.*;
import java.awt.*;
import java.awt.event.*;
import netscape.ldap.*;
import netscape.ldap.util.*;
import java.util.*;

/**
 * Frame to select filters from a filter file and do searches
 */

public class FilterSearchDialog extends Frame {

    /**
     * Launch a frame to do searches using a filter file
     *
     * @param args host, port, authDN, password, base
     */
    public static void main( String[] args ) {
        if ( (args.length != 4) &&
             (args.length != 6 ) ) {
            System.out.println( "Usage: java " +
                                "FilterSearchDialog " +
                                "<host> <port> " +
                                "<filterfile> <baseDN> " +
                                "[<authdn> <password>]" );
            System.out.println( "Example:" );
            System.out.println( "    java " +
                               "FilterSearchDialog " +
                               "localhost 389 " +
                               "filter.conf \"o=airius.com\"" );
            System.exit(1);
        }

        String host = args[0];
        int port = Integer.parseInt( args[1] );
        String conf = args[2];
```

```
        String base = args[3];
        String authid = "";
        String authpw = "";
        if ( args.length > 4 ) {
            authid = args[4];
            authpw = args[5];
        }

        Frame f = new FilterSearchDialog(
            "Graphical LDAP Search", host, port,
            authid, authpw, conf, base );
        f.setSize( 430,280 );
        f.show();
    }

    /**
     * Standard Frame constructor, plus connection parameters
     *
     * @param title window title
     * @param host host to search
     * @param port port number of server
     * @param authid DN to authenticate as (may be "")
     * @param authpw password for authentication (may be "")
     * @param conf name of filter configuration file
     * @param base base DN for subtree search
     */
    public FilterSearchDialog( String title,
                               String host, int port,
                               String authdn, String authpw,
                               String conf, String base ) {
        super( title );

        this.host = host;
        this.port = port;
        this.authdn = authdn;
        this.authpw = authpw;
        this.conf = conf;
        this.base = base;

        setLayout(null);
```

The following block of code handles disconnecting from the LDAP server when the user closes the window.

```
this.addWindowListener(new WindowAdapter() {
    public void windowClosing( WindowEvent e ) {
        // Disconnect from server
        if ( (ld != null) && ld.isConnected() ) {
            try {
                ld.disconnect();
            } catch ( LDAPException le ) {
                System.out.println( le.toString() );
            }
        }
        System.exit(0);
    }
});
```

The following code creates the GUI components and places them on the frame.

```
Label lbl1 = new Label( "Search for:" );
lbl1.setBounds( 10,36,75,26 );
add( lbl1 );
srch = new TextField();
Font font = new Font("Monospaced",Font.PLAIN,12);
srch.setFont( font );
srch.setBounds( 90,36,230,26 );
add( srch );

searchb = new Button( "Search" );
searchb.setBounds( 340,36,80,26 );
add( searchb );

output = new TextArea(12,3);
output.setFont( font );
output.setEditable( false );
output.setBounds( 10,70,410,200 );
add( output );
```

An action is associated with the Search button:

```
searchb.addActionListener(new ActionListener() {
    public void actionPerformed(ActionEvent e) {
        String srchstr = srch.getText();
        // If there is a search string, do a search
        if ( srchstr.length() > 0 ) {
            searchLDAP( srchstr );
        }
```

```
        }
    });
```

The following code handles reading the filter description file and creating a filter descriptor. If the file cannot be located, the program aborts, reporting an error to the console.

```
    // Read the filter description file
    // If not found, exit and report error to the console
    try {
        filterDesc =
            new LDAPFilterDescriptor(conf);
    } catch ( Exception e ) {
        System.out.println( "Cannot load " + conf +
                            " file" );
        System.out.println( "Exiting..." );
        System.exit( 1) ;
    }
}
```

The searchLDAP method takes the search string from the user and builds a filter with the aid of the filter descriptor. Once the proper search string has been built, an LDAP search is executed:

```
protected void searchLDAP( String srchString ) {
    int status = -1;
    String appendmsg = "";
    LDAPSearchResults res = null;
    LDAPFilterList filtlist = null;
    String  srchfilter = "(|";

    // Check if we are connected first
    if ( (ld == null) || (!ld.isConnected()) ) {
        connectServer();
    }

    // Use the filter descriptor to build a
    // search filter
    try {
        filtlist =
            filterDesc.getFilters("search", srchString);

        while ( filtlist.hasMoreElements() ) {
            LDAPFilter fline = filtlist.next();
            // The actual filter is next
```

```
        String fstr = fline.getFilter();
        srchfilter += fstr;
    }
    srchfilter += ")";
    if ( srchfilter.length() == 3 ) {
        // No filters found
        return;
    }

    // Now do the search
    res = ld.search( base,
                     scope,
                     srchfilter,
                     ATTRS,
                     false );

    // Display search filter
    String outres = "Filter=" + srchfilter + "\n" +
                    "-------\n";

    // Loop on results building each line
    while ( res.hasMoreElements() ) {
        try {
            // Next directory entry
            LDAPEntry entry = res.next();
            outres += format( entry );
            status = 0;
        } catch ( LDAPReferralException e ) {
            // Ignore referrals
            continue;
        } catch (LDAPException le) {
            int rc = le.getLDAPResultCode();
            if ( rc == le.SIZE_LIMIT_EXCEEDED ) {
                appendmsg =
                    "\nExceeded size limit";
            } else if ( rc ==
                        le.TIME_LIMIT_EXCEEDED ) {
                appendmsg =
                    "\nExceeded time limit";
            } else {
                appendmsg = le.toString();
            }
        }
    }
```

```
            outres += appendmsg;
            output.setText( outres ); // Display in text area

        } catch( Exception e ) {
            System.out.println( "Search error: " +
                                        e.toString() );
        }
    }
```

The connectServer method is called whenever we need to establish a connection to the LDAP server:

```
    protected void connectServer() {
        // Connect to the LDAP server
        if ( (ld == null) || (!ld.isConnected()) ) {
            try {
                ld = new LDAPConnection();
                ld.connect( host, port, authdn, authpw );
            } catch( LDAPException e ) {
                 System.out.println( "Connect error: " +
                                        e.toString() );
                System.exit( 1 );
            }
        }
    }
```

We are binding with the specified command-line credential information. If none is supplied, we simply bind anonymously.

The following two methods return a display string for the text box. They handle situations in which no value exists by substituting a dash for the value. The format method returns a String with each matching entry in tab-delimited format. The returned String is directly appended to the text box by the calling method.

```
    /**
     * Format a string with attribute values from an entry,
     * separated by tabs
     *
     * @param entry LDAP entry containing cn, telephoneNumber,
     * and mail
     */
    public String format( LDAPEntry entry ) {
        String outstr = "";

        // Get the data - hard-coded attribute names here!
        String name = getValue( entry, "cn" );
```

```
        String phone = getValue( entry, "telephoneNumber" );
        String email = getValue( entry, "mail" );

        // Limit the full name to 15 characters
        if ( name.length() > 15 ) {
            name = name.substring( 0, 15 );
        }

        outstr = name + "\t" + phone + "\t" + email + "\n";

        return outstr;
    }

    /**
     * Get first string value of an attribute from an entry
     * or '-' if not present
     *
     * @param entry LDAP entry containing the attribute
     * @param attrName name of attribute to retrieve
     * @return first value of attribute or '-'
     */
    protected String getValue( LDAPEntry entry,
                               String attrName ) {
        LDAPAttribute attr = entry.getAttribute( attrName );
        if ( attr == null ) {
            return "-";
        }
        Enumeration enumVals = attr.getStringValues();
        // Enumerate on values for this attribute
        boolean hasVals = false;
        if ( (enumVals == null) ||
             !enumVals.hasMoreElements() ) {
            return "-";
        }

        return (String)enumVals.nextElement();
    }

    private LDAPConnection ld = null;
    private String host;
    private int port;
    private String conf;
    private String base;
    private String authdn;
    private String authpw;
```

```
    private int scope = LDAPConnection.SCOPE_SUB;
    private TextArea output;
    private TextField srch;
    private Button searchb;
    // Attributes to display for each entry found
    private static final String[] ATTRS =
        {"cn","mail","telephoneNumber"};
    // Filter configuration file object
    private LDAPFilterDescriptor filterDesc = null;
}
```

This program is useful as an example of working with the results from a search and presenting them in a graphical environment. When the program is first started, a Connect button is displayed. Clicking this button will open a connection to the LDAP server and rename the button as Search. After a search string is entered, clicking the Search button will cause the search string to be parsed using a filter configuration file, and then the search will be submitted to the server. Search filter configurations provide other functionality as well, such as filter prefixing and suffixing.

Check the reference section of this book for details on these features. It should be evident that this functionality can make your code more dynamic in response to user input.

To execute the program, use the following command-line option:

```
java FilterSearchDialog localhost 389 filter.conf "o=airius.com"
```

This command will present a search screen, where you may issue searches against the directory. Issuing a search of 555 against the sample data file included on the CD-ROM that accompanies this book will result in the display shown in Figure 5-5.

Sorting

We now turn our attention to sorting the results returned from the server. As you may have noticed, the LDAP server does not always return results in a natural order. Human beings generally prefer to have information ordered so that it can be reviewed or browsed easily. The LDAP SDK provides two methods for sorting results: client-side sorting and server-side sorting. **Server-side sorting** is an LDAPv3 enhancement and is supported on many servers, including Netscape Directory Server. We will cover server-side sorting in detail in Chapter 16. **Client-side sorting** is the option to retrieve the data and sort it on the client machine before working with the results.

Client-side sorting has a couple of restrictions. First, the attributes on which you wish to sort must be among the attributes you request in your search results. You can-

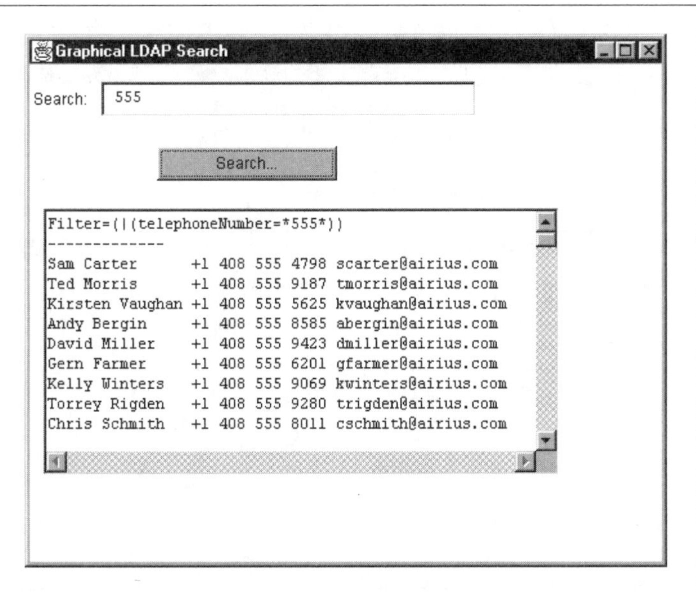

FIGURE 5-5. *Results of sample query with* `FilterSearchDialog`.

not, for instance, request just the `uid` and `telephoneNumber` for your search, and then try to sort by `cn`. Second, in client-side sorting, the sort will block until all records have been retrieved from the server. With these restrictions in mind, let's look at how we can add client-side sorting to the `FilterSearchDialog` program.

The client-side sort routine needs two arrays or two single values that indicate the attributes to sort and a flag for ascending or descending order. The following code snippet shows the modifications to the `FilterSearchDialog` code that are needed to sort by `cn` in ascending order.

```
res = ld.search( BASE, SCOPE, srchfilter, ATTRS, false;
// Since we are sorting by only one field, we do not need an array
res.sort ( new LDAPCompareAttrNames("cn",true) );
```

The `LDAPCompareAttrNames` constructor creates a comparator that looks at LDAP string values in the entries for sorting purposes. The `LDAPCompareAttrNames` constructor also takes a form with two arrays. For instance, to sort on both the `cn` and `telephoneNumber` attributes, the code would look like this:

```
String[] sortattr = {"cn", "telephoneNumber"};
boolean[] ascend = {true, true};
res.sort new ( LDAPCompareAttrNames(sortattr,ascend) );
```

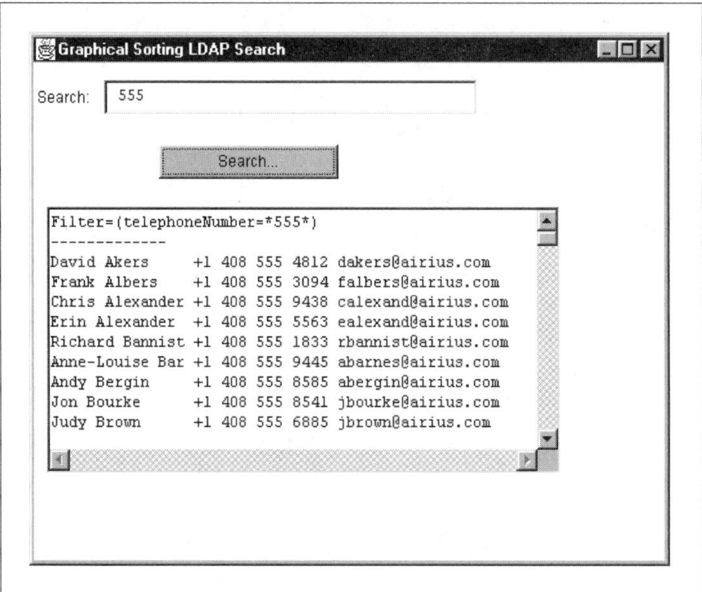

FIGURE 5-6. *Results with client-side sorting.*

The output from `FilterSearchDialogSort` (the sorting version of `FilterSearchDialog`) with the same search as earlier looks like Figure 5-6.

Authenticating for Searches

None of the examples presented so far in this chapter have involved authenticating to the directory. All connections have been anonymous (not using a DN or password). Most LDAP directories are configured to allow anonymous searching of at least some of the information in the system, but some attributes may have access control configured to prevent access. For instance, the corporate directory at Netscape Communications Corporation does not allow anonymous connections to retrieve the JPEG photo of an employee. Only security personnel or the employee corresponding to the entry may retrieve this attribute. The same usually is true for the `userPassword` attribute as well.

If you ask for one of the required or commonly used attributes and it is not returned, more than likely access control has been configured to prevent you from retrieving it. We will cover authenticating to the directory in Chapter 6, when we will be modifying data, but to peek ahead—for those who need to authenticate for a search or to retrieve a specific attribute—the additional method to call is shown here (indicated by bold):

```
ld = new LDAPConnection();
ld.connect( HOST, PORT ); // Connect to server
ld.authenticate( 3, authid, authpw );  // Bind by DN and password
```

The connect and authenticate steps can be combined:

```
ld.connect( 3, HOST, PORT, authid, authpw );
```

The optional first numerical parameter is the requested LDAP protocol version. You must specify 3 to take advantage of controls and other new features of LDAPv3. On the other hand, if the server supports only LDAPv2 and you specify 3 when authenticating, the server will refuse the connection. The default in the SDK is 2.

The value used to authenticate to the directory must be a DN of an existing entry. One DN in the server—the root DN (like the root user on UNIX)—has unlimited privileges and does not correspond to a physical entry. In Netscape Directory Server, the default root DN is `cn=Directory Manager`. The root DN is also often called the Directory Manager.

Typically the DN used to authenticate will be that of a user needing to perform an operation on his own entry. For example, if Sam Carter wanted to bind and retrieve his photograph, he would authenticate as follows:

```
String bindDN = "uid=scarter, ou=People, o=airius.com";
// Bind password is passed to us
if (bindpwd.length() > 0) {
    ld.authenticate(bindDN,bindpwd);
}
```

When authenticating, always validate that the password is not a blank string ("") or `null`. If a blank string is passed as the password, there will be no exception thrown to indicate an invalid authentication. Instead the operation will succeed but the connection will be anonymous. Later, when the program attempts to modify an entry, an exception may be thrown because anonymous users do not have the right to make modifications. We will cover authenticating in detail in Chapter 6.

Improving Directory Search Performance

As an application developer you can increase the performance of your search operations, reduce memory usage, and reduce the load on the server by observing a few rules of thumb:

- Use indexed attributes
- Specify an object class in your filter to get only entries of the desired type
- Retrieve only attributes you need
- Keep the DN handy
- Use `compare` where it makes sense

Use Indexed Attributes

The most significant way to get good performance from the directory when searching is to use only indexed attributes in your search requests. As a programmer you may need to work with your directory administrator to determine which attributes are indexed or to request that additional attributes be indexed. If you find you need to perform searches frequently on unindexed attributes, then it may make sense to index the particular attributes. With Netscape Directory Server, you can view the access logs and determine if searches are occurring against unindexed fields. The following is a sample of the access log. The text "notes=U" marks a search against an unindexed attribute.

```
[03/May/1999:09:24:29 -0400] conn=19 op=6 SRCH
base="ou=tony.home,o=NetscapeRoot" scope=2 filter="(objectclass=NsHost)"
      .
      .
[03/May/1999:09:24:29 -0400] conn=19 op=6 RESULT err=0 tag=101 nentries=1
etime=0 notes=U
```

Specify an Object Class to Get Only Entries of the Desired Type

If your application is working with particular types of records (for example, person records), it makes sense to include in your filter the object class you need. For instance, for all the records of people whose names begin with "barbara," use a filter such as `(&(objectclass=person)(cn=Barbara*))`. You can use a filter configuration file to set up a tag for finding entries that represent people. Include the filter component `objectclass=person` in the tag. The result may be that fewer records are returned to the client, and consequently that performance is improved, particularly if your directory stores many entries for objects other than people.

Retrieve Only Attributes You Need

Many programmers pass `null` as the attributes field for a `search` operation. The result is that all attributes for the indicated records are returned. For a large potential result set, the performance of both server and client can be severely affected. If you need only the name and phone number, then specify these in your search request. Keep in mind that if you are doing client-side sorting, you will also need to request the attributes by which you wish to sort.

Keep the DN Handy

If you are going to do anything else with a retrieved record, keep the DN. The DN can be used to find a record uniquely within the directory without invoking a new search. For instance, suppose you are displaying a list of names and want to allow the user to click on a name and get all the information about that person. Store the DN for each record in a nonvisible variable and use it to look up the record when the user clicks on it.

Use `compare` Where It Makes Sense

If you are interested only in whether an attribute exists and has a certain value, use `compare` rather than `search`. A `compare` is a lightweight transaction with very little client and server overhead. When entries are returned, access control must be evaluated for each attribute, and client memory usage increases according to the size of the entries returned.

Conclusion

The major use of an LDAP directory is to retrieve information. In this chapter we have presented samples of code to direct searches to LDAP directories. We have also covered the details of processing the results, along with many tips to make the most efficient use of the SDK. One of the key pieces of information to maintain during processing is the DN of the retrieved records. With this information, any other data can be obtained rapidly from the directory. We have also included in this chapter a discussion of techniques to minimize impact on the directory, the client application, and the network through efficient use of the SDK.

CHAPTER 6

Creating and Maintaining Information

Chapter 5 described various methods for retrieving and processing data under program control. This chapter will focus on placing data into the directory and manipulating it there, including entering new data, altering existing data, or deleting data that is no longer necessary.

In many cases software may need to update or alter the directory; for example, a user has changed her home phone number, a reorganization has caused the manager of a series of employees to change, or a user wants to alter her password. All these instances require the directory to be updated at some point. Another area of rapid growth is storing extranet or Web account preferences and selections in the directory. Once this information is stored, whenever the user returns she is greeted with a familiar environment—her own.

We will concentrate in this chapter on the code that is necessary to perform all these operations. By "updating" the directory, we mean adding new entries, modifying existing entries, or completely deleting an entire entry. We will also discuss the use of groups in the directory for simplifying access control and implementing mailing lists.

Before We Can Update: Authentication Basics

Before we can modify anything in an LDAP directory, generally we must authenticate. The directory uses this authentication information to determine whether we are authorized to make the particular changes we are requesting. Chapter 7 will cover authentication in detail.

Many LDAP servers have one identity that is a privileged account and can perform any operation. By default, this user is `cn=Directory Manager` for Netscape Directory Server. Other directory servers have their own designated privileged user or users. Typically this privileged account may request an unlimited number of entries returned on a search and is not affected by server-side settings such as the maximum number of results to return. Sometimes a particular operation may need to be performed as the Directory Manager because no other user has sufficient global rights. In this chapter we will be using **simple authentication**: passing a DN and password. If you do not want unencrypted passwords to be transmitted over the network, then you should use SSL or a SASL mechanism to secure the communications.

With simple authentication you must supply a full DN and a valid password, as the following code fragment illustrates.

```
LDAPConnection ld = new LDAPConnection();
try {
    ld.connect( HOST, PORT);
    ld.authenticate( "cn=Directory Manager", "PASSWORD" );
} catch ( LDAPException e ) {
}
```

If a blank password is passed, the authentication will succeed but it will be an anonymous authentication (authenticating as the anonymous user). Although the authentication process itself will not throw an error, anytime an operation that requires privileges is requested, an exception will be thrown. When your program accepts passwords as input, you should check that the supplied password is not blank. If the program requires authentication other than as anonymous, you should reject a DN or password that is blank.

You may issue another authenticate operation against an existing connection. The operation allows for changing authentication information after a connection has been established.

Finally, the user ID must be specified as a full DN. Users usually do not know the full DNs of their user IDs, so typically a search must be performed anonymously (or as a special user) to locate the DN corresponding to the user ID before the user can authenticate to the directory. Chapter 7 will provide sample code and discuss authentication in detail; the following code just provides the highlights of authentication with a user-supplied user ID and password.

```
import netscape.ldap.*;
import java.util.*;

/**
 * Given a uid and password, find the corresponding entry
 * and authenticate
 */

public class UidLogin {
```

```
/**
 * Search for the uid and then authenticate with the
 * password
 *
 * @param args host, port, uid, password
 */
public static void main( String[] args ) {

    if ( args.length != 5 ) {
        System.out.println( "Usage: java UidLogin " +
                            "<host> <port> <baseDN> " +
                            "<uid> <password>" );
        System.out.println( "Example:" );
        System.out.println( "    java UidLogin " +
                            "localhost 389 " +
                            "\"o=airius.com\" " +
                            "cathyp password" );
        System.exit(1);
    }

    String host = args[0];
    int port = Integer.parseInt( args[1] );
    String baseDN = args[2];
    String authid = args[3];
    String authpw = args[4];

    if ( (authid.length() == 0) ||
         (authpw.length() == 0) ||
         (authid.indexOf('*') >= 0) ) {
        System.out.println( "You must supply a uid and " +
                            "password" );
        System.exit(1);
    }

    boolean authed = false;
    LDAPConnection ld = new LDAPConnection();
    try {
        // Connect to server anonymously
        ld.connect( host, port );

        // Search for entries with a matching uid
        LDAPSearchConstraints cons =
            ld.getSearchConstraints();
             cons.setBatchSize( 0 );
```

```
            LDAPSearchResults results =
                ld.search( baseDN,
                           ld.SCOPE_SUB,
                           "uid=" + authid,
                           new String[] {ld.NO_ATTRS},
                           false,
                           cons );
            // There should be exactly one match
            if ( !results.hasMoreElements() ) {
                System.out.println( "uid not found" );
            } else if ( results.getCount() > 1 ) {
                System.out.println( "More than one matching " +
                                    "uid" );
            } else {
                LDAPEntry entry = results.next();
                String authDN = entry.getDN();
                System.out.println( "uid maps to: " +
                                    authDN );
                ld.authenticate( authDN, authpw );
                authed = true;
            }
        } catch( LDAPException e ) {
            System.out.println( e.toString() );
        }

        // Done, so disconnect
        if ( (ld != null) && ld.isConnected() ) {
            try {
                ld.disconnect();
            } catch ( LDAPException e ) {
                System.out.println( e.toString() );
            }
        }

        int rc = 0;
        if ( authed ) {
            System.out.println( "Authenticated!" );
        } else {
            System.out.println("Not Authenticated!");
            rc = 1;
        }
        System.exit(rc);
    }
}
```

Adding an Entry

You can add new entries to the directory by defining a DN for the entry, creating the attributes for the entry, and requesting that the LDAP server add the new entry.

Summary of Steps to Add a New Entry

Creating an entry in the directory requires the following steps:

1. Instantiate an `LDAPAttribute` object for each attribute that forms the entry.
2. Instantiate an `LDAPAttributeSet` object and use the `add` method to add each `LDAPAttribute` object from step 1.
3. Instantiate an `LDAPEntry` object that specifies the new DN and the `LDAPAttributeSet` from step 2.
4. Call the `LDAPConnection.add` method with the `LDAPEntry` object from step 3.

The `LDAPAttribute` class represents an attribute. An `LDAPAttribute` is used to build each attribute and the corresponding values for the entry. The following code fragment shows calls to create an `LDAPAttribute` for a single-valued attribute, a multivalued attribute, and an attribute that contains binary data.

```
LDAPAttribute attr1 = new LDAPAttribute( "cn", "Babs Jensen" );

String attrvals = { "Babs Jensen", "Barbara Jensen" };
LDAPAttribute attr2 = new LDAPAttribute( "cn", attrvals);

byte[] jpeg_data = readImage( "myimage.jpg" );
LDAPAttribute attr3 = new LDAPAttribute( "jpegPhoto", jpeg_data );
```

Once the attributes have been built, they are put into an `LDAPAttributeSet` using the `add` method on the `LDAPAttributeSet` object. An `LDAPEntry` object is then created with the `LDAPAttributeSet` and the `String` representing the DN. Figure 6-1 shows what is contained in an `LDAPEntry` object.

This `LDAPEntry` is passed to the `LDAPConnection.add` method, as illustrated in the following code, which adds a new person entry to the directory.

```
LDAPAttributeSet attrs = new LDAPAttributeSet();
String objclass[] = { "top", "person", "organizationalPerson",
```

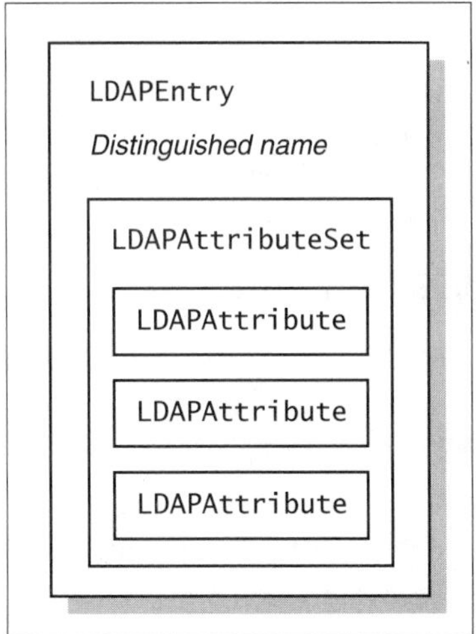

FIGURE 6-1. *Contents of an* `LDAPEntry` *object.*

```
                        "inetOrgPerson" };
attrs.add( new LDAPAttribute( "objectclass", objclass ) );
attrs.add( new LDAPAttribute( "cn", "Babs Jensen" ) );
attrs.add( new LDAPAttribute( "sn", "Jensen" ) );
attrs.add( new LDAPAttribute( "mail", "bjensen@airius.com" ) );
String dn = "uid=bjensen,ou=People,o=airius.com";
LDAPEntry theEntry = new LDAPEntry( dn, attrs );
try {
   // The add may fail for lack of privileges or other reasons
    ld.add( theEntry );
} catch ( LDAPException e ) {
}
```

You must include the required attributes for the specified object class as part of the entry. For `person` and its derived object classes, the required attributes are `objectclass`, `sn`, and `cn`. In the example just given, we are also adding an optional attribute—`mail`.

Note that not only `inetOrgPerson` should be specified as object class, but also its ancestors (`top`, `person`, and `organizationalPerson`). You must also be authenticated with credentials that allow adding entries to the directory at the point specified by the DN. In this case, you must have the right to add child entries to `ou=People, o=airius.com`. Finally, the parent entry—`ou=People, o=airius.com` in this case—must exist.

Inserting Records from a Data File

Often data from different systems needs to be imported into an LDAP directory. Although LDIF is the primary means of importing data files, Java's `StringTokenizer` class and the SDK make it easy to import custom files. The program that follows reads a comma-separated list of values from a file, builds an LDAP entry for each line, and inserts it into the directory.

The file to be imported is of the following format:

```
jdoe,John,Doe,650-555-1212
tsmith,Tom,Smith,650-555-1213
tmartin,Tim,Martin,650-555-1214
swright,Sally,Wright,650-555-1215
```

The program can be customized for other input formats.

```
import java.util.*;
import java.io.*;
import netscape.ldap.*;

/**
 * Class that reads a comma-delimited file of user records and
 * inserts the records into an LDAP directory at a specified
 * base DN
 */
public class MultiAdd {

    /**
     * Add entries from a comma-delimited file of user records
     *
     * @param args host, port, filename, dn, authdn,
     * password
     */
    public static void main( String[] args ) {

        if ( args.length != 6 ) {
            System.out.println( "Usage: java MultiAdd " +
                                "<host> <port> <filename> " +
                                "<dn> <authdn> <password> " );
            System.out.println( "Example:" );
            System.out.println( "    java MultiAdd " +
                                 "localhost 389 " +
                                      "records.csv " +
                                      "o=airius.com\" " +
```

```
                              "\"cn=Directory Manager\" " +
                              "password" );
        System.out.println( "The comma-delimited file " +
                              "should contain:");
        System.out.println("  uid,fname,lname,phone" );
        System.exit(1);
    }

    String host = args[0];
    int port = Integer.parseInt( args[1] );
    String filename = args[2];
    String basedn = args[3];
    String authid = args[4];
    String authpw = args[5];
```

The following two declarations determine which object class the records we are importing are stored as.

```
         // Object classes for a person entry
         String[] objclass = { "top","person",
                               "organizationalPerson",
                               "inetOrgPerson"};
        LDAPAttribute attrobj =
            new LDAPAttribute( "objectclass", objclass );
```

Then we connect to the directory, open the file, and loop on reading and parsing each line:

```
         BufferedReader in = null;
         int numAdded = 0;
         LDAPConnection ld = new LDAPConnection();
         try {
             // Connect to server and authenticate
             ld.connect( host, port, authid, authpw );
             System.out.println( "Connected to " + host );

             in = new BufferedReader(
                 new FileReader(filename));

             String line;
             while ( (line = in.readLine()) != null ) {
                 String uid = "";
                 String fname = "";
```

```
            String lname = "";
            String phone = "";
            // Parse the line
            try {
                StringTokenizer t =
                    new StringTokenizer(line,",");
                uid = t.nextToken();
                fname = t.nextToken();
                lname = t.nextToken();
                phone = t.nextToken();
            } catch (NoSuchElementException e) {
                System.err.println( "Missing fields in: " +
                                    line );
                continue;
            }
```

The next block of code builds the entry using the attribute values parsed from the input file. The DN is formed as the user ID from the comma-delimited file, prepended to the base DN that is provided by the user on the command line. Once the `LDAPAttributes` have been created and placed into an `LDAPAttributeSet`, an `LDAPEntry` object is created and added to the directory.

```
        String dn = "uid=" + uid + "," + basedn;
        LDAPAttributeSet attrs = new LDAPAttributeSet();
        attrs.add( attrobj );
        // Western composition: first name, last name
        String fullname = fname + " " + lname;
        attrs.add( new LDAPAttribute("cn", fullname) );
        attrs.add( new LDAPAttribute(
                       "givenName", fname) );
        attrs.add( new LDAPAttribute("sn",lname) );
        attrs.add( new LDAPAttribute(
                       "telephoneNumber", phone) );
        // Now add the record to the directory
        LDAPEntry theEntry = new LDAPEntry( dn, attrs );
        try {
            ld.add( theEntry );
            System.out.println("Added: " + dn);
            numAdded++;
        } catch ( LDAPException lda ) {
            System.out.println( lda.toString() );
            System.out.println("Failed to add: " + dn);
        }
    }
```

Any errors during the add will be caught by the following block of code. The program does not stop when it encounters an error, but instead reports the error to the console and continues with the next record. This way of handling errors prevents a single bad value from causing the remaining import to fail.

```
            } catch( Exception e ) {
                // Either IOException on reading the file or
                // LDAPException on connecting to LDAP server
                System.out.println( e.toString() );
            }

            // Done, so disconnect
            if ( (ld != null) && ld.isConnected() ) {
                try {
                    ld.disconnect();
                } catch ( LDAPException e ) {
                    System.out.println( e.toString() );
                }
            }
            if ( in != null ) {
                try {
                    in.close();
                } catch ( IOException e ) {
                }
            }
            System.out.println( numAdded + " entries added" );
            System.exit(0);
        }
    }
```

Adding an Organizational Unit

So far in this chapter we have looked at adding new user entries. An organizational unit, or ou, is just another type of entry. It is instructive to look at an LDIF representation of the organizational unit `ou=People, o=airius.com`:

```
dn: ou=People, o=airius.com
objectclass: top
objectclass: organizationalUnit
ou: People
... access control instructions omitted
```

An ou is simply an entry for which the DN specifies the full ou path, as well as the objectclass attributes of top and organizationalUnit. Similarly an o is identical except that the object class is organization instead. The following code snippet creates a new ou of Partners for Airius.com.

```
LDAPAttributeSet attrs = new LDAPAttributeSet();
String objclass[] = { "top","organizationalUnit" };
attrs.add( new LDAPAttribute("objectclass", objclass) );
attrs.add( new LDAPAttribute("ou", "Partners") );
String dn = "ou=Partners,o=airius.com";
LDAPEntry theEntry = new LDAPEntry( dn, attrs );
try {
    ld.add(theEntry);
} catch ( LDAPException e ) {
}
```

Upon execution of this code, the directory will contain a new ou. Once the ou has been created, new entries may be created under this branch. When entries are added to an LDAP directory, they may not reference a branch point for insertion that does not yet exist. For instance, you cannot add an entry with the DN uid=bjensen, ou=partners, o=airius.com if ou=partners, o=airius.com does not exist in the tree.

Processing Exceptions

An add operation will fail if the entry already exists (that is, if the DN exists). To avoid this situation you can execute the add method, and if an exception of LDAPException.ENTRY_ALREADY_EXISTS is caught, then use a modify. Modify is for changing values in the directory for entries that already exist; it will be covered in the next section. If the duplicate entry is an error condition and you do not want to overwrite an existing entry, then you can handle the exception in some other way, such as reporting an error and aborting. You will need to identify and process other exception types as well, in particular LDAPException.INSUFFICIENT_ACCESS_RIGHTS.

Modifying an Existing Entry

The preceding section outlined the steps necessary to add a new entry to the directory. This section will focus on altering entries that are already in the directory. To modify a single attribute of an entry, we use an LDAPModification object. We modify multiple attributes by using an LDAPModificationSet. Once the LDAPModification object has been built, the changes are written back via the modify method of LDAPConnection.

Modifying an attribute value can include adding a new value, changing a value, and/or removing a value. After a brief look at the general procedure for modifying an entry, we will examine each of these cases.

Summary of Steps to Modify an Existing Entry

Modifying an entry in the directory requires the following steps:

1. Instantiate an `LDAPAttribute` object for each attribute you want to modify.
2. Instantiate an `LDAPModificationSet` object and use the `add` method, specifying `LDAPModification.ADD`, `REPLACE`, or `DELETE` for each `LDAPAttribute` object from step 1, or construct a single `LDAPModification` if only one attribute is to be updated.
3. Call the `LDAPConnection.modify` method with the DN and the `LDAPModificationSet` or `LDAPModification` object from step 2.

Adding an Attribute

A value may be added to an attribute, making the attribute a **multivalued attribute.** Attributes such as `telephoneNumber` are defined in the schema as multivalued and can therefore have multiple values. The following code snippet adds an additional e-mail address for an entry. This code will add a `mail` attribute to the indicated entry if the attribute does not already exist. If the attribute does exist, the new value is appended to the existing values.

```
LDAPAttribute attr = new LDAPAttribute( "mail", "email@mycom.com" );
LDAPModification mod =
    new LDAPModification( LDAPModification.ADD, attr );
try {
    ld.modify( theDN, mod );  // write to the directory
} catch ( LDAPException e ) {
}
```

If the value already exists—that is, there already is a `mail` attribute with the value “email@mycom.com”—an exception is thrown for `LDAPException.ATTRIBUTE_OR_VALUE_EXISTS`.

Modifying an Attribute

To modify an existing attribute in the directory, construct an `LDAPAttribute` with the new values and then create an `LDAPModification` using the constant

LDAPModification.REPLACE. A replace will also function like an add if the attribute does not exist or contains no values. If the attribute is multivalued, a replace will replace all values with the new values. The section on multivalued attributes later in this chapter discusses how to modify a single value within a multivalued attribute.

The following snippet of code modifies the telephone number for an entry, replacing all preexisting values, if any.

```
LDAPAttribute attr = new LDAPAttribute( "telephoneNumber",
                                        "650-555-1212");
LDAPModification mod =
    new LDAPModification( LDAPModification.REPLACE, attr );
try {
    ld.modify( theDN, mod );
} catch ( LDAPException e ) {
}
```

Removing an Attribute

To remove an attribute entirely from an entry, you must perform a replace or delete on the attribute, and specify no values when constructing the LDAPAttribute object. Removing all values of an attribute removes the attribute itself. The following code will remove the telephoneNumber atttribute. Attributes that are mandatory for a particular object class cannot be removed.

```
LDAPAttribute attr = new LDAPAttribute( “telephoneNumber” );
LDAPModification mod =
    new LDAPModification( LDAPModification.DELETE, attr );
    //or you can use REPLACE
try {
    ld.modify( theDN, mod );
} catch ( LDAPException e ) {
}
```

An LDAPModification.DELETE operation with no values specified for the attribute will fail if the attribute does not exist in the entry. To avoid this situation (if you don't care if the attribute exists and has a value before you execute the operation), use LDAPModification.REPLACE rather than DELETE.

Modifications may also be cascaded as part of a single modification set to effect deletions, replacements, and additions in a single operation. The following code snippet will change the e-mail address of the entry, delete the telephone number, and add a facsimile number.

```
LDAPModificationSet mods = new LDAPModificationSet();
mods.add( LDAPModification.REPLACE,
          new LDAPAttribute("mail","myemail@abc.com") );
mods.add( LDAPModification.DELETE,
          new LDAPAttribute("telephoneNumber") );
mods.add( LDAPModification.ADD,
          new LDAPAttribute("facsimileTelephoneNumber",
                            "650-555-1111") );
try {
    ld.modify( theDN, mods );
} catch ( LDAPException e ) {
}
```

LDAP guarantees that the modify operation is atomic—that is, that when multiple operations (deleting, replacing, and adding attributes to a single record) are requested, as shown here, all the operations must succeed in order for any of them to take effect.

Updating Multivalued Attributes

To alter a particular value of a multivalued attribute, we use a combination of a delete operation that specifies the value(s) to be deleted, followed by an add operation that specifies the new values. Since the modify operation is atomic, the delete and add operations will succeed as a single operation or no change will occur. Let's examine some scenarios using the familiar Babs Jensen record, which was introduced in Chapter 4. The following lists a subset of the record:

```
dn: uid=bjensen, ou=People, o=airius.com
cn: Babs Jensen
sn: Jensen
givenName: Babs
objectclass: top
objectclass: person
objectclass: organizationalPerson
objectclass: inetOrgPerson
ou: People
uid: bjensen
mail: bjensen@airius.com
telephoneNumber: 408 555 1862
telephoneNumber: 408 555 2681
```

Note the multivalued `telephoneNumber` attribute in the original record. The following snippet of code *removes* the existing telephone number (408-555-1862) from the attribute and *adds* the new telephone number 650-555-1212.

```
LDAPAttribute dAttr =
    new LDAPAttribute( "telephoneNumber", "408 555 1862" );
LDAPAttribute aAttr =
    new LDAPAttribute( "telephoneNumber", "650 555 1212" );
LDAPModificationSet mods = new LDAPModificationSet();
mods.add( LDAPModification.DELETE, dAttr );
mods.add( LDAPModification.ADD, aAttr );
try {
    ld.modify( theDN, mods );
} catch(Exception e ) {
}
```

After this snippet of code is executed, the entry for Babs Jensen displays changes in the `telephoneNumber` attribute:

```
dn: uid=bjensen, ou=People, o=airius.com
...
telephoneNumber: 408 555 2681
telephoneNumber: 650 555 1212
```

If we had specified `REPLACE` for the new number instead of a `DELETE` followed by an `ADD`, as follows:

```
mods.add(LDAPModification.REPLACE, dAttr);
```

the entry would now have a single value for `telephoneNumber`:

```
dn: uid=bjensen, ou=People, o=airius.com
...
telephoneNumber: 650-555-1212
```

In this record all values of the multivalued attribute have been replaced by the new value.

Storing Binary Data

The LDAP SDK supports storing of binary data into attributes. This feature is useful for maintaining information that cannot be represented in a string format. Binary storage can be used to maintain photographs of people in the directory, thereby providing security personnel with up-to-date and accurate pictures of personnel, or to customize an online phone book entry. Another common use of binary data in LDAP directories is storage of digital certificates. The program that follows is a stand-alone Java application that stores and retrieves photographs in the directory. The program is executed by the following command (if your directory is on the same machine as the program, and if its port number is 389):

```
java JPEGLDAP localhost 389
```

```
import java.awt.*;
import java.awt.event.*;
import java.io.*;
import java.util.*;
import javax.swing.*;
import javax.swing.border.*;
import javax.swing.filechooser.FileFilter;
import java.net.*;
import netscape.ldap.*;

/**
 * A dialog for viewing and updating the jpegPhoto attribute
 * of an entry in a directory
 *
 * @version 1.0
 */
public class JPEGLDAP extends JFrame {

   /**
    * Launch a dialog
    *
    * @param args host and port of LDAP server
    */
   public static void main(String args[]) {
       try {
           if ( args.length != 2 ) {
               System.out.println( "Usage: java JPEGLDAP " +
                                   "<host> <port>" );
               System.exit( 1 );
           }
           String host = args[0];
           int port = Integer.parseInt( args[1] );

           // Enable the following code if you want the look
           // and feel to be set to the look and feel of the
           // native system.
           /*
           try {
                UIManager.setLookAndFeel(
```

```
                UIManager.getSystemLookAndFeelClassName());
        } catch (Exception e) {
        }
        */

        // Create a new instance of the application frame
        // and make it visible.
        JFrame frame = new JPEGLDAP( host, port );
        frame.pack();
        frame.setVisible(true);
    } catch (Exception e) {
        System.err.println( e );
        System.exit(1);
    }
}

 /**
  * Constructor
  *
  * @param host host name of LDAP server
  * @param port port number of LDAP server
  */
 public JPEGLDAP( String host, int port ) {
     super( "LDAP JPEG Photo Handler" );

     setDefaultCloseOperation(DO_NOTHING_ON_CLOSE);
     setVisible(false);

     DNEntryField = new JTextField();
     DNEntryField.setPreferredSize(
         new Dimension( 300, 24 ) );
     DNEntryField.setMaximumSize(
         new Dimension( 300, 24 ) );
     JLabel DNLabel = new JLabel( "DN: " );
     DNLabel.setHorizontalAlignment(SwingConstants.RIGHT);
     DNLabel.setLabelFor(DNEntryField);

     JLabel pswdFieldLbl = new JLabel( "Password: " );
     pswdFieldLbl.setHorizontalAlignment(
              SwingConstants.RIGHT);
     pswdFieldLbl.setLabelFor(passwordField);
     passwordField = new JPasswordField();
     passwordField.setPreferredSize(
                 new Dimension( 300, 24 ) );
```

```
passwordField.setMaximumSize(
    new Dimension( 300, 24 ) );

// Read the default images into memory for display.
noLDAP = getFileData("noldap.jpg");
noFile = getFileData("nofile.jpg");
if ( (noLDAP == null) || (noFile == null) ) {
    System.out.println("Unable to read default files");
    System.exit(1);
}

// JPEG image data for LDAP image
currentPhotoIcon =
    adjustImageSize( new ImageIcon(noLDAP), dim );
currentPhoto = new JLabel( currentPhotoIcon );
currentPhotoIcon.setImageObserver( currentPhoto );
currentPhoto.setPreferredSize( dim );
currentPhoto.setMaximumSize( dim );

// JPEG image data for file image
newPhotoIcon =
    adjustImageSize( new ImageIcon(noFile), dim );
newPhoto = new JLabel( newPhotoIcon );
newPhotoIcon.setImageObserver( newPhoto );
newPhoto.setPreferredSize( dim );
newPhoto.setMaximumSize( dim );

Dimension buttonSize = new Dimension( 110, 16 );
saveNewBtn = new JButton( "< Save" );
saveNewBtn.setPreferredSize( buttonSize );
saveNewBtn.setMinimumSize( buttonSize );
```

All the GUI elements have their own handlers to make the code easier to read and to localize the functions of each element:

```
saveNewBtn.addActionListener(new saveNewJPEG());
// Nothing to save yet
saveNewBtn.setEnabled(false);

JLabel currentPhotoLbl =
    new JLabel( "Current Photo" );
currentPhotoLbl.setHorizontalAlignment(
    SwingConstants.CENTER);
currentPhotoLbl.setLabelFor(currentPhoto);
```

```
JLabel newPhotoLbl = new JLabel( "New Photo" );
newPhotoLbl.setHorizontalAlignment(
    SwingConstants.CENTER);
newPhotoLbl.setLabelFor(newPhoto);

loadNewBtn = new JButton( "Select Photo" );
loadNewBtn.setPreferredSize( buttonSize );
loadNewBtn.setMinimumSize( buttonSize );
loadNewBtn.addActionListener(new GetNewJPEG());
loadNewBtn.setEnabled(false);  // Not valid yet

JButton retrieveBtn = new JButton( "Get Entry" );
retrieveBtn.setPreferredSize( buttonSize );
retrieveBtn.setMinimumSize( buttonSize );
retrieveBtn.addActionListener(new GetLDAPEntry());

// Now lay out all the components
Box pane = new Box( BoxLayout.Y_AXIS );
getContentPane().add( pane );

Box textBox = new Box( BoxLayout.X_AXIS );
Box DNBox = new Box( BoxLayout.X_AXIS );
DNBox.add( Box.createGlue() );
DNBox.add( DNLabel );
DNBox.add( DNEntryField );
Box passwordBox = new Box( BoxLayout.X_AXIS );
passwordBox.add( Box.createGlue() );
passwordBox.add( pswdFieldLbl );
passwordBox.add( passwordField );
Box inputBox = new Box( BoxLayout.Y_AXIS );
inputBox.add( DNBox );
inputBox.add( Box.createVerticalStrut( 3 ) );
inputBox.add( passwordBox );

textBox.add( inputBox );
textBox.add( Box.createHorizontalStrut( 6 ) );
textBox.add( retrieveBtn );

pane.add( Box.createGlue() );
pane.add( textBox );
pane.add( Box.createVerticalStrut( 6 ) );
pane.add( Box.createGlue() );

Box theRestBox = new Box( BoxLayout.X_AXIS );
pane.add( theRestBox );
```

```
        Box imageBox = new Box( BoxLayout.X_AXIS );
        Box currentBox = new Box( BoxLayout.Y_AXIS );
        currentBox.add( currentPhotoLbl );
        currentBox.add( currentPhoto );
        imageBox.add( currentBox );
        imageBox.add( Box.createHorizontalStrut( 6 ) );
        imageBox.add( saveNewBtn );
        imageBox.add( Box.createHorizontalStrut( 6 ) );
        Box newBox = new Box( BoxLayout.Y_AXIS );
        newBox.add( newPhotoLbl );
        newBox.add( newPhoto );
        imageBox.add( newBox );

        theRestBox.add( Box.createGlue() );
        theRestBox.add( imageBox );
        theRestBox.add( Box.createHorizontalStrut( 6 ) );
        theRestBox.add( Box.createGlue() );
        theRestBox.add( loadNewBtn );
        // Handle window-closing action
        addWindowListener(new WindowCloser());

        // Connect to server
        try {
            ld = new LDAPConnection();
            ld.connect( host, port );
        } catch (LDAPException e) {
            System.out.println("Connect error: "+ e.toString());
            System.exit(1);
        }
        System.out.println( "Connected to LDAP server " +
                            host );
    }
```

The getFileData method reads a JPEG file from the disk, returning the data as a byte array:

```
    /**
     * Read the contents of a file into memory
     *
     * @param fname name of the file
     * @return the contents of the file
     */
    public byte[] getFileData( String fname ) {
        byte[] data = null;
```

```
    RandomAccessFile rf = null;
    try {
        rf = new RandomAccessFile(fname,"r");
        data = new byte[(int)rf.length()];
        rf.readFully(data);
    } catch (IOException e) {
        e.printStackTrace();
    }
    try {
        if (rf != null) {
            rf.close();
        }
    } catch (IOException e) { }
    return data;
}
```

The adjustImageSize method resizes an image to fit within an image window:

```
/**
 * If the image is larger than the specified max, then scale it
 * down; otherwise return the input image
 *
 * @param icon input image
 * @param dim max width and height
 * @return scaled-down image, or original image
 */
private ImageIcon adjustImageSize( ImageIcon icon,
                                   Dimension dim ) {
    if ( (icon.getIconHeight() > dim.height) ||
         (icon.getIconWidth() > dim.width) ) {
        Image img = icon.getImage();
        float hRatio = (float)icon.getIconHeight() / dim.height;
        float wRatio = (float)icon.getIconWidth() / dim.width;
        int h, w;
        if ( hRatio > wRatio ) {
            h = dim.height;
            w = (int)(icon.getIconWidth() / hRatio);
        } else {
            w = dim.width;
            h = (int)(icon.getIconHeight() / wRatio);
        }
        img = img.getScaledInstance( w, h, img.SCALE_SMOOTH );
        return new ImageIcon( img );
    } else {
```

```
            return icon;
        }
    }
```

The handler for the Get New button presents the user with a file chooser that displays only JPEG files. We also save the name of the directory of the selected file so that we can return the user to this directory the next time a new file is to be selected:

```
    /**
     * Handler for New button
     */
    class GetNewJPEG implements ActionListener {
        /**
         * Called when a button is pressed
         *
         * @param e event from New button
         */
        public void actionPerformed(ActionEvent e) {
            // Select a file
            JFileChooser chooser = new JFileChooser(directory);
            // Make sure it is a JPEG file
            JPEGFileFilter jpgfilter = new JPEGFileFilter();
            chooser.setFileFilter(jpgfilter);
            int returnVal =
                chooser.showOpenDialog(JPEGLDAP.this);
            directory =
                chooser.getCurrentDirectory().getPath();
            if ( returnVal == JFileChooser.APPROVE_OPTION ) {
                File f = chooser.getSelectedFile();
                String fullname = f.getPath();
                // Load the JPEG data
                newFilePhoto = getFileData( fullname );
                if ( newFilePhoto == null ) {
                    System.out.println( "Unable to read " +
                                        "file " +
                                        fullname );
                    return;
                }
                // Create image object
                newPhotoIcon =
                    adjustImageSize(
                        new ImageIcon(newFilePhoto), dim );
                newPhoto.setIcon(newPhotoIcon);
```

```
                newPhoto.setPreferredSize( dim );
                newPhoto.setMaximumSize( dim );
                // There is now an image to save
                saveNewBtn.setEnabled( true );
                return;
            }
        }
    }
```

As the next block of code shows, the handler for the Get Entry button attempts to read the entry from the LDAP directory and locate the photo if present. An `LDAPConnection` object is reused; here we just reauthenticate with the new DN and password. We save the DN and password used to load this entry, in case the user enters a new one (without loading a new entry) and still wants to save the current image before clicking Get Entry.

```
    /**
     * Handler for Get button
     */
    class GetLDAPEntry implements ActionListener {
        /**
         * Called when a button is pressed
         *
         * @param e event from Get button
         */
        public void actionPerformed(ActionEvent e) {

            byte[] theLDAPPhoto = null;
            DNRead = DNEntryField.getText();
            DNPswd = new String(passwordField.getPassword());
            if ( (DNRead.length() == 0) ||
                 (DNPswd.length() == 0) ) {
                System.out.println("DN and Password must " +
                                   "be entered!");
                return;
            }
            // Go get the data
            try {
                // Authenticate with the credentials of the
                // owner of the photo
                ld.authenticate( DNRead, DNPswd );
                // Read the entry
                LDAPEntry entry = ld.read( DNRead, ATTRS );
```

```
        // Extract the jpegPhoto attribute
        LDAPAttribute attr =
            entry.getAttribute( ATTRS[0] );
        if ( attr != null ) {
```

The code that follows reads the `jpegPhoto` attribute and gets the values as an enumerated list using `getByteValues`, although we will use only the first one (if there is more than one value). Once the data is in a byte array, it can be treated just as if it had been read from the disk.

```
            // Get the values as byte arrays
            Enumeration enumVals =
                attr.getByteValues();
            // Get the first value - if there's more
            // than one
            if ( enumVals.hasMoreElements() ) {
                theLDAPPhoto = (byte[])enumVals.nextElement();
            }
        } else {
            System.out.println( "No photo in the " +
                                "directory for " +
                                DNRead );
        }
```

The following block of code deals with the situation in which the entry has no photo. We return the panels to the default images and prepare for the user to select a new image.

```
        if ( (attr == null) ||
             (theLDAPPhoto == null) ) {
            // Reset images to mark this condition
            currentPhotoIcon =
                adjustImageSize( new ImageIcon(noLDAP), dim );
            currentPhoto.setIcon(currentPhotoIcon);
            newPhotoIcon =
                adjustImageSize( new ImageIcon(noFile), dim );
            newPhoto.setIcon(newPhotoIcon);
            newFilePhoto = null;
            // Nothing to save now
            saveNewBtn.setEnabled(false);
            loadNewBtn.setEnabled(true);
        } else {
            // Show image from LDAP and clear right
```

```
                    // image
                    newFilePhoto = theLDAPPhoto;
                    currentPhotoIcon =
                        adjustImageSize(
                            new ImageIcon(newFilePhoto), dim );
                    currentPhoto.setIcon(currentPhotoIcon);
                    newPhotoIcon =
                        adjustImageSize( new ImageIcon(noFile), dim );
                    newPhoto.setIcon(newPhotoIcon);
                    loadNewBtn.setEnabled(true);
                }
                currentPhoto.setPreferredSize( dim );
                currentPhoto.setMaximumSize( dim );
                newPhoto.setPreferredSize( dim );
                newPhoto.setMaximumSize( dim );

            } catch ( LDAPException le ) {
                System.out.println( le.toString() );
            }
            return;
        }
    }
```

The method saveNewJPEG is responsible for writing the new photograph to the directory. We reauthenticate, construct an attribute for storing the photo, and then specify the LDAPModification.REPLACE modification type to overwrite an existing value or create a new one if it does not exist:

```
    /**
     * Handler for Save button
     */
    class saveNewJPEG implements ActionListener {
      /**
       * Called when a button is pressed
       *
       * @param e event from Save button
       */
        public void actionPerformed(ActionEvent e) {

            // Save the image in the directory
            try {
                // Authenticate with the credentials of the
                // owner of the photo
```

```
                ld.authenticate(DNRead,DNPswd);
                // Write image to directory
                LDAPAttribute attrphoto =
                    new LDAPAttribute(ATTRS[0],newFilePhoto);
                LDAPModification mod =
                    new LDAPModification(
                        LDAPModification.REPLACE,
                        attrphoto);
                ld.modify( DNRead,mod );

                // Show current (LDAP) image (same as right)
                currentPhotoIcon =
                    adjustImageSize(
                        new ImageIcon(newFilePhoto), dim );
                currentPhoto.setIcon(currentPhotoIcon);
                currentPhoto.setPreferredSize( dim );
                currentPhoto.setMaximumSize( dim );
                System.out.println("Photo saved to DN: " + DNRead);
            } catch ( LDAPException le ) {
                System.out.println( le.toString() );
            }
            return;
        }
    }
```

The following method handles requests to shut down the application. This code also disconnects from the LDAP server.

```
    /**
     * Handler for window closing events
     */
    class WindowCloser extends WindowAdapter {
        /** Close the window and application
         *
         * @param event event for window closing
         */
        public void windowClosing(WindowEvent event) {
            Window win = event.getWindow();
            win.setVisible(false);
            win.dispose();
            // Close down LDAP connection
            if ( (ld != null) && (ld.isConnected()) ) {
                try {
                    ld.disconnect();
```

```
            } catch (LDAPException e) {
                System.out.println( e.toString() );
            }
        }
        System.exit(0);
    }
}
```

A custom file filter is provided to restrain the file chooser to image files with the `jpg` extension:

```
/**
 * Helper class for JFileChooser to force selection of a
 * JPEG file
 */
class JPEGFileFilter extends FileFilter {
    /**
     * Validate a file name
     *
     * @param f a file name
     * @return true if it is a valid JPEG file name
     */
    public boolean accept( File f ) {
        if ( f == null ) {
            return false;
        }
        if ( f.isDirectory() ) {
            return true;
        }
        String name = (f.getName()).toLowerCase();
        return ( (name.endsWith("jpg")) ||
                 (name.endsWith("jpeg")) );
    }

    /**
     * Returns a description string for the file filter
     *
     * @return description field for file filter
     */
    public String getDescription() {
        return "JPEG Image Files (*.jpg, *.jpeg)";
    }
}
```

All class and instance members are declared:

```
    private LDAPConnection ld = null;
    static final private String[] ATTRS = {"jpegPhoto"};
    // Size of image
    static final private Dimension dim = new Dimension( 144, 156 );
    // Stores image for no LDAP photo
    private byte[] noLDAP;
    // Stores image for no file photo
    private byte[] noFile;
    // When user selects new file to send
    private byte[] newFilePhoto;
    // Track what we read for current display
    private String DNRead = "";
    private String DNPswd = "";
    // Get the working directory
    private String directory =
        System.getProperty("user.dir");
    private JTextField DNEntryField;
    private JPasswordField passwordField;
    private ImageIcon currentPhotoIcon;
    private JLabel currentPhoto;
    private JLabel newPhoto;
    private ImageIcon newPhotoIcon;
    private JButton saveNewBtn;
    private JButton loadNewBtn;
}
```

Execute the program, enter a DN and password, and click the Get Entry button. You will be greeted with the display shown in Figure 6-2. If the entry already has a photograph stored, it will be displayed in the left pane.

Select any JPEG file off the local hard disk and click the Save New button to place it into the directory. Images may also be displayed from the directory inside of a browser that can issue an LDAP query and display a JPEG photo that is returned (assuming security has not been set to prevent this viewing). After you save the entry, the screen will look like Figure 6-3.

After the photograph is stored in the directory, a standard query by the browser will show the photograph with the entry. Figure 6-4 shows the results of a sample browser query using an LDAP URL for the record used in Figures 6-2 and 6-3:

```
ldap://localhost:389/uid%3Dbjensen%2Cou%3Dpeople%2Co%3Dairius.com.
```

The LDAP URL format will be described in detail in Chapter 15. We must use URL encoding for commas and equal signs when pasting the LDAP URL into a browser.

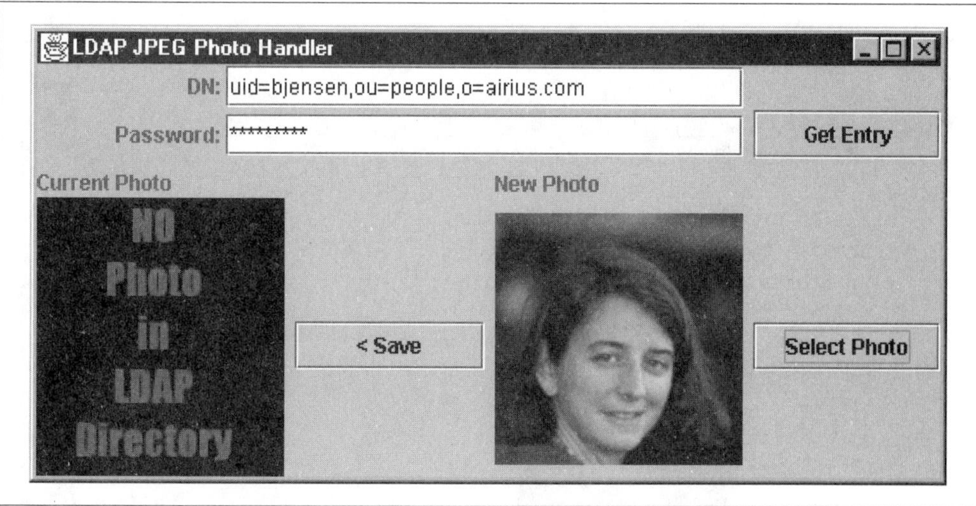

FIGURE 6-2. *LDAP JPEG Photo Handler.*

Storing Preferences and State

The Java language and its serialization model allow direct storage of Java objects within the directory. To "serialize" an object means to convert its state into a byte stream in such a way that the byte stream can be converted back into a copy of the object. Serialization is very useful if you want to persistently store a user's shopping cart or preferences for that user's browser session at your site.

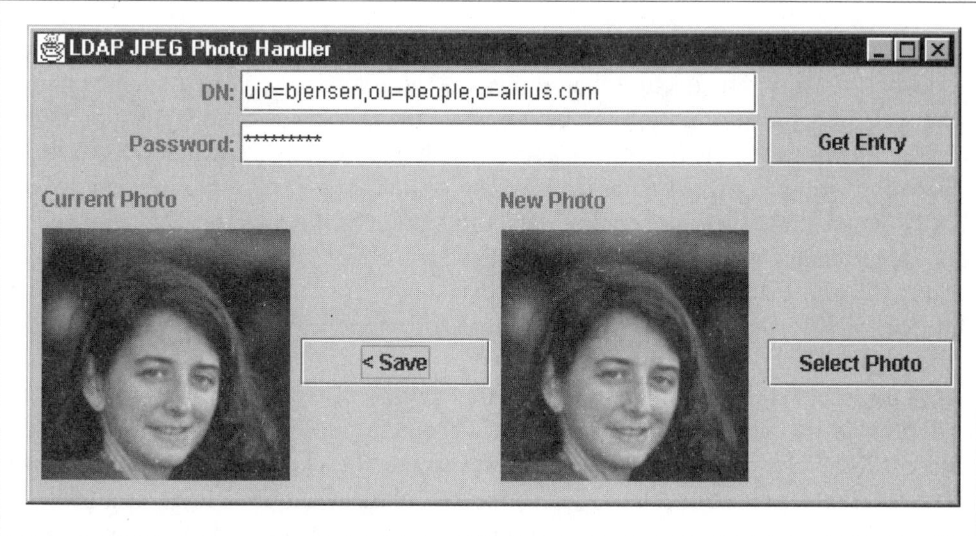

FIGURE 6-3. *After clicking Save New.*

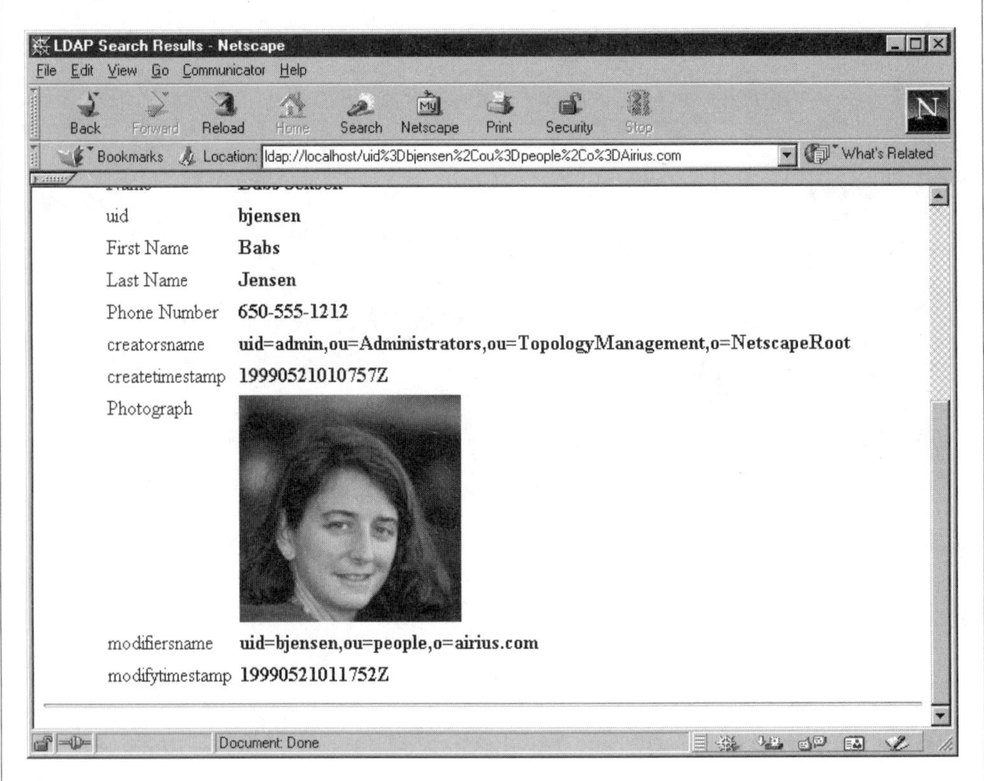

FIGURE 6-4. *Browser view of photograph.*

Servlets have become very popular for building applications on the Net. The servlet model has a session architecture that allows the developer to serialize this information. Once serialized, the information can be stored for the user inside the directory, and when the user returns to the site the previous session can be restored. We will develop a servlet application using LDAP in Chapter 13. The stand-alone Java program that follows shortly demonstrates how to serialize data and store it in the directory. Netscape Directory Server comes with a schema for storing Java objects. If your directory does not include this schema, you can use the file `jndi-object-schema.ldif` that comes with Directory SDK for Java (in the JNDI section) to add support for the schema elements that relate to Java object serialization.

This schema includes an object class, `javaSerializedObject`, that has the attributes `javaClassName` and `javaSerializedData`, among others, for storing this kind of data. The `javaClassName` attribute stores the class name of the serialized object so that applications may determine the class without first deserializing the object. The `javaSerializedData` attribute stores the serialized data. Even if we do not use the value of the javaClassName attribute in the following block of code, it is a mandatory attribute for objects of the object class javaSerializedObject.

The SavePrefs program that follows serializes and deserializes data to and from the directory. If the program is executed with the r option, it will read the data from the directory and deserialize it. Executing the program with the w option will serialize a preferences object and write it to the directory. The object written or read contains two integers and the current date and time.

```
import java.io.*;
import java.util.Date;
import java.util.*;
import netscape.ldap.*;

/**
 * Read or write the serialized form of a preferences object
 * to the directory
 */
public class SavePrefs {
    private static final int NONE = 0;
    private static final int READ = 1;
    private static final int WRITE = 2;

    // Where to store the preferences
    private static final String PREFS_DN =
        "cn=savePrefs,ou=People,o=airius.com";

    private static final String ATTR_CLASS =
        "javaClassName";
    private static final String ATTR_DATA =
        "javaSerializedData";

    // Object classes of the preferences object
    private static final String[] PREFS_OC =
        { "top", "javaContainer",
          "javaSerializedObject" };

    /**
     * Read or write the serialized form of a preferences
     * object to "cn=savePrefs,ou=People,o=airius.com"
     *
     * @param args host, port, dn, authdn, password,
     * [r] | [w, x, y]
     */
```

```
public static void main (String[] args) {

    int pgmOption = NONE;
    Prefs prefvals = null;
    String host = null;
    int port = -1;
    String authid = null;
    String authpw = null;
    int err = -1;

    if ( args.length > 4 ) {
        host = args[0];
        port = Integer.parseInt( args[1] );
        authid = args[2];
        authpw = args[3];
        if ( (args.length == 5) &&
             args[4].equalsIgnoreCase("r") ) {
            pgmOption = READ;
        } else if ( (args.length == 7) &&
                    args[4].equalsIgnoreCase("w") ) {
            prefvals =
                new Prefs( Integer.parseInt(args[5]),
                           Integer.parseInt(args[6]) );
            pgmOption = WRITE;
        }
    }
    if ( pgmOption == NONE ) {
        System.out.println( "Usage: java SavePrefs " +
                            "<host> <port> " +
                            "<authdn> <password> " +
                            "[r]|[w x y]" );
        System.out.println( "Examples:" );
        System.out.println( "    java SavePrefs " +
                            "localhost 389 " +
                            "\"cn=Directory Manager\" " +
                            "password r" );
        System.out.println( "    java SavePrefs " +
                            "localhost 389 " +
                            "\"cn=Directory Manager\" " +
                            "password w 35 62" );
        System.out.println("r reads values");
        System.out.println("w writes values x and y");
        System.exit(1);
    }
```

```
LDAPConnection ld = new LDAPConnection();
try {
    // Connect to server and authenticate
    ld.connect( host, port, authid, authpw );
} catch ( LDAPException e ) {
    System.out.println("Error: " + e.toString());
    System.exit(1);
}

if ( pgmOption == READ ) {
    // Read data from directory
    byte[] info = readBytes( ld, PREFS_DN, ATTR_DATA );
    if ( info == null ) {
        System.out.println( "Unable to read data " +
                            "from " + PREFS_DN );
    } else {
        // Deserialize the data into an object
        try {
            prefvals =
                (Prefs)deserializeObject( info );
            System.out.println( "a=" +
                                prefvals.geta() );
            System.out.println( "b=" +
                                prefvals.getb() );
            System.out.println( "Date created = " +
                                prefvals.getDate() );
            err = 0;
        } catch ( IOException e ) {
            System.out.println( e.toString() );
        }
    }

} else if ( pgmOption == WRITE ) {

    // Create the entry if it doesn't exist
    createEntry( ld );

    // Serialize the object
    try {
        byte[] info = serializeObject( prefvals );
        if (info == null) {
            System.out.println( "Unable to serialize " +
                                "object" );
        } else {
```

```
                System.out.println( "Object serialized... " +
                                    "Size = " +
                                        info.length +
                                    " bytes" );

                // Write to directory
                err = writeObject( ld, PREFS_DN,
                                   "thePrefs", info );
                if ( err != 0 ) {
                    System.out.println( "Error writing to " +
                                        PREFS_DN +
                                            ": " +
                                        err );
                } else {
                    System.out.println( "Object stored at " +
                                        PREFS_DN );
                }
            }
        } catch ( IOException e ) {
            System.out.println( e.toString() );
        }
    }

    // Done, so disconnect
    if ( (ld != null) && ld.isConnected() ) {
        try {
            ld.disconnect();
        } catch ( LDAPException e ) {
            System.out.println( e.toString() );
        }
    }
    System.exit( err );
}
```

The `createEntry` method creates an entry in the directory the first time we need to write the values to it:

```
/**
 * Create the entry if it doesn't exist
 *
 * @param ld active connection to the directory
 */
protected static void createEntry( LDAPConnection ld ) {
    try {
```

```
            // Construct the attributes of the entry
            LDAPAttributeSet attrs = new LDAPAttributeSet();
            attrs.add( new LDAPAttribute(
                "objectclass", PREFS_OC ) );
            attrs.add( new LDAPAttribute(
                "javaClassName", "Prefs") );
            byte[] info = serializeObject( new Prefs() );
            attrs.add( new LDAPAttribute(
                "javaSerializedData", info ) );
            attrs.add( new LDAPAttribute(
                "cn", "savePrefs") );
            // Construct an entry
            LDAPEntry entry = new LDAPEntry( PREFS_DN, attrs );
            // Add the entry to the directory
            ld.add( entry );
        } catch ( LDAPException e ) {
            if ( e.getLDAPResultCode() !=
                 e.ENTRY_ALREADY_EXISTS ) {
                System.out.println( e.toString() );
            }
        } catch ( IOException ioe ) {
            System.out.println( ioe.toString() );
        }
    }
```

The following method reads the entry from the directory. It makes use of the `getByteValues` method to return the attribute values as an enumerated list of `byte[]`. If more than one value is present, only the first value is used.

```
    /**
     * Read the first value of a single attribute from the
     * directory and return it as a byte array
     *
     * @param ld active connection to directory
     * @param dn DN of entry to read
     * @param attr name of attribute to read
     * @return value of the attribute as a byte array
     */
    public static byte[] readBytes( LDAPConnection ld,
                                    String dn,
                                    String attrName ) {
        byte[] attrVal = null;
        try {
            // Get the attribute from the directory
```

```
        LDAPEntry entry =
            ld.read( dn, new String[] { attrName } );
        LDAPAttribute attr =
            entry.getAttribute( attrName );
        // Get first value, if there's more than one
        Enumeration enumVals = attr.getByteValues();
        if ( enumVals.hasMoreElements() ) {
            attrVal = (byte[])enumVals.nextElement();
        }
    } catch ( LDAPReferralException e ) {
        // Ignore referrals
    } catch ( LDAPException e ) {
        System.out.println( e.toString() );
    }
    return attrVal;
}
```

The `writeObject` method that follows writes the serialized data to the directory. Note the use of the `LDAPModification.REPLACE` modification type to overwrite an existing value or create a new one if it does not exist.

```
/**
 * Write the serialized form of an object to the directory
 * as a byte array
 *
 * @param ld active connection to directory
 * @param dn DN of entry to write
 * @param className class of serialized object
 * @param data serialized object
 * @return 0 on success, 1 on error
 */
public static int writeObject( LDAPConnection ld,
                               String dn,
                               String className,
                               byte[] data ) {

    // Use an LDAPModification object to replace the
    // current values of the entry. If they do not
    // exist, they will be created.
    LDAPModificationSet mods = new LDAPModificationSet();
    mods.add( LDAPModification.REPLACE,
              new LDAPAttribute( ATTR_CLASS,
                                 "Prefs" ) );
    mods.add(LDAPModification.REPLACE,
```

```
                new LDAPAttribute( ATTR_DATA,
                                   data ) );

    try {
        // Write the entry to the directory
        ld.modify( dn, mods );
    } catch ( LDAPException e ) {
        System.out.println( e.toString() );
        return 1;
    }
    return 0;
}
```

The deserializeObject method takes a byte array and reconstitutes an object:

```
/**
 * Instantiate an object from its serialized form
 *
 * @param byteBuf serialized form of object
 * @return instantiated object
 * @exception IOException on failure
 */
protected static Object deserializeObject( byte[] byteBuf )
    throws IOException {

    ByteArrayInputStream bis = null;
    ObjectInputStream  objis = null;

    try {
        bis = new ByteArrayInputStream( byteBuf );
        objis = new ObjectInputStream( bis );
        return objis.readObject();
    } catch( Exception ex ) {
        throw( new IOException(
            "Failed to deserialize object" ) );
    } finally {
        if ( objis != null ) {
            objis.close();
        }
        if ( bis != null ) {
            bis.close();
        }
    }
}
```

The serializeObject method produces a byte array by serializing an object:

```
    /**
     * Convert an object to its serialized form
     *
     * @param obj object to be serialized
     * @return serialized form of object
     * @exception IOException on failure
     */
    protected static byte[] serializeObject( Object obj )
        throws IOException {

        ByteArrayOutputStream bos = null;
        ObjectOutputStream objos = null;

        try {
            bos = new ByteArrayOutputStream();
            objos = new ObjectOutputStream(bos);
            objos.writeObject(obj);
            objos.flush();
            return bos.toByteArray();
        } catch(Exception ex) {
            throw( new IOException(
                "Failed to serialize object" ) );
        } finally {
            if (objos != null) {
                objos.close();
            }
            if (bos != null) {
                bos.close();
            }
        }
    }
}
```

Most objects can easily be serialized; all that is required for simple objects is to declare that they extend java.io.Serializable:

```
/**
 * Trivial class to illustrate serialization and
 * deserialization
 */
class Prefs implements Serializable {
```

```
/**
 * Default constructor for deserialization
 */
public Prefs() {
    this( 0, 0 ); // Default values
}

/**
 * Constructor that initializes with values
 *
 * @param a an integer value
 * @param b another integer value
 */
public Prefs(int a, int b) {
    this.a = a;
    this.b = b;
    this.d = new Date();
}

/**
 * Return a
 *
 * @return a
 */
public int geta() { return a; }

/**
 * Return b
 *
 * @return b
 */
public int getb() { return b; }

/**
 * Return date of construction
 *
 * @return date of construction
 */
public Date getDate() { return d; }

/**
 * Assigns a
 *
 * @param a1 value for a
```

```
    */
    public void seta(int a1) { a = a1; }

    /**
     * Assigns b
     *
     * @param b1 value for b
     */
    public void setb(int b1) { b = b1; }

    /**
     * Assigns the construction date
     *
     * @param newDate value for date
     */
    public void setDate(Date newDate) { d = newDate; }

    private int a;
    private int b;
    private Date d = new Date();
}
```

The program that we have presented in this section on storing preferences and state is instructive in that it demonstrates serialization, shows how to modify attributes, and handles the case in which the attribute does not exist the first time. Note that you will need to specify the DN and password of an administrator (for example, the Directory Manager) to alter the attributes of the `SavePrefs` user. The reason is that the default access control does not allow a user to create or modify the `javaSerializedData` or `javaClassName` attributes. In Chapter 7 we will discuss the use of ACIs (access control instructions) to configure access control. Once you have configured access control to allow a user to modify these attributes, you can authenticate as the user instead of as an administrator.

Executing the program with the following commands will write the data to the directory and then read it back and display it.

```
java SavePrefs localhost 389 "cn=Directory Manager" "password" w 6 7
java SavePrefs localhost 389 "cn=Directory Manager" "password" r
```

`SavePrefs` demonstrates a way to maintain state and preferences on the network for your Java programs. Chapter 11 will cover storing program preferences in the directory in greater detail.

Deleting an Entry

The data in an LDAP directory must be kept up-to-date and valid. Eventually an entry will need to be removed. Deleting an entire entry from the directory is a simple process:

```
String theDN = "uid=bjensen, ou=People, o=airius.com";
try {
    ld.delete(theDN);
} catch ( LDAPException e ) {
}
```

The `LDAPConnection.delete` method takes a single argument: the DN of the record to be deleted. All that is needed to delete a leaf node is the DN and the proper authorization to delete the record. An `ou` or `o` entry may be deleted using the code just given, provided there are no entries underneath in the tree. A node that contains entries underneath it is a branch node, and it cannot be deleted using this method. This constraint is a limitation of the LDAP protocol.

The following code removes an entire branch by first removing all subentries underneath. The code will also delete a leaf node and can be used as a generic library routine for any form of deletion. The code contains the necessary warning, but it is worth repeating here: **Be very careful with this code and specify your starting point carefully!** The code is the equivalent of `rm -rf` in UNIX or `deltree -y *.*` in Windows.

```
import netscape.ldap.*;
import java.util.*;

/**
 * Delete a branch point and all records under it
 *
 * USE THIS PROGRAM WITH CARE. IT WILL ERASE YOUR ENTIRE
 * DIRECTORY IF YOU SET A START POINT OF THE ROOT AND HAVE
 * SUFFICIENT ACCESS RIGHTS.
 * !!!! YOU HAVE BEEN WARNED !!!!
 */
public class BranchDelete {

    /**
     * Delete an entry or subtree
     *
     * @param args host, port, dn, authdn, password, YES|N
     */
    public static void main( String[] args ) {
```

```
if ( args.length != 6 ) {
    System.out.println( "Usage: java BranchDelete " +
                        "<host> <port> " +
                        "<dn> <authdn> <password> " +
                        "YES|N" );
    System.out.println( "Example:" );
    System.out.println( "    java BranchDelete " +
                        "localhost 389 " +
                        "\"ou=notneeded," +
                        "o=airius.com\" " +
                        "\"cn=Directory Manager\" " +
                        "password YES" );
    System.out.println( "YES|N is a confirmation " +
                        "for actually doing the " +
                        "deletion");
    System.out.println( "YES must be in all caps " +
                        "and spelled out!" );
    System.exit(1);
}

String host = args[0];
int port = Integer.parseInt( args[1] );
String branch = args[2];
String authid = args[3];
String authpw = args[4];

boolean doDelete = false;
if ( args[5].equals( "YES" ) ) {
    System.out.println( "Deleting " + branch + '!' );
    doDelete = true;
} else {
    System.out.println( "Not deleting");
}

LDAPConnection ld = new LDAPConnection();
try {
    // Connect to server and authenticate
    ld.connect( host, port, authid, authpw );
    // Start deleting from the selected point
    delete( branch, ld, doDelete );
} catch( LDAPException e ) {
    System.out.println( e.toString() );
}
```

```
        // Done, so disconnect
        if ( (ld != null) && ld.isConnected() ) {
            try {
                ld.disconnect();
            } catch ( LDAPException e ) {
                System.out.println( e.toString() );
            }
        }
        System.exit(0);
    }
```

In the next block of code, we first determine if any entries are under the one being deleted. We use a search scope of LDAPConnection.SCOPE_ONE. We are requesting no attributes from the search because the only data we are interested in is the DNs of the entries we find. If there are any entries, we recursively call ourselves with the DNs of those entries to check the next level. If there are no entries, then we delete the entry using the standard LDAPConnection.delete method.

```
    /**
     * Delete an entry, recursing if the entry has children
     *
     * @param dn DN of the entry to delete
     * @param ld active connection to server
     * @param doDelete true if the entries really
     * are to be deleted
     */
    public static void delete( String dn,
                               LDAPConnection ld,
                               boolean doDelete ) {
        String theDN = "";

        try {
            LDAPSearchConstraints cons =
                ld.getSearchConstraints();
            // Retrieve all results at once
            cons.setBatchSize( 0 );

            // Find all immediate child nodes; return no
            // attributes
            LDAPSearchResults res =
                ld.search( dn,
                           ld.SCOPE_ONE,
```

```
                    "objectclass=*",
                    new String[] {LDAPv3.NO_ATTRS},
                    false,
                    cons );
// Recurse on entries under this entry
while ( res.hasMoreElements() ) {
    try {
        // Next directory entry
        LDAPEntry entry = res.next();
        theDN = entry.getDN();
        // Recurse down
        delete( theDN, ld, doDelete );
    } catch ( LDAPReferralException e ) {
        // Do not follow referrals; just list them
        System.out.println( "Search reference: " );
        LDAPUrl refUrls[] = e.getURLs();
        for ( int i = 0; i < refUrls.length; i++ ) {
           System.out.println(
                "  " + refUrls[i].getUrl() );
        }
        continue;
    } catch ( LDAPException e ) {
        System.out.println( e.toString() );
        continue;
    }
}

// At this point, the DN represents a leaf node,
// so stop recursing and delete the node
try {
    if ( doDelete ) {
        ld.delete( dn );
        System.out.println( dn + " deleted" );
    }
    else {
        System.out.println( dn +
                             " would be
                                 deleted" );
    }
} catch (LDAPException e) {
    System.out.println( e.toString() );
}
```

```
        } catch( LDAPException e ) {
            System.out.println( e.toString() );
        }

        return;
    }
}
```

The CD-ROM that accompanies this book includes an LDIF file that you can import into the directory to test the branch deletion code. Import the file `branchdelete.ldif` using the following command:

```
java LDAPModify -D "cn=directory manager" -w password -c -a -f
    branchdelete.ldif
```

This file will create a new `ou` entry called "People2" and place entries underneath it, including another `ou` entry.

Execute `BranchDelete` by typing the following:

```
java BranchDelete localhost 389 "ou=People2,o=airius.com"
    "cn=Directory Manager" "password" N
```

The `N` means you do not wish the deletions to be performed, but instead you want the entries that would be deleted to be displayed. When you are ready to try the actual deletion, reissue the command with the `YES` option instead.

The preceding block of code provides a generic library routine for universal deletions. It is not transactional, though, because LDAP does not support transactions or subtree deletions as a single operation. You may have permission to delete some entries in a subtree but not others, in which case `BranchDelete` will fail midway through the subtree deletion.

Renaming an Entry: Modifying the RDN

Renaming an entry means changing the relative distinguished name (RDN) of the entry. Suppose you would like to rename an entry with the DN `uid=bjensen, ou=People, o=airius.com` to have the DN `uid=babsjensen, ou=People, o=airius.com`. The RDN of the entry is `uid=bjensen`. The `LDAPConnection.rename` method invokes the LDAP operation to change the RDN of the entry. There are four forms of the `rename` method. We will look at two of these forms:

```
public void rename(String DN, String newRDN, boolean deleteOldRDN)
    throws LDAPException
```

```
public void rename(String DN, String newRDN, String newParentDN,
                   boolean deleteOldRDN) throws LDAPException
```

The first form of the `rename` method is for altering the RDN without moving the entry to a different branch node in the directory tree. The best way to understand how the rename operation works is to look at an entry before and after a rename has been issued. The entry in Figure 6-5 is one on which we wish to perform a rename.

A small Java program (`RenameRDN.java`) to test the `LDAPConnection.rename` method is provided on the CD-ROM that accompanies this book. This program takes some simple arguments and passes them directly to the `rename` method after setting up a connection to the directory. We will use it in the following examples.

Let's rename `bjensen` to `babsjensen` and not delete the old RDN. Execute the following command:

```
java RenameRDN localhost 389 "uid=bjensen,ou=People,o=airius.com"
    "uid=babsjensen" "cn=Directory Manager" "password" N
```

The new record for Babs Jensen looks like Figure 6-6. Note (1) that the DN is now `uid=babsjensen, ou=People, o=airius.com` and (2) that because we requested the rename operation not to delete the old RDN, there are two values for the `uid` attribute (the old value "bjensen" and the new value "babsjensen").

Let's execute the command again on the original record and specify `true` for the `deleteoldRDN` parameter:

```
java RenameRDN localhost 389 "uid=bjensen,ou=People,o=airius.com"
    "uid=babsjensen" "cn=Directory Manager" "password" Y
```

Figure 6-7 shows the result. The DN has been changed as in the previous example, and the `uid` field contains only the new value. This is the expected result of a rename operation and is the form that is most commonly used.

```
   dn: uid=bjensen, ou=People, 0=airius.com
   cn: Babs Jensen

...

   uid: bjensen
```

FIGURE 6-5. *The original Babs Jensen entry.*

```
dn:   uid=bjensen, ou=People, o=airius.com

      ...
cn:   Babs Jensen
uid:  bjensen
uid:  babsjensen
```

FIGURE 6-6. *The Babs Jensen entry after renaming without deleting the old RDN.*

Let's continue our investigation with the second form of the rename method, in which we alter the parent. Again, run RenameRDN on the original Babs Jensen entry depicted in Figure 6-5:

```
java RenameRDN "uid=bjensen,ou=People,o=airius.com" "uid=babsjensen"
   "ou=People2,o=airius.com" "cn=Directory Manager" "password" Y
```

As a result, the entry for bjensen is moved into a different part of the LDAP tree—namely, under ou=People2. This operation is not supported in most current LDAP directory implementations, including Netscape Directory Server, although it is defined as valid for LDAP version 3. Figure 6-8 shows the new entry after the rename.

The lack of support in the server for moving an entry to another parent makes the renaming of populated ou or o entries rather difficult. The following code provides a way to effectively move or rename an o or ou, while also moving or renaming all the entries under it. If you wish to delete the original entries at the same time, you can follow the move with a call to BranchDelete, which was presented in the previous section.

The user DN that is passed to the program for authentication purposes should have enough privileges to perform the moves and insertions in the new location of the

```
dn:   uid=bjensen, ou=People, o=airius.com
...
cn:   Babs Jensen
uid:  babsjensen
```

FIGURE 6-7. *The Babs Jensen entry after renaming and deleting the old RDN.*

```
dn:  uid=bjensen, ou=People, o=airius.com
...
cn:  Babs Jensen
uid: babsjensen
```

FIGURE 6-8. *The Babs Jensen entry after being moved to* People2.

directory tree. Operations of this type are normally performed by a highly privileged user (for Netscape Directory Server, typically cn=Directory Manager).

The following code implements a recursive algorithm to create a new entry at the desired location and then move all its subordinate children to the new location. It does not use the rename method, relying instead on the add and search methods that are supported by all LDAP servers.

```
import java.util.*;
import netscape.ldap.*;

/**
 * Class that will move a specified entry to a new location,
 * including any subentries under it.
 * Subentries that are leaf nodes will have their original
 * entry deleted before the new one is created. This is
 * to avoid constraint violations against duplicate uids
 * existing in two places in the tree at the same time.
 */
public class MoveNode {

    /**
     * Move an entry or subtree
     *
     * @param args host, port, dn, new location, authdn,
     * password, YES | N
     */
    public static void main( String[] args ) {

        if ( args.length != 7 ) {
            System.out.println( "Usage: java MoveNode " +
                                "<host> <port> " +
                                "<dn> <newlocation> " +
                                "<authdn> <password> " +
```

```
                                "YES|N" );
            System.out.println( "Example:" );
            System.out.println( "    java MoveNode " +
                                "localhost 389 " +
                                "\"ou=People," +
                                "o=airius.com\" " +
                                "\"ou=People," +
                                "\"ou=employees," +
                                "o=airius.com\" " +
                                "\"cn=Directory Manager\" " +
                                "password YES" );
            System.out.println( "  will move " +
                                "ou=People,airius.com to " +
                                "ou=People,ou=employees," +
                                "airius.com");
            System.out.println( "YES|N is a confirmation " +
                                "for actually doing the " +
                                "deletion");
            System.out.println( "YES must be in all caps " +
                                "and spelled out!" );
            System.out.exit(1);
        }

        String host = args[0];
        int port = Integer.parseInt( args[1] );
        String branch = args[2];
        String newDN = args[3];
        String authid = args[4];
        String authpw = args[5];


        boolean doMove = false;
        if (args[6].equals("YES") ) {
            System.out.println( "Moving " + branch + " to " +
                                     newDN + '!' );
                doMove = true;
            } else {
                System.out.println("Not doing the move");
            }

        LDAPConnection ld = new LDAPConnection();
            try {
                // Connect to server and authenticate
            ld.connect( host, port, authid, authpw );
```

```
            // Start recursively moving
            move( branch, newDN, ld, doMove );

            // If you want the old tree deleted, call the
            // BranchDelete.delete method here

        } catch( LDAPException e ) {
            System.out.println( e.toString() );
        }

        // Done, so disconnect
        if ( (ld != null) && ld.isConnected() ) {
            try {
                ld.disconnect();
            } catch ( LDAPException e ) {
                System.out.println( e.toString() );
            }
        }
        System.exit(0);
    }

    /**
     * Move an entry or a subtree to a new location
     *
     * @param dn entry or subtree to move
     * @param parentDN new parent location
     * @param ld active connection to directory
     * @param doMove true if the entries really
     * are to be moved
     * @exception LDAPException on failure
     */
    public static void move( String dn,
                             String parentDN,
                             LDAPConnection ld,
                             boolean doMove )
                             throws LDAPException {
        // Read all attributes of the entry
        LDAPEntry entry = ld.read( dn );
```

The following code takes the DN of the starting point and breaks it apart. The first element (given a DN of `ou=advertising, o=airius.com` that is being moved to `ou=mktg, o=airius.com`) is preprended to the new location, resulting in `ou=advertising, ou=mktg, o=airius.com`.

```
// Compose new DN of RDN plus new parent
String[] rdns =
    LDAPDN.explodeDN( entry.getDN(), false );
String newDN = rdns[0] + "," + parentDN;
// Create entry object with new DN and old attributes
LDAPEntry newEntry =
    new LDAPEntry( newDN, entry.getAttributeSet() );

// See if there are any children
LDAPSearchConstraints cons =
    ld.getSearchConstraints();
cons.setBatchSize( 0 );  // Get all at once
LDAPSearchResults res =
    ld.search( dn,
               ld.SCOPE_ONE,
               "objectclass=*",
               ATTRS,
               false,
               cons );
// Recurse on entries under this entry - if any
System.out.println( "Copying DN:" + dn +
                    " to -> " + newDN );
```

The following code handles single entry situations in which the original entry must be deleted to prevent a constraint violation.

```
if ( !res.hasMoreElements() ) {
    // Single entry, so delete original first to
    // avoid constraint violations (duplicate uid)
    if ( doMove ) {
        ld.delete( dn );
        try {
            ld.add( newEntry );
        } catch ( LDAPException ldape ) {
            // Error adding new entry, so put old
            // one back
            System.out.println( "Could not add " +
                                "new entry, " +
                                "restoring old " +
                                "one");
            ld.add(entry);
        }
    }
```

```
        } else {
            // This is a branch node, so copy it
            if ( doMove ) {
                ld.add(newEntry);
            }
            while ( res.hasMoreElements() ) {
                // Recurse on moving all children
                try {
                    LDAPEntry theEntry = res.next();
                    String theDN = theEntry.getDN();
                    move( theDN, newDN, ld, doMove );
                } catch ( LDAPReferralException e ) {
                    // Do not follow referrals; just list
                    // them
                    System.out.println( "Search " +
                                        "reference: " );
                    LDAPUrl refUrls[] = e.getURLs();
                    for ( int i = 0; i < refUrls.length;
                          i++ ) {
                        System.out.println(
                            "  " + refUrls[i].getUrl() );
                    }
                    continue;
                }
            }
        }
    }

    private final static String[] ATTRS = {LDAPv3.NO_ATTRS};
}
```

Managing Groups

Groups allow reference to numerous entries in the directory under a common heading. The primary use of groups has been to simplify access control to services. It is far simpler to say the `Accounting` group has access to a particular resource than to list twenty or so user IDs that have access. Groups are also used to manage and maintain mailing lists for e-mail distribution.

The basic type of group is the **static group**. A static group is an entry within the directory with the object class `groupOfUniqueNames`, which contains a multivalued attribute of `uniqueMember`, or one with the object class `groupOfNames`, which contains a multivalued attribute of `member`. The multivalued attribute contains the DN of each entry that is a member of the group. Figure 6-9 shows an example of a static group.

Netscape Directory Server supports an additional type of group: the **dynamic group**. A dynamic group does not store each entry within the group; rather it stores zero or more LDAP URLs in an attribute called `memberUrl`. Each LDAP URL contains a search expression, a base DN, and a scope, which are used to dynamically build the member list when the group is queried. For example, if we want a group for everyone located in Cupertino, we can build an LDAP URL that looks like this:

```
ldap:///o=airius.com??sub?(&(objectclass=person)(l=cupertino))
```

Note that no host or port is specified. A dynamic group is evaluated within the context of the server where it is defined.

A dynamic group has the object class `groupOfUrls` and a `memberUrl` attribute (Figure 6-10).

Although the two forms of group definition appear very flexible, there are some issues with each.

A static group can become large and unwieldy for many members. In addition, the smallest cache unit in many directory servers is an entry; therefore, the whole group must be brought into the server's cache for a search that involves a group or a search in which a group's members must be inspected to determine if the client has access rights derived from the group. For a group with more than a couple thousand members, this requirement can affect cache performance in a negative way. The other disadvantage is that the directory server cannot sort attribute values, but only entries. Therefore, the client must sort the members of a group.

Dynamic groups hold some promise in fixing these problems, but they do not help in the area of random subsets. For example, if you wanted to add just `bjensen`

```
dn: cn=static, ou=People, o=airius.com
objectclass: top
objectclass: groupOfUniqueNames
cn: static
uniqueMember: uid=bjensen, o=Airius.com
uniqueMember: uid=tdahbura, ou=People, o=airius.com
uniqueMember: uid=jackdoe, ou=People, o=airius.com
```

FIGURE 6-9. *A static group.*

```
dn: cn=dynamic, ou=People, o=airius.com
objectclass: top
objectclass: groupOfUrls
cn: dynamic
memberUrl: ldap:///o=airius.com??sub?(&(objectclass=person) (cn=*))
memberUrl: ldap:///o=airius.com??sub?(&(objectclass=person) (l=california*))
```

FIGURE 6-10. *A dynamic group.*

and `jackdoe` to a dynamic group, and no others, you could formulate an LDAP URL as follows:

```
ldap:///o=airius.com??sub?(|(uid=bjensen)(uid=jackdoe))
```

But if you wanted to add `tdahbura`, a third element would need to be added to the filter expression. If a dozen more individual members then needed to be added—well, you get the picture!

The way to work around this particular dilemma is to combine dynamic groups with the use of an attribute in user entries. There is no standard for such an attribute, but in this discussion we will call it `memberOf`. The `memberOf` attribute is a multivalued attribute that is placed on individual records and combines with the power of the LDAP URL to form concise dynamic groups. Let's look at an example.

User Babs Jensen is defined as shown in Figure 6-11. We now define our dynamic group as in Figure 6-12.

The granular control of user acceptance into the group (typical of a static group) is combined with the power to dynamically build the searches for group membership. Together these capabilities provide a flexible means of handling mail lists, access control, and any service in which the determining factor is not the individual user ID, but rather the role of the user.

The `memberOf` attribute is not a standard, and it is not defined for `inetOrgPerson`. In order to use it, you must add a definition of the attribute to the server, include the

```
dn: uid-bjensen, ou=People, o=airius.com
memberOf: mktg602
memberOf: sales754
```

FIGURE 6-11. *Babs Jensen defined as* `memberOf`.

```
dn: cn=mktg602, ou=Groups, o=airius.com
objectclass: top
objectclass: groupOfUrls
cn: mktg602
memberUrl: ldap:///o=airius.com??sub?(memberOf=mktg602)
```

FIGURE 6-12. *A dynamic group that uses* `memberOf`.

attribute in a new `objectclass` definition, and add the object class to any entry that is to become a member of a group. Some LDAP servers may already include the `memberOf` attribute.

Adding a User to a Group

The following code fragment adds a user to a static group.

```
LDAPAttribute mbr1 =
   new LDAPAttribute("uniqueMember",
                     "uid=bjensen,ou=People,o=airius.com");
LDAPModification mod =
    new LDAPModification( LDAPModification.ADD, mbr1 );
ld.modify("cn=static,ou=People,o=airius.com", mod );
```

The following code fragment adds a user to a dynamic group that is using the `memberOf` paradigm.

```
LDAPAttribute mbrgrp =
   new LDAPAttribute("memberOf",
                     "cn=dynamic,ou=People,o=airius.com");
LDAPModification mod =
    new LDAPModification( LDAPModification.ADD, mbrgrp );
ld.modify("uid=bjensen,ou=People,o=airius.com", mod );
```

Removing a User from a Group

To delete a user from a dynamic group, you must remove the group from the user's `memberOf` attribute. For example, if you wished to remove Babs Jensen from the `mktg602` group, you would use the following code:

```
LDAPAttribute mbrgrp =
   new LDAPAttribute("memberOf",
```

```
                    "cn=dynamic,ou=People,o=airius.com");
LDAPModification mod =
    new LDAPModification( LDAPModification.DELETE, mbrgrp );
ld.modify("uid=bjensen,ou=People,o=airius.com", mod );
```

To delete Babs Jensen from the static group `mktg`, you would perform a similar operation using the following code fragment:

```
LDAPAttribute mbr1 =
   new LDAPAttribute("uniqueMember",
                    "uid=bjensen,ou=People,o=airius.com");
LDAPModification mod =
    new LDAPModification( LDAPModification.DELETE, mbr1 );
ld.modify("cn=static,ou=People,o=airius.com", mod );
```

Using the `LDAPIsMember` Bean

We will discuss the use of JavaBeans in detail in Chapter 10. Here, however, the `LDAPIsMember` JavaBean can provide some useful services for our discussion of groups. `LDAPIsMember` is a nonvisual JavaBean for determining group membership. It can be run at the command line or used within your Java programs. You may want to read the source code for the Bean to see how it handles lookups of static and dynamic groups. To execute the Bean at the command prompt, use the following command:

```
java netscape.ldap.beans.LDAPIsMember <host> <port> <group DN> <user DN>
```

The following example checks whether Babs Jensen is a member of the group mktg602:

```
java netscape.ldap.beans.LDAPIsMember localhost 389 "cn=mktg602,
    ou=groups,o=airius.com" "uid=bjensen,ou=People,o=airius.com"
```

The output from the program is a simple string: either `Is a member` or `Not a member`, depending on group membership. The following code sample shows how the Bean is used within a Java application.

```
LDAPIsMember bean = new LDAPIsMember("localhost", 389,
   "uid=bjensen,ou=People,o=airius.com",
   "", "cn=VPs,ou=groups,o=airius.com");
if ( bean.isMember() )
   // is a member of the VP group
```

Conclusion

This chapter has demonstrated how to add, modify, and delete data in LDAP directories. We have presented some stand-alone examples of code for handling tasks such as inserting photographs into the directory. In addition, we have presented complete programs to move or delete an entire subtree. All these programs are strong tools in the arsenal of the LDAP programmer. The final discussion focused on the use of groups, both static and dynamic, for managing at a less granular but more powerful and expressive level than that of individual users. Armed with the information from this chapter, you should have no trouble writing applications that update and maintain LDAP directory content.

CHAPTER 7

Securing the Data

At this point you know how to write LDAP clients that perform most of the basic operations. You can write clients that search, add, modify, and delete entries in the directory.

You probably want most users to be able to make changes to only a subset of records, if any, rather than to the entire directory. To control access to the directory and restrict the permissions to add, modify, and delete entries, you can set up access control lists in the directory server. When LDAP clients authenticate to the server, the directory server can then determine whether or not the client is allowed to add, modify, or delete a particular entry.

You may also want to prevent outsiders from eavesdropping on communications between your LDAP clients and the directory server. You can configure the LDAP client and the directory server to communicate over a secure network connection.

In this chapter you will learn how to set up access control lists in your directory. You will also learn the different methods of authentication. Finally, you will learn how to set up communication over Secure Sockets Layer (SSL).

No Standards for Access Control

Access control in LDAP is an area not yet covered by a standards document, and each server vendor has its own way of expressing and configuring the rights that users have to directory entries. A working group in the IETF is developing a standard syntax for access control, as well as a protocol for querying the access rights that are applicable to a directory entry, but it will probably be years before LDAP servers from different vendors can exchange access control information.

Neither Novell Directory Services (NDS) nor Microsoft's Active Directory allows you to configure or query the state of access control over LDAP. Both require the use of proprietary APIs and protocols, or special administration tools, to view and update access control on the directory tree. OpenLDAP uses the same mechanism that the University of Michigan LDAP server used to define access rights: access control statements in a server configuration file.

Netscape Directory Server stores **access control instructions** (**ACIs**) inside the directory itself. Every entry can have a set of rules that define an ACI for that entry. An ACI appears as an attribute in the entry like any other one, so it can be retrieved over LDAP by searching, or it can be added, updated, or deleted with an LDAP modify operation. An ACI can appear in an LDIF file for import into a server, and it can be transmitted to another server during replication. In this chapter we will take a closer look at how this type of access control works and can be configured.

Although the syntax for expressing ACIs in Netscape Directory Server is different from the syntax that is currently under discussion in the IETF, the functionality is similar. The basic model for hierarchical access control evaluation described in the next section is valid for most directories, including those that do not store ACIs in the directory entries themselves.

Setting Up an Access Control List

An entry may have no ACIs, one ACI, or many ACIs. ACIs allow or deny permissions to entries. When the directory server processes an incoming request for that entry, the server uses the ACIs for the entry to determine whether or not the LDAP client has permission to perform the requested operation.

An ACI on an entry affects all the entries in the directory tree that are beneath that entry. For example, an ACI on the `o=airius.com` entry in the sample directory provided on the CD-ROM that accompanies this book affects all entries under that entry, including `ou=Groups, o=airius.com` and `uid=bjensen, ou=People, o=airius.com`.

If one ACI allows access to an entry and another ACI denies access, the ACI that denies access takes precedence. For example, suppose an LDAP client attempts to write to the `ou=Groups, o=airius.com` entry. If an ACI on `o=airius.com` denies write permission but an ACI on `ou=Groups, o=airius.com` allows write permission, the server complies with the former ACI, which denies permission, since "deny" overrides "allow."

An ACI specifies the following information:

- The *entry* (or group of entries) and the attributes affected by the ACI
- The *permissions* that are allowed or denied for the entry (for example, read or write permission)
- The *bind rule*, which identifies the LDAP client authenticating to the server and the means of authenticating to the server

The permissions for an ACI can be any combination of the following:

- **`read`** permissions allow the client to read the entry and any entries beneath that entry.
- **`write`** permissions allow the client to modify the entry and any entries beneath that entry. In other words, the client can add, modify, and delete the attributes in that entry.
- **`search`** permissions allow the client to search the entry and any entries beneath that entry. Note that in order to view search results, a client must have both `read` and `search` permissions.
- **`compare`** permissions allow the client to compare the entry (and any entries beneath that entry) against a value submitted in a query.
- **`selfwrite`** permissions allow the client to add or delete itself as the value of an attribute in an entry. This permission is applicable only for managing group memberships.
- **`delete`** permissions allow the client to delete the entry and any entries beneath that entry.
- **`add`** permissions allow the client to add new entries beneath the entry.
- **`proxy`** permissions allow the client to assume the identity of another user while executing an operation at or beneath the entry.

The bind rule ("bind" here refers to "binding," or authenticating, to the server) specifies the following types of authentication requirements:

- The users and groups that have access
- The methods of authentication allowed
- The hosts or domains that have access
- The period of time access is allowed (in other words, the starting and ending times for the client's access to the entry)

The bind rule, in conjunction with the permissions settings, defines access to the entry. For example, an ACI can allow `write` permissions only to clients that authenticate as members of the `HR Managers` group during the workday (9:00 A.M. to 5:00 P.M.). The ACI can also specify access only if the client's IP address falls within a certain subnet.

The set of ACIs under a suffix (such as the `o=airius.com` suffix for your sample directory) make up an access control list. You can use Directory Server Console to view and modify the ACIs in the access control list for your sample directory.

To see the ACIs for the sample directory, do the following:

1. Start Netscape Console, log in as the Directory Manager (for example, `cn=Directory Manager`), and launch Directory Server Console. For detailed steps, see Chapter 4 and the *Netscape Directory Server Administrator's Guide*.
2. Click the Directory tab to view the contents of the directory. The suffix for the sample directory (`o=airius.com`) should appear in the left pane.
3. Expand the `o=airius.com` node to display the `People` entry, right-click on the `People` entry, and choose Set Access Permissions to display the ACIs for the entry (see Figures 7-1 and 7-2).
4. Double-click on one of the ACIs to display the Set Access Permissions dialog box for that ACI (see Figure 7-3). This dialog box lists the rules in the ACI that define the permissions and bind information for the ACI. You can double-click on any cell to change the settings for that cell. For example, you can double-click on the Host cell for a rule to specify restrictions on the LDAP client's host name or IP address.

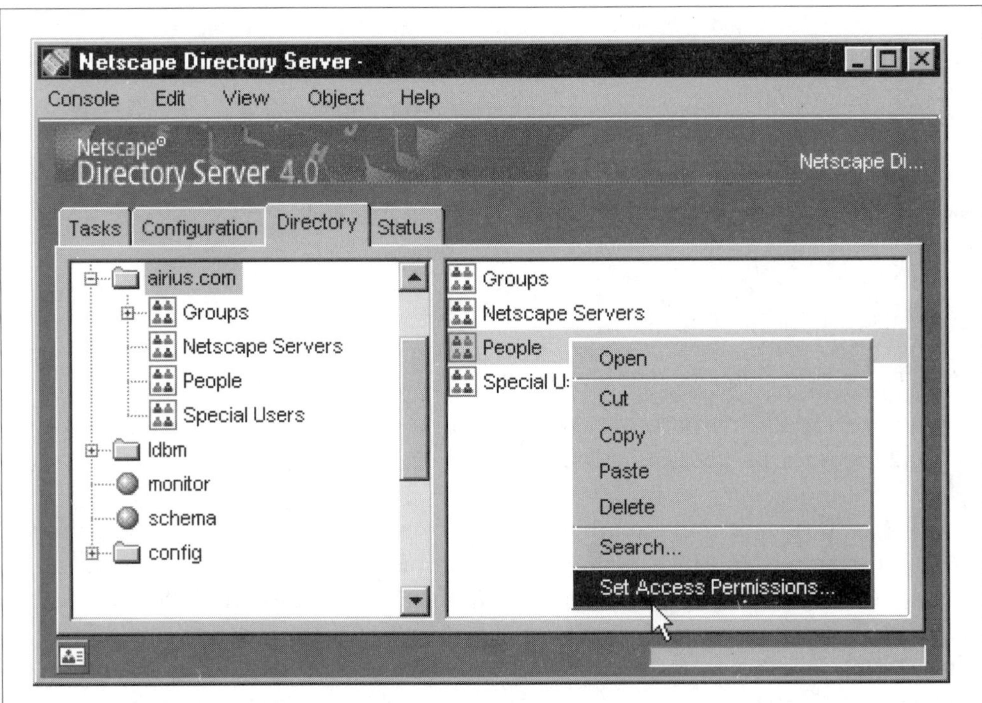

FIGURE 7-1. *Selecting an entry to view ACIs.*

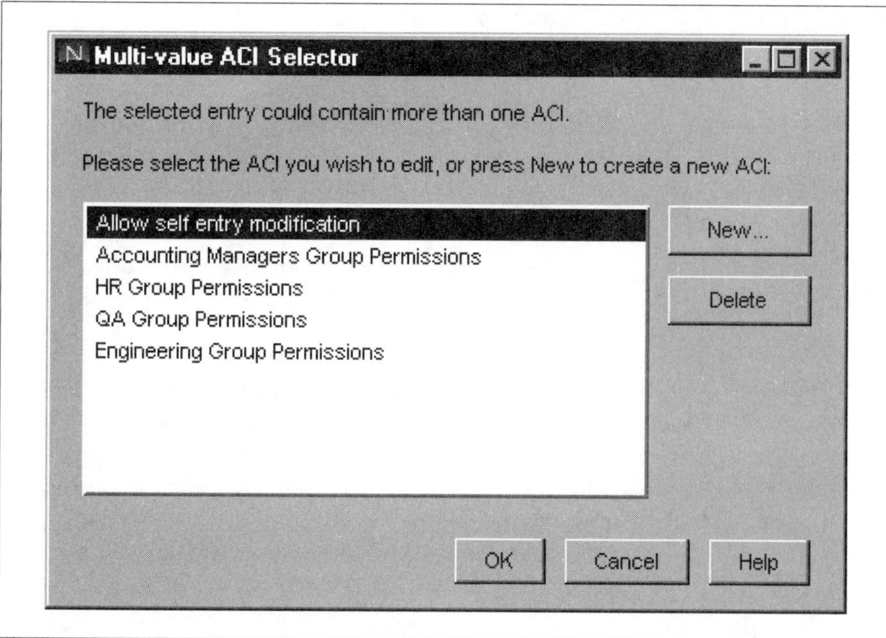

FIGURE 7-2. *Viewing the ACIs for an entry.*

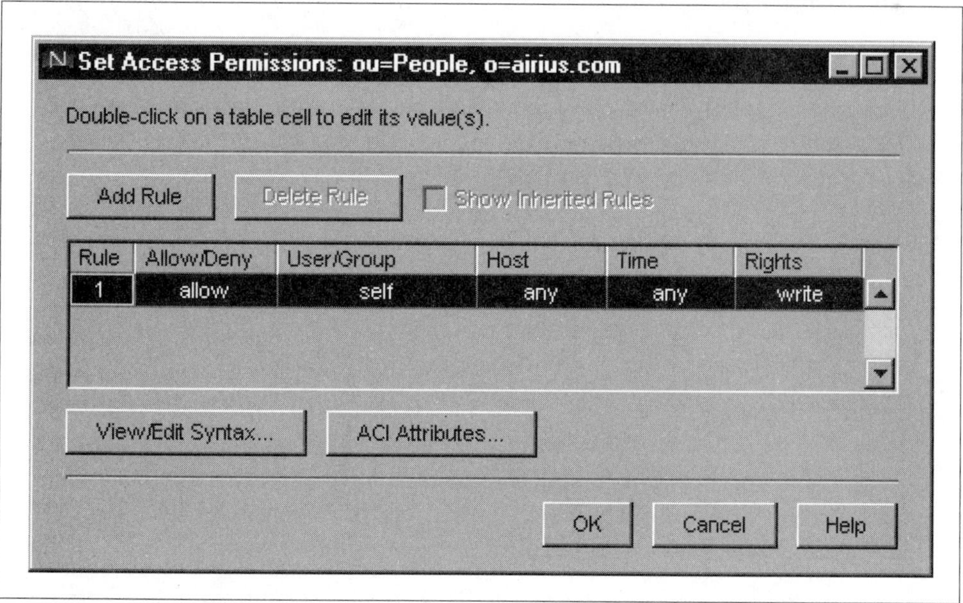

FIGURE 7-3. *Viewing an ACI.*

5. Click Cancel to close the dialog boxes.

In the sample database, most of the ACIs are set on branches in the directory tree, as opposed to individual entries in the tree. You should review the ACIs for `o=airius.com`; `ou=People, o=airius.com`; and other branches in the directory tree.

The ACIs for the `o=airius.com` entry include the following:

- An ACI that allows anyone `read`, `search`, and `compare` permissions to all attributes except the `userPassword` attribute (allowing any user to perform anonymous searches).
- An ACI that allows members of the `Directory Administrators` group (`ldap:///cn=Directory Administrators, ou=Groups, o=airius.com`) all permissions to all attributes (allowing the directory administrators to manage the directory). In the ACI, subjects of permissions are expressed with an LDAP URL. LDAP URLs will be discussed in detail in Chapter 15. When used in an ACI, an LDAP URL starts with the protocol specification "ldap://" followed immediately by another forward slash (since ACIs always apply to the server on which they are defined), and then the DN of a directory entry or one of the keywords `self`, `anyone`, or `all`. In this case, the DN is that of the `Directory Administrators` group.

The ACIs for the `ou=People, o=airius.com` entry include the following:

- An ACI that allows a user `write` permissions to the `userPassword`, `telephoneNumber`, and `facsimileTelephoneNumber` attributes of the user's entry. For example, the user bjensen can change the values of these attributes for the `uid=bjensen` entry.
- An ACI that allows members of the `Accounting Managers` group (`ldap:///cn=Accounting Managers, ou=Groups, o=airius.com`) `write` permissions to all attributes except `cn`, `sn`, and `uid` in the entries that have the attribute `ou=Accounting` (allowing the Accounting managers to modify entries that belong to the `Accounting` organizational unit).
- An ACI that allows members of the `HR Managers` group (`ldap:///cn=HR Managers, ou=Groups, o=airius.com`) `write` permissions to all attributes except `cn`, `sn`, and `uid` in the entries that have the attribute `ou=Human Resources` (allowing the Human Resources managers to modify entries that belong to the `Human Resources` organizational unit).
- An ACI that allows members of the `QA Managers` group (`ldap:///cn=QA Managers, ou=Groups, o=airius.com`) `write` permissions to all attributes

except cn, sn, and uid in the entries that have the attribute ou=Product Testing (allowing the Quality Assurance managers to modify entries that belong to the Product Testing organizational unit).

- An ACI that allows members of the PD Managers group (ldap:///cn=PD Managers, ou=Groups, o=airius.com) write permissions to all attributes except cn, sn, and uid in the entries that have the attribute ou=Product Development (allowing the Product Development managers to modify entries that belong to the Product Development organizational unit).

The ACIs for the cn=config entry include the following:

- An ACI that allows all permissions to all attributes to members of the Configuration Administrators group (ldap:///cn=Configuration Administrators, ou=Groups, ou=TopologyManagement, o=NetscapeRoot).
- An ACI that allows the Configuration Administrator (ldap:///uid=admin, ou=Administrators, ou=TopologyManagement, o=NetscapeRoot) all permissions to all attributes.
- An ACI that allows members of the Local Directory Administrators group (ldap:///ou=Directory Administrators, o=MyDomain.com) all permissions to all attributes.
- An ACI that allows members of the SIE (Server Instance Entry) group (ldap:///cn=slapd-MyHostName, cn=Netscape Directory Server, cn=Server Group, cn=MyHostName.MyDomain.com, ou=MyDomain.com, o=NetscapeRoot) all permissions to all attributes. This ACI is for the case in which more than one server is administered centrally, with information about each server stored in a particular directory server called the Configuration Directory. Each server has an SIE in the Configuration Directory that allows the delegation of administration rights for the server. An administrator can allow a user to administer a particular server by adding her DN to the SIE group.

In Netscape Directory Server, the cn=config entry stores critical configuration information. Modifying attributes of the entry generally causes the changed configuration to take effect immediately, allowing the server to be managed and administered over LDAP.

Note that the ACIs for each entry affect the given entry and any entries below that entry in the directory hierarchy. For example, suppose ACI 1 is applied to the o=airius.com entry and allows write permission to all attributes in all entries for members of the Directory Managers group. And suppose ACI 2 is applied to the

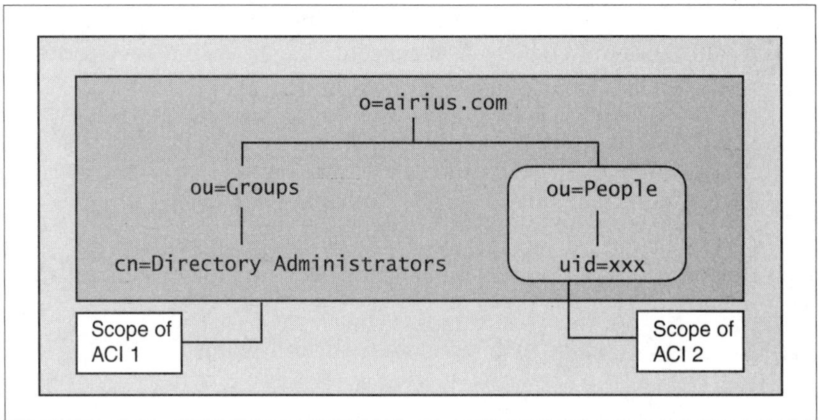

FIGURE 7-4. *Scope of ACIs in the sample directory.*

ou=People, o=airius.com entry and denies write permission to all attributes for members of the Directory Managers group. This means that directory managers can modify entries anywhere in the o=airius.com directory hierarchy except for the entries under ou=People, o=airius.com (see Figure 7-4).

For more information on setting up ACIs for entries in the directory, see the *Netscape Directory Server Administrator's Guide*.

Viewing Access Control Lists through LDAP

In Netscape Directory Server, the ACIs for an entry are defined in the aci attribute of the entry. For example, if you search the o=airius.com entry for the aci attribute using the command

```
java LDAPSearch -b "o=airius.com" -s base "objectclass=*" aci
```

the search returns the following lines:

```
dn: o=airius.com
aci: (target ="ldap:///o=airius.com")(targetattr !="userPassword")
 (version 3.0;acl "Anonymous read-search access";allow
 (read, search, compare)(userdn = "ldap:///anyone");)
aci: (target="ldap:///o=airius.com") (targetattr = "*")
 (version 3.0; acl "allow all Admin group"; allow(all)
 groupdn = "ldap:///cn=Directory Administrators, ou=Groups,
 o=airius.com";)
```

Note that this syntax is specific to Netscape Directory Server. No standards currently exist for ACIs in LDAP directories.

The value of the aci attribute has the following syntax:

```
aci: (<target>)(version 3.0;aci "<name>";<permissions><bind rule>;)
```

The keyword target identifies the entries and attributes that you want to control access to. You can specify the target with the following syntax:

```
(target = "ldap:///<dn of entry>")(targetattr [=|!=]
    "<attributes>")(targetfilter = "<LDAP search filter>")...
```

Use the keyword target to specify the top-level entry that you want to control. For example, to specify an ACI for all entries under ou=People, o=airius.com, define the target as follows:

```
aci: (target ="ldap:///ou=People, o=airius.com")...
```

If you want to apply the ACI to only some of the entries in the directory hierarchy, use the keyword targetfilter. For example, to specify an ACI for all entries under ou=People, o=airius.com that have the attribute ou=Accounting, define the target filter as follows:

```
aci: (target ="ldap:///ou=People, o=airius.com")...(targetfilter =
    "(ou=Accounting)")
```

To allow or deny access to specific attributes within an entry, use the keyword targetattr. Use the operator != if you want to specify all attributes except a selected few. To specify a list of attributes, use the || operator as a delimiter. For example, to apply the ACI to all attributes except cn, sn, and uid, specify the following target attributes:

```
aci: (target ="ldap:///ou=People, o=airius.com")
 (targetattr != "cn || sn || uid")
 (targetfilter = "(ou=Accounting)")
```

For keywords target, targetfilter, and targetattr, you can specify asterisks as wild cards (for example, target = "ldap://uid=*, ou=*, o=airius.com") except in the suffix (o=airius.com).

"Permissions" specifies the list of permissions that are allowed or denied by this ACI. The syntax for permissions is:

```
allow|deny (<list of permissions>)
```

The list of permissions can be `read`, `write`, `search`, `compare`, `selfwrite`, `delete`, `add`, `proxy`, or `all` (the last option is for all permissions except `proxy`, which must be granted explicitly). See the previous section for a description of these permissions. If you specify more than one permission, use a comma to delimit them.

For example, the following ACI allows `read`, `search`, and `compare` permissions to entries under `o=airius.com`, except for the `userPassword` attribute.

```
aci: (target ="ldap:///o=airius.com")(targetattr !="userPassword")
 (version 3.0;acl "Anonymous read-search access";
 allow (read, search, compare)
 (userdn = "ldap:///anyone");)
```

“Bind rule” specifies the authentication requirements for this ACI. Two of the common bind rules are rules based on user DNs and group DNs. Many of the ACIs in the sample directory allow access to only a specific user or group. To deny or allow access by user or group, use the keywords `userdn` and `groupdn`:

```
(userdn = ldap:///<dn>)
(groupdn = ldap:///<dn>)
```

For `userdn`, you can also specify the following values:

- **`ldap:///self`** applies the ACI to the user’s own entry. You can use this bind rule to write ACIs that allow users to modify their own entries.
- **`ldap:///all`** applies the ACI if the user has authenticated. You can use this bind rule to restrict access for users who do not authenticate.
- **`ldap:///anyone`** applies the ACI without requiring the user to authenticate. You can use this bind rule to set up anonymous access to entries (for example, to allow anonymous searches).

To apply the ACI to more than one DN, use the operator `||`. To apply the ACI to all DNs except the specified DN, use the operator `!=`.

The rest of this section illustrates ACIs in the sample directory. An explanation follows each example.

```
aci: (target="ldap:///o=airius.com") (targetattr = "*")
 (version 3.0; acl "allow all Admin group";
 allow(all) groupdn = "ldap:///cn=Directory Administrators,
 ou=Groups, o=airius.com";)
```

This ACI allows `all` permissions to users who authenticate as members of the `Directory Administrators` group. These users have all permissions to all attributes of all entries under `o=airius.com`.

```
aci: (target ="ldap:///ou=People, o=airius.com")
 (targetattr ="userPassword || telephoneNumber
 || facsimileTelephoneNumber")
 (version 3.0;acl "Allow self entry modification";
 allow (write)(userdn = "ldap:///self");)
```

This ACI allows users the permission to write to the `telephoneNumber`, `userPassword`, and `facsimileTelephoneNumber` attributes of their own entries.

```
aci: (target ="ldap:///ou=People, o=airius.com")
 (targetattr !="cn || sn || uid")
 (targetfilter ="(ou=Accounting)")
 (version 3.0;acl "Accounting Managers Group Permissions";
 allow (write)(groupdn = "ldap:///cn=Accounting
 Managers,ou=Groups,o=airius.com");)
```

This ACI allows members of the `Accounting Managers` group to modify all attributes (except `cn`, `sn`, and `uid`) of the entries under `o=airius.com` that have the attribute `ou=Accounting`.

For more information on ACI syntax, see the *Netscape Directory Server Administrator's Guide*.

Modifying Access Control Lists through LDAP

In Netscape Directory Server, since ACIs are defined in the `aci` attribute of entries, you can modify the ACIs for an entry by adding, modifying, or deleting values from the `aci` attribute.

The following section of code illustrates how you can use the `LDAPConnection.modify` method to add an ACI to an entry.

```
String ENTRYDN = "ou=People, o=Airius.com";
String ACI = "(target =\"ldap:///ou=People,o=airius.com\")" +
    "(targetattr =\"roomNumber\")" +
    "(targetfilter =\"(ou=Product Development)\")" +
    "(version 3.0;" +
    "acl \"Allow all to modify room number\";" +
    "allow (write) userdn = \"ldap:///all\";)";
LDAPConnection ld = new LDAPConnection();
try {
    // Connect to server
    ld.connect( 3, "localhost", 389,
                "cn=directory manager", "secret" );
    LDAPModification mod =
```

```
            new LDAPModification( LDAPModification.ADD,
                                  new LDAPAttribute( "aci", ACI ) );
        ld.modify( ENTRYDN, mods );
        System.out.println( "Entry modified"  );
    } catch( LDAPException e ) {
        System.out.println( "Unable to modify " + ENTRYDN + ", " + e  );
    }
```

Authenticating to the Directory

Now that you know how to set up access control on the directory server and have reviewed the existing ACIs in the sample directory, you can determine how you want your LDAP clients to authenticate to the directory.

You can authenticate using one of the following methods:

- *Simple, password-based authentication.* In this method, your client sends a DN and password to the directory server. Note that the DN and password are normally sent in the clear (unencrypted) over the network, so this method should be avoided if possible unless the network connection is secure (for example, if it uses SSL for encryption, or if it is an internal network).
- *Certificate-based authentication.* In this method, your client connects to the directory server over Secure Sockets Layer (SSL). Your client provides a digital certificate to the directory server as identification.
- *Authentication using SASL mechanisms.* **SASL (Simple Authentication and Security Layer)** is a proposed standard for pluggable authentication, including authentication based on means other than those used in simple authentication and certificate-based authentication.

Although all three types of authentication theoretically should work with any LDAP client SDK and any LDAP server that supports them, in reality there is very little interoperability with SSL authentication. Slight differences in protocol or configuration have so far prevented servers and clients from different vendors from authenticating with SSL. Simple authentication, on the other hand, works well with all servers and clients. SASL is not yet available widely enough to evaluate its interoperability.

With Netscape Directory Server, you can set up ACIs for entries to require certain methods of authentication. To set the method for an entry, do the following:

1. Under the Directory tab in Directory Server Console, right-click on a directory entry and choose Set Access Permissions to display the list of ACIs for the entry.

2. Double-click on an ACI or click New to display the Set Access Permissions dialog box.
3. Double-click on a cell under the User/Group column to display the Select Users And Groups dialog box. At the bottom of this dialog box is the Authentication Method pop-up menu, which allows you to specify the authentication method required for this rule.

The rest of this chapter will describe the different authentication methods in more detail.

Using Password-Based Authentication

The LDAP protocol provides a bind operation to allow clients to authenticate to the server. The simplest authentication method supported by the protocol is a method that allows the client to send a DN and password to the server.

In order to use the simple authentication method, you can invoke the `LDAPConnection.authenticate` method or an `LDAPConnection.connect` method variant that takes an authentication DN and password as parameters. Some of the possible exceptions that can be thrown include the following:

- **`LDAPException.NO_SUCH_OBJECT`**. This exception is thrown if the DN you specify does not correspond to an entry in the directory.
- **`LDAPException.INVALID_CREDENTIALS`**. This exception is thrown if the password you specify is not correct.

Below is a section of an application that uses simple authentication to authenticate to the directory server as the user `uid=bjensen, ou=People, o=airius.com`.

```
try {
    String MY_HOST = "localhost";
    int MY_PORT = 389;
    String MY_DN = "uid=bjensen,ou=People,o=airius.com";
    String MY_PASSWORD = "hifalutin";
    LDAPConnection ld = new LDAPConnection();
    // Connect to the directory server
    ld.connect(MY_HOST, MY_PORT);
    // Use simple authentication. The first argument
    // specifies the version of the LDAP protocol used.
    ld.authenticate(3, MY_DN, MY_PASSWORD);
```

```
        // Code to perform LDAP operations as the user bjensen
        ...
    } catch( LDAPException e ) {
        switch( e.getLDAPResultCode() ) {
            // The DN does not correspond to any existing entry
            case e.NO_SUCH_OBJECT:
                System.out.println(
                    "The specified user does not exist: " + MY_DN );
                break;
            // The password is incorrect
            case e.INVALID_CREDENTIALS:
                System.out.println( "Invalid password" );
                break;
            // Some other error occurred
            default:
                System.out.println( "Failed to authenticate as " +
                                    MY_DN + ", " + e );
                break;
        }
    }
```

You can call `authenticate` again to acquire a new identity without disconnecting and reconnecting. Many server applications use this technique to check the credentials of a client against the directory. They keep one or more connections open to the directory but attempt to authenticate over it each time a new client provides credentials.

The preceding example uses the `LDAPConnection.authenticate` method to authenticate to the server. You can also pass the DN and password as arguments to the `LDAPConnection.connect` method to both connect and authenticate:

```
ld.connect(3, MY_HOST, MY_PORT, MY_DN, MY_PASSWORD);
```

As with the `authenticate` method, the first argument in the `connect` method specifies the version of the LDAP protocol. The default is 2.

Note that this method of authentication sends the password in the clear over the network. Unless the client is using a secure network connection to the server, you may want to use a more protected method of authentication.

Communicating over Secure Sockets Layer

The Secure Sockets Layer (SSL) protocol is intended to provide privacy and integrity between two communicating applications. SSL is designed to sit above a transport protocol (such as TCP) and below application protocols (such as LDAP). As part of the SSL Handshake Protocol, a client and server can identify themselves to each other by using digital certificates. Note that the use of certificates for authentication is optional; a client and server can use SSL and still use the standard password-based method of authentication.

A standard has been defined for initiating an SSL session in LDAP. The standard specifies that a nonsecure session can become an SSL session if the client requests `startTLS`. TLS stands for Transport Layer Security, and it is the more recent term for SSL, as well as the one used in standards documents. Once an SSL session has been initiated, the session cannot revert to being nonsecure. However, `startTLS` has not been widely implemented at the time of this writing.

Netscape Directory Server can authenticate and encrypt a session with SSL, but it does so on a separate port from the nonsecure sessions. Whereas 389 is the standard port for nonsecure connections, 636 is the standard for SSL connections. In the following examples, the client immediately begins an SSL session with the server at the secure port when calling `LDAPConnection.connect`. There is no `startTLS` step.

To connect to the directory server over SSL, do the following:

1. Set up the directory server to accept connections over LDAPS (the LDAP protocol that runs over SSL).

   Netscape Directory Server supports LDAPS. To configure the directory server to use LDAPS, you will need to get a certificate for the server (either from a trusted certificate authority or from your own certificate server), install the certificate, and trust the certificate authority that issued the certificate. You will also need to specify the ciphers you want used for encryption.

   For information on setting up Netscape Directory Server to use LDAPS, see the *Netscape Directory Server Administrator's Guide*. For information on setting up LDAPS in other servers, see the Web site for each vendor (listed in Appendix A).

2. Obtain a Java class that implements SSL sockets (for example, Phaos Technology provides a class in their SSLava Toolkit: `crysec.SSL.SSLSocket`).

   Directory SDK for Java includes an interface for creating sockets (`LDAPSocketFactory`) and two classes that implement that interface for SSL sockets (`LDAPSSLSocketFactory` and `LDAPSSLSocketWrapFactory`).

   Note that these classes do not implement SSL sockets on their own. Both classes expect you to specify the name of a class that implements SSL sockets. `LDAPSSLSocketFactory` and `LDAPSSLSocketWrapFactory` use that specified class to construct an SSL socket. You must find and import a class that implements the `createSocket` method of the `javax.net.ssl.SSLSocket` abstract class.

   If the class that implements SSL sockets extends the `Socket` class, use the `LDAPSSLSocketFactory` class to create the SSL socket. If the class does not extend the Socket class (for example, if it extends the Object class), use the LDAPSSLSocketWrapFactory class instead.

Note that Netscape Navigator 4.05 and more recent versions include the netscape.net.SSLSocket class, which implements SSL sockets. If you are writing a Java applet that will run in Navigator, you can use this class.

To connect to the directory server over SSL, your LDAP client needs to do the following:

1. Construct a new LDAPSSLSocketFactory object or a new LDAPSSLSocketWrapFactory object. You need to specify the name of the class that implements SSL sockets. If you are writing a Java applet that runs in Netscape Navigator 4.05 or later, you can omit the class name. The netscape.net.SSLSocket class is used by default. Construct a new LDAPConnection object, passing in the LDAPSSLSocketFactory or LDAPSSLSocketWrapFactory object.
2. Invoke the LDAPConnection.connect method to establish a connection to the server over LDAPS.

For example, the following section of code uses the SSLava package from Phaos Technology to implement SSL sockets.

```
import netscape.ldap.*;
import crysec.SSL.*;
...
LDAPConnection ld = null;
try {
    Object cipherSuite = SSLParams.getCipherSuite();
    ld = new LDAPConnection(
        new LDAPSSLSocketFactory("crysec.SSL.SSLSocket",
                                 cipherSuite));
    ld.connect( "localhost", 636 );
    ld.authenticate( 3, "uid=bjensen,ou=People,o=airius.com",
                     "hifalutin" );
} catch ( LDAPException e ) {
    System.out.println( e );
}
```

In this case an SSL session was established, and then the client used simple password authentication. It was safe to pass the password over the wire because the session was encrypted.

When the client called ld.connect, the SSLava classes started SSL negotiations with the server. The server sent a certificate to assert its identity. However, the client (in this case) has not prepared a certificate database and appropriate callbacks for the SSLava classes so that it can validate the certificate against those it already knows about. The client is trusting the server to be what it says it is.

See `http://www.phaos.com/` for information on configuring SSLava to validate server certificates.

Using Certificate-Based Authentication

If you are connecting over SSL, you can use digital certificates to authenticate your LDAP client to the directory server. In certificate-based client authentication, the directory server requests a certificate from the client during the handshake portion of the protocol. The client sends a certificate that identifies itself (using a DN in the certificate) to the server. The server examines the certificate to determine if it trusts the certificate authority that issued the certificate. The server then determines if the DN in the certificate corresponds to a user in the directory. If these steps complete successfully, the client is authenticated.

As part of the SSL Handshake Protocol, the server can also send a certificate to identify itself back to the client. The client can then determine if it trusts the authority that issued the server's certificate.

Note that Directory SDK for Java supports certificate-based authentication when either of the following conditions is met:

- You are writing a Java applet that will run in a Netscape browser.
- You are using a class that implements the `LDAPSocketFactory` interface and that supports the use of certificate-based authentication.

If you are writing an applet that will run in Netscape Navigator, you use the classes `LDAPSSLSocketFactory` and `netscape.net.SSLSocket` to create SSL sockets. These classes use the browser's certificate database to provide authentication and to determine if the applet trusts the server's digital certificate. Be sure to do the following:

- In the client's certificate database, include the certificate of the directory server or the certificate of the certificate authority (CA) that issued the server's certificate. If there is a hierarchy of CAs above the CA that issued the server's certificate, you can include the certificate of any of the CAs. The CA certificate that you include in the certificate database should be marked as "trusted" by the browser.
- In the client's certificate database, you should also include the certificate for the client. This is the certificate that the applet will send to the directory server for authentication. The subject DN in the certificate should correspond to a user in the directory.

- In the certificate database for the directory server, make sure that the CA that issued the client certificate is marked as "trusted."
- Configure the directory server to map the subject DN from the certificate to an entry in the directory. As part of this process, you may also want to include the actual certificates of users in the directory. If you configure Netscape Directory Server to check the client's certificate against the certificate of the user in the directory, the server compares the client's certificate against the `userCertificate` attribute of the entry for the user.

For information on setting up the directory server to use certificate-based authentication, see the *Netscape Directory Server Administrator's Guide*.

After you set up the browser's certificate database and the directory server, you can enable your applet to use certificate-based authentication by doing the following:

1. Construct a new `LDAPSSLSocketFactory` object. You do not need to specify the name of a class that implements SSL sockets. By default, `LDAPSSLSocketFactory` uses the class `netscape.net.SSLSocket`, which is included in Netscape Navigator 4.05 and later versions of the browser.
2. Invoke the `LDAPSSLSocketFactory.enableClientAuth` method to set up the factory for certificate-based authentication.
3. Construct a new `LDAPConnection` object, passing in the `LDAPSSLSocketFactory` object.
4. Invoke the `LDAPConnection.connect` method to establish a connection to the directory server over LDAPS. As part of this process, the directory server (if set up correctly) requests a certificate from your applet. Your applet retrieves the certificate from the browser's certificate database and sends the certificate to the server.

```
LDAPSSLSocketFactory fac = new LDAPSSLSocketFactory();
fac.enableClientAuth();
LDAPConnection ld = new LDAPConnection( fac );
try {
    ld.connect( "localhost", 636 );
} catch ( LDAPException e ) {
}
```

Using SASL Authentication

RFC 2222 ("Simple Authentication and Security Layer") proposes a method for adding authentication support to connection-based protocols. The protocol (LDAP in this case) supports a command to identify and authenticate a user to the server.

The command requires that you specify the name of the mechanism to use for authentication. Netscape Directory Server supports the use of SASL mechanisms through server plug-ins. You can write a server plug-in that handles authentication through a SASL mechanism. SASL mechanisms are registered with the IANA (Internet Assigned Numbers Authority) and have names such as "CRAM-MD5," "GSSAPI," and "KERBEROS_V4." The same mechanism can be used with many protocols—LDAP, IMAP (Internet Message Access Protocol), ACAP (Application Configuration Access Protocol), and so on.

If the directory server supports the SASL mechanism, it can issue a challenge to the LDAP client. The client sends a response to the challenge. The server and client can continue to issue a series of server challenges and client responses. During this process, the directory server sends the LDAP result code `SASL_BIND_IN_PROGRESS` to the client. When authentication is completed, the server sends a different LDAP result code to the client: `SUCCESS` if authentication succeeded, and an error code such as `INVALID_CREDENTIALS` if it failed.

If authentication completes successfully, the client and server may agree on a security layer to protect the privacy of the session from that point on.

For more information on SASL, you can find RFC 2222 at this location: `http://www.ietf.org/rfc/rfc2222.txt`.

Authenticating with SASL in LDAP

In Directory SDK for Java, you can use SASL authentication by choosing one of the `LDAPConnection.authenticate` methods with an appropriate signature:

```
public void authenticate( String dn,
                          Hashtable props,
                          CallbackHandler cbh) throws LDAPException
public void authenticate( String dn,
                          String mechanism,
                          Hashtable props,
                          CallbackHandler cbh) throws LDAPException
public void authenticate( String dn,
                          String mechanisms[],
                          Hashtable props,
                          CallbackHandler cbh) throws LDAPException
```

Specify the arguments as follows:

- **`mechanism`**. The name of the SASL mechanism—for example, "GSSAPI."
- **`mechanisms`**. An array of names of acceptable SASL mechanisms—for example, { "GSSAPI", "KERBEROS_V4" }. If no mechanisms are specified, the SDK contacts the server to query its supported mechanisms.

- **props**. Any optional properties that apply to the mechanism—for example, the minimum acceptable encryption strength expressed as a number of bits, and the name of a package containing an implementation of `SaslClientFactory` that can produce a handler for the desired mechanism. The argument may be `null` if default properties are acceptable. Table 7-1 lists properties that can be specified in `props`.
- **cbh**. If the mechanism requires additional credentials or other information during the authentication process, it will call the `CallbackHandler` interface that you supply, if you supply a value other than `null`.

Callbacks in SASL

The `Callback` interface is defined in the `javax.auth.security.callback` package, which is provided with the SDK in `jaas.jar`. A current version of `jaas.jar` can be obtained from `http://java.sun.com`. The `javadoc` documentation for the interface provides the following description of `javax.auth.security.callback.CallbackHandler`.

An application implements a `CallbackHandler` and passes it to underlying security services so that they may interact with the application to retrieve specific authenti-

TABLE 7-1. *Properties for SASL authentication.*

PROPERTY NAME	MEANING
"javax.security.sasl.encryption.minimum"	Minimum key length; default "0" (no session protection); "1" means integrity protection only.
"javax.security.sasl.encryption.maximum"	Maximum key length; default "256."
"javax.security.sasl.server.authentication"	If server must authenticate to client, then "true"; default "false."
"javax.security.sasl.ip.local"	IP address in dotted decimal format, for Kerberos version 4; no default.
"javax.security.sasl.ip.remote"	IP address in dotted decimal format, for Kerberos version 4; no default.
"javax.security.sasl.maxbuffer"	Maximum size of security layer frames; default "0" (client will not use the security layer).
"javax.security.sasl.client.pkgs"	A space-separated list of package names to use when locating a `SaslClientFactory` interface.

cation data, such as user names and passwords, or to display certain information, such as error and warning messages.

CallbackHandler interfaces are implemented in an application-dependent fashion. For example, implementations for an application with a graphical user interface (GUI) may pop up windows to prompt for requested information or to display error messages. An implementation may also choose to obtain requested information from an alternate source without asking the end user.

Underlying security services make requests for different types of information by passing individual Callback objects to the CallbackHandler. The CallbackHandler implementation decides how to retrieve and display information depending on the Callback objects passed to it. For example, if the underlying service needs a user name and password to authenticate a user, it uses a NameCallback and PasswordCallback. The CallbackHandler can then choose to prompt for a user name and password serially, or to prompt for both in a single window.

A class that implemented CallbackHandler with support for several different Callback types in a command-line application environment could look like this:

```
class SampleCallbackHandler implements CallbackHandler {
    SampleCallbackHandler( String userName ) {
        _userName = userName;
    }
    /**
     * Invoke the requested Callback
     */
    public void invokeCallback(Callback[] callbacks)
        throws java.io.IOException,
               UnsupportedCallbackException {

        for (int i = 0; i < callbacks.length; i++) {
            if (callbacks[i] instanceof TextOutputCallback) {
                // display the message according to the specified STYLE
                TextOutputCallback toc = (TextOutputCallback)callbacks[i];
                switch (toc.getStyle()) {
                case TextOutputCallback.ERROR:
                    System.out.println("ERROR: " + toc.getMessage());
                    break;
                case TextOutputCallback.INFORMATION:
                    System.out.println(toc.getMessage());
                    break;
                case TextOutputCallback.WARNING:
                    System.out.println("WARNING: " + toc.getMessage());
                    break;
                }
```

```
                } else if (callbacks[i] instanceof TextInputCallback) {
                    // prompt the user for information
                    TextInputCallback tic = (TextInputCallback)callbacks[i];
                    // display the prompt like this:
                    //      prompt [default_reply]:
                    System.err.print(tic.getPrompt() +
                                    " [" +
                                    tic.getDefaultText() +
                                    "]: ");
                    System.err.flush();
                    BufferedReader reader =
                        new BufferedReader(
                            new InputStreamReader(System.in));
                    tic.setText(reader.readLine());
                } else if (callbacks[i] instanceof NameCallback) {
                    ((NameCallback)callbacks[i]).setName( _userName );
                } else if (callbacks[i] instanceof PasswordCallback) {
                    // prompt the user for sensitive information
                    PasswordCallback pc = (PasswordCallback)callbacks[i];
                    System.err.print(pc.getPrompt() + " ");
                    System.err.flush();
                    pc.setPassword(readPassword(System.in));
                } else if (callbacks[i] instanceof LanguageCallback) {
                    // get the language from the locale
                    LanguageCallback lc = (LanguageCallback)callbacks[i];
                    lc.setLocale( Locale.getDefault() );
                } else {
                    throw new UnsupportedCallbackException
                            (callbacks[i], "Unrecognized Callback");
                }
            }
        }
        /**
         * Reads user password from given input stream.
         */
        private char[] readPassword(InputStream in) {
            // insert code to read a user password from the input stream
        }
        private String _userName = null;
    }
```

The SASL Framework Classes

An Internet Draft proposes a standard Java API for SASL clients and servers to use and register mechanisms, and there is an identical proposal to Sun's Java Community

Process to add the API to the standard Java extensions. Eventually the framework classes will be available as `javax.security.auth.sasl` or something similar.

In the meantime, Directory SDK for Java includes `com.netscape.sasl`, the package that contains the classes and interfaces that make up the SASL framework. Sun provides the same interfaces with the LDAP Service Provider for JNDI in the package `com.sun.security.sasl`. The Netscape package includes only the mechanism `EXTERNAL`; the Sun package includes `EXTERNAL` and `CRAM-MD5`.

The `sasl` packages contain a factory class `Sasl`, with the static methods `createSaslClient` and `createSaslServer`. Protocol-specific clients, such as Directory SDK for Java, call `Sasl.createSaslClient` with several parameters to specify the desired SASL mechanism to use and other requirements for the authentication. The `SaslClient` object that is returned by the method can then be used by the SDK to negotiate authentication and optionally also a security layer.

The `Sasl` class may be aware of one or more implementations of the `SaslClientFactory` interface. Each implementation of `SaslClientFactory` can produce a `SaslClient` object for one or more SASL mechanisms. A savvy client may also specify a package in which `Sasl.createSaslClient` can find a `SaslClientFactory` interface—for example, a package developed by the vendor of the client. In general, though, the `Sasl` middleware layer will manage the choice of factory implementations itself.

The SASL implementation in the SDK consists of a bind module that calls the SASL package from certain versions of `LDAPConnection.authenticate`.

- To select the SASL mechanism or mechanisms you want to use, you can invoke the `LDAPConnection.authenticate` method from your application or applet. LDAPv3 servers publish the SASL mechanisms they support in the root entry (the entry with a blank DN):

```
java LDAPSearch -b "" -s base "objectclass=*" supportedsaslmechanisms
dn:
supportedsaslmechanisms: EXTERNAL
```

Generally a client will let the SDK obtain the list of mechanisms supported by the server, and let the SDK try each mechanism to find one supported by both the client SASL framework and the server; however, a client may want to allow authentication using only one or more specific mechanisms, in which case the mechanism or mechanisms are specified to `LDAPConnection.authenticate`.

- Internally, the SDK obtains a `SaslClient` object that can use the agreed-upon mechanism to negotiate authentication.
- The `SaslClient` object is responsible for generating an initial client request to the server and subsequent responses to challenges from the server. The

SaslClient object is also responsible for providing a security layer for encoding and decoding data exchanged with the server after completed authentication, if the client and server agree to use a security layer.

The following procedure and Figure 7-5 illustrate how the SASL framework processes an authentication request from the SDK.

1. Your LDAP client invokes the `LDAPConnection.authenticate` method, passing in the following information:
   - The DN of the user for authentication.
   - Optionally, the name(s) of the SASL mechanism(s) to use. If they are not provided, the server is contacted and its `supportedSaslMechanisms` list is used for authentication.

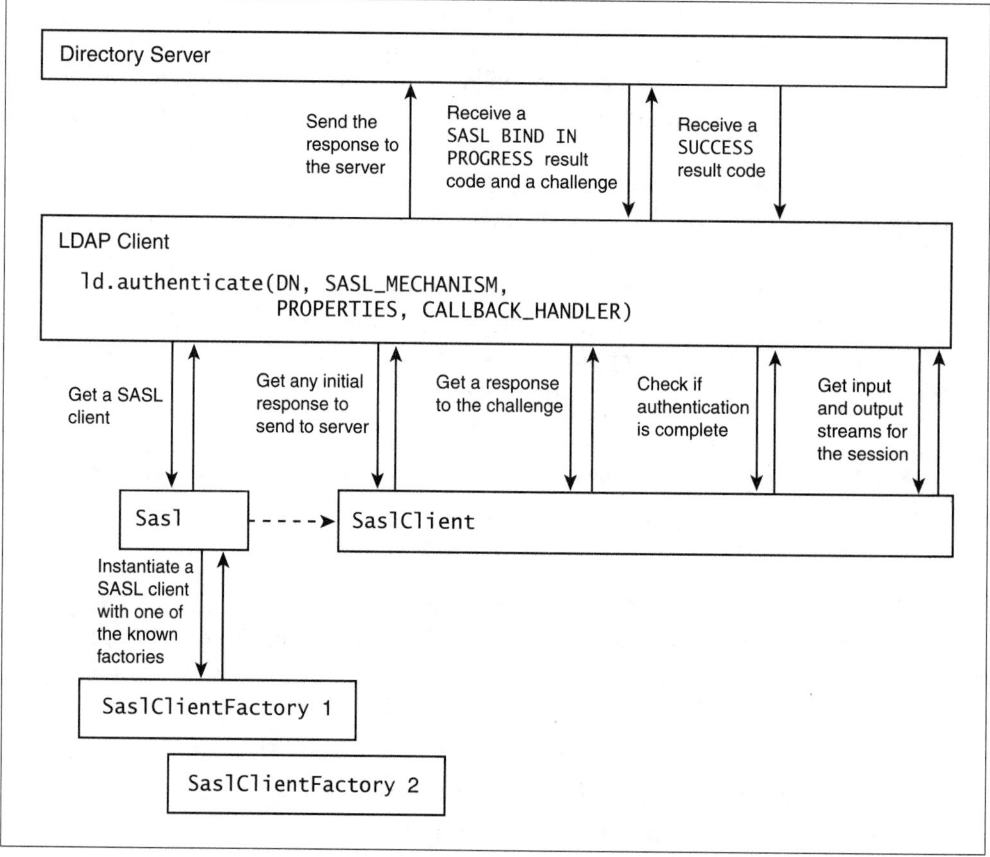

FIGURE 7-5. *How the SASL framework authenticates.*

- A set of properties that apply to the authentication mechanism. One of the properties may be the name of a package containing a `ClientFactory`.
- An object that implements the `javax.security.auth.callbacks.CallbackHandler` interface. It may be used by the SASL client to obtain credentials or other information required to complete the authentication process.

To obtain a SASL client object, the `authenticate` method invokes the static `createSaslClient` method of the `Sasl` class, passing in the DN, the set of properties, the callback handler, the protocol (always "ldap"), and the host name of the LDAP server. The host name is used only with certain mechanisms, such as `KERBEROS_V4`.

To generate the initial SASL request, the `authenticate` method invokes the `createInitialResponse` method of the SASL client. The `createInitialResponse` method returns the initial SASL authentication request, or it returns `null` if the mechanism does not prescribe an initial request from the client. The `authenticate` method sends this request to the server.

2. As the LDAP client receives server "challenges" (which are accompanied by the LDAP result code `SASL_BIND_IN_PROGRESS`), the `authenticate` method invokes the `evaluateChallenge` method of the SASL client to obtain an appropriate response and return it to the server.
3. The SASL client may invoke methods of the callback handler at any time during authentication to obtain additional required information.
4. When the server has finished authenticating the client, the server sends the LDAP result code `SUCCESS` to the client. The `authenticate` method invokes the `isComplete` method of the SASL client to verify that authentication has completed. If the `isComplete` method returns `true`, the SDK calls `getInputStream` and `getOutputStream` so that the SASL client can insert a security layer if one was negotiated.

Preparing to Use an Existing Mechanism

Directory SDK for Java includes a class for only one mechanism: `EXTERNAL`. Additional mechanisms are expected to become available as SASL is more widely used with LDAP. The `EXTERNAL` mechanism is used to validate that authentication has been negotiated by another means—for example, PPP (Point-to-Point Protocol) or SSL.

To use a SASL mechanism for authentication, you need to do the following:

- Ensure that your LDAP server supports the SASL mechanism that you intend to use. In Netscape Directory Server, you do this by writing a preoperation bind plug-in for the SASL mechanism. This plug-in should register the SASL mechanism, retrieve information from a SASL bind request, and create a SASL bind response to be sent back to the client. For more information, see the *Netscape Directory Server Plug-In Programmer's Guide*.

- Write (or find) a class that implements the `LDAPClientFactory` interface and can produce a `SaslClient` object that supports your SASL mechanism, and name the class `ClientFactory`. The `SaslClient` object may also be able to provide a security layer. Tell the `Sasl` class to use your factory in one of the following ways:
  - Call `Sasl.setClientFactory( "mypackage.sasl.ClientFactory" )`, substituting the full name of your factory. The factory must be in the `CLASSPATH` of the Java Virtual Machine.
  - Set the "javax.security.sasl.client.pkgs" property in the `props` argument to authenticate, assigning to it the name of the package (not including ".ClientFactory") containing your factory.

By calling one of the `LDAPConnection.authenticate` methods described earlier in the chapter, you can now use your SASL mechanism. The following LDAP client code asks the SDK to use the `GSSAPI` SASL mechanism to authenticate. The package containing the custom factory is specified in the `props` argument.

```
Hashtable props = new Hashtable();
props.put("javax.security.sasl.client.pkgs", "mypackage.sasl");
ld.authenticate("uid=bjensen,ou=People,o=airius.com", "GSSAPI",
                props, new SampleCallbackHandler("bjensen"));
```

The identity to be authenticated is `uid=bjensen, ou=People, o=airius.com`. The class `mypackage.sasl.ClientFactory` can produce an appropriate `SaslClient` object. No additional qualifiers are required in this case (the defaults are satisfactory). The `CallbackHandler` implementation described earlier in this chapter is used to provide additional credentials required during authentication.

The rest of this chapter will explain how to create and use your own `SaslClient` and `ClientFactory` classes.

Your Own `SaslClient` and `ClientFactory`

Your SASL client class must implement the `SASLClient` interface. You need to implement the following methods in your class:

- **`public String getMechanismName`** returns the IANA-registered mechanism name of this SASL client (for example, "CRAM-MD5", "GSSAPI").

- **`public byte[] createInitialResponse throws SaslException`** returns the initial authentication request that will be sent to the server. Not all mechanisms involve an initial request from the client. If there is no initial request, the method returns `null`.
- **`public byte[] evaluateChallenge(byte[] challenge) throws SaslException`** evaluates a server challenge and returns a response to the challenge. The return value should be `null` if (1) the challenge accompanied a SUCCESS status, (2) the challenge contains data only for the client to update its state, and (3) no response needs to be sent to the server.
- **`public boolean isComplete`** returns `true` if authentication has completed. The `isComplete` method should verify that authentication has completed. If the client still expects another challenge from the server, the `isComplete` method should return `false`. You need to implement this method to handle cases in which the server incorrectly assumes that the authentication process is done, and to prevent man-in-the-middle security attacks.
- **`public InputStream getInputStream(InputStream is) throws IOException`** retrieves an input stream for the session. It may return the same stream that is passed in, if no processing is to be done by the client object. If a security layer was negotiated, the returned object may incorporate an encoding or decoding step. This method can be called only if `isComplete` returns true. It throws an `IOException` if the authentication exchange has not completed or if an error occurred during retrieval of the stream.
- **`public OutputStream getOutputStream( OutputStream os ) throws IOException`** retrieves an output stream for the session. It may return the same stream that is passed in, if no processing is to be done by the client object. If a security layer was negotiated, the returned object may incorporate an encoding or decoding step. This method can be called only if `isComplete` returns `true`. It throws an `IOException` if the authentication exchange has not completed or if an error occurred during retrieval of the stream.

The following class provides support for the ANONYMOUS SASL mechanism. It is a trivial implementation, since in the ANONYMOUS authentication mechanism the client simply notifies the server that it wishes to use anonymous authentication but no challenge-response sequence follows.

```
package mypackage.sasl.mechanisms;

import java.io.*;
import com.netscape.sasl.*;
```

```
/**
 * This class provides the implementation of the ANONYMOUS mechanism driver.
 * This mechanism is passed in the SASL bind request to request anonymous
 * authentication with the server.
 */
public class Anonymous implements SaslClient {

    /**
     * Default constructor
     */
    public Anonymous() {
    }

    /**
     * Retrieves the initial response.
     *
     * @return null, because anonymous authentication
     * does not involve a challenge/response series
     * @exception SaslException If an error occurred while creating
     * the initial response.
     */
    public byte[] createInitialResponse() throws SaslException {
        // No initial response for anonymous authentication
        return null;
    }

    /**
     * Evaluates the challenge data and generates a response.
     *
     * @param challenge the non-null challenge sent from the server
     *
     * @return null, because anonymous authentication
     * does not involve a challenge/response series
     * @exception SaslException If an error occurred while processing
     * the challenge or generating a response.
     */
    public byte[] evaluateChallenge(byte[] challenge)
        throws SaslException {
        // There is no exchange of challenges and responses for
        // anonymous authentication
        return null;
    }

    /**
```

```
 * Returns the name of mechanism driver.
 * @return the mechanism name
 */
public String getMechanismName() {
    return MECHANISM_NAME;
}

/**
 * The method may be called at any time to determine if the
 * authentication process is finished.
 * @return true if authentication is complete.
 * For this class, it always returns true.
 */
public boolean isComplete() {
    return true;
}

/**
 * Retrieves an input stream for the session. It may return
 * the same stream that is passed in, if no processing is to be
 * done by the client object.
 * This method can be called only if isComplete() returns true.
 * @param is the original input stream for reading from the server
 * @return an input stream for reading from the server, which
 * may include processing the original stream. For this class, the
 * input parameter is always returned.
 * @exception IOException If the authentication exchange has not
 * completed or if an error occurred during retrieval of the stream.
 */
public InputStream getInputStream(InputStream is)
    throws IOException {
    return is;
}

/**
 * Retrieves an output stream for the session. It may return
 * the same stream that is passed in, if no processing is to be
 * done by the client object.
 * This method can be called only if isComplete() returns true.
 * @param is the original output stream for writing to the server
 * @return an output stream for writing to the server, which
 * may include processing the original stream. For this class, the
 * input parameter is always returned.
 * @exception IOException If the authentication exchange has not
```

```
     * completed or if an error occurred during retrieval of the stream.
     */
    public OutputStream getOutputStream(OutputStream os)
        throws IOException {
        return os;
    }

    private final static String MECHANISM_NAME = "ANONYMOUS";
}
```

Next we need a SaslClientFactory implementation that can produce an instance of the Anonymous class. It must be named ClientFactory. In this case, the implementation knows of only one mechanism that it can instantiate: ANONYMOUS.

```
package mypackage.sasl;

import java.util.Hashtable;
import javax.security.auth.callback.CallbackHandler;

/**
 * An interface for creating instances of <tt>SaslClient</tt>.
 *
 * @see SaslClient
 * @see Sasl
 */
public class ClientFactory implements SaslClientFactory {
    public ClientFactory() {
    }

    /**
     * Creates a SaslClient using the parameters supplied.
     *
     * @param mechanisms the non-null list of mechanism names to try.
     * Each is the IANA-registered name of a SASL mechanism (e.g.,
     * "GSSAPI", "CRAM-MD5").
     * @param authorizationId the possibly null authorization ID to
     * use. When the SASL authentication completes successfully, the
     * entity named by authorizationId is granted access.
     * @param protocol the non-null string name of the protocol for
     * which the authentication is being performed (e.g., "ldap")
     * @param serverName the non-null string name of the server to
     * which we are creating an authenticated connection.
     * @param props The possibly null properties to be used by the SASL
```

```
 * mechanisms to configure the authentication exchange. For example,
 * "javax.security.sasl.encryption.maximum" might be used to
 * specify the maximum key length to use for encryption.
 * @param cbh the possibly null callback handler to be used by the
 * SASL mechanisms to get further information from the
 * application/library to complete the authentication. For example,
 * a SASL mechanism might require the authentication ID and
 * password from the caller.
 * @return a possibly null <tt>SaslClient</tt> created using the
 * parameters supplied. If null, this factory cannot produce a
 * <tt>SaslClient</tt> using the parameters supplied.
 * @exception SaslException if it cannot create a
 * <tt>SaslClient</tt> because of an error.
 */
public SaslClient createSaslClient(
    String[] mechanisms,
    String authorizationId,
    String protocol,
    String serverName,
    Hashtable props,
    CallbackHandler cbh ) throws SaslException {

    String mechClass = null;
    // Check each of the mechanisms to see if any of them match
    // a mechanism we can produce
    for( int i = 0; (mechClass == null) &&
                    (i < mechanisms.length); i++ ) {
        if ( MECHANISM_NAME.equals( mechanisms[i] ) ) {
            mechClass = MECHANISM_CLASS;
        }
    }
    if ( mechClass != null ) {
        // Found a mechanism, so attempt to instantiate an
        // appropriate SaslClient object
        try {
            Class c = Class.forName( mechClass );
            return (SaslClient)c.newInstance();
        } catch ( Exception e ) {
            System.err.println(
                "SaslClientFactory.createSaslClient: " + e );
            throw new SaslException( mechClass, e );
        }
    }
    return null;
}
```

```
    /**
     * Returns an array of names of mechanisms supported by this
     * factory.
     * @return a non-null array containing IANA-registered SASL
     * mechanism names
     */
     public String[] getMechanismNames() {
         return new String[] { MECHANISM_NAME };
     }

    private final static String MECHANISM_NAME = "ANONYMOUS";
    private final static String MECHANISM_CLASS =
        "mypackage.sasl.mechanisms.Anonymous";
}
```

After you have defined and compiled the SASL client class and a factory that can produce it, you can use the `LDAPConnection.authenticate` methods to authenticate to the server, as described earlier. Specify your factory either with `Sasl.setClientFactory` or by setting the "javax.security.sasl.client.pkgs" property in the `props` argument to `authenticate`.

Conclusion

In this chapter we have discussed the ways in which directory data and client sessions can be protected. Directory data is subject to access control. There is no standard yet for defining and publishing the access control of an LDAP server, but we have looked closely at how it is published and configured in Netscape Directory Server.

Three authentication types are published in Internet standards-track documents: simple password authentication, TLS (SSL), and SASL. All LDAP servers support simple password authentication, but not many support the proposed standard for TLS (although many support SSL over a dedicated connection). SASL is more widely supported in principle, but not many mechanisms are available yet for most servers or clients.

SSL is the only widely used protocol for session privacy. SASL offers a means for negotiating a security layer, but mechanisms to support a security layer are not yet available for most servers or clients.

PART III

GETTING DOWN AND DIRTY

CHAPTER 8

More Power to the Browser: An Applet That Speaks LDAP

One of the advantages of using Java is that you can write an LDAP client that runs as an applet within a browser. Because LDAP clients need to communicate with an LDAP server (which is typically running on a machine other than the one that hosts the Web server), your applet will need to request privileges to connect to the LDAP server. If you sign your applet digitally, the user can determine who created the applet and can make an intelligent decision about whether or not to allow your applet to connect to the LDAP server. In this chapter we will explain the differences between writing an LDAP client as an applet and writing it as a stand-alone application.

Note that although this chapter contains some information on setting up certificates and on signing an applet, it is not intended as a comprehensive guide to applet security. For more information on applet security, visit the Netscape (`http://developer.netscape.com/tech/security/`), Microsoft (`http://www.microsoft.com/security/`), and Sun Microsystems (`http://java.sun.com/security/`) Web sites on security.

What's So Different about an Applet?

Java applets run within browsers and have additional restrictions that do not apply to stand-alone Java applications. Typically, browsers restrict the capabilities of an applet to prevent potential security problems (for example, to prevent a rogue applet from damaging files on the system or from making unwarranted connections to sites on the Internet and passing information to those sites). These restrictions or boundaries are typically referred to as the sandbox (as in "applets can work only within the sandbox").

One of the main restrictions of the sandbox is that an applet cannot make network connections to other systems. This limitation presents a problem for developers who want to create applets that are LDAP clients. The applet typically must be capable of connecting to an LDAP server on a machine other than the Web server that hosts the applet; however, browsers restrict applets from making network connections.

Fortunately, both Netscape Navigator and Microsoft Internet Explorer have trust-based security models that allow "trusted" applets to work outside the sandbox. Trusted applets need to be signed to identify the creator of the applet. To sign an applet, you need a digital certificate that identifies you as a software publisher—an object-signing certificate.

Certificates and Signed Applets

The purpose of signing an applet is to allow the browser to identify the author of the applet and determine if the applet has been tampered with since it was signed.

To understand how digital signatures work, you need to understand public-key cryptography. In public-key cryptography, a unique pair of keys is used to encrypt and decrypt data. The keys are related mathematically; the data encrypted by one of the keys in the pair can be decrypted only by the other key.

Each individual, or entity (for example, a software publisher), has a unique pair of keys. The entity makes one of the keys available to the public and keeps the other key private. The public key allows anyone to encrypt data to send to the entity. Since the corresponding private key is the only key that can decrypt this data, the sender can be confident that the data can be decrypted only by the entity (who has exclusive access to the private key).

Similarly, the entity is the only one who can encrypt data with the private key. If a recipient gets encrypted data from the entity, the recipient can use the public key to decrypt the data in order to verify that the data came from the entity. If the public key decrypts the data successfully, the data must have been encrypted by the private key. Since the private key can be used only by the entity, the entity must have sent the data. In this situation the key pair authenticates that data was sent from the entity. Figure 8-1 illustrates how the public-private key pair is used to verify the authenticity of the sender.

Digital certificates provide the means to verify that an entity owns a given pair of keys. These certificates are issued by a certificate authority (CA). The entity sends a public key to the CA and requests a certificate for the key. The CA is responsible for verifying that the entity is the owner of the key pair. If the CA can attest to the ownership, the CA issues a certificate to the entity.

The certificate contains the name of the entity and a bit-string representation of the public key of the entity. It certifies that the entity with this name is the owner of this key. The certificate also contains the name of the CA who issued the certificate, the time period within which the certificate is valid, the serial number of the certificate, and some additional information. The CA signs all this data with a private key

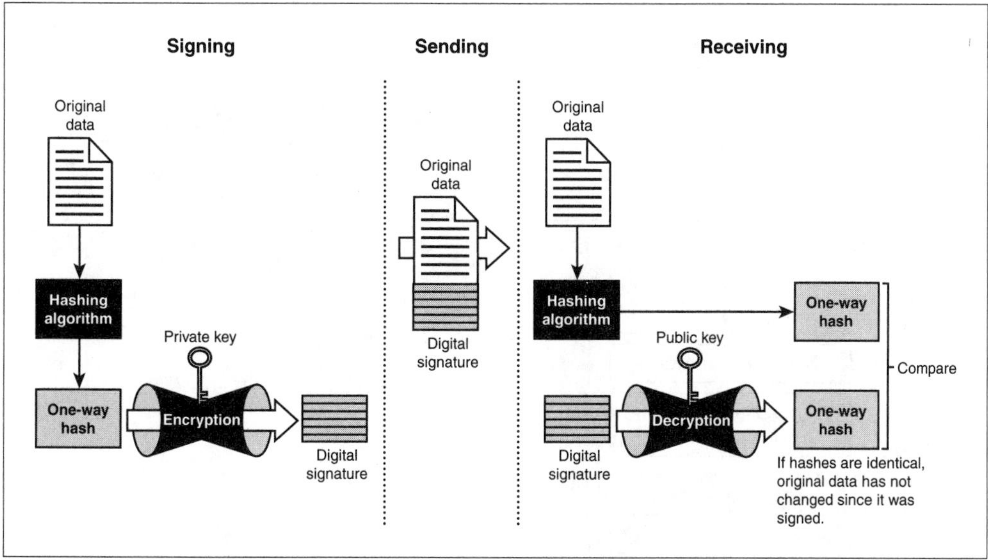

FIGURE 8-1. *Encryption with public-key cryptography.*

and includes the data, the algorithm used to sign the data, and the digital signature in the certificate. Upon receiving a certificate, a recipient can use this digital signature to verify that the certificate was issued by the CA.

The following general description is a simple overview of the signing process and does not describe in detail how the Netscape, Microsoft, and Sun signing tools work. These details are covered later in this chapter in the relevant sections on those signing tools.

A digital signature is generated from the private key and the data to be signed (your Java classes). First, a hash function is applied to the data (typically referred to as the message). From the message, the hash function generates a unique, fixed-length string, which is called the message digest. The hash function should be a one-way function; that is, it should be computationally infeasible to recover the message from the message digest. Examples of hash functions include `MD5` and `SHA1`. The private key is used to encrypt the message digest. The encrypted message digest is the digital signature.

The signing tool also includes the certificate (which contains the public key) with the signed code. At this point the signed code can be posted on a Web server for download, as illustrated in Figure 8-2.

When downloading the signed file, the browser uses the public key (found in the certificate included with the signed code) to check the digital signature. The browser decrypts the encrypted message digest (the digital signature) and then generates its own message digest from the files (using the same hash function). Then the browser

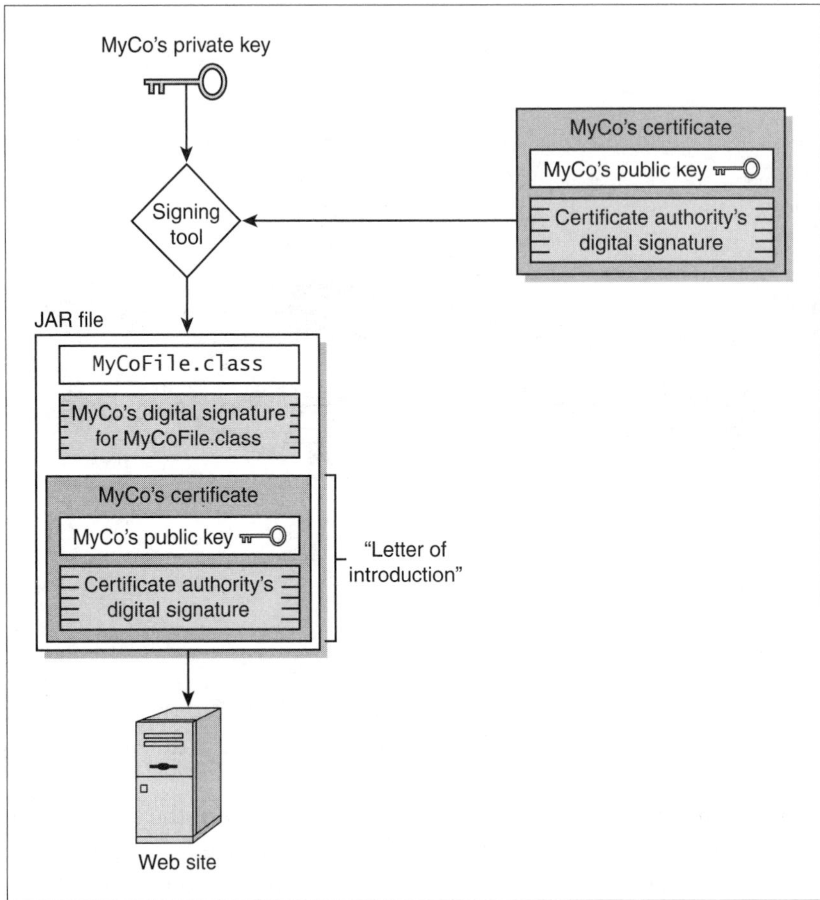

FIGURE 8-2. *Creating a signed JAR file.*

compares the two message digests. If the message digests are the same, the encrypted message digest was decrypted successfully using the public key. The message digest must have been signed by the private key associated with the public key that was included with the code. The comparison of the message digests also verifies that the files have not been modified since they were signed (since the message digests were generated from the files).

Now that the browser has verified that the files were signed by the private key corresponding to this public key, the browser can examine the certificate for the public key. The browser attempts to determine if it trusts the CA who issued the certificate. The browser typically has a database of CA certificates, which are marked as trusted or untrusted. If necessary, the browser presents this identification to the user so that the user can determine whether or not to trust the applet. Some browsers may simply ask the user if the certificate issuer can be trusted; others may have a more fine-grained model and ask the user if the applet signed by the certificate issuer can be trusted to execute a particular privileged operation—for example, to establish a network connection. Figure 8-3 provides an illustration of how the browser determines the authenticity of the signer of a JAR file.

In summary, if you want to write an applet that is an LDAP client, your applet will need to get permissions to work outside the sandbox to connect to the LDAP server. You need to generate a public-private key pair and a digital certificate that certifies that key pair. The certificate must identify you as a software publisher. You need to use the private key to sign your applet, which identifies you as the creator of the applet.

If your company has its own certificate server, you can get the digital certificate from your company's certificate authority. Typically, this certificate is valid only within the company. Otherwise you can get a digital certificate from an independent certificate authority, such as VeriSign.

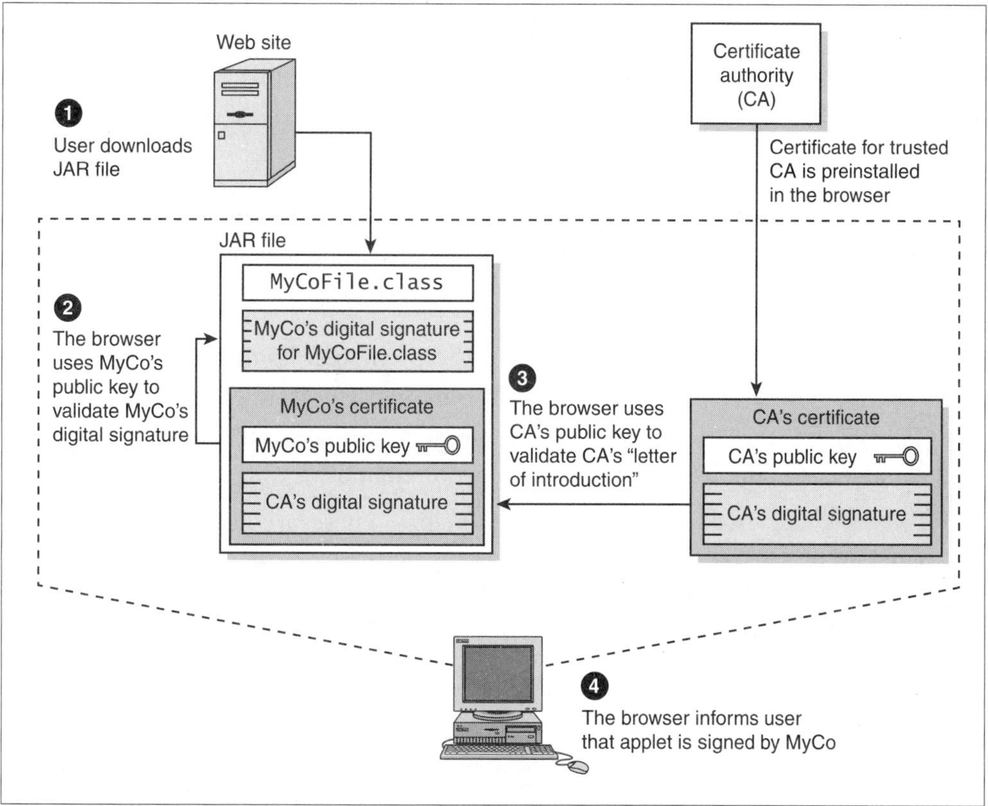

FIGURE 8-3. *How a browser validates a signed JAR file.*

The rest of this chapter describes the details of writing and signing applets for the different browsers.

Writing LDAP Applets for Netscape Navigator

To use your applet with Netscape Navigator, you need to create a JAR file that contains the class files for your applet and the digital signatures for each class file. You create the digital signatures by using an object-signing certificate.

When the browser downloads the JAR file (during the loading of the applet), Netscape Navigator checks the digital signatures for the class files in the JAR file to verify that the classes have not been modified since they were signed. The browser also gets the public key of the certificate authority (who signed your certificate) from its local database of certificates, and it validates the authority's signature on your digital certificate.

If the applet requests special privileges to run outside the sandbox, the browser presents your identification to the user. The browser also reports any problems that occurred during this process (for example, if the browser failed to validate the digital signatures). At this point the user can choose to let the applet run.

The rest of this section explains how to set up your applet for use in Netscape Navigator.

Requesting Connection Privileges

Netscape Navigator uses a capabilities model to determine which applets have which privileges. This model consists of principals, targets, and privileges:

- The *principal* is the entity requesting the privileges. In the case of your applet, the principal is the digital certificate that you used to sign the files.
- The *target* is the permissions being requested. In this case, the target is the capability to establish a network connection to another system.
- *Privileges* are associated with each principal. These privileges determine whether or not the principal is allowed access to a particular target. In this case, a privilege indicates whether or not your applet (code signed by your digital certificate) is allowed to establish a network connection to another machine.

The Privilege Manager in Navigator keeps track of the privileges for each principal. If a principal requests a privilege that has not been granted, the browser prompts the user with a message indicating that the applet is requesting additional privileges. The user can choose to grant or deny that request.

To request the privilege to connect over the network, invoke the static `enablePrivilege` method of the `netscape.security.PrivilegeManager` class, passing in the target `"UniversalConnect"`:

```
netscape.security.PrivilegeManager.enablePrivilege("UniversalConnect");
```

The first time you request the privilege (that is, if the privilege has not been granted before), the browser prompts the user with a message indicating that your applet is requesting this privilege (see Figure 8-4). The user can click the Certificate button to see the details about the object-signing certificate that was used to sign the applet (see Figure 8-5). If the user clicks the Grant button in the Security dialog box to grant the privilege, the Privilege Manager notes that the privilege has been granted. The next time you invoke `enablePrivilege` for the same target, the Privilege Manager will not prompt the user, since that particular privilege has already been granted. If the user refuses to grant the request, the browser throws a `ForbiddenTargetException`.

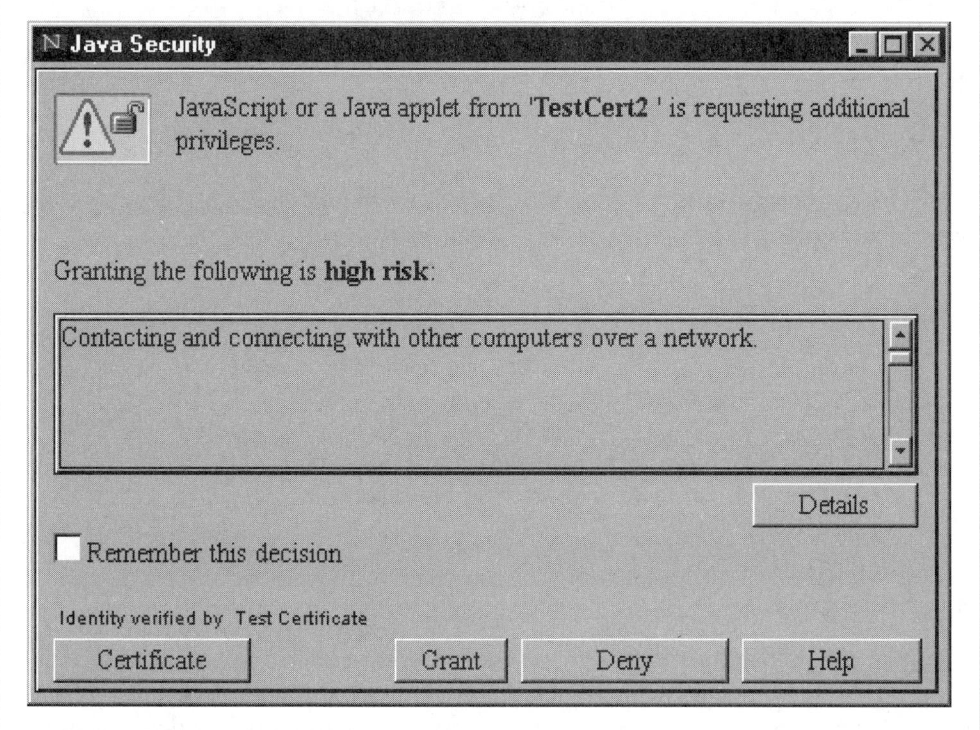

FIGURE 8-4. *Java Security dialog box in Navigator.*

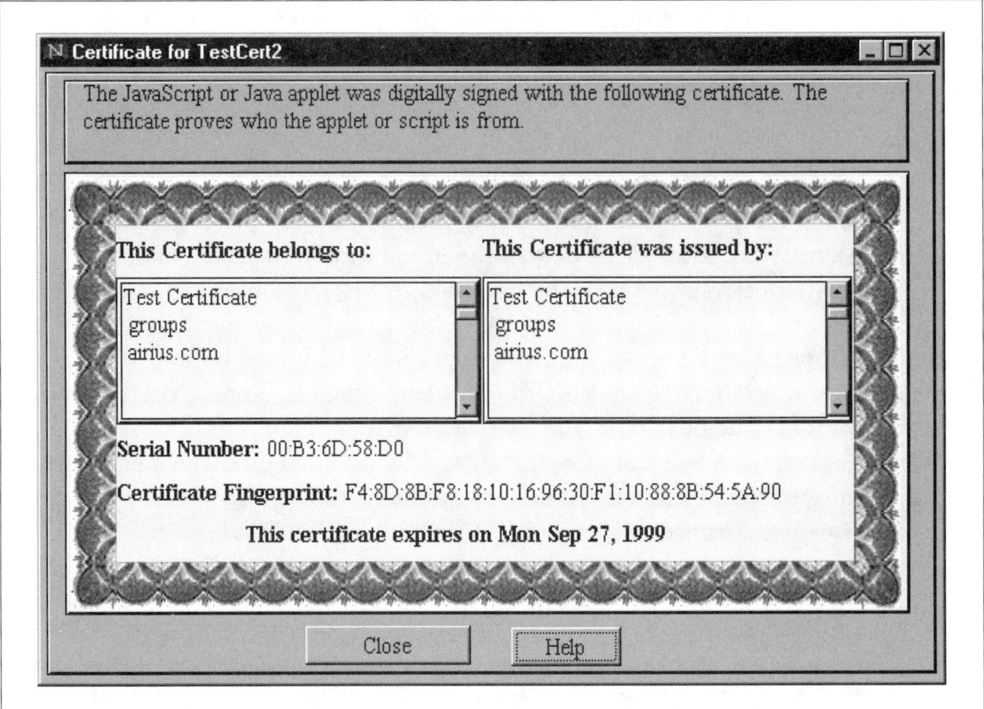

FIGURE 8-5. *Certificate dialog box in Navigator.*

The following section of code illustrates how to enable the privilege to connect over the network.

```
...
try {
    netscape.security.PrivilegeManager.enablePrivilege(
        "UniversalConnect");
...
} catch (netscape.security.ForbiddenTargetException e) {
    /* The user refused to grant the privilege. */
} catch (Exception e) {
    /* A different error occurred. */
}
```

You can invoke the `enablePrivilege` method right before you need to connect to the LDAP server, or you can invoke the method when the applet loads (within the `init` method). The place in your code where you enable the privilege determines when the user is prompted to grant privileges. In the former case, the user will be prompted to grant privileges when your applet needs to connect to the LDAP server. In the latter case, the user will be prompted to grant privileges when the applet loads.

The `netscape.security.PrivilegeManager` class is in the `java40.jar` file that comes with Netscape Navigator. To compile code that references the class, you will need to add the JAR file to your CLASSPATH. In Windows NT, for example, use the following command:

```
set CLASSPATH=%CLASSPATH%;"c:\Program
Files\Netscape\Communicator\Program\Java\Classes\java40.jar"
```

You can also have your code invoke `enablePrivilege` dynamically (using reflection) to avoid including `java40.jar` in your CLASSPATH:

```
    java.lang.reflect.Method getEnabler()
                          throws ClassNotFoundException {
        SecurityManager sec = System.getSecurityManager();

        if ( (sec == null) ||
             sec.toString().startsWith(
                 "java.lang.NullSecurityManager") ) {
            /* Not an applet; we can do what we want to */
            return null;
        } else if (sec.toString().startsWith(
            "netscape.security.AppletSecurity")) {
            /* Running as applet. PrivilegeManager around? */
            Class c = Class.forName(
                      "netscape.security.PrivilegeManager");
            java.lang.reflect.Method[] m = c.getMethods();
            for( int i = 0; i < m.length; i++ ) {
                if ( m[i].getName().equals("enablePrivilege") ) {
                    return m[i];
                }
            }
        }
        return null;
    }
...
...
// Time to request network connection privileges
try {
    java.lang.reflect.Method m = getEnabler();
    if (m != null) {
        Object[] args = new Object[1];
```

```
        args[0] = new String("UniversalConnect");
        m.invoke( null, args);
    } catch (Exception ie) {
            System.err.println( "Invoking enablePrivilege: " +
                                ie.toString() );
    }
```

Be careful where you invoke the `enablePrivilege` method. You should not invoke this method within a public "helper" method (for example, a public method to open network connections) that another applet could subvert.

If you want to restrict the amount of your code that allows network connections, you can invoke the `revertPrivilege` method of the `PrivilegeManager` class after you are done with the network connection. After you invoke this method, the privilege is no longer enabled. Note, however, that the privilege is still granted by the user, which means that you can invoke the `enablePrivilege` method again without prompting the user again for permission.

The Privilege Manager inserts security information into the stack of the caller. This means that the application retains any privileges only until it returns from the method where they were acquired. If you create a method that just calls `netscape.security.PrivilegeManager.enablePrivilege` and then returns, the privileges will have been relinquished by the time the caller of the method regains control:

```
void callEnable() {
    netscape.security.PrivilegeManager.enablePrivilege(
                                        "UniversalConnect" );
}
void mainMethod() {
...
    callEnable(); // Request privileges
    try {
        ldc.connect( "myhost.airius.com", 389 );
        // The call will fail with a Navigator exception
        // because the privileges were released on return from
        // callEnable()
```

For more information on privileges and the capabilities model, see the following references:

- "Introduction to the Capabilities Classes" (at `http://developer.netscape.com/docs/manuals/signedobj/capabilities/index.html`)
- "Netscape System Targets" (at `http://developer.netscape.com/docs/manuals/signedobj/targets/index.htm`)

Packaging Your Applet

When you are ready to test your applet, you should sign your code with your digital certificate and package your code with the digital signatures and certificates into a JAR file. To sign your code, you need the following:

- An object-signing certificate and the corresponding private key (you can request the certificate from your company's certificate authority or from an independent authority, such as VeriSign)
- The certificate of the certificate authority who issued your object-signing certificate
- Netscape Signing Tool (download from `http://developer.netscape.com/software/signedobj/index.html?content=jarpack.html`)

There is valuable information on using the SigningTool in "Signing Software with the Netscape Signing Tool." Before you sign your code, read the documentation at `http://developer.netscape.com/docs/manuals/signedobj/signtool/index.htm`.

If you have not received your object-signing certificate but you want to test your applet, you have the following options:

- You can use Netscape Signing Tool to generate a test public-private key pair and a self-signed certificate for object signing.
- You can set up your copy of Netscape Navigator to allow the codebase of the applet (the HTTP or file URL) to serve as the principal (rather than the signing certificate). If you do this, you do not need to use Netscape Signing Tool to sign your code. For more details, see the section "Using the Codebase as a Principal" later in the chapter.

Generating a Test Certificate

To generate a test certificate, do the following:

1. Exit from Netscape Navigator if it is running.
2. Make a backup copy of the `key3.db` and `cert7.db` files, which are located in your Netscape user's directory (the `Program Files\Netscape\Users\<username>` directory in Windows and the `~/.netscape` directory in UNIX).
3. Set up a password for the key and certificate databases, if you have not already done so. When you run `signtool`, you will be prompted to enter

this password. To set up a password, choose the Communicator/Tools/Security Info menu item, and click the Passwords link on the left. Follow the directions in this dialog box to set your password.

4. Run the `signtool` command with the `-G <name of certificate>` and `-d <location of key and certificate databases>` options. When prompted, enter the appropriate information for your object-signing certificate.

The following is an example of running `signtool`. The information you need to enter is highlighted in bold.

```
D:\>signtool -G TestCertificate -d "D:\Program
    Files\Netscape\Users\myusername"
using certificate directory: D:\Program
Files\Netscape\Users\myusername

Enter certificate information.  All fields are optional. Acceptable
characters are numbers, letters, spaces, and apostrophes.
certificate common name: Object Signing Certificate for Testing
organization: My Company
organization unit: My Division
state or province: California
country (must be exactly 2 characters): US
username: myusername
email address: myemail@mydomain.com
Enter Password or Pin for "Communicator Certificate DB": My Password
generated public/private key pair
certificate request generated
certificate has been signed
certificate "TestCertificate" added to database
Exported certificate to x509.raw and x509.cacert.
```

Running `signtool` generates a test certificate for object signing. This test certificate is self-signed. Although most certificates are signed by a separate certificate authority, this test certificate serves as its own certificate authority and signs its own certificate. If you start Netscape Navigator, choose Communicator/Tools/Security Info and click the Signers link on the left. The new certificate should be listed as a certificate authority, as in Figure 8-6. A self-signed certificate cannot be used in a production environment, because clients will not be able to verify the issuer.

Signing Your Code

Now that you have an object-signing certificate, you can use Netscape Signing Tool (`signtool`) to sign your code and package everything in a JAR file.

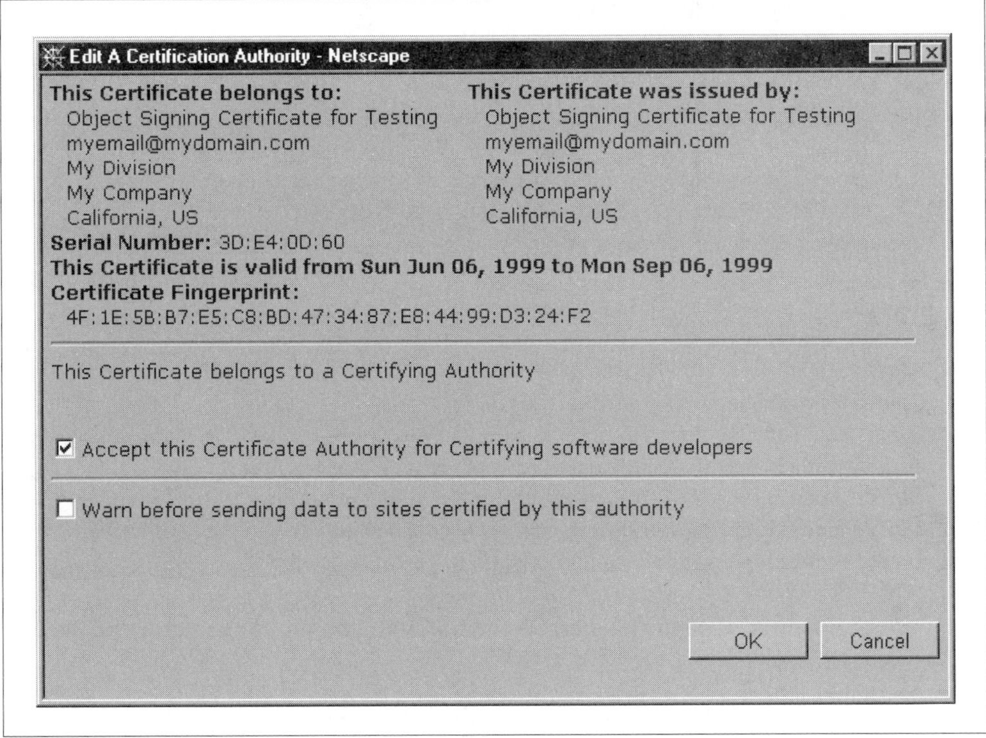

FIGURE 8-6. *Listing a test certificate in Navigator.*

Use the following syntax for the `signtool` executable:

```
signtool -d <cert_dir> -k <cert_name> -Z <jar_file> <code_dir>
```

where

- `<cert_dir>` specifies the location of your certificate database and your key database. For example, in Windows NT this is typically `C:\Program Files\Netscape\Users\<yourname>`.
- `<cert_name>` specifies the object-signing certificate.
- `<jar_file>` specifies the JAR file you want to create.
- `<code_dir>` specifies the directory that contains the code files you want to sign.

The following example demonstrates how to sign your code. The example uses the "TestCertificate" certificate to sign the `LDAPApplet.class` file, which is located in the `D:\sourcefiles\codefiles` directory. The example also creates a JAR file named `LDAPApplet.jar`. The example expects to find the certificate and key databases in the `D:\Program Files\Netscape\Users\myname` directory. The information you need to enter is highlighted in bold.

```
D:\sourcefiles>signtool -d "D:\Program Files\Netscape\Users\myname" -k
    TestCertificate -Z LDAPApplet.jar codefiles
using key "TestCertificate"
using certificate directory: D:\Program Files\Netscape\Users\myname
Generating codefiles/META-INF/manifest.mf file..
-> LDAPApplet.class
adding codefiles/LDAPApplet.class to LDAPApplet.jar...(deflated 44%)
Generating zigbert.sf file..
Enter Password or Pin for "Communicator Certificate DB": MyPassword
adding codefiles/META-INF/manifest.mf to LDAPApplet.jar...(deflated 15%)
adding codefiles/META-INF/zigbert.sf to LDAPApplet.jar...(deflated 27%)
adding codefiles/META-INF/zigbert.rsa to LDAPApplet.jar...(deflated 45%)
tree "codefiles" signed successfully
```

In this example, `signtool` generates the following files in the directory `META-INF`:

- A manifest file (`manifest.mf`)
- A signature instruction file (`zigbert.sf`)
- A digital signature file (`zigbert.rsa`)

The manifest file contains a list of files to be signed. For each file, the manifest file lists the file name and the message digests of the file (using `MD5` and `SHA1`):

```
Manifest-Version: 1.0
Created-By: Signtool (signtool 1.0)
Comments: PLEASE DO NOT EDIT THIS FILE. YOU WILL BREAK IT.

Name: DirBrowser$1.class
Digest-Algorithms: MD5 SHA1
MD5-Digest: PYjS+BxHowayyFXC2zneEQ==
SHA1-Digest: 0NEKcktsn9HZelX/GF6dCHQ7quQ=

Name: DirBrowser$2.class
Digest-Algorithms: MD5 SHA1
MD5-Digest: O9bVKN4s1XZv61YXvUD6Tg==
SHA1-Digest: j7b3+ueHUvC6huTVr9JelRELDU8=

Name: DirBrowser.class
Digest-Algorithms: MD5 SHA1
```

```
MD5-Digest: 8XhQaKaVIRIzu83x/WNQcg==
SHA1-Digest: as5dt4GoADFRSm4SS5EFcCFBwgc=
```

The signature instruction file contains message digests of the entries in the manifest file. For each section that specifies the name and message digest of a file, the signature instruction file contains a message digest of that section:

```
Signature-Version: 1.0
Created-By: Signtool (signtool 1.0)
Comments: PLEASE DO NOT EDIT THIS FILE. YOU WILL BREAK IT.
Digest-Algorithms: MD5 SHA1
MD5-Digest: AS2/p3IMG4G4R8ngJZMXYg==
SHA1-Digest: K+5iG58pGOawiYucrif0fQDkU8g=

Name: DirBrowser$1.class
Digest-Algorithms: MD5 SHA1
MD5-Digest: AoZ/ajkQpon7YtmS8vj9ww==
SHA1-Digest: hH0UCdwgWKA6a/3MBPEpz8+8nus=

Name: DirBrowser$2.class
Digest-Algorithms: MD5 SHA1
MD5-Digest: CJW1d+60OUI/yFg8setPzw==
SHA1-Digest: hsIH+/+cUtnqO5VvrqJ7GAtk6k4=

Name: DirBrowser.class
Digest-Algorithms: MD5 SHA1
MD5-Digest: MY9zMx2XR+5y7KhyJTsquQ==
SHA1-Digest: ff03BtltOU2rdQ/rUL4VNA89DQk=
```

The message digest of the signature instruction file is signed and placed in the digital signature file. The digital signature file also contains the certificate for the key pair used to sign the files. The utility `signtool` puts all the files into the JAR file (`LDAPApplet.jar` in this example).

To verify that your files have been signed correctly, use the following syntax for the `signtool` executable:

```
signtool -d <cert_dir> -v <jar_file>
```

where

- `<cert_dir>` specifies the location of your certificate database and your key database. For example, in Windows NT this is typically `C:\Program Files\Netscape\Users\<yourname>`).
- `<jar_file>` specifies the JAR file you have just created.

The following example demonstrates how to verify that your code has been signed correctly. The example expects to find the certificate and key databases in the `D:\Program Files\Netscape\Users\myname` directory. The information you need to enter is highlighted in bold.

```
D:\sourcefiles>signtool -d "D:\Program Files\Netscape\Users\myname" -v
    LDAPApplet.jar
using certificate directory: D:\Program Files\Netscape\Users\myname
archive "LDAPApplet.jar" has passed crypto verification.

          status   path
          ------   ----------
        verified   LDAPApplet.class
```

For more information on the JAR format as used by Netscape, see the Netscape documentation at `http://developer.netscape.com/docs/manuals/signedobj/jarfile/index.html`. For more information on using Netscape Signing Tool, see the manual *Signing Software with Netscape Signing Tool 1.1* at

`http://developer.netscape.com/docs/manuals/signedobj/signtool/index.htm.`

Testing Your Applet

Next you need to import the CA certificate into the browser that you will use to test the applet (if you are testing the applet from a different system). To import the CA certificate into other browsers, you need to set up a Web page to serve the certificate, and you need to configure your Web server to send the certificate with a specified MIME type. Follow these steps:

1. Create a Web page that contains a link pointing to the file `x509.cacert`. This file was exported when you generated your test certificate. For example,

   ```
   <a href="x509.cacert">Import the Test Certificate</a>
   ```

2. Place the Web page and the `x509.cacert` file in a document directory under your Web server.
3. Configure your Web server to use the `MIME type application/x-x509-ca-cert` when serving files with the extension `.cacert`.
4. Load the Web page in the browser, and click the link to import the certificate.

5. Netscape Navigator presents a wizard for importing a CA certificate. Be sure to indicate that you trust this CA for issuing object-signing certificates.

   Now create a Web page for your applet, and load the Web page in your browser.

Using the Codebase as a Principal

If you do not want to generate a test certificate, you can still test your applet by configuring Netscape Navigator to use as a principal the codebase (that is, the file URL or HTTP URL) rather than a signed certificate. Note that this configuration is intended for development use only. Your users should not configure the browser in this way.

You also need to be cautious when downloading applets from the Internet. When an unknown applet attempts to enable a privilege, the browser prompts you to grant or deny the privilege. Be wary of any codebase principal that appears here, since you cannot verify the identity of the applet creator or the integrity of the applet.

To set up the browser to use codebase principals, exit Netscape Navigator and open the file `prefs.js` in a text editor. Like the key and certificate database files, the `prefs.js` file is located in the Netscape user's directory. Add the following line:

```
user_pref("signed.applets.codebase_principal_support", true);
```

Writing LDAP Applets for Microsoft Internet Explorer

To use your applet with Microsoft Internet Explorer, you need to create a CAB (cabinet) file that contains the class files for your applet, your digital certificate, and the digital signatures for the CAB file. The certificate must be a software publishing certificate (SPC).

When a user downloads the CAB file (when loading someone else's applet), Internet Explorer checks the digital signatures for the class files in the CAB file to verify that the classes have not been modified since they were signed. The browser also checks the signature for permission information and compares the requested permissions against the security zones (which are defined in the next section) set up by the user. If the requested permissions exceed the permissions allowed for the current zone, the browser prompts the user to allow or deny the permissions. The browser also displays information from the certificate to the user.

To develop an applet and sign the CAB file, you need Microsoft SDK for Java. You can download this SDK from the Microsoft Web site

```
(http://www.microsoft.com/java/sdk/32/default.htm).
```

The rest of this section explains how to set up your applet for use in Internet Explorer.

Requesting Connection Privileges

Internet Explorer uses a model that combines permission requests with security zones to determine which applets have which permissions.

Zones allow users to set up security policies for different groups of sites. Internet Explorer groups Web sites into four zones:

1. *Local intranet.* These are sites in the network of the user's company.
2. *Trusted sites.* These are sites the user trusts, and they require only a low level of security when downloading and running files.
3. *Internet.*
4. *Restricted sites.* These are sites the user does not trust, and they require a medium or high level of security.

The user can assign one of the following security levels to each zone:

- *High security.* This security level allows Java applets to run within the sandbox without prompting the user for permission.
- *Medium security.* This security level allows Java applets to run within the sandbox and to use up to 1MB of scratch space on the local system.
- *Low security.* This security level allows Java applets to run outside of the sandbox as fully trusted applets.
- *Custom security.* This option allows the system administrator or the user to set up a custom security level.

The security zones and levels are described in more detail in the documentation for Microsoft SDK for Java and in the online help for Internet Explorer.

CAB files containing Java classes can also be signed with security levels. For example, if a Java applet needs to use scratch space on the local machine, the CAB file for the applet can be signed with the medium security level. This designation indicates that the applet will be requesting permissions to operate under the medium security level or lower.

If a CAB file from a given zone requests a permission higher than the permissions allowed for that zone, the user is prompted to grant or deny the permission. For example, suppose a user assigns the high security level to the Internet zone. If the user downloads a CAB file from the Internet that is signed with the medium security level, the browser will prompt the user to grant or deny the permissions to run at the medium security level.

If you expect your applet to be used by Internet Explorer 4.01 and more recent browsers, you can sign the CAB file with specific permissions to access computers on the network (rather than as a fully trusted applet with the low security level). For more details, see the section "Signing Your Code" later in this discussion of applets in Internet Explorer.

Even though the user grants permissions before downloading and running your applet, you still need to ask for ("assert," in Internet Explorer parlance) permission to connect to the network. When running the applet, the Microsoft Virtual Machine crawls the call stack to verify that all callers are trusted to perform the operation. During this verification process, the Security Manager throws a `SecurityException [Host]` if your code did not assert permission to connect to the network before attempting to connect.

To assert permission to connect to other machines over the network, invoke the following method:

```
import com.ms.security.*;
...
PolicyEngine.assertPermission(PermissionID.NETIO);
```

This method prevents the Security Manager from crawling the call stack. Note that before you decide to assert permissions, you should make sure any untrusted members of the call stack cannot use the permissions to damage or cause potential problems with the user's machine. Typically this means that you will call the method at the lowest method level at which permissions are needed in your application. After you are done interacting with the LDAP server over the network, you can invoke the `revertPermission` method to negate the effect of the permission.

For more information on permissions and the policy engine, see the documentation for Microsoft SDK for Java.

Packaging Your Applet

When you are ready to test your applet, you should package your code in a CAB file and sign your code with your digital certificate. You can use the `cabarc` utility (provided with Microsoft SDK for Java) to create the CAB file. To sign the CAB file, you need the following:

- A software publishing certificate (SPC) and the corresponding private key (you can request the certificate from your company's certificate authority or from an independent authority, such as VeriSign)
- The certificate of the certificate authority who issued your SPC
- The `signcode` utility, which is included with Microsoft SDK for Java

If you have not received your SPC but you want to test your applet, you can use the makecert and cert2spc utilities (provided with Microsoft SDK for Java) to generate a test SPC.

Generating a Test Certificate

To generate a test certificate, do the following:

1. Run the makecert utility to generate the public-private key pair and the certificate:

   ```
   makecert -sk <key_name> -n <subject_dn> <cert_file>.cer
   ```

   where

   - <key_name> specifies the container for your public-private key pair. The makecert utility generates this name automatically if it does not exist.
   - <subject_dn> specifies your DN as a software publisher—for example, cn=My Software Publisher Name.
   - <cert_file> specifies the file that will contain the generated certificate.

2. Run the cert2spc utility to convert the generated certificate to an SPC:

   ```
   cert2spc <cert_file>.cer <spc_file>.spc
   ```

   where

   - <cert_file> specifies the file that contains the generated test certificate.
   - <spc_file> specifies the file that will contain the generated SPC.

Signing Your Code

Now that you have an SPC, you can set up the permissions for your applet and sign the CAB file.

Rather than setting up your applet to request a low security level, you can define a custom set of permissions that includes only the permission to connect to the network (and not any of the other permissions allowed by a low security level). The signcode utility allows you to define a set of custom permissions in an .ini file. To create and modify this .ini file, you can use the piniedit utility, which is included with Microsoft SDK for Java. Use the following syntax:

```
piniedit <ini_file>
```

The `piniedit` utility displays a warning message if the `.ini` file does not exist. You can click OK to dismiss this message, and the utility will display the main window.

In the main window (see Figure 8-7), click the Network tab and choose the Connect access type. Use the Include Host text box and the Ports text box to specify the name and port of your LDAP server, respectively, and click Add to add your server to the list. Save your changes and exit the utility.

The `piniedit` utility generates an `.ini` file that defines the permissions to connect to your LDAP server. You can use that `.ini` file with the `signcode` utility to sign the CAB file:

```
signcode -j javasign.dll -jp <ini_file> -spc <spc_file>.spc -k
    <key_name> <cab_file>
```

where

- `<ini_file>` specifies the `.ini` file that contains your custom permissions.
- `<spc_file>` specifies the file that contains the generated SPC.

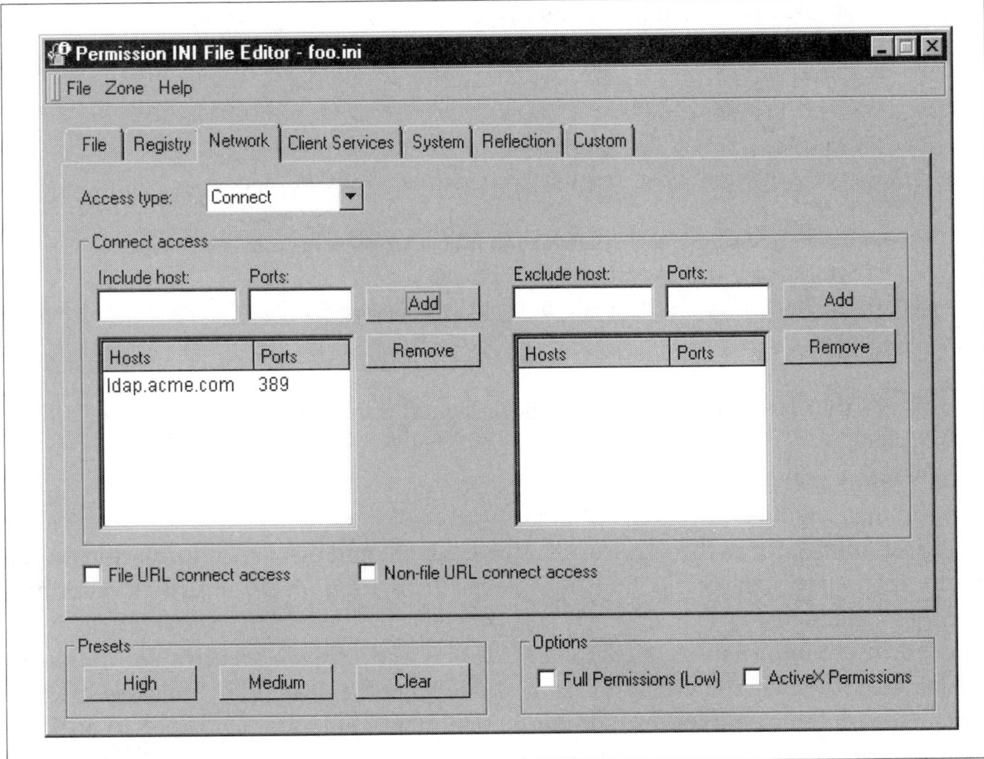

FIGURE 8-7. *Permission INI File Editor for Internet Explorer.*

- `<key_name>` specifies the container for your public-private key pair in the registry.
- `<cab_file>` specifies the CAB file that contains the code files you want to sign.

The following example demonstrates how to generate a test certificate and sign your CAB file. The example does the following:

- Generates a public-private key pair in the container named `MyKeys` (in the registry)
- Generates a certificate file named `TestCertificate.cer`
- Converts this generated certificate to an SPC in the file named `TestSPC.spc`
- Uses the `piniedit` utility to create a `permissions.ini` file that defines custom permissions and uses that file (along with the generated SPC) to sign the CAB file named `LDAPApplet.cab`

The example assumes that your DN (as a software publisher) is `cn=My Software Publisher Name`. The information you need to enter is highlighted in bold.

```
D:\sourcefiles>makecert -sk MyKeys -n "CN=My Software Publisher Name"
    TestCertificate.cer
Succeeded
D:\sourcefiles>cert2spc TestCertificate.cer TestSPC.spc
Succeeded
D:\sourcefiles>signcode -j javasign.dll -jp permissions.ini -spc
    TestSPC.spc -k MyKeys LDAPApplet.cab
Warning: This file is signed, but not timestamped.
Succeeded
```

To verify that your CAB file has been signed correctly, use the `chkjava` utility:

```
chkjava <cab_file>
```

The utility verifies the signature on the CAB file and displays information on the certificate used to sign the file. It also displays information on the security level or permissions requested.

For more information on signing CAB files and on Java security, see the documentation for Microsoft SDK for Java. Note that the Java LDAP classes are not included with Internet Explorer, so to use them in an applet you will need to package them and provide them in a CAB file.

Creating a Web Page for the Applet

The fact that Netscape Navigator ignores the `CABBASE` applet parameter (used by Internet Explorer to locate the CAB file of an applet) and Microsoft Internet Explorer ignores the `ARCHIVE` tag (used by Navigator to identify the JAR file of an applet) is fortunate because it means you can have a single Web page that makes both a signed CAB file and a signed JAR file available for users of both browsers:

```
<APPLET CODE="snazzy.class"
        CODEBASE="jars"
        ARCHIVE="snazzy.jar"
        WIDTH=100 HEIGHT=100>
        <PARAM NAME="cabbase" VALUE="snazzy.cab">
</APPLET>
```

If the CAB or JAR file is not already present on the user's system when the Web page is loaded, the browser downloads the appropriate file and starts the applet.

Writing LDAP Applets for Java Plug-In Software

If you are writing an applet that uses Java Foundation Classes (JFC), your browser needs to be able to run JFC applets. If the browser is not configured to run JFC applets out of the box, you can choose one of the following options:

- If you have a recent version of a browser (Internet Explorer 4.01 or later, or Netscape Communicator 4.5 or later), you can configure the browser or the Java virtual machine to include the JFC classes in the `CLASSPATH` environment variable. See the instructions on the `java.sun.com` Web site at `http://java.sun.com/products/jfc/tsc/web/applets/applets.html` for more information.
- You can use Sun's Java Plug-in Software to run the applet in Netscape Navigator or in Internet Explorer. See the instructions on the `java.sun.com` Web site at `http://java.sun.com/products/plugin/` for more information.

Java Plug-in Software (starting from version 1.2) supports applets signed using the Java 2 security tools. If a signed applet is trusted, that applet is allowed full permission, which includes permissions to connect to other systems on the network.

Note that in Java Plug-in Software 1.2.2, Sun introduced support for applets signed with RSA keys. This means you can use Netscape's `signtool` utility to sign applets for Java Plug-in Software. If you use this method for signing your applet, you do not need to install the certificate manually on each user's machine. If you use the Java 2 security tools to sign the applet, you will need to install the certificate manually on each machine. For details on using `signtool`, see the previous section on writing applets for Netscape Navigator.

The section that follows explains how to use the Java 2 security tools to sign an LDAP applet.

Packaging Your Applet

When you are ready to test your applet, you should sign your code with your digital certificate and package your code with the digital signatures into a JAR file. To sign your code, you need the following:

- A certificate and the corresponding private key (you can request the certificate from your company's certificate authority or from an independent authority, such as VeriSign)
- The certificate of the certificate authority who issued your certificate
- The Java 2 security tools (which are included with Java 2)

You can generate a public-private key pair and issue a request for a certificate by using the `keytool` utility, which is provided with Java 2. The `keytool` utility puts the keys and certificate in a database called a keystore. Each entry in the keystore (an entry contains the key and certificate) is assigned a unique alias. You access the entry for the key and certificate by specifying the alias for the entry.

Before you sign your code, read the documentation on security in Java 2, which is available at

`http://java.sun.com/products/jdk/1.2/docs/guide/security/index.html.`

If you have not received your certificate but you want to test your applet, you can use the JDK security tools to generate a test public-private key pair and a self-signed certificate.

Generating a Key Pair and Self-signed Certificate

When you use the `keytool` utility to generate a public-private key pair, the utility automatically wraps the generated public key in a self-signed certificate. To generate a key pair and self-signed certificate, use the following syntax:

```
keytool -genkey -alias <key_alias> -dname <your_publisher_dn>
```

Use the `-alias` option to specify an alias for the generated key pair and self-signed certificate. You will use this alias to access the keys and certificate from the keystore to sign your code. Use the -dname option to specify your DN as a software publisher.

After you enter this command, you will be prompted for a password for the new private key and a password for the keystore. After the command completes, verify that the new certificate is in your keystore. Run the following command:

```
keytool -list
```

This command prints out information about the keys and certificates in your keystore:

```
D:\>keytool -list
Enter keystore password:Password

Keystore type: jks
Keystore provider: SUN

Your keystore contains 1 entry:

testcert, Sat Jun 19 19:02:52 PDT 1999, keyEntry,

Certificate fingerprint (MD5):
4C:4F:40:86:9A:7B:8C:70:DB:24:C2:01:CC:C5:51:6F
```

Signing Your Code

Now that you have a certificate, you can package your classes in a JAR file and then use the jarsigner tool to sign your code. Use the following syntax:

```
jarsigner -signedjar <signed_jar_file> <jar_file> <cert_alias>
```

where

- <signed_jar_file> specifies the signed JAR file that this tool will create.
- <jar_file> specifies the existing JAR file you want to sign.
- <cert_alias> specifies the alias of your certificate.

The jarsigner tool generates the following files in the directory META-INF:

- A manifest file (manifest.mf)
- A signature instruction file (<certifcate_name>.sf)
- A digital signature file (<certificate_name>.dsa)

The manifest file contains a list of files to be signed. For each file, the manifest file lists the file name and the message digest of the file (generated using `SHA1`):

```
Manifest-Version: 1.0
Created-By: 1.2.1 (Sun Microsystems Inc.)

Name: DirBrowser$1.class
SHA1-Digest: 5UiaGsXc0LLlt/IEotcH+9bHfRA=

Name: DirBrowserBeanInfo.class
SHA1-Digest: kn0rZcyhzcCDRfZtlxQw0LcKoWo=

Name: DirBrowser$2.class
SHA1-Digest: gXHmfkFrucvmIL/53ejCV1LjU3w=

Name: DirBrowser.class
SHA1-Digest: JK4rqsxJFDRNWizMGibfTiTVjqg=
```

The signature instruction file contains message digests of the entries in the manifest file. For each section that specifies the name and message digest of a file, the signature instruction file contains a message digest of that section:

```
Signature-Version: 1.0
SHA1-Digest-Manifest: QOxxxZ9giDJs3QjiXiXSFWz92Eg=
Created-By: 1.2.1 (Sun Microsystems Inc.)

Name: DirBrowser$1.class
SHA1-Digest: L/zgZtORHeFNrmAaWqsqgkdOmA4=

Name: DirBrowserBeanInfo.class
SHA1-Digest: Mag4zERGXJPG6H3TKxRBA8h9UU4=

Name: DirBrowser$2.class
SHA1-Digest: JCVDgrSr/ypDdfaSOy0XX6di4rg=

Name: DirBrowser.class
SHA1-Digest: PgWvUCWWOmGpDz0C1JoF+YeVjso=
```

The message digest of the signature instruction file is signed and placed in the digital signature file. The digital signature file also contains the certificate for the key pair used to sign the files.

To verify that your files have been signed correctly, use the following syntax for the `jarsigner` tool:

```
jarsigner -verify -verbose <signed_jar_file>
```

For example,

```
D:\sourcefiles>jarsigner -verify -verbose sDirBrowser.jar

          433 Tue Jul 06 08:43:22 PDT 1999 META-INF/TESTCERT.SF
          950 Tue Jul 06 08:43:22 PDT 1999 META-INF/TESTCERT.DSA
            0 Tue Jul 06 08:38:58 PDT 1999 META-INF/
smk       901 Tue Jul 06 08:38:30 PDT 1999 DirBrowser$1.class
smk      1094 Tue Jul 06 08:38:30 PDT 1999 DirBrowser$2.class
smk      5473 Tue Jul 06 08:38:30 PDT 1999 DirBrowser.class
smk       235 Tue Jul 06 08:38:30 PDT 1999 DirBrowserBeanInfo.class

  s = signature was verified
  m = entry is listed in manifest
  k = at least one certificate was found in keystore
  i = at least one certificate was found in identity scope

jar verified.
```

Setting Up the End User's System

Next you need to verify that your code can be executed on an end user's system. You need to set up a keystore on the end user's system, and you need to import your certificate into the keystore as a trusted certificate.

To make your public certificate available in a file, use the `keytool` utility with the following syntax:

```
keytool -export -alias <key_alias> -file <output_filename>.cer
```

Use the `-alias` option to specify the alias for your self-signed certificate. Use the `-file` option to specify the name of a file in which to store your certificate (for example, `softwarepub.cer`). Copy the file that contains the certificate to the end user's machine.

On the end user's machine, install Java Plug-In Software. You can download a copy from `http://java.sun.com/products/plugin/index.html`. The plug-in software is part of Java Runtime Environment (JRE). After you install the plug-in software, make sure that the `bin` directory of JRE is in the path, and use the `keytool` utility to set up a keystore that contains your SPC. Use the following syntax:

```
keytool -import -alias <certificate_alias> -file <certificate_
    file>.cer
```

When prompted, indicate that the certificate is trusted:

```
C:\>keytool -import -alias testcert -file e:\shared\testcert.cer
Enter keystore password:  MyPassword
Owner: CN=My Software Publisher, OU="Information Technology o=Airius.com"
Issuer: CN=My Software Publisher, OU="Information Technology o=Airius.com"
Serial number: 376c4bc8
Valid from: Sat Jun 19 19:02:48 PDT 1999 until: Fri Sep 17 19:02:48 PDT
    1999
Certificate fingerprints:
         MD5:  4C:4F:40:86:9A:7B:8C:70:DB:24:C2:01:CC:C5:51:6F
         SHA1: FA:43:A1:60:ED:35:2E:2C:66:7B:D7:D5:62:9E:09:FD:E7:24:1D:1F
Trust this certificate? [no]:  y
Certificate was added to keystore
```

Next you need to set up a policy file to allow the signed applet to connect to the LDAP server. From a command prompt, enter `policytool` to display the Policy Tool dialog box (see Figure 8-8). Choose the Change KeyStore command from the Edit menu.

In the New KeyStore URL text box of the Keystore dialog box (see Figure 8-9), enter the file URL that points to the keystore you just created. By default, the `keytool` command creates the keystore as the `.keystore` file in the user's home directory (the directory specified by the "user.home" system property). In Windows NT, for example, the default keystore is the file `C:\winnt\profiles\<username>\.keystore`. Click OK to use the specified keystore.

To create a new policy, click the Add Policy Entry button in the Policy Tool dialog box (see Figure 8-8). The Policy Entry window (Figure 8-10) will be displayed. In the CodeBase text box, enter the URL to the codebase for your applet. In the SignedBy text box, enter the alias for your certificate. Then click Add Permission to define the permissions for connecting to the LDAP server. The Permissions dialog box (Figure 8-11) will be displayed.

In the Permissions combo box, choose SocketPermission. In the Target Name text box, enter the host name of the LDAP server. In the Actions combo box, choose connect. Click OK to add the permissions. Figure 8-12 shows what the Policy Entry dialog box looks like after the socket permission has been added.

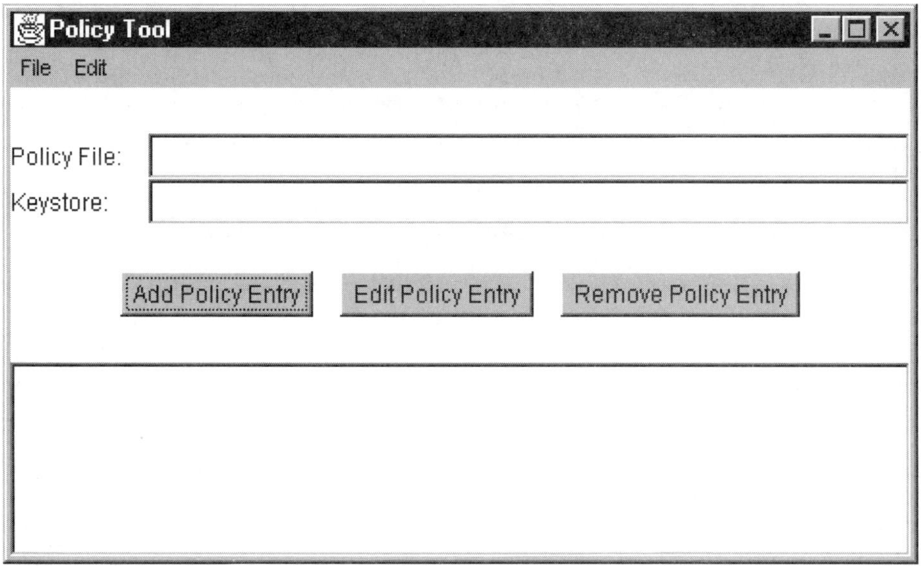

FIGURE 8-8. *Policy Tool dialog box of Java Plug-In Software.*

Click Done to close any open windows. From the main Policy Tool window (see Figure 8-8), choose Save As on the File menu, and save the policy file as a file named `.java.policy` in the user's home directory.

For more information on the Java 2 security tools, see the documentation at `http://java.sun.com/products/jdk/1.2/docs/guide/security/index.html`.

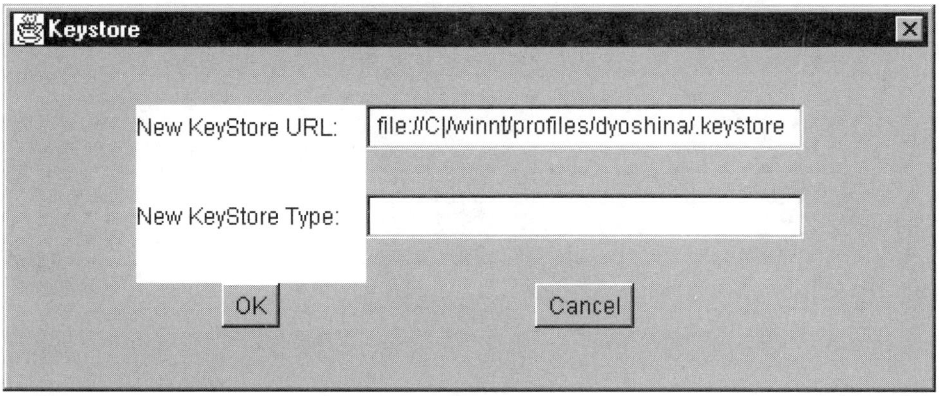

FIGURE 8-9. *Keystore dialog box of Java Plug-In Software.*

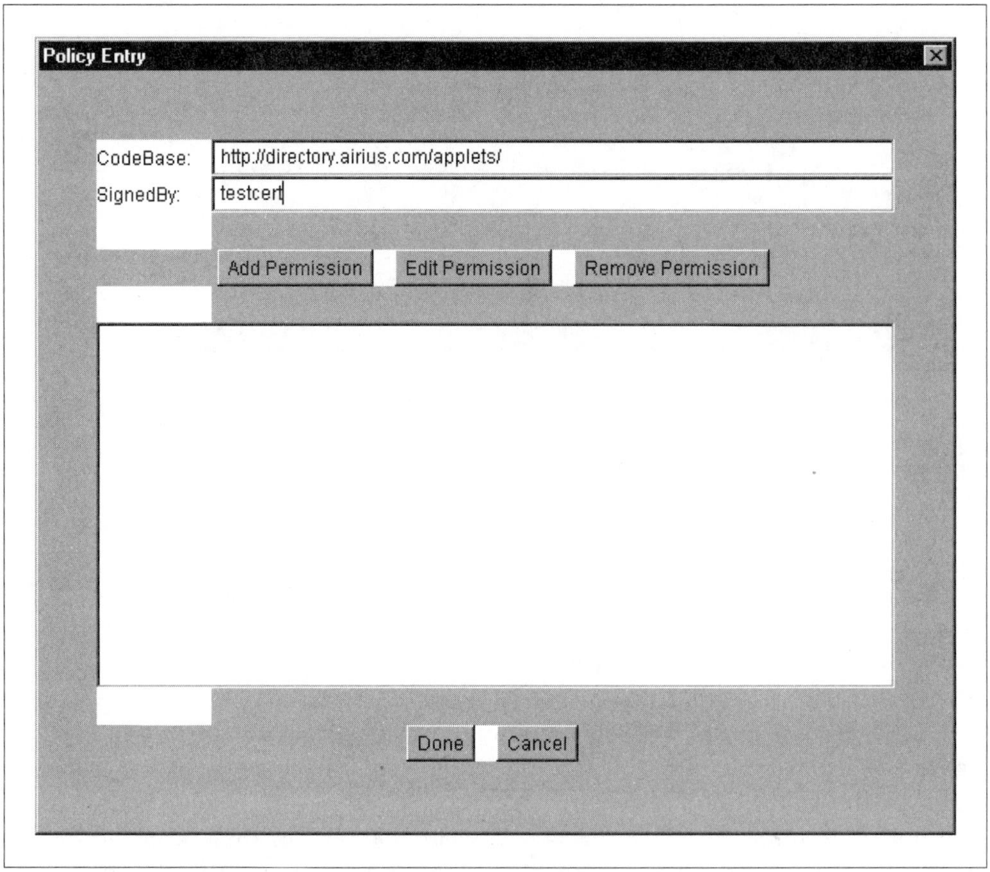

Policy Entry

CodeBase: http://directory.airius.com/applets/
SignedBy: testcert

Add Permission | Edit Permission | Remove Permission

Done | Cancel

FIGURE 8-10. *Specifying the codebase and signer with Java Plug-In Software.*

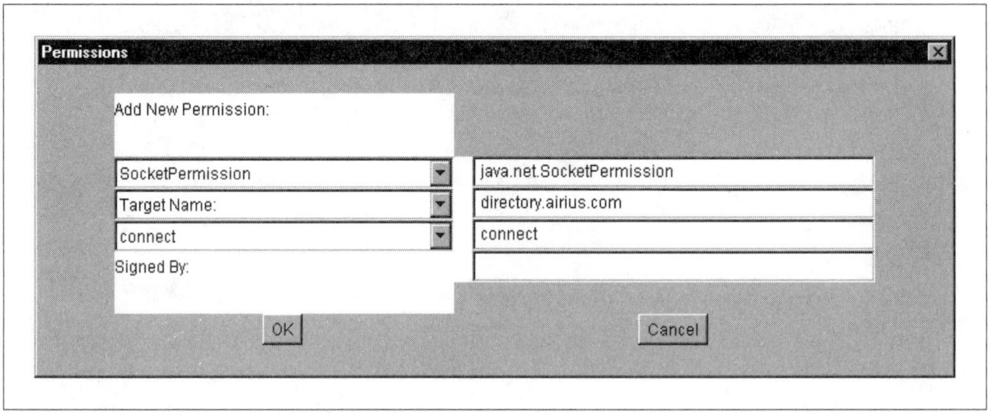

Permissions

Add New Permission:

SocketPermission | java.net.SocketPermission
Target Name: | directory.airius.com
connect | connect
Signed By:

OK | Cancel

FIGURE 8-11. *Permissions dialog box of Java Plug-In Software.*

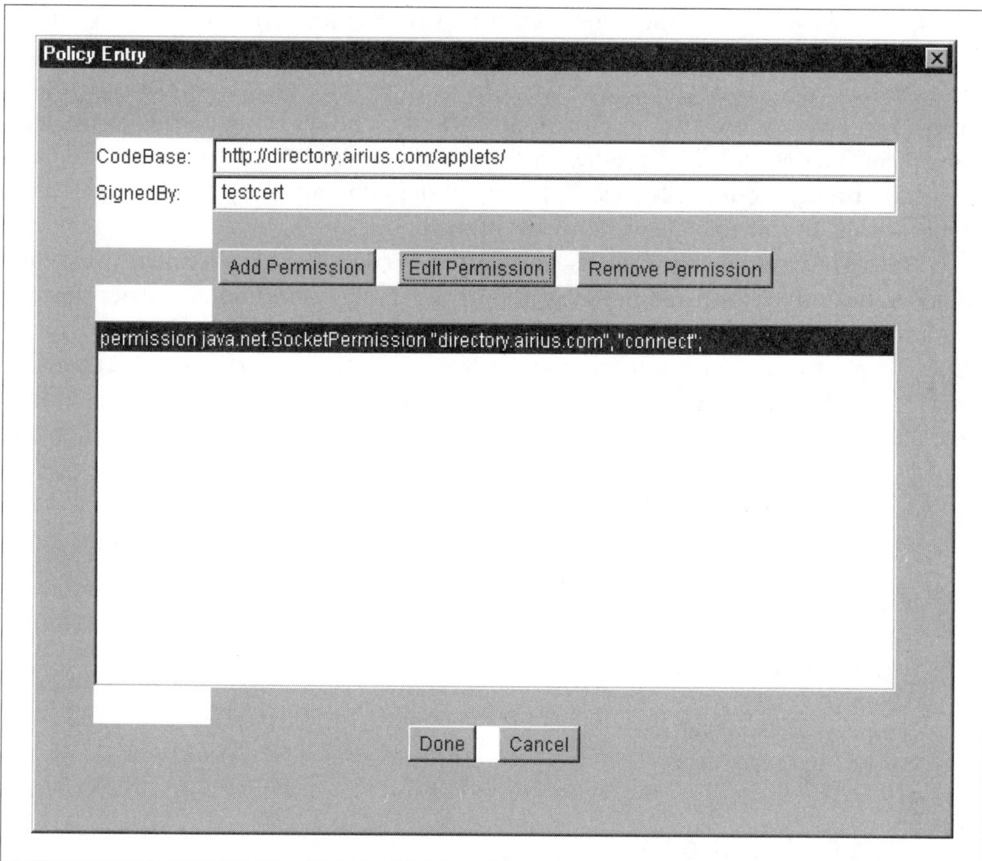

FIGURE 8-12. *Policy Entry dialog box after adding socket permission.*

A Directory Viewer Applet

This section provides a simple example of an applet for displaying entries and attributes in the sample directory on the CD-ROM that accompanies this book. This rudimentary example is presented here mainly to explain how to set up applets; more full-featured examples are provided in subsequent chapters of this book.

A Simple Example for Java Plug-In Software

The `DirBrowser` class, a simple applet, uses a `JTree` component to display the entries in the directory hierarchy and a `JTextArea` component to display the attributes of the selected entry. The `JTree` and `JTextArea` components are in a `JSplitPane` component.

Each node or leaf in the tree represents an LDAP entry in the directory. When the user selects a node, the applet displays the attributes for the entry corresponding to the selected node. When the user expands a node in the tree, the applet queries for entries two levels below the selected node and adds the resulting entries to the tree. The applet queries two levels below (rather than one level) to determine if the child entries are branch nodes or leaves. If the applet queried only one level down, all child entries would appear to be leaves and not branch nodes.

The `init` method that follows sets up the `JTree`, `JTextArea`, and `JSplitPane` components and performs an initial search of the directory to find all entries that are two levels below the root node. The method adds these entries as nodes to the tree. It also sets up a tree expansion listener and a tree selection listener. The tree expansion listener searches the directory for additional levels of entries when a tree node is expanded. The tree selection listener searches the directory for the selected entry and displays the attributes of the entry in the text area.

```
import java.io.*;
import java.util.*;
import javax.swing.*;
import javax.swing.event.*;
import javax.swing.tree.*;
import java.awt.*;
import java.awt.event.*;
import netscape.ldap.*;

/**
 * Applet that displays a tree view of a directory
 */
public class DirBrowser extends JApplet {

    /**
     * Default constructor
     */
    public DirBrowser() {
        /* Netscape Communicator and Internet Explorer 4.0
           unconditionally print an error message to the
           Java console when an applet attempts to access
           the AWT system event queue. */
        getRootPane().putClientProperty(
            "defeatSystemEventQueueCheck",
            Boolean.TRUE);
    }

    /**
```

```
     * Constructor with explicit parameters, for calling
     * as an application
     *
     * @param host host name of directory server
     * @param port port number of directory server
     * @param base base DN of DIT to display
     */
    public DirBrowser( String host, int port, String base ) {
        this.host = host;
        this.port = port;
        this.base = base;
        isApplet = false;
    }


    /**
     * Standard applet entry point; create the tree view
     */
    public void init() {
        /* Get parameters from applet tags if present */
        String s = getParameter( "host" );
        if ( (s != null) && (s.length() > 0) ) {
            host = s;
        }
        s = getParameter( "base" );
        if ( (s != null) && (s.length() > 0) ) {
            base = s;
        }
        s = getParameter( "port" );
        if ( (s != null) && (s.length() > 0) ) {
            port = Integer.parseInt( s );
        }
        /* Create the root of the tree and
           get the entries beneath the root. */
        DefaultMutableTreeNode root =
            new DefaultMutableTreeNode( base );
        addChildren( root );
        /* Set up the area for displaying attributes. */
        attributeListing = new JTextArea();
        attributeListing.setEditable(false);
        JScrollPane attributePane =
            new JScrollPane(attributeListing);
        attributePane.setVerticalScrollBarPolicy(
            JScrollPane.VERTICAL_SCROLLBAR_ALWAYS);
        attributePane.setHorizontalScrollBarPolicy(
```

```
    JScrollPane.HORIZONTAL_SCROLLBAR_ALWAYS);
Dimension dim = new Dimension(300, 150);
attributePane.setMinimumSize(dim);
attributePane.setPreferredSize(dim);
/* Create the tree for displaying entries
   in the directory hierarchy. */
final JTree tree = new JTree( root );
tree.getSelectionModel().setSelectionMode
    (TreeSelectionModel.SINGLE_TREE_SELECTION);
tree.addTreeExpansionListener(
    new TreeExpansionListener() {
    /* If the tree is expanded, get the
       children of the expanded entry. */
    public void treeExpanded(TreeExpansionEvent e) {
        DefaultMutableTreeNode entry =
            (DefaultMutableTreeNode)
            e.getPath().getLastPathComponent();
        addChildren(entry);
    }
    public void treeCollapsed(TreeExpansionEvent e) {
    }
});
tree.addTreeSelectionListener(
    new TreeSelectionListener() {
    /* If a node or leaf is selected, display
       the attributes of that entry. */
    public void valueChanged(TreeSelectionEvent e) {
        DefaultMutableTreeNode entry =
            (DefaultMutableTreeNode)
            e.getNewLeadSelectionPath().
            getLastPathComponent();
        String attributeString =
            flattenAttributes(entry);
        attributeListing.setText(attributeString);
        attributeListing.setCaretPosition(0);
    }
});
JScrollPane treeView = new JScrollPane(tree);
dim = new Dimension(300, 150);
treeView.setMinimumSize(dim);
treeView.setPreferredSize(dim);
/* Set up the tree and text area components
   in a split pane. */
JSplitPane twoPanes =
```

```
            new JSplitPane(JSplitPane.VERTICAL_SPLIT);
        twoPanes.setTopComponent(treeView);
        twoPanes.setBottomComponent(attributePane);
        twoPanes.setDividerLocation(150);
        /* Add the split pane to the main content pane. */
        getContentPane().add(twoPanes,
                             BorderLayout.CENTER);
    }

    /**
     * Display the entries one level
     * below a selected entry. The parent argument
     * identifies the node to be expanded.
     */
    protected void addChildren(
        DefaultMutableTreeNode parent ) {
        DefaultMutableTreeNode entry = null;
        DefaultMutableTreeNode subEntry = null;
        LDAPEntry childEntry, grandchildEntry;
        String childEntryDN;

        try {
            LDAPConnection conn = getConnection();
            if ( conn == null ) {
                return;
            }
            /* Get only the cn attribute. */
            String[] attrNames = { "cn" };
            /* If the node is the root node, query the
               directory to get the child entries.*/
            if ( parent.isRoot() ) {
                /* Search all entries that are
                   one level below the current entry.*/
                LDAPSearchResults results =
                    conn.search( base,
                                 conn.SCOPE_ONE,
                                 "(objectclass=*)",
                                 attrNames,
                                 false );
                /* Get the DN for each result, and use
                    the DN as the string value of the node. */
                while ( results.hasMoreElements() ) {
                    childEntry = results.next();
                    entry = new DefaultMutableTreeNode(
```

```
            childEntry.getDN());
        /* Add the new node as a child of the
            top-level node. */
        parent.add(entry);
        /* Search for entries that are one level
           beneath the child entry to determine
           if the child entry is a leaf or a node.*/
        LDAPSearchResults resUnderEntry =
            conn.search( childEntry.getDN(),
                         conn.SCOPE_ONE,
                         "(objectclass=*)",
                         attrNames,
                         false );
        /* Get the DN of each result and add the DN
            as a "grandchild" node under the child
            node.*/
        while (resUnderEntry.hasMoreElements()) {
            grandchildEntry = resUnderEntry.next();
            subEntry =
                new DefaultMutableTreeNode(
                    grandchildEntry.getDN());
            entry.add(subEntry);
        }
    }
    /* If the node passed in is not the root node,
       the child entries (in the tree) should
       already exist (from the previous query). Use
       the tree hierarchy to get the child entries,
       and then query each child entry to get the
       "grandchild" entries. (This determines
       whether or not the child entry is a leaf or
       a node.) */
} else {
    /* Get the child entries in the tree. */
    Enumeration childEntries = parent.children();
    while (childEntries.hasMoreElements()) {
        entry = (DefaultMutableTreeNode)
            childEntries.nextElement();
        /* Each existing child entry in the tree
           contains the DN of that entry. Get the
           DN. */
        childEntryDN =
            (String)entry.getUserObject();
        /* Use this "child" DN to find the
```

```
                   "grandchild" entries. */
                LDAPSearchResults resUnderEntry =
                    conn.search( childEntryDN,
                                 conn.SCOPE_ONE,
                                 "(objectclass=*)",
                                 attrNames,
                                 false);
                /* Add each "grandchild" entry to the
                   tree.*/
                while ( resUnderEntry.hasMoreElements() ) {
                    grandchildEntry = resUnderEntry.next();
                    subEntry =
                        new DefaultMutableTreeNode(
                            grandchildEntry.getDN());
                    entry.add( subEntry );
                }
            }
        }
    } catch( Exception e ) {
        /* Any errors - connecting or searching - end up
           here and terminate the expansion */
        System.out.println( e.toString() );
    }
}

/**
 * "Flatten" the list of attributes as a string.
 * Instead of using LDAPEntry.toString(), which results in
 * a long string containing all attributes and values,
 * this method queries the directory for the entry and
 * returns a string containing newline-delimited attribute
 * names and values.
 */
private String flattenAttributes(
    DefaultMutableTreeNode entry ) {
    String entryDN, attributeString;
    try {
        LDAPConnection conn = getConnection();
        if ( conn == null ) {
            return "";
        }
        /* Get the DN from the tree node. */
        entryDN = (String)entry.getUserObject();
        /* Get the corresponding LDAP entry from
```

```
               the directory.*/
            LDAPEntry fullEntry = conn.read( entryDN );
            /* Get the attributes for the entry. */
            LDAPAttributeSet attributeSet =
                fullEntry.getAttributeSet();
            Enumeration enumAttrs =
                attributeSet.getAttributes();
            attributeString = "Attributes:";
            /* Build a string containing the attribute names
               and values. Delimit the names and values with
               newline characters.*/
            while ( enumAttrs.hasMoreElements() ) {
                LDAPAttribute anAttr =
                    (LDAPAttribute)enumAttrs.nextElement();
                String attrName = anAttr.getName();
                attributeString =
                    attributeString + "\n  " + attrName;
                Enumeration enumVals =
                    anAttr.getStringValues();
                while ( enumVals.hasMoreElements() ) {
                    String aVal =
                        (String)enumVals.nextElement();
                    attributeString =
                        attributeString + "\n    " + aVal;
                }
            }
            attributeString += "\n";
            return attributeString;
        } catch( Exception e ) {
            System.out.println(e.toString());
        }
        return "";
    }

    /**
     * Connect to server, if not already done
     *
     * @return connection to directory server
     */
    protected LDAPConnection getConnection() {
        if ( connection == null ) {
            try {
                /* Connect to the LDAP server. */
                connection = new LDAPConnection();
```

```
                connection.connect( host, port );
            } catch ( LDAPException ex ) {
                System.out.println( ex.toString() );
                connection = null;
            }
        }
        return connection;
    }

    public static void main( String[] args ) {
      if ( args.length != 3 ) {
            System.out.println( "Usage: java DirBrowser " +
                                "<host> <port> <baseDN>" );
            System.exit( 1 );
        }
        String host = args[0];
        int port = Integer.parseInt( args[1] );
        String baseDN = args[2];
        DirBrowser browser = new DirBrowser( host,
                                             port,
                                             baseDN );
        browser.init();
        JFrame frame = new JFrame( "Directory Browser" );
        frame.addWindowListener( new WindowAdapter() {
            public void windowClosing(WindowEvent e) {
                Window win = e.getWindow();
                win.setVisible(false);
                win.dispose();
                System.exit(0);
            }
        } );
        frame.getContentPane().add( browser );
        frame.pack();
        // Center frame
        Dimension screenSize =
            Toolkit.getDefaultToolkit().getScreenSize();
        Dimension size = frame.getSize();
        screenSize.height = screenSize.height/2;
        screenSize.width = screenSize.width/2;
        size.height = size.height/2;
        size.width = size.width/2;
        int y = screenSize.height - size.height;
        int x = screenSize.width - size.width;
        frame.setLocation(x, y );
```

```
        frame.show();
    }

    /* JTextArea for displaying attributes of an entry. */
    private JTextArea attributeListing;
    /* Connection to directory */
    private LDAPConnection connection = null;
    private String host = "localhost";
    private int port = 389;
    private String base = "o=airius.com";
    private boolean isApplet = true;
}
```

To set up the applet for use with Java Plug-In Software, you need to use the JDK security tools to sign the applet.

Before you package the applet and sign the file, you need to create a `BeanInfo` file for your applet because of a known problem with Java Plug-In Software and Internet Explorer. If the applet is served by Microsoft Internet Information Server or Microsoft Personal Web Server, Java Plug-In Software and Internet Explorer expect to find a `BeanInfo` class for your applet, even though your applet is not a JavaBean. If no `BeanInfo` class is present, the `AppletClassLoader` may crash with a `NullPointerException`.

You can derive your `BeanInfo` class from the `SimpleBeanInfo` class:

```
import java.beans.*;

public class DirBrowserBeanInfo extends SimpleBeanInfo {
    public DirBrowserBeanInfo() {
        super();
    }
}
```

After you create this file, compile your classes and create a JAR file:

```
D:\>jar cvf DirBrowser.jar *.class

added manifest
adding: DirBrowser$1.class (in=901) (out=485) (deflated 46%)
adding: DirBrowser$2.class (in=1094) (out=579) (deflated 47%)
adding: DirBrowser.class (in=4842) (out=2379) (deflated 50%)
adding: DirBrowserBeanInfo.class (in=235) (out=180) (deflated 23%)
```

Next run the `jarsigner` tool to create a signed JAR file. The following example creates a signed JAR file named `sDirBrowser.jar` by signing the JAR file `DirBrowser.jar` with the certificate `testcert`.

```
D:\>jarsigner -signedjar sDirBrowser.jar DirBrowser.jar testcert
Enter Passphrase for keystore: YourPassword
```

Copy the JAR file (along with the `ldapjdk.jar` JAR file for Netscape Directory SDK) to your Web server. Set up an HTML page to load your applet. Since the applet should be loaded by Java Plug-In Software and not by the browser's default Java virtual machine, you need to set up the Web page to use Java Plug-In Software. An example follows.

```
<html>
<head>
<title>DirBrowser</title>
</head>
<body BGCOLOR="#ffffff" LINK="#000099">
<!- The OBJECT tag specifies the use of
    Java Plug-In Software. If the user does not have
    the software loaded (as identified by the class ID),
    the codebase attribute identifies the location of the
    CAB file that contains Java Plug-In Software. ->
<OBJECT classid="clsid:8AD9C840-044E-11D1-B3E9-00805F499D93"
    width="300" height="300" align="baseline"
    codebase="
    http://java.sun.com/products/plugin/1.2/
        jinstall-12-win32.cab#Version=1,2,0,0">
  <!- These parameters identify your applet and
      the JAR files required by your applet. ->
  <PARAM NAME="code" VALUE="DirBrowser.class">
  <PARAM NAME="archive" VALUE="ldapjdk.jar, sDirBrowser.jar"
  <PARAM NAME="type" VALUE="application/x-java-applet;version=1.2">
  <PARAM NAME="host" VALUE="directory.airius.com">
  <PARAM NAME="port" VALUE="389">
  <PARAM NAME="base" VALUE="o=airius.com">
  <!-  Since IE ignores any statements between the COMMENT tags,
      you can use these statements for Netscape Navigator. ->
  <COMMENT>
      <!- The EMBED tag specifies that Java Plug-In
          Software should load your applet. The type identifies
          Java Plug-In Software, the code and archive
          attributes specify your applet, and the pluginspage
          attribute specifies the location where Java Plug-In
          Software can be installed (if it is not already installed
          on the user's system. ->
      <EMBED type="application/x-java-applet;version=1.2" width="300"
        height="300" align="baseline" code="DirBrowser.class"
```

```
        archive="ldapjdk.jar, sDirBrowser.jar"
        pluginspage="
            http://java.sun.com/products/plugin/1.2/plugin-install.html"
        host="directory.airius.com"
        port="389"
        base="o=airius.com">
      <NOEMBED>
            No JDK 1.2 support for APPLET!!
      </NOEMBED>
      </EMBED>
  </COMMENT>
</OBJECT>
</body>
</html>
```

Figure 8-13 shows the applet running in Internet Explorer, using Java Plug-In Software.

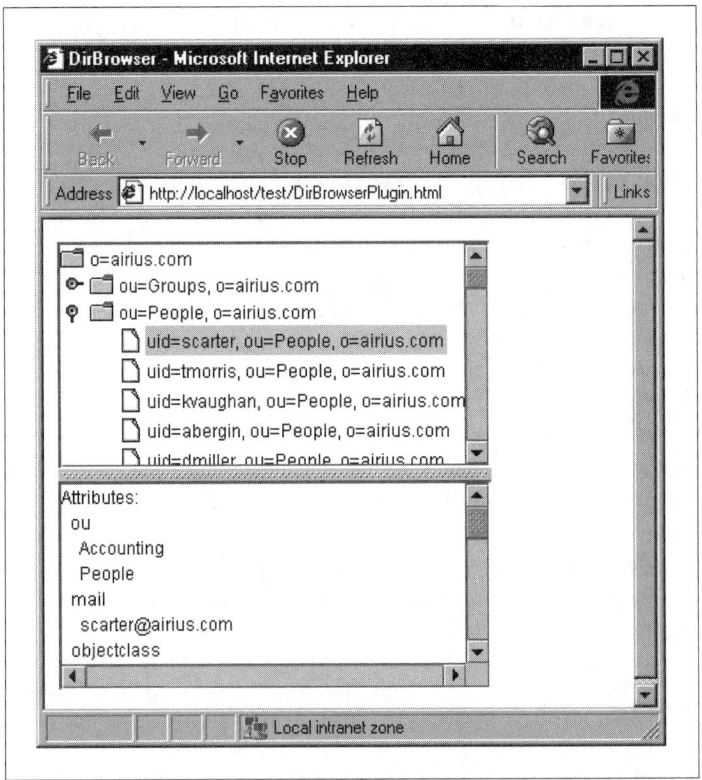

FIGURE 8-13. *Directory browser applet in Internet Explorer with Java Plug-In Software.*

Conclusion

Writing an applet rather than a stand-alone application to access the directory has some benefits:

- Users do not need to install and configure the application. They can just load the applet from the Web server.
- When you update your code, you just need to replace the applet on the Web server. You do not need to reinstall or upgrade an application on every user's machine.

Because of the sandbox restrictions on applets that run within browsers, you need to sign your applet and use the appropriate browser-specific calls to request permission to connect to the LDAP server on the network. In this chapter we have discussed the different procedures for doing this in Netscape Navigator, in Microsoft Internet Explorer, and in any browser using Sun's Java Plug-In Software.

CHAPTER 9

Scripting LDAP: JavaScript and Java

Both Netscape Navigator and Microsoft Internet Explorer allow JavaScript developers to invoke methods in Java applets. This means that an HTML page can use JavaScript to take advantage of the classes in Directory SDK for Java. For example, you can set up an HTML form that queries your directory server.

Netscape Navigator also allows you to create and manipulate Java objects directly in JavaScript. Internet Explorer requires that you wrap them in COM (Component Object Model) objects first.

This chapter explains how to access methods in an LDAP-powered Java applet, as well as how to access the Java LDAP classes directly, from JavaScript in an HTML page.

Accessing Java Applets from JavaScript

Netscape Navigator 3.0 and more recent versions use a technology called LiveConnect to enable Java, JavaScript, and browser plug-ins to interact. To be accessed from JavaScript, the methods in a Java applet must be public methods. As mentioned in Chapter 8, try to minimize any potential security risks when writing your public methods. For example, do not write a public method that simply writes to the file system or connects to the network.

After you write an applet with the public methods that you want exposed to JavaScript code, request permissions to connect to the network (if your LDAP server is not on the same machine as your Web server) and sign your applet. For more information on requesting privileges and signing applets, see Chapter 8.

Then, in your JavaScript code, use the `document.applets` property to access the Java methods. For example, if you named the applet "DirApplet" (using the <APPLET>

tag), you can invoke the public method named `search` in the applet by using the following JavaScript code:

```
document.applets.DirApplet.search();
```

You can also access the applet by its index (for example, `document.applets[0]`).

Similarly, when you run a Java applet in Internet Explorer, most of the public methods and variables in the applet are available to scripting languages that support the ActiveX scripting protocol (for example, JavaScript).

You can write a Java applet that exposes public methods for searching the directory and include the applet in an HTML page with JavaScript code that invokes those methods. In your applet, be sure to assert the permission to connect to the LDAP server (if the server is running on a different machine from your Web server), and be sure to sign the CAB file that contains your applet. For details on asserting permissions and signing CAB files, see Chapter 8.

The following applet code defines a public method `search` that searches an LDAP directory. The HTML example that follows this applet code demonstrates how to invoke `search` from JavaScript. The applet is invisible; that is, it does not include a GUI.

Note that this example reads the `java.vendor` system property to determine which browser is loading the applet. Before signing your CAB file for Internet Explorer, run the `piniedit` utility to edit your permissions `.ini` file, and include the permission to read the `java.vendor` system property. If you don't, a `SecurityException` will be thrown.

To compile this example, you will need to have both the Navigator and the Internet Explorer system JAR files in your `CLASSPATH`. In Windows, use the following command:

```
set CLASSPATH=%CLASSPATH%;"c:/program files/netscape/communicator/
    program/java/classes/java40.jar";c:/winnt/java/classes/
classes.zip
```

In UNIX the command is

```
setenv CLASSPATH $CLASSPATH\:/usr/netscape/communicator/program/java/
    classes/java40.jar:/home/me/classes.zip
```

The sample applet code follows.

```
import java.io.*;
import java.util.*;
```

```
import java.awt.*;
import java.applet.*;
import netscape.ldap.*;
// Must have Navigator's java40.jar in the CLASSPATH
import netscape.security.PrivilegeManager;
// Must have Internet Explorer's classes.zip in the CLASSPATH
import com.ms.security.*;


/**
 * Invisible applet that searches a directory and returns a
 * single string with all results, formatted with line feeds.
 * The host, port, and base (base DN for search) are read from
 * applet parameter tags.
 */
public class DirApplet extends Applet {
    /**
     * Standard applet entry point
     */
    public void init() {
        super.init();
        // Get parameters from applet tags if present
        String s = getParameter( "host" );
        if ( (s != null) && (s.length() > 0) ) {
            host = s;
        }
        s = getParameter( "base" );
        if ( (s != null) && (s.length() > 0) ) {
            base = s;
        }
        s = getParameter( "port" );
        if ( (s != null) && (s.length() > 0) ) {
            port = Integer.parseInt( s );
        }
        // Detect the browser version
        try {
            String vendor =
                System.getProperty("java.vendor");
            if (vendor.indexOf("Netscape") != -1) {
                browser = NETSCAPE;
            } else if (vendor.indexOf("Microsoft")
                != -1) {
                browser = MICROSOFT;
            }
        } catch (SecurityException e) {
```

```
            System.out.println(e.toString());
        }
    }

    /**
     * Searches the directory and returns the
     * results as a single string. Entries,
     * attributes, and values are delimited
     * by newline characters.
     *
     * @param filter an LDAP search filter expression
     * @return a string containing all search results, or
     * an error message with stack trace on error
     */
    public String search(String filter) {
        String str = new String();
        try {
            // Get permission to connect to the network
            if ( browser == NETSCAPE ) {
                PrivilegeManager.enablePrivilege(
                    "UniversalConnect" );
                PrivilegeManager.enablePrivilege(
                    "UniversalThreadAccess" );
            } else if ( browser == MICROSOFT ) {
                PolicyEngine.assertPermission(
                    PermissionID.NETIO );
            }
            // Connect to the LDAP server
            connection = new LDAPConnection();
            connection.connect( host, port );
            // Perform the search
            LDAPSearchResults results
                = connection.search( base,
                                     LDAPConnection.SCOPE_SUB,
                                     filter, null, false );
            // Revert the privileges so that
            // they are no longer enabled
            if ( browser == NETSCAPE ) {
                PrivilegeManager.revertPrivilege(
                    "UniversalConnect" );
                PrivilegeManager.revertPrivilege(
                    "UniversalThreadAccess" );
            } else if ( browser == MICROSOFT ) {
                PolicyEngine.revertPermission(
                    PermissionID.NETIO );
```

```
        }
        str = "Entries:\n";
        // Loop through the results
        while ( results.hasMoreElements() ) {
            LDAPEntry entry = results.next();
            // Start each result with the DN
            str += entry.getDN() + "\n";
            // Get the attributes for the entry
            LDAPAttributeSet attributeSet =
                entry.getAttributeSet();
            Enumeration enumAttrs =
                attributeSet.getAttributes();
            str += "Attributes:\n";
            // Delimit the attribute names
               and values with newline characters
            while ( enumAttrs.hasMoreElements() ) {
                LDAPAttribute anAttr =
                    (LDAPAttribute)enumAttrs.nextElement();
                String attrName = anAttr.getName();
                str += "  " + attrName + "\n";
                Enumeration enumVals =
                    anAttr.getStringValues();
                // Get the values of the attribute
                while ( enumVals.hasMoreElements() ) {
                    String aVal =
                        (String)enumVals.nextElement();
                    str += "    " + aVal + "\n";
                }
            }
            str += "\n";
        }
    } catch ( Exception e ) {
        PrintWriter pWriter =
            new PrintWriter( new CharArrayWriter() );
        e.printStackTrace( pWriter );
        str += e.toString() + ":\n\t"
            + pWriter.toString();
        return str;
    }
    return str;
}

// Connection to directory
private LDAPConnection connection = null;
// Default parameters for connection and search base
```

```
        private String host = "localhost";
        private int port = 389;
        private String base = "o=airius.com";
        // Browser type
        private static final int NETSCAPE = 0;
        private static final int MICROSOFT = 1;
        private int browser = -1;
}
```

The following HTML page uses JavaScript code to invoke the `search` method in the applet `DirApplet`. The applet has been signed and packaged in the JAR file `DirApplet.jar` and in the CAB file `DirApplet.cab` (using the `signtool` and `signcode` utilities, respectively). The HTML page contains a text box for entering search criteria and a text area for displaying the results.

If you click the Search button or submit the form, the JavaScript function `searchDirectory` (which is set up as an `onClick` and `onSubmit` event handler for the button and form) invokes the `search` method, passing in the value in the text box. The JavaScript code gets the return value of this method (the results formatted as a single string) and displays the results in the text area.

```
<HTML>
<HEAD>
<TITLE>Example Using JavaScript Code to Access DirApplet</TITLE>
<SCRIPT LANG="JavaScript">
function searchDirectory() {
    document.LDAPSearch.results.value =
document.applets.DirApplet.search(document.LDAPSearch.filter.value);
    return false;
}
</SCRIPT>
</HEAD>
<BODY BGCOLOR="#ffffff" LINK="#000099">
<APPLET NAME="DirApplet" HEIGHT="1" WIDTH="1"
CODE="DirApplet.class" ARCHIVE="DirApplet.jar"
CABBASE="DirApplet.cab">
<PARAM NAME="host" VALUE="localhost">
<PARAM NAME="port" VALUE="389">
<PARAM NAME="base" VALUE="o=airius.com">
</APPLET>

<FORM NAME="LDAPSearch"
ONSUBMIT="searchDirectory(); return false">
<P>Enter the search criteria:</P>
```

```
<INPUT TYPE="text" NAME="filter" SIZE=60>
<INPUT TYPE="button" VALUE="search"
ONCLICK="searchDirectory()">
<P>Results: </P>
<TEXTAREA NAME="results" ROWS=5 COLS=50 WRAP="OFF">
</TEXTAREA>
</FORM>
</BODY>
</HTML>
```

The page appears in the browser as in Figure 9-1.

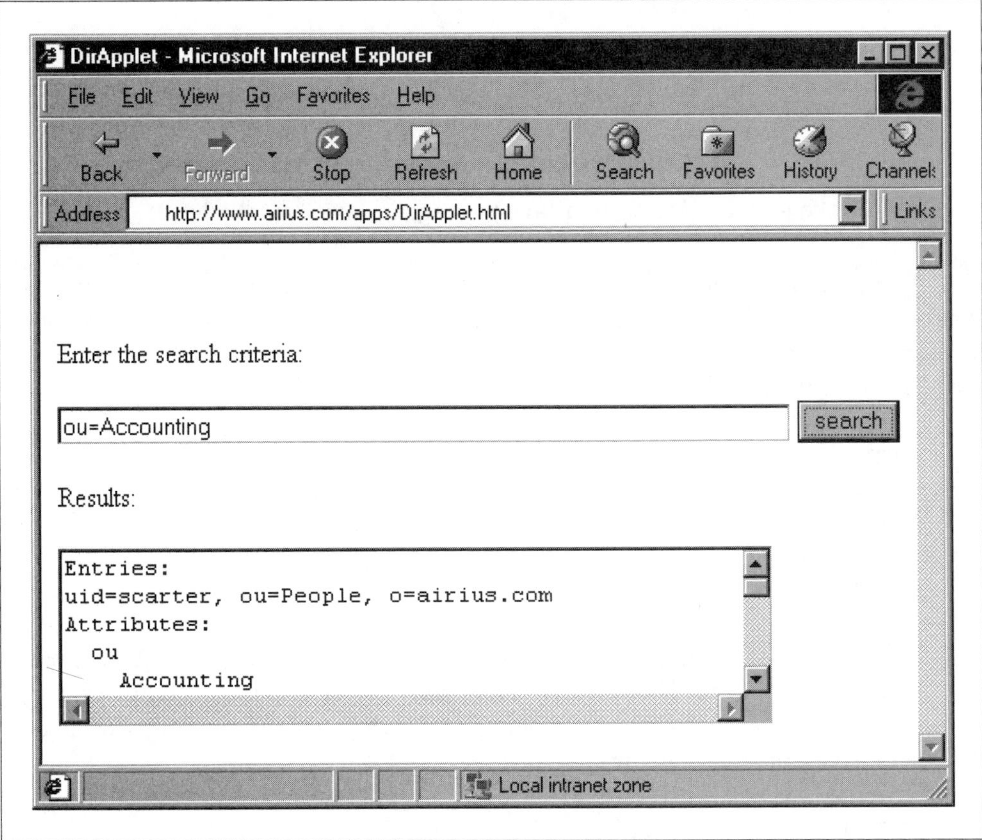

FIGURE 9-1. *Accessing an invisible LDAP applet from JavaScript.*

Chapter 10 will discuss how to access non-applet JavaBeans from JavaScript. The main differences are in how applets are declared in HTML, compared to components that are not applets, and in how applets are initialized or launched.

Accessing Java Objects from JavaScript

In Netscape Navigator you can use the LiveConnect technology to access Java packages, classes, methods, and variables directly from JavaScript code. You do not need to write an applet with public functions in order to access Java.

When you invoke the constructor for a Java class in JavaScript, LiveConnect creates a wrapper object for that Java object. Invoking methods and accessing properties for the wrapper object causes methods to be invoked and properties to be accessed in the Java object.

Behind the scenes, the following special LiveConnect objects are used as wrappers for Java objects:

- **`JavaArray`** is a wrapped Java array that you access from JavaScript code.
- **`JavaClass`** is a reference to a Java class in JavaScript code.
- **`JavaObject`** is a wrapped Java object that you access from JavaScript code.
- **`JavaPackage`** is a reference to a Java package in JavaScript code.

The JavaScript engine converts the data types in Java to corresponding data types in JavaScript. For example, the following line of JavaScript code creates a variable, `connection`, that is a `JavaObject`. This `JavaObject` contains an instance of an `LDAPConnection` Java object:

```
<SCRIPT LANG="JavaScript">
var connection = new netscape.ldap.LDAPConnection();
connection.connect("directory.airius.com", 389);
...
</SCRIPT>
```

Note that if the Java class does not belong to the `java`, `sun`, or `netscape` packages, you must access the class through the JavaScript `Packages` object. For example, if you define a class `MyLDAP` in the package `MyPackage`, you can construct a new `MyLDAP` object in the following way:

```
<SCRIPT LANG="JavaScript">
var x = new Packages.MyPackage.MyLDAP();
```

```
</SCRIPT>
```

If your class is not in a package but is in the CLASSPATH, you can omit the package name:

```
<SCRIPT LANG="JavaScript">
var x = new Packages.MyLDAP();
</SCRIPT>
```

The HTML file `jsldap.html` illustrates how to search a directory and how to read and present all attributes of an entry.

The doSearch JavaScript function shown in the following block of code creates an `LDAPConnection` object, extracts various parameters from the HTML form elements, and then does a subtree search. Depending on the user's selection of one of two radio buttons, either the DN or the common name of each entry found is displayed in an HTML text area.

```
<HTML>
<HEAD>
   <TITLE>Searching in LDAP with LiveConnect</TITLE>
</HEAD>

<SCRIPT LANGUAGE="JavaScript" ARCHIVE="JSLDAPHTML.jar" ID="1">
// Do a subtree search
function doSearch() {
    // Check if DNs or CNs are to be displayed
    for (var i = 0; i < document.LDAPForm.AttrChoice.length; i++ ) {
        if ( document.LDAPForm.AttrChoice[i].checked )
            break;
    }
    // Create a connection
    conn = new LDAPConnection();
    java.lang.System.out.println( "SDK version: " +
                        conn.getProperty("version.sdk") );
    // Ask the user for permission to establish a remote
    // connection
    netscape.security.PrivilegeManager.enablePrivilege(
            "UniversalConnect");
    netscape.security.PrivilegeManager.enablePrivilege(
            "UniversalPropertyRead");
    // Connect to selected host
    conn.connect( 3, // LDAPv3
```

```
                        document.LDAPForm.host.value,
                        parseInt(document.LDAPForm.port.value),
                        "", // Anonymous
                        "" );
    res = conn.search(
            document.LDAPForm.searchbase.value, // search base
            2,  // = SCOPE_SUB, search whole subtree
            document.LDAPForm.searchfilter.value, //filter
            null, // return all attributes
            false ); // return values as well as attribute names
    // Concatenate all results to be printed in a String
    str = new java.lang.String();
    while( res.hasMoreElements() ) { // Iterate on entries
        entry = res.next();
        // Get the distinguished name of the entry
        if ( document.LDAPForm.AttrChoice[i].value == "" ) {
            str += entry.getDN() + "\r\n";
        } else {
            // Get the common name attribute
            attr = entry.getAttribute( "cn" );
            // Get the values of the attribute
            vals = attr.getStringValues();
            while( vals.hasMoreElements() ) {
                str += vals.nextElement() + "\r\n";
            }
        }
    }
    // Display the results
    document.LDAPForm.searchresults.value = str;
}
```

The function doRead starts off the same, but it reads a specific entry:

```
// Do a base search for all attributes of an entry.
function doRead() {
    // Create a connection
    conn = new LDAPConnection();
    // Ask the user for permission to establish a remote
    // connection
    netscape.security.PrivilegeManager.enablePrivilege(
            "UniversalConnect");
    netscape.security.PrivilegeManager.enablePrivilege(
            "UniversalPropertyRead");
    // Connect to selected host
```

```
    conn.connect( 3, // LDAPv3
                  document.LDAPForm.host.value,
                  parseInt(document.LDAPForm.port.value),
                  "", // Anonymous
                  "" );
    // If we wanted to modify or delete an entry, we would
    // authenticate here as a real user.
    // Read the entry
    entry = conn.read(document.LDAPForm.textbox.value);
    // Concatenate all results to be printed in a String
    str = new java.lang.String();
    res = entry.getAttributeSet().getAttributes();
    // Iterate on attributes
    while( res.hasMoreElements() ) {
        attr = res.nextElement();
        vals = attr.getStringValues();
        if ( vals != null ) {
            // Iterate on values of the attribute
            while( vals.hasMoreElements() ) {
                str += attr.getName() + ": " +
                        vals.nextElement() + "\r\n";
            }
        }
    }
    // Display the results
    document.LDAPForm.result.value= str;
}
</SCRIPT>
```

Parameters for the LDAP server to which a connection should be made and for the search that is to be performed are provided through standard HTML form elements: text fields and radio buttons. Two buttons have `onClick` event handlers to call `doSearch` and `doRead`:

```
Search base <INPUT TYPE=text NAME="searchbase" SIZE=40
             VALUE="o=airius.com">
<P>
Search filter <INPUT TYPE=text NAME="searchfilter" SIZE=40
               VALUE="cn=a*">
<P>
<INPUT TYPE="radio" NAME="AttrChoice" VALUE="" CHECKED>
Show Distinguished names
<INPUT TYPE="radio" NAME="AttrChoice" VALUE="cn">
Show Common names
```

```
<P>
<INPUT TYPE=button VALUE="search"
 onClick="doSearch()" ID="2">
<P>
<TEXTAREA NAME="searchresults" WRAP="virtual" ROWS=15 COLS=65>
</TEXTAREA>
<P>
<H3>Reading an entry</H3>
<P>
To read an entry and list all attributes, enter a distinguished
name and press "readDN". An example of an entry in the demo
database is:
<P>
<PRE>
uid=tmorris,ou=People,o=airius.com
</PRE>
<P>
Distinguished name <INPUT TYPE=text NAME="textbox" SIZE=50
 VALUE="uid=tmorris,ou=People,o=Airius.com">
<P>
<INPUT TYPE=button VALUE="readDN"
 onClick="doRead()" ID="3">
<P>
<TEXTAREA NAME="result" WRAP="virtual" ROWS=15 COLS=65></TEXTAREA>
</FORM>
```

The `doSearch` output on the HTML page for the default parameters is presented in Figure 9-2, and the output of `doRead` in Figure 9-3.

JavaScript Gotchas

Because of the differences between the Java language and the JavaScript language, you need to consider the following when using LiveConnect:

- Because the versions of JavaScript prior to 1.4 do not support exceptions, you need to write a wrapper Java class to trap any potential exceptions. Otherwise, if there is an exception (for example, if a server is not available at the specified host and port), your script will abort. Navigator posts a discrete message in the status bar, as Figure 9-4 shows. If you type "javascript:" in the URL field of the browser, a dialog box appears and displays information about the error, as in Figure 9-5.

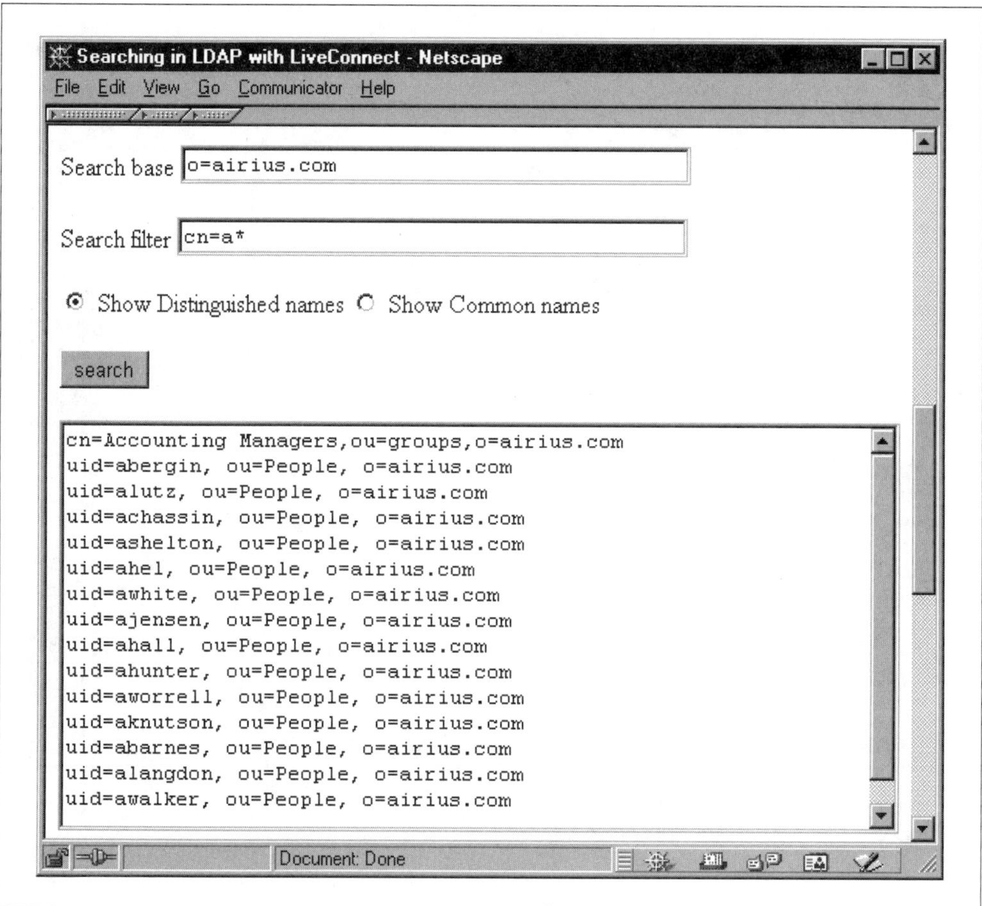

FIGURE 9-2. *Search results from JavaScript.*

- Because LDAP attributes have multiple values, you may want to pass the values of an attribute between your Java classes and JavaScript code as an array of strings. To do this, you can write a JavaScript function that will create a JavaScript array to convert the Java `String` array. Java `String` arrays are not interchangeable with JavaScript arrays of strings.
- If the LDAP server is not running on the same machine as the Web server, you need to request permission to connect to the LDAP server. You also need to sign your JavaScript code.

The rest of the chapter explains these points in more detail. For more information on LiveConnect, see the *Core JavaScript Guide* (`http://developer.netscape.com/docs/manuals/js/core/jsguide/index.htm`).

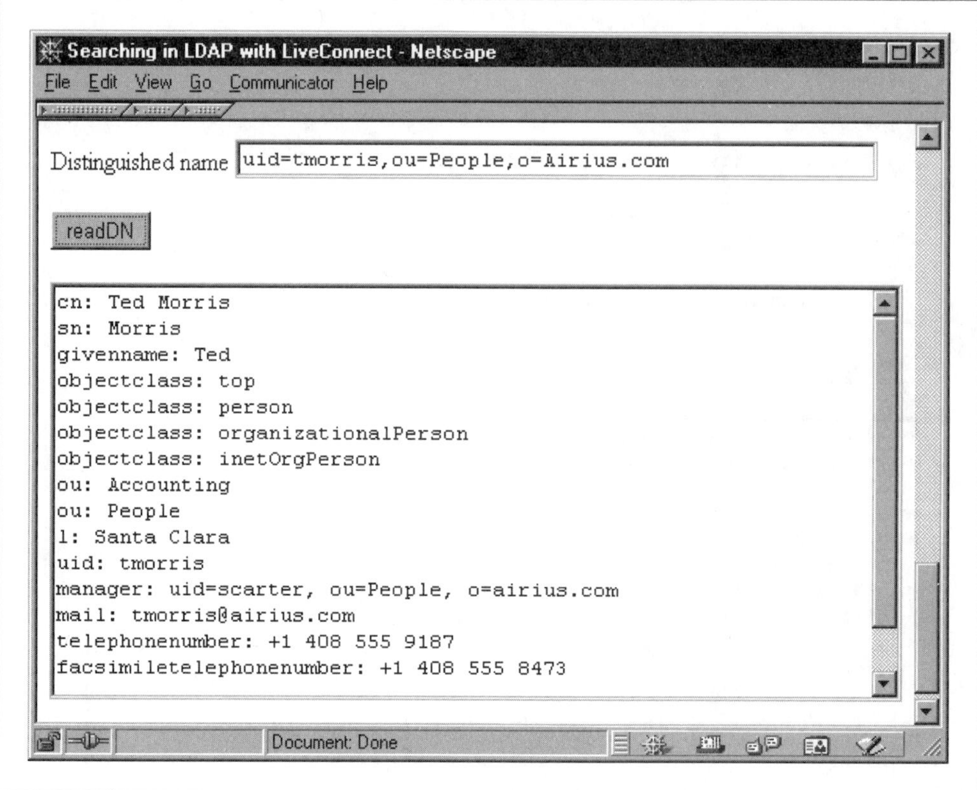

FIGURE 9-3. *Reading attributes with JavaScript.*

Handling Java Exceptions in JavaScript

With JavaScript 1.4, you can throw and catch exceptions using the new `throw` and `try...catch` statements. If Java code throws an exception, the exception is passed on to your JavaScript code. At the time of this writing, however, the latest versions of Netscape Navigator (4.08 through 4.61) support only JavaScript 1.3, which provides no statements for handling Java exceptions.

To handle exceptions, you need to write a wrapper Java class with methods that (1) catch the exceptions, (2) possibly print out error messages about the exceptions, and (3) return status codes to indicate the success or failure of the operation.

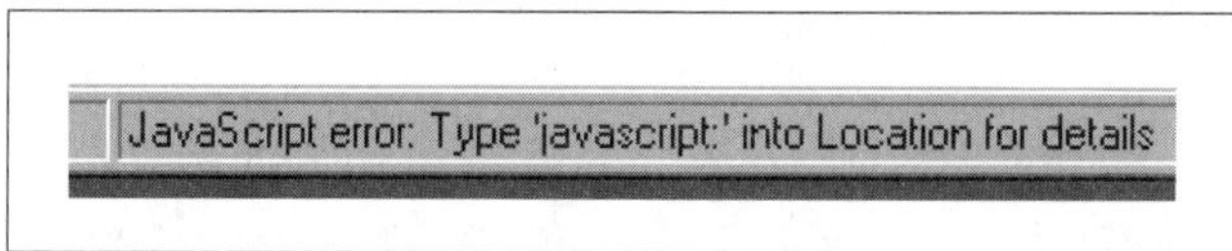

FIGURE 9-4. *Navigator message on Java exception.*

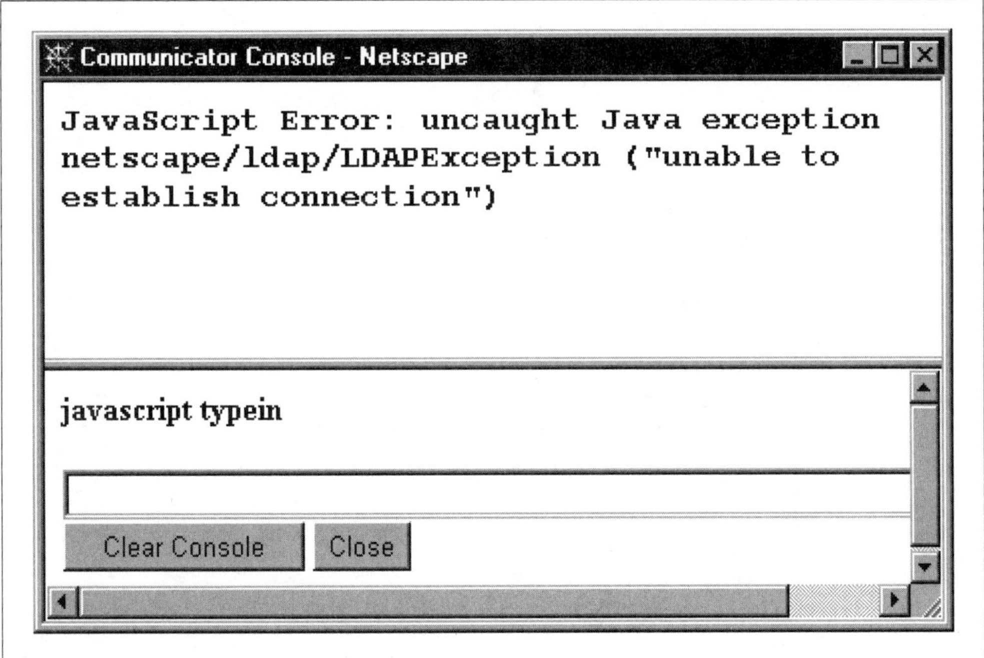

FIGURE 9-5. *JavaScript message dialog box.*

The following Java code in the wrapper class `JSLDAPConnection` provides a method (`safeConnect`) for trapping exceptions when connecting to the LDAP server and a corresponding method for disconnecting.

```
public class JSLDAPConnection extends LDAPConnection {
  public JSLDAPConnection() {
     super();
      }

      /**
       * Connect to LDAP server
       *
       * @return 0 on success, an LDAP error code failure
       */
      public int safeConnect( int version, String host, int port,
                              String authdn, String authpw ) {
         try {
                connect( version, host, port, authdn, authpw );
         } catch( LDAPException e ) {
              return (_errorCode = e.getLDAPResultCode());
```

```
          }
          _errorCode = 0;
          return 0;
     }
       /**
        * Disconnect from LDAP server
        *
        * @return 0 on success, an LDAP error code failure
        */
       public int safeDisconnect() {
          try {
               disconnect();
          } catch( LDAPException e ){
             return (_errorCode = e.getLDAPResultCode());
          }
          _errorCode = 0;
             return 0;
     }
}
```

Your JavaScript code can construct a new `JSLDAPConnection` object and invoke the `safeConnect` method to connect to the LDAP server:

```
<SCRIPT LANG="JavaScript">
var connection = new Packages.JSLDAPConnection();
var isConnected = connection.safeConnect( 3, "directory.airius.com",
                                           389, "", "" );
</SCRIPT>
```

`JSLDAPConnection` also has wrappers for searching and reading, and a method to get the latest status code from an LDAP operation:

```
    /**
     * Performs the search specified by the criteria you enter.
     * This method also allows you to specify constraints for the search
     * (such as the maximum number of entries to find or the
     * maximum time to wait for search results). <P>
     *
     * @param base base distinguished name from which to search
     * @param scope scope of the entries to search
     * @param filter search filter specifying the search criteria
     * @param attrs list of attributes you want returned in the search
     * results
```

```
 * @param cons constraints specific to this search (e.g., the
 * maximum number of entries to return)
 * @param attrsOnly If true, returns the names but not the values of the
 * attributes found. If false, returns the names and values for
 * attributes found.
 * @return JSLDAPSearchResults The results of the search,
 * or null on failure. If null, call
 * getErrorCode() to get the LDAP error code.
 */
public JSLDAPSearchResults
    safeSearch( String base,
                int scope,
                String filter,
                String[] attrs,
                boolean attrsOnly,
                LDAPSearchConstraints cons ) {

    try {
      LDAPSearchResults res = search( base, scope,
                             filter, attrs,
                             attrsOnly, cons );
        _errorCode = 0;
        return new JSLDAPSearchResults( res );
    } catch( LDAPException e ) {
      _errorCode = e.getLDAPResultCode();
        return null;
    }
  }

/**
 * Reads the entry for the specified distiguished name (DN)
 * and retrieves all attributes for the entry.
 *
 * @param DN distinguished name of the entry you want
 * to retrieve
 * @return the specified entry, or null if the entry is not
 * found
 */
public LDAPEntry safeRead ( String DN ) {
   try {
        LDAPEntry entry = read( DN );
        _errorCode = 0;
        return entry;
   } catch( LDAPException e ) {
```

```
                _errorCode = e.getLDAPResultCode();
                return null;
            }
        }
        /**
         * Get latest LDAP error code
         *
         * @return latest LDAP error code
         */
        public int getErrorCode() {
            return _errorCode;
        }

    private int _errorCode = 0;;
}
```

We can now write a new version of the HTML page: `jsldapsafe.html`. It calls the wrapper methods and processes any errors returned:

```
    // Create a connection
    var conn = new Packages.JSLDAPConnection();
...
    // Connect to selected host
    err = conn.safeConnect( 3, // LDAPv3
                            document.LDAPForm.host.value,
                            parseInt(document.LDAPForm.port.value),
                            "", // Anonymous
                            "" );
    if ( err != 0 ) {
        alert( "Failed to connect to " +
               document.LDAPForm.host.value +
               ":" + document.LDAPForm.port.value );
        return;
    }
```

If the specified LDAP server is not accessible, the user now sees a more helpful error dialog box, as in Figure 9-6. Now that we have control of exceptions, we can do more sophisticated things, as we will see in the remainder of this chapter.

Iterating on search results with `LDAPSearchResults.next` can also throw an exception (for example, if more results were requested than the server is configured to return). The `JSLDAPSearchResults` class wraps `LDAPSearchResults` to allow safe enumeration in JavaScript. It doesn't extend `LDAPSearchResults`, because there is no

FIGURE 9-6. *Application-controlled error dialog box on Java exception.*

easy way for an extension class to access the contents of `LDAPSearchResults`; rather it keeps a reference to one `LDAPSearchResults` in a member variable: `_results`. If calling `next` throws an exception, `JSLDAPSearchResults` returns `null` instead and stores the error code for retrieval by the client:

```
/**
 * Returns the next LDAP entry from the search results
 * or null if the next result is an
 * exception (including a referral). If null,
 * the LDAP result code is available with getErrorCode.
 * @return the next LDAP entry in the search results
 */
public LDAPEntry next() {
    try {
        LDAPEntry entry = _results.next();
        _errorCode = 0;
        return entry;
    } catch( LDAPException e ) {
        _errorCode = e.getLDAPResultCode();
        return null;
    }
}
```

The JavaScript code can now detect and process an exception during the iteration of search results:

```
while( res.hasMoreElements() ) { // Iterate on entries
```

```
        entry = res.next();
        if ( res == null ) {
            alert( "Error processing search results; error code = " +
                   res.getErrorCode() );
            return;
        }
```

Handling Arrays of Strings

In LDAP, attributes can have multiple values. You can represent the multiple values in Java and in JavaScript as an array of strings. If you plan to pass a multivalued attribute as an array of strings from your Java code to your JavaScript code, you need to convert the Java `String` array to a JavaScript array of strings. The following JavaScript function illustrates one way to do this. The `javaArray` parameter is assumed to be a Java `String` array returned from a call to a Java object.

```
function javaToJS(javaArray){
    // Declare an array of JavaScript strings
    var jsArray = new Array();
    for( var i = 0; i < javaArray.length; i++ ) {
        jsArray[i] = javaArray[i];
    }
    return (jsArray);
}
```

Requesting Privileges and Signing Your JavaScript Code

If the LDAP server is running on a different machine from your Web server, you need to request permission to connect to the LDAP server. Chapter 8 covers permissions in detail (see the section on writing LDAP applets for Netscape Navigator in that chapter for more information). The following excerpt from `jsldap.html` illustrates how to request permission to connect to the LDAP server.

```
    // Create a connection
    conn = new LDAPConnection();
    // Ask the user for permission to establish a remote
    // connection
    netscape.security.PrivilegeManager.enablePrivilege(
            "UniversalConnect");
    netscape.security.PrivilegeManager.enablePrivilege(
            "UniversalPropertyRead");
    // Connect to selected host
    conn.connect( 3, // LDAPv3
```

```
                    document.LDAPForm.host.value,
                    parseInt(document.LDAPForm.port.value),
                    "", // Anonymous
                    "" );
```

Next you need to sign your JavaScript code. Netscape's `signtool` utility allows you to sign inline JavaScript code. For details on signing code, getting certificates, and using `signtool`, see Chapter 8.

In the `<SCRIPT>` tag that surrounds your JavaScript functions, set the `ARCHIVE` attribute to the name of a JAR file (`signtool` will create this JAR file as part of the process of signing the scripts), and set the `ID` attribute to a unique identifier for each script section in the file. This ID will identify the signed script segments in the generated JAR file:

```
<SCRIPT LANGUAGE="JavaScript" ARCHIVE="JSLDAPHTML.jar" ID="1">
// Do a subtree search
function doSearch() {
...
}
</SCRIPT>
```

If you have event handlers for a tag (for example, a function to be called when a button is clicked), you also need to include an `ID` attribute in the tag. You do not need to specify separate `ARCHIVE` attributes for event handlers, as long as they are preceded by a script with the `ARCHIVE` attribute. These event handler scripts will be placed in the same JAR file as the preceding script:

```
<INPUT TYPE=button VALUE="search" onClick="doSearch()" ID="2">
```

When you run `signtool`, it creates subdirectories named `<jarfile>.arc` and `<jarfile.arc>\inlineScripts`. For each tag with an ID, `signtool` extracts the inline JavaScript code to a file named after the ID. The `signtool` utility places these files into the `inlineScripts` directory.

As with signed Java applets (see Chapter 8), `signtool` creates a `META-INF` subdirectory, as well as a `manifest.mf` file (containing the name and a hash of each file to be signed), a `zigbert.sf` signature instruction file (containing a hash of each section in `manifest.mf`), and a `zigbert.rsa` digital signature file (containing a hash of the `zigbert.sf` file encrypted with the private key, as well as the certificate for that key). The `signtool` utility puts the contents of the `META-INF` and `inlineScripts` directories in a JAR file and removes the `.arc` directory and all temporary files.

To sign inline JavaScript code with `signtool`, use the following syntax:

```
signtool -d <cert_dir> -k <cert_name> -J <code_dir>
```

where

- `<cert_dir>` specifies the location of your certificate database and your key database. For example, in Windows this is typically

  `C:\Program Files\Netscape\Users\<yourname>.`

- `<cert_name>` specifies the object-signing certificate.
- `<code_dir>` specifies the directory containing the HTML files that have JavaScript code you want to sign.

The following example demonstrates how to sign your code. The example uses the "TestCertificate" certificate to sign the JavaScript code in any HTML files located in the `html` directory. If you place `jsldap.html` in that directory, `signtool` will create a JAR file named `JSLDAPHTML.jar` (as specified by the `ARCHIVE` attribute of the `SCRIPT` tag in `jsldap.html`). The example expects to find the certificate and key databases in the directory `D:\Program Files\Netscape\Users\username`. The information you need to enter is highlighted in bold.

```
D:\sourcefiles>signtool -k TestCertificate -d "D:\Program
    Files\Netscape\Users\username" -J html
using key "TestCertificate"
using certificate directory: D:\Program Files\Netscape\Users\username

Generating inline signatures from HTML files in: html
Processing HTML file: jsldap.html

signing: html/JSLDAPHTML.jar
Generating html/JSLDAPHTML.arc/META-INF/manifest.mf file..
-> inlineScripts/1
-> inlineScripts/2
-> inlineScripts/3
Generating zigbert.sf file..
adding html/JSLDAPHTML.arc/META-INF/manifest.mf to html/
JSLDAPHTML.jar...(deflated 46%)
adding html/JSLDAPHTML.arc/META-INF/zigbert.sf to html/
JSLDAPHTML.jar...(deflated 41%)
adding html/JSLDAPHTML.arc/META-INF/zigbert.rsa to html/
JSLDAPHTML.jar...(deflated 38%)
jarfile "html/JSLDAPHTML.jar" signed successfully
removing: html/JSLDAPHTML.arc
Directory html signed successfully.
```

Note that if you make any changes to the HTML file (even adding or deleting spaces), you need to sign the file and generate the JAR file again.

Copy the HTML files and the JAR file, as well as any wrapper classes, to your Web server.

Accessing the LDAP Classes from JScript in Internet Explorer

Internet Explorer does not make Java classes available automatically to scripts written in JScript or Visual Basic. To use JScript or Visual Basic with the LDAP classes or any other classes that you add to Internet Explorer, you must create COM wrappers for them. Microsoft Visual J++ allows you to select classes that require COM wrappers, and then it generates them for you.

Another option may be to use the open-source JavaScript interpreter Rhino, which is written in Java and available at `http://www.mozilla.org`.

Conclusion

In this chapter we have discussed how to access applets and built-in Java objects from JavaScript in a safe and efficient way. JavaScript is an effective glue for tying together Java applets on a Web page or for binding Java applets to HTML-type form elements. In Netscape Navigator, you can also use JavaScript to access any built-in Java classes and objects, such as the Java LDAP classes. If not a lot of processing needs to be done, then having all the client code in JavaScript rather than in Java may make your HTML page appear more quickly, since no applets need to be downloaded. In addition, JavaScript does not need be compiled before use.

However, JavaScript has certain limitations compared to Java, and the Java LDAP classes can be made more JavaScript-friendly by being wrapped in a thin layer that catches exceptions and passes status codes instead. As with applets, JavaScript must be signed if it makes calls that imply a connection to a machine other than that of the Web server.

CHAPTER 10

Don't Redo It, Reuse It: LDAP JavaBeans

Java is an object-oriented language that lends itself well to encapsulating functionality as components. The JavaBeans specification takes this encapsulation a step further, defining how a component publishes its properties and methods and how other components can discover and access those properties and methods. Many Java development environments support the JavaBeans specification. Because of this support, you can write a component that complies with the specification, and that component can be dropped into the component palette of any of these Java development environments. The component you write can be used again in future projects or by other developers, who need no knowledge about the component's implementation.

Directory SDK for Java includes a few sample JavaBeans. Although each Java Bean does very little, each one provides a single piece of commonly used directory functionality. The JavaBeans also encapsulate some of the implementation details of LDAP, which means that developers can use these JavaBeans without knowing very much about LDAP.

Invisible LDAP JavaBeans

The first set of JavaBeans we'll look at are "invisible Beans." These JavaBeans wrap subsets of the SDK functionality, but they provide no GUI interface.

All these invisible JavaBeans extend the common base class `LDAPBasePropertySupport`, illustrated in Figure 10-1. This class provides standard methods for accessing SDK properties, a method for connecting to the directory, and an event dispatcher for property change events. Property change events are the simplest and probably the most common events used by JavaBeans to notify other components of significant changes. Let's take a look at the implementation of the `LDAPBasePropertySupport` class.

```
LDAPBasePropertySupport
(from beans)

$ OK : int = 0
$ INVALID_PARAMETER : int = 1
$ CONNECT_ERROR : int = 2
$ AUTHENTICATION_ERROR : int = 3
$ PROPERTY_NOT_FOUND : int = 4
$ AMBIGUOUS_RESULTS : int = 5
$ NO_SUCH_OBJECT : int = 6
_debug : boolean = false
_errCode : int = 0
_port : int = 389
_scope : int = LDAPConnection.SCOPE_SUB

LDAPB asePropertySupport()
getHost() : String
setHost(theHost : String) : void
getPort() : int
setPort(thePort : int) : void
getBase() : String
setBase(theBase : String) : void
getAuthDN() : String
setAuthDN(authDN : String) : void
getAuthPassword() : String
setAuthPassword(authPassword : String) : void
getUserName() : String
setUserName (name : String) : void
getUserlD() : String
setUserlD(name : String) : void
getScope() : int
setScope(scope : int) : void
getFilter() : String
setFilter(filter : String) : void
getDebug() : boolean
setDebug(on : boolean) : void
getErrorCode() : int
setErrorCode(code : int) : void
addPropertyChangeListener(listener : PropertyChangeListener) : void
removePropertyChangeListener(listener : PropertyChangeListener) : void
firePropertyChange(propName : String , oldValue : Object, newValue :
   Object) : void
printDebug(s : String) : void
connect(conn : LDAPConnection, host : String, port : int) : void
setDefaultReferralCredentials(conn : LDAPConnection) : void
convertToString(aResuit : String[]) : String
```

FIGURE 10-1. LDAPBasePropertySupport.

LDAPBasePropertySupport

One of the requirements of a JavaBean is that it must be serializable; that is, the object must be able to be written to disk or transferred over a network and then reconstituted. In addition, the JavaBean must have a public constructor that takes no parameters. These two requirements are related: a JavaBean object can be stored persistently (which requires it to be serializable) and restored later (which requires a constructor with no parameters). The `LDAPBasePropertySupport` class fulfills both of these requirements:

```
public class LDAPBasePropertySupport implements Serializable {
    /**
     * Constructor with no parameters
     */
    public LDAPBasePropertySupport() {}
```

Next, accessor methods are declared for the properties used to connect to the directory and to search the directory. These properties include the host name and port number of the LDAP server, the DN and password used for authentication, and the base DN, scope, and filter used for the search. Only the accessors for the host name property are included in the block of code shown here; the others are similar.

```
    /**
     * Returns the host to search at
     * @return DNS name or dotted IP name of host to search at
     */
    public String getHost() {
        return _host;
    }

    /**
    * Sets host string.
    * @param theHost host name
    */
    public void setHost( String theHost ) {
        _host = theHost;
    }
```

The invisible JavaBeans provided with the SDK use property change events to notify other components of the results of operations. The base class provides support for registering interest in property change events and for "firing" them:

```
/**
 * Add a client to be notified when an authentication result is in
 * @param listener a client to be notified of changes
 */
public void addPropertyChangeListener(
                          PropertyChangeListener listener ) {
    System.out.println( "Adding listener " + listener );
    m_propSupport.addPropertyChangeListener( listener );
}

/**
 * Remove a client that had requested notification on authentication
 * @param listener a client not to be notified of changes
 */
public void removePropertyChangeListener(
                          PropertyChangeListener listener ) {
    m_propSupport.removePropertyChangeListener( listener );
}

/**
 * Support for bound property notification
 * @param propName name of changed property
 * @param oldValue previous value of property
 * @param newValue new value of property
 */
public void firePropertyChange(
                          String propName,
                          Object oldValue,
                          Object newValue ) {

    if (m_propSupport == null)
        m_propSupport = new PropertyChangeSupport( this );

    m_propSupport.firePropertyChange( propName, oldValue, newValue );
}
```

The `LDAPBasePropertySupport` class also defines two utility methods, shown in the block of code that follows. The `printDebug` method prints out debugging information, and the `convertToString` method converts a `String` array to a single `String` (with line feeds delimiting the fields in the single String). The convertToString method is useful if you are using this class in JavaScript (through LiveConnect). You can use convertToString to supply results as a single String (JavaScript does not support arrays as return values). This method is not declared static, because JavaScript in earlier browsers doesn't handle inheritance of static methods properly.

```
    protected void printDebug( String s ) {
        if ( _debug )
            System.out.println( s );
    }

    /**
     * Utility method to convert a String array to a single String
     * with line feeds between elements.
     * @param aResult the String array to convert
     * @return a String with the elements separated by line feeds
     */
    public String convertToString( String[] aResult ) {
        String sResult = "";
        if ( null != aResult ) {
            for ( int i = 0; i < aResult.length; i++ ) {
                sResult += aResult[i] + "\n";
            }
        }
        return sResult;
    }
```

Finally, a method to connect to a directory is defined. It is protected, since it is to be used by derived Beans and not by external components. The connect method, shown in the block of code that follows, checks if the Bean is running as an applet in Netscape Navigator, and if so, requests permission to make network connections. We discussed the need to request permission to establish network connections in Chapter 8.

The method also sets up automatic following of referrals using the same credentials that were supplied for the original connection. Referral processing will be discussed in detail in Chapter 16.

```
    /**
     * Sets up basic connection privileges for Navigator if necessary,
     * and connects
     * @param host host to connect to
     * @param port port number
     * @exception LDAPException from connect()
     */
```

```
protected void connect( LDAPConnection conn, String host, int port )
    throws LDAPException {
    boolean needsPrivileges = true;
    /* Running stand-alone? */
    SecurityManager sec = System.getSecurityManager();
    printDebug( "Security manager = " + sec );
    if ( sec == null ) {
        printDebug( "No security manager" );
        /* Not an applet; we can do what we want to */
        needsPrivileges = false;
    /* Cannot do instanceof on an abstract class */
    } else if ( sec.toString().startsWith(
        "java.lang.NullSecurityManager") ) {
        printDebug( "No security manager" );
        /* Not an applet; we can do what we want to */
        needsPrivileges = false;
    } else if ( sec.toString().startsWith(
        "netscape.security.AppletSecurity" ) ) {

        /* Connecting to the local host? */
        try {
            if ( host.equalsIgnoreCase(
                java.net.InetAddress.getLocalHost().getHostName() ) )
                needsPrivileges = false;
        } catch ( java.net.UnknownHostException e ) {
        }
    }

    if ( needsPrivileges ) {
        /* Running as applet. Is PrivilegeManager around? */
        String mgr = "netscape.security.PrivilegeManager";
        try {
            Class c = Class.forName( mgr );
            java.lang.reflect.Method[] m = c.getMethods();
            if ( m != null ) {
                for( int i = 0; i < m.length; i++ ) {
                    if ( m[i].getName().equals(
                        "enablePrivilege" ) ) {
                        try {
                            Object[] args = new Object[1];
                            args[0] =
                                new String( "UniversalConnect" );
                            m[i].invoke( null, args );
```

```
                                        printDebug(
                                            "UniversalConnect enabled" );
                                    } catch ( Exception e ) {
                                        printDebug( "Exception on invoking " +
                                                    "enablePrivilege: " +
                                                    e.toString() );
                                        break;
                                    }
                                    break;
                                }
                            }
                        }
                    } catch ( ClassNotFoundException e ) {
                        printDebug( "no " + mgr );
                    }
                }

            conn.connect( host, port );
            setDefaultReferralCredentials( conn );
        }
```

The `setDefaultReferralCredentials` method, illustrated in the block of code that follows, creates and configures an object used to handle any referrals encountered during a search. The object holds the DN and password used to authenticate to the original server. When the Bean is "referred" to another LDAP server, the DN and password in the object are used to authenticate to the new server.

```
    protected void setDefaultReferralCredentials(
        LDAPConnection conn ) {
        final LDAPConnection m_conn = conn;
        LDAPRebind rebind = new LDAPRebind() {
            public LDAPRebindAuth getRebindAuthentication(
                    String host,
                    int port ) {
                return new LDAPRebindAuth(
                    m_conn.getAuthenticationDN(),
                    m_conn.getAuthenticationPassword() );
            }
        };
        LDAPSearchConstraints cons = conn.getSearchConstraints();
        cons.setReferrals( true );
        cons.setRebindProc( rebind );
    }
```

In the following block of code, error codes are defined for use by derived classes as well as by clients. Clients do not need to know about the extensive list of error codes in `LDAPException`.

```
/*
 * Variables
 */
/* Error codes from search operations, etc. */
public static final int OK = 0;
public static final int INVALID_PARAMETER = 1;
public static final int CONNECT_ERROR = 2;
public static final int AUTHENTICATION_ERROR = 3;
public static final int PROPERTY_NOT_FOUND = 4;
public static final int AMBIGUOUS_RESULTS = 5;
public static final int NO_SUCH_OBJECT = 6;
```

Finally, variables storing the Bean properties are declared:

```
private boolean _debug = false;
private int _errCode = 0;
private String _host = new String("localhost");
private int _port = 389;
private int _scope = LDAPConnection.SCOPE_SUB;
private String _base = new String("");
private String _filter = new String("");
private String _authDN = new String("");
private String _authPassword = new String("");
private String _userName = new String("");
private String _userID = new String("");
transient private PropertyChangeSupport m_propSupport =
          new PropertyChangeSupport( this );
```

LDAPSimpleAuth

Many applications, particularly server-side applications, use a directory solely to authenticate a user (to determine if a user is who he says he is). We've already looked at authenticating to the directory, starting in Chapter 6. Not much to it. So why do we need a JavaBean to do authentication? The answer will become apparent very soon.

`LDAPSimpleAuth`, illustrated in Figure 10-2, is a JavaBean for LDAP authentication.

As with all other JavaBeans, `LDAPSimpleAuth` is serializable and has a constructor with no parameters. For convenience, it also has constructors to allow setting

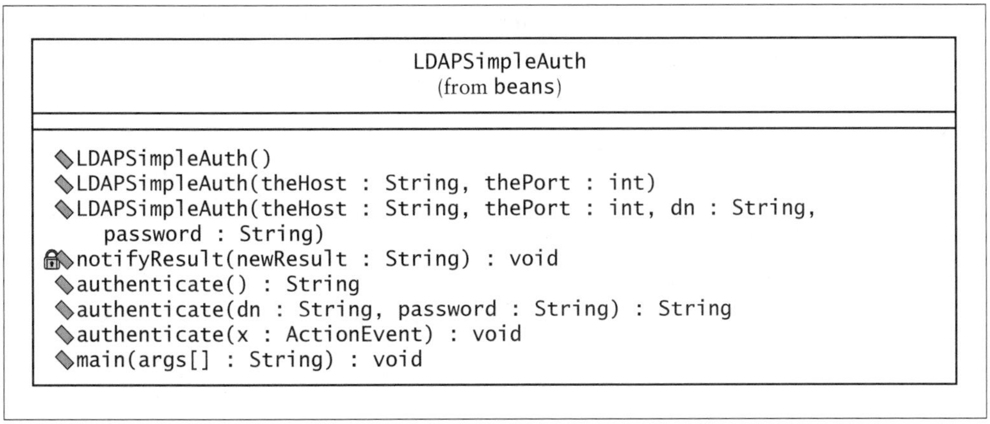

```
LDAPSimpleAuth
(from beans)

LDAPSimpleAuth()
LDAPSimpleAuth(theHost : String, thePort : int)
LDAPSimpleAuth(theHost : String, thePort : int, dn : String,
   password : String)
notifyResult(newResult : String) : void
authenticate() : String
authenticate(dn : String, password : String) : String
authenticate(x : ActionEvent) : void
main(args[] : String) : void
```

FIGURE 10-2. LDAPSimpleAuth.

some or all parameters in one shot, rather than through the methods for setting individual properties:

```
public class LDAPSimpleAuth extends LDAPBasePropertySupport
                            implements Serializable {

    /**
     * Constructor with no parameters
     */
    public LDAPSimpleAuth() {}

    /**
    * Constructor with host and port initializers
    * @param theHost host string
    * @param thePort port number
    */
    public LDAPSimpleAuth( String theHost,
                           int thePort ) {
        setHost( theHost );
        setPort( thePort );
    }

    /**
    * Constructor with all required authentication parameters
    * @param theHost host string
    * @param thePort port number
```

```
    * @param dn fully qualified distinguished name to authenticate
    * @param password password for authenticating the DN
    */
    public LDAPSimpleAuth( String theHost,
                           int thePort,
                           String dn,
                           String password ) {
        setHost( theHost );
        setPort( thePort );
        setAuthDN( dn );
        setAuthPassword( password );
    }
```

The only public method (aside from a `main` method, which you can use to verify that the JavaBean works) is `authenticate`, which has two signatures. One signature has no parameters and relies on the properties you set by using the accessor methods. The other signature allows you to pass in the DN and the password you want to use for authentication. To facilitate use with JavaScript in a browser or on a Web server, `authenticate` returns a `String`. The `authenticate` method, shown in the following block of code, also notifies clients of results by firing property change events.

```
    /**
     * Connect to LDAP server using parameters specified in
     * constructor and/or by setting properties, and attempt to
     * authenticate.
     * @return "Y" on successful authentication, "N" otherwise
     */
    public String authenticate() {
        LDAPConnection m_ldc = null;
        String result = "N";
        try {
            m_ldc = new LDAPConnection();
            System.out.println("Connecting to " + getHost() +
                               " " + getPort());
            connect( m_ldc, getHost(), getPort());
        } catch (Exception e) {
            System.out.println( "Failed to connect to " + getHost() +
                                ": " + e.toString() );
        }
        if ( m_ldc.isConnected() ) {
            System.out.println( "Authenticating " + getAuthDN() );
            try {
                m_ldc.authenticate( getAuthDN(), getAuthPassword() );
```

```
            result = "Y";
        } catch (Exception e) {
            System.out.println( "Failed to authenticate to " +
                                getHost() + ": " + e.toString() );
        }
    }

    try {
        if ( (m_ldc != null) && m_ldc.isConnected() )
            m_ldc.disconnect();
    } catch ( Exception e ) {
    }

    notifyResult( result );
    return result;
}

/**
 * Connect to LDAP server using parameters specified in
 * constructor and/or by setting properties, and attempt to
 * authenticate.
 * @param dn fully qualified distinguished name to authenticate
 * @param password password for authenticating the DN
 * @return "Y" on successful authentication, "N" otherwise
 */
public String authenticate( String dn,
                            String password ) {
    setAuthDN( dn );
    setAuthPassword( password );
    return authenticate();
}
```

The `String` return value makes it easy to use this Bean in JavaScript. In the following sample section of a Web page, the parameters are taken from HTML text fields in an HTML form called "input," and the result is displayed in a JavaScript alert dialog box.

```
<SCRIPT LANGUAGE="JavaScript">
function checkAuthentication() {
    auth = new Packages.netscape.ldap.beans.LDAPSimpleAuth();
    auth.setHost( document.input.host.value );
    auth.setPort( parseInt(document.input.port.value) );
    auth.setAuthDN( document.input.dn.value );
```

```
    auth.setAuthPassword( document.input.password.value );
    // Must request rights to do network connections
    netscape.security.PrivilegeManager.enablePrivilege("UniversalConnect");
    // And for property reads, to get LDAP error strings
    netscape.security.PrivilegeManager.enablePrivilege(
        "UniversalPropertyRead");
    result = auth.authenticate();
    if ( result == "N" )
        msg =  "Incorrect password";
    else
        msg = "Successful login";
    alert( msg );
}
</SCRIPT>
```

Clients that prefer to listen for a property change event rather than checking the return value of `authenticate` are notified through `notifyResult`:

```
private void notifyResult( String newResult ) {
    firePropertyChange( "result", result, newResult );
    result = newResult;
    }
```

LDAPGetEntries

When searching for a user entry in a directory, a typical user might enter part of the name or ID of the desired user and expect to select from a list of matching users. After selecting a name from the list, the user might then expect to see some properties of that entry. The `LDAPGetEntries` JavaBean (Figure 10-3) helps with the first part. It will accept part of a full name (`cn`), part of a user ID (`uid`), or both; search for all matching entries; and return a list of DNs. The full name and/or user ID may contain wild cards—for example, "john*" or "*ramer*."

As with `LDAPSimpleAuth`, `LDAPGetEntries` has a constructor with no parameters (for deserialization), as well as constructors to allow setting some or all parameters at once, rather than through the methods for setting individual properties:

```
public class LDAPGetEntries extends LDAPBasePropertySupport
                             implements Serializable {

    /**
     * Constructor with no parameters
     */
```

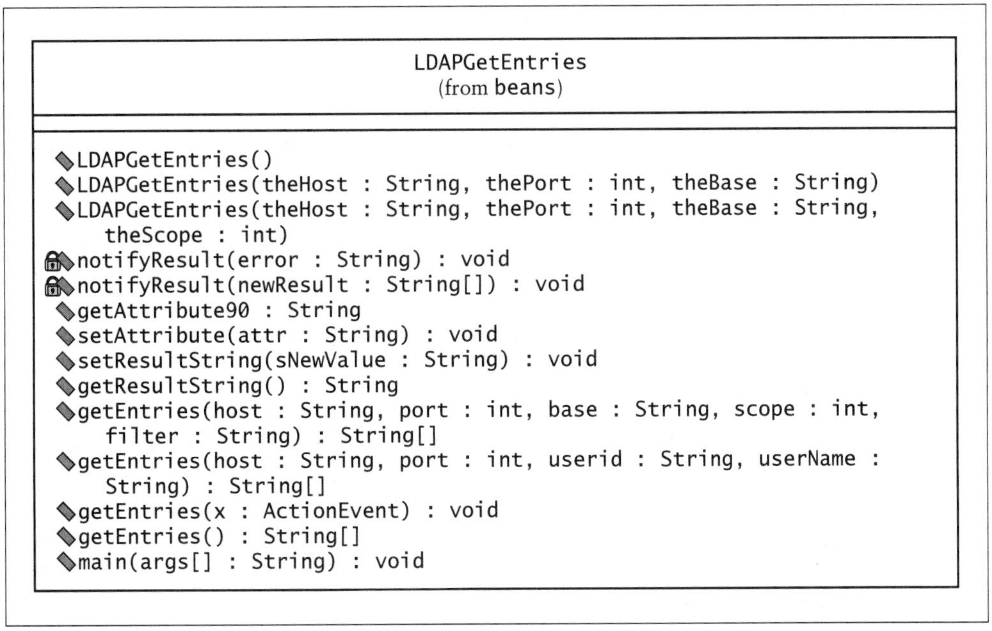

```
LDAPGetEntries
(from beans)

LDAPGetEntries()
LDAPGetEntries(theHost : String, thePort : int, theBase : String)
LDAPGetEntries(theHost : String, thePort : int, theBase : String,
   theScope : int)
notifyResult(error : String) : void
notifyResult(newResult : String[]) : void
getAttribute90 : String
setAttribute(attr : String) : void
setResultString(sNewValue : String) : void
getResultString() : String
getEntries(host : String, port : int, base : String, scope : int,
   filter : String) : String[]
getEntries(host : String, port : int, userid : String, userName :
   String) : String[]
getEntries(x : ActionEvent) : void
getEntries() : String[]
main(args[] : String) : void
```

FIGURE 10-3. LDAPGetEntries.

```
public LDAPGetEntries() {
    super();
}

/**
* Constructor with host, port, and base initializers
* @param theHost host string
* @param thePort port number
* @param theBase directory base string
*/
public LDAPGetEntries( String theHost, int thePort, String theBase ) {
    setHost( theHost );
    setPort( thePort );
    setBase( theBase );
}

/**
* Constructor with host, port, base, and scope initializers
* @param theHost host string
* @param thePort port number
* @param theBase directory base string
```

```
    * @param theScope one of LDAPConnection.SCOPE_BASE,
    * LDAPConnection.SCOPE_SUB, LDAPConnection.SCOPE_ONE
    */
    public LDAPGetEntries( String theHost,
                           int thePort,
                           String theBase,
                           int theScope ) {
        setHost( theHost );
        setPort( thePort );
        setBase( theBase );
        setScope( theScope );
    }
```

As with LDAPSimpleAuth, clients can be notified when results are ready with a PropertyChangeEvent (delivered by firePropertyChange):

```
private void notifyResult( String error ) {
    firePropertyChange( "error", _errorMsg, error );
    _errorMsg = error;
    }

    private void notifyResult( String[] newResult ) {
        String sNewResult = convertToStrings( newResult );
        firePropertyChange( "result", result, newResult );
        _sResult = sNewResult;
        result = newResult;
    }
```

There are accessors for the results:

```
public void setResultString( String sNewValue ) {
        _sResult = sNewValue;
    }

    public String getResultString() {
        return _sResult;
    }
```

The most important method in this JavaBean is getEntries, shown in the following block of code. This is the method called by a client to begin the search. Parameters can be supplied with the method, or they can be assumed to be already provided with the constructor or using the accessors.

```
/**
 * Searches and returns values for a specified attribute
 * @param host host string
 * @param port port number
 * @param base directory base string
 * @param scope one of LDAPConnection.SCOPE_BASE,
 * LDAPConnection.SCOPE_SUB, LDAPConnection.SCOPE_ONE
 * @param filter search filter
 * @param attribute name of property to return values for
 * @return array of values for the property
 */
public String[] getEntries( String host,
                            int port,
                            String base,
                            int scope,
                            String filter) {
    setHost( host );
    setPort( port );
    setBase( base );
    setScope( scope );
    setFilter( filter );
    return getEntries();
}

/**
 * Searches and returns values for a specified attribute
 * @param host host string
 * @param port port number
 * @param base directory base string
 * @param scope one of LDAPConnection.SCOPE_BASE,
 * LDAPConnection.SCOPE_SUB, LDAPConnection.SCOPE_ONE
 * @param userName the user name
 * @param userid the user ID
 * @return array of DNs
 */
public String[] getEntries( String host,
                            int port,
                            String base,
                            int scope,
                            String userid,
                            String userName) {
    setHost( host );
    setPort( port );
```

```
        setBase( base );
        setScope( scope );
        if (userName == null)
            userName = new String("");
        setUserName( userName );
        if (userid == null)
            userid = new String("");
        setUserID( userid );
        return getEntries();
    }

    // Added this method in order to get exposed in BDK
    public void getEntries(ActionEvent x) {
        getEntries();
    }

    /**
     * Searches and returns values of a previously registered property,
     * using previously set parameters
     * @return array of values for the property
     */
    public String[] getEntries() {
        boolean invalid = false;
        if ((getUserName().length() < 1) && (getUserID().length() < 1) &&
            (getFilter().length() < 1)) {
            printDebug("No user name or user ID");
            invalid = true;
        } else if ( (getHost().length() < 1) || (getBase().length() < 1) ) {
            printDebug( "Invalid host name or search base" );
            invalid = true;
        }
        if ( invalid ) {
            setErrorCode( INVALID_PARAMETER );
            notifyResult( (String)null);
            return null;
        }

        if (getFilter().length() < 1) {
            String filter = new String("");
            if ((getUserName().length() > 1) && (getUserID().length() > 1)) {
                filter = "(|(cn="+getUserName()+")(uid="+getUserID()+"))";
            } else if (getUserName().length() > 1) {
                filter = "cn="+getUserName();
            } else if (getUserID().length() > 1) {
```

```
            filter = "uid="+getUserID();
        }
        setFilter(filter);
    }

    String[] res = null;
    LDAPConnection m_ldc = new LDAPConnection();
    try {
        try {
            printDebug("Connecting to " + getHost() +
                       " " + getPort());
            connect( m_ldc, getHost(), getPort());
        } catch (Exception e) {
            printDebug( "Failed to connect to " + getHost() + ": " +
                        e.toString() );
            setErrorCode( CONNECT_ERROR );
            notifyResult( (String)null );
            m_ldc = null;
            throw( new Exception() );
        }

        // Authenticate?
        if ( (!getAuthDN().equals("")) &&
             (!getAuthPassword().equals("")) ) {

            printDebug( "Authenticating " + getAuthDN() );
            try {
                m_ldc.authenticate( getAuthDN(), getAuthPassword() );
            } catch (Exception e) {
                printDebug( "Failed to authenticate: " + e.toString() );
                setErrorCode( AUTHENTICATION_ERROR );
                notifyResult( (String)null );
                throw( new Exception() );
            }
        }

        // Search
        try {
            printDebug("Searching " + getBase() +
                       " for " + getFilter() + ", scope = " + getScope());
            String[] attrs = null;
            LDAPSearchResults results = m_ldc.search( getBase(),
                                                      getScope(),
                                                      getFilter(),
```

```
                                                attrs,
                                                false);

            // Create a vector for the results
            Vector v = new Vector();
            LDAPEntry entry = null;
            while ( results.hasMoreElements() ) {
                try {
                    entry = (LDAPEntry)results.next();
                } catch (LDAPReferralException e) {
                    if (getDebug()) {
                        notifyResult("Referral URLs: ");
                        LDAPUrl refUrls[] = e.getURLs();
                        for (int i = 0; i < refUrls.length; i++)
                            notifyResult(refUrls[i].getUrl());
                    }
                    continue;
                } catch (LDAPException e) {
                    if (getDebug())
                        notifyResult(e.toString());
                    continue;
                }
                String dn = entry.getDN();
                v.addElement( dn );
                printDebug( "... " + dn );
            }
            // Pull out the DNs and create a string array
            if ( v.size() > 0 ) {
                res = new String[v.size()];
                for( int i = 0; i < v.size(); i++ )
                    res[i] = (String)v.elementAt( i );
                setErrorCode( OK );
            } else {
                printDebug( "No entries found for " + getFilter() );
                setErrorCode( PROPERTY_NOT_FOUND );
            }
        } catch (Exception e) {
            printDebug( "Failed to search for " + getFilter() + ": " +
                        e.toString() );
            setErrorCode( PROPERTY_NOT_FOUND );
        }
    } catch (Exception e) {
    }
```

```
        try {
            if ( (m_ldc != null) && m_ldc.isConnected() )
                m_ldc.disconnect();
        } catch ( Exception e ) {
        }

        notifyResult( res );
        return res;
    }
```

You can verify the functionality of the Bean from the command line as follows:

```
java netscape.ldap.beans.LDAPGetEntries localhost 389 "o=airius.com" sub
    "cn=*"
       ou=Directory Administrators, o=mcom.com
       cn=Accounting Managers,ou=groups,o=mcom.com
       cn=HR Managers,ou=groups,o=mcom.com
       cn=QA Managers,ou=groups,o=mcom.com
       cn=PD Managers,ou=groups,o=mcom.com
```

The following is a simple example of using the LDAPGetEntries Bean in a Web page.

```
<FORM NAME=input>
<TABLE WIDTH="300" >
  <TR>
    <TD>Host:</TD>
    <TD><INPUT TYPE=text NAME="host" VALUE="manta" SIZE=40></TD>
  </TR>
  <TR>
    <TD>Port:</TD>
    <TD><INPUT TYPE=text NAME="port" VALUE=389 SIZE=40></TD>
  </TR>
  <TR>
    <TD>Directory base:</TD>
    <TD><INPUT TYPE=text NAME="base" VALUE="o=Airius.com" SIZE=40></TD>
  </TR>
  <TR>
    <TD>Filter:</TD>
    <TD><INPUT TYPE=text NAME="filter" VALUE="objectclass=groupOfUniqueNames"
    SIZE=40></TD>
  </TR>
```

```
</TABLE>
<P><INPUT TYPE=button VALUE="Get entries"
 onClick="getEntries()" ARCHIVE="LDAPGetEntries.jar" ID="2">
</FORM>

<P><FORM NAME=output>

<TEXTAREA NAME="results" ROWS=10 COLS=70></TEXTAREA>

</FORM>

<SCRIPT LANGUAGE="JavaScript" ARCHIVE="LDAPGetEntries.jar" ID="3">
function showError(err) {
    var pkg = netscape.ldap.beans.LDAPGetEntries;
    if ( err == pkg.INVALID_PARAMETER )
        errString = "Invalid parameter";
    else if ( err == pkg.CONNECT_ERROR )
        errString = "Unable to connect to server";
    else if ( err == pkg.AUTHENTICATION_ERROR )
        errString = "Unable to authenticate to server";
    else if ( err == pkg.PROPERTY_NOT_FOUND )
        errString = "Entry or property not found";
    else
        errString = "Unexpected error " + err;

    alert( "Error fetching entries: " + errString );
}

var getter;
function getEntries() {
    if ( document.input.filter.value.length < 1 ) {
        alert( "Must enter a value for Filter" );
    }
    var getter = new netscape.ldap.beans.LDAPGetEntries();
    // Get parameters from form fields
    getter.setHost( document.input.host.value );
    getter.setPort( parseInt(document.input.port.value) );
    getter.setBase( document.input.base.value );
    getter.setFilter( document.input.filter.value );
    // Do the search
    netscape.security.PrivilegeManager.enablePrivilege("UniversalConnect");
    values = getter.getEntries();
    // Display the results, converted to a single string with line feeds
    if ( values != null ) {
        document.output.results.value=getter.convertToString( values );
```

```
    } else {
        var err = getter.getErrorCode();
        showError( err );
    }
}
</SCRIPT>
```

A search for "objectclass=person" in the sample Airius database produces results as in Figure 10-4.

Directory-Based Authentication in JavaScript

`LDAPGetEntries` and `LDAPSimpleAuth` can be hooked up to provide simple authentication using a user ID and password. Recall that `LDAPSimpleAuth` requires a full DN, which users generally do not know (or at least they find difficult to type in). We'll use

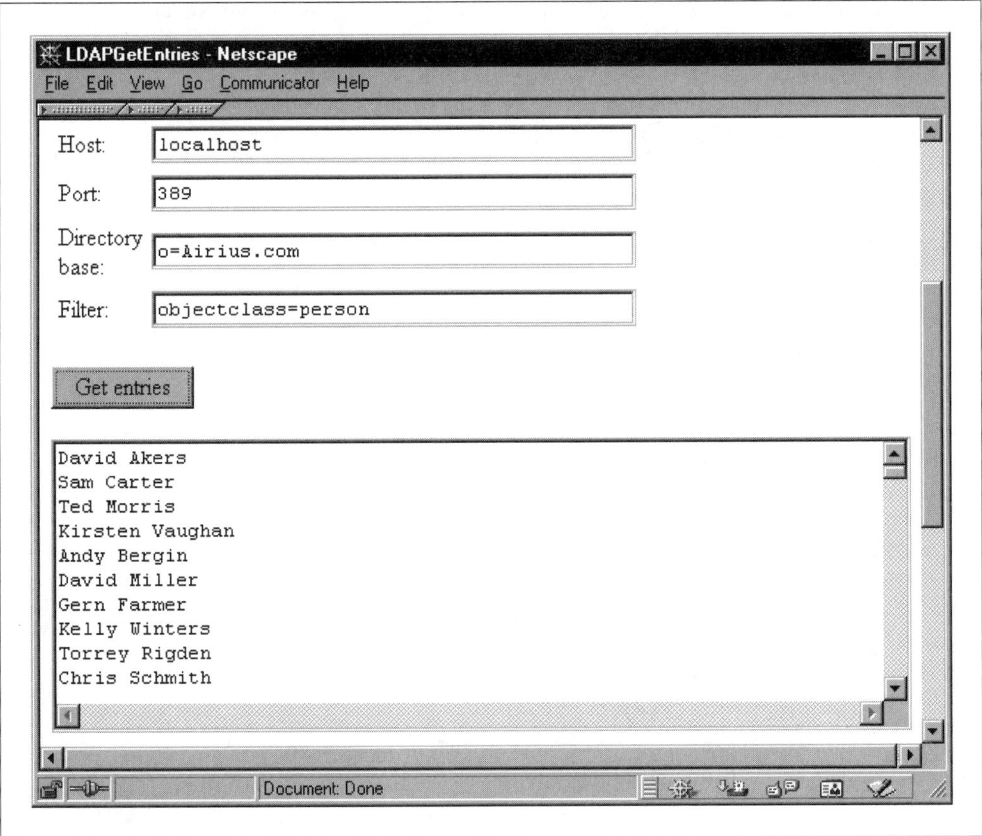

FIGURE 10-4. `LDAPGetEntries` *in a simple Web page.*

LDAPGetEntries to find the DN corresponding to the user ID entered by a user, and then LDAPSimpleAuth to validate the password supplied by the user for the DN.

The HTML page login.html demonstrates use of the two Beans to validate a user. The validated DN is available in the variable userDN:

```
<SCRIPT>
var userDN = "";
function doLogin() {
    // Create an instance of the LDAPGetEntries Bean
    var getter = new netscape.ldap.beans.LDAPGetEntries();
    // Get parameters from form fields
    getter.setHost( document.input.host.value );
    getter.setPort( parseInt(document.input.port.value) );
    getter.setBase( document.input.base.value );
    getter.setFilter( "uid="+document.input.userid.value );
    // Must request rights to do network connections
    netscape.security.PrivilegeManager.enablePrivilege("UniversalConnect");
    // And for property reads, to get LDAP error strings
    netscape.security.PrivilegeManager.enablePrivilege(
        "UniversalPropertyRead");
    // Do the search
    values = getter.getEntries();
    var result;
    // No matching entries?
    if ( (values == null) || (values.length < 1) ) {
        result = getter.getErrorCode();
        if ( result == 0 ) {
            result = getter.NO_SUCH_OBJECT;
        }
    // Too many matching entries?
    } else if ( values.length > 1 ) {
        result = TOO_MANY_MATCHES;
    // Good - just one match
    } else {
        userDN = values[0];
        auth = new Packages.netscape.ldap.beans.LDAPSimpleAuth();
        auth.setHost( document.input.host.value );
        auth.setPort( parseInt(document.input.port.value) );
        auth.setAuthDN( userDN );
        auth.setAuthPassword( document.input.password.value );
        result = auth.authenticate();
    }
    showResult( result );
}
</SCRIPT>
```

Using PropertyChangeEvent Notifications

So far in this chapter our examples have used the LDAP JavaBeans in a synchronous manner—calling a method and receiving the results as the return value of the method. However, JavaBeans are often connected to each other and to a client through event notification, which can be implemented very simply. In the following TestBean example, an anonymous object is created inline. This object is set up to be notified when results are available. When the property change event fires, the object prints out the results.

```
public class TestBean {
    public static void main( String[] args ) {
        // Create an instance of the Bean
        LDAPGetEntries getter = new LDAPGetEntries();
        // Create an object that listens for results and prints
        // them out
        getter.addPropertyChangeListener( new PropertyChangeListener() {
            public void propertyChange(PropertyChangeEvent evt) {
                String[] results = (String[])evt.getNewValue();
                for( int i = 0; i < results.length; i++ ) {
                    System.out.println( results[i] );
                }
            }
        } );

        // Do the search
        getter.getEntries( HOST, PORT, BASE, SCOPE, FILTER );
    }

    private static final String HOST = "localhost";
    private static final int PORT = 389;
    private static final String BASE = "o=airius.com";
    private static final int SCOPE = LDAPConnection.SCOPE_SUB;
    private static final String FILTER = "objectclass=groupofuniquenames";
}
```

A more useful and common scenario for JavaBeans is a visual development environment, in which components are combined and connected with a layout tool and no explicit programming is required. TestBeanApplet is an applet that contains only a TextArea. It has methods to set the font and background and foreground colors either through property accessors or through PARAM declarations in the APPLET tag, but these methods are omitted here for brevity.

The page TestBeanApplet.html demonstrates connecting the LDAPGetEntries JavaBean with a TestBeanApplet object through property change events. You can use a visual development environment like Visual JavaScript to lay out, connect, and configure the two components without having to write any code.

TestBeanApplet.java is very simple, if we set aside for now the parsing and processing of color and font specifications:

```
public class TestBeanApplet extends Applet
                              implements PropertyChangeListener {
      public void init() {
            super.init();
            setLayout(null);
            addNotify();
            int w = Integer.parseInt(getParameter("width"));
            int h = Integer.parseInt(getParameter("height"));
            resize(w+10,h+10);
            textField1 = new java.awt.TextArea(4, 40);
            textField1.setBounds(0,0,w,h);
            parseParameters();
            add(textField1);
      }
      private java.awt.TextArea textField1;
}
```

TestBeanApplet.html, shown below, is almost the same as LDAPGetEntries.html. Instead of a text area for displaying results, a TestBeanApplet is placed on the page and added as a PropertyChangeListener to the LDAPGetEntries JavaBean.

```
<APPLET code="TestBeanApplet.class" NAME="TestBeanApplet"
    MAYSCRIPT="true" width=450 height=200>
</APPLET>
var getter;
function getEntries() {
    // Get parameters from form fields
    getter.setHost( document.input.host.value );
    getter.setPort( parseInt(document.input.port.value) );
    getter.setBase( document.input.base.value );
    getter.setFilter( document.input.filter.value );
    getter.setAttribute( "cn" );
    // Must request rights to do network connections
    netscape.security.PrivilegeManager.enablePrivilege(
        "UniversalConnect");
    // Do the search
    values = getter.getEntries();
```

```
    if ( values == null ) {
        var err = getter.getErrorCode();
        showError( err );
    }
}

// Instantiate the Bean and hook it up to the applet
function doWire() {
    // Create an instance of the Bean
    getter = new netscape.ldap.beans.LDAPGetEntries();
    // Hook it up to the applet
    getter.addPropertyChangeListener( document.TestBeanApplet );
    // Set some interesting colors and font for the applet
    document.TestBeanApplet.setBackgroundColor( "yellow" );
    document.TestBeanApplet.setForegroundColor( "blue" );
    document.TestBeanApplet.setTextFont( "Helvetica-bolditalic-20" );
}
window.onload=doWire()
```

The Java `TextArea` can be easily customized with colors and fonts, as in Figure 10-5.

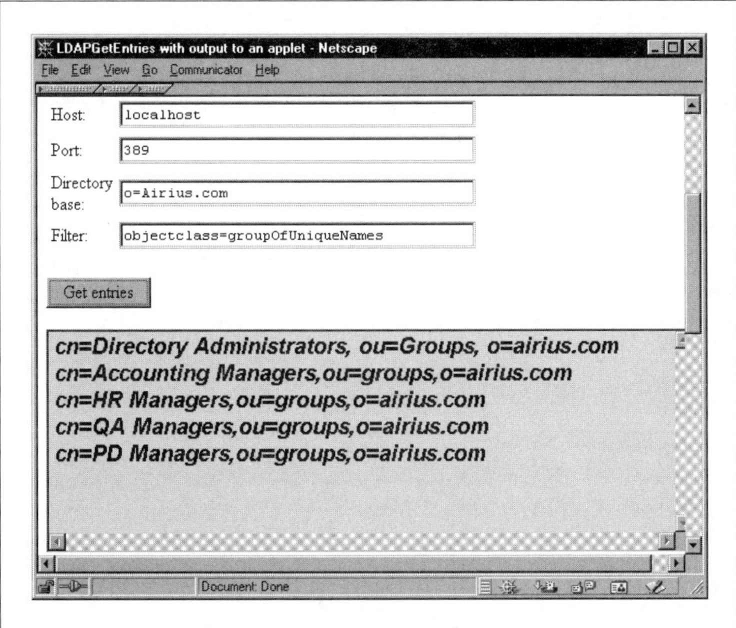

FIGURE 10-5. `LDAPGetEntries` *with JavaBean text area.*

Graphical LDAP JavaBeans

Now that we've investigated typical properties of an LDAP JavaBean, we can take a look at graphical components that can be plugged into a graphical user interface (GUI).

A Directory Browser

A component that displays the contents of a directory as a tree can be useful in many ways. It could be used simply to explore the directory. It could be invoked as a pop-up in places in an application where a user must enter a DN. Later in this chapter we'll hook it up to a table component to make a simple directory explorer, similar to Windows Explorer.

To simplify use of the Bean in a JFC (Java Foundation Classes) environment, we'll have it extend `javax.swing.JPanel`.

The `TreePanel` Bean (Figure 10-6) uses several utility classes, which are presented in Appendix C:

- **`Debug`** for conditional printout of error statements
- **`DateUtil`** for converting LDAP date strings to a localized date format

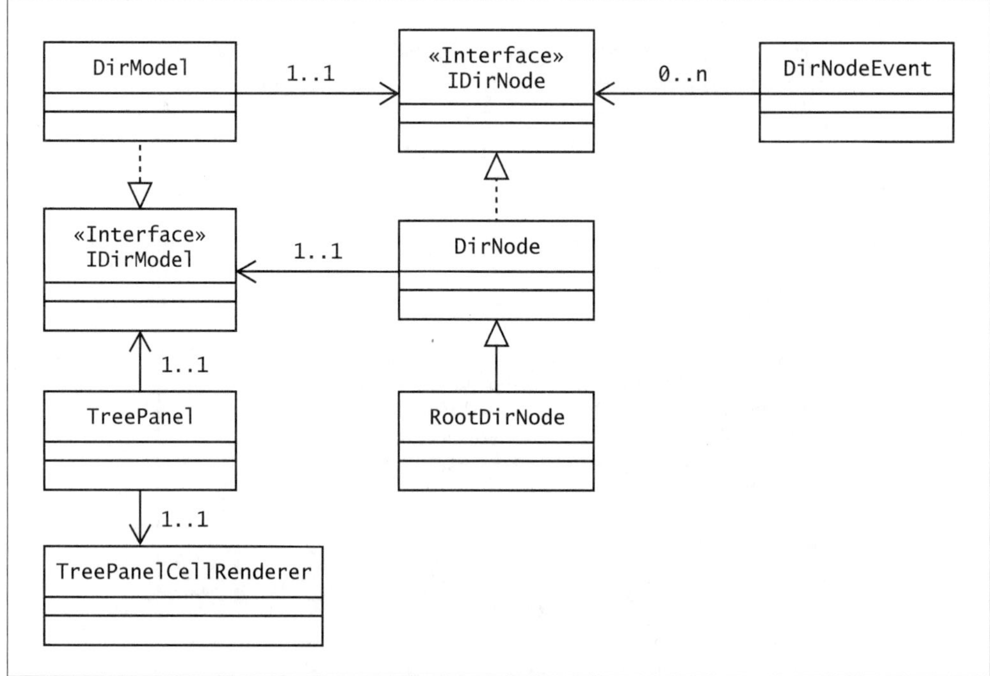

FIGURE 10-6. `TreePanel` *and supporting classes.*

- **DirUtil** to simplify connecting to a server (optionally using SSL)
- **ImageUtil** for remote or local loading of image files
- **ResourceSet** for reading properties from properties files
- **SortUtil** for sorting

TreePanel is supplied with data from an object that implements IDirModel. The level of indirection provided by the IDirModel interface allows us to substitute other implementations in the future, and it clarifies the interfaces used.

IDirModel

IDirModel (Figure 10-7) extends TreeModel, which is the basic JFC model interface for supporting a JTree. It adds methods for getting and setting various additional properties related to how the directory is to be searched.

```
public interface IDirModel extends javax.swing.tree.TreeModel {
    /**
     * Get a connection to the directory instance
     *
     * @return a connection to the server
     */
    public LDAPConnection getLDAPConnection();
```

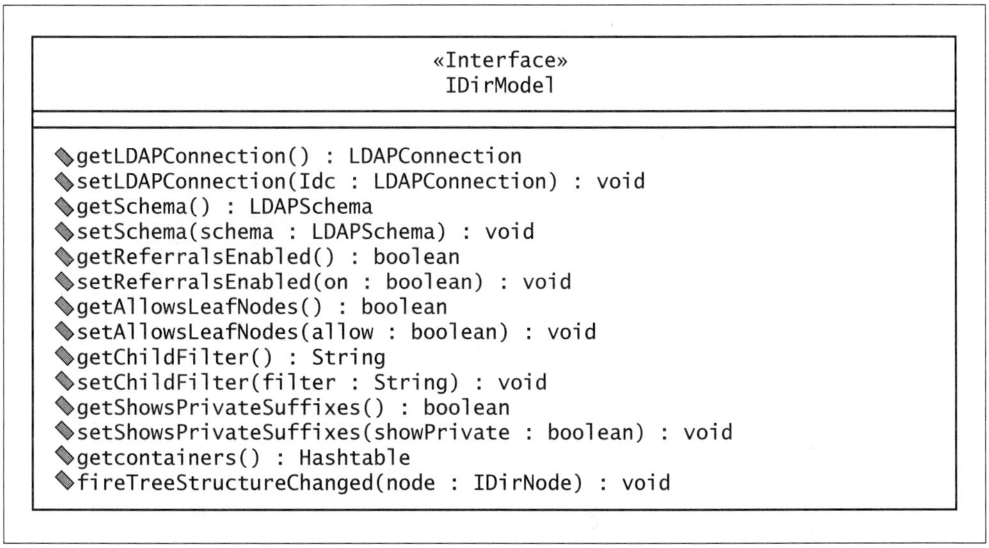

```
«Interface»
IDirModel

getLDAPConnection() : LDAPConnection
setLDAPConnection(ldc : LDAPConnection) : void
getSchema() : LDAPSchema
setSchema(schema : LDAPSchema) : void
getReferralsEnabled() : boolean
setReferralsEnabled(on : boolean) : void
getAllowsLeafNodes() : boolean
setAllowsLeafNodes(allow : boolean) : void
getChildFilter() : String
setChildFilter(filter : String) : void
getShowsPrivateSuffixes() : boolean
setShowsPrivateSuffixes(showPrivate : boolean) : void
getcontainers() : Hashtable
fireTreeStructureChanged(node : IDirNode) : void
```

FIGURE 10-7. IDirModel.

```
/**
 * Sets the server connection used to populate the tree
 *
 * @param ldc the server connection used to populate the tree
 */
public void setLDAPConnection( LDAPConnection ldc );

/**
 * Get the schema of the directory instance
 *
 * @return a reference to a schema object
 */
public LDAPSchema getSchema();

/**
 * Sets a reference to the schema of the directoryinstance
 *
 * @param schema a reference to a schema object
 */
public void setSchema( LDAPSchema schema );

/**
 * Get the parameter that determines if the
 * ManagedSAIT control is sent with each search. If the
 * control is sent, referral entries are returned as
 * normal entries and not followed.
 *
 * @return true if referrals are to be followed
 */
public boolean getReferralsEnabled();

/**
 * Set a parameter for future searches that determines if the
 * ManagedSAIT control is sent with each search. If referrals are
 * disabled, the control is sent and you will receive the referring
 * entry back.
 *
 * @param on true (the default) if referrals are to be followed
 */
public void setReferralsEnabled( boolean on );

/**
 * Reports if the model is currently configured to show leaf (as well as
 * container) nodes
```

```
 *
 * @return true if the model is currently configured to show leaf
 * (as well as container) nodes
 */
public boolean getAllowsLeafNodes();

/**
 * Determines if the model is to show leaf (as well as container) nodes
 *
 * @param allow true if the model is to show leaf (as well as container)
 * nodes
 */
public void setAllowsLeafNodes( boolean allow );

/**
 * Used between DirNode and DirModel, to manage the search filter used to
 * find children of a node
 *
 * @return the search filter to be used to find direct children
 */
public String getChildFilter();

/**
 * Set the search filter used to find children of a node
 *
 * @param filter the search filter to be used to find direct children
 */
public void setChildFilter( String filter );

/**
 * Report if the model will show private suffixes.
 * If true (the default), private suffixes will appear.
 *
 * @return true if private suffixes are to be displayed in the tree
 */
public boolean getShowsPrivateSuffixes();

/**
 * Determines if the model will supply node objects for tree nodes.
 * If false (the default), only container nodes will appear.
 *
 * @param allow true if leaf nodes are to be displayed in the tree
 */
public void setShowsPrivateSuffixes( boolean showPrivate );
```

```
    /**
     * Used between DirNode and DirModel, to manage the list of object classes
     * that are to be considered containers
     *
     * @return a hash table containing object classes to be considered
     containers
     */
    public Hashtable getContainers();

    /**
     * Informs the tree that a particular node's structure
     * has changed and its view needs to be updated
     *
     * @param node the node that has changed
     **/
    public void fireTreeStructureChanged( IDirNode node );
}
```

TreePanel

TreePanel (Figure 10-8) catches and handles mouse, key, and tree selection events on the JTree it manages:

```
public class TreePanel extends JPanel
                       implements TreeSelectionListener,
                                  MouseListener,
                                  KeyListener,
                                  Serializable {
```

TreePanel uses a special node renderer—TreePanelCellRenderer—to work around bugs in the JFC default implementation and to provide better selection indication. There is a default constructor as well, for deserialization:

```
    /**
     * Construct tree using the data model specified
     *
     * @param model a directory model
     */
    public TreePanel( IDirModel model ) {
        super();
        _treeRenderer = new TreePanelCellRenderer();
        _model = model;
        setLayout(new BorderLayout());
        setBorder(new EmptyBorder(0, 0, 0, 0));
```

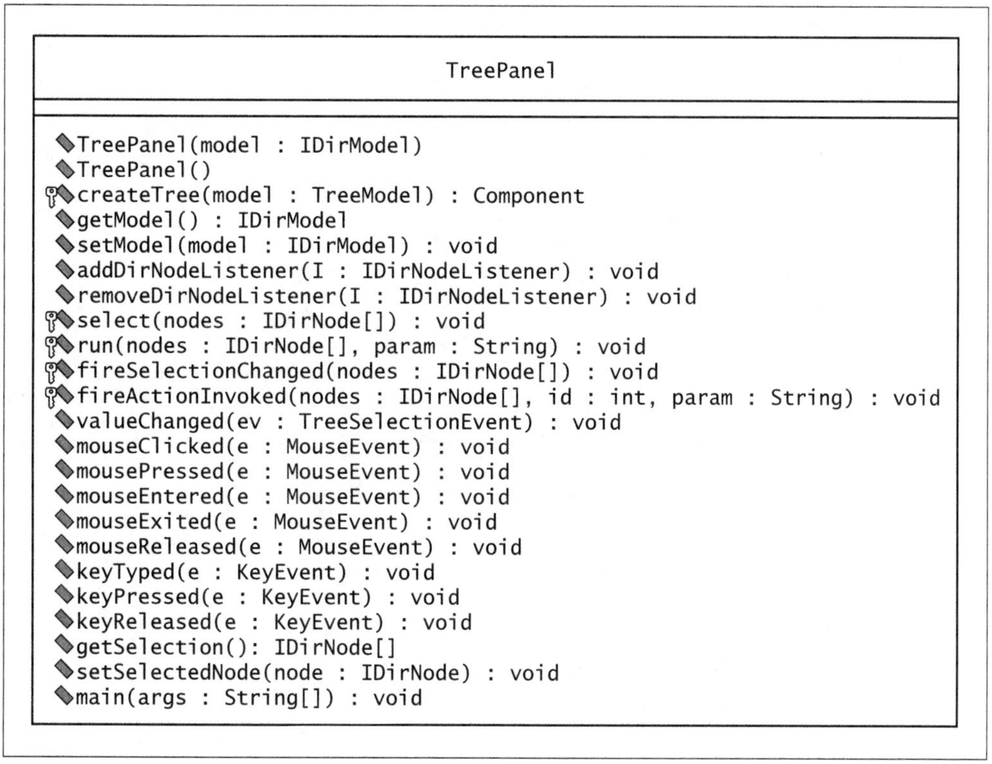

```
TreePanel
---
TreePanel(model : IDirModel)
TreePanel()
createTree(model : TreeModel) : Component
getModel() : IDirModel
setModel(model : IDirModel) : void
addDirNodeListener(I : IDirNodeListener) : void
removeDirNodeListener(I : IDirNodeListener) : void
select(nodes : IDirNode[]) : void
run(nodes : IDirNode[], param : String) : void
fireSelectionChanged(nodes : IDirNode[]) : void
fireActionInvoked(nodes : IDirNode[], id : int, param : String) : void
valueChanged(ev : TreeSelectionEvent) : void
mouseClicked(e : MouseEvent) : void
mousePressed(e : MouseEvent) : void
mouseEntered(e : MouseEvent) : void
mouseExited(e : MouseEvent) : void
mouseReleased(e : MouseEvent) : void
keyTyped(e : KeyEvent) : void
keyPressed(e : KeyEvent) : void
keyReleased(e : KeyEvent) : void
getSelection(): IDirNode[]
setSelectedNode(node : IDirNode) : void
main(args : String[]) : void
```

FIGURE 10-8. TreePanel.

```
        Component tree = createTree( model );
        add( tree );
    }

    /**
     * Default constructor for deserialization
     */
    public TreePanel() {
        this( null );
    }
```

The JTree is created and configured:

```
    /**
     *  Returns a Component that contains the tree
     *
```

```
     * @return a Component that contains the tree
     */
    protected Component createTree( TreeModel model ) {
        _tree = new JTree(model);
        // Lines between nodes, as in Windows
        _tree.putClientProperty( "JTree.lineStyle", "Angled" );
        // For now, single selection only
        _tree.getSelectionModel().setSelectionMode(
            TreeSelectionModel.SINGLE_TREE_SELECTION );
        _tree.addFocusListener(new FocusListener() {
            // This causes ALL tree nodes to repaint, which
            // is needed to change colors for selected tree nodes
            public void focusGained(FocusEvent e) {
                JTree tree = (JTree)e.getSource();
                tree.validate();
                tree.repaint();
            }
            public void focusLost(FocusEvent e) {
                JTree tree = (JTree)e.getSource();
                tree.validate();
                tree.repaint();
            }
        });
        // Special cell renderer
        _tree.setCellRenderer(_treeRenderer);
        // Catch all events
        _tree.addTreeSelectionListener(this);
        _tree.addMouseListener(this);
        _tree.addKeyListener(this);

        _treePanel = new JScrollPane();
        _treePanel.getViewport().add(_tree);
        _treePanel.setBorder( new BevelBorder(BevelBorder.LOWERED,
                UIManager.getColor("controlHighlight"),
                UIManager.getColor("control"),
                UIManager.getColor("controlDkShadow"),
                UIManager.getColor("controlShadow")));
        _treePanel.setPreferredSize(new Dimension(200, 200));
        _treePanel.setMinimumSize(new Dimension(1, 1));
        return _treePanel;
    }
```

In some cases a client will want to access the model directly:

```
/**
 *  Return tree model
 *
 *  @return the tree model
 */
public IDirModel getModel() {
    return _model;
}

/**
 * Set the model
 *
 * @param model the model
 */
public void setModel( IDirModel model ) {
    _model = model;
}
```

TreePanel dispatches events to objects implementing the IDirNodeListener interface that have registered an interest:

```
/**
 * Adds a listener that is interested in receiving
 DirNodeListener events
 *
 * @param l an object interested in receiving DirNodeListener
 * events
 */
public void addDirNodeListener( IDirNodeListener l ) {
    _listenerList.add( IDirNodeListener.class, l );
}

/**
 * Removes a listener that is interested in receiving
 * DirNodeListener events
 *
 * @param l an object interested in receiving DirNodeListener
 * events
 */
public void removeDirNodeListener( IDirNodeListener l ) {
    _listenerList.remove( IDirNodeListener.class, l );
}
```

```
/**
 * Dispatch selection events to listeners
 *
 * @param nodes currently selected nodes
 */
protected void select( IDirNode[] nodes ) {
    fireSelectionChanged( nodes );
}

/**
 * Dispatch "run" event to listeners
 *
 * @param nodes currently selected nodes
 * @param param optional additional event info
 */
protected void run( IDirNode[] nodes, String param ) {
    fireActionInvoked( nodes, DirNodeEvent.RUN, param );
}

/**
 * Dispatch selection events to listeners, using the
 * EventListenerList
 *
 * @param nodes currently selected nodes
 */
protected void fireSelectionChanged( IDirNode[] nodes ) {
    // Guaranteed to return a non-null array
    Object[] listeners = _listenerList.getListenerList();
    // Process the listeners last to first, notifying
    // those that are interested in this event
    for ( int i = listeners.length - 2; i >= 0; i -= 2 ) {
        if ( listeners[i] == IDirNodeListener.class ) {
            IDirNodeListener l = (IDirNodeListener)listeners[i + 1];
            l.selectionChanged( nodes );
        }
    }
}

/**
 * Dispatch events to listeners, using the
 * EventListenerList
 *
 * @param nodes currently selected nodes
```

```
     * @param id identifier of the type of event
     * @param param optional additional event info
     */
    protected void fireActionInvoked( IDirNode[] nodes,
                                      int id,
                                      String param ) {
        // Guaranteed to return a non-null array
        Object[] listeners = _listenerList.getListenerList();
        DirNodeEvent e = null;
        // Process the listeners last to first, notifying
        // those that are interested in this event
        for ( int i = listeners.length - 2; i >= 0; i -= 2 ) {
            if ( listeners[i] == IDirNodeListener.class ) {
                // Lazily create the event:
                if (e == null)
                    e = new DirNodeEvent( nodes, id, param );
                IDirNodeListener l = (IDirNodeListener)listeners[i + 1];
                l.actionInvoked( e );
            }
        }
    }
```

Then we have the implementations of the mouse, key, and tree selection interfaces. On tree selection events, clients of this object are notified of selection events. On mouse events with double-click or on key events in which the Enter key is pressed, clients are notified of a RUN event:

```
    /**
     * Implements TreeSelectionListener. Called when an object is selected
     * in the tree.
     *
     * @param ev event provided by JTree
     */
    public void valueChanged(TreeSelectionEvent ev) {
        Debug.println( 9, "Tree.valueChanged: " +
                       ev.getPath().getLastPathComponent() );
        IDirNode[] selection = getSelection();
        if ( selection != null ) {
            Debug.println( 9, "Tree.valueChanged: selection = " +
                           selection[0] );
            select( selection );
        }
    }
```

```
/**
 * Implements MouseListener. Called when a mouse button is pressed
 * and released in the tree.
 *
 * @param e mouse event
 */
public void mouseClicked(MouseEvent e) {
    IDirNode[] selection = getSelection();
    if (selection != null) {
        if (e.getClickCount() == 2) { // double click
            run( selection, "" );
        }
    }
}

/**
 * Implements MouseListener. Called when a mouse button is pressed
 * in the tree.
 *
 * @param e mouse event
 */
public void mousePressed(MouseEvent e) {
}

/**
 * Implements MouseListener
 *
 * @param e mouse event
 */
public void mouseEntered(MouseEvent e) {
}

/**
 * Implements MouseListener
 *
 * @param e mouse event
 */
public void mouseExited(MouseEvent e) {
}

/**
 * Implements MouseListener. Called when a mouse button is released
 * in the tree.
 *
```

```
     * @param e mouse event
     */
    public void mouseReleased(MouseEvent e) {
    }

    /**
     * Implements KeyListener
     *
     * @param e key event
     */
    public void keyTyped(KeyEvent e) {
    }

    /**
     * Implements KeyListener. Called when a key is pressed.
     *
     * @param e key event
     */
    public void keyPressed(KeyEvent e) {
        if (e.getKeyCode() == KeyEvent.VK_ENTER) {
            IDirNode[] selection = getSelection();
            if (selection != null) {
                run( selection, "" );
            }
        }
    }

    /**
     * Implements KeyListener. Called when a key is released.
     *
     * @param e key event
     */
    public void keyReleased(KeyEvent e) {
    }
```

Finally, there are two utility methods—`getSelection` and `setSelectedNode`—that other components can use to force selection of a particular node or to find out which nodes are selected at any time:

```
    /**
     * Returns array of selected nodes
     *
     * @param return array of selected nodes
```

```
     */
    public IDirNode[] getSelection() {
        IDirNode[] selection = null;
        TreePath path[] = _tree.getSelectionPaths();
        if ((path != null) && (path.length > 0)) {
            selection = new IDirNode[path.length];
            for (int index = 0; index < path.length; index++) {
                selection[index] =
                    (IDirNode)path[index].getLastPathComponent();
            }
        }
        return selection;
    }

    /**
     * Make a node selected and visible
     *
     * @param node node to make visible
     */
    public void setSelectedNode( IDirNode node ) {
        if ( node != null ) {
            TreePath path =
                new TreePath(
                    ((DefaultMutableTreeNode)node).getPath() );
            _tree.expandPath( path );
            _tree.makeVisible( path );
            _tree.scrollPathToVisible( path );
            _tree.repaint();
            _tree.setSelectionPath( path );
        }
    }
```

The member variables of `TreePanel` are declared as follows:

```
    protected IDirModel _model;
    protected JTree _tree = null;
    protected TreeCellRenderer _treeRenderer;
    protected JScrollPane _treePanel;
    // Use an EventListenerList to manage different types of
    // listeners
    protected EventListenerList _listenerList =
        new EventListenerList();
```

DirModel

DirModel (Figure 10-9) implements the IDirModel interface to provide data for the JTree inside TreePanel. It also implements IDirContentListener so that it can be notified if the directory has changed and the model must be reinitialized.

```
DirModel
---------------------------------------------
_followReferrals : boolean = true
_allowLeafNodes : boolean = false
_showPrivateSuffixes : boolean = true
---------------------------------------------
DirModel()
DirModel(ldc : LDAPConnection)
DirModel(root : Object , ldc : LDAPConnection)
initializeChildFilter() : String
getAllowsLeafNodes() : boolean
setAllowsLeafNodes(allow : boolean) : void
getChildFilter() : String
setChildFilter(filter : String) : void
initialize(root : Object) : void
getChild(node : Object, index : ins) : Object
getChildCount(node : Object) : int
getindexOfChild(parent : Object, child : Object) : int
addTreeModelListener(l : TreeModelListener) : void
removeTreeModelListener(l : TreeModelListener) : void
fireTreeNodeChanged(node : DirNode) : void
fireTreeStructureChanged(node : IDirNode) : void
valueForPathChanged(path : TreePath, newValue : Object) : void
isLeaf(node : Object) : boolean
contentChanged() : void
repaintObject(node : IDirNode) : void
newTree() : void
refreshNode(node : IDirNode) : void
refreshTree() : void
getLDAPConnection() : LDAPConnection
setLDAPConnection(ldc : LDAPConnection) : void
getRoot() : Object
setRoot(root : Object) : void
getReferralsEnabled() : boolean
setReferralsEnabled(on : boolean) : void
getSchema() : LDAPSchema
setSchema(schema : LDAPSchema) : void
getShowsPrivateSuffixes() : boolean
setShowsPrivateSuffixes(showPrivate : boolean) : void
initContainerNames() : Hashtable
addContainerName(name : String) : void
getContainers() : Hashtable
```

FIGURE 10-9. DirModel.

```
public class DirModel implements IDirModel,
                                 IDirContentListener,
                                 Serializable {

    /**
     * Default constructor for deserialization
     */
    public DirModel() {
        setChildFilter( initializeChildFilter() );
    }

    /**
     * Constructor of the model that doesn't populate the tree. You must
     * call initialize() to populate it.
     *
     * @param ldc connection to LDAP server
     */
    public DirModel( LDAPConnection ldc ) {
        this();
        setLDAPConnection( ldc );
    }

    /**
     * Constructor of the model with the root object passed in.
     * Suffix nodes are retrieved and added to the tree.
     *
     * @param root root object
     * @param ldc connection to LDAP server
     */
    public DirModel( Object root, LDAPConnection ldc ) {
        this( ldc );
        initialize( root );
    }
```

The child filter is the search filter used to find children of a node. It is initialized to search for all entries that contain any object classes considered to be containers, as well as any entries that have children of their own. There are methods to switch between this mode and the mode in which all children are searched:

```
    /**
     * Set default filter, which causes only container nodes to be
     * displayed in the tree
     */
```

```
private String initializeChildFilter() {
    Hashtable containers = getContainers();
    /* "numSubordinates>=1" is not indexed, but
       "(&(numSubordinates=*)(numSubordinates>=1))" is, in DS 4.0
    */
    String filter = "(|(&(numSubordinates=*)(numSubordinates>=1))";
    Enumeration e = containers.keys();
    while( e.hasMoreElements() )
        filter += "(objectclass=" + (String)e.nextElement() + ")";
    filter += ")";
    Debug.println( "DirModel.initializeChildFilter: " +
                   filter );
    return filter;
}

/**
 * Report if the model will supply node objects for tree nodes.
 * If false (the default), only container nodes will appear.
 *
 * @return true if leaf nodes are to be displayed in the tree
 */
public boolean getAllowsLeafNodes() {
    return _allowLeafNodes;
}

/**
 * Determines if the model will supply node objects for tree nodes.
 * If false (the default), only container nodes will appear.
 *
 * @param allow true if leaf nodes are to be displayed in the tree
 */
public void setAllowsLeafNodes( boolean allow ) {
    if ( allow ) {
        setChildFilter( "objectclass=*" );
    } else {
        setChildFilter( initializeChildFilter() );
    }
    _allowLeafNodes = allow;
    contentChanged();
}

/**
 * Used between DirNode and DirModel, to manage the search
 * filter used to find children of a node
```

```
     *
     * @return the search filter to be used to find direct children
     */
    public String getChildFilter() {
        return _childFilter;
    }

    /**
     * Set the search filter used to find children of a node
     *
     * @param filter the search filter to be used to find
     * direct children
     */
    public void setChildFilter( String filter ) {
        _childFilter = filter;
    }
```

The `initialize` method creates the root node, which fetches all public and optionally all private suffixes and adds them as children. It is necessary to explicitly enumerate the suffixes because the root entry in LDAP has no children. Extra work is required to figure out what the public and private suffixes of the directory are, in order to retrieve them and present them as children.

```
    /**
     * Create root node and a node for each suffix
     *
     * @param root root node for the tree. If null, a new root node
     * will be created and the root entry will be searched for suffixes.
     */
    public void initialize( Object root ) {
        if ( root == null ) {
            root = new RootDirNode( this, getShowsPrivateSuffixes() );
            Debug.println(9, "DirModel.initialize: new root");
        } else {
            ((DirNode)root).setModel( this );
            Debug.println(9, "DirModel.initialize: old root=" +
                          root);
        }
        setRoot( root );
    }
```

Many methods are called by—or call back to—the `JTree` object. Most of these methods delegate the responsibility to the `IDirNode` involved:

```
/**
 *  Get a child node of a node
 *
 * @param node parent node
 * @param index position of the child
 * @return the child of the specified node
 */
public Object getChild(Object node, int index) {
    IDirNode sn = (IDirNode) node;
    return sn.getChildAt(index);
}

/**
 *  Return the number of children
 *
 * @param node node to be checked
 * @return number of children of the specified node
 */
public int getChildCount(Object node) {
    IDirNode sn = (IDirNode) node;
    return sn.getChildCount();
}

/**
  * Returns the index of a particular child node
  * @param parent parent node
  * @param child child node
  * @return position of the child
  */
public int getIndexOfChild(Object parent, Object child) {
    return ((IDirNode) parent).getIndex(
            (IDirNode) child);
}

/**
 *  Check whether the node is a leaf node or not
 *
 * @param node node to be checked
 * @return true if the node is leaf, false otherwise
 */
public boolean isLeaf( Object node ) {
    IDirNode sn = (IDirNode) node;
    return ( sn.isLeaf() );
}
```

The model provides the expected methods for managing listeners:

```
/**
 * Adds a listener that is interested in receiving TreeModelListener
 * events. Called by JTree.
 *
 * @param l an object interested in receiving TreeModelListener
 * events
 */
public void addTreeModelListener(TreeModelListener l) {
    _listenerList.add(TreeModelListener.class, l);
}

/**
 * Removes a listener that is interested in receiving
 * TreeModelListener events. Called by JTree.
 *
 * @param l an object interested in receiving TreeModelListener
 * events
 */
public void removeTreeModelListener(TreeModelListener l) {
    _listenerList.remove(TreeModelListener.class, l);
}

/**
  * Informs the tree that a particular node has changed
  *
  * @param node the node that changed
  * @see EventListenerList
  */
public void fireTreeNodeChanged( DirNode node ) {
    // Guaranteed to return a non-null array
    Object[] listeners = _listenerList.getListenerList();
    TreeModelEvent e = null;
    // Process the listeners last to first, notifying
    // those that are interested in this event
    for ( int i = listeners.length - 2; i >= 0; i -= 2 ) {
        if ( listeners[i] == TreeModelListener.class ) {
            // Lazily create the event:
            if (e == null)
                e = new TreeModelEvent( this, node.getPath() );
            ((TreeModelListener)listeners[i + 1]).treeNodesChanged(e);
        }
    }
}
```

```
/**
 * Informs tree that a particular node's structure has changed
 * and its view needs to be updated.
 * @param node the node at the root of the changes
 * @see EventListenerList
 */
public void fireTreeStructureChanged( IDirNode node ) {
    // Guaranteed to return a non-null array
    Object[] listeners = _listenerList.getListenerList();
    TreeModelEvent e = null;
    // Process the listeners last to first, notifying
    // those that are interested in this event
    for ( int i = listeners.length - 2; i >= 0; i -= 2 ) {
        if ( listeners[i] == TreeModelListener.class ) {
            // Lazily create the event:
            if (e == null)
                e = new TreeModelEvent(this, ((DirNode)node).getPath());
            TreeModelListener l = (TreeModelListener)listeners[i + 1];
            l.treeStructureChanged( e );
        }
    }
}

/**
 * Called when user has altered the value for the item identified
 * by path to newValue. Called by JTree.
 *
 * @param path path to the changed node
 * @param newValue new value of the node
 */
public void valueForPathChanged(TreePath path,
                                Object newValue) {
}
```

The method `contentChanged` is called when another component with which `DirModel` has registered an interest in changes in directory contents wishes to notify `DirModel`. A few helper methods cause regeneration of part or all of the tree:

```
/**
 * Called when the tree structure has changed radically; read a new
 * tree from the server
 */
public void contentChanged() {
    newTree();
}
```

```
void repaintObject( IDirNode node ) {
    Debug.println( "DirModel.repaintObject: " +
                   node );
    fireTreeStructureChanged( (DirNode)node );
}

private void newTree() {
    DirNode root = new RootDirNode( this, "",
                                    getShowsPrivateSuffixes() );
    Debug.println(9, "DirModel.newTree: new root");
    setRoot( root );
    refreshTree();
}

private void refreshNode( IDirNode node ) {
    node.load();
    repaintObject( node );
}

private void refreshTree() {
    refreshNode( (IDirNode)getRoot() );
}
```

All nodes share the LDAP connection of the model, which they access through `getLDAPConnection`, as the following block of code shows. It is also possible to set the connection after object instantiation—for example, on deserialization.

```
/**
 * Returns the server connection used to populate the tree
 *
 * @return the server connection used to populate the tree
 */
public LDAPConnection getLDAPConnection() {
    return _ldc;
}

/**
 * Sets the server connection used to populate the tree
 *
 * @param ldc the server connection used to populate the tree
 */
public void setLDAPConnection( LDAPConnection ldc ) {
    _ldc = ldc;
}
```

There are several accessors for properties of the model:

```
/**
 * Returns root node of the tree.
 *
 * return Root node of the tree
 */
public Object getRoot() {
    return _root;
}

/**
 * Sets root node of the tree
 *
 * @param root root node for the tree
 */
public void setRoot(Object root) {
    _root = (IDirNode) root;
}

/**
 * Get the parameter that determines if the
 * ManageDsaIT control is sent with each search
 *
 * @returns true if referrals are to be followed
 */
public boolean getReferralsEnabled() {
    return _followReferrals;
}

/**
 * Set a parameter for future searches that determines if the
 * ManageDsaIT control is sent with each search. If referrals are
 * disabled, the control is sent and you will receive the referring
 * entry back.
 *
 * @param on true (the default) if referrals are to be followed
 */
public void setReferralsEnabled( boolean on ) {
    _followReferrals = on;
}

/**
 * Get the schema of the directory instance
```

```
     *
     * @return a reference to a schema object
     */
    public LDAPSchema getSchema() {
        if ( _schema == null ) {
            _schema = new LDAPSchema();
            try {
                _schema.fetchSchema( getLDAPConnection() );
            } catch ( LDAPException e ) {
                Debug.println( "DirModel.getSchema: " + e );
                _schema = null;
            }
        }
        return _schema;
    }

    /**
     * Sets a reference to the schema of the directory instance
     *
     * @param schema a reference to a schema object
     */
    public void setSchema( LDAPSchema schema ) {
        _schema = schema;
    }

    /**
     * Report if the model will show private suffixes.
     * If true (the default), private suffixes will appear.
     *
     * @return true if private suffixes are to be displayed in the tree
     */
    public boolean getShowsPrivateSuffixes() {
        return _showPrivateSuffixes;
    }

    /**
     * Determines if the model will supply node objects for tree nodes.
     * If false (the default), only container nodes will appear.
     *
     * @param allow true if leaf nodes are to be displayed in the tree
     */
    public void setShowsPrivateSuffixes( boolean showPrivate ) {
        _showPrivateSuffixes = showPrivate;
        contentChanged();
    }
```

Some methods manage the definitions of the object classes that are to be considered containers:

```
/**
 * Get object classes that are to be considered containers
 * from a properties file
 *
 */
private static Hashtable initContainerNames() {
    Hashtable h = new Hashtable();
    String items = _resource.getString( _section, "containers" );
    Debug.println( "DirModel.initContainerNames" );
    if ( items != null ) {
        StringTokenizer st = new StringTokenizer( items, " " );
        int i = 0;
        while ( st.hasMoreTokens() ) {
            String name = st.nextToken().toLowerCase();
            Debug.println( "  added container type " + name );
            h.put( name, name );
        }
    }
    return h;
}

/**
 * Add the name of an object class to be considered a container
 *
 * @param name name of an object class to be considered a container
 */
public void addContainerName( String name ) {
    _cContainers.put( name, name );
}

/**
 * Used between DirNode and DirModel, to manage the list of
 * object classes that are to be considered containers
 *
 * @return a hash table containing object classes to be
 * considered containers
 */
public Hashtable getContainers() {
    if ( _cContainers == null )
        _cContainers = initContainerNames();
        return _cContainers;
    }
```

Finally, member variables are declared:

```
// Properties for this component (strings)
static ResourceSet _resource =
    new ResourceSet( "dirtree" );
// Section of the properties file to use
private static final String _section = "EntryObject";

// Active connection to directory
private LDAPConnection _ldc;
// Schema definitions
private LDAPSchema _schema = null;
// Control to use if referrals are not to be followed
private static LDAPControl _manageDSAITControl =
        new LDAPControl( LDAPControl.MANAGEDSAIT, true, null );
// Root node of the tree
private IDirNode _root = null;
private boolean _followReferrals = true;
private boolean _allowLeafNodes = false;
// List of possible container object classes
private Hashtable _cContainers = null;
// Filter string to search for immediate children
private String _childFilter;
// Helper object to manager event listeners
protected EventListenerList _listenerList =
    new EventListenerList();
// Set this to false to NOT show private suffixes
private boolean _showPrivateSuffixes = true;
```

IDirNode

DirModel delegates much of its work to DirNode (Figure 10-10), which implements the IDirNode interface (in addition to extending DefaultMutableTreeNode).

```
public interface IDirNode extends javax.swing.tree.TreeNode,
                                  javax.swing.tree.MutableTreeNode {

    /**
     * Specifies the name for this object, displayed in tree, right of icon
     *
     * @return a string representing the object's name
     */
    public String getName();
```

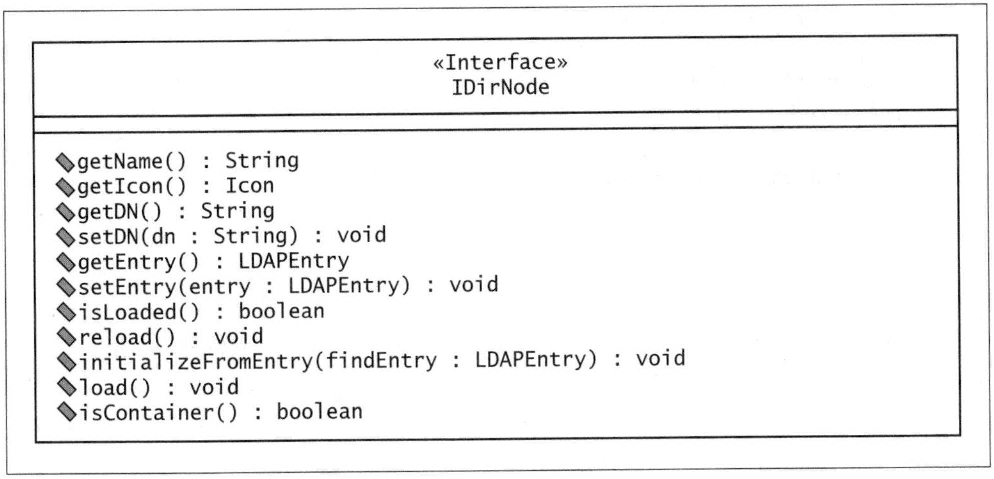

```
«Interface»
IDirNode
-----------------------------------------------
getName() : String
getIcon() : Icon
getDN() : String
setDN(dn : String) : void
getEntry() : LDAPEntry
setEntry(entry : LDAPEntry) : void
isLoaded() : boolean
reload() : void
initializeFromEntry(findEntry : LDAPEntry) : void
load() : void
isContainer() : boolean
```

FIGURE 10-10. IDirNode.

```
/**
 * Specifies an icon for this object, displayed in tree, left of name.
 * The recommended size for this icon is 16_16 pixels.
 *
 * @return an icon representing the object's icon
 */
public Icon getIcon();

/**
 * Get the DN of the entry corresponding to this node
 *
 * @return the DN of the node
 */
public String getDN();

/**
 * Set the DN of the node
 *
 * @param dn the new DN of the node
 */
public void setDN( String dn );

/**
 * Report the entry associated with this node. If the entry has not been
```

```
     * retrieved from the directory yet, it is done now.
     *
     * @return the entry associated with this node. Only a few attributes are
     * retrieved in the entry.
     */
    public LDAPEntry getEntry();

    /**
     * Set the entry for this node
     *
     * @param entry the new entry. May be null to force reinitialization.
     */
    public void setEntry( LDAPEntry entry );

    /**
     * Returns true if the node has read its entry from the directory
     *
     * @return true if the node has read its entry from the directory
     */
    public boolean isLoaded();

    /**
     *  Create all the one-level child nodes
     */
    public void reload();

    /**
     * Initialize the node from data in an entry
     *
     * @param entry an entry initialized with data
     */
    public void initializeFromEntry( LDAPEntry findEntry );

    /**
     *  Check if there are children to this node
     */
    public void load();

    /**
     * Report if this node is considered a container. This is true if it is
     * one of a defined list of object classes, or if it has children.
     *
     * @return true if the node is considered a container
```

```
     */
    public boolean isContainer();
}
```

DirNode

DirNode (Figure 10-11) is a fairly large class. We won't go into its complete definition here, but we'll discuss the main things that distinguish it from a standard JFC DefaultMutableTreeNode.

RootDirNode (Figure 10-12) is derived from DirNode. The main difference is that the root node in a directory—called the root DSE (the special entry with the empty DN)—returns nothing if you do a one-level search on it. To get the public and private suffixes of the directory, you have to look elsewhere. RootDirNode overrides the method to get children of itself, and it is set up to retrieve the suffixes on instantiation.

DirNode maintains its own image and display label. Appropriate images for various object classes are defined in a properties file, and additional images can be added there. The properties file entries are as follows:

```
EntryObject-person-icon=alluser16n.gif
EntryObject-organization-icon=folder.gif
EntryObject-organizationalunit-icon=ou16.gif
EntryObject-groupofuniquenames-icon=allgroup16n.gif
EntryObject-default-icon=genobject.gif
EntryObject-default-folder-icon=folder.gif
```

When a node is initialized from a directory entry, an appropriate image and label are selected:

```
    /**
     * Initialize the node from data in an entry
     *
     * @param entry an entry initialized with data
     */
    public void initializeFromEntry( LDAPEntry entry ) {
        _fLoaded = ( entry.getAttribute( SUBORDINATE_ATTR ) != null );
        _objectClasses = checkObjectClasses( entry );
        _fContainer = checkIfContainer();
        setIcon( checkIcon( _objectClasses, !isContainer() ) );
        _sCn = checkCn( entry );
        if ( _sCn != null ) {
            setName( _sCn );
        }
    }
```

```
DirNode
---------------------------------------------------------------
_fLoaded : boolean = false
_iChildren : int = -1
_fContainer : boolean = false
_objectCode : long = 0
_isBogus : boolean = false
---------------------------------------------------------------
DirNode()
DirNode(isBogus : boolean)
DirNode(model : IDirModel, dn : String, displayName : String)
DirNode(model : IDirModel, dn : String)
DirNode(dn : String)
DirNode(model : IDirModel, entry : LDAPEntry()
initialize(model : IDirModel, dn : String, displayName : String) : void
getModel() : IDirModel
setModel(model : IDirModel) : void
getName() : String
setName(name : String) : void
geticon() : Icon
seticon(icon : Icon) : void
getAllowLeafNodes() : boolean
getEntry() : LDAPEntry
setEntry(entry : LDAPEntry() : void
initDefaultIconName() : String
initDefaultFolderIconName() : String
getDN() : String
setDN(dn : String) : void
getLDAPConnection() : LDAPConnection
load() : void
readEntry(dn : String, attrs: String[]) : LDAPEntry
isContainer() : boolean
reload() : void
getChildList() : Vector
countChildren(all : boolean) : int
isLoaded() : boolean
getCountFromEntry(entry : LDAPEntry() : int
getCountFromEntry() : int
initializeFromEntry(entry : LDAPEntry() : void
hasChildren() : boolean
hasCheckedForChildren() : boolean
checkObjectClasses(entry : LDAPEntry() : Hashtable
checkIfContainer() : boolean
checkIcon(objectClasses : Hashtable, isLeafNode : boolean) : ImageIcon
getFirstValue(entry : LDAPEntry, attrName : String) : String
checkCn(entry : LDAPEntry() : String
getChildAt(index : ins) : TreeNode
getChildCount() : int
removeAllChildren() : void
isLeaf() : boolean
toString() : String
childExists(node : IDirNode) : boolean
getBogusEntryObject() : DirNode
isRootDSE(dn : String) : boolean
getChildFilter() : String
```

FIGURE 10-11. DirNode.

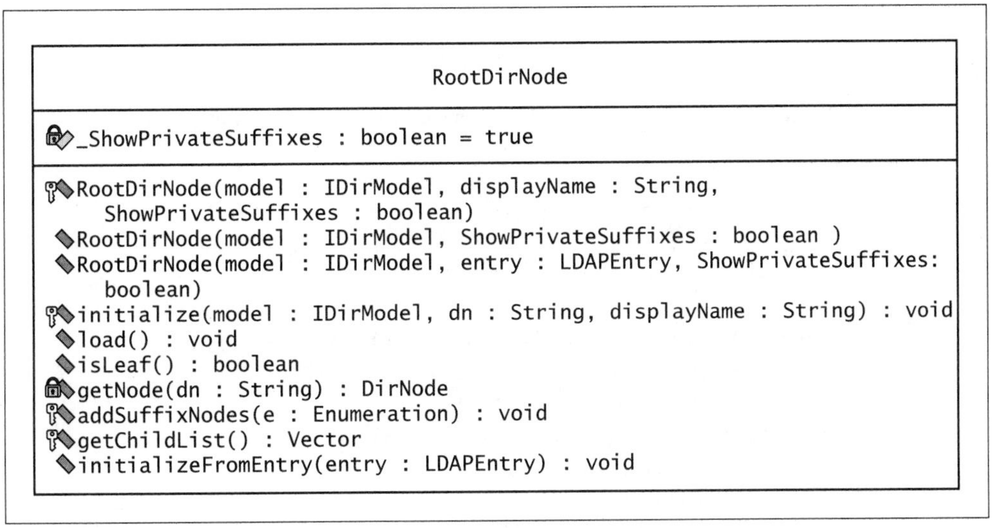

```
RootDirNode
_ShowPrivateSuffixes : boolean = true
RootDirNode(model : IDirModel, displayName : String,
    ShowPrivateSuffixes : boolean)
RootDirNode(model : IDirModel, ShowPrivateSuffixes : boolean )
RootDirNode(model : IDirModel, entry : LDAPEntry, ShowPrivateSuffixes:
    boolean)
initialize(model : IDirModel, dn : String, displayName : String) : void
load() : void
isLeaf() : boolean
getNode(dn : String) : DirNode
addSuffixNodes(e : Enumeration) : void
getChildList() : Vector
initializeFromEntry(entry : LDAPEntry) : void
```

FIGURE 10-12. RootDirNode.

```
/**
 * Create hash table of object classes from the entry
 *
 * @param entry entry containing at least object classes
 * @return a hash table of the object classes
 */
protected Hashtable checkObjectClasses( LDAPEntry entry ) {
    if ( _objectClasses != null )
        return _objectClasses;
    Hashtable objectClasses = new Hashtable();
    LDAPAttribute attr = entry.getAttribute(
        "objectclass" );
    String[] names = { "top" };;
    /* attr should never be null, but there is a bug in
       "cn=monitor,cn=ldbm" */
    if ( attr != null ) {
        Enumeration e = attr.getStringValues();
        while ( e.hasMoreElements() ) {
            String name = (String)e.nextElement();
            objectClasses.put( name.toLowerCase(), name );
        }
    }
    return objectClasses;
}
```

```
/**
 * Report if this node is to be considered a container
 *
 * @return true if the node has children or is of container
 * type
 */
protected boolean checkIfContainer() {
    if ( getCountFromEntry() > 0 ) {
        return true;
    }
    Hashtable containers = getModel().getContainers();
    Enumeration e = _objectClasses.elements();
    while ( e.hasMoreElements() ) {
        String s = (String)e.nextElement();
        if ( containers.get( s ) != null ) {
            return true;
        }
    }
    return false;
}

/**
 * Find an appropriate image for a node, based on the
 * object classes specified and whether or not it is a
 * leaf node
 *
 * @param objectClasses hash table containing object classes
 * for which to look for an icon
 * @param isLeafNode true if this is for a leaf node
 * @return an appropriate image
 */
static ImageIcon checkIcon( Hashtable objectClasses,
                            boolean isLeafNode ) {
    String iconName = "";
    Enumeration e = objectClasses.keys();
    while ( e.hasMoreElements() ) {
        String s = ((String)e.nextElement()).toLowerCase();
        iconName = (String)_icons.get( s );
        if ( iconName == null ) {
            iconName = _resource.getString( _section,
                                            s+"-icon" );
            if ( iconName == null )
                iconName = "";
            _icons.put( s, iconName );
        }
```

```
            if ( !iconName.equals( "" ) )
                break;
        }
        if ( iconName.equals( "" ) ) {
            if ( isLeafNode )
                iconName = _defaultImageName;
            else
                iconName = _defaultFolderImageName;
        }
        return ImageUtil.getPackageImage( iconName );
    }
```

`DirModel` delegates most messages from `JTree` to `DirNode`. Of special interest is how `DirNode` handles the `isLeaf`, `getChildCount`, and `getChildAt` methods. We don't want to populate the whole tree when it is instantiated. That might take a long time and use a lot of memory. We want to read only as much as is necessary to render the parts of the tree that the user has traversed.

With Netscape Directory Server or MessagingDirect LDAP Server, you can determine if a particular node has children and how many children it has by reading the `numSubordinates` operational attribute. For the case in which all nodes are to be displayed in the tree, the `numSubordinates` operational attribute is checked. If only container nodes are to be displayed, it is necessary to do a one-level search of the directory to see if there are any child entries of the container type. However, this search has been optimized in the following block of code: if `numSubordinates` is 0, then the number of container children must also be 0, and the search is not performed.

Netscape Directory Server also provides the `hasSubordinates` operational attribute, which indicates whether or not a node has child entries, but not how many. Other LDAP servers may provide similar attributes with other names.

```
    /**
     * Create a vector of all the one-level subnodes. The nodes
     * are also added as subnodes to this node.
     *
     * @return a Vector of all direct child nodes
     */
    protected Vector getChildList() {
        String dn = getDN();
        Debug.println(9, "DirNode.getChildList: <" + dn +
                      ">, " + getChildFilter() );
        Vector v = null;
        removeAllChildren();

        try {
            LDAPConnection ldc = getLDAPConnection();
```

```
if ( ldc == null ) {
    Debug.println( "DirNode.getChildList: " +
                   "no LDAP connection" );
    return new Vector();
}
LDAPSearchConstraints cons =
    ldc.getSearchConstraints();
// Unlimited search results
cons.setMaxResults( 0 );
LDAPControl[] controls;
if ( !getModel().getReferralsEnabled() ) {
    // If not following referrals, send the
    // manageDSAIT control, which tells the server
    // to return referral entries as ordinary
    // entries
    controls = new LDAPControl[2];
    controls[0] = _manageDSAITControl;
} else {
    controls = new LDAPControl[1];
}
// Ask the server to sort the results, by
// specifying a sort control
String[] sortOrder =
    { "sn", "givenName", "cn", "ou", "o" };
LDAPSortKey[] keys =
    new LDAPSortKey[sortOrder.length];
for( int i = 0; i < sortOrder.length; i++ ) {
    keys[i] = new LDAPSortKey( sortOrder[i] );
}
controls[controls.length-1] =
    new LDAPSortControl( keys, false );
cons.setServerControls( controls );
// Search for immediate children
LDAPSearchResults result =
    ldc.search( dn, ldc.SCOPE_ONE,
                getChildFilter(),
                _baseAttrs, false, cons );
Debug.println(9, "DirNode.getChildList: <" + dn +
              "> searching" );

int found = 0;
while ( result.hasMoreElements() ) {
    try {
        // Add each entry found to the tree
        LDAPEntry entry = result.next();
```

```
                    Debug.println(7, "DirNode.getChildList: " +
                                  "adding <" +
                                  entry.getDN() + ">" );
                    DirNode node =
                        new DirNode( getModel(), entry );
                    insert( node, super.getChildCount() );
                    found++;
                } catch (LDAPException e) {
                    Debug.println( "DirNode.getChildList: " +
                                   "<" + dn + ">: " + e );
                }
                if ( (found % 100) == 0 ) {
                    Debug.println(5, "DirNode.getChildList: " +
                                  "added " + found );
                }
            }
            _iChildren = super.getChildCount();
            Debug.println(9, "DirNode.getChildList: <" +
                          dn + "> found " + found);
        } catch (LDAPException e) {
            Debug.println( "DirNode.getChildList: " +
                           "<" + dn + "> " + e );
        }
        return children;
    }

    /**
     *  Count the number of children of this node that are containers
     *
     * @return the number of children that are containers
     */
    protected int countContainerChildren() {
        String dn = getDN();
        int count = 0;
        try {
            LDAPConnection ldc = getLDAPConnection();
            if ( ldc == null ) {
                Debug.println(
                    "DirNode.countChildren: " +
                    "no LDAP connection" );
                return count;
            }
            LDAPSearchConstraints cons =
                ldc.getSearchConstraints();
            cons.setMaxResults( 0 );
```

```
            if ( !getModel().getReferralsEnabled() ) {
                cons.setServerControls( _manageDSAITControl );
            }
            String[] attrs = { "dn" }; // Pseudo-attribute
            String filter = (all) ? _allFilter :
                getChildFilter();
            Debug.println(9, "DirNode.countChildren: " +
                          "<" + dn + "> , " + filter );
            LDAPSearchResults result =
                ldc.search( dn, ldc.SCOPE_ONE,
                            filter,
                            attrs, false, cons );

            while ( result.hasMoreElements() ) {
                try {
                    LDAPEntry entry = result.next();
                    Debug.println(9,"DirNode.countChildren: " +
                                  "<" + entry.getDN() + ">" );
                    count++;
                } catch (LDAPException e) {
                    // This is for inline exceptions and
                    // referrals
                    Debug.println( "DirNode.countChildren: " +
                                   "<" + dn + ">  " + e );
                }
            }
        } catch (LDAPException e) {
            // This is for exceptions on the search request
            Debug.println( "DirNode.countChildren: " +
                           "<" + dn + ">: " + e );
        }
        return count;
    }

    /**
     * Return the value of the numSubordinates attribute in an
     * entry, or -1 if the attribute is not present
     *
     * @param entry the entry containing the attribute
     * @return the number of children, or -1
     */
    static int getCountFromEntry( LDAPEntry entry ) {
        String s = getFirstValue( entry, SUBORDINATE_ATTR );
        if ( s != null ) {
```

```
            int count = Integer.parseInt( s );
            if ( _verbose ) {
                Debug.println( "DirNode.getCountFromEntry: <" +
                               entry.getDN() + "> = " + count );
            }
            return count;
        }
        return -1;
    }

    /**
     * Return the value of the numSubordinates attribute in the
     * entry of this node, or -1 if the attribute is not present
     *
     * @return the number of children, or -1
     */
    protected int getCountFromEntry() {
        return getCountFromEntry( getEntry() );
    }

    /**
     * Report the number of children (containers only) of this
     * node
     *
     * @return the number of container nodes that are children
     * of this node
     */
    public int getChildCount() {
        /* If there are no children at all, ... */
        if ( !hasCheckedForChildren() ) {
            if ( !isLoaded() ) {
                load();
            }
            int count = getCountFromEntry();
            if ( count < 1 ) {
                _iChildren = 0;
            }
        }

        if ( _iChildren < 0 ) {
            if ( getModel().getAllowsLeafNodes() ) {
                _iChildren = getCountFromEntry();
            } else {
                _iChildren = countContainerChildren();
            }
```

```
    }
     return _iChildren;
}

/**
 * Check whether or not the node is a leaf node. Since this
 * is used by JTree to determine whether or not to put an
 * expander on the tree, return true if the node currently
 * has no children.
 *
 * @return true if the node is leaf, false otherwise
 */
public boolean isLeaf() {
    int count = getChildCount();
    Debug.println( 9, "DirNode.isLeaf: <" + getDN() +
                       ">  : " + count +
                   " children" );
    return ( count == 0 );
}

/**
 * Return a specific child of this node, by index. This
 * currently assumes that all nodes in the tree are
 * explicitly managed by JFC (and not by a virtual tree
 * where we supply the contents).
 *
 * @param index zero-based index of child to return
 * @return the node at the requested index, or null
 */
public TreeNode getChildAt( int index ) {
    TreeNode node = null;
    Debug.println( 9, "DirNode.getChildAt: <" +
                   getDN() + "> index " + index );

    /* Search for and collect all children, if not already done */
    int count = getChildCount();
    if ( count > super.getChildCount() ) {
        reload();
    }

    try {
        node = super.getChildAt( index );
    } catch ( Exception e ) {
        // Request for node outside of range
        Debug.println( "DirNode.getChildAt: " + count +
                       " children " +
```

```
                            "available, number " + index +
                            " requested: " + e );
        }
        Debug.println( 9, "DirNode.getChildAt: found <" +
                        ((DirNode)node).getDN() + ">" );
        return node;
    }
```

Put It All Together, What Do You Get?

Using the Bean is as simple as

```
LDAPConnection ldc = DirUtil.getLDAPConnection( "manta.mcom.com",
                                                389,
                                                "cn=directory manager",
                                                "password" );
TreePanel tree = new TreePanel( new DirModel( ldc ) );
```

Figure 10-13 shows `TreePanel` in the mode in which only container entries are displayed. `TreePanel` is displayed in the application `TestTree`, which allows selection of various options from the command line:

- Display leaf nodes or only container nodes
- Show private suffixes or only public suffixes

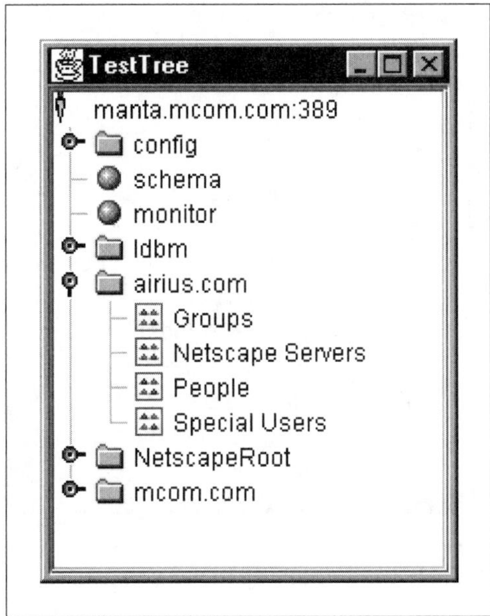

FIGURE 10-13. `TreePanel` *with only containers.*

- Follow referrals or not
- Show only the tree or the tree together with a table of child entries

If we want to display all nodes, including leaf nodes, then instantiation and initialization have to be done separately:

```
LDAPConnection ldc = DirUtil.getLDAPConnection( "manta.mcom.com",
                                                389,
                                                "cn=directory manager",
                                                "password" );
DirModel model = new DirModel( ldc );
model.setAllowsLeafNodes( true );
model.initialize( null );
TreePanel tree = new TreePanel( model );
```

In Figure 10-14, both container entries and leaf entries are displayed.

To compile the code examples, you will need to have the `bin` directory of your Java 2 installation in your `PATH`, and the LDAP JAR file `ldapjdk.jar`, as well as the

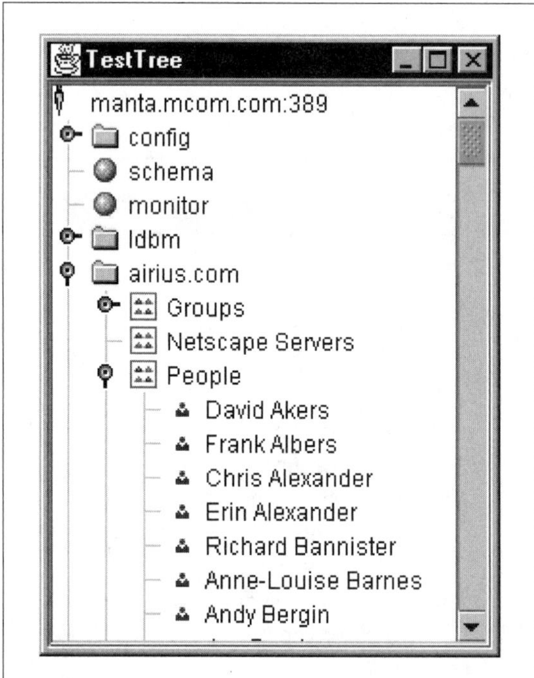

FIGURE 10-14. `TreePanel` *with all nodes.*

current working directory, in your CLASSPATH, as described in Chapter 3. You can compile the examples in the source code directory for Chapter 10 using the following command:

```
javac *.java
```

You can run TreePanel as an application using the command

```
java TreePanel localhost 389 "cn=directory manager" password
```

Substitute the host name of the machine where the directory is installed (if it is not on the same machine where you are running the application), the port number of the directory, a valid distinguished name, and a password for that DN. You can use any valid DN and password, including anonymous, but a nonprivileged user will not be able to see any of the private suffixes. The command looks like this for anonymous access:

```
java TreePanel localhost 389 "" ""
```

Figure 10-15 illustrates TreePanel with only public suffixes displayed (because it is executed as a nonprivileged user).

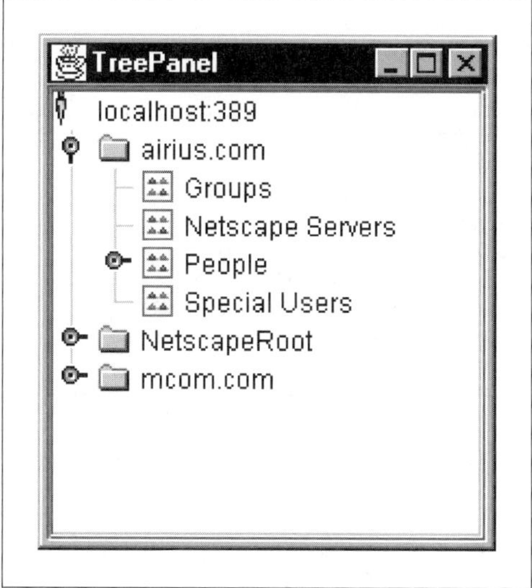

FIGURE 10-15. *Tree viewed by anonymous user.*

A Directory Lister

Displaying all the nodes of the directory in a tree has some disadvantages:

- It is hard to find a particular entry if a particular node contains many entries.
- You may end up with a large number of entries in memory when the user expands a node with many children.
- If you want to display attributes of entries, and not just the DNs or names, you can display only one at a time.

It is common to display only container nodes in a tree, and then show children of a selected node in a list or table. The list or table may display several attributes of each child. The next JavaBean (`SimpleTable`) is a table with sorting, and an adapter to hook up the `TreePanel` Bean with the table Bean.

`SimpleTable` (Figure 10-16) is a `JPanel` containing a simple extension of `JTable`. It adds support for sorting by clicking on the column headers, and for easily changing the headers and data dynamically. It is not LDAP-aware; that's the purpose of the adapter. It is also not suitable for very large numbers of entries. In Chapter 16 we will discuss the use of Virtual List View to handle the display of large databases.

```
SimpleTable

SimpleTable()
addRow(v : Vector) : void
removeAllRows() : void
SetColumnNames(names : String[]) : void
SetHeaderRenderer(renderer : TableCellRenderer) : void
SetColumnWidths(ColumnWidth : int[]) : void
fireTableDataChanged() : void
fireTableStructureChanged() : void
```

FIGURE 10-16. `SimpleTable`.

`SimpleTable` offers the following methods of interest, dispatching to the table:

```
/**
 * Add a row to the table model without triggering an event to notify
 * the table to update itself. After finishing adding all rows,
 * fireTableDataChanged should be called to notify the table.
 *
 * @param v a row to add
 */
public void addRow( Vector v ) {
    _tableModel.getDataVector().addElement( v );
}

/**
 * Remove all rows from the model and notify the table
 */
public void removeAllRows() {
    Vector v = _tableModel.getDataVector();
    v.removeAllElements();
    _tableModel.fireTableDataChanged();
}

/**
 * Set the column header labels and attach the sorting header
 * renderer
 *
 * @param names array of one label for each column
 */
public void setColumnNames( String[] names ) {
    _tableModel.setColumnIdentifiers( names );
    setHeaderRenderer( _renderer );
}

/**
 * Attach the sorting header renderer to each column
 */
public void setHeaderRenderer( TableCellRenderer renderer ) {
    TableColumnModel model = _table.getColumnModel();
    for ( int i = model.getColumnCount() - 1; i >= 0; i- ) {
        model.getColumn(i).setHeaderRenderer( renderer );
    }
}

/**
 * Set the column widths of the table
```

```
     *
     * @param columnWidth array of one width for each column
     */
    public void setColumnWidths( int[] columnWidth ) {
        TableColumnModel model = _table.getColumnModel();
        for (int i = 0; i < columnWidth.length; i++) {
            model.getColumn(i).setPreferredWidth(columnWidth[i]);
        }
        _table.sizeColumnsToFit( -1 );
    }

    /**
     * Notify the table that all the data has changed
     */
    public void fireTableStructureChanged() {
        _tableModel.fireTableStructureChanged();
        _tableModel.getIndexes();
    }
```

EntryListAdapter (Figure 10-17) acts on selection events from TreePanel and searches the directory to provide data for SimpleTable:

```
/**
 * The selection changed
 *
 * @param nodes array of selected tree nodes
 */
public void selectionChanged( IDirNode[] nodes ) {
    String dn = nodes[0].getDN();
    Debug.println( "EntryListAdapter.selectionChanged: " + dn );
    _table.removeAllRows();
    try {
        LDAPSearchConstraints cons =
            (LDAPSearchConstraints)_ldc.getSearchConstraints().clone();
        cons.setMaxResults( 0 );
        LDAPControl[] controls = new LDAPControl[1];
        String[] sortOrder = { "sn", "givenName", "cn", "ou", "o" };
        LDAPSortKey[] keys = new LDAPSortKey[sortOrder.length];
        for( int i = 0; i < sortOrder.length; i++ ) {
            keys[i] = new LDAPSortKey( sortOrder[i] );
        }
        controls[controls.length-1] =
            new LDAPSortControl( keys, true );
        cons.setServerControls( controls );
        LDAPSearchResults result =
            _ldc.search( dn, _ldc.SCOPE_ONE, "objectclass=*",
```

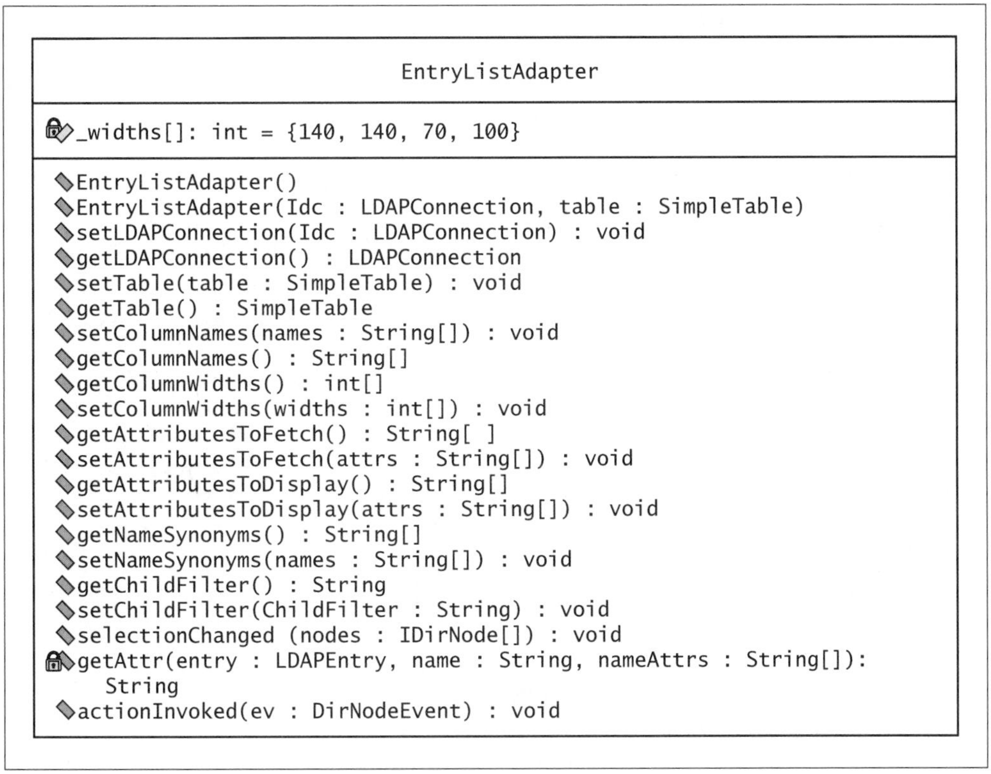

```
EntryListAdapter
---------------------------------------------------------------
_widths[]: int = {140, 140, 70, 100}
---------------------------------------------------------------
EntryListAdapter()
EntryListAdapter(ldc : LDAPConnection, table : SimpleTable)
setLDAPConnection(ldc : LDAPConnection) : void
getLDAPConnection() : LDAPConnection
setTable(table : SimpleTable) : void
getTable() : SimpleTable
setColumnNames(names : String[]) : void
getColumnNames() : String[]
getColumnWidths() : int[]
setColumnWidths(widths : int[]) : void
getAttributesToFetch() : String[ ]
setAttributesToFetch(attrs : String[]) : void
getAttributesToDisplay() : String[]
setAttributesToDisplay(attrs : String[]) : void
getNameSynonyms() : String[]
setNameSynonyms(names : String[]) : void
getChildFilter() : String
setChildFilter(ChildFilter : String) : void
selectionChanged (nodes : IDirNode[]) : void
getAttr(entry : LDAPEntry, name : String, nameAttrs : String[]):
   String
actionInvoked(ev : DirNodeEvent) : void
```

FIGURE 10-17. EntryListAdapter.

```
                      getAttributesToFetch(), false, cons );
    LDAPEntry entry;
    Vector all = new Vector();
    String[] displayAttrs = getAttributesToDisplay();
    String[] nameAttrs = getNameSynonyms();
    while ( result.hasMoreElements() ) {
        Vector v = new Vector();
        entry = result.next();
        v.removeAllElements();
        for( int i = 0; i < displayAttrs.length; i++ ) {
            v.addElement( getAttr( entry, displayAttrs[i],
                                   nameAttrs ) );
        }
        _table.addRow( v );
    }
    _table.fireTableStructureChanged();
    _table.setColumnNames( getColumnNames() );
    _table.setColumnWidths( getColumnWidths() );
```

```
        } catch (LDAPException e) {
            System.err.println( "EntryLister.selectionChanged" +
                                " cannot get entry <" + dn + ">" );
        }
    }

    private String getAttr( LDAPEntry entry, String name,
                            String[] nameAttrs ) {
        String value = "         ";
        LDAPAttribute attr = null;
        // For the special cn case, check several possible
        // attributes
        if ( name.equals( "cn" ) ) {
            for( int i = 0;
                 (attr == null) && (i < nameAttrs.length); i++ ) {
                attr = entry.getAttribute( nameAttrs[i] );
            }
        } else {
            attr = entry.getAttribute( name );
        }
        if ( attr != null ) {
            Enumeration en = attr.getStringValues();
            if ( (en != null) && (en.hasMoreElements()) ) {
                value = (String)en.nextElement();
            }
        }
        return value;
    }
```

EntryListAdapter has accessor methods to configure what attributes are displayed, how the columns should be labeled, and so on:

```
    /**
     * Headings to display on columns. The default is:
     * { "Name", "Email", "User ID", "Phone" }
     *
     * @return headings to display on columns
     */
    public String[] getColumnNames() {
        return _names;
    }
    public void setColumnNames( String[] names ) {
        _names = names;
    }
```

```
    /**
     * Widths of columns. The default is:
     * { 140, 140, 60, 100 }
     *
     * @return widths of columns
     */
    public int[] getColumnWidths() {
        return _widths;
    }
    public void setColumnWidths( int[] widths ) {
        _widths = widths;
    }

    /**
     * Attributes to search for. The default is:
     * { "cn", "mail", "uid", "telephoneNumber", "ou",
     *   "o", "displayName" }
     *
     * @return attributes to search for
     */
    public String[] getAttributesToFetch() {
        return _attrs;
    }
   public void setAttributesToFetch( String[] attrs ) {
        _attrs = attrs;
    }

    /**
     * Attributes to display. The default is: { "cn", "mail",
     * "uid", "telephoneNumber" }
     *
     * @return attributes to display
     */
    public String[] getAttributesToDisplay() {
        return _displayAttrs;
    }
     public void setAttributesToDisplay( String[] attrs ) {
        _displayAttrs = attrs;
    }

    /**
     * Attributes that may be used to display in the cn column,
     * in priority order. The default is:
     * { "displayName", "cn", "ou", "o" }.
```

```
     *
     * @return attributes that may be used to display in the cn
column
     */
    public String[] getNameSynonyms() {
        return _nameAttrs;
    }
    public void setNameSynonyms( String[] names ) {
        _nameAttrs = names;
    }
```

`TreePanel` *and* `SimpleTable` *Join Forces*

It doesn't take much code to hook up the two Beans:

```
LDAPConnection ldc = DirUtil.getLDAPConnection( "manta.mcom.com",
                                                389,
                                                "cn=directory manager",
                                                "secretdog" );
TreePanel tree = new TreePanel( new DirModel( ldc ) );
SimpleTable table =  new SimpleTable();
EntryListAdapter lister = new EntryListAdapter( ldc,
                                                tree,
                                                table );
// EntryListAdapter could add itself as a listener, but we'll
// do it here just to demonstrate
tree.addDirNodeListener( lister );
JSplitPane splitPane = new JSplitPane(JSplitPane.HORIZONTAL_SPLIT,
                                      sp, table);
splitPane.setBorder( new EmptyBorder(6, 6, 6, 6) );
frame.getContentPane().add( splitPane );
```

Figure 10-18 shows `TreePanel` and `SimpleTable` connected and functioning as a directory browser.

Figure 10-19 demonstrates that the data can be sorted by any column and in either ascending or descending order.

`SimpleTable` also offers events on selection, so it can be used to trigger other actions—for example, to launch a user editor for a selected user, or to delete the selected user.

You can run the `TestTree` application using the following command:

```
java TestTree localhost 389 "cn=directory manager" password
```

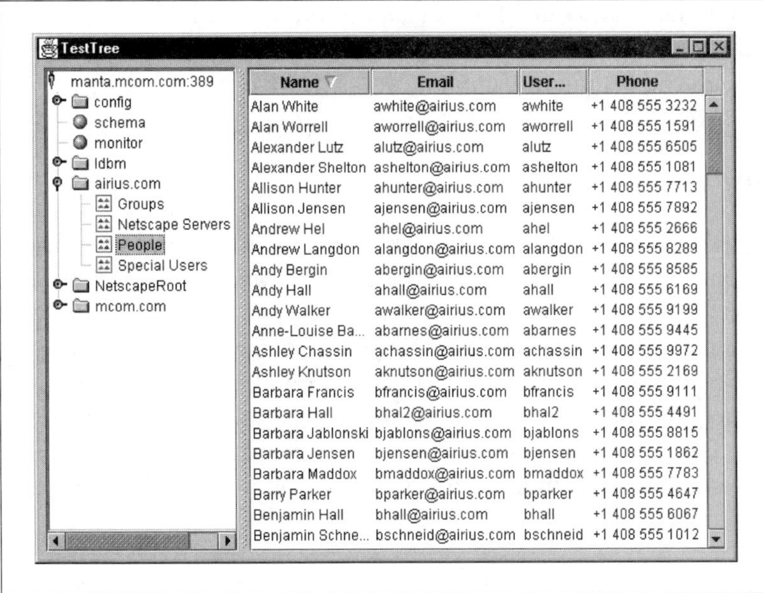

FIGURE 10-18. `TreePanel` *and* `SimpleTable`.

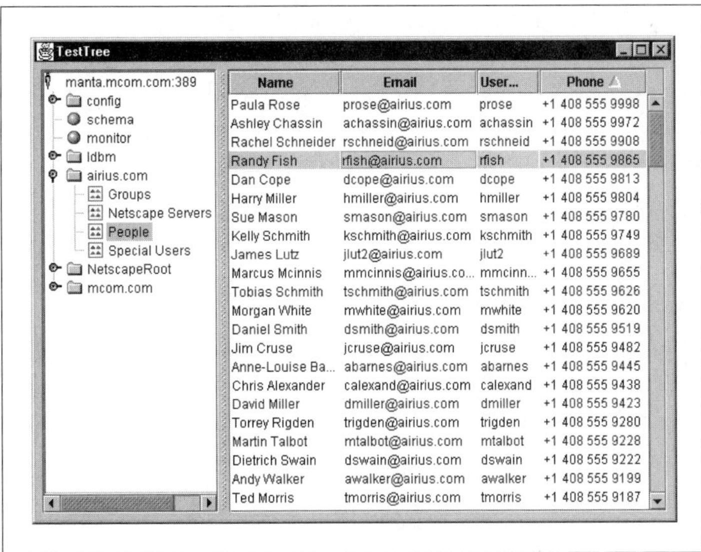

FIGURE 10-19. *Selecting a different sort column and direction.*

Substitute the host name of the machine where the directory is installed (if it is not on the same machine where you are running the application), the port number of the directory, a valid distinguished name, and a password for that DN.

Conclusion

In this chapter we have looked at several JavaBeans for LDAP programming. Some are invisible and simply encapsulate subsets of the functionality of the class library; others capture and render directory contents in graphical form and allow the user to interact with them. LDAP JavaBeans can be combined easily, using a small amount of Java or JavaScript glue code. The Beans can be configured and the glue code generated in an IDE (integrated development environment) that understands JavaBeans, without additional coding. A complete application or applet can be composed of one or more LDAP JavaBeans that communicate through a listener interface.

CHAPTER 11

Make Your Application Location-Independent

Most applications store user preferences or configuration information. For example, some applications store the size and positions of windows used, directories selected for importing and exporting files, and other default values. Because these preferences are saved, the user does not have to reenter them when using the application again.

Remembering the user's preferences becomes more complicated if the application is shared (for example, if the application is accessed from a network file system) and if the application may be run by many users. In such a scenario, the application may need to keep a database of preferences for each user or store the preferences in the home directory of each user (as is the case with many UNIX applications).

Maintaining individual user preferences becomes much more complicated if the application is Web based and a user may be accessing the application from many different machines. Perhaps she uses it from work most of the time, but she also frequently uses it from a home machine, and sometimes from a cybercafe when away from home. Now a database is definitely required. The application doesn't have access to the same set of preferences when running on the computer at home, the computer at work, and the computer at the cybercafe. Preferences cannot be stored on a user's computer or in the user's home directory; the computers are different, and there is no home directory on the Web.

One solution is to store the preferences in a directory that is accessible from all computers the user might be using. We mentioned one such directory in Chapter 3: the Netcenter membership directory at `ldap://memberdir.netscape.com:389/ou=member_directory.o=netcenter.com`. Netcenter members can have their bookmarks and address books stored there rather than locally by Netscape Communicator, and then have access to them from wherever they access their Netcenter home page.

In this chapter we'll show how an application can be made to store and retrieve user preferences using LDAP.

The Teex Multicharacter-Set Text Editor

You've got Notepad, vi, or emacs. But do these text editors handle the UTF8 character set? How about shift-jis and EUC? It's a brave new world of applications localized in many languages and character sets, and in the world of LDAP the common character set is UTF8.

If you are responsible for writing a directory-enabled application that can handle character sets other than good old latin-1, you may have to verify that it will work with double-byte data for languages such as Japanese, Chinese, or Korean. When you import LDIF files into an LDAP server, the LDIF files must use the UTF8 character set, not a local character set such as shift-jis (a common encoding for Japanese). This constraint means you can no longer use your favorite text editor or word processor to create or edit your LDIF files (well, you *can* use them, as long as you then run the output through a converter).

The simple text editor Teex will let you read, debug, and edit your files in many character sets, including UTF8, and it will let you save the results in a character set of your choice. In addition, Teex understands the peculiarities of the LDIF file format, and it does the appropriate line continuation and base64 encoding or decoding automatically if LDIF "encoding" is selected.

In the next section we'll introduce Teex, and then we'll see how its configuration and preferences can be stored in an LDAP directory.

The Teex JavaBean

"Teex" stands for Text Editor and Translator. It was born out of necessity at Netscape to help debug problems with the handling of double-byte character sets (for example, the Asian languages) on importing and exporting data to a directory. It doesn't do much, but it has helped Netscape developers quash numerous bugs, and you may also find it useful.

Because it extends `JPanel`, Teex is easy to embed in an application or an applet. However, Teex is itself a full application, with its own menu bar. It includes a `main` method so that it can be run from the command line as follows:

```
java Teex
```

When invoked with no parameters, Teex uses the default character set of the Java environment and starts with no file open for editing (see Figure 11-1).

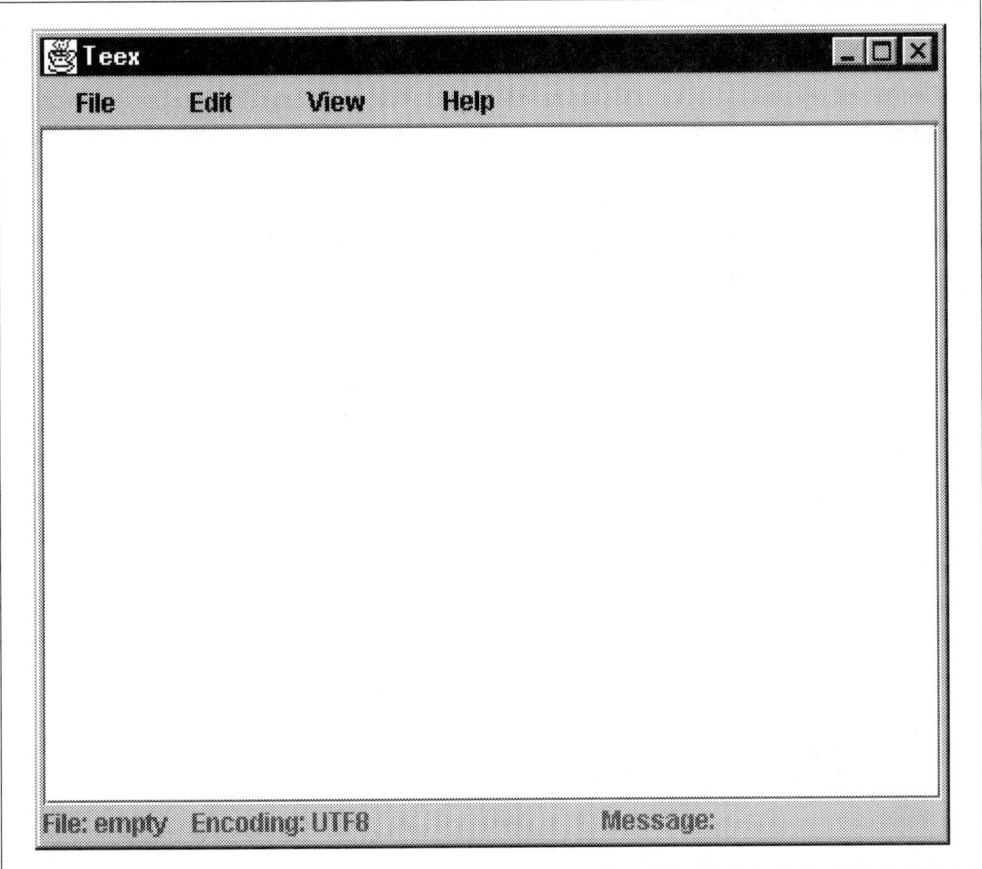

FIGURE 11-1. *Teex with no file loaded.*

Teex has a few settings that can be selected from the View menu:

- Foreground color
- Background color
- Font size
- Tab size
- Line wrap on or off

The settings are not saved when the program exits, but they will be by the time we finish this chapter.

A Class for User Preferences

First we'll define a general-purpose class for managing preference settings in memory: `Preferences` (Figure 11-2). It is an abstract class. We must extend the class to provide persistence. This book is concerned with LDAP, but another extension class could store the preferences persistently in a file system, a database, or somewhere else.

The `Preferences` class extends `Hashtable` rather than implementing its own internal storage and indexes. It also declares itself `Serializable` in case a `Preferences` object or a derived object is to be used as a JavaBean:

```
public abstract class Preferences extends Hashtable
                                   implements Serializable {
    /**
     * Blank constructor for deserialization
     */
    public Preferences() {
    }
```

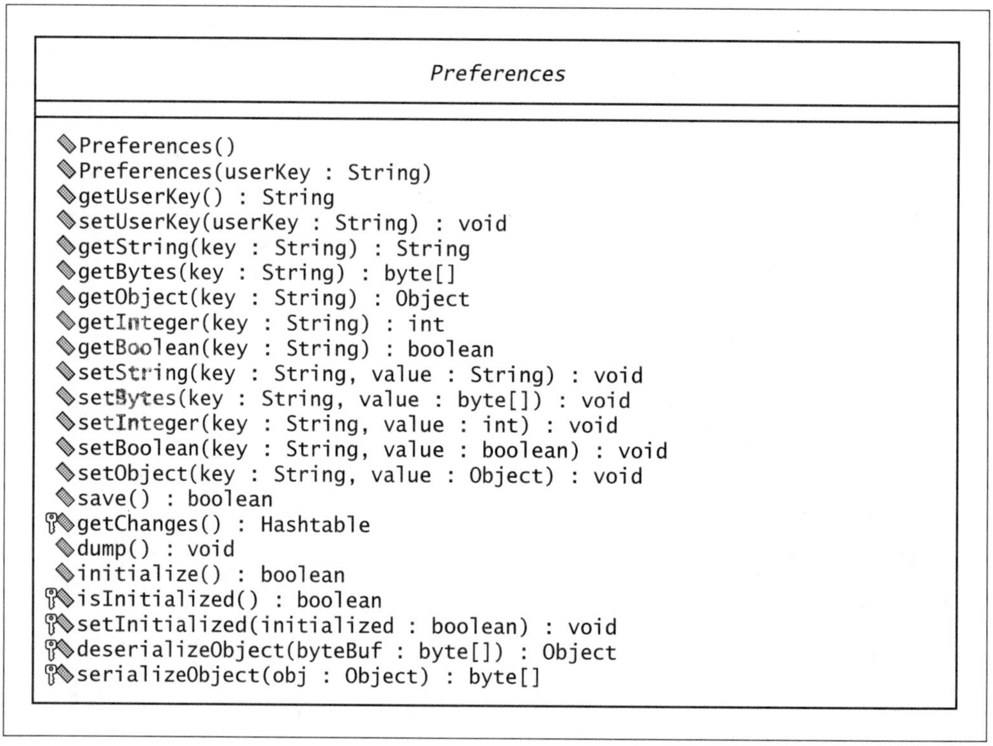

```
Preferences
-----------------------------------------------
Preferences()
Preferences(userKey : String)
getUserKey() : String
setUserKey(userKey : String) : void
getString(key : String) : String
getBytes(key : String) : byte[]
getObject(key : String) : Object
getInteger(key : String) : int
getBoolean(key : String) : boolean
setString(key : String, value : String) : void
setBytes(key : String, value : byte[]) : void
setInteger(key : String, value : int) : void
setBoolean(key : String, value : boolean) : void
setObject(key : String, value : Object) : void
save() : boolean
getChanges() : Hashtable
dump() : void
initialize() : boolean
isInitialized() : boolean
setInitialized(initialized : boolean) : void
deserializeObject(byteBuf : byte[]) : Object
serializeObject(obj : Object) : byte[]
```

FIGURE 11-2. `Preferences`.

A `String` is used to identify the owner of the preferences. Usually the key will be a user ID of some kind:

```
/**
 * Normal constructor specifying user ID of some kind for
 * identifying the user's preferences
 *
 * @param userKey user ID or another unique identifier
 */
public Preferences( String userKey ) {
    setUserKey( userKey );
}

/**
 * Report the user ID or other key to the user's preferences
 *
 * @return user ID
 */
public String getUserKey() {
    return _userKey;
}

/**
 * Set the user ID or other key to user preferences
 *
 * @param userKey user ID
 */
public void setUserKey( String userKey ) {
    _userKey = userKey;
}
```

Our `Preferences` class will store all data internally as byte arrays. A byte array presentation happens to be a good match for an LDAP directory, but it makes a good common denominator as well. The accessors for getting and setting preference values are responsible for the appropriate data conversions. For `String` conversions, UTF8 is assumed for the character set.

The lowest accessors are the ones that set and return byte arrays. The `setBytes` method also keeps track of changes in the value, so that the changed values can be saved without all preferences having to be saved. Note that `getBytes` calls `initialize`, so that preferences may be read from persistent storage when they are first needed in an application:

```
    /**
     * Retrieve a single raw preference value, just as stored in the
     * directory
     *
     * @param key key for the particular preference
     * @return value of the preference
     * @exception MissingResourceException if not found
     */
    public byte[] getBytes( String key ) {
        if ( !isInitialized() ) {
            if ( !initialize() ) {
                return null;
            }
        }
        byte[] value = (byte[])get( key.toLowerCase() );
        if ( value != null ) {
            return value;
        }
        throw new MissingResourceException(
            "Missing value", "Preferences", key );
    }

/**
     * Set a single raw preference value
     *
     * @param key key for the particular preference
     * @param value value for the particular preference
     */
    public void setBytes( String key, byte[] value ) {
        key = key.toLowerCase();
        byte[] old = (byte[])get( key );
        boolean different = ( (old == null) ||
                              (old.length != value.length) );
        int i = value.length - 1;
        while( (i >= 0) && !different ) {
            different = (value[i] != old[i]);
            i-;
        }
        if ( different ) {
            put( key, value );
            _changed.put( key, value );
        }
    }
```

Then there are accessors for the common data types:

```
/**
 * Retrieve a single String-valued preference value
 *
 * @param key key for the particular preference
 * @return value of the preference
 * @exception MissingResourceException if not found
 */
public String getString( String key ) {
    byte[] val = getBytes( key );
    String s = null;
    if ( val != null ) {
        try {
            s = new String( val, "UTF8" );
        } catch ( UnsupportedEncodingException e ) {
        }
    }
    return s;
}

/**
 * Retrieve a single preference value of integer type
 *
 * @param key key for the particular preference
 * @return value of the preference
 * @exception MissingResourceException if not found
 */
public int getInteger( String key )  {
    String s = getString( key );
    if ( s != null ) {
        return Integer.valueOf(s).intValue();
    }
    // Will never get this far, because there will be a
    // MissingResourceException or NumberFormatException
    // on error
    return -1;
}

/**
 * Retrieve a single preference value of boolean type
 *
 * @param key key for the particular preference
```

```
     * @return value of the preference
     * @throw MissingResourceException if not found
     */
    public boolean getBoolean( String key )  {
        String s = getString( key );
        if ( s != null ) {
            return Boolean.valueOf( s ).booleanValue();
        }
        // Will never get this far, because there will be a
        // MissingResourceException on error
        return false;
    }

    /**
     * Set a single String-valued preference
     *
     * @param key key for the particular preference
     * @param value value for the particular preference
     */
    public void setString( String key, String value ) {
        setBytes( key, value.getBytes() );
    }

    /**
     * Set a single integer-valued preference
     *
     * @param key key for the particular preference
     * @param value value for the particular preference
     */
    public void setInteger( String key, int value ) {
        String s = Integer.toString( value );
        setString( key, s );
    }

    /**
     * Set a single boolean-valued preference
     *
     * @param key key for the particular preference
     * @param value value for the particular preference
     */
    public void setBoolean( String key, boolean value ) {
        String s = new Boolean( value ).toString();
        setString( key, s );
    }
```

There are also methods for storing and retrieving Java objects as preferences. The object is serialized before storing and deserialized when retrieved:

```
/**
 * Retrieve a single preference value, instantiated as a Java class
 *
 * @param key key for the particular preference
 * @return a deserialized object
 * @exception MissingResourceException if not found
 * @exception IOException on failure to deserialize
 */
public Object getObject( String key ) throws IOException {
    byte[] val = getBytes( key );
    return deserializeObject( val );
}

/**
 * Serialize an object
 *
 * @param key key for the particular preference
 * @param value object to serialize
 * @throw IOException on failure to serialize
 */
public void setObject( String key, Object value )
    throws IOException {
    byte[] val = serializeObject( value );
    setBytes( key, val );
}

/**
 * Deserializes an object - creates an object from a byte array
 *
 * @param byteBuf serialized form of object
 * @return deserialized object
 * @throw IOException on failure to deserialize
 */
protected static Object deserializeObject( byte[] byteBuf )
    throws IOException {

    ByteArrayInputStream bis = null;
    ObjectInputStream  objis = null;

    try {
        bis = new ByteArrayInputStream(byteBuf);
```

```
            objis = new ObjectInputStream(bis);
            return objis.readObject();
        } catch( Exception ex ) {
            throw( new IOException("Failed to deserialize object") );
        } finally {
            try {
                if (objis != null) {
                    objis.close();
                }
                if (bis != null) {
                    bis.close();
                }
            }
            catch (Exception ex) {}
        }
    }


    /**
     * Serializes an object - converts it to a byte array
     *
     * @param obj object to serialize
     * @return serialized form of object
     * @throw IOException on failure to serialize
     */
    protected static byte[] serializeObject( Object obj )
        throws IOException {

        ByteArrayOutputStream bos = null;
        ObjectOutputStream objos = null;

        try {
            bos = new ByteArrayOutputStream();
            objos = new ObjectOutputStream(bos);
            objos.writeObject(obj);
            objos.flush();
            return bos.toByteArray();
        } catch( Exception ex ) {
            throw( new IOException(
                "Failed to serialize object " + obj ) );
        } finally {
            try {
                if (objos != null) {
                    objos.close();
                }
```

```
                if (bos != null) {
                    bos.close();
                }
            }
            catch (Exception ex) {}
        }
    }
```

Derived classes are responsible for implementing the save and initialize methods to store and restore persistent state:

```
    /**
     * Save any changed preferences
     *
     * @return true on success
     */
    abstract public boolean save();

    /**
     * Initialize the preferences (e.g., from persistent storage)
     *
     * @return true if the preferences were
     * successfully initialized
     */
    abstract protected boolean initialize();
```

A few utility methods help derived classes keep track of changes and of whether or not the in-memory state is consistent with the state of persistent storage:

```
    /**
     * Report if the preferences have been initialized (e.g., from
     * persistent storage)
     *
     * @return true if the preferences have been
     * initialized
     */
    protected boolean isInitialized() {
        return _isInitialized;
    }

    /**
     * Set the internal-state flag to show whether or not the preferences
```

```
     * have been initialized (e.g., from persistent storage)
     *
     * @param initialized true if the preferences
     * have been initialized
     */
    protected void setInitialized( boolean initialized ) {
        _isInitialized = initialized;
    }

    /**
     * Get the hash table containing attributes that have changed
     *
     * @return the hash table of changed attributes
     */
    protected Hashtable getChanges() {
        return _changed;
    }
```

Another method helps debug the applications that are using the preferences:

```
    /**
     * Debugging utility method: dumps the contents of the
     * preferences
     *
     */
    public void dump() {
        if ( !isInitialized() ) {
            initialize();
        }
        Enumeration e = keys();
        while( e.hasMoreElements() ) {
            String s = (String)e.nextElement();
            System.out.println( "    " + s + ": " + getString( s ) );
        }
    }
```

Finally, the variables to be shared across classes that extend the class `Preferences` are declared:

```
    private String _userKey = null;
    private boolean _isInitialized = false;
    private Hashtable _changed = new Hashtable();
```

Storing Preferences as Attributes in User Entries

A natural place to store user preferences in the directory is the entry of each user (see Figure 11-3). Users are often allowed to modify certain attributes in their own entries in a directory but not in anyone else's entry.

We are using attribute names like `teexTabSize` for the user preferences for Teex. They are not valid attributes for the `inetOrgPerson` object class, and in a standard directory installation they are not even defined attributes. If we attempted to assign values to these attributes in a standard directory configuration, the server would respond with a schema violation error message.

First we must add definitions for the new attributes and for the new object class to the schema of the directory. We will discuss ways to read and update the schema programmatically in Chapter 16. For now, we will use `LDAPModify` to add definitions from an LDIF file:

```
java LDAPModify -D "cn=directory manager" -w password -f teexschema.ldif
```

FIGURE 11-3. *User preferences in user entries.*

Our LDAPPreferences1 class (Figure 11-4) will retrieve values from these attributes and save values to them, as the following block of code shows. An LDAPPreferences1 object requires a URL that identifies the base DN of the subtree where user preferences are stored, a user ID, and a password for the user. The user ID and the URL will be used to locate the entry where preferences are stored, and the password is required for updating the entry when the preferences change.

```
/**
 * Normal constructor specifying user ID or some such key for
 * identifying the user's preferences, a URL identifying
 * where user entries for preferences are to be found,
 * and a password for the user
 *
 * @param userKey user ID or another unique identifier
 * @param url LDAP URL indicating the host, port, and base DN
 * from where to search for the user
 * @param password password for the user
 */
public LDAPPreferences1( String url, String userKey,
                         String password ) {
    super( userKey );
```

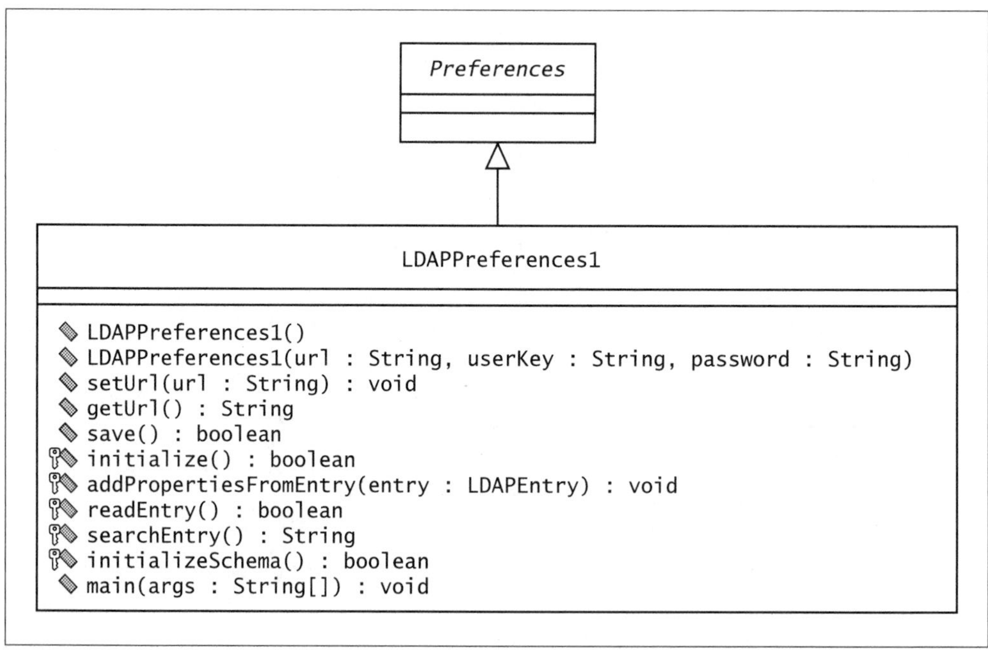

FIGURE 11-4. LDAPPreferences1.

```
        try {
            setUrl( url );
        } catch ( java.net.MalformedURLException e ) {
        }
        _password = password;
    }
```

The URL and base DN are used together with the user ID to construct a search URL. The search filter in the URL checks the `uid` attribute against the user ID:

```
    /**
     * Set the host, port, and base DN through an LDAP URL
     *
     * @param url LDAP URL indicating the host, port, and base DN
     * from where to search for the user
     */
    public void setUrl( String url )
        throws java.net.MalformedURLException {
        _url = null;
        try {
            LDAPUrl inUrl = new LDAPUrl( url );
            // Make a complete LDAPUrl, including a search
            // filter for uid matching userKey
            String[] attrs = { "dn" }; // No attributes
            _searchUrl = new LDAPUrl( inUrl.getHost(),
                                      inUrl.getPort(),
                                      inUrl.getDN(), attrs,
                                      LDAPConnection.SCOPE_SUB,
                                      "uid=" + getUserKey() );
        } catch ( java.net.MalformedURLException e ) {
            System.err.println( "Incorrect URL syntax: " + url );
            throw e;
        }
    }

    /**
     * Report the host, port, and base DN through an LDAP URL
     *
     * @return LDAP URL indicating the host, port, and base DN
     * from where to search for the user
     */
    public String getUrl() {
        return (_url != null) ? _url.getUrl() : null;
    }
```

When the object is to be initialized from persistent storage, the search URL is evaluated. If one—and only one—matching entry is found, then a new, exact URL is composed to read from that entry. We don't want to write to attributes other than the preference attributes (for example, the `cn` attribute), so at this point we also read the schema of the directory and identify which attributes are part of the `teexPreferences` object class:

```
/**
 * Read preferences from directory
 *
 * @return true if successful
 */
protected boolean initialize() {
    clear();
    setInitialized( false );

    if ( _searchUrl == null ) {
        System.err.println( "Incorrect URL syntax" );
        return false;
    }

    // Search for a single matching entry
    if ( _url == null ) {
        String dn = searchEntry();
        if ( dn != null ) {
            // Found it
            String[] attrs = null; // Inefficient...
            // URL to read one entry
            _url = new LDAPUrl( _searchUrl.getHost(),
                                _searchUrl.getPort(),
                                dn, attrs,
                                LDAPConnection.SCOPE_BASE,
                                "objectclass=*" );
            System.out.println( "URL: " + _url.getUrl() );
            if ( !initializeSchema() ) {
                return false;
            }
        }
    }

    // Now we know the entry containing the preferences
    boolean success = readEntry();
    if ( success ) {
```

```
            setInitialized( true );
        } else {
            clear();
        }

        return success;
    }

    /**
     * Get the preference values from an entry and store them
     * internally
     *
     * @param entry an LDAP entry containing preference attributes
     */
    protected void addPropertiesFromEntry( LDAPEntry entry ) {
        // Get the attributes
        Enumeration en = entry.getAttributeSet().getAttributes();
        while ( en.hasMoreElements() ) {
            LDAPAttribute attr = (LDAPAttribute)en.nextElement();
            String attrName = attr.getName().toLowerCase();
            if ( _allowed.contains( attrName ) ) {
                // Assume only one value each
                Enumeration valsEn = attr.getByteValues();
                // Get the values
                if ( valsEn.hasMoreElements() ) {
                    byte[] value = (byte[])valsEn.nextElement();
                    put( attrName, value );
                }
            }
        }
    }

    /**
     * Get the preference values from the directory and store
     * them internally
     *
     * @return true if the values could be read
     */
    protected boolean readEntry() {
        clear();
        try {
            System.out.println( "LDAPPreferences.readEntry: " +
                                "reading " +  _url.getUrl() );
            LDAPEntry entry = LDAPConnection.read( _url );
```

```
                addPropertiesFromEntry( entry );
                // Check if the entry has the preferences object class
                Enumeration en =
                    entry.getAttribute( "objectclass" ).
                        getStringValues();
                while( en.hasMoreElements() ) {
                    String val = (String)en.nextElement();
                    System.out.println( "objectclass: " + val );
                    if ( val.equalsIgnoreCase( PREFERENCES_OC ) ) {
                        _hasOc = true;
                        break;
                    }
                }
                return true;
            } catch ( LDAPException e ) {
                System.err.println( "LDAPPreferences.readEntry: " + e );
            }
            return false;
        }

        /**
         * Get the preference values from the directory and store
         * them internally
         *
         * @return true if the values could be read
         */
        protected boolean readEntry() {
            clear();
            try {
                System.out.println( "LDAPPreferences.readEntry: " +
                                    "reading " + _url.getUrl() );
                LDAPEntry entry = LDAPConnection.read( _url );
                addPropertiesFromEntry( entry );
                // Check if the entry has the preferences object class
                Enumeration en =
                    entry.getAttribute( "objectclass" ).
                        getStringValues();
                while( en.hasMoreElements() ) {
                    String val = (String)en.nextElement();
                    System.out.println( "objectclass: " + val );
                    if ( val.equalsIgnoreCase( PREFERENCES_OC ) ) {
                        _hasOc = true;
                        break;
                    }
```

```
            }
            return true;
        } catch ( LDAPException e ) {
            System.err.println( "LDAPPreferences.readEntry: " + e );
        }
        return false;
    }

    /**
     * Get the names of the attributes that are preferences by
     * reading the directory schema
     *
     * @return true if the schema could be read
     */
    protected boolean initializeSchema() {
        if ( _allowed == null ) {
            try {
                LDAPSchema schema = new LDAPSchema();
                LDAPConnection ldc = new LDAPConnection();
                ldc.connect( _url.getHost(), _url.getPort() );
                schema.fetchSchema( ldc );
                LDAPObjectClassSchema oc =
                    schema.getObjectClass( PREFERENCES_OC );
                if ( oc == null ) {
                    System.err.println(
                        "LDAPPreferences.initializeSchema: "
                        + "no object class in schema - " +
                        PREFERENCES_OC );
                    return false;
                }
                _allowed = new Hashtable();
                Enumeration e = oc.getRequiredAttributes();
                while( e.hasMoreElements() ) {
                    String name = (String)e.nextElement();
                    if ( !name.equalsIgnoreCase( "objectclass" ) ) {
                        _allowed.put( name.toLowerCase(), name );
                    }
                }
                e = oc.getOptionalAttributes();
                while( e.hasMoreElements() ) {
                    String name = (String)e.nextElement();
                    if ( !name.equalsIgnoreCase( "objectclass" ) ) {
                        _allowed.put( name.toLowerCase(), name );
                    }
```

```
                }
            } catch ( LDAPException e ) {
                System.err.println(
                    "LDAPPreferences.initializeSchema: " + e );
                return false;
            }
        }
        return true;
    }
```

When it is time to save the preferences, only preferences that are new or that have changed are written to the directory. Note that the directory will reject any values for the Teex attributes if the entry does not include the object class `teexPreferences`. The save method adds the `teexPreferences` object class if it is not already present:

```
    /**
     * Save any changed preferences
     *
     * @return true on success
     */
    public boolean save() {
        try {
            Enumeration keys = getChanges().keys();
            // Any changes to save?
            if( !keys.hasMoreElements() ) {
                return true;
            }
            LDAPConnection ldc = new LDAPConnection();
            ldc.connect( _url.getHost(), _url.getPort() );
            ldc.authenticate( _url.getDN(), _password );
            LDAPModificationSet mods = new LDAPModificationSet();
            // Do we need to add the preferences object class?
            if ( !_hasOc ) {
                mods.add( LDAPModification.ADD,
                          new LDAPAttribute( "objectclass",
                                             PREFERENCES_OC ) );
            }
            while( keys.hasMoreElements() ) {
                String name = (String)keys.nextElement();
                byte[] value = (byte[])getChanges().get( name );
                LDAPAttribute attr =
                    new LDAPAttribute( name, value );
```

```
                mods.add( LDAPModification.REPLACE, attr );
            }
            System.out.println( "LDAPPreferences.save: " + mods );
            ldc.modify( _url.getDN(), mods );
            _hasOc = true;
            getChanges().clear();
            return true;
        } catch ( LDAPException e ) {
            System.err.println( "LDAPPreferences.save: " + e );
        }
        return false;
    }
```

LDAPPreferences1 has a few member variables of its own:

```
    public final String PREFERENCES_OC = "teexPreferences";

    private LDAPUrl _searchUrl = null; // Host, port, base DN
    private LDAPUrl _url = null; // Complete URL of user entry
    private String _password = null; // User password
    private Hashtable _allowed = null; // Preference attributes
    private boolean _hasOc = false;
```

Now we are ready to use our Preferences class with Teex.

The Teex class has the following constructors (other than the blank constructor for deserialization):

```
public Teex( javax.swing.JFrame frame )
public Teex( javax.swing.JFrame frame, String filePath,
             String encoding)
```

We'll add a parameter to each for a Preferences object:

```
public Teex( javax.swing.JFrame frame, Preferences prefs )
public Teex( javax.swing.JFrame frame, String filePath,
             String encoding, Preferences prefs )
```

In the following block of code, the constructors fetch any preferences that are in the object and copy them to internal variables. Any preferences not available from the object are ignored, and initial default values are used. Note that the first call to get a value from the object will cause it to be initialized from the directory because the Preferences object we are passing is actually an instance of LDAPPreferences1.

```
    public Teex( javax.swing.JFrame frame, Preferences prefs ) {
...
        initializePreferences( prefs );
...
    }

    /**
     * Get the values we need from the preferences object
     *
     * @param prefs an object containing application preferences
     */
    protected void initializePreferences( Preferences prefs ) {
        g_prefs = prefs;
        if ( g_prefs == null ) {
            return;
        }

        String key = "teexbackground";
        try {
            int i = g_prefs.getInteger( key );
            textAreaBackground = new Color( i );
        } catch ( Exception e ) {
            // If the value was not there, stick with the default
            System.out.println( "Teex: no preference " + key );
        }
        key = "teexforeground";
        try {
            int i = g_prefs.getInteger( key );
            textAreaForeground = new Color( i );
        } catch ( Exception e ) {
            System.out.println( "Teex: no preference " + key );
        }
        key = "teextabsize";
        try {
            int i = g_prefs.getInteger( key );
            tabSize = i;
        } catch ( Exception e ) {
            System.out.println( "Teex: no preference " + key );
        }
        key = "teexfontsize";
        try {
            int i = g_prefs.getInteger( key );
            fontSize = i;
        } catch ( Exception e ) {
```

```
            System.out.println( "Teex: no preference " + key );
        }
        key = "teexlinewrap";
        try {
            boolean wrap = g_prefs.getBoolean( key );
            lineWrap = wrap;
        } catch ( Exception e ) {
            System.out.println( "Teex: no preference " + key );
        }
    }
```

The internal variables are then used to initialize and configure the Teex panels, just as before. When the user changes preferences by interacting with the View menu, the changes are also recorded in the preferences object. For example, when line wrap is enabled or disabled, the corresponding value is recorded as a boolean:

```
        wrapMenu = new JMenuItem(lineWrap ? "Do Not Wrap Lines" :
                                 "Wrap Lines");
        wrapMenu.addActionListener (new ActionListener() {
            public void actionPerformed(ActionEvent e) {
                lineWrap = !lineWrap;
                textArea.setLineWrap(lineWrap);
                wrapMenu.setText(lineWrap ? "Do Not Wrap Lines" :
                                 "Wrap Lines");
                g_prefs.setBoolean( "teexlinewrap", lineWrap );
            };
        });
        viewMenu.add(wrapMenu);
```

When the user selects Exit from the File menu, the preferences are saved before the application terminates:

```
        JMenuItem exitMenu = new JMenuItem("Exit");
        exitMenu.addActionListener (new ActionListener() {
            public void actionPerformed( ActionEvent e ) {
                g_frameCount--;
                if ( g_frameCount <= 0 ) {
                    g_prefs.save();
                    g_frame.dispose();
                    System.exit(0);    // close the application
                }
            }
        });
```

The `main` method was modified to take optional arguments for the LDAP URL, user ID, and password for an `LDAPPreferences1` object. If all three are provided, an object is instantiated; otherwise a `null` preferences object is passed to the `Teex` constructors and no persistent preferences are used:

```
static public void main(String args[]) {
    int i = 0;
    String filePath = null;
    String encoding = null;
    String url = null;
    String uid = null;
    String password = null;

    while (i < args.length) {
        if (args[i].compareTo("-encoding") == 0) {
            if ((i + 1) < args.length) {
                encoding = args[i+1];
                i ++;
            }
        } else if (args[i].compareTo("-u") == 0) {
            if ((i + 1) < args.length) {
                url = args[i+1];
                i ++;
            }
        } else if (args[i].compareTo("-D") == 0) {
            if ((i + 1) < args.length) {
                uid = args[i+1];
                i ++;
            }
        } else if (args[i].compareTo("-w") == 0) {
            if ((i + 1) < args.length) {
                password = args[i+1];
                i ++;
            }
...
    Preferences prefs = null;
    if ( (url != null) && (password != null) && (uid != null) ) {
        prefs = new LDAPPreferences1( url, uid, password );
    }

    Teex t;
    if ( filePath != null ) {
        t = new Teex(frame, filePath, encoding, prefs);
    } else {
```

```
            t = new Teex(frame, prefs);
        }
```

We can now run the application and specify LDAP preferences, using the following command:

```
java Teex -u "ldap://localhost:389/o=airius.com" -D dakers -w integument
```

The first time through there will be no preferences in the directory. But if settings are changed, they will be saved on program exit and restored the next time the application is run.

Saving Preferences as an Object in the Directory

Storing each preference value as a unique attribute is convenient. It is easy to use `LDAPSearch` or any other LDAP client to inspect and adjust the values if necessary, and more than one application can share certain preferences.

However, there is also a major disadvantage: whenever you add a new preference to your application, you must define a new attribute and add it to the directory schema. You must also modify the object class definition for the preferences object class to include the new attribute. Generally, only privileged users have permission to change the directory schema. With a corporate directory, application developers may not be allowed to make random changes to the schema. There may also be problems with interoperability if data is synchronized between the directory and other data sources, or replicated to other directories. Every schema change must be carefully copied to each participant in replication agreements with the server.

One way to ensure flexibility for adding new preference values in the future is to store all values in a single object. The schema needs to be modified only once to allow this compound attribute. `LDAPPreferences2` (Figure 11-5) implements the compound object model by serializing a `Hashtable` with all preferences and storing the serialized value as a single attribute in the user entry. In other respects `LDAPPreferences2` is identical to `LDAPPreferences1`, so only the differences will be presented here.

`LDAPPreferences2.initialize` specifies a single attribute to read from the user entry, rather than `null` (for all attributes):

```
String[] attrs = { PREFERENCES_ATTR };
 // URL to read one entry
 _url = new LDAPUrl( _searchUrl.getHost(),
                     _searchUrl.getPort(),
                     dn, attrs,
                     LDAPConnection.SCOPE_BASE,
                     "objectclass=*" );
```

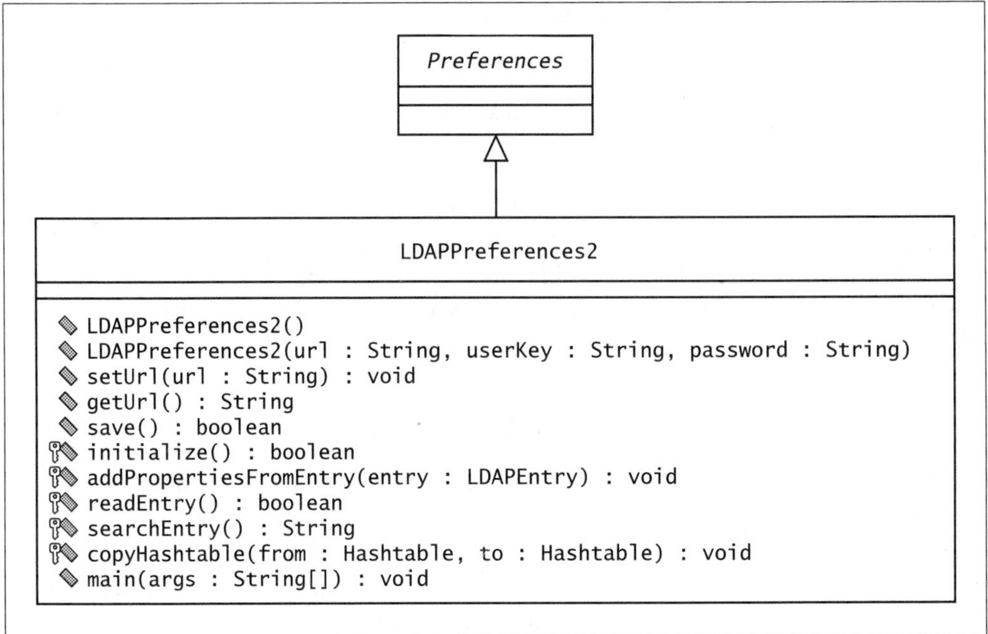

FIGURE 11-5. `LDAPPreferences2`.

Instead of multiple discrete attributes (defined by the `teexPreferences` object class) being pulled out of the user entry, a single attribute is extracted. It is deserialized into a `Hashtable`, and the contents are copied into the preferences object:

```
protected void addPropertiesFromEntry( LDAPEntry entry ) {
    // Get the attribute with a serialized Hashtable
    LDAPAttribute attr = entry.getAttribute( PREFERENCES_ATTR );
    if ( attr == null ) {
        System.out.println(
            "LDAPPreferences.addPropertiesFromEntry: " +
            "no attribute - " + PREFERENCES_ATTR );
        return;
    }
    Enumeration valsEn = attr.getByteValues();
    // Get the values
    if ( valsEn.hasMoreElements() ) {
        byte[] value = (byte[])valsEn.nextElement();
        Hashtable ht = null;
        try {
            ht = (Hashtable)deserializeObject( value );
```

```
            } catch ( IOException ex ) {
                System.err.println(
                    "LDAPPreferences.addPropertiesFromEntry: " + ex );
                return;
            }
            copyHashtable( ht, this );
        } else {
            System.err.println(
                "LDAPPreferences.addPropertiesFromEntry: " +
                "no value for attribute " + PREFERENCES_ATTR );
        }
    }
```

Similarly, when saving the preferences, all values (not just those that have changed) are copied to a `Hashtable`. The `Hashtable` is serialized and saved as a single attribute:

```
    public boolean save() {
        try {
            Enumeration keys = getChanges().keys();
            // Any changes to save?
            if( !keys.hasMoreElements() ) {
                return true;
            }
            LDAPConnection ldc = new LDAPConnection();
            ldc.connect( _url.getHost(), _url.getPort() );
            ldc.authenticate( _url.getDN(), _password );
            // Copy all values to new Hashtable
            Hashtable ht = new Hashtable();
            copyHashtable( this, ht );
            // Put it into serialized form
            byte[] val;
            try {
                val = serializeObject( ht );
            } catch ( IOException ex ) {
                System.err.println( "LDAPPreferences.save: " + ex );
                return false;
            }
            LDAPModification mod =
                new LDAPModification(
                    LDAPModification.REPLACE,
                    new LDAPAttribute( PREFERENCES_ATTR,
                                       val ) );
            System.out.println( "LDAPPreferences.save: " + mod );
```

```
            ldc.modify( _url.getDN(), mod );
            getChanges().clear();
            return true;
        } catch ( LDAPException e ) {
            System.err.println( "LDAPPreferences.save: " + e );
        }
        return false;
    }
```

`LDAPPreferences2` defines a few member variables:

```
    public final String PREFERENCES_ATTR = "teexPreferencesObject";
    private LDAPUrl _searchUrl = null; // Host, port, base DN
    private LDAPUrl _url = null; // Complete URL of user entry
    private String _password = null; // User password
    private Hashtable _allowed = null; // Preference attributes
```

To begin using `LDAPPreferences2` instead of `LDAPPreferences1`, we must do two things:

- Add a definition of the new attribute to the directory schema
- Change one line in `Teex.main` to use `LDAPPreferences2`

We can use `teexschema2.ldif` to add the new attribute and modify the `teexPreferences` object class definition. The old object class definition is deleted, and then a new one is added that allows `teexPreferencesObject` in addition to the other Teex attributes. We accomplish all this in a single modify operation in the LDIF file:

```
java LDAPModify -D "cn=directory manager" -w password -f teexschema2.ldif
```

The change required to `Teex.main` is to replace `LDAPPreferences1` with `LDAPPreferences2`:

```
prefs = new LDAPPreferences2( url, uid, password );
```

You can then compile `Teex.java` and run it from the command line, just as before. There is no visible difference in the behavior, but after changing preferences there is a new binary attribute in the user entry:

```
dn: uid=dakers, ou=People, o=airius.com
teexPreferencesObject:: rO0ABXNyABNqYXZhLnV0aWwuSGFzaHRhYmxlE7sPJSFK5LgDAAJGA
Apsb2FkRmFjdG9ySQAJdGhyZXNob2xkeHA/QAAAAAAAS3cIAAAAZQAAAAR0AAt0ZWV4dGFic216Z
```

```
XVyAAJbQqzzF/gGCFTgAgAAeHAAAAABNHQADnRlZXhiYWNrZ3JvdW5kdXEAfgADAAAABC0yMDV0A
h0ZWV4Zm9udHVxAH4AAwAAAAdjb3VyaWVydAAJdGVleGNvbG9ydXEAfgADAAAABGJsdWV4
```


Using Directory Structure to Model Attributes

We lost a couple of things when we started storing attributes as a compound object:

- It is no longer possible to do a search based on the value of one of the attributes.
- It is much more difficult to interpret the values in the user entry for debugging.

In this concluding section on user preferences we will look at a third way to store the values. This time each preference will be stored in a separate entry under the user entry (see Figure 11-6).

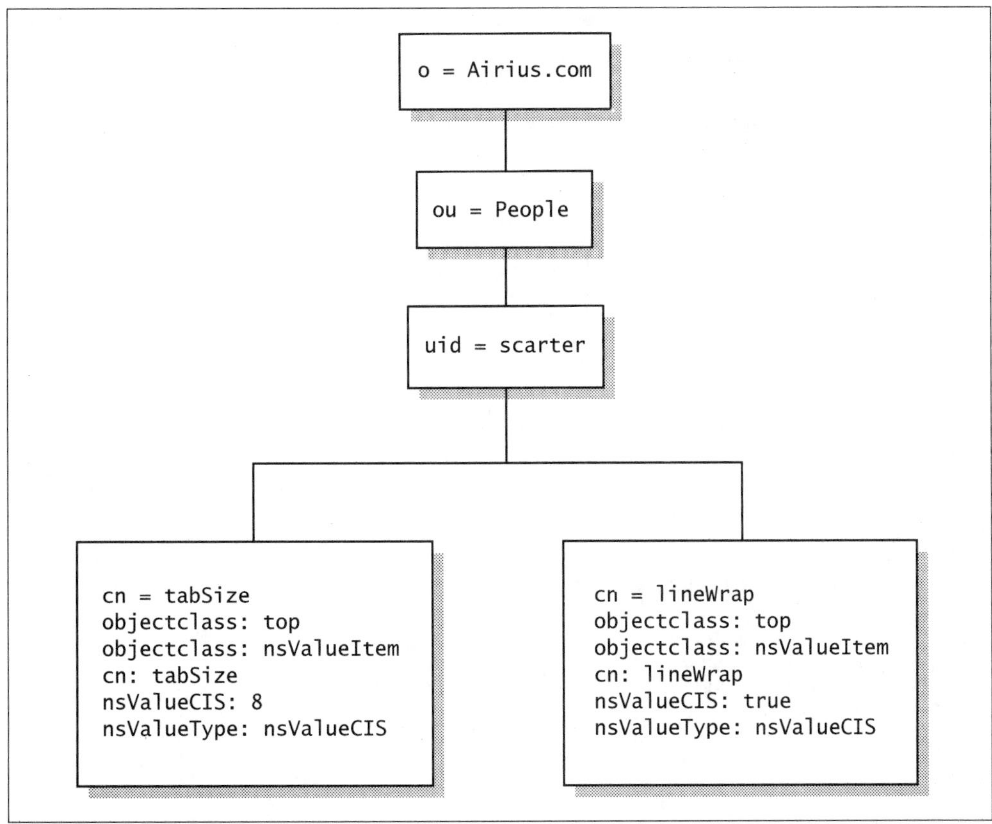

FIGURE 11-6. *Preferences as individual entries.*

We are now using special schema elements for generic attributes. The schema is predefined in Netscape Directory Server. An entry containing one or more preference values includes the object class `nsValueItem`. There are several allowed attributes for this object class, the name of each attribute indicating its syntax. The `cn` value of the entry is the name of the preference value. In Figure 11-6, the user entry for Sam Carter has two preference entries underneath it. Each one contains a single preference value. Both values are of type `cis` ("case-insensitive string"). The DN of the `tabSize` entry is `cn=tabSize,uid=scarter,ou=People,o=Airius.com`.

Since the schema is provided with Netscape Directory Server, we don't have to add a schema of our own if we are using it. For a different directory, we would have to provide the schema only once. An LDIF file is provided for this purpose: `generic.ldif`. We can add new preferences by creating new entries under the user entries, without defining additional new schema elements.

`LDAPPreferences3` (Figure 11-7) is similar to `LDAPPreferences1` and `LDAPPreferences2`. The differences are in how preferences are read from the directory and how they are saved.

When reading preferences, we must now read all children of the user entry, rather than reading the user entry itself:

```
protected boolean initialize() {
    ...
```

```
Preferences
    △
LDAPPreferences3

LDAPPreferences3()
LDAPPreferences3(url : String, userKey : String, password : String)
setUrl(url : String) : void
getUrl() : String
save() : boolean
initialize() : boolean
addPropertiesFromEntry(entry : LDAPEntry) : void
readChildren() : boolean
searchEntry() : String
main(args : String[]) : void
```

FIGURE 11-7. `LDAPPreferences3`.

```
    // Search for a single matching entry
    if ( _url == null ) {
        String dn = searchEntry();
        if ( dn != null ) {
            // Found it
            String[] attrs = null;
            // URL to read children of this entry
            _url = new LDAPUrl( _searchUrl.getHost(),
                                _searchUrl.getPort(),
                                dn, attrs,
                                LDAPConnection.SCOPE_ONE,
                                "objectclass=nsValueItem" );
            System.out.println( "URL: " + _url.getUrl() );
        }
    }

    // Now we know the entry containing the preferences
    boolean success = readChildren();
```

For each child found, retrieve the preference value. The cn of the entry is the preference name. An entry with the object class nsValueItem may have an attribute nsValueType, which indicates the data type of the preference value. If nsValueType is present, we use it to determine which of the possible attribute types to look for in the entry. If it is not present, we look in turn for each of the possible types:

```
/**
 * Get the preference values from the directory and store
 * them internally
 *
 * @return true if the values could be read
 */
protected boolean readChildren() {
    clear();
    LDAPSearchResults res = null;
    try {
        System.out.println( "LDAPPreferences.readChildren: " +
                            "reading " + _url.getUrl() );
        res = LDAPConnection.search( _url );
    } catch ( LDAPException e ) {
        System.err.println( "LDAPPreferences.readChildren: " +
                            e );
        return false;
    }
    while ( res.hasMoreElements() ) {
```

```
            try {
                LDAPEntry entry = res.next();
                addPropertiesFromEntry( entry );
                System.out.println(
                    "LDAPPreferences.readChildren: found " +
                    entry.getDN() );
            } catch ( LDAPException e ) {
                System.err.println(
                    "LDAPPreferences.readChildren: " + e );
                continue;
            }
        }
        return true;
    }

    /**
     * Get the preference values from an entry and store them
     * internally
     *
     * @param entry an LDAP entry containing preference attributes
     */
    protected void addPropertiesFromEntry( LDAPEntry entry ) {
        // Get the name of the attribute
        LDAPAttribute attr = entry.getAttribute( "cn" );
        String name = (String)attr.getStringValues().nextElement();
        Object value = null;
        // Get the type of the attribute
        String type = null;
        if ( (attr = entry.getAttribute( "nsValueType" )) != null ) {
            // Is the type specified?
            type = (String)attr.getStringValues().nextElement();
            if ( (attr = entry.getAttribute( type )) != null ) {
               value = attr.getByteValues().nextElement();
            }
        }
        // If type was not specified, look for all possible types
        for( int i = 0; (value == null) && (i < ATTRS.length); i++ ) {
            if ( (attr = entry.getAttribute( ATTRS[i] )) != null ) {
                value = attr.getByteValues().nextElement();
            }
        }
        if ( value != null ) {
            put( name, value );
        }
```

```
    }
    // Possible attribute types for nsValueItem
    private final static String[] ATTRS = { "nsValueBin",
                                            "nsValueCIS",
                                            "nsValueCES",
                                            "nsValueInt",
                                            "nsValueDN",
                                            "nsValueTel" };
```

The `nsValueItem` object class allows a few additional attributes to specify a default attribute value, a description, a help URL, a syntax, and flags. We won't be using them in this example.

When the preferences are to be saved, an entry must be created or modified for each new or changed preference, as the following code shows. Storing all values as strings will allow searching based on preference values, which might be useful in a future application.

```
        String[] oclasses = { "top", "nsValueItem" };
        while( keys.hasMoreElements() ) {
            String name = (String)keys.nextElement();
            String value = "";
            try {
                value =
                    new String( (byte[])getChanges().get( name ),
                                "UTF8" );
            } catch ( UnsupportedEncodingException e ) {
            }
            // Create a DN for each preference
            String dn = "cn="+name + "," + _url.getDN();
            LDAPAttributeSet set = new LDAPAttributeSet();
            set.add( new LDAPAttribute( "objectclass",
                                        oclasses ) );
            // Save the value as a string
            set.add( new LDAPAttribute( "nsValueType",
                                        "nsValueCIS" ) );
            set.add( new LDAPAttribute( "nsValueCIS",
                                        value ) );
            set.add( new LDAPAttribute( "cn",
                                        name ) );
            LDAPEntry entry = new LDAPEntry( dn, set );
            System.out.println( "LDAPPreferences.save: " +
                                entry );
            try {
```

```
                ldc.add( entry );
            } catch ( LDAPException ex ) {
                System.err.println( "LDAPPreferences.save: " + ex );
                // If the entry already exists, replace it
                if ( ex.getLDAPResultCode() ==
                     ex.ATTRIBUTE_OR_VALUE_EXISTS ) {
                    LDAPModification mod =
                        new LDAPModification(
                            LDAPModification.REPLACE,
                            new LDAPAttribute( "nsValueCIS",
                                               value ) );
                    ldc.modify( dn, mod );
                }
            }
        }
```

Change `LDAPPreferences2` to `LDAPPreferences3` in `Teex.java` and recompile to use the new class. Again, the user cannot tell the difference, but behind the scenes data is being saved in a new way in the directory.

Using directory structure to model preferences instead of using entry content has several advantages:

- Preferences can be extended, deleted, or modified without schema changes.
- Adding or removing preferences does not affect replication or synchronization partners.
- Preferences can be self-describing, have defaults, and have links to meta-information.
- If each user has a very large number of preferences, or each preference contains a lot of data, then server performance will be better if the data is split among several entries.

There are also a couple of disadvantages:

- Users must have permission to create child entries under their own entries. This is less of an issue for server-side applications.
- Other LDAP client applications that share the same user directory may be confused if they find child entries under the user entries. Some applications may assume that user entries are leaf nodes. A well-written application will include an object class such as `person` or `inetOrgPerson` in its search filter when looking up users to avoid confusing user entries with other entries.

Conclusion

If application and user preferences are stored in a directory, they can be shared easily. A user or application can re-create a previous state from a different location or computer, as long as there is network access for LDAP. Preferences can be stored as individual values or as a Java object. They can be identified by unique attribute names or by using the tree structure of the directory along with metainformation. If the number and types of preferences are variable and growing, it may be difficult to maintain unique attributes for each type. This chapter has presented three different strategies for storing a user's application preferences with LDAP; determining which one is appropriate for your application is left to you.

CHAPTER 12

Modeling Relationships

In Chapter 10 we developed a tree browser component for exploring directory data. The structure of the data presented in the browser mirrored the organization of the data in the directory. However, directory information may embody other relationships between entries, beyond their structural organization into a tree. In this chapter we will discuss the mechanisms for representing and interpreting these relationships, develop components for representing a reporting hierarchy, and add a property browser for directory entries to the collection of LDAP JavaBeans that we started in Chapter 10.

Mirroring an Organizational Structure

When designing a directory structure for an organization, the first thing that comes to mind is to represent each division, department, and other organizational unit in the tree as a directory entry and to place each person entry under the department to which the person belongs. A division entry might have many department entries as child nodes, and a department entry might have additional department entries and/or individual person entries underneath it.

The directory structure maps exactly to the structure of the organization, and the DN of a person entry describes the full chain of the person's affiliation in the organization. The structure of a particular directory content is often called a **Directory Information Tree**, or **DIT**. Figure 12-1 illustrates a DIT that corresponds exactly to the structure of the hypothetical corporation Acme. In Figure 12-1, Gern Farmer's DN is `uid=gfarmer, ou=Payroll, ou=Accounting, ou=Internet Products, o=Acme.com`, which precisely identifies where Gern works.

In recent years this type of DIT has become much less commonly used, primarily because of the difficulty of maintenance. Most organizations experience organizational

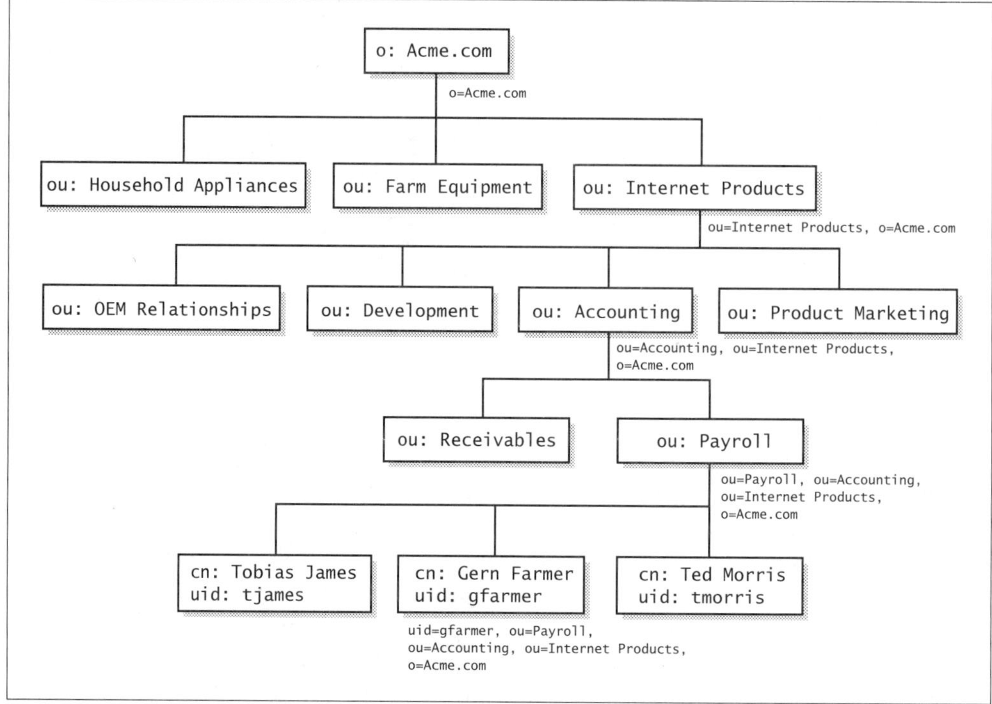

FIGURE 12-1. *A DIT for organizational mapping.*

changes over time, with employees moving from one department to another or with departments and divisions being reorganized or renamed. For large organizations, changes such as these may be frequent enough to generate significant extra work for the administrators who are responsible for maintaining the directory contents.

However, the new element that has definitively tipped the scales against having the DIT mirror the organizational structure is the growing use of certificates for user authentication. A certificate contains the owner's DN, or at least a DN that can be easily mapped to the user's DN in the directory. If the DN contains the full hierarchy of the user's position in the organization, then any change in the hierarchy—even a simple renaming of a department—will require revoking all the certificates of every user in that department and issuing new ones. This is clearly not feasible.

Attributes as Pointers

To preserve organizational affiliation information while allowing for change, many companies and institutions are now choosing a fairly flat DIT for user entries and using attributes of the user entries to maintain the organizational relationships. All person entries are in a single pool or a small number of pools. Each person entry has an attribute indicating the organization to which the person belongs.

Figure 12-2 shows the Acme DIT restructured to use attributes to represent the organizational hierarchy. In this example, all employees are in a single pool. If there is little possibility of change between divisions, then Acme might decide to have one pool for each division instead. With the directory organization of Figure 12-2, Gern Farmer can change departments, or departments can change names, and all that needs to happen to Gern's account is that the `ou` attribute be updated. His DN remains `uid=gfarmer, ou=People, o=Acme.com`, and his certificates are still valid.

If an application needs to represent Gern's chain of affiliation, it cannot do so simply by decomposing his DN; rather it must search for the entry to which his `ou` attribute points. In this case, a subtree search from `o=Acme.com` for "ou=Payroll" will return `ou=Payroll, ou=Accounting, ou=Internet Products, o=Acme.com`.

In the remainder of this chapter we will develop components that demonstrate how to illustrate reporting relationships from directory information. Similar techniques may be used to extract other types of relationships.

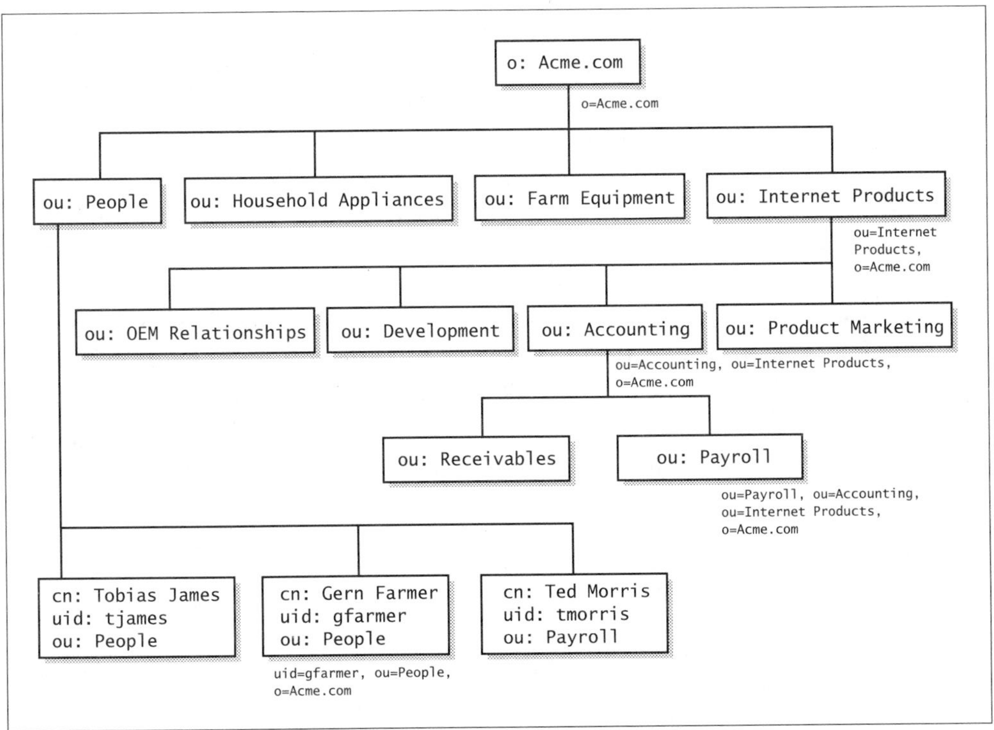

FIGURE 12-2. *DIT using the* `ou` *attribute to represent affiliation.*

Parsing the Reporting Relationships in a Directory

The commonly used `inetOrgPerson` object class includes an optional attribute `manager`. The `ManagementParser` class that will be developed in this chapter assumes that the `manager` attribute is used to indicate reporting relationships.

The attribute syntax for `manager` is `dn`, and it should point to another entry in the directory. Having `dn` syntax rather than `cis` (case-insensitive string) syntax means that a search for a particular DN will succeed even if there is an extra space or two after the comma that separates RDNs, because the server normalizes away differences that are not relevant to DNs.

`ManagementParser` (Figure 12-3) follows the `manager` values as pointers to create a tree of nodes, using the JFC class `DefaultMutableTreeNode` for each entry. `ManagementParser` uses the following algorithm:

1. Find all person entries that do not have a `manager` attribute and save them in a root list. These entries are assumed to represent either top-level executives (with direct reports) or individuals who are not part of any organization.
2. Find all person entries that do have a `manager` attribute and save them in a subordinate list. Record each `manager` value found in a hash table.
3. Check each `manager` value against the root list and the subordinate list. If the value is not found in either list, then the directory information has not been kept up-to-date and any person entries reporting to the manager cannot be placed in the reporting hierarchy (we don't know who they really report to).
4. Starting with the members of the root list, search the subordinate list recursively for all entries reporting to a particular entry.

`ManagementParser` has one main public method, with two variants. The first variant of `parseTree` takes an active connection to a directory and a base DN as arguments. The second variant takes as an additional parameter the DN of a manager. If the DN corresponds to a directory entry, then the return value of the method will be the node that contains the entry, rather than the top-level node or nodes found:

```
static public DefaultMutableTreeNode
parseTree( LDAPConnection ldc,
           String base ) throws LDAPException {

static public DefaultMutableTreeNode
parseTree( LDAPConnection ldc,
           String base,
           String rootDN ) throws LDAPException {
```

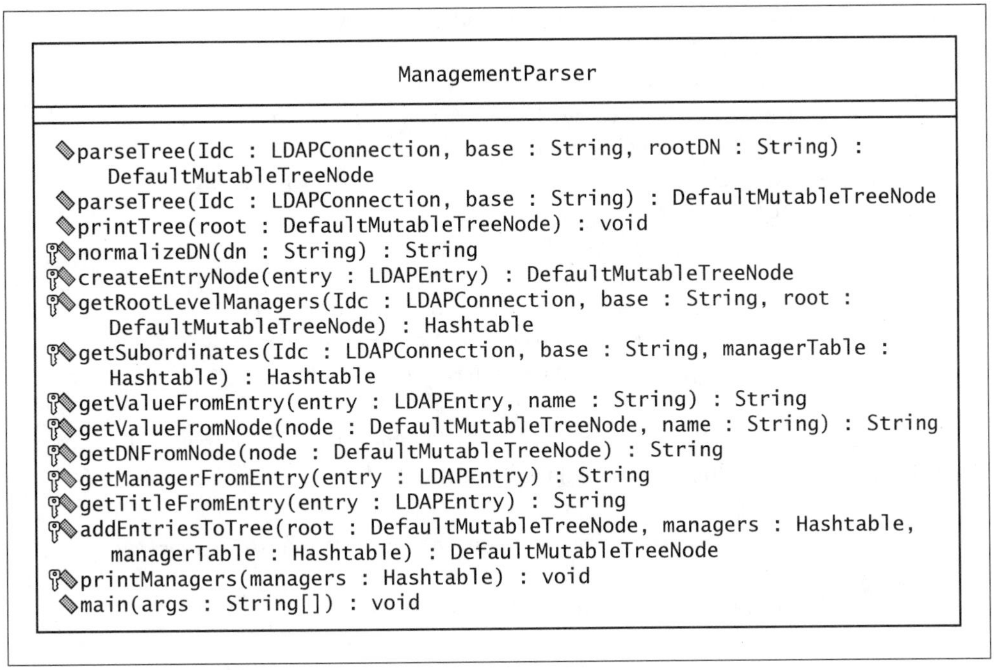

```
ManagementParser

parseTree(ldc : LDAPConnection, base : String, rootDN : String) :
    DefaultMutableTreeNode
parseTree(ldc : LDAPConnection, base : String) : DefaultMutableTreeNode
printTree(root : DefaultMutableTreeNode) : void
normalizeDN(dn : String) : String
createEntryNode(entry : LDAPEntry) : DefaultMutableTreeNode
getRootLevelManagers(ldc : LDAPConnection, base : String, root :
    DefaultMutableTreeNode) : Hashtable
getSubordinates(ldc : LDAPConnection, base : String, managerTable :
    Hashtable) : Hashtable
getValueFromEntry(entry : LDAPEntry, name : String) : String
getValueFromNode(node : DefaultMutableTreeNode, name : String) : String
getDNFromNode(node : DefaultMutableTreeNode) : String
getManagerFromEntry(entry : LDAPEntry) : String
getTitleFromEntry(entry : LDAPEntry) : String
addEntriesToTree(root : DefaultMutableTreeNode, managers : Hashtable,
    managerTable : Hashtable) : DefaultMutableTreeNode
printManagers(managers : Hashtable) : void
main(args : String[]) : void
```

FIGURE 12-3. ManagementParser.

The method parseTree starts by creating an empty root node and then creating a Hashtable of all entries that do not have a manager attribute. It prints a message indicating the number found:

```
/**
 * Read person entries in a directory subtree, and
 * sort the results by reporting relationships
 *
 * @param ldc connected and authenticated LDAPConnection
 * object
 * @param base base DN from which to search for entries
 * @param rootDN DN of the top manager node to return
 * @return the root node of a tree, or null
 * on failure
 * @throws LDAPException on failure in searching
 */
static public DefaultMutableTreeNode
parseTree( LDAPConnection ldc,
           String base,
           String rootDN ) throws LDAPException {
```

```
// Get root-level managers and add them to the root;
// keep references in a Hashtable. We consider a root-
// level manager to be anyone who doesn't have a
// manager. In reality, some of the entries without managers may be
// highly placed individual contributors, and some
// may just not have their directory info up-to-date.
DefaultMutableTreeNode root =
    new DefaultMutableTreeNode();
Hashtable rootEntries =
    getRootLevelManagers( ldc, base, root );
System.out.println( rootEntries.size() + " entries " +
                    "do not have a manager" );
```

The `getRootLevelManagers` method searches for all entries that match `rootFilter`, which in this case is declared as follows:

```
// Filter string to retrieve users not reporting to anyone
private static String _rootFilter =
    "(&(objectclass=person)(!(manager=*)))";
```

You may need to customize `_rootFilter` for your site. The attributes to be returned are declared as follows:

```
// Attributes to retrieve on search
private static String[] _fetchAttrs =
    { "cn", "title", "manager", "description", "ou" };
```

The `cn` value will be used to display the name of each person found. The `manager` value will be used to evaluate the reporting relationships. For managers, we would also like to display a title, so we request the `title` attribute. However, some managers may not have a `title` value assigned, so the `description` and `ou` attributes are requested as well, to use if there is no `title` value.

For each entry found, a node is created and added to the root node. In addition, the node is added to the `rootEntries` `Hashtable` to be returned by the method. The key for each node is the normalized DN of the entry.

```
/**
 * Get all person entries that do not have a manager;
 * assume they are top-level managers or free entities
 * at the top, and add them to the root node.
 *
 * @param ldc active connection to directory
 * @param base base DN from which to do a subtree search
```

```
 * @param root root node to which to add the entries found
 * @return a Hashtable with all entries found
 */
static protected Hashtable
getRootLevelManagers( LDAPConnection ldc,
                      String base,
                      DefaultMutableTreeNode root )
    throws LDAPException {
    // Get all person entries that do not have a manager;
    // assume they are top-level managers or free entities
    Hashtable rootEntries = new Hashtable();
    LDAPSearchConstraints cons =
        ldc.getSearchConstraints();
    cons.setMaxResults( 0 );
    LDAPSearchResults res =
        ldc.search( base,
                    ldc.SCOPE_SUB,
                    _rootFilter,
                    _fetchAttrs,
                    false,
                    cons );
    while ( res.hasMoreElements() ) {
        try {
            LDAPEntry entry = res.next();
            // Add this top-level manager
            DefaultMutableTreeNode node =
                createEntryNode( entry );
            root.add( node );
            rootEntries.put(
                getDNFromNode( node ), node );
        } catch ( LDAPReferralException ref ) {
            // Just ignore referrals
        }
    }
    return rootEntries;
}
```

Next, `parseTree` creates a `Hashtable` to track all managers found (the value of the `manager` attribute of all entries) and passes it to `getSubordinates`, which returns a `Hashtable` containing nodes for all entries that have a `manager` attribute:

```
        // Now get everyone who reports to someone. Some
        // of them are managers themselves.
        // Keep track of all managers in a Hashtable.
```

```
Hashtable managerTable = new Hashtable();
Hashtable allEntries =
    getSubordinates( ldc, base, managerTable );
```

The method getSubordinates creates a node for each entry found and stores it in a new Hashtable to be returned by the method. The key is the normalized DN of the entry. It also creates a Vector for all entries reporting to a particular manager and stores the Vector in the managers Hashtable. The search filter for finding entries with a manager is defined as follows:

```
// Filter to retrieve users reporting to someone
private static String _subordinateFilter =
    "(&(objectclass=person)(manager=*))";
```

The definition of _SubordinateFilter may need customization to work at your site—for example, to include additional attributes that must be present or must not be present to distinguish manager entries from nonmanager entries.

```
/**
 * Get all entries that have a manager. Keep track of all
 * referenced managers.
 *
 * @param ldc active connection to directory
 * @param base base DN from which to do a subtree search
 * @param managerTable Hashtable to store DNs and
 * nodes of managers
 * @return a Hashtable mapping all employee DNs to nodes
 */
static protected Hashtable
getSubordinates( LDAPConnection ldc,
                 String base,
                 Hashtable managerTable )
    throws LDAPException {
    LDAPSearchConstraints cons =
        ldc.getSearchConstraints();
    cons.setMaxResults( 0 );
    Hashtable allEntries = new Hashtable();
    // Find all person entries with a manager.
    // Retrieve each one's name, title, and manager.
    LDAPSearchResults res =
        ldc.search( base,
                    ldc.SCOPE_SUB,
                    _subordinateFilter,
```

```
                        _fetchAttrs,
                        false,
                        cons );
        int numReadEntries = 0;
        while ( res.hasMoreElements() ) {
            try {
                // Found an entry. Normalize the DN and use it
                // as the key in the allEntries Hashtable.
                LDAPEntry entry = res.next();
                String dn = normalizeDN( entry.getDN() );
                DefaultMutableTreeNode node =
                    createEntryNode( entry );
                allEntries.put( dn, node );
                // Get the manager DN and normalize it
                String managerDN =
                    getValueFromNode( node, "manager" );
                // Keep track of all managers' direct reports
                Vector v =
                    (Vector)managerTable.get( managerDN );
                if ( v == null ) {
                    v = new Vector();
                }
                v.addElement( node );
                managerTable.put( managerDN, v );
            } catch ( LDAPReferralException ref ) {
                // Just ignore referrals
            }
        }
        return allEntries;
    }
```

In some organizations—and in the sample LDIF file `airiusplus.ldif` supplied on the CD-ROM that accompanies this book—all manager information is always up-to-date, and all person entries except for those of the top executives have a `manager` attribute. However, that is not the case for many real-life organizations. The next thing `parseTree` does is to validate all the entries from the `rootEntries` table against the table of managers. If an entry is not found, the user corresponding to the entry neither has a manager nor has anyone reporting to her (if the directory data is to be believed):

```
        // Check how many root-level entries really are
        // managers
        int nRootManagers = 0;
```

```
Enumeration en = rootEntries.keys();
while( en.hasMoreElements() ) {
    String dn = (String)en.nextElement();
    if ( managerTable.containsKey( dn ) ) {
        nRootManagers++;
    }
}
System.out.println( nRootManagers + " top-level " +
                    "managers found" );

System.out.println( allEntries.size() + " people " +
                    "who report to someone" );
```

Person entries that report a manager who is not in the directory cannot be processed. Perhaps the manager is no longer with the organization, but the entries of her direct reports have not been updated to reflect the change by pointing to a different manager, or perhaps a data entry error occurred during creation or updating of the person entries. Code within the following section of `parseTree` prints out all such invalid managerial relationships, but this code is commented out. It may be useful to enable this code when debugging inconsistent directory contents.

```
        // Remove any invalid manager pointers
        int nInvalid = 0;
        en = managerTable.keys();
        while( en.hasMoreElements() ) {
            String dn = (String)en.nextElement();
            // If the manager DN doesn't exist in either the
            // root manager table or the subordinates table,
            // then we can't place any subordinates with that
            // manager.
            if ( !allEntries.containsKey( dn ) &&
                 !rootEntries.containsKey( dn ) ) {
//                  System.err.println( "No manager found: " +
//                                      dn + "; had these " +
//                                      "reports: " );
//                  Vector v = (Vector)managerTable.get( dn );
//                  for( int i = 0; i < v.size(); i++ ) {
//                      DefaultMutableTreeNode node =
//                          (DefaultMutableTreeNode)v.elementAt( i );
//                      System.out.println(
//                          "  " + getDNFromNode( node ) );
//                  }
                nInvalid++;
```

```
                managerTable.remove( dn );
            }
        }
        System.out.println( nInvalid + " managers no " +
                            "longer present" );
```

The managers table will map DNs to nodes. It is used later to select a node to return to the caller, if the caller used the second variant of parseTree. The method addEntriesToTree is called for each top-level node (under the virtual root node), to recursively add all entries from managerTable that report to the user corresponding to the node:

```
        // Create a cross-reference from DNs to nodes
        Hashtable managers = new Hashtable();
        // Add all subordinates to tree
        en = root.children();
        while( en.hasMoreElements() ) {
            DefaultMutableTreeNode node =
                (DefaultMutableTreeNode)en.nextElement();
            addEntriesToTree( node, managers,
                              managerTable );
        }
```

The method addEntriesToTree extracts the DN of the root node it receives and looks in the managerTable Hashtable for any nodes pointing to it. If there are any direct reports, a Vector is obtained from the table and each member of the Vector is added to the root node. If a member is listed in managerTable, then it has direct reports itself, so addEntriesToTree calls itself recursively to add all reports of that member.

The method can print out statistics on the relationships found for each node, but the relevant code is commented out in the block of code that follows. It may be useful to enable the printouts if you are having trouble interpreting the hierarchy found by the class, but the printouts are voluminous.

```
    /**
     * Add all entries in a Hashtable to a tree, sorting by
     * manager
     *
     * @param root the root node of the tree to add to. If it
     * is null, it is allocated in the method.
     * @param toAdd a Hashtable of directory entries
     * @param managers a Hashtable that on return maps DNs
     * to tree nodes
     * @return the root node of the tree
```

```
     */
    static protected DefaultMutableTreeNode addEntriesToTree(
        DefaultMutableTreeNode root,
        Hashtable managers,
        Hashtable managerTable ) {

        int childLess = 0;
        int childRich = 0;
        // Get all entries that have this manager
        String dn = getDNFromNode( root );
        Vector v = (Vector)managerTable.get( dn );
        if ( v != null ) {
            Enumeration children = v.elements();
            while( children.hasMoreElements() ) {
                DefaultMutableTreeNode nextNode =
                    (DefaultMutableTreeNode)
                    children.nextElement();
                String childDN = getDNFromNode( nextNode );
                // Recurse if this node is a manager
                if ( managerTable.containsKey( childDN ) ) {
                    childRich++;
                    addEntriesToTree( nextNode,
                                      managers,
                                      managerTable );
                } else {
                    childLess++;
                }
                // Add this child to the tree
                root.add( nextNode );
            }
            // Update manager Hashtable to point to this
            // node for the DN
            managers.put( dn, root );
        }
//          System.out.println( dn + " has " + childRich +
//                              " managers and " + childLess +
//                              " non-managers reporting" );
        return root;
    }
```

At this point we have the entire directory contents represented in a tree of `DefaultMutableTreeNode` objects. The only thing left to do is to decide which node to return to the caller:

```
        if ( rootDN != null ) {
            rootDN = normalizeDN( rootDN );
            Object o = managers.get( rootDN );
            return (DefaultMutableTreeNode)o;
        } else {
            return root;
        }
    }
```

You can have `ManagementParser` print the tree it has constructed to standard output. If you have installed the `airiusplus.ldif` file on your server, you will see a printout as in Figure 12-4. The higher a manager is in the hierarchy, the more indented her DN is in the display.

`ManagementParser` includes several internal utility methods. For example, a DN is normalized and changed to all lowercase with `normalizeDN`:

```
java ManagementParser-b "o=airius.com"

1 entries do not have a manager
1 top-level managers found
149 people who report to someone
0 managers no longer present
uid=tmorris, ou=people, o=airius.com
uid=dmiller, ou=people, o=airius.com
uid=gfarmer, ou=people, o=airius.com
uid=jwallace, ou=people, o=airius.com

...
uid=phun2, ou=people, o=airius.com
uid=dcope, ou=people, o=airius.com
uid=charvey, ou=people, o=airius.com
uid=alangdon, ou=people, o=airius.com
uid=bparker, ou=people, o=airius.com
uid=cnewport, ou=people, o=airius.com
      uid=kwinters, ou=people, o=airius.com
      uid=jvedder, ou=people, o=airius.com
```

FIGURE 12-4. *Tree printout from* `ManagementParser`.

```
/**
 * Normalize a DN (spacing)
 *
 * @param dn String to be normalized
 * @return a normalized DN String
 */
static protected String normalizeDN( String dn ) {
    return new DN( dn ).toString().toLowerCase();
}
```

The `createEntryNode` method in the following block of code creates a node from an `LDAPEntry`. The `UserObject` of a node is a `Hashtable` that contains various attribute values of the entry. If additional attributes are to be tracked and rendered using the nodes, then the `fetchAttrs` list should be extended and `createEntryNode` modified to store them.

```
/**
 * Create a tree node from info in an entry
 *
 * @param entry a directory entry with "cn" and optionally
 * also "title"
 * @return a tree node
 */
static protected DefaultMutableTreeNode createEntryNode(
    LDAPEntry entry ) {
    String mgr = normalizeDN(
        getManagerFromEntry( entry ) );
    String name = getValueFromEntry( entry, "cn" );
    String title = getTitleFromEntry( entry );
    String dn = normalizeDN( entry.getDN() );
    Hashtable ht = new Hashtable();
    if ( name != null ) {
        ht.put( "name", name );
    }
    if ( title != null ) {
        ht.put( "title", title );
    }
    if ( mgr != null ) {
        ht.put( "manager", mgr );
    }
    ht.put( "dn", dn );
    return new DefaultMutableTreeNode( ht );
}
```

In addition, utility methods extract values from an LDAPEntry or from a node:

```
/**
 * Get a single String attribute value from an entry
 *
 * @param entry a directory entry
 * @param name name of the attribute
 * @return the attribute value, or null if
 * the attribute is not present
 */
static protected String getValueFromEntry( LDAPEntry entry,
                                           String name ) {
    // Get the value from the entry
    LDAPAttribute attr = entry.getAttribute( name );
    if ( attr != null ) {
        Enumeration en = attr.getStringValues();
        if ( (en != null) && en.hasMoreElements() ) {
            return (String)en.nextElement();
        }
    }
    return null;
}

/**
 * Get a single String attribute value from a node
 *
 * @param node a tree node
 * @param name name of the attribute
 * @return the attribute value, or null if
 * the attribute is not present
 */
static protected String getValueFromNode(
    DefaultMutableTreeNode node,
    String name ) {
    Hashtable nodeEntry =
        (Hashtable)node.getUserObject();
    if( nodeEntry == null ) {
        return null;
    }
    return (String)nodeEntry.get( name );
}

/**
 * Get the DN from a node
```

```
 *
 * @param node a tree node
 * @return the DN value, or null if
 * the node doesn't have values
 */
static protected String
getDNFromNode( DefaultMutableTreeNode node ) {
    return getValueFromNode( node, "dn" );
}

/**
 * Get the manager DN from an entry
 *
 * @param entry a directory entry
 * @return the manager DN value, or null if
 * the manager attribute is not present
 */
static protected String
getManagerFromEntry( LDAPEntry entry ) {
    // Get the manager DN from the entry
    return getValueFromEntry( entry, "manager" );
}

/**
 * Get a title value from an entry
 *
 * @param entry a directory entry
 * @return String to use for title
 */
static protected String
getTitleFromEntry( LDAPEntry entry ) {
    for( int i = 0; i < _titleAttrs.length; i++ ) {
        String val =
            getValueFromEntry( entry, _titleAttrs[i] );
        if ( val != null ) {
            return val;
        }
    }
    return _defaultTitle;
}
```

An Alternative Strategy for Management Parsing

The CD-ROM that accompanies this book includes an alternative class for parsing the management relationships: `ManagementParser2` (see Figure 12-5). It builds the tree of nodes by starting at the top and doing a search at each node for entries that have the node as a manager, rather than doing a single search and then parsing the relationships in memory, as is done in `ManagementParser`. The intention is to demonstrate a top-down, search-as-you-go algorithm.

`ManagementParser2.parseTree` starts off just as `ManagementParser`: by creating a table of all top-level nodes. Then it searches for all person entries that have a `manager` attribute, as in `ManagementParser`, but it keeps only the table of managers and not the table of all employees:

```
        // Now get all managers
        Hashtable managerTable = getAllManagers( ldc, base );
```

The method `getAllManagers` is interested in only the `manager` attribute of each entry:

```
    // Filter string to retrieve users with a manager
    private static String _managerFilter =
        "(&(objectclass=person)(manager=*))";
...
```

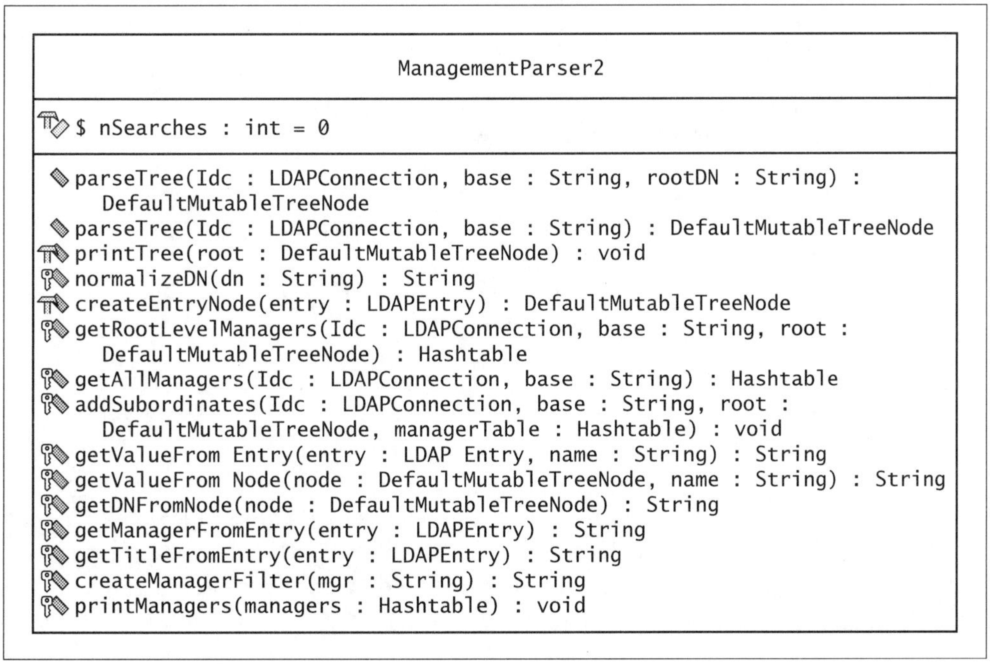

```
ManagementParser2

$ nSearches : int = 0

parseTree(ldc : LDAPConnection, base : String, rootDN : String) :
    DefaultMutableTreeNode
parseTree(ldc : LDAPConnection, base : String) : DefaultMutableTreeNode
printTree(root : DefaultMutableTreeNode) : void
normalizeDN(dn : String) : String
createEntryNode(entry : LDAPEntry) : DefaultMutableTreeNode
getRootLevelManagers(ldc : LDAPConnection, base : String, root :
    DefaultMutableTreeNode) : Hashtable
getAllManagers(ldc : LDAPConnection, base : String) : Hashtable
addSubordinates(ldc : LDAPConnection, base : String, root :
    DefaultMutableTreeNode, managerTable : Hashtable) : void
getValueFrom Entry(entry : LDAP Entry, name : String) : String
getValueFrom Node(node : DefaultMutableTreeNode, name : String) : String
getDNFromNode(node : DefaultMutableTreeNode) : String
getManagerFromEntry(entry : LDAPEntry) : String
getTitleFromEntry(entry : LDAPEntry) : String
createManagerFilter(mgr : String) : String
printManagers(managers : Hashtable) : void
```

FIGURE 12-5. `ManagementParser2`.

```
/**
 * Get all managers by searching for all entries that
 * have a manager attribute.
 *
 * @param ldc active connection to directory
 * @param base base DN from which to do a subtree search
 * @return a Hashtable with all manager DNs found
 */
static protected Hashtable
getAllManagers( LDAPConnection ldc,
                String base )
    throws LDAPException {
    // Get all person entries that have a manager
    Hashtable managers = new Hashtable();
    LDAPSearchConstraints cons =
        (LDAPSearchConstraints)ldc.getSearchConstraints().
        clone();
    cons.setMaxResults( 0 );
    LDAPSearchResults res =
        ldc.search( base,
                    ldc.SCOPE_SUB,
                    _managerFilter,
                    new String[] { "manager" },
                    false,
                    cons );
    while ( res.hasMoreElements() ) {
        try {
            LDAPEntry entry = res.next();
            // Extract the manager value
            String mgr =
                normalizeDN( getManagerFromEntry( entry ) );
            managers.put( mgr, mgr );
        } catch ( LDAPReferralException ref ) {
            // Just ignore referrals
        }
    }
    return managers;
}
```

To create the tree of nodes recursively, `ManagementParser2.addSubordinates` searches at each node for any entries pointing to it, if the node is known to be a manager node from the previous step. A static variable, `nSearches`, keeps track of the number of search operations completed:

```
/**
 * Get all entries that have a manager. Keep track of all
 * referenced managers.
 *
 * @param ldc active connection to directory
 * @param base base DN from which to do a subtree search
 * @param managerTable Hashtable to store DNs and
 * nodes of managers
 * @return a Hashtable mapping all employee DNs to nodes
 */
static protected void
addSubordinates( LDAPConnection ldc,
                 String base,
                 DefaultMutableTreeNode root,
                 Hashtable managerTable )
    throws LDAPException {

    // Get all entries that have this manager
    String dn = getDNFromNode( root );
    LDAPSearchConstraints cons =
        (LDAPSearchConstraints)ldc.getSearchConstraints().
        clone();
    cons.setMaxResults( 0 );
    // Find all person entries with this manager.
    // Retrieve each one's name, title, and manager.
    LDAPSearchResults res =
        ldc.search( base,
                    ldc.SCOPE_SUB,
                    createManagerFilter( dn ),
                    _fetchAttrs,
                    false,
                    cons );
    nSearches++;
    while ( res.hasMoreElements() ) {
        try {
            // Found an entry. Check if it is a manager.
            LDAPEntry entry = res.next();
            String childDN = normalizeDN( entry.getDN() );
            DefaultMutableTreeNode node =
                createEntryNode( entry );
            // Recurse if this is a manager
            if ( managerTable.containsKey( childDN ) ) {
                addSubordinates( ldc, base, node,
```

```
                                        managerTable );
                }
                root.add( node );
            } catch ( LDAPReferralException ref ) {
                // Just ignore referrals
            }
            if ( numReadEntries == 0 ) {
                managerTable.put( dn, root );
            }
        }
    }
```

The end results are the same as with `ManagementParser`, but performance is much worse if the organization contains a large number of managers, since each one is searched separately against the directory. However, the technique used here—progressively expanding the tree by doing a search—is useful in many cases. If an application expands a subtree lazily (only when a user clicks on a particular node, for example), then the technique may be efficient.

An Organizational Chart Tree Component

In Chapter 10 we used the `JTree` component from JFC to render the relationships of directory entries. `JTree` takes a `DefaultMutableTreeNode` as parameter, so we can use the output of `ManagementParser.parseTree` (or `ManagementParser2.parseTree`) to render reporting relationships with no effort. However, we would like to display the title of each manager along with the name inside a box, and we would like a tooltip to show the full DN of a node when a user places the cursor over it.

`OrgChartTreeCellRenderer` (Figure 12-6) replaces the default renderer for nodes. It contains a label for an icon, some space below it, and below that a compo-

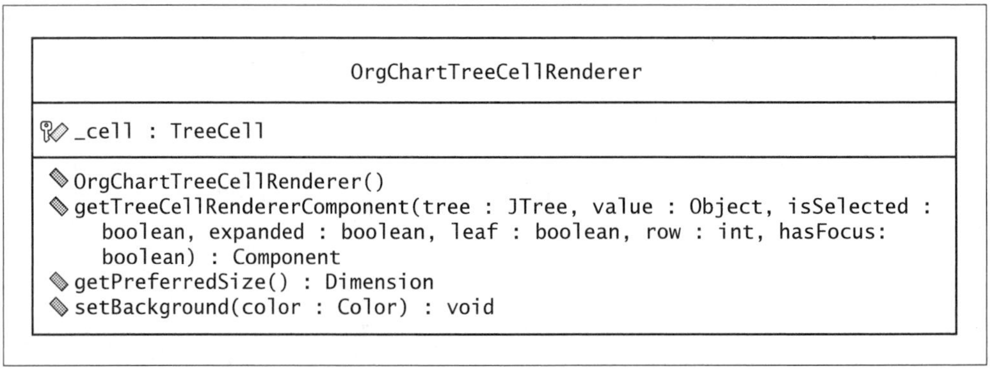

```
OrgChartTreeCellRenderer
------------------------
_cell : TreeCell
------------------------
OrgChartTreeCellRenderer()
getTreeCellRendererComponent(tree : JTree, value : Object, isSelected :
    boolean, expanded : boolean, leaf : boolean, row : int, hasFocus:
    boolean) : Component
getPreferredSize() : Dimension
setBackground(color : Color) : void
```

FIGURE 12-6. `OrgChartTreeCellRenderer`.

nent that will either display just the name of the person to which the node corresponds, or a name and title inside a box:

```
public class OrgChartTreeCellRenderer extends JPanel
                                    implements TreeCellRenderer {

    /**
     * Default constructor
     */
    public OrgChartTreeCellRenderer() {
        // Icon, and under that a TreeCell
        setLayout( new BoxLayout(this,BoxLayout.X_AXIS) );
        _icon = new JLabel() {
            public void setBackground( Color color ) {
                if( color instanceof ColorUIResource ) {
                    color = null;
                }
                super.setBackground( color );
            }
        };
        add( _icon );
        add( Box.createHorizontalStrut(4) );
        add( _cell = new TreeCell() );
    }
```

A `TreeCellRenderer` is required to provide only one public method—`getTreeCellRendererComponent`—to produce a component to display for a particular node. In this case the code for the method is completely standard except for setting a tooltip for the node based on information in the user object of the node:

```
    /**
     * TreeCellRenderer interface implementation
     */
    public Component getTreeCellRendererComponent(
        JTree tree,
        Object value,
        boolean isSelected, boolean expanded,
        boolean leaf, int row, boolean hasFocus) {
        setEnabled( tree.isEnabled() );
        _cell.setValue( value );
        _cell.setSelected( isSelected );
        _cell.setFocus( hasFocus );
        if ( leaf ) {
```

```
            _icon.setIcon(UIManager.getIcon("Tree.leafIcon"));
        } else if ( expanded ) {
            _icon.setIcon(UIManager.getIcon("Tree.openIcon"));
        } else {
            _icon.setIcon(UIManager.getIcon("Tree.closedIcon"));
        }
        DefaultMutableTreeNode node =
            (DefaultMutableTreeNode)value;
        Hashtable info = (Hashtable)node.getUserObject();
        setToolTipText( (String)info.get( "dn" ) );
        return this;
    }
```

The renderer must also override `JLabel.getPreferredSize`, or the manager boxes will be truncated on the right:

```
    /**
     * Calculate the size required as the sum of the icon and
     * the TreeCell
     *
     * @return the combined size of the icon and TreeCell
     */
    public Dimension getPreferredSize() {
        Dimension iconD = _icon.getPreferredSize();
        Dimension cellD = _cell.getPreferredSize();
        int height = Math.max( iconD.height, cellD.height );
        return new Dimension(iconD.width + cellD.width, height);
    }
```

The `TreeCell` class (Figure 12-7) is responsible for rendering all text, as well as a box if the node corresponds to a manager:

```
    /**
     * Panel containing name and title
     */
    class TreeCell extends JPanel {
        TreeCell() {
            setLayout( new BoxLayout( this, BoxLayout.Y_AXIS ) );
            setOpaque(true);
        }
```

The main overridden method in `TreeCell` is `setValue`. Information is pulled from the user object of the node to set the name and title. The title is rendered in italics. The member variable `_lines` keeps track of how many lines of text have been ren-

```
TreeCell
(from OrgChartTreeCellRenderer)

_lines : int = 0

TreeCell()
setBackground(color : Color) : void
setPreferredSize(d : Dimension) : void
getPreferredSize() : Dimension
setValue(o : Object) : void
setSelected(isSelected : boolean) : void
setFocus(hasFocus : boolean) : void
```

FIGURE 12-7. TreeCell.

dered. It is used to determine the size of the node and later to decide if a box is required around the text:

```
/**
 * Set the text contents and fonts based on info in the
 * user object of the tree node
 *
 * @param o a tree node with a Hashtable as UserObject
 */
public void setValue(Object o) {
    DefaultMutableTreeNode node =
        (DefaultMutableTreeNode)o;
    Hashtable info = (Hashtable)node.getUserObject();
    int maxWidth = 0;
    int height = 0;
    _lines = 0;
    removeAll();
    JLabel label =
        new JLabel( (String)info.get( "name" ) );
    add( label );
    Dimension dim = label.getPreferredSize();
    height += dim.height;
    if (maxWidth < dim.width) {
        maxWidth = dim.width;
    }
    _lines++;
    // Check if this is a container node
    if ( node.getChildCount() > 0 ) {
```

```
                label =
                    new JLabel( (String)info.get( "title" ) );
                add( label );
                dim = label.getPreferredSize();
                height += dim.height;
                if (maxWidth < dim.width) {
                    maxWidth = dim.width;
                }
                // Same font but italics for title
                Font font = label.getFont();
                font = new Font( font.getName(), font.ITALIC,
                                 font.getSize() );
                label.setFont( font );
                _lines++;
            }
            int margin = (_lines > 1) ? 2 : 0;
            setPreferredSize(
                new Dimension(maxWidth + 6 + 2*margin,
                              height + 2*margin));
        }
```

`TreeCell.setFocus` is called by `OrgChartTreeCellRenderer.getTreeCellRendererComponent`. If the node corresponds to a manager node (more than one line of text), it always applies a black border. If not, it uses the standard border color if the node has focus and no border if it doesn't:

```
        /**
         * Set the appropriate visuals for if the item has focus
         * or not.
         *
         * @param hasFocus true if the item has
         * focus
         */
        protected void setFocus( boolean hasFocus ) {
            int lineWidth = 1;
            // Put a black border around the cell if it contains
            // more than one line (i.e., it contains a title)
            if ( _lines > 1 ) {
                setBorder(BorderFactory.createLineBorder(
                    Color.black, lineWidth));
            } else {
                if ( hasFocus ) {
                    Color lineColor =
                        UIManager.getColor(
```

```
                              "Tree.selectionBorderColor");
                    setBorder(BorderFactory.createLineBorder(
                        lineColor));
                } else {
                    setBorder(BorderFactory.createEmptyBorder(
                        1,1,1,1));
                }
            }
        }
```

`OrgChartTree` (Figure 12-8) is a driver class for displaying a tree using `ManagementParser` and `OrgChartTreeCellRenderer`. It extends `JTree`, and it takes `DefaultMutableTreeNode` as a constructor argument and passes it to the `JTree` superclass constructor.

To handle the case in which there is a virtual root node (that is, more than one top-level node), `OrgChartTree` hides the root node if it doesn't contain a user object. Then it sets its cell renderer, and it is ready to go. It can be placed and displayed just as any other `JTree`:

```
public class OrgChartTree extends JTree {
    /**
     * Constructor
     *
     * @param root root node of a tree of DefaultMutableTreeNode
     */
    public OrgChartTree( DefaultMutableTreeNode root ) {
        super( root );
        if ( root.getUserObject() == null ) {
            // Must be a virtual root
            setRootVisible( false );
        }
```

OrgChartTree
$ _debug : boolean = false
OrgChartTree(root : DefaultMutableTreeNode, ldc : LDAPConnection) enableToolTips(state : boolean) : void main(args : String[]) : void

FIGURE 12-8. `OrgChartTree`.

```
        setCellRenderer( new OrgChartTreeCellRenderer() );
    }
```

JTree doesn't normally display tooltips, so OrgChartTree provides a method to turn them on or off. Tooltips are truncated by the frame of the application or applet, and DNs tend to be long. If the tree is to be displayed in a small window, it may be visually more appealing to turn the tooltips off.

```
    /**
     * Enable or disable tooltips
     *
     * @param state true to enable tooltips
     */
    public void enableToolTips( boolean state ) {
        ToolTipManager mgr = ToolTipManager.sharedInstance();
        if ( state ) {
            // Enable tooltips
            mgr.registerComponent( this );
        } else {
            mgr.unregisterComponent( this );
        }
    }
```

The main method parses command-line arguments, creates and connects an LDAPConnection object, and then uses ManagementParser to create a tree of directory nodes:

```
        // Get a tree of users, organized by reporting
        // structure
        DefaultMutableTreeNode root = null;
        try {
            root = ManagementParser.parseTree( ldc, base,
                                               rootDN );
        } catch ( LDAPException e ) {
            System.err.println( e );
            System.exit( 1 );
        }
```

The root node returned by ManagementParser is then provided to the consructor OrgChartTree, the top-level node is expanded, tooltips are enabled, and the tree is displayed in a dialog box:

```
        // Create a tree component with the nodes found
        OrgChartTree tree = new OrgChartTree( root, ldc );
```

```
        tree.expandPath( tree.getPathForRow( 0 ) );
        tree.enableToolTips( true );

        // Create frame
        Dimension dim = new Dimension( 300, 400 );
        new SimpleDialog( "OrgChartTree " + base, tree, 0, 0,
                          dim, true ).show();
```

The command-line options are as follows:

```
OrgChartTree -b BASEDN [-D AUTHDN] [-w AUTHPASSWORD]
[-r ROOTMANAGERDN] [-h HOST] [-p PORT]
```

If you have a server running on your local machine at port 389, and you have installed the `airiusplus.ldif` file supplied on the CD-ROM that accompanies this book, you can display the tree with the following command:

```
java OrgChartTree -b "o=airius.com"
```

The tree shown in Figure 12-9 will be displayed.

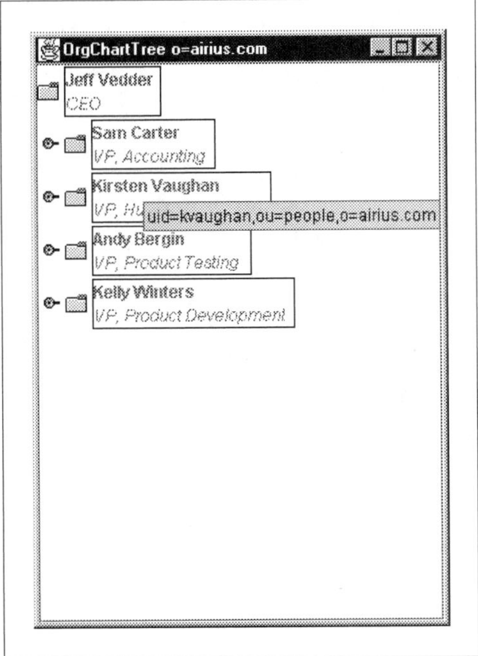

FIGURE 12-9. `OrgChartTree`.

The tree can be expanded to display any part of the organization, as illustrated in Figure 12-10.

A More Traditional Organizational Chart Component

The vertical tree view takes a little getting used to as an organizational chart. In addition to `OrgChartTree`, the CD-ROM that accompanies this book contains `OrgChartPanel` (Figure 12-11), a `JPanel` with nested vertically and horizontally oriented panels to render a hierarchy in a more familiar way.

The `OrgChart` class is a driver application for the panel. Its `main` method parses command-line parameters and invokes `ManagementParser.parseTree` in the same way as `OrgChartTree` does, but then it creates an `OrgChartPanel` instead of a `JTree`:

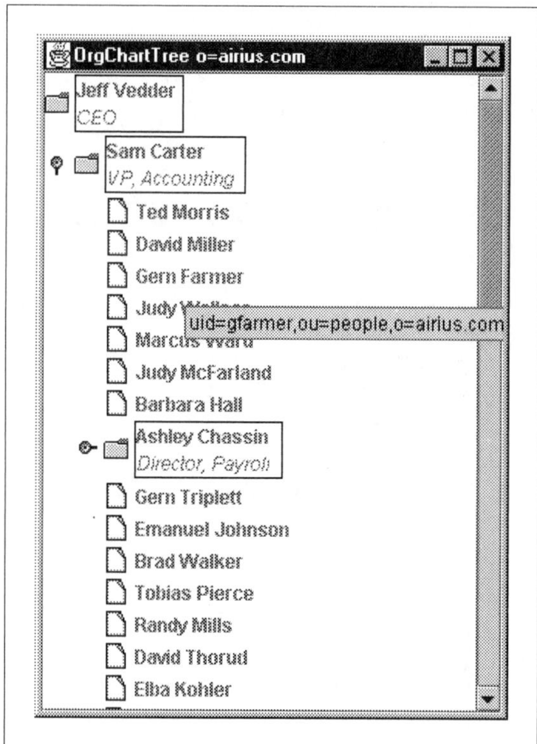

FIGURE 12-10. *Expanded* `OrgChartTree`.

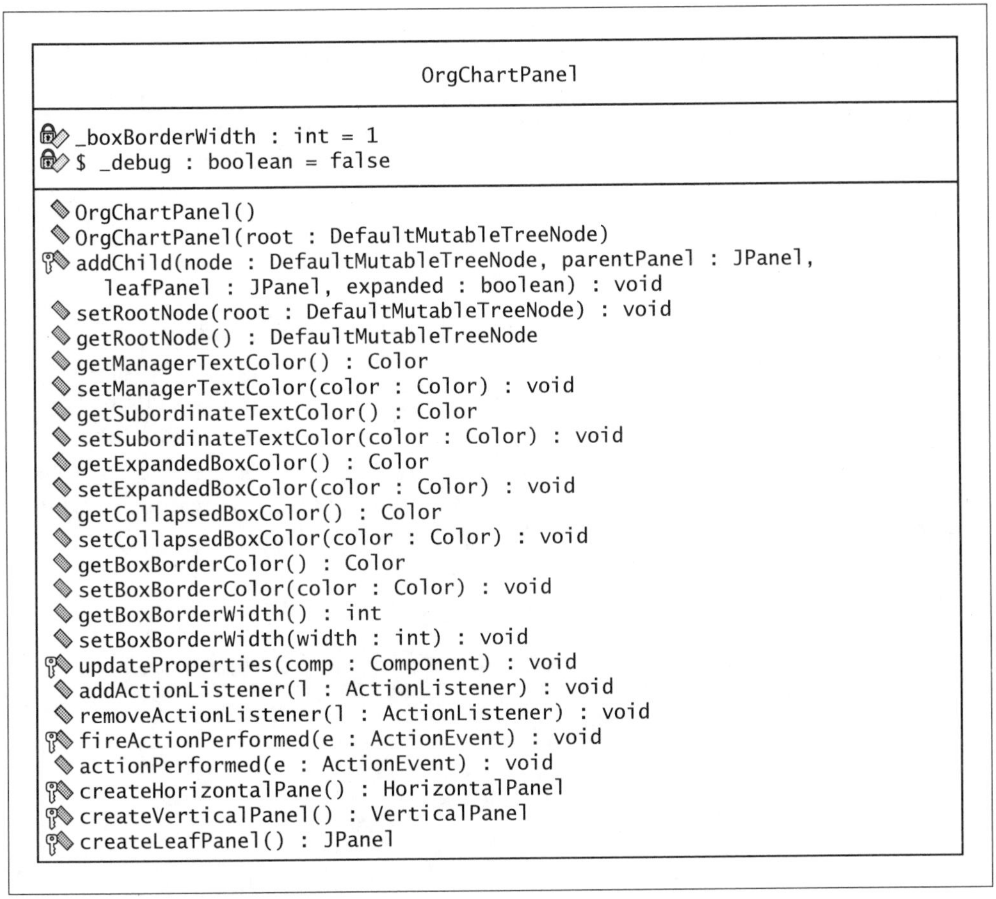

```
OrgChartPanel
-------------------------------------------------------------
_boxBorderWidth : int = 1
$ _debug : boolean = false
-------------------------------------------------------------
OrgChartPanel()
OrgChartPanel(root : DefaultMutableTreeNode)
addChild(node : DefaultMutableTreeNode, parentPanel : JPanel,
    leafPanel : JPanel, expanded : boolean) : void
setRootNode(root : DefaultMutableTreeNode) : void
getRootNode() : DefaultMutableTreeNode
getManagerTextColor() : Color
setManagerTextColor(color : Color) : void
getSubordinateTextColor() : Color
setSubordinateTextColor(color : Color) : void
getExpandedBoxColor() : Color
setExpandedBoxColor(color : Color) : void
getCollapsedBoxColor() : Color
setCollapsedBoxColor(color : Color) : void
getBoxBorderColor() : Color
setBoxBorderColor(color : Color) : void
getBoxBorderWidth() : int
setBoxBorderWidth(width : int) : void
updateProperties(comp : Component) : void
addActionListener(l : ActionListener) : void
removeActionListener(l : ActionListener) : void
fireActionPerformed(e : ActionEvent) : void
actionPerformed(e : ActionEvent) : void
createHorizontalPane() : HorizontalPanel
createVerticalPanel() : VerticalPanel
createLeafPanel() : JPanel
```

FIGURE 12-11. OrgChartPanel.

```
// Get a tree of users, organized by reporting structure
DefaultMutableTreeNode root = null;
try {
    root = ManagementParser.parseTree( _ldc, base, rootDN );
} catch ( LDAPException e ) {
    System.err.println( e );
    System.exit( 1 );
}

// Create a panel component with the nodes found
OrgChartPanel org = new OrgChartPanel( root );
```

The panel is then displayed in a dialog box in the same way that `OrgChartTree` displays its `JTree`. Manager boxes have a different color and a different tooltip when expanded and when collapsed. To expand a box, you click on it. The initial view when using `airiusplus.ldif` shows only the single top-level node, as in Figure 12-12. Tooltips display the DNs of each node. Display the organizational chart with the following command:

```
java OrgChart -b "o=airius.com"
```

Nonmanagers reporting to each manager are listed vertically, to the right of any reporting managers. Any individuals who have neither a manager nor anyone reporting to them appear in a vertical listing to the right of any top-level managers (see Figure 12-13).

`OrgChartPanel` offers several properties for customization, shown in Table 12-1, to be accessed using the standard JavaBean conventions of `getProperty` and `setProperty`. It also provides an interface for `ActionListeners` to be notified when a user clicks on any name. We will get back to this interface later in the chapter.

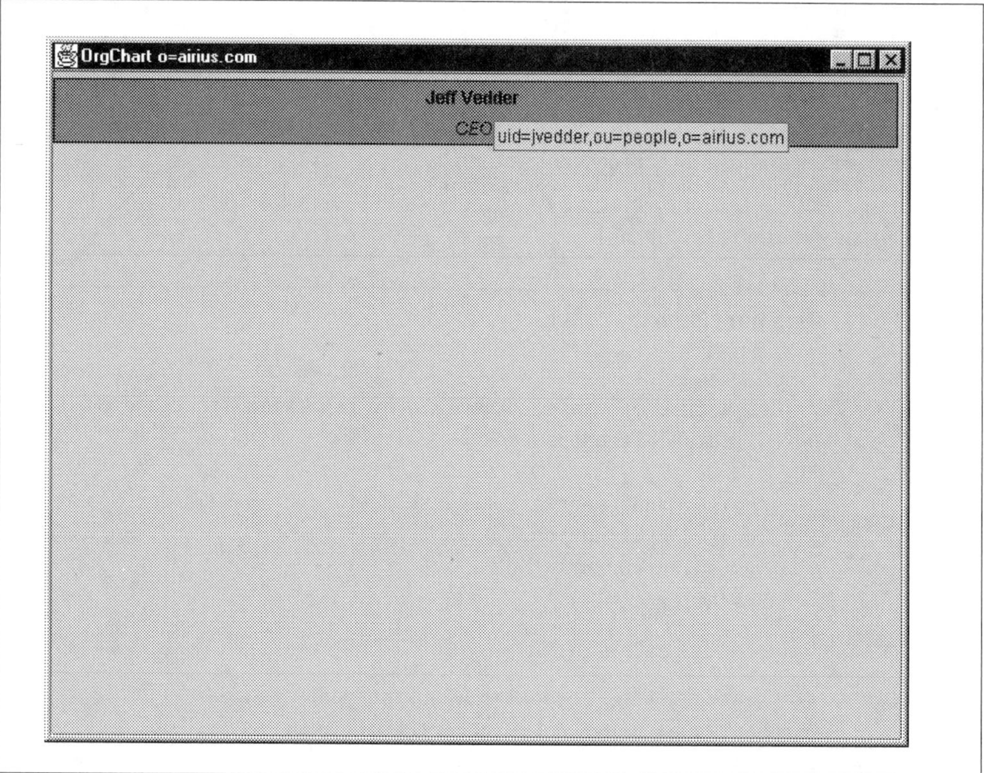

FIGURE 12-12. *Initial view of* `OrgChart`.

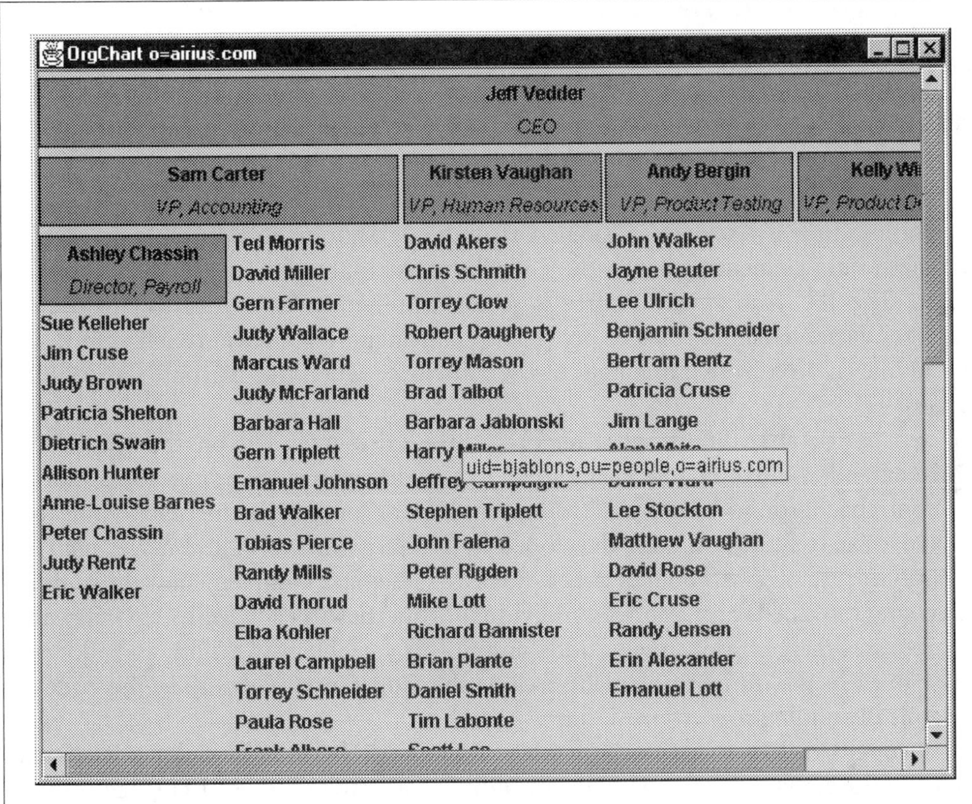

FIGURE 12-13. `OrgChart` *with a few nodes expanded.*

TABLE 12-1. `OrgChartPanel` *properties.*

PROPERTY NAME	DESCRIPTION
`managerTextColor`	Color of the text in a manager box
`subordinateTextColor`	Color of the labels for nonmanagers
`expandedBoxColor`	Color of the manager boxes when expanded
`collapsedBoxColor`	Color of the manager boxes when collapsed
`boxBorderColor`	Color of the borders of manager boxes
`boxBorderWidth`	Width in pixels of the borders of manager boxes

Inspecting Properties of an Entry

Regardless of how a tree or a list of directory entries is organized or displayed, individual attributes of an entry often need to be examined and sometimes updated. The CD-ROM that accompanies this book includes a component (`PropertyTable`) that extends `JTable` and can be used to display the contents of a directory entry.

Unlike most relational data views, a directory view of an entry must be able to present multiple values for a single attribute. It should also be able to display odd-sized data elements, such as the `jpegPhoto` attribute of a user, and not just text values. The JFC component `JTable` is severely limited in both regards. It does not allow for variable-height rows or provide for concatenating adjacent table cells (as we would like to do for the name field of each attribute when the attribute has multiple values).

`PropertyTable` builds on `FlexibleTable` (also included on the CD-ROM), which extends `JTable` in addressing these two issues, as well as in providing individual font, background color, and foreground color properties for each table cell. `FlexibleTable` builds on code developed by Nobuo Tamemasa and made available by him at `http://www.codeguru.com/java/`. Tamemasa's implementation supports coalescing table cells and applying individual properties to each cell. `FlexibleTable` incorporates these improvements, adds support for variable row height, and addresses a few bugs in the initial implementation at the CodeGuru Web site in the code for dynamically adding rows to the table.

`PropertyTable` is a `FlexibleTable` (Figure 12-14) that populates itself with data from a directory entry. The most useful constructor takes an LDAP connection and a DN as parameters and uses the connection to populate the table from the entry corresponding to the DN.

The data is supplied to the table by an `LDAPTableModel` object (Figure 12-15). `LDAPTableModel` extends `FlexibleTableModel`, which extends `DefaultTableModel`:

```
/**
 * Constructor to read content from a directory
 * entry
 *
 * @param ldc an active directory connection
 * @param dn DN of the entry to read
 */
public PropertyTable( LDAPConnection ldc, String dn ) {
    this( new LDAPTableModel( ldc, dn ) );
    _ldc = ldc;
    _dn = dn;
}
```

FlexibleTable
FlexibleTable(model : TableModel)
getVariableCellRect(row : int, column : int, include Spacing : boolean) : Rectangle
getCellRect(row : int, column : int, includeSpacing : boolean) : Rectangle
adjustRowColumn(corner : int[], cellAtt : CellAttribute, doBoth : boolean) : void
rowColumnAtPoint(point : Point) : int[]
rowAtPoint(point : Point) : int
columnAtPoint(point : Point) : int
columnSelectionChanged(e : ListSelectionEvent) : void
valueChanged(e : ListSelectionEvent) : void
tableChanged(e : TableModelEvent) : void
tableRowsInserted(e : TableModelEvent) : void
tableRowsDeleted(e : TableModelEvent) : void
getRowHeight(row : int) : int
setRowHeight(row : int, height : int) : void
resetRowHeight(row : int) : void
resetRowHeight() : void
dumpCellSpans() : void
PropertyTable
$ _colWidths[] : int = {150,320}
_toolTipsEnabled : boolean = false
PropertyTable()
PropertyTable(model : TableModel)
PropertyTable(ldc : LDAPConnection, dn : String)
initialize() : void
setDN(dn : String) : void
getDN() : String
setLDAPConnection(ldc : LDAPConnection) : void
getLDAPConnection() : LDAPConnection
setToolTipsEnabled(on : boolean) : void
getToolTipsEnabled() : boolean
isCellEditable(row : int, column : int) : boolean
getToolTipCell(event : MouseEvent) : int[]
getToolTipText(event : MouseEvent) : String
getToolTipLocation(event : MouseEvent) : Point
setColumnWidths(widths : int[]) : int
main(args : String[]) : void

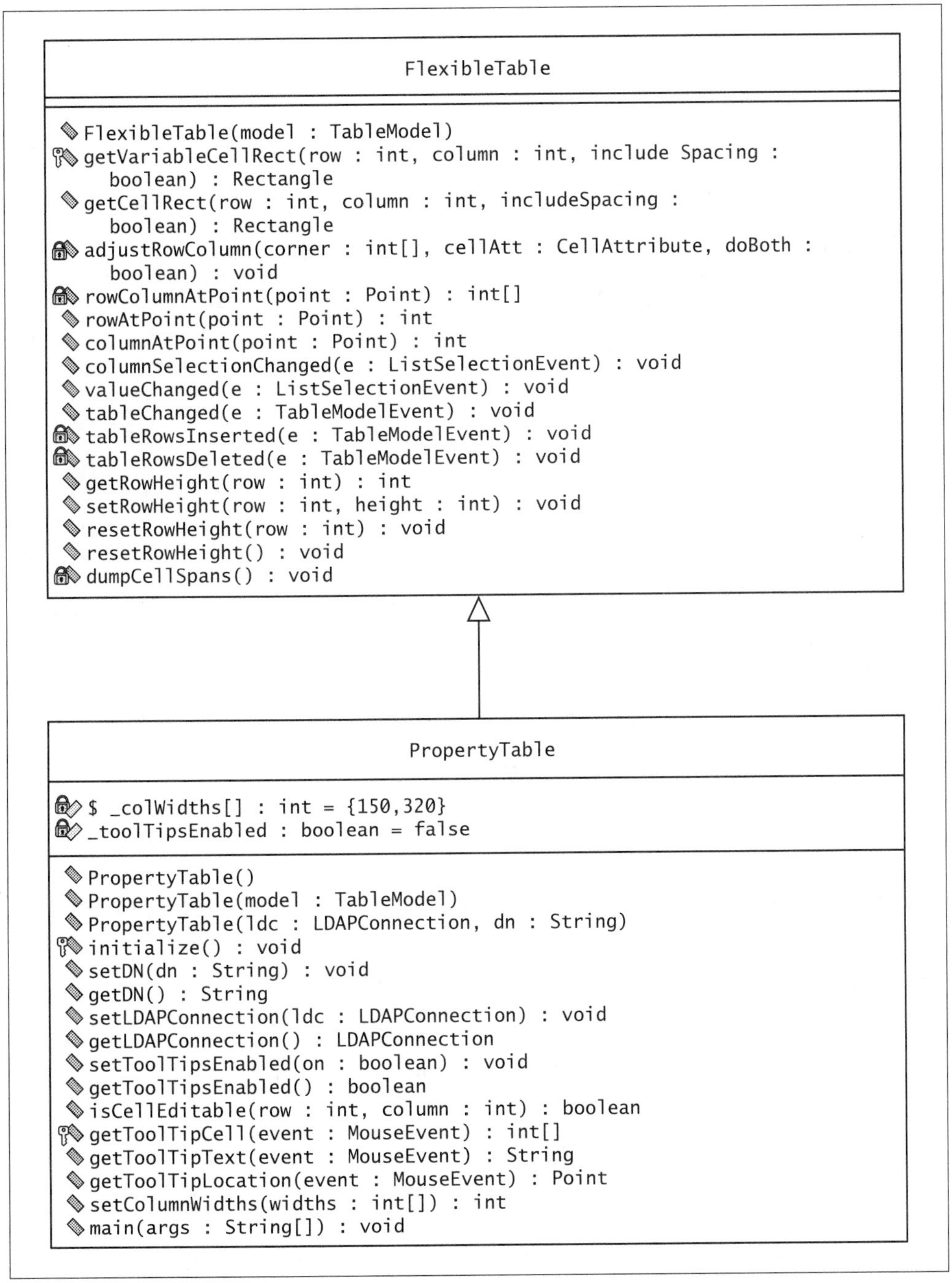

FIGURE 12-14. FlexibleTable *and* PropertyTable.

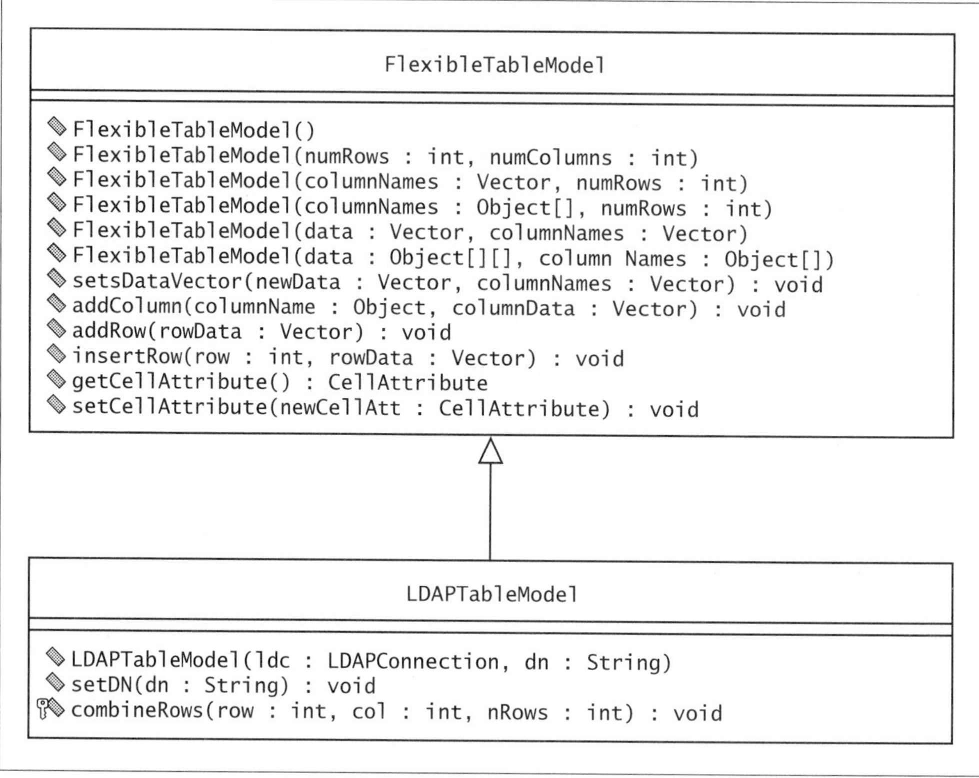

FIGURE 12-15. `FlexibleTableModel` *and* `LDAPTableModel`.

The class has a `setDN` method to change the DN. Calling `setDN` results in the internal creation of a new data model and repopulation of the table. A single table object can be quickly refreshed with new directory data in this way:

```
/**
 * Set the DN of the model; repopulate the table from
 * the specified directory entry
 *
 * @param dn the DN of the entry to read
 */
public void setDN( String dn ) {
    setModel( new LDAPTableModel( _ldc, dn ) );
    initialize();
}
```

PropertyTable allows the default column widths to be changed with setColumnWidths. An individual row height can be set with the setRowHeight method of FlexibleTable.

All the action in LDAPTableModel is in the setDN method, which reads data from the directory in the usual way but puts the results in a Vector of Vectors (one for each row), which is the format used by the JFC DefaultTableModel:

```
/**
 * Reads and parses directory entry
 *
 * @param dn DN of entry to read
 */
public void setDN( String dn ) {
    if ( _ldc == null ) {
        System.err.println( "No LDAP connection" );
        return;
    }
    _dn = dn;
    if ( _dn == null ) {
        return;
    }
    try {
        LDAPEntry entry = _ldc.read( dn );
        Enumeration attrs =
            entry.getAttributeSet().getAttributes();
        // Starting row of the next attribute
        int row = 0;
        while( attrs.hasMoreElements() ) {
            LDAPAttribute attr =
                (LDAPAttribute)attrs.nextElement();
            int nVals = 0;
            Enumeration vals = attr.getStringValues();
            while( (vals != null) &&
                   vals.hasMoreElements() ) {
                // Each table row is a Vector with two
                // elements
                Vector v = new Vector();
                v.addElement( attr.getName() );
                v.addElement( (String)vals.nextElement() );
                nVals++;
                addRow( v );
            }
            // Combine the name column for all values of
```

```
                // the same attribute
                if ( nVals > 1 ) {
                    combineRows( row, 0, nVals );
                }
                row += nVals;
            }
        } catch ( LDAPException e ) {
            System.err.println( "LDAPTableModel.setDN: " + e );
        }
    }
```

The only unusual thing here is that if an attribute has more than one value, the table cells for the name of the attribute are combined into one, using the `CellAttribute` object of the model. A `CellAttribute` object (see Figure 12-16) manages the colors

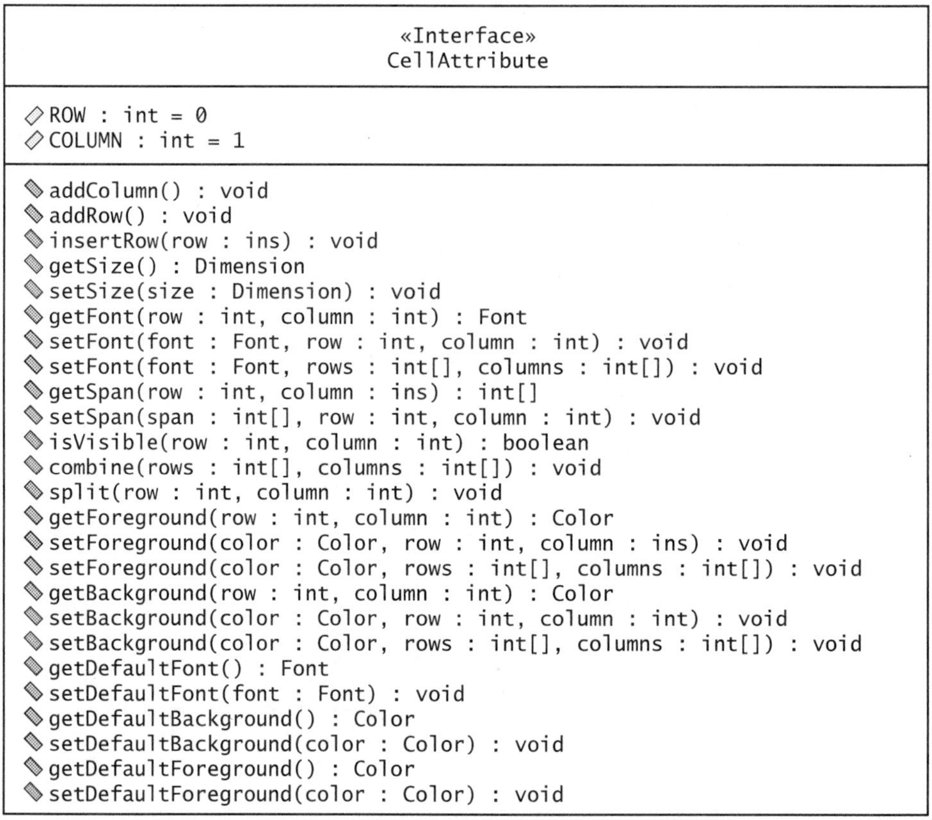

```
«Interface»
CellAttribute
---
ROW : int = 0
COLUMN : int = 1
---
addColumn() : void
addRow() : void
insertRow(row : ins) : void
getSize() : Dimension
setSize(size : Dimension) : void
getFont(row : int, column : int) : Font
setFont(font : Font, row : int, column : int) : void
setFont(font : Font, rows : int[], columns : int[]) : void
getSpan(row : int, column : ins) : int[]
setSpan(span : int[], row : int, column : int) : void
isVisible(row : int, column : int) : boolean
combine(rows : int[], columns : int[]) : void
split(row : int, column : int) : void
getForeground(row : int, column : int) : Color
setForeground(color : Color, row : int, column : ins) : void
setForeground(color : Color, rows : int[], columns : int[]) : void
getBackground(row : int, column : int) : Color
setBackground(color : Color, row : int, column : int) : void
setBackground(color : Color, rows : int[], columns : int[]) : void
getDefaultFont() : Font
setDefaultFont(font : Font) : void
getDefaultBackground() : Color
setDefaultBackground(color : Color) : void
getDefaultForeground() : Color
setDefaultForeground(color : Color) : void
```

FIGURE 12-16. `CellAttribute`.

and fonts of individual cells of a model and controls which cells are to be treated as a single, merged cell:

```
/**
 * Ask the CellAttribute of this model to combine several
 * table cell rows into one
 *
 * @param row starting row
 * @param col column to combine
 * @param nRows number of row cells to combine
 */
protected void combineRows( int row, int col, int nRows ) {
    CellAttribute cellAtt =
        (CellAttribute)getCellAttribute();
    int[] r = new int[nRows];
    for( int i = 0; i < nRows; i++ ) {
        r[i] = row + i;
    }
    int[] c = { col };
    cellAtt.combine( r, c );
}
```

PropertyTable has a main method that parses command-line arguments, creates and connects an LDAPConnection object, and then creates a PropertyTable. It sets the font of the left column (attribute names) to bold and then displays the table in a dialog box:

```
PropertyTable table = null;

// Connect to server
LDAPConnection ldc = new LDAPConnection();
try {
    ldc.connect( host,
                 port,
                 authDN,
                 authPassword );
    table = new PropertyTable( ldc, dn );
    // Bold for attribute names
    FlexibleTableModel m =
        (FlexibleTableModel)table.getModel();
    CellAttribute cellAtt =
        (CellAttribute)m.getCellAttribute();
    Font font = cellAtt.getFont( 0, 0 );
    font = new Font( font.getName(), font.BOLD,
```

```
                              font.getSize() );
            for( int j = 0; j < m.getRowCount(); j++ ) {
                cellAtt.setFont( font, j, 0 );
            }
        } catch ( LDAPException e ) {
            System.err.println( e );
            System.exit( 1 );
        }

        Dimension dim = new Dimension( 550, 300 );
        new SimpleDialog( "PropertyTable " + dn, table, 0, 0,
                          dim, true ).show();
```

The command-line arguments are similar to those of the other applications:

```
java PropertyTable [-D AUTHDN] [-w AUTHPASSWORD] [-h HOST]
[-p PORT] DN
```

We can display the contents of Jeff Vedder's directory entry by entering the following command:

```
java PropertyTable "uid=jvedder,ou=people,o=airius.com"
```

The dialog box displays the entry as in Figure 12-17.

`PropertyTable` is read-only. It prevents editing of table cells by overriding `JTable.isCellEditable`:

```
    /**
     * Override DefaultTableModel.isCellEditable to disallow
     * editing.
     *
     * @param row the row of the cell being queried
     * @param column the column of the cell being queried
     * @return true if the cell is editable
     */
    public boolean isCellEditable( int row,
                                   int column ) {
        if ( column == 0 ) {
            // Never allow editing the attribute name
            return false;
        }
        // For now, do not allow editing the values either
```

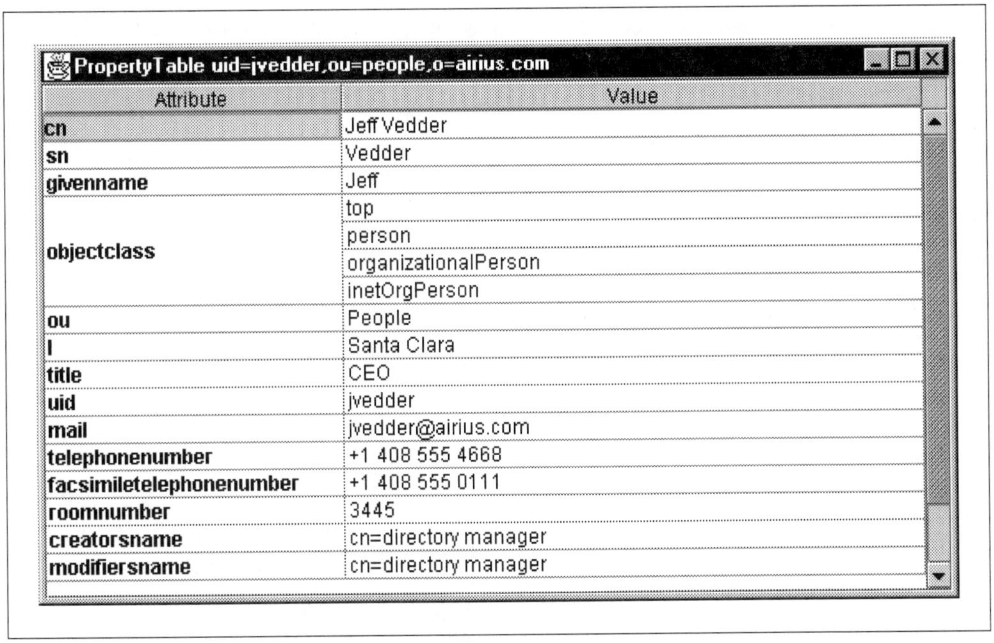

PropertyTable uid=jvedder,ou=people,o=airius.com

Attribute	Value
cn	Jeff Vedder
sn	Vedder
givenname	Jeff
objectclass	top
	person
	organizationalPerson
	inetOrgPerson
ou	People
l	Santa Clara
title	CEO
uid	jvedder
mail	jvedder@airius.com
telephonenumber	+1 408 555 4668
facsimiletelephonenumber	+1 408 555 0111
roomnumber	3445
creatorsname	cn=directory manager
modifiersname	cn=directory manager

FIGURE 12-17. `PropertyTable` *for Jeff Vedder.*

```
        return false;
    }
```

This is where we offer the unavoidable exercise for the reader: extend `PropertyTable` to become a full-fledged property editor for directory entries. Doing this would require changing the return value from `isCellEditable` to `true` for column 1, and then handling any changes made by the user. Changed values would need to be written to the directory. We would need a way to add values and to delete them. And finally, the editor would have to be able to display, or at least handle, binary values.

Connecting the Property Table and the Directory Viewers

Let's see how to instantiate a `PropertyTable` from the various directory viewers we have developed in Chapters 10 and 12.

`OrgChartTree` *and* `PropertyTable`

To launch a `PropertyTable` view when a node is double-clicked in an `OrgChartTree`, we need to do two things: pass an `LDAPConnection` object to its constructor and have the `OrgChartTree` object listen for mouse events. If there is a double-click event, then the DN of the node is extracted from its user object and a PropertyTable is created and placed in a dialog box:

```
/**
 * Constructor
 *
 * @param root root node of a tree of DefaultMutableTreeNode
 * @param ldc an active connection to a directory
 */
public OrgChartTree( DefaultMutableTreeNode root,
                     LDAPConnection ldc ) {
    super( root );
    _ldc = ldc;
    if ( root.getUserObject() == null ) {
        // Must be a virtual root
        setRootVisible( false );
    }
    setCellRenderer( new OrgChartTreeCellRenderer() );
    addMouseListener( new MouseAdapter() {
        public void mouseClicked(MouseEvent e) {
            if (e.getClickCount() == 2) { // double click
                TreePath path =
                    getPathForLocation( e.getX(),
                                        e.getY() );
                if ( path == null ) {
                    return;
                }
                DefaultMutableTreeNode node =
                    (DefaultMutableTreeNode)
                    path.getLastPathComponent();
                Hashtable ht =
                    (Hashtable)node.getUserObject();
                String dn = (String)ht.get( "dn" );
                if ( dn != null ) {
                    JTable table =
                        new PropertyTable( _ldc, dn );
                    Dimension dim =
                        new Dimension( 500, 350 );
                    new SimpleDialog( dn, table, 20, 20,
                                      dim, false ).show();
                }
            }
        }
    } );
}
```

Figure 12-18 illustrates the results of double-clicking on the node for David Miller.

`OrgChart` *and* `PropertyTable`

We mentioned earlier that `OrgChartPanel` can supply an `ActionListener` with events. Whenever a user clicks on a name in the panel, all registered `ActionListeners` are called with an `ActionEvent`. The action command is the DN of the corresponding directory entry. To receive and process this event, the `OrgChart` application must register itself as an `ActionListener` with the `OrgChartPanel` and implement the `actionPerformed` method of the `ActionListener` interface:

```
public class OrgChart implements ActionListener {
    public OrgChart( String[] args ) {
...
        // Create a panel component with the nodes found
        OrgChartPanel org = new OrgChartPanel( root );
        org.setSubordinateTextColor( Color.blue );
        org.addActionListener( this );
```

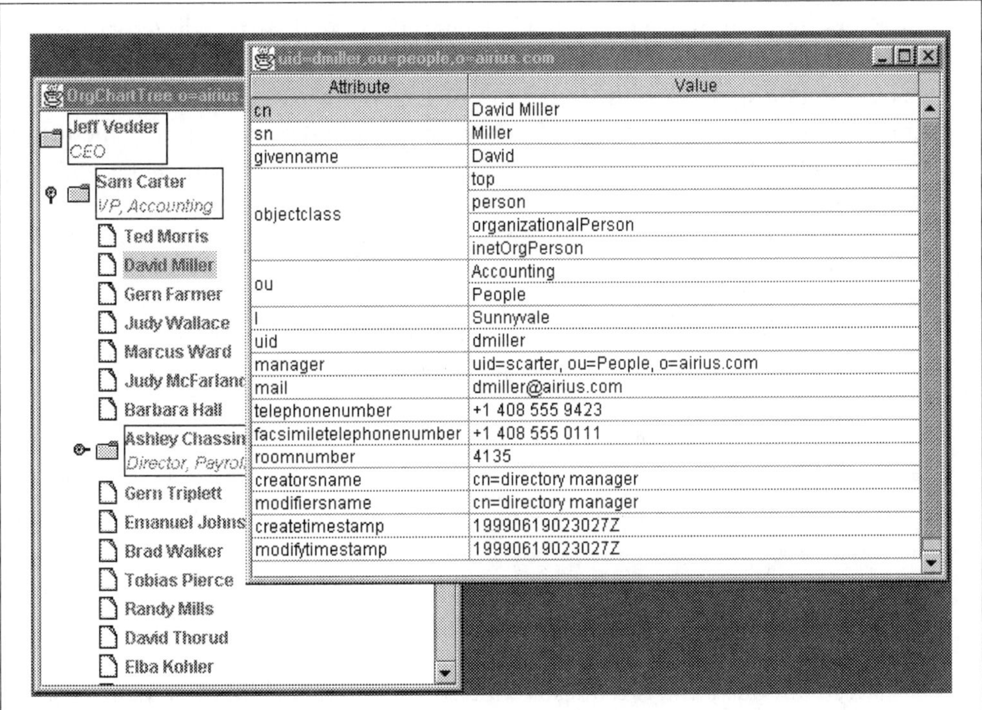

FIGURE 12-18. *Popping up a* `PropertyTable` *from* `OrgChartTree`.

```
    ...
    }
        /**
         * Handle events from clicking on a user node
         *
         * @param e event from a button; the action command
         * is the DN of the user entry
         */
        public void actionPerformed( ActionEvent e ) {
            if ( e.getSource() instanceof JButton ) {
                String dn = e.getActionCommand();
                System.out.println( dn );
                // The action command is the DN of an entry to view
                JTable table = new PropertyTable( _ldc, dn );
                Dimension dim = new Dimension( 500, 300 );
                new SimpleDialog( dn, table, 20, 20,
                                  dim, false ).show();
            }
        }
```

TestTree *and* PropertyTable

The TestTree application we presented in Chapter 10 can display a directory tree as a JTree, and optionally also as a table that presents a few attributes each of all child entries of the node selected in the tree. For our concluding example of LDAP component integration, we will extend TestTree to optionally request a third pane to present all attributes of the entry selected in the child table. The third pane will be a PropertyTable.

In parsing command-line arguments, TestTree will now allow the values 1 through 3 for the number of panes, rather than 1 through 2:

```
} else if ( args[i].compareTo("-panes" ) == 0 ) {
    if ( (i + 1) < args.length ) {

        nPanes = Integer.parseInt(args[i+1]);

        invalid = ( (nPanes < 1) || (nPanes > 3) );

        i++;

    }
```

If more than one pane is requested, a tree panel and a child table panel are created and inserted into a horizontal splitter pane as before. If more than two panes are requested, a PropertyTable object is created as well. The horizontal splitter pane and the `PropertyTable` object are added to a vertical splitter pane. `TestTree` creates a listener for selection events in the child table. When a row is selected, the DN of the corresponding directory entry is obtained from the child table and the `PropertyTable` object is asked to refresh itself from the new DN:

```
if ( nPanes > 1 ) {
    // Show both a tree and a table
    final SimpleTable table = new SimpleTable();
    // Hook the table to the tree with an adapter
    EntryListAdapter lister =
        new EntryListAdapter( ldc,
                              table );
    tree.addDirNodeListener( lister );
    // A panel is required to keep the background
    // the right color
    JPanel tablePanel =
        addTableToScrollPanel( table );

    JSplitPane splitPane =
        new JSplitPane(JSplitPane.HORIZONTAL_SPLIT,
                       treeSp, tablePanel);
    splitPane.setBorder(
        new EmptyBorder(6, 6, 6, 6) );

    if ( nPanes > 2 ) {
        // Add a property table to show all
        // properties of a selected table row
        final PropertyTable ptable =
            new PropertyTable( ldc, "" );
        tablePanel =
            addTableToScrollPanel( ptable );

        // A vertical splitter pane, with the
        // property table at the bottom
        JSplitPane triPane =
            new JSplitPane(
                JSplitPane.VERTICAL_SPLIT,
                splitPane, tablePanel);
        triPane.setBorder(
            new EmptyBorder(6, 6, 6, 6) );
        triPane.setDividerLocation( 200 );
        frame.getContentPane().add( triPane );
        frame.setSize( new Dimension( 650, 450 ) );
        // Listen for selection changes in the
```

```
                // simple table and notify the property
                // table
                ListSelectionModel m =
                    table.getSelectionModel();
                m.addListSelectionListener(
                    new ListSelectionListener() {
                        public void valueChanged(
                            ListSelectionEvent e) {
                            int index =
                                table.getSelectedRow();
                            String dn =(String)
                                table.getKeyAt( index );
                            ptable.setDN( dn );
                        }
                });
            } else {
                // Two panes
                frame.getContentPane().add( splitPane );
                frame.setSize( new Dimension( 650, 300 ) );
            }
        } else {
            // One pane - just show the tree
            frame.getContentPane().add( treeSp );
            frame.setSize( new Dimension( 200, 300 ) );
        }
```

You can now request three panes, using the following command:

```
java TestTree -panes 3
```

As you click through the tree, the table on the right is updated (Figure 12-19). As you click on a row in the table on the right, the table below is updated with all attributes for the entry.

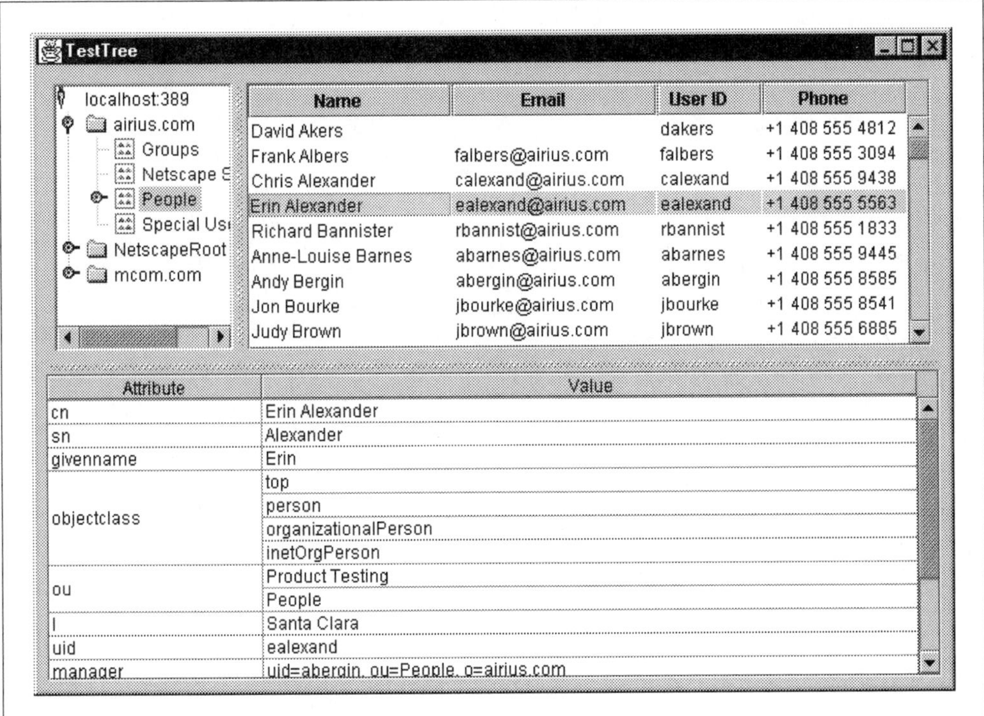

FIGURE 12-19. *Three-pane directory browser.*

Conclusion

In this chapter we have discussed alternative views of directory relationships, investigated ways to capture these relationships in an internal tree structure, and given examples of the alternative structures with two different components for rendering an organizational chart from directory data.

We continued our exploration of LDAP GUI components with a property table viewer and demonstrated how to connect it to other GUI components with standard JavaBean event interfaces. Our collection of reusable LDAP JavaBeans is now substantial, and most importantly, we know how to create new ones and how to integrate them into applications.

CHAPTER 13

Servlets and LDAP

Most of the examples and discussion in the book so far have pertained to using the LDAP SDK in a client application or applet. This chapter will focus on using the SDK in server applications. We will build a general-purpose server-side phone book application that can be used to provide HTML access to an LDAP directory. The application will be built as a Java servlet and provide digital certificate (X.509v3) lookup and the ability to view someone's photograph. The servlet also supports the concept of internal and external users.

Server-side applications typically are exposed to much higher bandwidth requirements than client-side programs, and we will look closely at squeezing maximal performance from the SDK. Let's begin the journey into server-side use of the SDK.

Overview of Servlets

A basic understanding of the architecture of Java servlets is important to the application that will be developed in this chapter. A **servlet** at its simplest level can be thought of as a Java application written to reside on a server and provide data back to clients. These clients do not have to be HTTP clients, although our discussion will focus on Web clients. The servlet runs either on a Web server that hosts servlets natively or through the use of a servlet engine that extends the functionality of a Web server. Servlets also provide the added benefit of being platform neutral: you can have the servlet running in Solaris, Linux, NT, or any other operating system that has a servlet engine. Servlets provide the same functionality as CGI scripts, but they have many features that make them superior to CGIs. They are written in Java, which makes them portable across server architectures; they are loaded once by the servlet engine, which makes them very fast; and they persist across multiple client requests.

Servlets communicate with browser-based clients using the following flow model. Note that some commercial Web servers include a servlet engine and do not require an external engine.

The client requests a page from the Web server.

The Web server invokes the servlet engine (externally or internally).

The servlet is loaded (if not already loaded by the system).

If it is a fresh load, then the `init` method of the servlet is invoked.

The `doPost` or `doGet` method of the servlet is invoked with client data.

The servlet processes the data.

The results are returned to the caller (Web server).

The Web server returns the results to the client.

The `init` method allows us to prepare the environment for future calls to the servlet. Servlets persist between multiple connections and can maintain information across them. This is one significant advantage over standard CGIs, which require a new invocation for each request. The `init` method also lets us do some of the more CPU-intensive tasks before our clients begin requesting use of the servlet. In this chapter we will develop a pooling architecture to alleviate performance bottlenecks in the phone book servlet. Without the `init` method and the load-once characteristic of the servlet architecture, we would not be able to take advantage of a connection pool.

Many books more fully describe servlet architecture. The Sun Web site (at `http://java.sun.com/products/servlet/index.html`) contains literature on this important architecture. The site also provides the latest version of `jsdk.jar`, the main library for compiling and implementing Java servlets.

Uses of LDAP in Servlets

Before delving into the implementation of our phone book servlet, it is worthwhile to look at some of the primary areas where LDAP can serve the needs of the servlet developer. The LDAP directory can provide the authentication source for servlets. The ability to code your own custom security policy in your servlet and take advantage of the LDAP directory for storage of authentication details provides a powerful model for today's applications.

Furthermore, the combination of authentication information in the LDAP directory and an HTML presentation can provide universal and user-friendly access to Internet-based applications. The standard Web server authentication mechanism that merely asks for a user ID and password can be replaced with a graphically rich and

Airius Corporation
Welcome to the time-off request system. We know you are looking forward
to your vacation, so please log in and you will be on your way!
Corporate ID:
This is the standard access ID for all your services!
Password:
If you cannot remember your password, click the hint button and we will help you out.
Hint - Help!
If you have errors or questions, contact the HR department by e-mail or at 650-555-1212.

FIGURE 13-1. *Friendly authentication screen.*

friendly interface. Of course, the standard Web server authentication can also be utilized, and the server will pass the authentication details on to the servlet. The authenticated user ID is then available with the `HttpServletRequest.getRemoteUser` method. Figure 13-1 shows a sample interface for requesting authentication information.

The directory also stores the user hint information as an additional attribute. Additional uses of the directory for servlet developers include storing shopping cart or purchasing preferences for each user within the directory. We discussed in Chapter 6 how to serialize Java object classes and store them in the directory. Servlets can store entire session objects and other pertinent information about a user. When the user returns to the application, the servlet retrieves this information and restores all the preferences. The directory, which servlets can access through the Java LDAP SDK, also serves as a resource for managing information about users.

Designing the LDAP Servlet

Before you begin work on the servlet itself, your machine configuration needs to be updated for compiling servlets. If you are using the servlet engine in Netscape Enterprise

Server (which is included on the CD-ROM with this book), you already have the Java Servlet Development Kit (JSDK): `bin/https/jar/servlets.jar`. If you are using a different servlet engine, you may need to install the JSDK, which includes the file `jsdk.jar`. Either `servlets.jar` or `jsdk.jar` must be added to the `CLASSPATH` of your javac compiler. Chapter 3 included instructions for installing the LDAP SDK; follow the instructions for adding the SDK to your `CLASSPATH` also to add the `jsdk.jar` file to your `CLASSPATH`. The second step is to include the `ldapjdk.jar` file in your servlet engine's `CLASSPATH`. Many different servlet engines are available on the market, and each has its own method of setting up the `CLASSPATH`. Refer to the documentation provided with your servlet engine to configure the `CLASSPATH`. Instructions for configuring Netscape Enterprise Server to include a JAR file in the `CLASSPATH` of its Java Virtual Machine (JVM) and for enabling and installing servlets are at `http://home.netscape.com/eng/server/webserver/4.0/index.html`.

After compiling and installing the phone book servlet, you may receive the error shown in Figure 13-2 in your browser when trying to access the servlet. The error message indicates that the servlet engine could not locate the LDAP SDK JAR file `ldapjdk.jar`. The servlet engine generally uses its own `CLASSPATH` rather than the one you have set up for your compiler.

Location of Files

Each servlet engine has its own location for storing the class files. Again, consult the documentation and store your compiled class files in this directory. Netscape

FIGURE 13-2. *Error message for misconfigured* CLASSPATH *on servlet engine.*

Enterprise Server allows you to specify any directory you choose for storing servlets; see `http://home.netscape.com/eng/server/webserver/4.0/servlets/1-intro.htm#532740`. You should not store your Java source files in the servlet engine directory. Servlets are accessed with a URL of the form `http://webserver_hostname/servlet/NameOfServlet`. Many servlet engines are case-sensitive when specifying the servlet name. Our phone book servlet is accessed with the URL `http://localhost/servlet/Phonebook`.

Our Phone Book Servlet

Our servlet is designed to provide a lightweight phone book application that can be used by anyone inside or outside of the organization to locate people and resources in the LDAP directory. These are the requirements for our servlet:

- Provide phone book lookups
- Be accessible with a simple browser
- Utilize the corporate LDAP directory
- Be customizable
- Have several search attributes (phone number, e-mail address, etc.)
- Be useful both for an intranet and an extranet, and present data specific to each
- Allow user self-administration
- Pool connections and cache data for optimal performance
- Be accessible over SSL (Secure Sockets Layer)

Phone Book Lookups

The servlet will function as the internal corporate white pages. It will serve as an external face to the organization by allowing lookup of limited employee information, such as phone number. Since the corporate directory is the authoritative source for user data, this information will always be current.

Accessibility with a Simple Browser

Requests to the servlet will use HTTP, and all of its output will be in standard HTML. Small pieces of cross-platform JavaScript will be utilized to enhance the user experience. The output must be compatible with a wide range of browsers, since the application will be accessed by outside users.

Utilizing the Corporate LDAP Directory

The reason for utilizing the corporate directory is obvious: it is a maintained and reliable data source. In many deployment scenarios there are options for the topology of the LDAP servers. The directory server could be a replicated copy of the master server with specific settings for the efficient and safe provision of data to the phone book application. A special replicated copy of the directory could be placed outside the firewall with minimal data available for external users.

Customizability

The servlet is customizable or extensible to meet the needs of the corporation. This application is fully customizable because the entire source code is provided on the CD-ROM that accompanies the book. If you want to implement a different view or provide other interactions, the model is simple to enhance or extend.

Search Attributes

The search interface of the application offers several options. You can search for someone by name, phone number, or e-mail address. You can add additional search schemes by editing the pull-down menu contents and adding a code snippet to the search handler. One major advantage of having the code on the server instead of on the client is that these changes can be made and put online without users of the application being required to upgrade or reconfigure. The search code makes use of wild card characters to return as many matches as possible for a given target string.

Intranet and Extranet

A module within the servlet determines if the caller is inside the company or outside. This module can be fully customized to meet specific network requirements, and it can even utilize other data sources to determine these needs. The servlet also enforces a restriction that "outside" clients cannot perform certain operations, such as lookup of complete records or of employee photographs.

User Self-administration

One area in which many corporations are seeing great savings is employee self-administration. The phone book servlet allows employees to change certain information about themselves, such as home phone numbers, mobile phone numbers, or passwords. This self-administration by employees frees up the administrative staff to deal with larger issues.

Connection Pooling and Data Caching

Because the servlet has the potential to be called by many users simultaneously, much thought went into maximizing its performance. A connection-pooling model was developed to provide fast turnaround of data to users. The entire connection-pooling class will be presented and reviewed shortly. This class takes advantage of the `init` method of servlets and allocates connections at start-up. The built-in caching services of the SDK are utilized as well to minimize repeated hits to the directory.

Accessibility over SSL

Because servlets are called from the Web server, it is easy to add the extra protection of SSL for the data transport between the client and the server by enabling SSL on the Web server. The servlet requires no special code to take advantage of this powerful secure transport. The servlet can also be made to communicate with the LDAP server using SSL, but that feature is not implemented in the code example provided in this chapter.

Connection-Pooling Class

The benefits of connection pooling are most fully realized with server-side processes. As noted throughout the book, the time to set up an LDAP connection can be an order of magnitude larger than the time for the transaction that follows. Our connection-pooling class has the following constructors:

```
public LDAPConnectionPool( int min, int max, String host,
                          int port, String authid, String authpw )
public LDAPConnectionPool( int min, int max, String host, int port )
public LDAPConnectionPool( String host, int port )
```

The constructor arguments define the characteristics of the pool. The `min` argument is the minimum number of connections for the pool to open to the directory server. The `max` argument is the number of connections to which the pool will grow when all connections are in use. The `host` and `port` arguments determine the server host and port number. The `authdn` and `authpw` arguments specify the credentials of the user to authenticate as. The `authdn` is a full distinguished name (`uid=bjensen, ou=people, o=airius.com`, for example).

Once the connection pool has been allocated, LDAP connections are requested with the `getConnection` method. The following code snippet shows setting up a connection pool and obtaining a connection.

```
LDAPConnectionPool ldapPool =
    new LDAPConnectionPool( 40, 60, "localhost", 389);
LDAPConnection ld = ldapPool.getConnection();
```

When you have finished with the connection, it should be returned to the pool using the `close` method:

```
    ldapPool.close( ld );
```

Other than the methods for obtaining the connection and returning it to the pool, you can use the acquired `LDAPConnection` object just like any other `LDAPConnection`. Other methods of interest in the `LDAPConnectionPool` class are as follows:

- `printPool` prints the contents of the pool to standard output (`stdout`).
- `setDebug` turns debug printouts on or off.
- `getDebug` returns the current debug setting.

The class is made available to the servlet engine by the placing of all class files in the `CLASSPATH` of the servlet engine or by placing them directly in the servlet directory. The following class files are part of the pooling package:

- `LDAPConnectionPool.class`
- `LDAPConnectionPool$LDAPConnectionObject.class`

The code for the pooling class follows.

```
import java.util.*;
import netscape.ldap.*;

public class LDAPConnectionPool {

    /**
     * Constructor for specifying all parameters
     *
     * @param min initial number of connections
     * @param max maximum number of connections
     * @param host host name of LDAP server
```

```
 * @param port port number of LDAP server
 * @param authdn DN to authenticate as
 * @param authpw password for authentication
 * @exception LDAPException on failure to create connections
 */
public LDAPConnectionPool( int min, int max,
                           String host, int port,
                           String authdn, String authpw )
    throws LDAPException {

    this.poolSize = min;
    this.poolMax = max;
    this.host = host;
    this.port = port;
    this.authdn = authdn;
    this.authpw = authpw;
    this.debugMode = false;
    createPool();
}

/**
 * Constructor for specifying all parameters, anonymous
 * identity
 *
 * @param min initial number of connections
 * @param max maximum number of connections
 * @param host host name of LDAP server
 * @param port port number of LDAP server
 * @exception LDAPException on failure to create connections
 */
public LDAPConnectionPool( int min, int max,
                           String host, int port)
    throws LDAPException {
    this( min, max, host, port, "", "");
}

/**
 * Constructor for using default parameters,
 * anonymous identity
 *
 * @param host host name of LDAP server
 * @param port port number of LDAP server
 * @exception LDAPException on failure to create connections
 */
```

```
public LDAPConnectionPool( String host, int port )
    throws LDAPException {
    // poolsize=10,max=20,host,port,
    // noauth,nopswd
    this( 10, 20, host, port, "", "" );
}

/**
 * Destroy the whole pool - called during a shutdown
 */
public void destroy() {
    for ( int i = 0; i < pool.size(); i++ ) {
        disconnect(
            (LDAPConnectionObject)pool.elementAt(i) );
    }
    pool.removeAllElements();
}
```

The `getConnection` method retrieves an available `LDAPConnection` from the pool:

```
/**
 * Get a connection from the pool
 *
 * If no connections are available, the pool will be
 * extended if the number of connections is less than
 * the maximum; if the pool cannot be extended, the method
 * blocks until a free connection becomes available.
 *
 * @return an active connection
 */
public LDAPConnection getConnection() {
    LDAPConnection con;

    while( (con = getConnFromPool()) == null ) {
        synchronized( pool ) {
            try {
                pool.wait();
            } catch ( InterruptedException e ) {
            }
        }
    }
    return con;
}
```

```
/**
 * Get a connection from the pool
 *
 * If no connections are available, the pool will be
 * extended if the number of connections is less than
 * the maximum; if the pool cannot be extended, the method
 * returns null.
 *
 * @return an active connection or null
 */
protected synchronized LDAPConnection getConnFromPool() {
    LDAPConnection con = null;
    LDAPConnectionObject ldapconnobj = null;

    int pSize = pool.size();

    // Get an available connection
    for ( int i = 0; i < pSize; i++ ) {

        // Get the ConnectionObject from the pool
        LDAPConnectionObject conn =
            (LDAPConnectionObject)pool.elementAt(i);

        if ( conn.isAvailable() ) {
            ldapconnobj = conn;
            break;
        }
    }

    if ( ldapconnobj == null ) {
        // If there were no conns in pool, can we grow
        // the pool?
        if ( (poolMax < 0) ||
             ( (poolMax > 0) &&
               (pSize < poolMax)) ) {

            // Yes we can grow it
            int i = addConnection();

            // If a new connection was created, use it
            if ( i >= 0 ) {
                ldapconnobj =
                    (LDAPConnectionObject)pool.elementAt(i);
            }
```

```
            } else {
                debug("All pool connections in use",true);
            }
        }

        if ( ldapconnobj != null ) {
            ldapconnobj.setInUse( true );
            con = ldapconnobj.getLDAPConn();
        }
        return con;
    }
```

The `close` method, which follows, is what users of the pool invoke to close down (or return to the pool) a connection. We do not actually shut down the connection, but we mark it as available for reuse. Once we return a connection to the pool, a notification is sent to any thread waiting for a new connection.

```
    /**
     * This is our soft close; all we do is mark
     * the connection available for others to use
     *
     * @param ld a connection to be returned to the pool
     */
    public synchronized void close( LDAPConnection ld ) {

        int index = find( ld );
        if ( index != -1 ) {
            LDAPConnectionObject co =
                (LDAPConnectionObject)pool.elementAt(index);
            co.setInUse( false );  // Mark as available
            synchronized( pool ) {
                pool.notifyAll();
            }
        }
    }

    /**
     * Debug method to print the contents of the pool
     */
    public void printPool(){
        System.out.println("-LDAPConnectionPool-");
        for ( int i = 0; i < pool.size(); i++ ) {
            LDAPConnectionObject co =
                (LDAPConnectionObject)pool.elementAt(i);
```

```
            System.out.println( "" + i + "=" + co );
        }
    }

    /**
     * Physically disconnect a connection object and set its
     * reference to null
     *
     * @param ld a connection to be discarded
     */
    private void disconnect(
        LDAPConnectionObject ldapconnObject ) {
        if ( ldapconnObject != null ) {
            if (ldapconnObject.isAvailable()) {
                LDAPConnection ld = ldapconnObject.getLDAPConn();
                if ( (ld != null) && (ld.isConnected()) ) {
                    try {
                        ld.disconnect();
                    } catch (LDAPException e) {
                        debug("disconnect: "+e.toString());
                    }
                }
                ldapconnObject.setLDAPConn(null); // Clear conn
            }
        }
    }
```

The `createPool` method is called by the constructors and starts the pool setup. It validates the arguments and resets any that are not acceptable. The method then calls `setUpPool` to build the connections:

```
    private void createPool() throws LDAPException {
        // Called by the constructors
        if ( poolSize <= 0 ) {
            throw new LDAPException("LDAPConnectionPoolSize invalid");
        }
        if ( poolMax < poolSize ) {
            debug("ConnectionPoolMax is invalid, set to " +
                  poolSize);
            poolMax = poolSize;
        }

        debug("****Initializing LDAP Pool****",true);
        debug("LDAP host = "+host+" on port "+port,true);
        debug("Number of connections="+poolSize,true);
```

```
        debug("Maximum number of connections="+poolMax,true);
        debug("******",true);

        pool = new java.util.Vector(); // Create pool vector
        setUpPool( poolSize ); // Initialize it
    }

    private int addConnection() {
        int index = -1;

        debug("adding a connection to pool...");
        try {
            int size = pool.size() + 1; // Add one connection
            setUpPool( size );

            if ( size == pool.size() ) {
                // New size is size requested?
                index = size - 1;
            }
        } catch (Exception ex) {
            debug("Adding a connection: "+ex.toString(),true);
        }
        return index;
    }

    private synchronized void setUpPool( int size )
        throws LDAPException {
        // Loop on creating connections
        while( pool.size() < size ) {
            LDAPConnectionObject co =
                new LDAPConnectionObject();
            // Make LDAP connection
            co.setLDAPConn(new LDAPConnection());
            try {
                co.getLDAPConn().connect( host, port,
                                          authdn, authpw);
            } catch ( LDAPException le ) {
                debug("Creating pool:"+le.toString(),true);
                debug("aborting....",true);
                throw le;
            }
            co.setInUse( false ); // Mark not in use
            pool.addElement( co );
```

```
    }
}
private int find( LDAPConnection con ) {
    // Find the matching connection in the pool
    if ( con != null ) {
        for ( int i = 0; i < pool.size(); i++ ) {
            LDAPConnectionObject co =
                (LDAPConnectionObject)pool.elementAt(i);
            if ( co.getLDAPConn() == con ) {
                return i;
            }
        }
    }
    return -1;
}

/**
  * Set the debug printout mode
  *
  * @param mode debug mode to use
  */
public synchronized void setDebug( boolean mode ) {
    debugMode = mode;
}

/**
  * Report the debug printout mode
  *
  * @return debug mode in use
  */
public boolean getDebug() {
    return debugMode;
}

private void debug( String s ) {
    if ( debugMode )
        System.out.println("LDAPConnectionPool ("+
                           new Date()+") : " + s);
}

private void debug(String s, boolean severe) {
    if ( debugMode || severe ) {
        System.out.println("LDAPConnectionPool ("+
                           new Date()+") : " + s);
```

```
        }
    }
```

The LDAPConnectionObject inner class manages a connection object. It encapsulates an LDAPConnection and adds a boolean value marking whether or not the connection is currently in use:

```
    /**
     * Wrapper for LDAPConnection object in pool
     */
    class LDAPConnectionObject {

        /**
         * Returns the associated LDAPConnection
         *
         * @return the LDAPConnection
         *
         */
        LDAPConnection getLDAPConn() {
            return this.ld;
        }

        /**
         * Sets the associated LDAPConnection
         *
         * @param ld the LDAPConnection
         *
         */
        void setLDAPConn( LDAPConnection ld ) {
            this.ld = ld;
        }

        /**
         * Marks a connection in use or available
         *
         * @param inUse true to mark in use, false to mark available
         *
         */
        void setInUse( boolean inUse ) {
            this.inUse = inUse;
        }

        /**
```

```
         * Returns whether the connection is available
         * for use by another user
         *
         * @return true if available
         */
        boolean isAvailable() {
            return !inUse;
        }

        /**
         * Debug method
         *
         * @return a user-friendly rendering of the object
         */
        public String toString() {
            return "LDAPConnection=" + ld + ",inUse=" + inUse;
        }

        private LDAPConnection ld; // LDAP Connection
        private boolean inUse; // In use? (true = yes)
    }

    private int poolSize; // Min pool size
    private int poolMax; // Max pool size
    private String host; // LDAP host
    private int port;    // Port to connect at
    private String authdn;  // Identity of connections
    private String authpw;  // Password for authdn
    private java.util.Vector pool;  // The actual pool
    private boolean debugMode;
}
```

Servlet Request-Response Model

The servlet is self-contained and relies on static files only for icons. State is maintained between accesses using <HIDDEN> tags in the HTML documents—the most lightweight means for both the server and the client. The state model for the program is as follows:

On initial or invalid request, transmit a fresh search page.

On incoming search page, generate a search results page.

From the search results page, go to one of the following:

- Detail view
- Retrieval of a certificate
- Retrieval of a photograph

From detail view, do one of the following:

- Change password
- Edit user information

All these actions are controlled through string constants declared at the top of the module. All fields that are sent back to the client are also named using these constants. The main search window is shown in Figure 13-3.

Besides the connection pool, the `Phonebook` object uses the `CParseRFC1867` and `CBlobInputStream` classes to parse a multipart MIME document and to read raw data from a binary part. The parsing of multipart data is greatly simplified by the `CParseRFC1867` java class courtesy of Peter English at `english@quiknet.com`. Figure 13-4 illustrates the relationships of the classes of the application.

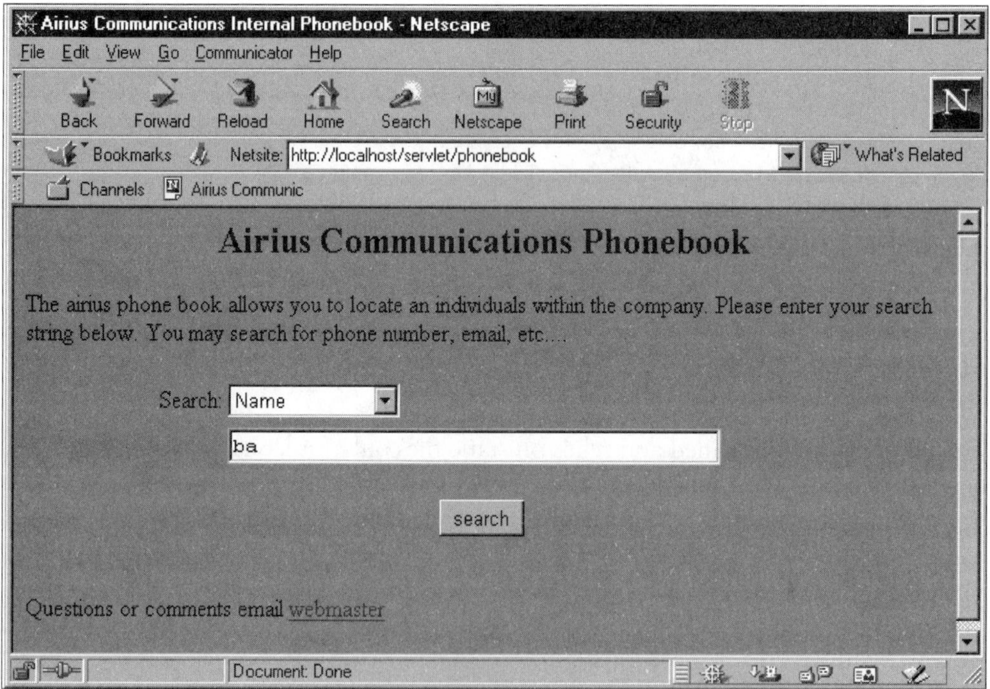

FIGURE 13-3. *Main entry point to our phone book.*

Phonebook
getServletInfo() : String
init(sc : ServletConfig) : void
destroy() : void
doPost(req : HttpServletRequest, res : HttpServletResponse) : void
doGet(req : HttpServletRequest, res : HttpServletResponse) : void
searchLDAP(req : HttpServletRequest, out : PrintWriter, isInternal : boolean) : void
binaryLDAP(req : HttpServletRequest, res : HttpServletResponse, attr : String, name : String, mime : String) : void
errorMessage(out : PrintWriter, errmsg : String) : void
checkInside(req : HttpServletRequest) : boolean
getLDAPConn() : LDAPConnection
closeConnection(ld : LDAPConnection) : void
getValue(entry : LDAPEntry, attrN : String) : String
getValue(entry : LDAPEntry, attrN : String, defVal : String) : String
getBinaryValue(entry : LDAPEntry, attrN : String) : byte[]
getScope(scope : String) : int
prettyDN(theDN : String) : String
readFormData(req : HttpServletRequest, fdname : String) : String
buildAttr(attrN : String, attrV : String) : LDAPAttribute
modifyPwd(req : HttpServletRequest, out : PrintWriter) : void
modifyEntry(req : HttpServletRequest, out : PrintWriter) : void
sendSrchPage(out : PrintWriter, isInternal : boolean, uri : String) : void
sendPwdPage(req : HttpServletRequest, out : PrintWriter, isInternal : boolean) : void
generateRow(out : PrintWriter, color : String, attrs : String[], entry : LDAPEntry, uri : String, url : String, isInternal : boolean) : void
detailEdit(req : HttpServletRequest, out : PrintWriter, detail : boolean) : void
CBlobInputStream
CParseRFC1867
1..1
1..1
LDAPConnectionPool
LDAPConnectionPool(min : int, max : int, host : String, port : int, authdn : String, authpw : String)
LDAPConnectionPool(min : int, max : int, host : String, port : int)
LDAPConnectionPool(host : String, port : int)
destroy() : void
getConnection() : LDAPConnection
getConnFromPool() : LDAPConnection
close(ld : LDAPConnection) : void
printPool() : void
disconnect(ldapconnObject : LDAPConnectionObject) : void
createPool() : void
addConnection() : int
setUpPool(size : int) : void
find(con : LDAPConnection) : int
setDebug(mode : boolean) : void
getDebug() : boolean
debug(s : String) : void
debug(s : String, severe : boolean) : void

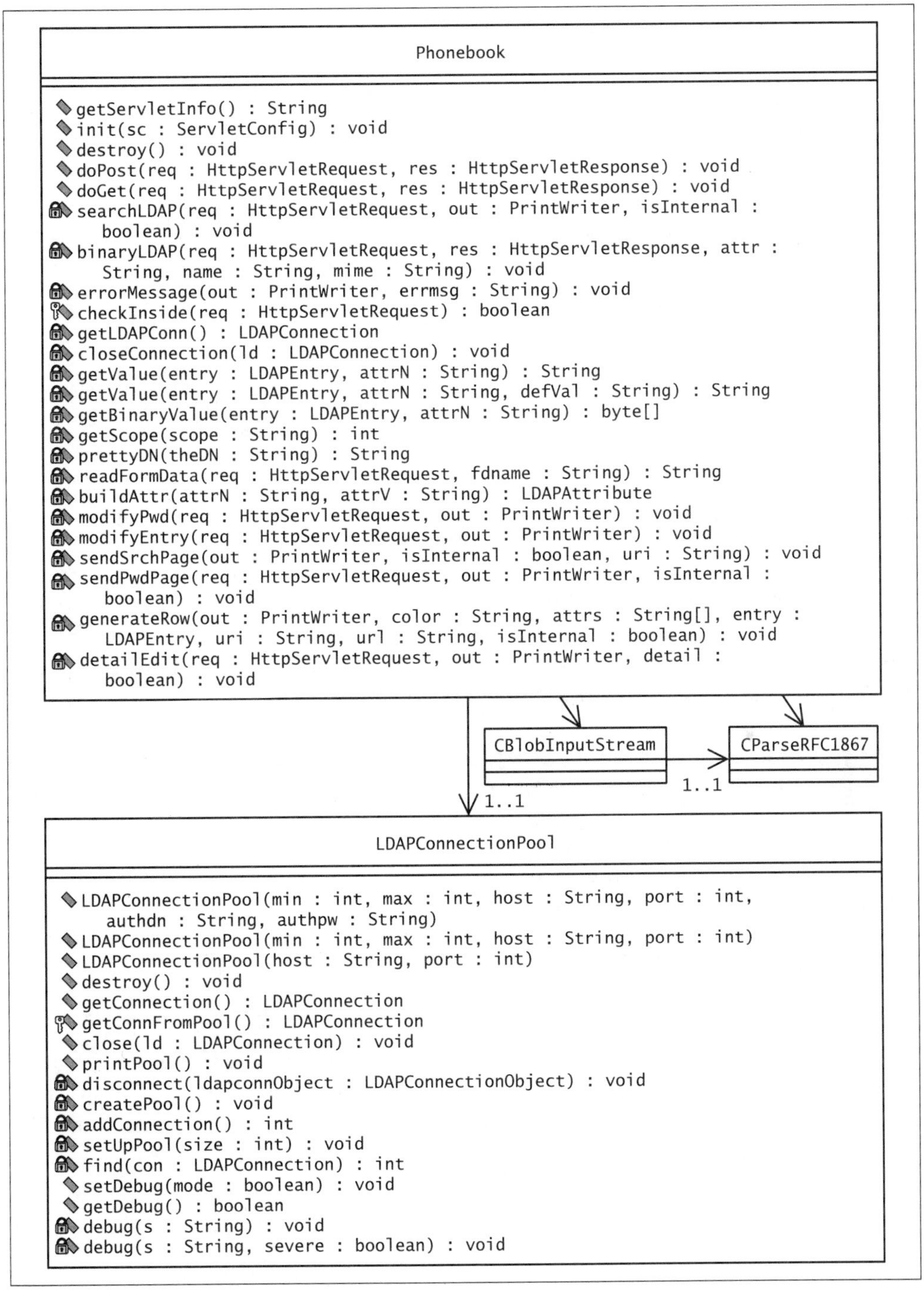

FIGURE 13-4. Phonebook *classes*

The Phonebook servlet code is presented here:

```
import java.io.*;
import java.util.*;
import javax.servlet.*;
import javax.servlet.http.*;
import netscape.ldap.*;
import netscape.ldap.util.*;
import netscape.ldap.controls.*;

/**
 * Phonebook servlet
 *
 *
 * @version 1.0
 * @author tdahbura
 **/
public class Phonebook extends HttpServlet {
```

The following settings may need customization for your site. These, as well as many other settings, can be set using the phone book properties file described later in this chapter, in the section on how to set up the servlet. They are standard LDAP values that have been described elsewhere in the book.

```
    // The following values are defaults.  They
    // can all be set using the properties file.
    // ----------------------
    protected static String host = "localhost";
    protected static int    port = 389;
    protected static String srchRoot = "o=airius.com";
    static String orgName = "Airius Communications";
    static String ownMail = "webmaster@airius.com";
    static int maxPhotoSize = 50000;
```

The following declaration is the Web server URL for the static graphic images used to display the pages. In this configuration we are storing the images in the directory phonebook/images under our main Web server document root. This setting should be made in the properties file and is dependent on your Web server's configuration.

```
    String imagesURL = "/phonebook/images/";

    //The following values may all be customized for look and feel
    // Colors for listings lines
```

```
final static String[] LIST_COLOR = {"#00CCCC","#009999"};
// Colors for initial search page
final static String srchPageColors =
    "\"#999999\" text=\"#000000\""+
    " link=\"#0000FF\" vlink=\"#FF00FF\""+
    " alink=\"#FF0000\"";
// Colors for output of search
final static String srchOutColors =
    "\"#999999\" text=\"#000000\""+
    " link=\"#0000FF\" vlink=\"#FF00FF\""+
    " alink=\"#FF0000\"";
// End of customizable values --------------

protected static int scope = LDAPConnection.SCOPE_SUB;
private LDAPConnectionPool ldapPool;
private LDAPCache readCache = null;

final static String certAttr = "userCertificate;binary";
final static String photoAttr = "jpegPhoto";
// Window dimensions for photos
final static int photoWinHeight = 100;
final static int photoWinWidth = 100;
final static String[] intAttrs = {"cn","telephoneNumber",
                                  "mail",
                                  certAttr,photoAttr,
                                  "givenName","sn"};

final static String[] extAttrs = {"cn","telephoneNumber",
                                  "mail",
                                  certAttr,photoAttr,
                                  "givenName","sn"};

private String hostIP = "127.0.0.1";
```

Next we declare the command and field names. By using these throughout the code, we can minimize errors on command parsing.

```
final static String ACTION_FIELD = "cmd";
final static String ACTION_SEARCH = "search";
final static String ACTION_DETAIL = "getdetail";
final static String ACTION_GETCERT = "getcert";
final static String ACTION_GETPHOTO = "getphoto";
final static String ACTION_EDIT = "editrecord";
final static String ACTION_DOEDIT = "editsubmit";
```

```
    final static String ACTION_PWD = "editpwd";
    final static String ACTION_DOPWD = "pwdsubmit";

    final static String FLDNAME_SRCHKIND = "searchkind";
    final static String FLDNAME_SRCHSTRING = "searchstring";
    final static String FLDNAME_DN = "dn";
    final static String FLDNAME_OLDPW = "oldpwd";
    final static String FLDNAME_NEWPW1 = "newpwd1";
    final static String FLDNAME_NEWPW2 = "newpwd2";
    final static String FLDNAME_NEWPHOTO = "newphoto";

    /**
      * return some descriptive information about us
      *
      * @return descriptive information
      */
    public String getServletInfo() {
        return "A servlet that handles phone book lookup " +
            "using LDAP";
   }

    /**
     * Initialize the servlet. This is called once at start-up.
     * Properties are read and prepared for future operations.
     * The LDAPConnectionPool and the LDAPCache instances are
     * prepared. The host IP address is stored for later use
     * by the inside/outside firewall checks.
      *
      * @param sc the servlet configuration
      * @exception ServletException on
      * failure to read properties or initialization of pool
      */
    public void init( ServletConfig sc )
        throws ServletException {

        super.init(sc);
```

The next block of the `init` method handles reading the properties file, where configuration is stored. The location to store a properties file depends on the servlet server. If we cannot locate the file, a file is created. The first time the servlet is run, a warning message will be generated; look for the file `phonebook.properties` and store properties there. Any errors in converting integers or reading property values will cause the servlet to throw an exception. Fix the indicated value and restart the servlet.

```
// Read properties from the properties file.
// If not found, then create a placeholder file.
Properties props = new Properties();
File f = new File("phonebook.properties");
if ( !f.exists() ) {
    System.out.println(f.getPath() + "not found");
    try {
        FileWriter fwout = new FileWriter(f);
        fwout.write("#Store your phone book properties
            here");
        fwout.close();
        throw new ServletException
            ("Cannot locate properties in ->"+f.getPath());
    } catch (IOException ie) {
        System.out.println(
           "Cannot write properties file");
        throw new ServletException(
           "Cannot write properties file");
    }
}

try {
    InputStream is = new BufferedInputStream(
                        new FileInputStream(f));
    props.load(is);
    is.close();
} catch (IOException e) {
    throw new ServletException
        ("Cannot load properties in ->"+f.getPath());
}

// Read and save properties
host = props.getProperty("host",host);
try {
    port = Integer.parseInt(
        props.getProperty("port",String.valueOf(port)));
} catch ( Exception ex ) {
    System.out.println("Invalid port");
    throw new ServletException(
        "Invalid port in properties file");
}
srchRoot = props.getProperty("srchroot",srchRoot);
orgName = props.getProperty("orgname",orgName);
ownMail = props.getProperty("ownmail",ownMail);
```

```
imagesURL = props.getProperty("imgurl",imagesURL);
int initPool=0;
int maxPool=0;
String authdn="";
String authpw="";
int cacheSize=0;
int cacheTime=0;

try {
    initPool = Integer.parseInt(
        props.getProperty("initpool","10"));
    maxPool = Integer.parseInt(
        props.getProperty("maxpool","20"));
    authdn = props.getProperty("authdn","");
    authpw = props.getProperty("authpw","");
    cacheSize = Integer.parseInt(
        props.getProperty("cachesize","250000"));
    cacheTime = Integer.parseInt(
        props.getProperty("cachetime","3600"));
    maxPhotoSize = Integer.parseInt(
        props.getProperty("maxphotosize","50000"));
} catch (NumberFormatException ne) {
    throw new ServletException(
        "Invalid integer value in properties file");
}
```

The following code sets up and initializes the cache and connection pool. The `LDAPConnectionPool` class is important for the phone book servlet's performance. Another feature contributing to the performance of the servlet is the use of the cache mechanism of the Java LDAP SDK (the SDK cache mechanism is fully described in Chapter 15). Our phone book servlet utilizes a 256K cache to pool repeated search requests.

```
try {
    // Create connection pool
    ldapPool = new LDAPConnectionPool(
        initPool,maxPool,host,port,authdn,authpw);
    if ( cacheSize > 0 ) {
        readCache = new LDAPCache(cacheTime,cacheSize);
    }
} catch (Exception ex) {
    ex.printStackTrace();
    throw new ServletException
```

```
                ("Unable to initialize LDAP connection pool");
        }

        // Get our IP address and trim last octet
        try {
            hostIP =
                java.net.InetAddress.getLocalHost().
                getHostAddress();
        } catch (java.net.UnknownHostException he) {
            hostIP = "127.0.0.1";
        }
        System.out.println("Servlet server IP="+hostIP);
        int i = hostIP.lastIndexOf( '.' );
        hostIP = hostIP.substring( 0, i );
    }

    /**
     * Destroy the servlet - called during an unload/shutdown
     */
    public void destroy() {
        if ( ldapPool != null ) {
            ldapPool.destroy();  // Release all connections
        }
        super.destroy();
    }

    /**
     * Handle HTTP posts.
     * Check size of request and pass the request off to the
     * doGet handler if not too large.<BR>
     * If it is too large, respond with an HTML error page.<BR>
     *
     * @param req the HTTP request
     * @param res the HTTP response
     *
     * @exception ServletException<BR>
     * @exception IOException<BR>
     *
     */
    public void doPost( HttpServletRequest req,
                        HttpServletResponse res )
        throws ServletException, IOException {
        // Value chosen to limit denial of service attacks
        int limit = maxPhotoSize+1*1024;
```

```
        if ( maxPhotoSize==0 ) {
            limit = 20*1024;  //Still within reason?
        }
        if (req.getContentLength() > limit) {
            res.setContentType("text/html");
            PrintWriter out = res.getWriter();
            out.println("<HTML><HEAD><TITLE>Too big</TITLE></HEAD>");
            out.println("<BODY><H1>Error - content length &gt;"+
                limit+"k not allowed.");
            out.println("</H1></BODY></HTML>");
        } else {
            doGet(req, res);
        }
    }
```

The doGet method is the main handler of the servlet. All inbound get and post requests are routed through this routine. The doPost handler calls into this routine. First we determine if the caller is an internal or an external user and allow or deny the call based on that determination. Requests for certificates or photographs are processed and return a result type of application/x-x509-email-cert or image/jpeg, respectively. The transition from one state to another is also handled within this block.

```
    /**
      * Handles HTTP gets<BR>
        * Main logic processing for our servlet.  We look at the
        * arguments (form elements or URL elements) and dispatch
        * to the servlet methods to handle these.<BR>
      *
      * @param req the HTTP request
        * @param res the HTTP response
        * <BR>
        * Exceptions can be thrown by servlet methods:
        * @exception ServletException<BR>
        * @exception IOException
        *
      */
    public void doGet( HttpServletRequest req,
                       HttpServletResponse res )
        throws ServletException, IOException {

        PrintWriter out = null;
        boolean isInternal = checkInside(req);
        String cmd = readFormData(req,ACTION_FIELD);
```

```
// Set output content type to text/html; change later
// if necessary
res.setContentType("text/html");

// All routines output HTML except cert and photo
if ( (!cmd.equals(ACTION_GETCERT)) &&
     (!cmd.equals(ACTION_GETPHOTO)) ) {
    out = res.getWriter();
}

//Dispatch to the proper handler
if (cmd.equals(ACTION_SEARCH)) {
    //Set response not to be cached
    res.setHeader("Expires","Tues, 01 Jan 1980 00:00:00 GMT");
    searchLDAP(req,out,isInternal);
} else if (cmd.equals(ACTION_DETAIL)) {
    if (!isInternal) {
        errorMessage(out,"Not authorized!");
    } else {
        detailEdit(req,out,true);  //display only
    }
} else if (cmd.equals(ACTION_GETCERT)) {
    binaryLDAP (req, res, certAttr, "Certificate",
                "application/x-x509-email-cert" );
} else if (cmd.equals(ACTION_GETPHOTO)) {
    if (!isInternal) {
        res.setContentType("text/html");
        out = res.getWriter();
        errorMessage(out,"Not authorized!");
    } else {
        binaryLDAP (req, res, photoAttr, "Photograph",
                "image/jpeg" );
    }
} else if (cmd.equals(ACTION_EDIT)) {
    if (!isInternal) {
        res.setContentType("text/html");
        out = res.getWriter();
        errorMessage(out,"Not authorized!");
    } else {
        detailEdit(req,out,false);  //Edit mode
    }
} else if (cmd.equals(ACTION_DOEDIT)) {
    // Process user values
    modifyEntry(req,out);
```

```
        } else if (cmd.equals(ACTION_PWD)) {
            sendPwdPage(req,out,isInternal);
        } else if (cmd.equals(ACTION_DOPWD)) {
            modifyPwd(req,out);
        } else {
            res.setContentType("text/html");
            sendSrchPage(out,isInternal,req.getRequestURI());
        }
        return;
}
```

The following routine is the handler for all search requests. It parses the search string and determines the type of search (by name, telephone number, etc.). The search strings are also modified to include an asterisk at the end to allow matches with values that begin with the search string. The search by name also includes an LDAP "sounds like" search: "~=" (see Table 5-1). Once the search filter is validated and constructed, we obtain a connection from the pool and issue the search request. The search utilizes server-side sorting (if supported by the server) and calls `generateRow` to build each row of the result set.

```
/**
 * Handle search requests to the servlet.<BR>
 * Retrieve arguments from the req and transmit HTML
 * back to the client. Build an LDAP search request
 * using server-side sorting when possible. If not
 * possible, do client-side sorting (in the servlet).
  *
  * @param req the HTTP request
  * @param out stream back to the client
  * @param isInternal true if client
  *  is internal to organization
  */
private void searchLDAP( HttpServletRequest req,
                         PrintWriter out,
                         boolean isInternal ) {

    // Get search arguments
    String srchType =
        readFormData(req,FLDNAME_SRCHKIND).toLowerCase();
    String srchString = readFormData(req,FLDNAME_SRCHSTRING);
    LDAPSearchResults res=null;
    LDAPConnection ld;
    String appendmsg = "";
```

```
String srch = "";
String[] myAttrs;
String uri = req.getRequestURI();
boolean ssort = true; // Use server-side sorting

// Build full URL
String url = req.getScheme()+ "://" +
    req.getServerName();
// Assume standard port numbers. If not, uncomment below.
    //         + ":" + req.getServerPort();

myAttrs = isInternal ? intAttrs : extAttrs;

// Use the attribute name for telephone number in case the
// external number is in a different attribute from
// the internal one
// myAttrs[1] is the telephone number attribute name

if ( srchType.equals("all") ) {
    srch = "(|(cn=" + srchString + "*)" +
           "(sn=" + srchString + "*)" +
           "(givenName=" + srchString+ "*)" +
           "("+myAttrs[1]+"=" + srchString + "*)" +
           ")";
} else if ( srchType.equals("cn") ) {
    srch = "(|(cn=" + srchString + ")(cn=" +
           srchString + "*)" +
           "(cn~="+srchString+"))";
} else if ( srchType.equals("mail") ) {
    srch = "(|(mail="+srchString+")" +
           "(mail="+srchString+"*)" +
           ")";
} else if ( srchType.equals("telephoneNumber") ) {
    srch = "(|("+myAttrs[1]+"="+srchString+")" +
           "("+myAttrs[1]+"="+srchString+"*)" +
           ")";
} else if ( srchType.equals(
    "facsimiletelephoneNumber") ) {
    srch = "(|(facsimiletelephoneNumber="+
           srchString+")" +
           "(facsimiletelephoneNumber="+srchString+"*)" +
           ")";
}
if ( (srch.length() == 0) || srchString.length() == 0) {
```

```
                // Not a valid search type
                sendSrchPage(out,isInternal,req.getRequestURI());
                return;
            }

            ld = getLDAPConn();
            try {
                LDAPSearchConstraints cons =
                         ld.getSearchConstraints();
                // Block until all results are in
                cons.setBatchSize( 0 );

                if ( ssort ) {
                    // Use server-side sorting
                    LDAPSortKey sortL = new LDAPSortKey("sn");
                    LDAPSortKey sortF = new LDAPSortKey("givenName");
                    LDAPSortKey sortC = new LDAPSortKey("cn");
                    LDAPSortKey[] sortOrder = {sortL,sortF,sortC};
                    //Create the server control
                    LDAPSortControl sortCtl =
                            new LDAPSortControl(sortOrder,false);
                    cons.setServerControls(sortCtl);
                }

                res = ld.search( srchRoot,
                                 scope,
                                 srch,
                                 myAttrs,
                                 false,
                                 cons);

                // If sorting on server, then check if sort worked
                if ( ssort ) {
                    LDAPControl[] rControls =
                        ld.getResponseControls();
                    if ( rControls != null ) {
                        // Was there a server-side sort error?
LDAPSortControl response = null;
for( int i = 0; i < rControls.length;
     i++ ) {
  if ( rControls[i] instanceof
       LDAPSortControl ) {
       response =
           (LDAPSortControl)rControls[i];
       break;
  }
```

```
}
If ( response != null ) {
   int resCode =
      response.getResultCode();
   if ( resCode !=
        LDAPException.SUCCESS ) {
        System.err.println(
           "Server side sort failed!");
        ssort = false; // Do client sort
   }
}
            }

            if ( !ssort ) {
                // Need to sort locally
                // Sort by sn, given name, and common name in
                // ascending order
                String[] sortattr = {"sn", "givenName", "cn"};
                boolean[] ascend = {true, true, true};
                res.sort( new LDAPCompareAttrNames(
                    sortattr,ascend) );
            }
        } catch ( LDAPException le ) {
            int rc = le.getLDAPResultCode();
            if (rc == LDAPException.SIZE_LIMIT_EXCEEDED) {
                appendmsg = "\nExceeded size limit";
            } else if (rc == LDAPException.TIME_LIMIT_EXCEEDED) {
                appendmsg = "\nExceeded time limit";
            } else {
                appendmsg = le.toString();
            }
        }

        if (res.getCount() == 0) {
            // Send an error message
            errorMessage(out,"No entries matching "
                         + srchString + " found.");
            closeConnection(ld);
            return;
        }

        out.println("<HTML>");
        out.println("<HEAD>");
        // JavaScript to display picture
        out.println("<SCRIPT Language=\"JavaScript\">");
```

```
out.println("winopen = null;");
out.println("");
out.println("function displayPic(picName) {");
out.print("   if ( (winopen != null) && ");
out.println("(!winopen.closed) ) {");
out.println("     winopen.location = picName;");
out.println("     return winopen;");
out.println("   }");
out.println("   else {");
out.print("     winopen = window.open(picName,'photo',");
out.print(" 'toolbar=no,scrollbars=no,resizable=yes,");
out.print("width="+photoWinWidth);
out.println(",height="+photoWinHeight+"');");
out.println("     return winopen;");
out.println("   }");
out.println("}");
out.println("");
out.println("function winClose() {");
out.println("  if(winopen != null) winopen.close();");
out.println("}");

out.println("function doNothing() {}");
out.println("</SCRIPT>");
out.println("");

out.println("<TITLE>"+orgName+" "+
                (isInternal ? "Internal" : "")+
                " Phonebook</TITLE>");
out.println("</HEAD>");
out.println("<BODY BGCOLOR="+srchOutColors+
                "\"onUnload=\"winClose()\">");
out.println("<CENTER><H1>"+orgName+" Search "+
                "Results</H1></CENTER>");
out.println("<BR><BR>");
out.println("<TABLE WIDTH=\"100%\" BORDER=\"0\" "+
                "CELLSPACING=\"0\">");
out.println("<TR>");
out.println("<TH><DIV ALIGN=\"LEFT\">Name</DIV></TH>");
out.println("<TH><DIV ALIGN=\"LEFT\">Phone</DIV></TH>");
out.println("<TH><DIV ALIGN=\"LEFT\">Email</DIV></TH>");
out.println("<TH><DIV ALIGN=\"LEFT\"></DIV></TH>");
out.println("</TR>");

int rowcnt = 0;
while ( res.hasMoreElements() ) {
```

```
            try {
                // Next directory entry
                LDAPEntry entry = res.next();
                generateRow( out,LIST_COLOR[++rowcnt%2],myAttrs,
                           entry,uri,url,isInternal);
            } catch ( LDAPReferralException e ) {
                ; // Ignore referrals
            } catch ( LDAPException e ) {
                System.err.println( "Entry read error: " +
                                    e.toString() );
                // There may be valid results as well
                continue;
            }
        }
        out.println("</TABLE>");
        if ( appendmsg.length() > 0 ) {
            out.println("Search error:"+appendmsg);
            out.println("<BR>");
        }
        out.println("<BR><BR>");
        out.println("<P>Questions or comments email <A HREF=\""+
                    "mailto:"+ownMail+"\">webmaster</A>"+
                    "</P>");
        out.println("</BODY>");
        out.println("</HTML>");

        closeConnection(ld);
        return;
    }
```

There are many references in the servlet code to a JavaScript function called `doNothing`. This function is there to allow a result to be returned from clicking on a URL or Submit button. It does not perform any function other than to prevent the action from occurring. We intercept the action and call JavaScript functions instead.

A sample of the output from a search is shown in Figure 13-5. The photograph icon next to the entry for Barbara Jensen indicates that she has stored a photo in the directory. Clicking on this icon will open a separate window with the photograph. This action is handled by the routine that follows, which we use for all binary data types.

```
    /**
     * Return binary data in an HTTP stream;
     * retrieve arguments from the req
     *
     * @param req the HTTP request
```

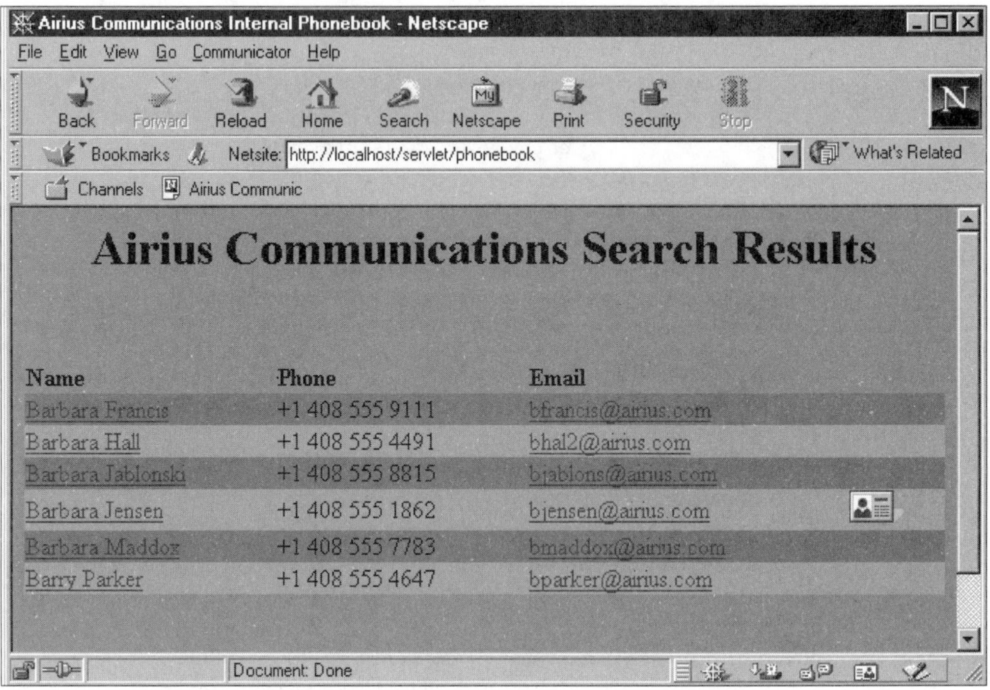

FIGURE 13-5. *Sample search results.*

```
 * @param res the HTTP response
 * @param attr name of attribute in the LDAP directory to
 *  return
 * @param name "friendly" name of the attribute to use for
 *  transmitting an error message
 * @param mime MIME type for this binary data
 * @exception ServletException<BR>
 * @exception IOException<BR>
 */
private void binaryLDAP( HttpServletRequest req,
                         HttpServletResponse res,
                         String attr,
                         String name, String mime )
    throws ServletException, IOException {
    LDAPConnection ld;
    LDAPEntry theEntry = null;
    String[] attrs = {attr};
    int err = 0;
    byte[] theData = null;
```

```
        // Get form arguments
        String theDN =
            readFormData(req,FLDNAME_DN).toLowerCase();
        if ( theDN.length() == 0 ) {
            PrintWriter out = res.getWriter();
            errorMessage(out,"Error with Distingushed Name");
            return;
        }
        theDN = LDAPUrl.decode(theDN);
        ld = getLDAPConn();
        try {
            theEntry = ld.read(theDN,attrs);
            theData = getBinaryValue(theEntry,attr);
            if ( theData == null ) {
                PrintWriter out = res.getWriter();
                errorMessage(out, name + " for " + theDN +
                             " not found!");
                err = 1;
            }
        } catch ( LDAPException e ) {
            PrintWriter out = res.getWriter();
            errorMessage(out,"Entry:" + theDN+" not found!");
            err = 1;
        } finally {
            closeConnection(ld);
        }

        if ( err == 1 ) {
            return;
        }

        // Prepare to transmit binary data
        res.setContentType(mime);
        // Set to pre-expire
        res.setHeader( "Expires",
                       "Tues, 01 Jan 1980 00:00:00 GMT");
        res.setContentLength(theData.length);
        ServletOutputStream sout = res.getOutputStream();
        sout.write(theData,0,theData.length);
        sout.flush();
        sout.close();

        return;
    }
```

```
/**
  * Builds an error HTML response page<BR>
  * @param out a stream back to client
  * @param errmsg the error message
  */
private void errorMessage( PrintWriter out, String errmsg ) {
    out.println("<HTML><HEAD>");
    out.println("<TITLE>Phonebook Error</TITLE>");
    out.println("</HEAD>");
    out.println("<BODY><BR><BR>");
    out.println("<CENTER><H1>Error</H1></CENTER><BR>");
    out.println(errmsg);
    out.println("<BR>Use the back button to correct");
    out.println("</BODY></HTML>");
    return;
}
```

The `checkInside` method considers any machine for which the first three octets match those of the servlet host to be internal. Using part of the IP address to determine if the caller is from the outside is very site specific, since your location may have different criteria for an internal versus external user. The following code looks at the IP source address to decide.

```
/**
 * Report if client is inside or outside the firewall<BR>.
 * This routine must be customized for each particular
 * site. Currently it just matches the first three octets
 * of an IP address to determine if someone is inside the
 * company.
 * @param req the HTTP request
 * @return true if inside firewall
 */
protected boolean checkInside( HttpServletRequest req ) {
    String clientIP = req.getRemoteAddr();
    boolean isInside = clientIP.startsWith( hostIP );
    return isInside;
}
```

The following method is responsible for returning an `LDAPConnection` to the servlet. It requests the connection from the pool we allocated at initialization and attaches the cache to the connection (if the cache is initialized). If no connections are available in the pool, then the pool will block until one becomes available. There will also be a message in the log that the pool ran out of connections.

```
/**
 * Get an LDAPConnection from the pool,
 * and assign the LDAP cache to this connection
 *
 * @return a valid LDAPConnection
 */
private LDAPConnection getLDAPConn() {
    // Get connection from pool
    LDAPConnection ld = ldapPool.getConnection();
    if ( readCache != null ) {
        ld.setCache( readCache );
    }
    return ld;
}


/**
 * Return an LDAPConnection to the pool
 *
 * @param ld the connection to return to the pool
 */
private void closeConnection( LDAPConnection ld ) {
    if ( ld != null ) {
        ldapPool.close( ld );
    }
}


/**
 * Returns the string representation of an LDAP attribute
 * from the specified entry.
 * If the attribute is not present or has a zero length
 * value, then return "-". If the attribute has more than
 * one value, then just return the first one.
 *
 * @param entry an LDAP entry
 * @param attrN name of the attribute (e.g., "cn")
 * @return value of attribute or -
 */
private String getValue( LDAPEntry entry, String attrN ) {
    return getValue( entry, attrN, "-" );
}


/**
 * Return the string representation of an LDAP attribute
```

```
     * from the specified entry.
     * If the attribute is not present or has a zero length value,
     * then return the default. If the attribute has more than one
     * value, then just return the first one.
     *
     * @param entry an LDAP entry
     * @param attrN name of the attribute (e.g., "cn")
     * @param defVal value to return if attribute does not
     *  exist
     * @return value of attribute or defVal
     */
    private String getValue( LDAPEntry entry,
                             String attrN,
                             String defVal) {
        LDAPAttribute attr = entry.getAttribute( attrN );
        if ( attr == null ) {
            return defVal;
        }
        Enumeration enumVals = attr.getStringValues();
        // Enumerate on values for this attribute
        if ( (enumVals == null) ||
             !enumVals.hasMoreElements() ) {
            return defVal;
        }
        String theValue = (String)enumVals.nextElement();
        if ( (theValue == null) ||
             (theValue.length() == 0) ) {
            return defVal;
        }
        return theValue;
    }

    /**
     * Return the binary representation of an LDAP attribute
     * value from the specified entry.
     * If the attribute is not present, then return null. If the
     * attribute has more than one value, then just return
     * the first one.
     *
     * @param entry an LDAP entry
     * @param attrN name of the attribute (e.g., "cn")
     * @return value of attribute as byte[] or null
     */
    private byte[] getBinaryValue( LDAPEntry entry,
```

```
                                 String attrN ) {
        LDAPAttribute attr = entry.getAttribute( attrN );
        if ( attr == null ) {
            return null;
        }
        Enumeration enumVals = attr.getByteValues();
        if ( (enumVals == null) ||
             (!enumVals.hasMoreElements()) ) {
            return null;
        }
        return (byte[])enumVals.nextElement();
    }

    /**
     * Return the LDAP scope constant for a string
     * value of "SCOPE_BASE", "SCOPE_ONE" or
     * "SCOPE_SUB".
     *
     * @param scope String representation of scope
     * @return LDAPConnection constant for the scope
     */
    private static int getScope( String scope ) {
        if ( scope.equalsIgnoreCase("SCOPE_BASE") ) {
            return LDAPConnection.SCOPE_BASE;
        } else if ( scope.equalsIgnoreCase("SCOPE_ONE") ) {
            return LDAPConnection.SCOPE_ONE;
        } else {
            return LDAPConnection.SCOPE_SUB;
        }
    }

    /**
     * Return a String without attribute types in the format
     * "bjensen, people, airius.com" from a DN like
     * "uid=bjensen,ou=people,o=airius.com"
     *
     * @param theDN a fully formed DN
     * @return a simplified DN without attribute types
     */
    private String prettyDN( String theDN ) {
        String[] dn = LDAPDN.explodeDN(theDN,true);
        String dncomps = "";
        for ( int i=0; i<dn.length; i++ ) {
            dncomps += (i==0 ? "" : ", ") + dn[i];
```

```
        }
        return dncomps;
    }

    /**
     * Return the String representing the HTML form value
     * from the specified post or get.
     * If form value does not exist or has no value,
     * then return an empty String.
     *
     * @param req HTTPServletRequest
     * @param fdname name of the field in the HTML form,
     * (e.g., "password")
     * @return value of field, or "" if not present
     */
    private String readFormData( HttpServletRequest req,
                                 String fdname )  {
        String d = req.getParameter(fdname);
        if ( d == null ) {
            return "";
        }
        return d.trim();
    }

    /**
     * Build an LDAPAttribute with the specified attribute
     * name and value. If no value is specified, then the
     * attribute will be deleted with an LDAP replace operation.
     *
     * @param attrN name of attribute (e.g., "cn")
     * @param attrV value for attribute (e.g., "Tom Jones"); pass
     * null for none
     * @return an LDAP attribute
     *
     */
    private LDAPAttribute buildAttr( String attrN,
                                     String attrV ) {
        if ( attrV == null ) {
            return new LDAPAttribute( attrN );
        } else {
            return new LDAPAttribute( attrN, attrV );
        }
    }
```

The `modifyPwd` method handles requests by users to change their passwords. It accepts two copies of the new password (one for confirmation), and the old password. The connection for this operation is allocated outside the normal pool of search connections because it will use different credentials. The credentials are validated by authenticating, and then the `userPassword` attribute is modified.

```
/**
 * Handle requests for password modification by the user.
 * Validate that both new passwords are OK and that the
 * old password is correct (by binding to the directory).
 *
 * @param req HTTPServletRequest
 * @param out output stream
 * @exception ServletException or IOException on reading
 * or writing form data
 */
private void modifyPwd( HttpServletRequest req,
                        PrintWriter out )
    throws ServletException, IOException {

    LDAPConnection ld = null;
    String theDN;
    String oldpw;
    String newpw1;
    String newpw2;
    int err = 0;

    // Get detail arguments (the DN)
    theDN = readFormData(req,FLDNAME_DN).toLowerCase();
    if ( theDN.length() == 0 ) {
        errorMessage(out,"Invalid Distingushed Name");
        return;
    }
    theDN = LDAPUrl.decode(theDN);
    oldpw = readFormData(req,FLDNAME_OLDPW);
    newpw1 = readFormData(req,FLDNAME_NEWPW1);
    newpw2 = readFormData(req,FLDNAME_NEWPW2);

    // The passwords must pass the following tests:
    //   old must be valid and nonzero length
    //   new1 and new2 must match and be nonzero length
```

```
if ( (!newpw1.equals(newpw2)) ||
     (newpw1.length()==0) ) {
    errorMessage(out,"Invalid new password");
    return;
}

if ( oldpw.length() == 0 ) {
    errorMessage(out,"Old password is invalid");
    return;
}

// Attempt to write change.
// Do not use the pool for this operation because it
// requires special credentials.

try {
    ld = new LDAPConnection();
    ld.connect( host, port, theDN, oldpw );
    LDAPAttribute pw =
        new LDAPAttribute("userPassword",newpw1);
    LDAPModification mod =
        new LDAPModification(LDAPModification.REPLACE,
                             pw);
    ld.modify( theDN, mod );
} catch (LDAPException e) {
    err = 1;
    int num =  e.getLDAPResultCode();
    if (num == LDAPException.INVALID_CREDENTIALS) {
        errorMessage(out,"Invalid old password.");
    } else {
        errorMessage(out,e.toString());
    }
}
```

If using an NDS (Novell Directory Services) directory with an LDAP client, then a password change request must be handled a bit differently: the same operation must specify the old password for deletion and the new password for addition. The following code demonstrates this technique for NDS:

```
LDAPModificationSet mods = new LDAPModificationSet();
mods.add( LDAPModification.DELETE,
          new LDAPAttribute("userPassword",oldpw) );
mods.add( LDAPModification.ADD,
          new LDAPAttribute("userPassword", newpw1) );
ld.modify( theDN, mods );
```

```
        if ( (ld!= null) && (ld.isConnected()) ) {
            try {
                ld.disconnect();
            } catch (LDAPException e) {}
        }
        if (err != 0) {
            return;
        }

        out.println("<HTML>");
        out.println("<HEAD>");
        out.println("<TITLE>"+orgName+"</TITLE>");
        out.println("<SCRIPT Language=\"JavaScript\">");
        out.println("function doNothing() {}");
        out.println("</SCRIPT>");
        out.println("");
        out.println("</HEAD>");
        out.println("<BODY BGCOLOR=\"white\">");
        out.println("Thank you for changing your password!");
        out.println("<BR>");
        out.print("<a href=\"javascript:doNothing()\" ");
        out.print("onclick=\"window.close();\">");
        out.println("Click Here</a>");
        out.println("</BODY>");
        out.println("</HTML>");

        return;
    }
```

The modifyEntry method handles the case in which a user wants to update certain information about herself. Users are allowed to update their mobile phone numbers, pager numbers, and home phone numbers in this example. They are also allowed to upload new JPEG photographs for themselves. To support uploading a file, we use the encoding type of multipart/form-data. Included on the CD-ROM that accompanies this book is a Java class, CParseRFC1867, that makes parsing data in this format relatively simple. Multipart form data is treated basically as a raw input stream, with each element inside of a properly coded boundary marker. Full details about the format and structure can be found in RFC 1867. Customize the attribute selection to fit the self-administration policies of your organization.

```
/**
  * Handle editing of an individual entry.
  * Remove attributes with no value, and add or replace
  * attributes with new or different values.
  * Use the java class
  * CParseRFC187 to parse multipart forms.
  * Multipart forms allow users to send new photographs
  * for their entries.
  *
  * @param req HTTPServletRequest
  * @param out output stream
  * @exception ServletException or IOException on writing
  * changes to the directory or writing output
  */
private void modifyEntry( HttpServletRequest req,
                          PrintWriter out )
    throws ServletException, IOException {

    LDAPConnection ld = null;
    String theDN = "";
    String thepw = "";
    String pager = "" ;
    String mobile = "";
    String homePhone = "";
    byte[] newPhoto = null;
    int err = 0;

    String conType = req.getContentType().toLowerCase();
    if (conType.indexOf("multipart/form-data") == -1) {
        // Standard form submit, no picture
        // Get form elements
        theDN = readFormData(req,FLDNAME_DN).toLowerCase();
```

```
        thepw = readFormData(req,FLDNAME_OLDPW);
        pager = readFormData(req,"pager");
        mobile = readFormData(req,"mobile");
        homePhone = readFormData(req,"homePhone");
    } else {
        CParseRFC1867 parse = new CParseRFC1867(req);
        while (parse.hasMoreContent()) {
            parse.getContent();
            int nType = parse.getContentType();
            switch (nType) {
                case CParseRFC1867.PARAMETER :
                    String fldname =
                        parse.getParameterName().
                        toLowerCase();
                    String fldval =
                        parse.getParameterValue();
                    if ( fldval == null ) {
                        fldval = "";
                    }
                    if ( fldname.equals(FLDNAME_DN) ) {
                        theDN = fldval;
                    } else if ( fldname.equals(
                        FLDNAME_OLDPW) ) {
                        thepw = fldval;
                    } else if ( fldname.equals(
                        "pager") ) {
                        pager = fldval;
                    } else if ( fldname.equals(
                        "mobile") ) {
                        mobile = fldval;
                    } else if ( fldname.equals(
                        "homephone") ) {
                        homePhone = fldval;
                    } else {
                        System.err.println(
                            "invalid field->"+fldname);
                    }
                    break;
                case CParseRFC1867.FILE :
                    String fname =
                        parse.getFileName().trim();
                     CBlobInputStream instream =
                         parse.getBlobInputStream();
                    if ( (fname != null) &&
```

```
                          (!fname.equals("")) ) {
                          instream.preFetch();
                          int sizePic =
                              instream.getTotalBytes();
                          if ( (sizePic <= maxPhotoSize) ||
                               (maxPhotoSize == 0) ) {
                              // If pic size within limits
                              newPhoto = new byte[sizePic];
                              for ( int i=0;i<sizePic;i++ ) {
                                  newPhoto[i] =
                                      (byte)instream.read();
                              }
                          }
                          instream.close();
                      } else {
                          parse.readToNextBoundary();
                      }
                      break;
              } // switch
          } // while
      }

      if ( theDN.length() == 0 ) {
          errorMessage(out,"Invalid Distingushed Name");
          return;
      }
      if ( thepw.length() == 0 ) {
          errorMessage(out,"Password cannot be blank");
          return;
      }
      theDN = LDAPUrl.decode(theDN);

      // Build a modification set
      LDAPModificationSet mods = new LDAPModificationSet();
      LDAPAttribute attr1 = buildAttr("pager",pager);
      LDAPAttribute attr2 = buildAttr("mobile",mobile);
      LDAPAttribute attr3 = buildAttr("homePhone",homePhone);

      mods.add(LDAPModification.REPLACE,attr1);
      mods.add(LDAPModification.REPLACE,attr2);
      mods.add(LDAPModification.REPLACE,attr3);
      if ( newPhoto != null ) {
          LDAPAttribute attr4 =
              new LDAPAttribute(photoAttr,newPhoto);
```

```
        mods.add(LDAPModification.REPLACE,attr4);
    }

    // Attempt to write change.
    // Do not use the pool for this operation because
    // special credentials are required.
    try {
        ld = new LDAPConnection();
        ld.connect( host, port, theDN, thepw );
        ld.modify( theDN, mods );
        if ( readCache != null ) {
            readCache.flushEntries( theDN,
                                    ld.SCOPE_BASE );
        }
    } catch (LDAPException e) {
        err = 1;
        int num = e.getLDAPResultCode();
        if ( num == LDAPException.INVALID_CREDENTIALS ) {
            errorMessage(out,"Invalid Password.");
        } else {
            errorMessage(out,e.toString());
        }
    }

    if ( (ld!= null) && (ld.isConnected()) ) {
        try {
            ld.disconnect();
        } catch (LDAPException e) {}
    }
    if (err != 0) {
        return;
    }

    out.println("<HTML>");
    out.println("<HEAD>");
    out.println("<TITLE>"+orgName+"</TITLE>");
    out.println("<SCRIPT Language=\"JavaScript\">");
    out.println("function doNothing() {}");
    out.println("</SCRIPT>");
    out.println("");
    out.println("</HEAD>");
    out.println("<BODY BGCOLOR=\"white\">");
    out.println("Thank you for keeping your information " +
                "current!");
```

```
        out.println("<BR>");
        out.print("<A HREF=\"javascript:doNothing()\" ");
        out.print("onclick=\"window.close();\">");
        out.println("Click Here</a>");
        out.println("</BODY>");
        out.println("</HTML>");

        return;
    }

    /**
     * Handles requests for search page or requests that
     * are not valid (we send the search page)
     *
     * @param out output stream
     * @param isInternal true if internal user
     * @param uri the servlet's uniform resource identifier
     *
     */
    private void sendSrchPage( PrintWriter out,
                               boolean isInternal,
                               String uri ) {
        // Dump the search page

        out.println("<HTML>");
        out.println("<HEAD>");
        out.println("<TITLE>"+orgName+" "+
                    (isInternal ? "Internal" : "")+
                    " Phonebook</TITLE>");
        out.println("</HEAD>");
        out.println("<BODY BGCOLOR="+srchPageColors+">");
        out.println("<H2 ALIGN=\"center\">"+orgName+
                    " Phonebook</H2>");
        out.println("<P>The "+orgName+" Phone Book allows you"+
                    " to locate an individual within the "+
                    "company.");
        out.println("Please enter your search ");
        out.println("string below. You may search for phone "+
                    "number, email, etc....</P>");
        out.print("<FORM METHOD=\"post\" action=\""+ uri + "?");
        out.println(ACTION_FIELD+"="+ACTION_SEARCH+"\">");

        out.println("<CENTER>");
        out.println("<TABLE WIDTH=\"75%\" BORDER=\"0\">");
```

```
    out.println("<TR>");
    out.println("<TD>");
    out.println("<DIV ALIGN=\"right\">Search:</DIV>");
    out.println("</TD>");
    out.println("<TD>");
    out.println("<SELECT NAME="+FLDNAME_SRCHKIND+">");
    out.println("<OPTION VALUE=\"all\">Anything</OPTION>");
    out.println("<OPTION VALUE=\"cn\" selected>"+
                "Name</OPTION>");
    out.println("<OPTION VALUE=\"mail\">"+
                "Electronic Mail</OPTION>");
    out.println("<OPTION VALUE=\"telephoneNumber\">"+
                "Phone Number</OPTION>");
    out.println("<OPTION VALUE=\""+
                "facsimiletelephoneNumber\">"+
                "Fax Number</OPTION>");
    out.println("</SELECT>");
    out.println("</TD>");
    out.println("</TR>");
    out.println("<TR>");
    out.println("<TD> </TD>");
    out.println("<TD>");
    out.println("<INPUT TYPE=\"text\" name="+
                FLDNAME_SRCHSTRING+" size=\"40\""+
                " maxlength=\"60\">");
    out.println("</TD>");
    out.println("</TR>");
    out.println("</TABLE>");
    out.println("</CENTER>");
    out.println("<BR>");
    out.print("<CENTER><INPUT TYPE=\"submit\" ");
    out.println("name=\"Submit\" value=\"Search\">"+
                "</CENTER>");
    out.println("</FORM>");

    out.println("<BR>");
    out.println("<P>Questions or comments email "+
                "<A HREF=\"mailto:"+ownMail+"\">"+
                "webmaster</A></P>");
    out.println("</BODY>");
    out.println("</HTML>");

    return;
}
```

```
/**
 * Handles requests for password change page
 *
 * @param req HttpServletRequest
 * @param out output stream
 * @param isInternal true if internal user
 * @exception throws ServletException or IOException for
 * invalid URL or error on writing output
 *
 */
private void sendPwdPage( HttpServletRequest req,
                          PrintWriter out,
                          boolean isInternal )
        throws ServletException, IOException {

    String theDN;
    String theDNd;
    String uri = req.getRequestURI();

    // Get the DN of the record we are altering
    theDN = readFormData(req,FLDNAME_DN).toLowerCase();
    theDN = LDAPUrl.decode(theDN);
    if ( theDN.length() == 0 ) {
        errorMessage(out,"Error with Distingushed Name");
        return;
    }

    out.println("<HTML>");
    out.println("<HEAD>");
    out.println("<TITLE>"+orgName+"</TITLE>");

    out.println("<SCRIPT Language=\"JavaScript\">");
    out.println("function doNothing() {}");
    out.println("</SCRIPT>");
    out.println("");

    out.println("</HEAD>");
    out.println("<BODY BGCOLOR=\"white\">");
    out.print("<FORM METHOD=POST name=\"PwdModForm\"");
    out.print("action=\""+uri+"?"+ACTION_FIELD+"=");
    out.println(ACTION_DOPWD+"\">");
    out.print("<INPUT TYPE=\"hidden\" name=\""+FLDNAME_DN);
    out.println("\" value=\""+LDAPUrl.encode(theDN)+"\">");
```

```
String dncomps = prettyDN(theDN);
out.println("<FONT SIZE=\"+2\">"+dncomps+"</FONT><BR>");
out.println("<BR>");

out.print("<TABLE CELLSPACING=\"2\" ");
out.println("BORDER BGCOLOR=#F2F2F2 WIDTH=60%>");
out.println("<TR>");
out.print("<TD BGCOLOR=#006666>");
out.print("<FONT FACE=ARIAL,HELVETICA COLOR=WHITE>");
out.println(" New Password</FONT></TD>");
out.println("</TR>");
out.println("<TR>");
out.println("<TD VALIGN=\"TOP\" NOWRAP>");
out.print("<INPUT TYPE=\"password\" name=");
out.print(FLDNAME_NEWPW1+" size=\"20\" ");
out.println("MAXLENGTH=\"20\">");
out.println("</TD>");
out.println("</TR>");
out.println("<TR>");
out.println("<TD VALIGN=\"TOP\" NOWRAP>");
out.print("<INPUT TYPE=\"password\" NAME=");
out.print(FLDNAME_NEWPW2+" size=\"20\" ");
out.println("MAXLENGTH=\"20\">");
out.println("Confirm New Password</TD>");
out.println("</TR>");
out.println("</TABLE>");
out.println("<BR>");
out.print("<TABLE CELLSPACING=\"2\" BORDER ");
out.println("BGCOLOR=#F2F2F2 WIDTH=60%>");
out.println("<TR>");
out.print("<TD BGCOLOR=#006666>");
out.print("<FONT FACE=ARIAL,HELVETICA COLOR=WHITE>");
out.println(" Old Password");
out.println("</FONT></TD>");
out.println("</TR>");
out.println("<TR>");
out.println("<TD VALIGN=\"TOP\" NOWRAP>");
out.print("<INPUT TYPE=\"password\" NAME=");
out.print(FLDNAME_OLDPW+" SIZE=\"20\" ");
out.println("MAXLENGTH=\"20\">");
out.println("</TD>");
out.println("</TR>");
out.println("</TABLE>");
out.println("<BR>");
```

```
        out.print("<CENTER><INPUT TYPE=\"submit\" NAME=\"");
        out.print("submit\" VALUE=\"Change Password");
        out.println("\"></CENTER>");
        out.println("</FORM>");
        out.println("<BR>");
        out.print("<A HREF=\"javascript:doNothing()\" ");
        out.print("onclick=\"window.close();\">");
        out.println("Cancel Password Modify</A>");

        out.println("</BODY>");
        out.println("</HTML>");

        return;
    }

    /**
     * Generates a single row for the search results page.
     *
     * @param out PrintWriter for output stream
     * @param color background color for this row
     * @param attrs the names of the attributes for this row
     *  for each of the five columns
     * @param entry containing the data for this row
     * @param uri the servlet's uniform resource identifier
     * @param url complete URL to get back to servlet
     * @param isInternal true if internal user
     *
     */
    private void generateRow( PrintWriter out, String color,
                              String[] attrs, LDAPEntry entry,
                              String uri, String url,
                              boolean isInternal ) {
        // Generate one row of output data
        String theDN = LDAPUrl.encode(entry.getDN()); // Encode
        String theName = getValue(entry,attrs[0]);
        String thePhone = getValue(entry,attrs[1]);
        String theMail = getValue(entry,attrs[2]);
        String certimg = " ";
        String photoimg = " ";
        String nameurl = theName;

        // Most of this is building the custom line based on
        // whether the caller is an external or internal user.
        // External users are not allowed to click on the name for
```

```
        // details, among other things.
        byte[] theCert = getBinaryValue(entry,certAttr);
        if ( theCert != null ) { // Has cert so give url
            certimg = "<A HREF=\""+uri+"?"+ACTION_FIELD+"="+
                ACTION_GETCERT+
                "&"+FLDNAME_DN+"="+theDN+"\"><IMG SRC=\""+
                imagesURL+
                "cert.gif\" WIDTH=24 HEIGHT=21 BORDER=0 " +
                "alt=\"Get digital certificate\"></A>";
        }

       byte[] thePhoto = getBinaryValue(entry,attrs[4]);
        if (thePhoto != null && isInternal) {
            photoimg = "<A HREF=\"javascript:doNothing()\" " +
                "onclick=\"winopen=displayPic('"+url+uri+"?"+
                ACTION_FIELD+"="+ACTION_GETPHOTO+"&"+
                FLDNAME_DN+"="+theDN+"');\"><IMG SRC=\""+imagesURL+
                "photo.gif\" WIDTH=37 HEIGHT=21 BORDER=0 " +
                "alt=\"Look at Photograph\"></A>";
        }

        if (isInternal) {
            nameurl = "<A HREF=\""+uri+"?"+ACTION_FIELD+"="+
                 ACTION_DETAIL+
                "&"+FLDNAME_DN+"="+theDN+"\">"+theName+"</A>";
        }

        //Colors are either "#666600" or "#009999"
        out.println("<TR BGCOLOR=\""+color+"\">");
        out.println("<TD>"+nameurl+"</TD>");
        out.println("<TD>"+thePhone+"</TD>");
        if (theMail.equals("-")) {
            out.println("<TD> - </TD>");
        } else {
            out.println("<TD><A HREF=\"mailto:" + theMail + "\">" +
                theMail + "</A></TD>");
        }
        out.println("<TD>"+certimg+" "+photoimg+"</TD>");
        out.println("</TR>");
    }
```

The detailEdit routine, which follows, is used to handle both detail views and preparation of the edit record for an individual entry. A detail view of Barbara Jensen is shown in Figure 13-6. The edit view shown in Figure 13-7 is similar, with fields for

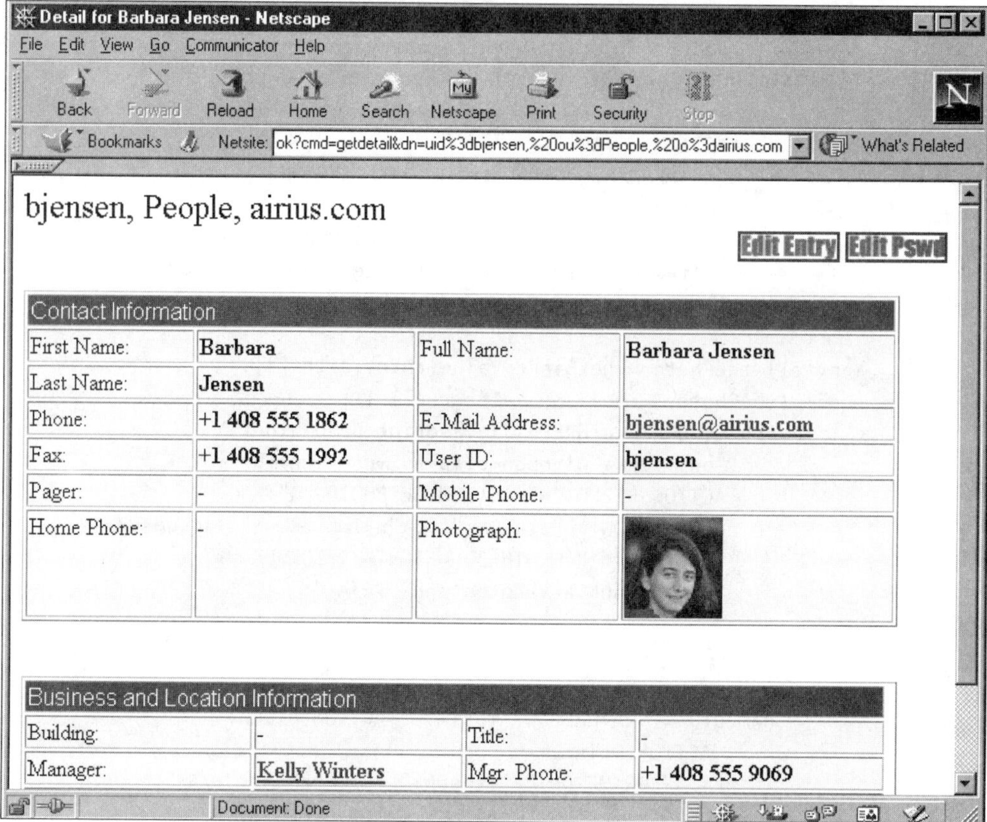

FIGURE 13-6. *Sample detail view.*

editing shown as standard HTML input tags. The user is also allowed to upload a new photo if desired.

```
  /**
   * Handles requests for detail view and edit pages
   *
   * @param req HttpServletRequest
   * @param out PrintWriter
   * @param detail true if detail view;
   * (view only) if edit page
   * @exceptions ServletException or IOException on reading
   * from directory or writing output
   *
 */
```

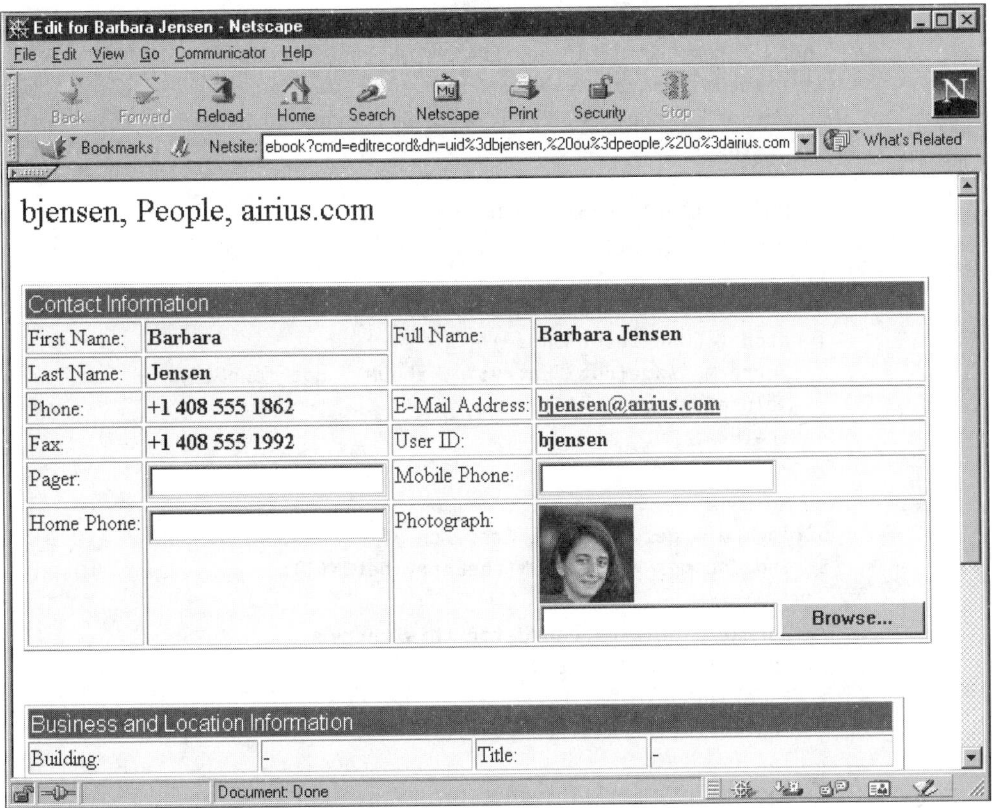

FIGURE 13-7. *Overview of edit screen.*

```
private void detailEdit( HttpServletRequest req,
                         PrintWriter out,
                         boolean detail )
    throws ServletException, IOException {

    LDAPConnection ld;
    LDAPEntry theEntry = null;
    String theDN;
    int err = 0;
    String uri = req.getRequestURI();
    String imgURL = "";

    // If detail is true, then show the record and
    // allow editing of certain fields
```

```
// Get detail arguments (the DN)
theDN = readFormData(req,FLDNAME_DN).toLowerCase();
if ( theDN.length() == 0 ) {
    errorMessage(out,"Error with Distingushed Name");
    return;
}
theDN = LDAPUrl.decode(theDN);
ld = getLDAPConn();
try {
    theEntry = ld.read(theDN);  // Read entry
} catch ( LDAPException e ) {
    errorMessage(out,"Entry:" + theDN+" not found!");
    closeConnection(ld);
    return;
}

String cn = getValue(theEntry,"cn");
String dncomps = prettyDN(theEntry.getDN());

// Format a detail record for this entry
out.println("<HTML><HEAD>");
if ( detail ) {
    out.println("<TITLE>Detail for "+cn+"</TITLE>");
} else {
    out.println("<TITLE>Edit for "+cn+"</TITLE>");
}
out.println("</HEAD>");
out.println("<BODY BGCOLOR=\"#FFFFFF\">");
out.println("<FONT SIZE=\"+2\">"+dncomps+"</FONT>");
out.println("<BR>");
//If edit, put a form tag in there
if ( !detail ) {
    out.print("<FORM METHOD=\"post\" ACTION=\"");
    out.print(uri+"?"+ACTION_FIELD+"="+ACTION_DOEDIT);
    out.println("\" ENCTYPE=\"multipart/form-data\">");
}

if ( detail ) {
    out.println("<DIV ALIGN=\"right\">");
    out.println("<A HREF=\""+uri+"?"+ACTION_FIELD+"="+
                ACTION_EDIT+"&"+FLDNAME_DN+"="+
                LDAPUrl.encode(theDN)+"\" "+
                "TARGET=\"_blank\">"+
                "<IMG SRC=\""+imagesURL+
```

```
                    "edit.gif\" alt=\"Edit this entry.\">"+
                    "</A>");
        out.println("<A HREF=\""+uri+"?"+ACTION_FIELD+"="+
                    ACTION_PWD+"&"+FLDNAME_DN+"="+
                    LDAPUrl.encode(theDN)+"\" "+
                    "TARGET=\"_blank\">"+
                    "<IMG SRC=\""+imagesURL+
                    "pwd.gif\" alt=\"Change password.\">"+
                    "</A></DIV>");
    }

    out.println("<BR>");
    out.println("<TABLE CELLSPACING=\"2\" " +
                    "BORDER BGCOLOR=#F2F2F2 WIDTH=95%>");
    out.println("<TR>");
    out.println("<TD BGCOLOR=#006666 COLSPAN=4>"+
                "<FONT FACE=ARIAL,HELVETICA COLOR=WHITE>"+
                "Contact Information</FONT></TD>");
    out.println("</TR>");

    out.println("<TD VALIGN=\"top\" NOWRAP>First Name:"+
                "</TD>");
    out.println("<TD VALIGN=\"top\" NOWRAP><B>"+
                getValue(theEntry,"givenName")+
                "</B></TD>");
    out.println("<TD VALIGN=\"top\" NOWRAP ROWSPAN=\"2\""+
                ">Full Name:</TD>");
    out.println("<TD VALIGN=\"top\" NOWRAP ROWSPAN=\"2\""+
                "><B>"+cn+"</B></TD></TR>");

    out.println("<TR>");
    out.println("<TD VALIGN=\"top\" NOWRAP>Last Name:"+
                "</TD>");
    out.println("<TD VALIGN=\"top\" NOWRAP><B>"+
                getValue(theEntry,"sn")+"</B></TD></TR>");

    out.println("<TR>");
    out.println("<TD VALIGN=\"TOP\">Phone:</TD>");
    out.println("<TD VALIGN=\"TOP\" NOWRAP><B>"+
                getValue(theEntry,"telephoneNumber")+
                "</B></TD>");
    out.println("<TD VALIGN=\"TOP\" NOWRAP>"+
                "E-Mail Address:</TD>");
```

```
String email = getValue(theEntry,"mail");
if ( !email.equals("-") ) {
    email = "<A HREF=mailto:"+email+">"+email+"</A>";
}
out.println("<TD VALIGN=\"TOP\" NOWRAP><B>"+
            email+"</B></TD></TR>");

out.println("<TR>");
out.println("<TD VALIGN=\"TOP\">Fax:</TD>");
out.println("<TD VALIGN=\"TOP\" nowrap><B>"+
            getValue(theEntry,"facsimiletelephoneNumber")
            +"</B></TD>");
out.println("<TD VALIGN=\"TOP\" nowrap>User ID:</TD>");
out.println("<TD VALIGN=\"TOP\" nowrap><B>"+
            getValue(theEntry,"uid")+"</B></TD></TR>");

out.println("<TR>");
out.println("<TD VALIGN=\"TOP\" nowrap>Pager:</TD>");

out.println("<TD VALIGN=\"TOP\" nowrap><B>");

if ( detail ) {
    out.println(getValue(theEntry,"pager")+"</B></TD>");
} else {
    out.println("<input type=\"text\" name=\"pager\" "+
                "size=\"20\" maxlength=\"20\" value=\""+
                getValue(theEntry,"pager","")+"\"></B></TD>");
}

out.println("<TD VALIGN=\"TOP\" nowrap>Mobile Phone:"+
                "</TD>");

out.println("<TD VALIGN=\"TOP\" nowrap><B>");
if ( detail ) {
    out.println(getValue(theEntry,"mobile")+"</B></TD></TR>");
} else {
    out.println("<input type=\"text\" name=\"mobile\" "+
                "size=\"20\" maxlength=\"20\" value=\""+
                getValue(theEntry,"mobile","")+"\">"+
                "</B></TD></TR>");
}

out.println("<TR>");
out.println("<TD VALIGN=\"TOP\" nowrap>Home Phone:</TD>");
```

```
out.println("<TD VALIGN=\"TOP\" nowrap><B>");
if ( detail ) {
    out.println(getValue(theEntry,"homePhone")+"</B>"+
                "</TD>");
} else {
    out.println("<input type=\"text\" name=\"homePhone\" "+
                "size=\"20\" maxlength=\"20\" value=\""+
                getValue(theEntry,"homePhone","")+"\">"+
                "</B></TD>");
}
// Display photograph if present
out.println("<TD VALIGN=\"TOP\" nowrap>Photograph:</TD>");
out.print("<TD VALIGN=\"TOP\" nowrap>");
if ( getBinaryValue(theEntry,photoAttr) != null ) {
    imgURL = "<IMG SRC=\""+uri+"?"+ACTION_FIELD+"="+
    ACTION_GETPHOTO+"&"+FLDNAME_DN+"="+
    LDAPUrl.encode(theDN)+"\" width=\"70\" height=\"70\">";
} else {
    imgURL = "<B>-</B>";
}

if ( !detail ) {
    //Put a browse-for-new-picture button
    imgURL += "<BR><INPUT TYPE=FILE NAME="+
        FLDNAME_NEWPHOTO+">";
}

imgURL += "</TD>";
out.println(imgURL);
out.println("</TABLE>");
out.println("<BR><BR>");

// Business and location information in this section
out.println("<TABLE CELLSPACING=\"2\" " +
            "BORDER BGCOLOR=#F2F2F2 WIDTH=95%>");
out.println("<TR>");
out.println("<TD BGCOLOR=#006666 COLSPAN=4>"+
            "<FONT FACE=ARIAL,HELVETICA COLOR=WHITE>"+
            "Business and "+
            "Location Information</FONT>"+
            "</TD>");
out.println("</TR>");

out.println("<TR>");
out.println("<TD VALIGN=\"TOP\">Building:</TD>");
```

```
out.println("<TD VALIGN=\"TOP\" nowrap><B>"+
            getValue(theEntry,"buildingName")+
            "</B></TD>");
out.println("<TD VALIGN=\"TOP\">Title:</TD>");
out.println("<TD VALIGN=\"TOP\" nowrap><B>"+
            getValue(theEntry,"title")+"</B></TD>");
out.println("</TR>");

out.println("<TR>");
out.println("<TD VALIGN=\"TOP\">Manager:</TD>");

String mgr = getValue(theEntry,"manager");
String mgrPhone = "-";

if (!mgr.equals("-")) {
    String[] mgrAttrs = {"cn","telephoneNumber"};
    try {
        LDAPEntry mgrEntry = ld.read(mgr,mgrAttrs);
        String mgrdn = LDAPUrl.encode(mgr);
        String mgrName = getValue(mgrEntry,mgrAttrs[0]);
        mgrPhone = getValue(mgrEntry,mgrAttrs[1]);
        mgr = "<A HREF=\""+uri+"?"+ACTION_FIELD+"="+
              ACTION_DETAIL+"&"+FLDNAME_DN+"="+
              mgrdn+"\">"+mgrName+"</A>";
    } catch (LDAPException e) {
        mgr = "-";
    }
}

out.println("<TD VALIGN=\"TOP\" NOWRAP><B>"+
            mgr+"</B></TD>");
out.println("<TD VALIGN=\"TOP\">Mgr. Phone:</TD>");
out.println("<TD VALIGN=\"TOP\" NOWRAP><B>"+
            mgrPhone+"</B></TD>");
out.println("</TR>");

out.println("<TR>");
out.println("<TD VALIGN=\"TOP\">City:</TD>");
out.println("<TD VALIGN=\"TOP\"><B>"+
            getValue(theEntry,"l")+"</B></TD>");
out.println("<TD VALIGN=\"TOP\">State:</TD>");
out.println("<TD VALIGN=\"TOP\"><B>"+
            getValue(theEntry,"st")+"</B></TD>");
```

```
        out.println("</TR>");

        out.println("<TR>");
        out.println("<TD VALIGN=\"TOP\">Mailing Address:</TD>");
        out.println("<TD VALIGN=\"TOP\" COLSPAN=\"4\" "+
                    "NOWRAP><B>");
        String postAddr = getValue(theEntry,"l","")+", "+
                          getValue(theEntry,"st","")+" "+
                          getValue(theEntry,"postalCode","");
        if (postAddr.length() < 5) { //none stored
            postAddr = "";
        }
        out.println(getValue(theEntry,"postalAddress")+"<BR>");
        out.println(postAddr+"</B></TD>");
        out.println("</TR>");

        out.println("</TABLE>");

        if (!detail) {
            // Prompt for password
            out.println("<BR> Password: ");
            out.println("<INPUT TYPE=\"password\" name=\""+
                        FLDNAME_OLDPW+"\" size=\"20\""+
                        " maxlength=\"20\"><BR>");

            out.println("<BR><CENTER>");
            out.println("<INPUT TYPE=\"submit\" NAME=\"Submit\""+
                        " VALUE=\"Submit\">");
            out.println("<INPUT TYPE=\"reset\" NAME=\"Reset\""+
                        " VALUE=\"Reset\">");
            out.println("</CENTER><BR>");
            out.print("<INPUT TYPE=\"hidden\" NAME=\""+
                      FLDNAME_DN);
            out.println("\" VALUE=\""+LDAPUrl.encode(theDN)+
                        "\">");
            out.println("</FORM>");
        }

        out.println("</BODY></HTML>");
        closeConnection(ld);
    }

}
```

Setting Up and Using the Servlet

The servlet classes should be placed in the directory where your servlet engine expects class files. You will also need to place the `CParseRFC1867.class`, `CBlobInputStream.class`, `LDAPConnectionPool.class`, and `LDAPConnectionPool$LDAPConnectionObject.class` files in this directory. Next, place the images files in a directory that is available from your Web server. The path to this location should be set in the `phonebook.properties` file. Execute the servlet by accessing the URL for your servlet engine; in your Web browser you will most likely receive the message shown in Figure 13-8.

Locate the file `phonebook.properties` on the hard drive of your server. The JRun engine from Live Software, for example, looks for properties files in the `/jrun/jsm-default` directory. Add your properties to the `phonebook.properties` file. It is a standard resource bundle text file. A sample follows:

```
# Properties for Phonebook servlet

# host name, port, and search root of directory server
host=localhost
port=389
srchroot=o=airius.com
```

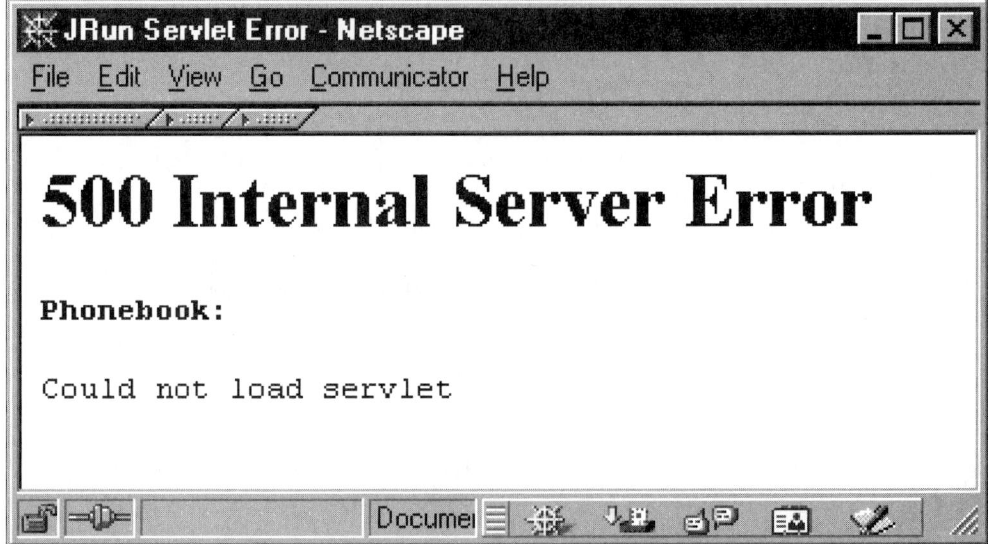

FIGURE 13-8. *Message indicating that the properties file could not be found.*

```
# name for header on pages
orgname=Airius Communications

# e-mail address of owner of service
ownmail=webmaster@airius.com

# URL for graphics - if local then specify off HTTP root
imgurl = /phonebook/images/

# initial size of connection pool
initpool=10

# maximum size of connection pool
maxpool=20

# connection authentication DN
authdn=

# connection authentication password
authpw=

# max photograph size in bytes
maxphotosize=100000

# cache size in bytes (max=1000000 = 1MB); 0=no caching
cachesize=1000000

# cache timeout in seconds
cachetime=3600
```

This file is consulted by the servlet upon start-up and can be used to alter specific values without modifying the source code. Two particular settings that may need adjustment are the initial pool size and the maximum size. When making changes to these settings, the servlet will need restarting to read the new values.

The servlet wraps most of the LDAP SDK functionality into a few key methods and makes heavy use of the pool. One characteristic of connection-pooling systems on most servlet engines is that the initial user of the system experiences a significant delay as the connection pool is constructed. Subsequent users do not see this delay. Some newer servlet engines (including JRun and Netscape's Enterprise Server 4.0) support preloading of servlets, prior to the first request from a client.

Servlet performance should be monitored by review of the logs. If users are complaining of not being able to access the system, more than likely the connection pool needs to be increased. Anytime a connection pool needs to be enlarged, there will be a message on the servlet console. The initial pool allocation is 10 connections, with a maximum of 20. The `LDAPConnectionPool` class also supports a debug mode that will send more messages to the console; enable debug printouts sparingly, since the debug mode decreases performance.

Tips for Servlet Developers

Maximizing servlet performance requires techniques somewhat different from those used to maximize the performance of stand-alone programs. One important step is to avoid having to connect to the LDAP server for each request. The connection-pooling model presented in this chapter solves this problem.

Another step to increase performance is to make use of the caching module of the SDK to avoid having to go out on the wire to satisfy repetitive searches. The cache object can be queried to see how many requests are being satisfied from the cache versus going to the directory. See Chapter 15 for details on how and when to use `LDAPCache`.

Finally, keep the DN of each record around to use as a key for direct access to a user's entry, instead of doing additional searches to find the entry when user attributes are needed.

Conclusion

This chapter has introduced the use of the Java LDAP SDK as a key component of a substantial server-side application. A connection-pooling class will benefit the development of almost any servlet involving LDAP. Directory SDK for Java 4.0 includes the class `netscape.LDAP.ConnectionPool` for this purpose. A servlet can allocate multiple connection pools for different purposes—for example, one for each LDAP server it connects to. The phone book servlet also demonstrates the dynamic creation of HTML based on LDAP queries and data.

PART IV

BEYOND THE BASICS

CHAPTER 14

Options and Constraints

In this chapter we will focus on the many different options and settings that you can impose on LDAP operations. These settings affect how results are returned, how the client deals with these results, and how much work needs to be done on the receiving end to process the requested data. Understanding the options and constraints settings available in the SDK is essential for efficient use of an LDAP directory.

How Do They Affect Me?

Options and constraints indicate to the SDK and the server how you want data and limits to be handled. For example, a search of an LDAP directory can result in the return of a referral rather than the actual entry meeting the search criteria. This referral names another host LDAP directory that holds the actual data. Instead of writing code to examine the results and follow referrals to additional servers, you can have the SDK follow referrals for you. If you set the option for automatic referral following, the SDK will connect to the referred-to server and obtain the data. This is just one example of how awareness of the available options can simplify your programming tasks.

For the most part within this chapter we will use the terms "options" and "constraints" interchangeably. They refer to the same thing: settings that affect a single or many LDAP operations. The SDK uses the `LDAPConstraints` and `LDAPSearchConstraints` classes to encapsulate constraints and options.

Options can be set for a connection. When an option is set on a connection, it affects all operations issued over that connection. Furthermore, any connections that are cloned from this connection will have the same constraints as the original connection. An option that is specified by a constraints parameter supplied to a particular operation, such as a search, overrides the default options of the connection for that operation only.

A View into Options

If you want to set a default option for a connection object, use the `setOption` method of `LDAPConnection`. Once the option has been set, any operations with this connection will use this option, unless you specifically override the option by supplying a constraints object when invoking the operation. The `setOption` method takes an integer argument to indicate which option is being set, and an `Object` argument for the value. The constant integer values for options are defined in `LDAPConnection`. Settings that are not `Object` arguments must be wrapped in an `Object` when calling `setOption`. For example, to set the maximum number of search results to return on any operation, you can use the following code:

```
ldc.setOption( ldc.SIZELIMIT, new Integer( 20 ) );
```

You can query the value of any option in an `LDAPConnection` object with `getOption`—for example:

```
int sizeLimit = ( (Integer)ldc.getOption( ldc.SIZELIMIT ) ).intValue();
```

You can also set many options at once with the `setConstraints` method of `LDAPConnection`. The `setConstraints` method takes an `LDAPConstraints` object as its parameter. An `LDAPConstraints` object is constructed using one of the following:

```
LDAPConstraints cons = new LDAPConstraints();
LDAPConstraints cons =
   new LDAPConstraints( int msLimit,
                         boolean doReferrals,
                         LDAPRebind reauth,
                         int hop_limit );
LDAPConstraints cons =
   new LDAPConstraints( int msLimit,
                        boolean doReferrals,
                        LDAPBind binder,
                        int hop_limit );
LDAPConstraints cons = ldc.getConstraints();
```

The constructor with no parameters implies using the default values, which are listed in Table 14-1. Referrals can be processed automatically in two ways: one uses an `LDAPBind` object; the other uses `LDAPRebind`. There are therefore different constructors for the two cases. A convenient way to create a constraints object is by obtaining a copy from an `LDAPConnection`, as in the final variant above, ensuring that the object starts off with any settings that have been applied to the connection up to that point.

TABLE 14-1. OPTIONS IN LDAPCONSTRAINTS.

PROPERTY	DATA TYPE	DEFAULT VALUE	LDAPCONNECTION OPTION
TimeLimit	int	0 (no limit)	TIMELIMIT
Referrals	boolean	false	REFERRALS
BindProc	LDAPBind	null	REFERRALS_BIND_PROC
RebindProc	LDAPRebind	null	REFERRALS_REBIND_PROC
HopLimit	Int	10	REFERRALS_HOP_LIMIT

After the object is created, the settings may be applied to a connection as follows:

```
ldc.setConstraints( cons );
```

The parameters used with LDAPConstraints will be explained shortly. An individual option for an LDAPConnection may be altered or retrieved by using the setOption and getOption methods for that option, as summarized in Table 14-1. The corresponding property in LDAPConstraints is accessed with the get and set methods for the property—for example, getTimeLimit to get the TimeLimit property.

To have the client wait only 10 milliseconds for results back from the directory server for all operations on this connection, use the following:

```
ldc.setOption( ldc.TIMELIMIT, new Integer( 10 ) );
```

To prepare a constraints object for use with one or more operations, use the setTimeLimit method:

```
cons.setTimeLimit( 10 );
```

Let's examine what each of these options does for a connection.

TimeLimit

The TimeLimit value specifies the maximum time in milliseconds to wait for results from the server. If an operation does not complete within the designated time interval, an LDAPException with a result code of TIME_LIMIT_EXCEEDED will be thrown. If a value of 0 is specified, then no limit will be set on the time to wait. This limit is enforced by the SDK, not by the server. The default value for this setting within the SDK is 0 (no limit).

Referrals

A server that does not hold requested information may return a referral on an LDAP operation. The client must then connect to the referred-to server to obtain the real information. The options that control the processing of referrals are discussed in detail in Chapter 16. The default value for this setting is `false` (not to follow referrals).

BindProc

This property allows you to specify an object that will manage authentication during the processing of a referral. The object must implement the `bind` method:

```
public void bind ( LDAPConnection ldc ) throws LDAPException
```

`LDAPConnection` will call this method when authenticating while following a referral. The application is responsible for reconnecting the connection object if necessary and for authenticating, using whatever credentials are required. See Chapter 16 for details on using `LDAPBind`. The default value for this setting is `null` (which indicates that a `RebindProc` should be used for reauthentication, if specified, or that referrals should be followed using anonymous authentication).

ReBindProc

This property specifies an object that implements the `LDAPRebind` interface. It is used when the following of a referral requires more than an anonymous bind to authenticate, but it will use a DN and password (not a SASL mechanism). If you set referral handling to `true` and use `null` for both the `BindProc` and the `RebindProc` properties, the SDK will use anonymous authentication. The default value for this setting is `null`.

HopLimit

If a referral is encountered during the execution of an operation, and referral handling is true, the SDK will make a new temporary connection to the referred-to server if necessary and continue the operation there. Every reference to a different server is considered an additional hop. The `HopLimit` option tells the SDK how many different connections it should follow before throwing an `LDAPException` with a result code of `REFERRAL_LIMIT_EXCEEDED`. The following instruction will set the hop limit for a particular constraints object to three:

```
cons.setHopLimit( 3 );
```

The main purposes of the limit are to prevent endless loops (if a server is misconfigured so that a referral points back to itself, for example) and to allow a client to limit the network activity of an application within a complicated referral environment. The default value for this setting is 10.

Constraints for Searching

The `LDAPSearchConstraints` object extends `LDAPConstraints` by adding options that apply only to search operations. You can use an `LDAPSearchConstraints` object anywhere you can use an `LDAPConstraints` object, but the options that are specific to searching will be ignored for all operations other than search. Construct an `LDAPSearchConstraints` object with one of the following:

```
   public LDAPSearchConstraints ();
   public LDAPSearchConstraints ( int msLimit,
                                  int serverTimeLimit,
                                  int dereference,
                                  int maxResults,
                                  boolean doReferrals,
                                  int batchSize,
                                  LDAPRebind reauth,
                                  int hop_limit );
   public LDAPSearchConstraints ( int msLimit,
                                  int serverTimeLimit,
                                  int dereference,
                                  int maxResults,
                                  boolean doReferrals,
                                  int batchSize,
                                  LDAPBind bind,
                                  int hop_limit );
LDAPSearchConstraints cons = ldc.getSearchConstraints();
```

Search constraints can be applied to a connection or supplied as a parameter to a search operation.

The properties in boldface in Table 14-2 are identical to the properties in the superclass `LDAPConstraints`. For example, the `TimeLimit` property has the same functionality whether applied to an individual search or to the connection.

TABLE 14-2. *Search options.*

PROPERTY	DATA TYPE	DEFAULT VALUE	LDAPCONNECTION OPTION
TimeLimit	int	0 (no limit)	**TIMELIMIT**
ServerTimeLimit	int	0 (no limit)	SERVERTIMELIMIT
Dereference	int	DEREF_NEVER	DEREFERENCE
MaxResults	int	1000	MAXRESULTS
Referrals	boolean	**false**	**REFERRALS**
BatchSize	int	1	BATCHSIZE
BindProc	**LDAPBind**	**null**	**REFERRALS_BIND_PROC**
RebindProc	**LDAPRebind**	**null**	**REFERRALS_REBIND_PROC**
HopLimit	int	10	**REFERRALS_HOP_LIMIT**
MaxBackLog	int	100	MAXBACKLOG

Let's examine how to retrieve the current settings from an LDAPConnection and add an additional setting for a search:

```
// ldc is an LDAPConnection
LDAPSearchConstraints cons =
    (LDAPSearchConstraints)ldc.getSearchConstraints();
// Retrieve all results at once (block when enumerating the
// search results)
cons.setBatchSize( 0 );
// cons can be passed to the search method
// and affects only this particular operation
LDAPSearchResults res = ldc.search( base, int scope,
                                    filter, attrs,
                                    false,
                                    cons );
```

We could have constructed the search constraints manually using the LDAPSearchConstraints constructor, but it is often useful to obtain the current settings and tweak one or two values for a particular operation.

Let's examine each of the new settings that are available as part of the LDAPSearchConstraints. We will not examine the settings that have already been defined for the connection constraints, because they have the same functionality. The additional settings that are part of the LDAPSearchConstraints are ServerTimeLimit, Dereference, MaxResults, BatchSize, and MaxBackLog.

ServerTimeLimit

The server time limit specifies the maximum amount of time, in seconds, that the server should spend on returning results to the client. The server may have been configured with its own limit. If so, the value used by the server for the operation will be the lesser of the value specified by the client and the value configured for the server. If the search operation requires more time to complete than is allowed, an LDAPException with a result code of TIME_LIMIT_EXCEEDED will be thrown. If a value of 0 is specified, then no limit will be set on the time to wait for results (except for any limit configured for the server itself).

With Netscape Directory Server, the Directory Manager is not subject to the time or size limits configured for other users. If you are doing a search that would take the server longer than its configured time limit to process fully or would produce more results than it is configured to return, you will need to authenticate as the Directory Manager to receive all results. The default value for this setting is 0 (no limit).

In most cases when you receive an exception because the size or time limit was exceeded, you would still like to process the results that were returned. The following code illustrates how to note the exception but continue processing any results that were received.

```
// Loop on results until complete
while ( res.hasMoreElements() ) {
    try {
        // Next directory entry
        LDAPEntry entry = res.next();
        prettyPrint( entry, ATTRS );
    } catch ( LDAPReferralException e ) {
        // Ignore referrals
        continue;
    } catch ( LDAPException e ) {
        int errCode = e.getLDAPResultCode();
        if ( errCode ==
                LDAPException.SIZE_LIMIT_EXCEEDED ) {
            System.out.println( "Size limit exceeded!" );
        } else if ( errCode ==
```

```
                    LDAPException.TIME_LIMIT_EXCEEDED ) {
                System.out.println("Time limit exceeded!" );
            } else {
                System.out.println( e.toString() );
            }
            continue;
        }
    }
```

Some may argue that continuing on an error is unusual, but when returning search results, for instance, it often makes sense to show the ones returned prior to the error. For example, if a user enters a search criterion that returns 10,000 records, it may be appropriate to show the first 100 returned entries and suggest that the user narrow the scope of the search.

The sample program `SearchWithLimits` in this chapter lets you experiment with different settings for time limit and size limit:

```
java SearchWithLimits <host> <port> <authdn> <password> <baseDN>
      <filter><server time> <size limit>
```

Examples:

```
java SearchWithLimits localhost 389 "" "" "o=airius.com"
     "(|(cn=sam*)(cn=b*))" 5 2
DN: uid=scarter, ou=People, o=airius.com
cn: Sam Carter
mail: scarter@airius.com
telephoneNumber: +1 408 555 4798
----------
DN: uid=bhall, ou=People, o=airius.com
cn: Benjamin Hall
mail: bhall@airius.com
telephoneNumber: +1 408 555 6067
----------
Size limit exceeded!
```

or

```
java SearchWithLimits slow.acme.com 60000 "" "" "o=acme.com"
       "objectclass=*" 1 10000
DN: o=mcom.com
cn not present
mail not present
```

```
telephoneNumber not present
...
----------
DN: cn=PD Managers,ou=groups,o=mcom.com
cn: PD Managers
mail not present
telephoneNumber not present
----------
Time limit exceeded!
```

Dereference

This setting determines how aliases will be handled. An **alias** is an entry that points to another entry, possibly on another server. Alias entries are similar in function to symbolic links (UNIX) or shortcuts (Windows). An alias entry is of the object class `alias` and has an attribute named `aliasedObjectName`, which contains the DN of the entry that contains the real data. The use of aliases can affect server performance, and not all directory servers support this function. Netscape Directory Server does not support aliases and will ignore this setting. The following are valid options for this setting:

- `DEREF_NEVER` specifies that aliases are never dereferenced.
- `DEREF_FINDING` specifies that aliases are dereferenced when finding the starting point for the search (but not when searching under that starting entry).
- `DEREF_SEARCHING` specifies that aliases are dereferenced when searching the entries beneath the starting point of the search (but not when finding the starting entry).
- `DEREF_ALWAYS` specifies that aliases are always dereferenced.

The default value is `DEREF_NEVER`.

To have a search operation follow all aliases, you could set the corresponding property in a search constraints object and pass the object as a parameter to the search:

```
cons.setDereference( LDAPConnection.DEREF_ALWAYS );
```

MaxResults

This setting determines the maximum number of results that should be returned from the search. The server may also be configured to return not more than a certain number of entries. If the server is configured with a limit, then the actual limit for a particular operation will be the lesser of the client and the server limits. Again, the privileged Directory Manager user is not subject to these limits. If more entries satisfy the request than the limit allows, an `LDAPException` will be thrown with a result code of `SIZE_LIMIT_EXCEEDED`. Specifying 0 indicates that there should be no limit. The default value for this setting is 1,000 entries.

`BatchSize`

This setting determines how many results should be delivered to the client at a time. A value of 0 indicates that the client wishes to wait until all entries have been returned before processing any results. When the client calls `LDAPSearchResults.next` or `LDAPSearchResults.nextElement`, the call will block until all results are available. If the value 1 is specified, the client can process each entry as soon as it is returned by the server. The method `next` or `nextElement` will block only until one additional result is available. Note that if you are doing client-side sorting, you will need to retrieve all entries before sorting. The default value for this setting is 1.

`MaxBackLog`

This setting determines the size of the queue of search results, when `BatchSize` is not 0. When the queue fills up, the client must process search results with `next` or `nextElement` before the SDK continues to receive and buffer additional results. `MaxBackLog` is discussed in detail in Chapter 16.

Conclusion

This chapter has discussed the various options for LDAP operations and how they can be applied. These options allow the programmer to tune operations individually or to configure a connection for all operations. Although the default options may be satisfactory for many applications, choosing the right options may be critical for others.

CHAPTER 15

Odds and Ends

We have covered all the basics for writing LDAP applications and applets. In the sample applications, we've touched on a few advanced or less commonly used features. In this chapter we will investigate some of the areas off the beaten track and look at some of the coding choices that will affect the performance of your application.

LDAP URLs

In Chapter 11 we used an `LDAPUrl` object as a compact representation of an LDAP query. Let's take a closer look at the composition and use of an LDAP URL.

An IETF Standard

An LDAP URL, defined by RFC 2255, is represented by the `LDAPUrl` class and composed of the following:

```
"ldap://" [ hostName [":" portNumber] ] "/" baseDN
    ["?" attributeList ["?" scope "?" filterString ["?" extensions ] ] ]
```

where

- All text enclosed by quotation marks is literal.
- `hostName` and `portNumber` identify the location of the LDAP server.
- `baseDN` specifies the name of an entry within the given directory (the entry represents the starting point of the search).
- `attributeList` contains a comma-delimited list of attributes to retrieve (if not specified, fetch all attributes).

- `scope` is one of the following:
  - "base"indicates that this is a search only for the specified entry.
  - "one" indicates that this is a search for matching entries one level under the specified entry (and not including the entry itself).
  - "sub" indicates that this is a search for matching entries at all levels under the specified entry (including the entry itself).

If not specified, the scope is base by default.

- `filterString` is a human-readable representation of the search filter, of the same type as is used as the search filter parameter in the `LDAPConnection.search` methods. This value is used only for one-level or subtree searches.

- `extensions` is an optional list of comma-separated extensions to the information provided by the other components. RFC 2255 defines one such extension, `bindname`, for specifying a DN to authenticate as. This extension is not widely used, because a corresponding password cannot be provided with the URL (the RFC advises against passing a reusable password for URL processing, for security reasons). Any other extensions must be prefixed with "X-" or "x-". An extension may have a value: for example, `bindname=uid=paul%2cou=people%2co=acme.com`. Note that commas must be URL-encoded in an extension value because they separate extensions. Each extension may be prefixed with an exclamation point, in which case the client (the SDK or the application) should consider the extension mandatory and not execute the search if it cannot process the extension. For example, `ldap:///ou=people,o=acme.com??sub?(sn=jensen)?!X-QUICKSEARCH`.

Note that if `scope` and `filterString` are not specified, an LDAP URL identifies exactly one entry in the directory.

Encoding rules similar to those for other URLs (for example, HTTP) apply for LDAP URLs. Specifically, any "illegal" characters are escaped with `%HH`, where `HH` represents the two hex digits that correspond to the ASCII value of the character. Characters that do not require encoding in LDAP URLs are the ASCII letters and numbers and the following characters: $ - _ . + ! * ' ( ). Encoding is legal (and necessary) only on the DN and filter portions of the URL.

The following are examples of LDAP URLs:

- `ldap://localhost:389/o=Airius.com`. This URL refers to the single entry `o=Airius.com` and is used to return all of its attributes (except for operational attributes).

- `ldap://localhost:389/o=Airius.com?o`. This is the same as the previous example, except that only the `o` (organization) attribute is requested.
- `ldap://localhost:389/o=Airius.com??one`. This URL expresses a request for all immediate children of `o=Airius.com` (but not `o=Airius.com` itself) and to return all attributes of the entries found (except for operational attributes).
- `ldap://localhost:389/ou=People,o=Airius.com?cn,mail?sub?(cn=a*)`. This URL expresses a request for all entries under and including `ou=People,o=Airius.com` that have a common name starting with the letter A, and to return only the common name and e-mail attributes of each entry found.

Some Web browsers allow you to type in an LDAP URL instead of an HTTP URL and will execute a search and display the results. You can try out the URLs described so far with Netscape Navigator or Microsoft Internet Explorer.

Using LDAP URLs in Java

You can create and use an `LDAPUrl` object for a search as in the following example:

```
LDAPUrl url = new LDAPUrl(
    "ldap://myhost.acme.com:389/ou=People,o=Airius.com?cn,mail?(cn=adam*)" );
try {
    LDAPSearchResults res = LDAPConnection.search( url );
    // Process the results...
} catch ( LDAPException e ) {
}
```

You can also specify the components of the LDAP URL individually when constructing the `LDAPUrl` object:

```
String[] attrs = { "cn", "mail" };
LDAPUrl url = new LDAPUrl( "myhost.acme.com", 389,
                           "ou=People,o=Airius.com",
                           attrs, LDAPConnection.SCOPE_SUB,
                           "(cn=adam*)" );
```

One advantage to using the constructor that takes individual components is that the `baseDN` and `filterString` fields are automatically encoded if necessary. For example, `o=Acme Parts = Us` is encoded internally as `o=Acme%20Parts%20%3D%20Us`.

There are methods to extract the various components of the LDAP URL:

```
String[] getAttributeArray()
String getDN()
```

```
String getFilter()
String getHost()
int getPort()
int getScope()
String getUrl() - this returns a String that is encoded for use as an
LDAP URL
```

There are also utility methods to encode or decode any `String` for use as an LDAP URL:

```
static String decode( String encodedString )
static String encode( String unencodedString )
```

Not Your Average URL

If you have done Internet programming in Java before, you may be familiar with the `java.net.URL` and the `java.net.URLConnection` classes. With those standard classes you can do things such as the following:

```
URL url = new URL( "http://java.sun.com/index.html" );
InputStream in = url.getURLConnection().getInputStream();
OutputStream in = url.getURLConnection().getOutputStream();
```

You can then write to and read from the streams. You can also let the standard content handler classes read from the URL and instantiate an appropriate object if the server supplies type information and there is a handler available for the content type:

```
Object o = url.getContent();
```

LDAP URLs are more limited. An LDAP URL can be used only to express a search and not any kind of update, and it does not imply a connection that can supply a stream to the application for reading or writing. Executing `LDAPConnection.search(LDAPUrl url)` causes a connection to be established, used for the single search operation, and then closed. LDAP URLs do not provide a means to supply authentication credentials, so any search operation will be unauthenticated (anonymous) when using the SDK.

Despite these limitations, you may find an `LDAPUrl` convenient for expressing a search. If authentication is required, you can unpack the `LDAPUrl` components and use your already authenticated `LDAPConnection` object to do a search:

```
// ld is an LDAPConnection that has been connected and authenticated
// earlier
```

```
// url is an LDAPUrl that was created earlier
try {
    LDAPSearchResults res = ld.search( url.getDN(), url.getScope(),
                                       url.getFilter(),
                                       url.getAttributeArray(),
                                       false );
    while ( res.hasMoreElements() ) {
        // Process the results...
    }
} catch ( LDAPException e ) {
}
```

A Rose by Any Other Name . . .

Directory users in the United States may never have to reflect on the fact that string data can be represented in many different character sets. Directory servers that comply with LDAPv3 transmit all string data in the UTF8 character set, a variant of Unicode. UTF8 has the pleasant characteristic that the ASCII characters are represented with the same 7-bit values (one character per byte) as in ASCII. That means that ASCII text can easily be added to a directory, searched, and updated; the data is the same in the UTF8 character set.

Things are trickier beyond the ASCII characters. Programmers and users in some European countries may expect to be able to use characters from the latin-1 character set—for example, å, ä, ö, é—and users in Japan might want to input data in shift-jis or EUC. The good news is that UTF8 can accommodate all the characters anyone can come up with for all these character sets; the bad news is that any data in those character sets must be converted to UTF8 before being stored in the server, and it must be converted back when reading from the server.

Suppose you have an LDIF file with data you would like to add to a directory. If the data was typed in with a German-language or Japanese-language word processor, it will most likely contain characters that are not valid in UTF8. You can add the contents of the file to the directory with `java LDAPModify`, but you will not be able to search for values containing those characters; if you search for something else and receive attribute values containing the characters, most likely the results will be truncated. The solution is to run the LDIF file through a converter (to UTF8) before adding it.

Clients of the C LDAP API are expected to convert their string data to UTF8 (if it is not in ASCII) before passing it to any API function, and to convert it back when receiving data from the server. Users of the Java LDAP API are much more fortunate. Character sets are handled in the Java language, the Java class libraries, and Directory SDK for Java as follows:

- The Java language uses UCS2—a variant of Unicode that represents each character as two bytes—internally for `String` and character data. Transformations between UTF8 and UCS2 are easy.
- By default, the Java class libraries expect data that is typed in at the keyboard or read from a file to be in the local character set (for which the computer is configured), so they convert the data on the fly to UCS2. When string data is written or displayed, it is automatically converted to the local character set first.
- The standard Java input and output stream reader and writer classes, as well as the `String` class, have methods that take a character set specification as a parameter. You can use these methods to convert the streams or strings to or from an arbitrary character set, not just the default local character set. For example,

```
InputStreamReader reader = new InputStreamReader( is, "UTF8" );
```

creates an input stream reader that will convert from UTF8 to UCS2 when reading data. A program to read a file in the local character set and output it in UTF8 may be as simple as the following:

```
import java.io.*;

public class ToUTF8 {
    public static void main( String[] args ) {
        try {
            InputStreamReader reader =
                new InputStreamReader(
                    new FileInputStream( args[0]) );
            OutputStreamWriter writer =
                new OutputStreamWriter(
                    new FileOutputStream( args[1]), "UTF8" );
            char[] buf = new char[1024];
            int nRead;
            while( (nRead = reader.read( buf, 0, buf.length )) > 0 ) {
                writer.write( buf, 0, nRead );
            }
            writer.close();
        } catch ( IOException e ) {
            System.err.println( e );
        }
    }
}
```

If the input data is not in the local character set, you can specify its character set when creating the `InputStreamReader`. For example, if the input file is in shift-jis, use the following:

```
InputStreamReader reader =
      new InputStreamReader(
          new FileInputStream( args[0]), "SJIS" );
```

- The Java LDAP SDK converts between UTF8 and UCS2 automatically when you create attributes or extract the values of an attribute as strings, and when a message is sent off to the server or received from the server. Most likely, your code will not need to concern itself with conversions between UTF8 and UCS2 unless it is reading data from an external source (as already discussed).
- One exception to this rule that we have run into is in making internationalized Web-based applications work with older browsers (Internet Explorer 3 and Netscape Navigator 3). These older browsers do not handle UTF8 well at all. If your application must handle non-ASCII character sets and it must work well with the older browsers, you will probably end up with code that explicitly converts between character sets, perhaps based on the Accept-Language header from the browser.

  Another exception to the rule is for certain platforms, such as Japanese Windows NT 4.0, that truncate or corrupt UTF8 data entered at the command line. For example, if you want to specify a base DN for a search as a command-line argument, Japanese Windows NT 4.0 will truncate or corrupt the DN before it gets to your program if the DN contains characters that are not in the local character set.

When What You Read Is Not What You Wrote

One of the real strengths of LDAP and many servers that implement it is the ability to replicate widely. Replication means that the directory contents, or parts of it, are copied to another server. There are many reasons to replicate directories—for example:

- A large number of users may want to access the same directory data, causing a heavy load on a server. One or more replicas are created, and the client programs of the users are configured to use one of the replicas rather than having all of them direct their requests to a single server.
- A company may have operations in several countries or widely dispersed geographical areas between which the network links are relatively slow.

The company creates a replica in each country, or perhaps a replica for several adjacent countries. Users access the server that is geographically closest and enjoy high bandwidth and little contention.

- A company may want to make some of its directory data available to partners outside the company firewall. It creates a replica that is accessible to the partners and configures the replication to copy only certain attributes of each entry, or only certain entries, to the replica.
- A replica may be maintained as a "hot standby." If the main server goes down, clients can be redirected to use the replica instead.

When a change is made to data in one server, the change may be propagated immediately to the other one, or the servers may be configured to propagate changes at regular intervals—for example, once an hour. The servers may be configured to do all the replication at night. Eventually, all the servers involved in replication will contain identical data (if replication was configured to keep the entire contents in synch). At any given moment, however, that may not be the case.

Why do we, as developers of client applications for directories, care? We should never assume that all clients of all servers in a replicated environment have the same view of the directory at all times. In particular, we cannot assume that a change made by a program to data in one server will be visible to all users immediately. If replication is configured to happen only once a day, it may be many hours before the change has propagated to all servers; in the meantime, other changes may have been introduced that negate the original change.

One particularly common programming paradigm simply does not work in many replicated scenarios: writing data to the server and then reading it back to verify that it was successfully stored. Often, a replica is configured to be read-only. The vast majority of LDAP operations are searches or reads, and the replica responds to the search and read requests just as if it were an independent directory and not a copy. But when it receives a write request, it returns a referral—pointing to the master (or source) directory—instead of returning search results. Referrals are discussed in detail in Chapter 16.

When the client receives the referral, it contacts the referred-to server and presents the write request there. That work may be done transparently by the SDK, such that the user or application is not aware that she or it is talking to more than one server. If the application then attempts to read from the server to verify the data, the request will be fulfilled by the replica. But the replica has most likely not yet been notified of the change in the data of the master, so the client may draw the conclusion that the write failed.

How can you keep your application functioning sanely when updates are being referred to a server that is different from the one to which the program originally connected? The first rule is to cache the changes in the client rather than reading an entry immediately after writing it (if the write succeeded). If relying on a cached copy is not possible (that is, if your application must immediately verify that a write succeeded by reading the same data), then you will have to make sure that the application connects to the master server and not to a read-only replica. You may even want to turn off automatic referral following during updates and have the SDK throw an exception if referrals are received instead, so that you can notify the user that the application needs to be reconfigured to point to the master server.

Once the IETF has adopted standards for multimaster replication, there will be an increasing number of LDAP servers configured so that more than one server may contain writable copies of the same data. In a multimaster environment, changes may be made to the same entry at the same time on different servers. Depending on how the servers resolve the differences when they compare the changes (and perhaps on whether or not the system clocks of the servers are perfectly synchronized), the change made on one server may erase the change made on another server, or the end result may be a combination of both changes. In either case, the client making a change to directory data cannot assume that the change will appear the same to other users or even to itself later—even if the client has sole access to one server.

In directory or database terms, this paradigm is called loose consistency. Eventually all servers will converge on a single view of the data, but at any given point in time they may differ.

Sometimes One Thread Is Not Enough

Java makes it easy to do more than one thing at once with the `Thread` class. In many traditional programming environments, you have to do tricks with asynchronous I/O or with message queues to prevent an application from apparently freezing while waiting for an operation to complete. With Java, you can create a thread to perform a task involving lengthy computations or synchronous I/O. The user interface thread continues to update the user interface elements so that screens can be repainted and the application appears responsive to the user. There may be a list or table that is continuously updated as the results of a search become available.

The Java LDAP classes are all thread safe. You can launch several threads that simultaneously execute search or update operations on a single `LDAPConnection` object. Synchronization is at the method level or lower. A thread that is excecuting an LDAP operation will typically block other threads only for as long as it takes to hand off a message to the internal `LDAPConnection` thread (which manages the socket to the server).

The following code creates a single connection and authenticates, and then launches one thread to do a search and process the results, and another thread to change the common name of an entry. There is no risk that the operations will interfere with each other.

```
public class TestMultiple {
    LDAPConnection ld = new LDAPConnection(); // Shared among threads
    TestMultiple( String[] args ) {
        if ( args.length < 4 ) {
            System.err.println( "Usage: TestMultiple HOST PORT " +
                                "DN PASSWORD" );
            System.exit( 1 );
        }
        try {
            // Connect and authenticate on behalf of all tasks
            ld.connect( args[0], Integer.parseInt(args[1]) );
            ld.authenticate( args[2], args[3] );
        } catch( LDAPException e ) {
            System.out.println( "Error: " + e.toString() );
            System.exit( 1 );
        }
        // Create and start a task to process all person entries under
        // "ou=People,o=Airius.com"
        DoASearch search = new DoASearch( "ou=People,o=Airius.com",
                                          "objectclass=person" );
        Thread th1 = new Thread(search, "searchPeople");
        th1.start();
        // Create and start a task to change Babs's common name
        ChangeName change =
            new ChangeName( "uid=bjensen,ou=People,o=Airius.com",
                            "Babs B. Jensen" );
        Thread th2 = new Thread(change, "changeBabs");
        th2.start();
        // At this point, both tasks are running in parallel.
        // Wait for both to finish, and then exit.
        try {
            th1.join();
            th2.join();
        } catch ( InterruptedException e ) {
        }
        System.exit( 0 );
    }

    public static void main( String[] args ) {
        new TestMultiple();
    }
```

```
// A command class - instantiate it in a thread to do a search
class DoASearch implements Runnable {
    String base, filter;
    DoASearch( String base, String filter ) {
        this.base = base;
        this.filter = filter;
    }
    public void run() {
        LDAPSearchResults res;
        try {
            // Use the LDAPConnection object of the outer class
            res = ld.search( base,
                             ld.SCOPE_SUB,
                             filter,
                             null,
                             false );
        } catch ( LDAPException e ) {
            System.out.println( "Error: " + e.toString() );
            return;
        }
        while ( res.hasMoreElements() ) {
            try {
                LDAPEntry entry = res.next(); // next directory entry
                System.out.println( entry.getDN() );
                // Do something with the entry...
            } catch ( LDAPException ex ) {
                System.out.println( "Error: " + ex.toString() );
                continue;
            }
        }
    }
}

// A command class - instantiate it in a thread to change the
// common name of an entry
class ChangeName implements Runnable {
    String dn, newName;
    ChangeName( String dn, String newName ) {
        this.dn = dn;
        this.newName = newName;
    }
    public void run() {
        try {
            // Use the LDAPConnection object of the outer class
```

```
                ld.modify( dn, new LDAPModification(
                                LDAPModification.REPLACE,
                                new LDAPAttribute( "cn", newName ) ) );
                System.out.println( "Changed name of " + dn + ": "
                                 + newName );
            } catch ( LDAPException e ) {
                System.out.println( "Error: " + e.toString() );
            }
        }
    }
}
```

This is a simple example. Both operations use the connection object without changing any options or setting any controls. In most real-life projects, the code will not reside in a single file, as is the case here. More than one programmer may be working on classes that collaborate and share a single connection. It becomes difficult to keep track of just how the connection is being used in various parts of the code.

Don't Step on My Settings

When options or controls are applied to a connection, they affect all threads sharing the object. Changing authentication also affects all threads because an LDAP connection has only one set of credentials at any given time. Consider the `TestMultiple` code from the previous example, with the following change to `DoASearch`:

```
try {
    // Use the LDAPConnection object of the outer class
    ld.authenticate( "uid=sadams,ou=People,o=Airius.com",
                     "password" );
    res = ld.search( base,
                     ld.SCOPE_SUB,
                     filter,
                     null,
                     false );
} catch ( LDAPException e ) { }
```

We now have a race condition. If the `DoASearch` thread does the `authenticate` before the `ChangeName` thread does its `modify`, the latter will have unexpected credentials and may fail. This is a bad situation. If `DoASearch` and `ChangeName` were defined in separate files, a programmer working on `DoASearch` might decide that changing authentication is a good thing to do when executing the `ou=People` search, and not even be aware that another thread was doing something that required other credentials.

Similar considerations apply to connection options. One thread may want to have referrals followed automatically, while for another thread it would be an error condition for a referral to be encountered during an operation. For the latter thread, rather than following the referral, an exception should be reported to the user and the operation should be discontinued. If one thread does one of the following:

```
ld.setOption( ld.REFERRALS, true );
```

or

```
LDAPSearchConstraints cons = ld.getSearchConstraints();
cons.setReferrals( true );
ld.setSearchConstraints( cons );
```

then all threads sharing the connection will find that referrals are being followed automatically.

Controls may also be specified as options. Some controls are valid only with certain operations. For example, a thread may specify an `LDAPVirtualListControl` for a connection or for the search constraints of a connection prior to executing a search. The `LDAPVirtualListControl` is not valid for any operations other than search, so another thread (or the same thread executing another part of the code later) will receive an exception when trying to do an add or modify if the control is still present in the connection.

There is a workaround for connection options and constraints: you can get a copy of the current constraints of the connection, modify the copy, and supply the copied constraints to the `LDAPConnection` methods that take an `LDAPConstraints` or `LDAPSearchConstraints` parameter. For example, do the following:

```
LDAPSearchConstraints cons = ld.getSearchConstraints();
cons.setReferrals( true );
ld.modify( dn, mod, cons );
```

instead of

```
LDAPcons = ld.getSearchConstraints ( );
cons.setReferrals(true);
ld.setSearchConstraints (cons );
```

or

```
ld.setOption( ld.REFERRALS, true );
ld.modify( dn, mod );
```

Copying constraints is an inexpensive operation, unless the constraints contain controls with a very large amount of data. None of the controls defined in the SDK involve large quantities of data.

A Cloned Connection Is a Safe Connection

Creating a copy of the connection constraints to modify for each operation (if particular options are desired for the operation) is a good thing, because then you don't have to worry about what other parts of the code might be doing with the options.

However, we still have the problem with authentication. The LDAP protocol defines authentication as an operation, not an option to an operation. Authenticating changes the state of the connection, and the credentials presented remain in effect for all subsequent operations until there is a new authentication. Chapter 16 discusses a special control that can be used to bypass this restriction in some cases, but for now we will present a general-purpose way to share connections without risk of affecting other threads or other code segments: cloned connections.

When you call `LDAPConnection.clone`, you receive an object that shares a physical connection with an LDAP server (if a connection has been established at that point) but has its own state. Any changes you make to the options or constraints of the original object or of any clone will affect only that individual object.

In the following example, for instance, `conn1` will continue to follow referrals automatically, and `conn2` won't.

```
LDAPConnection conn1 = new LDAPConnection();
conn1.getSearchConstraints().setReferrals( true );
LDAPConnection conn2 = (LDAPConnection)conn1.clone();
conn2 setOption(conn2.REFERRALS, false);
//... somewhere in one thread
res1 = conn1.search(...);
//... somewhere in another thread
res2 = conn2.search();
```

You could have used `conn1` for both search operations and protected the operations from affecting each other by copying the constraints and passing the modified constraints to each search operation as described earlier. But cloning the connection provides complete insulation and a safety net for client programming.

Cloning the connection also provides a unique benefit when an application must use more than one set of credentials while running: if any object sharing a physical connection calls `authenticate`, that object is transparently dissociated from the others and acquires its own physical connection. Consider the following:

```
LDAPConnection conn1 = new LDAPConnection();
try {
    conn1.connect( "localhost", 389 );
    conn1.authenticate( "uid=sadams,ou=People,o=Airius.com" );
} catch ( LDAPException e ) {
```

```
}
LDAPConnection conn2 = (LDAPConnection)conn1.clone();
```

At this point, conn2 is sharing a physical connection with conn1, and therefore necessarily sharing credentials.

```
try {
    conn2.authenticate( "uid=bjensen,ou=People,o=Airius.com" );
} catch ( LDAPException e ) {
}
```

Now conn2 has its own physical connection to the same server as conn1, but with different credentials.

```
LDAPConnection conn3 = (LDAPConnection)conn1.clone();
try {
    conn1.authenticate( "uid=bsimpson,ou=People,o=Airius.com" );
} catch ( LDAPException e ) {
}
```

Initially conn3 shared a physical connection with conn1. But then conn1 dissociated itself from the physical connection by authenticating. Now there are three physical connections, with three unique sets of credentials.

If we know that the application will constantly be reauthenticating with different credentials, obviously we haven't gained anything by cloning the connection and we should do something different—for example, create a pool of connections to share. But many applications maintain a connection for a long time and change credentials infrequently. For example, most of the time the application may be doing searches anonymously or as a single user, but sometimes the directory is to be updated and special credentials must be used to authenticate first. That part of the code can have its own clone of the shared connection and freely change authentication whenever necessary without worrying about disconnecting, reconnecting, or affecting other parts of the code.

When a clone calls `disconnect`, it is dissociated from the physical connection. If it is the last object using the physical connection, the physical connection is shut down.

This is the lowdown on connection cloning:

- If the connection to be cloned is not yet connected, the clone won't be either (of course). If the clone connects, the original object will not be affected (that is, it will remain disconnected).
- A clone continues to share a physical connection with its source connection object until it calls `disconnect` or `authenticate`. If it calls `authenticate`,

the object is dissociated from the others and acquires its own physical connection. If it calls `disconnect`, the other connection objects remain connected; if there are no other objects sharing the physical connection, the physical connection is terminated.

- All objects sharing a physical connection are symmetrical. It doesn't matter which one disconnects or reauthenticates first.
- All connection options, including referral settings, limits, and controls, are private to each object. Initially, a clone has options identical to those of the original object.

Cloning a connection is a very lightweight operation. Don't hesitate to use it!

Performance, and How to Get It

Most applications have performance concerns. Some do very infrequent LDAP operations. In those cases, it may be that nothing you can do in the code that calls the Java LDAP SDK will have any noticeable effect on the overall speed of the application. At the other end of the spectrum are many server-side programs, such as Web-based applications that use LDAP to authenticate every visitor to a Web site, or to retrieve the preferences of each visitor. Even modest speed increases in LDAP operations may have a big impact on the bandwidth that the site can handle.

Besides speed, memory usage is a concern in most sizable Java programs. In the following discussion we will present ways to minimize memory requirements and maximize speed when using the SDK.

Breaking Up Is Hard to Do: Avoid Unnecessary Connections

Establishing a connection to an LDAP server can be slower than a search or an authentication operation by an order of magnitude or more (if only a limited number of results are returned on the search). If possible, try to keep the connection alive and reuse it, rather than disconnecting and reconnecting on every search. Even if each search is done with different credentials (that is, it is preceded by an authentication operation), there is generally a substantial gain to avoiding a new connect. Besides time spent on the wire and in the server, a connect involves a DNS lookup (unless an IP address was specified instead of a host name).

Pool the Connections

If you expect to be changing credentials often, or supporting many threads doing operations with unique credentials, you may benefit from creating a pool of connections.

If you have a finite and reasonably small number of credentials that are to be used in different operations, you can preallocate a connection object for each identity (DN) and keep a reference to each object in a Hashtable, using the identity as the key. When the application needs a connection with a particular identity, the corresponding object can be retrieved from the Hashtable. If its isAuthenticated method returns false, the object can be authenticated at that time.

```
Hashtable ht = null;
String HOST = "myhost.acme.com";
int PORT = 4040;
String[] identities = { "uid=bjensen,ou=People,o=Airius.com",
                        "uid=sadams,ou=People,o=Airius.com",
                        "uid=jfoster,ou=People,o=Airius.com" };
protected void initializePool() throws LDAPException {
    ht = new Hashtable();
    for( int i = 0; i < identities.length; i++ ) {
        LDAPConnection ld = new LDAPConnection();
        ld.connect( HOST, PORT );
        ht.put( identities[i], ld );
    }
}

protected LDAPConnection getConnection( String dn, String password )
                                        throws LDAPException {
    // We need a connection with the right credentials
    LDAPConnection ld = (LDAPConnection)ht.get( dn );
    if ( (ld != null) && !ld.isAuthenticated() ) {
        ld.authenticate( dn, password );
    }
    return ld;
}
```

The preceding example assumes that the identity can be only one of the predefined DNs. If it is not a given that all identities will be used while the application is running, it may be better to postpone connecting the objects until inside getConnection, to avoid unnecessary work and resource usage.

You might use the pool in this way:

```
final static String[] ATTRS = { "mail" };
protected String getEmailAddress( String dn, String password )
                                  throws LDAPException {
    // Error checking skipped for now. We might get a null connection
    // if this is an unexpected DN, or the entry might not exist.
```

```
        LDAPConnection ld = getConnection( dn, password );
        LDAPEntry entry = ld.read( dn, ATTRS );
        return (String)entry.getAttribute().
            getStringValues().nextElement();
    }
```

If the number of identities to be used for authenticating is large, or if the identities are not known in advance, you can create a queue of connection objects instead, and have each thread wait for an object to be available. In this case, no assumptions should be made about the credentials of the connection. You can call `getAuthenticationDN` on the object to find out if reauthentication is required for the operation or if the previous operation left the object with the appropriate credentials.

Fewer But Better Searches

Chapter 5 introduced a few rules of thumb for increasing performance and reducing memory consumption while searching. To reiterate the two most important rules:

- Use indexed attributes
- Retrieve only attributes you need

Another useful technique is to combine searches, where possible, so that one operation can replace several. For example, if the application needs to know both the structure of an organization and the title of each manager, it may be possible to retrieve both sets of information with one search and parse the results in the client. The search filter might look like this, if only managers are assigned titles in this subtree:

```
(|(objectclass=organizationalUnit)(title=*))
```

To Cache or Not to Cache

The SDK includes a cache mechanism, which is not used by default. It is a search-level cache, not an entry-level cache. Results will be retrieved from the cache rather than from the LDAP server if and only if all of the following apply:

- The cache is enabled.
- The host and port of the connection match a cache entry.
- The credentials of the connection match those of the cache entry.
- Any controls in the request match those of the cache entry.

- The scope and search filter match those of the cache entry.
- The requested attribute list matches that of the cache entry.

Some applications do repeated identical searches, and using this cache will significantly improve their performance. We have benchmarked a 17-fold speed increase when the server is on the same machine as the client, or when the two are connected on a LAN. If the connection is slower—for example, if it is a modem connection—the relative gain will be even greater.

However, maintaining a cache incurs runtime overhead in performance and memory. If your application does a large number of unique searches or does searches with varying credentials, you will pay the price for this overhead but not see much benefit. In this case you are better off keeping a simple entry-level cache as a `Hashtable` in the application, or not using a cache at all. The same is true if you will be doing many different searches that each return a very large number of entries, because a large result set may fill the cache and force previous results to be expunged.

A cache is shared by all objects that share the same physical connection—that is, by all connection clones. The cache can also be used by multiple independent `LDAPConnection` objects, but there is no benefit if the objects are connected to different servers.

To enable the search-level cache, construct an `LDAPCache` object and apply it to the connection:

```
LDAPCache cache = new LDAPCache( 3600, 1000000 );
ld.setCache( cache );
```

The first parameter—`TTL` (time to live)—specifies the number of seconds before a cache entry expires; the second parameter—`maxSize`—specifies the maximum size in bytes of all cache entries together. An entry is purged from the cache if it is older than the `TTL` or if adding a new entry would cause the total cache size to be greater than `maxSize`.

The SDK does not maintain consistency between the cache and the directory. In other words, if an operation changes the directory contents after a search has completed, the cached search results may no longer be valid. If the same application is doing both the cached searching and the directory updates, then the application can flush the corresponding cache entries after updating the directory:

```
ld.getCache().flush( "ou=People,o=Airius.com", ld.SCOPE_ONE );
```

or

```
ld.getCache().flush( "uid=bjensen,ou=People,o=Airius.com",
    ld.SCOPE_BASE );
```

The first parameter is the base DN for the purge. If it is `null`, the whole cache is purged. The second parameter indicates whether only the specified DN is to be purged, only the children of the DN, or the DN along with all descendants.

In Chapter 16 we will present the persistent search control. It allows a thread to register its interest in any changes to an area of the directory you specify. When there are changes, the thread receives a search result and can flush the cache entries using the DN of the result.

Conclusion

This chapter has discussed the `LDAPUrl` class for representing an anonymous search, issues with storing non-ASCII string data, how to share a single connection among multiple threads, when and how to use the search-level cache class, and a few techniques to squeeze more performance out of your LDAP-enabled application. Chapter 16 will explore a few of the more advanced features of the SDK.

CHAPTER 16

Advanced Topics

In this chapter we will explore some of the less followed paths through the SDK, including managing the schema, using Virtual List Views, and handling password expiration. We'll take a look at the built-in controls of the SDK for accessing LDAP server functionality beyond what is defined by the protocol standards, how to write your own control, how to manage referrals, how to access extended operations, and how to use the asynchronous interface.

Information about Information: Managing the Schema

We ran into the schema earlier in this book. Chapter 2 introduced a few of the most commonly used object classes and attributes. We addressed the constraints imposed by the schema in Chapter 11, when we wanted to add values for various user preferences to the user's directory entry. If schema enforcement is enabled in a server, you can add values only for attributes that are defined as mandatory or optional for the object classes of the entry.

Programmatic Access through the Schema Classes

In Chapter 2 we looked at the notation used by Netscape and many others for schema configuration files (not a standard, but a commonly used format). The configuration files define the schema of the server when it starts up. In this chapter we will see how the schema can be discovered, read, and updated dynamically.

Version 3 of the LDAP protocol specifies that the schema can be read and updated using the same operations you would use to read and update any data in the directory. The steps are as follows:

1. Read the subSchemaSubEntry attribute from any entry in the directory.
2. Use the value of the subSchemaSubEntry attribute as the DN of an entry from which to access the schema; specify objectclass=subSchema as the filter.
3. Read or update the attributes of the entry to access or modify the schema.

For example:

```
java LDAPSearch -b "" -s base "objectclass=*" subSchemaSubentry
dn:
subSchemaSubentry: cn=schema

java LDAPSearch -b "cn=schema" -s base "objectclass=subSchema"
dn: cn=schema
objectclass: top
objectclass: subschema
cn: schema
objectclasses: ( 2.5.6.0 NAME 'top' DESC 'Standard ObjectClass'
 MUST ( object class )  MAY ( aci ) )
objectclasses: ( 2.5.6.1 NAME 'alias' DESC 'Standard ObjectClass' SUP
'top'  MUST ( objectclass $ aliasedobjectname )  MAY ( aci ) )
...
attributetypes: ( 2.16.840.1.113730.3.1.95 NAME 'accountUnlockTime'
 DESC 'Standard Attribute' SYNTAX '1.3.6.1.4.1.1466.115.121.1.15' )
attributetypes: ( 2.16.840.1.113730.3.1.74 NAME 'administratorContactInfo'
 DESC 'Standard Attribute' SYNTAX '1.3.6.1.4.1.1466.115.121.1.15' )
...
matchingrules: ( 2.16.840.1.113730.3.3.2.0.1 NAME
 'caseIgnoreOrderingMatch-default' DESC '' SYNTAX
 '1.3.6.1.4.1.1466.115.121.1.15' )
matchingrules: ( 2.16.840.1.113730.3.3.2.0.1.6 NAME
'caseIgnoreSubstringMatch-default' DESC '' SYNTAX
'1.3.6.1.4.1.1466.115.121.1.15' )
```

The format of the schema declarations is defined in RFC 2252, and it conforms to the format used by X.500. Each object class is defined in a value of the attribute objectClasses. Each attribute is defined in a value of the attribute attributeTypes. Each matching rule is defined in a value of the attribute matchingRules. There may also be an attribute matchingRuleUse, in which each value lists the attributes for which one particular matching rule may be used. A matching rule that is supported by a particular server may be specified as part of a search filter.

Each definition starts with the OID of the schema element and its name. The name and the OID of a schema element can generally be used interchangeably in the LDAP protocol and in the SDK.

Object class definitions declare the object class from which they derive ("SUP") and list the attributes that are required ("MUST") and the attributes that are allowed ("MAY") in entries containing the object class.

Attribute definitions declare the syntax that is used to compare and sort them; matching-rule definitions declare the syntax of attributes for which they may be used. The OID for caseIgnoreString syntax is 1.3.6.1.4.1.1466.115.121.1.15, which RFC 2252 also specifies as the OID for Directory String syntax, meaning that it must be in UTF8 format. Attribute definitions also include the qualifier "SINGLE-VALUE" if the attribute is allowed to have only one value.

With the Java LDAP SDK, you can use LDAPSchemaElement.cis as a constant to indicate case-insensitive string syntax rather than specifying the OID. Other syntax constants are LDAPSchemaElement.ces (case-exact string), LDAPSchemaElement.dn (compare as a DN), LDAPSchemaElement.telephone (normalize and compare as telephone numbers), LDAPSchemaElement.integer, and LDAPSchemaElement.binary.

Some additional schema element qualifiers are defined in RFC 2252 but not widely supported in LDAP servers: "OBSOLETE," "COLLECTIVE," "NO-USER-MODIFICATION," "USAGE," "EQUALITY," "ORDERING," and "SUBSTRING." The last three are used to specify special matching rules to use for equality comparisons, sorting, and substring evaluation. "USAGE" may have any of the following values: "userApplications," "directoryOperation," "distributedOperation," or "dSAOperation."

In the example given earlier, we read the schema for the root DSE (the special entry with the empty DN). In Netscape Directory Server and many other LDAP servers, you will get the same results for any entry for which you read the schema because the schema is global to the whole server. However, LDAP allows the schema to be defined for a particular subtree. In the future it may become common for directories to support different schema definitions for different subtrees.

Although you are free to read and change these values with LDAPConnection.search and LDAPConnection.modify, the Java LDAP API provides classes that parse and construct the declarations, making it easy to interpret and update the schema. To obtain the schema of a directory, follow these steps:

1. Instantiate an LDAPSchema object.
2. Execute its fetch method, supplying an LDAPConnection object.
3. Enumerate or extract object class, attribute, and matching-rule definition objects.

For example:

```
// Construct a new LDAPSchema object to get the schema.
 // ld is an LDAPConnection that is connected and authenticated.
LDAPSchema dirSchema = new LDAPSchema();
try {
    // Get the schema from the directory
    dirSchema.fetchSchema( ld );
} catch ( Exception e ) {
    System.err.println( e.toString() );
    System.exit( 1 );
}

// Get and print the inetOrgPerson object class description
LDAPObjectClassSchema objClass = dirSchema.getObjectClass(
                 "inetOrgPerson" );
if ( objClass != null ) {
    System.out.println("inetOrgPerson := " + objClass.toString());
}

// Get and print the definition of the userPassword attribute
LDAPAttributeSchema attrType = dirSchema.getAttribute(
                 "userPassword" );
if ( attrType != null ) {
    System.out.println("userPassword := " + attrType.toString());
}

// Get and print the definitions of all matching rules
Enumeration en = dirSchema.getMatchingRules();
while( en.hasMoreElements() ) {
    LDAPMatchingRuleSchema matchRule =
        (LDAPMatchingRuleSchema )en.nextElement();
    System.out.println("matchingRule := " + matchRule.toString());
}
```

We used LDAPSchema.fetchSchema(LDAPConnection ld) in this example to retrieve the schema associated with the root DSE of the server. There is an overloaded method, LDAPSchema.fetchSchema(LDAPConnection ld, String dn), to retrieve the schema associated with an arbitrary entry. As previously mentioned, Netscape Directory Server and most other LDAP servers will return the same results for any valid DN, but a server could return a different schema for each different part of the directory tree.

Once the schema has been obtained from the directory by the LDAPSchema object, you can extract individual schema elements by name, or obtain Enumerations for all schema elements. In the preceding example we used LDAPSchema.getObjectClass ("inetOrgPerson") to extract a single object class definition. We could have used LDAPSchema.getObjectClasses if we wanted to list or browse all object class definitions.

The LDAPObjectClassSchema, LDAPAttributeSchema, and LDAPMatchingRuleSchema classes all derive from LDAPSchemaElement, which defines many of the common members and methods.

You can add, modify, or remove a schema definition using the methods by the same names on a particular schema element object. The following example adds the new object class "Experiment." It then changes the definition of "hairColor" and deletes "Experiment." The OIDs in the example are fictitious; for production, your OIDs should be based on one obtained from the IANA (Internet Assigned Numbers Authority), to guarantee uniqueness.

```
// Construct a new LDAPSchema object to get the schema.
//  ld is an LDAPConnection that is connected and
// authenticated.
// Add a new object class.
String[] requiredAttrs = {"cn", "mail"};
String[] optionalAttrs = {"sn", "phoneNumber"};
LDAPObjectClassSchema newObjClass = new LDAPObjectClassSchema(
                   "newInetOrgPerson", "1.2.3.4.5.6.7", "top",
                   "Experiment", requiredAttrs, optionalAttrs );
// Add the new object class to the schema
newObjClass.add( ld );

// Create a new attribute type "hairColor"
LDAPAttributeSchema newAttrType = new LDAPAttributeSchema(
                   "hairColor", "1.2.3.4.5.4.3.2.1",
                   "Blonde, red, etc",
                   LDAPAttributeSchema.cis, false );
// Add the new attribute type to the schema
newAttrType.add( ld );
// Create a modified attribute definition for "hairColor"
LDAPAttributeSchema modAttrType = new LDAPAttributeSchema(
                   "hairColor", "1.2.3.4.5.4.3.2.1",
                   "Blue, green, etc",
                   LDAPAttributeSchema.cis, false );
// Modify the existing attribute type in the schema. This
// removes the previous definition and adds the new one in
// one atomic operation.
newAttrType.modify( ld, modAttrType );

// Remove the "Experiment" object class from the schema
newObjClass.remove( ld );
```

As with LDAPSchema.fetchSchema, each of the LDAPSchemaElement methods—add, modify, and remove—has an overloaded method that takes a DN as an additional parameter, for any LDAP server that supports a subtree-specific schema. With most servers you can specify any valid DN, but the operations always affect the global schema for the whole server.

A Pretty Printer for Schema Contents

The schema element classes have accessors for the commonly used (mandatory) qualifiers:

```
public String LDAPSchemaElement.getDescription
public String LDAPSchemaElement.getName
public String LDAPSchemaElement.getOID
public String LDAPSchemaElement.getValue, which returns a String that
is formatted for adding to an LDAP server (compliant with RFC 2252)
public String LDAPAttributeSchema.getSyntax
public boolean LDAPAttributeSchema.isSingleValued
public Enumeration LDAPObjectClassSchema.getOptionalAttributes
public Enumeration LDAPObjectClassSchema.getRequiredAttributes
public String LDAPObjectClassSchema.getSuperior
```

`LDAPSchemaElement` also has methods to access any additional qualifiers beyond those commonly used, and constants for the qualifiers defined in RFC 2252. Many LDAP servers will ignore the additional qualifiers if you attempt to use them when adding an attribute definition.

```
public void LDAPSchemaElement.setQualifier( String name, String value )
public String []LDAPSchemaElement.getQualifier( String name )
public Enumeration LDAPSchemaElement.getQualifierNames()
public static final String EQUALITY
public static final String ORDERING
public static final String SUBSTR
public static final String COLLECTIVE
public static final String NO_USER_MODIFICATION
public static final String USAGE
```

The next program retrieves the schema from a directory and prints out the definitions in a clear and readable format. Object classes are printed in a format similar to that used in the schema configuration files of many LDAP servers, but sorted and then ordered and indented to indicate inheritance. Then all attribute and matching-rule definitions are printed. You can optionally specify any number of individual schema elements to print; if you do, the program exits after printing them.

The program begins by parsing the command-line arguments for the required host name and port number and for any options specifying particular schema elements to print:

```
/**
 * Fetch the schema from the LDAP server at the specified
 * host and port, and print out the schema (including descriptions
 * of its object classes, attribute types, and matching rules).
 * The schema is printed in an easily readable format (not the
 * same as the format expected by an LDAP server).  For example,
 * you can enter the following command to print the schema:
 * <PRE>
 * java netscape.ldap.LDAPSchema myhost.mydomain.com 389
 * </PRE>
 * Options are:<BR>
 * -D AUTHDN         Use this DN to authenticate<BR>
 * -w AUTHPASSWORD  Use this password to authenticate<BR>
 * -o OBJECTCLASS   Print the definition of an object class<BR>
 * -a ATTRIBUTE     Print the definition of an attribute<BR>
 * -m MATCHINGRULE  Print the definition of a matching rule<BR>
 *<BR>
 * The default is to print all schema elements.<BR>
 *
 * @param args the host name and the port number of the LDAP server
 * (e.g., netscape.ldap.LDAPSchema directory.netscape.com 389)
 */
public static void main( String[] args ) {

    String host = null;
    int port = -1;
    String authDN = null;
    String authPassword = null;
    Vector attrList = new Vector();
    Vector ocList = new Vector();
    Vector matchList = new Vector();
    for( int i = 0; i < args.length; i++ ) {
        if ( args[i].startsWith( "-" ) ) {
            if ( i > (args.length - 2) ) {
                doUsage();
                System.exit( 1 );
            }
            if ( args[i].equals( "-a" ) ) {
                i++;
                attrList.addElement( args[i] );
```

```
                } else if ( args[i].equals( "-o" ) ) {
                    i++;
                    ocList.addElement( args[i] );
                } else if ( args[i].equals( "-m" ) ) {
                    i++;
                    matchList.addElement( args[i] );
                } else if ( args[i].equals( "-D" ) ) {
                    i++;
                    authDN = args[i];
                } else if ( args[i].equals( "-w" ) ) {
                    i++;
                    authPassword = args[i];
                } else {
                    doUsage();
                    System.exit( 1 );
                }
            } else if ( host == null ) {
                host = args[i];
            } else if ( port == -1 ) {
                port = Integer.parseInt( args[i] );
            } else {
                doUsage();
                System.exit( 1 );
            }
        }
        if ( (host == null) || (port <= 0) ) {
            doUsage();
            System.exit( 1 );
        }
```

Then the schema is retrieved from the directory:

```
        LDAPConnection ld = new LDAPConnection();
        try {
            // Connect and get schema
            ld.connect( host, port );
            if ( (authDN != null) && (authPassword != null) ) {
                ld.authenticate( authDN, authPassword );
            }
            LDAPSchema schema = new LDAPSchema();
            schema.fetchSchema( ld );
            ld.disconnect();
```

If any schema elements are requested on the command line, print them and exit:

```
// Print any specific schema elements that were requested
Enumeration en = ocList.elements();
while( en.hasMoreElements() ) {
    String name = (String)en.nextElement();
    System.out.println( "" );
    printOC( schema, name, 0 );
}
en = attrList.elements();
while( en.hasMoreElements() ) {
    String name = (String)en.nextElement();
    LDAPAttributeSchema attr =
        schema.getAttribute( name );
    if ( attr == null ) {
        break;
    }
    System.out.println( "" );
    printAttribute( attr );
}
en = matchList.elements();
while( en.hasMoreElements() ) {
    String name = (String)en.nextElement();
    LDAPMatchingRuleSchema match =
        schema.getMatchingRule( name );
    if ( match == null ) {
        break;
    }
    System.out.println( "" );
    printMatchingRule( match );
}
// If specific elements were requested, we're done
if ( (attrList.size() > 0) ||
     (ocList.size() > 0) ||
     (matchList.size() > 0) ) {
    System.exit( 0 );
}
```

If no schema elements are requested on the command line, sort the object classes by inheritance and print them out followed by the attributes and matching rules:

```
// Sort the object classes by inheritance, and print them
// as tree
Hashtable tree = sortObjectClasses( schema );
printOC( schema, "top", 0 );
printTree( schema, tree, 1 );
```

```
            // Sort the attributes and print them
            en = schema.getAttributes();
            LDAPSchemaElement[] elements = sortElements( en );
            for( int i = 0; i < elements.length; i++ ) {
                System.out.println( "" );
                printAttribute( (LDAPAttributeSchema)elements[i] );
            }

            // Sort the matching rules and print them
            en = schema.getMatchingRules();
            elements = sortElements( en );
            for( int i = 0; i < elements.length; i++ ) {
                System.out.println( "" );
                printMatchingRule( (LDAPMatchingRuleSchema)elements[i] );
            }

            System.exit( 0 );
        } catch ( LDAPException e ) {
            System.err.println( e );
        }
    }
```

The print method for object classes uses the accessors of LDAPObjectClassSchema:

```
    /**
     * Print the qualifiers of an object class definition, in a format
     * similar to what is used in slapd.oc.conf
     *
     * @param schema a complete collection of schema definitions
     * @param ocName name of the object class to print
     * @param level indentation level
     */
    private static void printOC( LDAPSchema schema,
                                 String ocName,
                                 int level ) {
        LDAPObjectClassSchema oc = schema.getObjectClass( ocName );
        if ( oc == null ) {
            return;
        }

        String tabs = "";
        for( int i = 0; i < level; i++ ) {
```

```
            tabs += '\t';
        }
        System.out.println( '\n' + tabs + ocName );
        System.out.println( tabs + '\t' + "OID" );
        System.out.println( tabs + "\t\t" + oc.getOID() );
        System.out.println( tabs + '\t' + "Superior" );
        System.out.println( tabs + "\t\t" + oc.getSuperior() );
        System.out.println( tabs + '\t' + "Description" );
        System.out.println( tabs + "\t\t" + oc.getDescription() );
        System.out.println( tabs + '\t' + "Required" );
        Enumeration vals = oc.getRequiredAttributes();
        while( vals.hasMoreElements() ) {
            String s = (String)vals.nextElement();
            System.out.println( tabs + "\t\t" + s );
        }
        System.out.println( tabs + '\t' + "Optional" );
        vals = oc.getOptionalAttributes();
        while( vals.hasMoreElements() ) {
            String s = (String)vals.nextElement();
            System.out.println( tabs + "\t\t" + s );
        }
    }
```

The attribute printer is similar but prints a user-friendly version of the syntax specifier instead of the dotted decimal OID:

```
    /**
     * Print the qualifiers of an attribute definition, in a format
     * similar to what is used in slapd.at.conf
     *
     * @param attr the attribute schema object
     */
    private static void printAttribute( LDAPAttributeSchema attr ) {
        System.out.println( attr.getName() );
        System.out.println( '\t' + "OID" );
        System.out.println( "\t\t" + attr.getOID() );
        System.out.println( '\t' + "Description" );
        System.out.println( "\t\t" + attr.getDescription() );
        System.out.println( '\t' + "Syntax" );
        System.out.println( "\t\t" + getSyntax( attr ) );
        if ( attr.isSingleValued() ) {
            System.out.println( '\t' + "single-valued" );
        } else {
```

```
            System.out.println( '\t' + "multi-valued" );
        }
        Enumeration en = attr.getQualifierNames();
        while( en.hasMoreElements() ) {
            String qualifier = (String)en.nextElement();
            String value = attr.getQualifier( qualifier );
            System.out.println( '\t' + qualifier );
        }
    }

    /**
     * Get a string representation of an attribute syntax
     *
     * @param attr an attribute schema definition
     * @return a user-friendly String describing the syntax
     */
    private static String getSyntax( LDAPAttributeSchema attr ) {
        int syntax = attr.getSyntax();
        if ( syntax == attr.cis ) {
            return "case-insensitive string";
        } else if ( syntax == attr.binary ) {
            return "binary";
        } else if ( syntax == attr.integer ) {
            return "integer";
        } else if ( syntax == attr.ces ) {
            return "case-exact string";
        } else if ( syntax == attr.telephone ) {
            return "telephone";
        } else if ( syntax == attr.dn ) {
            return "distinguished name";
        } else {
            return attr.getSyntaxString();
        }
    }
```

Matching rules have a simpler structure:

```
    /**
     * Print the qualifiers of a matching-rule definition,
     * in a format similar to what is used in slapd.at.conf
     *
     * @param match the matching-rule schema object
     */
```

```
private static void printMatchingRule(
                   LDAPMatchingRuleSchema match ) {
    System.out.println( match.getName() );
    System.out.println( '\t' + "OID" );
    System.out.println( "\t\t" + match.getOID() );
    System.out.println( '\t' + "Description" );
    System.out.println( "\t\t" + match.getDescription() );
    System.out.println( '\t' + "Attributes" );
    String[] attrs = match.getAttributes();
    if( attrs != null ) {
        for( int i = 0; i < attrs.length; i++ ) {
            System.out.println( "\t\t" + attrs[i] );
        }
    }
}
```

If all schema definitions are to be printed, the object class definitions must first be sorted by superior:

```
/**
 * Create a Hashtable for all object classes with a
 * common superior, and a Hashtable containing all these Hashtables
 *
 * @param schema a complete set of all schema definitions
 *
 * @return a Hashtable containing other Hashtables with
 * schema definitions
 */
private static Hashtable sortObjectClasses(
                         LDAPSchema schema ) {
    Hashtable htOC = new Hashtable();
    Enumeration en = schema.getObjectClasses();
    while( en.hasMoreElements() ) {
        // Sort the object classes by parent
        LDAPObjectClassSchema oc =
            (LDAPObjectClassSchema)en.nextElement();
        String sup = oc.getSuperior();
        Hashtable table =
           (Hashtable)htOC.get( sup.toLowerCase() );
        if( table == null ) {
            table = new Hashtable();
        }
        table.put( oc.getName().toLowerCase(), oc );
```

```
            htOC.put( sup.toLowerCase(), table );
        }
        Hashtable tree = new Hashtable();
        // Recursively add children, starting at "top"
        addChildren( htOC, tree, "top" );
        return tree;
    }

    /**
     * Find and add object classes that directly inherit
    * from sup to level
     *
     * @param htOC a table containing all object class
    * definitions
     * @level Table to which to add the children
     * @sup Name of superior of children to add
     */
    private static void addChildren( Hashtable htOC,
                                     Hashtable level,
                                     String sup ) {
        Hashtable ht =
           (Hashtable)htOC.get( sup.toLowerCase() );
        Enumeration en = ht.keys();
        while( en.hasMoreElements() ) {
            String name = (String)en.nextElement();
            Hashtable table =
               (Hashtable)htOC.get( name.toLowerCase() );
            if ( table != null ) {
                level.put( name.toLowerCase(), table );
                addChildren( htOC, table, name );
            } else {
                level.put( name,
                           ht.get( name.toLowerCase() ) );
            }
        }
    }
```

The output of the program might look like this:

```
java PrintSchema localhost 389

top
        OID
```

```
                2.5.6.0
        Superior

        Description
                Standard ObjectClass
        Required
                objectclass
        Optional
                aci

        account
                OID
                        0.9.2342.19200300.100.4.5
                Superior
                        top
                Description
                        Standard ObjectClass
                Required
                        objectclass
                        uid
                Optional
                        aci
                        description
                        host
                        l
                        o
                        ou
                        seealso
...
accountUnlockTime
        OID
                2.16.840.1.113730.3.1.95
        Description
                Standard Attribute
        Syntax
                case-insensitive string
        multi-valued
...
caseExactOrderingMatch-en
        OID
                2.16.840.1.113730.3.3.2.11.3
        Description
                en
        Attributes
```

Microsoft's Active Directory requires authentication to read the schema, so in the following example we provide an administrative DN and password.

```
java PrintSchema  -D
     "CN=Administrator,CN=Users,DC=myhost,DC=airius,DC=com"
     -w admin -o groupOfNames myhost.airius.com 389
```

```
groupOfNames
        OID
                2.5.6.9
        Superior
                top
        Description

        Required
                cn
                member
        Optional
                o
                ou
                businessCategory
                owner
                seeAlso
```

Controls: An Essential Extension

One of the innovations of version 3 of the LDAP protocol is the concept of controls that modify or extend the functionality of the standard protocol operations. The intent is to allow LDAP to be extended and meet the needs of developers and consumers without requiring another major revision of the protocol. A control is an arbitrary (that is, it needs to make sense only to the particular client and server) piece of data supplied by the client or the server along with any other data that is part of a standard protocol operation, such as search or delete.

Client controls are intended for local use by the SDK; they are not to be sent to the server. Server request controls are to be sent to the server, and server response controls may be sent by the server to a client. The Java LDAP SDK does not define or process any client controls at this time, but it leaves the door open for incorporation of any client controls that may be defined in standards documents in the future.

A directory server vendor is free to define proprietary controls. Often an Internet Draft is published to describe a control that may be of more general interest. The Virtual List View (VLV) control described in this chapter has been adopted by many or most LDAP server vendors. A server must publish in the root DSE any controls that it supports. Netscape Directory Server 4.1 reports the following:

```
java LDAPSearch -b "" -s base -h localhost -p 389 "objectclass=*"
     supportedcontrol
dn:
supportedcontrol: 2.16.840.1.113730.3.4.2
supportedcontrol: 2.16.840.1.113730.3.4.3
supportedcontrol: 2.16.840.1.113730.3.4.4
supportedcontrol: 2.16.840.1.113730.3.4.5
supportedcontrol: 1.2.840.113556.1.4.473
supportedcontrol: 2.16.840.1.113730.3.4.9
supportedcontrol: 2.16.840.1.113730.3.4.12
```

The OIDs reported here are defined in the header file ldap.h, which comes with the C LDAP SDK:

```
#define LDAP_CONTROL_MANAGEDSAIT       "2.16.840.1.113730.3.4.2"
#define LDAP_CONTROL_SORTREQUEST       "1.2.840.113556.1.4.473"
#define LDAP_CONTROL_PERSISTENTSEARCH "2.16.840.1.113730.3.4.3"
#define LDAP_CONTROL_VLVREQUEST        "2.16.840.1.113730.3.4.9"
/* Password information sent back to client */
#define LDAP_CONTROL_PWEXPIRED         "2.16.840.1.113730.3.4.4"
#define LDAP_CONTROL_PWEXPIRING        "2.16.840.1.113730.3.4.5"
#define LDAP_CONTROL_PROXYAUTH         "2.16.840.1.113730.3.4.12"
```

Although there are no restrictions on what the data in a control should look like, a control intended for general use (by more than one vendor) most often has its data encoded using the Basic Encoding Rules (BER) described in Chapter 2.

Too Much Data: A Virtual List View

A common task in LDAP applications is to list all the entries that match a particular search filter—for example, in response to a user's typing in part of a name to look up. Another common feature is to display the contents of a directory as a tree that can be browsed by the user. Both cases may be problematic if the number of entries to display is very large. There may not be enough memory available to hold the entire list at once. It may take a long time for the list to be received, and in the meantime the user is waiting at an unresponsive user interface. The number of search results may be higher than the server is configured to return on any one request, in which case the client will get an exception.

The VLV control was designed to allow clients to request arbitrary subsets of the search results. For example, clients may request 100 at a time while progressing through the results, or they may jump back and forth in response to a user's scrolling through a list. The entire set of results that would have been returned on each search without the control is called the virtual result set. The control allows the client to specify the starting point of the subset either as an absolute index into the virtual result set or as a string to be matched. The number of results before and after the first result are specified individually, offering an easily configurable window into the data. A client can implement typedown—jumping to an entry in the virtual list in response to a user's typing in the first letters of a name—by accumulating user keystrokes and sending a VLV control that requests the first entry matching the characters typed in so far.

An application that uses VLV can present the user with a scrolling list that works just as well with a user database of 10 million entries as with a database of 1,000 entries.

A VLV request control has two constructors, corresponding to the two ways to specify the starting point of the desired window into the result set. It may seem odd that the client specifies `contentCount`—the size of the virtual result set—when creating a control to access a window from a specific index. The server uses the number provided by the client as a hint when determining the actual window, in case the client's perception of the size of the virtual result set is radically different from the server's perception. Generally, `contentCount` is set to 0 on the first VLV search request. The VLV response control contains the real number at the time of the search, and it is used by the client on subsequent VLV requests involving the same search parameters:

```
LDAPVirtualListControl(int startIndex,
                       int beforeCount,
                       int afterCount,
                       int contentCount)
LDAPVirtualListControl(String jumpTo,
                       int beforeCount,
                       int afterCount)
```

Some servers (Novell Directory Services, for one) can process a request more efficiently if they are supplied with a context cookie. A cookie is returned by the server in a VLV response, and it should be provided in subsequent requests involving the same VLV search:

```
public LDAPVirtualListControl(int startIndex,
                              int beforeCount,
                              int afterCount,
                              int contentCount,
                              String context)
```

The class has accessors that can be used to get the current settings or to change them after the object has been constructed:

```
int getAfterCount
int getBeforeCount
int getIndex
int getListSize
void setListSize(int listSize)
void setRange(int startIndex, int beforeCount, int afterCount)
void setRange(String jumpTo, int beforeCount, int afterCount)
public String getContext
public void setContext(String context)
```

The server will include a VLV response control along with results from a search that included a VLV request control. The VLV response control has methods to determine what the returned window is (it may be smaller than the requested window if results were requested beyond the end of the result set) or if there was an error in producing the results:

```
int getContentCount()
int getFirstPosition()
int getResultCode()
public String getContext()
```

Note that the the offset reported by `getFirstPosition` may not be exact. The Internet Draft on VLV allows a server to report an approximate offset. In addition, the directory content may change between searches. An LDAP server is generally not a single-user system.

For the server to process a VLV request, a sort control must also be provided to indicate how the results are to be ordered. The following code snippet shows one way to do a VLV search and process the results.

```
LDAPControl[] pageControls = new LDAPControl[2];
// VLV requests also require a sort control; sort by common name
pageControls[0] = new LDAPSortControl( new LDAPSortKey("cn"),
                                       true );
// Do an initial search to get the virtual list size.
// Keep one page before and one page after the start.
beforeCount = pageSize;
afterCount = pageSize;
selectedIndex = -1;
// Create the initial VLV request control; we don't know the
// virtual list size, so we specify 0 for the size parameter
```

```
LDAPVirtualListControl vlc;
pageControls[1] = vlc =
            new LDAPVirtualListControl( 0, beforeCount,
                                        afterCount, 0 );
LDAPSearchConstraints cons =
    (LDAPSearchConstraints )ld.getSearchConstraints();
cons.setServerControls( pageControls );
// Do a search
try {
    String[] attrs = { "cn" };
    LDAPSearchResults result =
            ld.search( base, ld.SCOPE_SUB, filter, attrs,
                       false, cons );
```

The search results are processed in the same way as for an ordinary search, but the application should check if a VLV response control was returned. The VLV response control will contain the size of the whole virtual list in entries, and the size should be used in subsequent operations involving the same search. The server uses the parameter on receipt in a VLV request control to better accommodate the desired window of results.

```
// Check if we have a control returned
LDAPControl[] c = ld.getResponseControls();
if ( c != null ) {
    for( int i = 0; i < c.length; i++ ) {
        if ( c[i] instanceof LDAPVirtualListResponse ) {
            LDAPVirtualListResponse response =
                (LDAPVirtualListResponse)c[i];
            selectedIndex =
               response.getFirstPosition() - 1;
            top =
               Math.max( 0, selectedIndex - beforeCount );
            // Now we know the total size of the virtual
            // list
            size = response.getContentCount();
            vlc.setListSize( size );
        }
    }
}
if ( selectedIndex < 0 ) {
    System.out.println( "No VLV response control" );
}
```

If pageSize is 50, then 51 results are returned (if there are at least that many search results) because 0 was specified as the first index and there can be no results before that index. If the search is repeated after the desired window is adjusted with

```
vlc.setRange( 100, pageSize, pageSize );
```

then entries corresponding to indexes 50 through 150 will be returned.

VLV and Indexes: Defining a VLV Search and Filter for Netscape

Given all that VLV can do, why not use it on every search and page through the results by making repeated calls to the directory? The answer is that the VLV Internet Draft defines the protocol to use but not the server implementation, and LDAP servers generally cannot provide random subsets of search results for an arbitrary query. Some servers may have certain predefined queries that can always be serviced on a VLV search. Others—including Netscape Directory Server—can provide VLV results for any query, but they can do so efficiently only if a special index exists for the query.

Netscape Directory Server attempts to sort all search results in memory to return a requested window of entries if no index exists. This means that even if you request only five entries in your VLV control, the server will read all entries of the virtual result list into memory and sort them before returning the five results. If the query results in a virtual list size of more than one or two thousand entries, a lot of memory is used by the server to process the request and the response time degrades.

If the virtual list size is just a thousand or so entries, we haven't gained much compared to just reading all results and buffering them on the client. To allow efficient browsing of millions of entries, we must create an index for the particular search we are doing. The following steps are required with Netscape Directory Server to create a new VLV index:

- Create a VLV search entry in the directory under cn=config,cn=ldbm. The entry defines the base DN, scope, and search filter of the query.
- Create one or more VLV index entries under the search entry. Each entry defines a sort order for the results.
- Stop the server or make it read-only.
- Run the vlvindex script to generate a new index or indexes.
- Restart the server or make it read/writeable.

The following is an example of creating an index for a search for any person entry under o=Airius.com, sorted by last name, first name.

```
java LDAPModify -D "cn=directory manager" -w password -a
dn: cn=Find all persons, cn=config, cn=ldbm
objectclass: top
objectclass: vlvSearch
cn: Find all persons
vlvbase: o=Airius.com
vlvfilter: objectclass=person
vlvscope: 2

dn: cn=LastNameFirstName, cn=Find all persons, cn=config, cn=ldbm
objectclass: top
objectclass: vlvIndex
cn: LastNameFirstName
vlvsort: sn givenName
ctrl-D (Unix) or ctrl-Z (Windows)
cd /usr/netscape/server4/slapd-foo
stop-slapd
vlvindex "LastNameFirstName"
start-slapd
```

Note that the search scope must be specified with numerals (0 for base, 1 for one-level, and 2 for subtree). We have now created an index for all entries in the directory that match our query. When entries are added to the directory or modified, the index will automatically be kept up-to-date. Any VLV search that exactly matches the query will be serviced quickly and efficiently. This can be verified with `LDAPSearch`. We must use exactly the same base DN, scope, search filter, and sorting attributes that we specified when creating the index:

```
java LDAPSearch -D "uid=scarter, ou=People, o=airius.com" -w sprain
    -b "o=Airius.com" -s sub -S "sn givenName" -x -G 2:2:10:0
         "objectclass=person" cn

dn: uid=jbourke, ou=People, o=airius.com
cn: Jon Bourke

dn: uid=jbrown, ou=People, o=airius.com
cn: Judy Brown

dn: uid=jburrell, ou=People, o=airius.com
cn: James Burrell

dn: uid=jcampai2, ou=People, o=airius.com
cn: Jeffrey Campaigne
```

```
dn: uid=jcampaig, ou=People, o=airius.com
cn: Jody Campaigne

Server indicated results sorted OK
Server indicated virtual list positioning OK
index 10 content count 150
```

The -x option to turn on server-side sorting is required when using VLV. The -G option specifies the `beforeCount`, `afterCount`, and `firstIndex` of the desired window and the size (if known) of the virtual list.

The Internet Draft on VLV does not define how access control is to be assigned for using VLV. A subtree search with VLV will tell the caller how many entries exist under that node, even if the caller does not have access rights to read those entries. That may be an unacceptable security breach in many organizations. Netscape Directory Server declares VLV as a feature with its own directory entry, so any access control desired can be applied to it. The default access control for VLV searches is to allow them for any authenticated user (but not for anonymous users). The access control can be modified by changing or adding to the `aci` attribute in the entry `oid=2.16.840.1.113730.3.4.9, cn=features,cn=config`. Other servers may not allow setting access control on VLV searches, or they may require setting it in another way.

A VLV-Based Directory Lister with Typedown

We'll pull all this information together in `VListPanel` (Figure 16-1), a JavaBean that extends `JList` and presents the results of a VLV search. To test-drive the Bean, we will place it in a dialog box with a text field for typedown. As you type into the field, the list contents are updated or scrolled.

All JavaBeans must have a blank constructor for deserialization, but it is convenient also to have one in which you can set all parameters at once:

```
/**
 * A JavaBean that extends JList and contains a list of sorted
 * names from a directory. It is a property change listener for
 * string changes - the list updates itself and scrolls to the
 * first name matching the characters in a supplied string.
 * This is for typedown support.
 */
public class VListPanel extends JList
                        implements PropertyChangeListener,
                                   Serializable {

    public VListPanel() {
        super();
    }
```

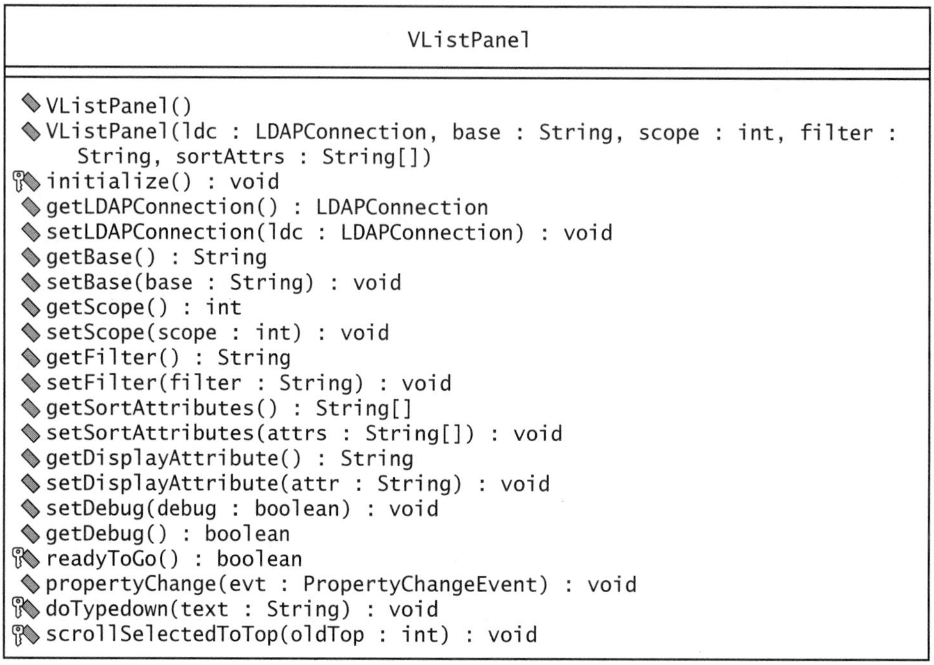

```
VListPanel
-----------------------------------------------------------------------
VListPanel()
VListPanel(ldc : LDAPConnection, base : String, scope : int, filter :
   String, sortAttrs : String[])
initialize() : void
getLDAPConnection() : LDAPConnection
setLDAPConnection(ldc : LDAPConnection) : void
getBase() : String
setBase(base : String) : void
getScope() : int
setScope(scope : int) : void
getFilter() : String
setFilter(filter : String) : void
getSortAttributes() : String[]
setSortAttributes(attrs : String[]) : void
getDisplayAttribute() : String
setDisplayAttribute(attr : String) : void
setDebug(debug : boolean) : void
getDebug() : boolean
readyToGo() : boolean
propertyChange(evt : PropertyChangeEvent) : void
doTypedown(text : String) : void
scrollSelectedToTop(oldTop : int) : void
```

FIGURE 16-1. VListPanel.

```
public VListPanel( LDAPConnection ldc, String base,
                   int scope, String filter,
                   String[] sortAttrs ) {
    super();
    _ldc = ldc;
    _base = base;
    _scope = scope;
    _filter = filter;
    _sortAttrs = sortAttrs;
    initialize();
}
```

The `initialize` method can be called more than once. If any of the Bean properties change, then `initialize` is called again to create a new virtual list model to supply data:

```
/**
 * Create model and user interface
```

```
     */
    protected void initialize() {
        // We don't want the JList implementation to compute
        //  the width or height of all the list cells,
        // so we give it a String that's as big as we'll need for
        // any cell.  It uses this to compute values for
        // the fixedCellWidth and fixedCellHeight properties.
        setPrototypeCellValue("1234567890123456789012345678 9");

        _model = new VListModel( _ldc, _base, _scope,
                                 _filter, _sortAttrs );
        setModel( _model );
        _model.setPageSize( getVisibleRowCount() );
    }
```

There are accessors for all the properties—LDAPConnection, base, scope, filter, sort attributes, display attribute, debug state—but we will not list them here.

The Bean is a listener for property changes. If the typedown property changes, then it notifies the virtual list model that it must update itself and scrolls so that the selected item is visible:

```
    /**
     * On a property change event, do typedown to the new
     * string value
     *
     * @param evt an event indicating a changed typedown
     * string
     */
    public void propertyChange( PropertyChangeEvent evt ) {
        if ( evt.getPropertyName().equals( "typedown" ) ) {
            String newVal = "";
            Object obj = (Object)evt.getNewValue();
            if ( (obj != null) && (obj instanceof String) ) {
                newVal = (String)obj;
            }
            doTypedown( newVal );
        }
    }

    /**
     * Tell the model to do typedown, and then scroll the list
     * so that the selected index is visible
```

```
 */
protected void doTypedown( String text ) {
    int top = _model.getFirstIndex();
    _model.typedown( text );
    scrollSelectedToTop( top );
}
```

The scrolling behavior is more attractive if we take into account the direction in which we are scrolling:

```
/**
 * Scroll so that the user-selected first index is visible
 *
 * @param oldTop the top index before we make any changes
 */
protected void scrollSelectedToTop( int oldTop ) {
    int index = _model.getSelectedIndex();
    // If scrolling down, make sure the selected index
    // becomes the topmost one
    if ( _model.getFirstIndex() > oldTop )
        index += getVisibleRowCount() - 1;
    ensureIndexIsVisible( index );
}
```

`VListModel` (Figure 16-2) does the real work of interacting with the directory when the list needs data to display:

```
class VListModel extends AbstractListModel {
/**
 * All parameters of the model are passed in to the
 * constructor
 *
 * @param ldc a sufficiently authenticated connection to a
 * server
 * @param base the base DN for the search
 * @param scope the search scope
 * @param filter the search filter
 * @param sortAttrs one or more attributes to sort by
 */
VListModel( LDAPConnection ldc, String base, int scope,
            String filter, String[] sortAttrs ) {
    _base = base;
    _scope = scope;
    _filter = filter;
```

```
        _sortAttrs = sortAttrs;
        _ldc = ldc;
        _cons = _ldc.getSearchConstraints();

    }
```

JList asks its model how many list items there are, and then when it needs to display a particular range of items—because the user has clicked on the scroll bar or because the JList has become visible after having previously been covered by another GUI component—it asks the model for each item in turn.

The first time the model is asked for the list size, it does a VLV search to find the answer. To avoid having to do a search every time it gets a request for an item, the model retrieves a cache of one page before and two pages after a requested item (if the item is not already in the cache). A "page" is the number of items that are visible in the list without scrolling. The getSize method fills the cache starting at index 0 if the model hasn't already been initialized:

```
    /**
     * Called by JList to get virtual list size. The vertical scroll-
```

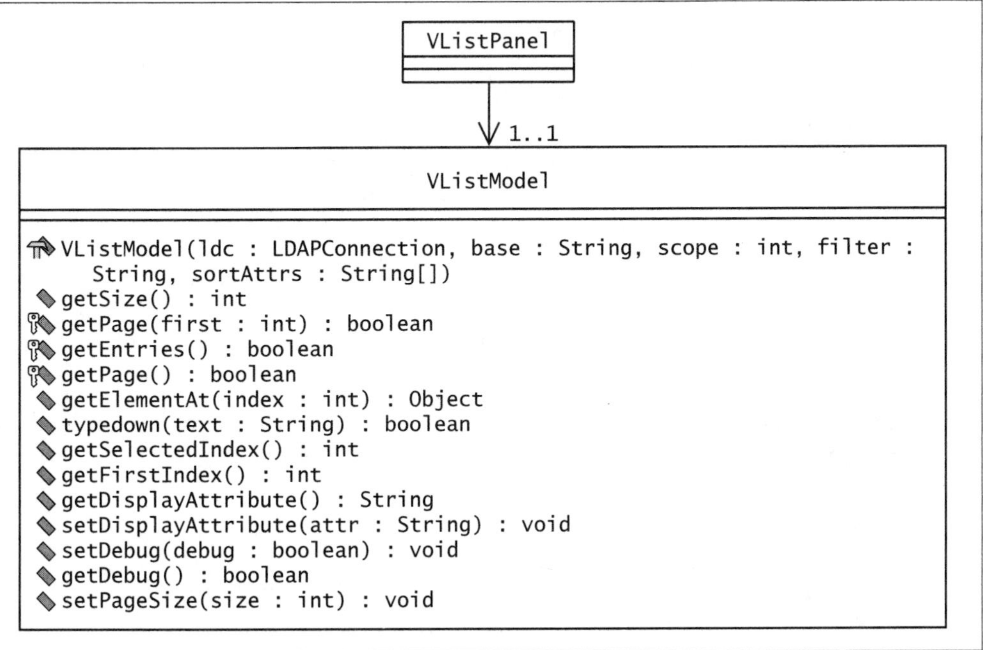

FIGURE 16-2. VListModel.

```
         * bar is sized using the return value.
         *
         * @return the size of the virtual list
         */
        public int getSize() {
            if ( !_initialized ) {
                _initialized = true;
                _pageControls = new LDAPControl[2];
                // VLV also require a sort control
                LDAPSortKey[] keys =
                    new LDAPSortKey[_sortAttrs.length];
                for( int i = 0; i < keys.length; i++ ) {
                    keys[i] = new LDAPSortKey( _sortAttrs[i] );
                }
                _pageControls[0] =
                    new LDAPSortControl( keys, true );
                // Do an initial search to get the virtual list
                // size. Keep one page before and two pages after
                // the start.
                _beforeCount = _pageSize;
                _afterCount = _pageSize * 2;
                // Create the initial paged results control
                _vlc =
                    new LDAPVirtualListControl( 0, _beforeCount,
                                                _afterCount, 0 );
                _pageControls[1] = _vlc;
                // Specify necessary controls for VLV
                _cons.setServerControls( _pageControls );
                // Bump the max results requested to unlimited
                _cons.setMaxResults( 0 );
                getPage( 0 );
            }
            return _size;
        }
```

On filling the cache from the directory, the VLV response control is examined to determine the exact window into the virtual list that was returned:

```
        /**
         * Get a page starting at a specified index (although we
         * may also fetch some preceding entries to our buffer)
         *
         * @param first the index of the first entry required
         * @return true if entries could be retrieved
```

```
 */
protected boolean getPage( int first ) {
    _vlc.setRange( first, _beforeCount, _afterCount );
    if ( _debug ) {
        System.out.println( "Setting requested range to " +
                            first + ", -" + _beforeCount +
                            ", +" + _afterCount );
    }
    return getPage();
}

/**
 * Fetch a buffer
 *
 * @return true if entries could be retrieved
 */
protected boolean getPage() {
    // Get the actual entries
    if ( !getEntries() )
        return false;

    // Check if we have a control returned
    LDAPControl[] c = _ldc.getResponseControls();
    LDAPVirtualListResponse response = null;
    if ( c != null ) {
        for( int i = 0; i < c.length; i++ ) {
            if ( c[i] instanceof LDAPVirtualListResponse ) {
                response = (LDAPVirtualListResponse)c[i];
                break;
            }
        }
    }
    if ( response != null ) {
        _selectedIndex = response.getFirstPosition() - 1;
        _top = Math.max( 0, _selectedIndex - _beforeCount );
        // Now we know the total size of the virtual list
        // box
        _size = response.getContentCount();
        _vlc.setListSize( _size );
        if ( _debug ) {
            System.out.println( "Virtual window: " + _top +
                                ".." +
                                (_top+_entries.size()-1) +
                                " of " + _size );
```

```
            }
        } else {
            System.out.println( "Null response control" );
        }
        return true;
    }
```

The getEntries method composes the search operation from the properties that were set when the model was constructed. A user-specified attribute is cached for each entry found. The displayAttribute property can be set to "dn" if the DN is to be presented instead of an attribute:

```
    /**
     * Fill the buffer with entries from a search
     *
     * @return true if entries could be retrieved
     */
    protected boolean getEntries() {
        // Empty the buffer
        _entries.removeAllElements();
        // Do a search
        try {
            String[] attrs = { _displayAttr };
            LDAPSearchResults res =
                _ldc.search( _base,
                             _scope,
                             _filter,
                             attrs,
                             false,
                             _cons );
            while ( res.hasMoreElements() ) {
                try {
                    LDAPEntry entry = res.next();
                    // Allow the user to specify that the DN
                    // should be displayed
                    if ( _displayAttr.equalsIgnoreCase(
                           "dn" ) ) {
                        _entries.addElement( entry.getDN() );
                    } else {
                        LDAPAttribute attr =
                            entry.getAttribute( attrs[0] );
                        if ( attr != null ) {
                            Enumeration en =
                                attr.getStringValues();
```

```
                        while( en.hasMoreElements() ) {
                            String name =
                                (String)en.nextElement();
                            _entries.addElement( name );
                        }
                    }
                }
            } catch ( LDAPException ex ) {
                System.out.println( ex + ", enumerating" );
            }
        }
    } catch ( LDAPException e ) {
        System.out.println( e + ", searching" );
        return false;
    }
    if ( _debug ) {
        System.out.println( "Returning " +
                            _entries.size() + " entries" );
    }
    return true;
}
```

When `JList` asks for a particular list item, the model checks its cache first. If the item is not found, the cache is refilled from the directory:

```
/**
 * Called by JList to fetch data to paint a single list item
 *
 * @param index the index of the item to return
 * @return the list item at the requested index
 */
public Object getElementAt(int index) {
    if ( _debug ) {
        System.out.println( "need entry " + index );
    }
    if ( (index < _top) ||
         (index >= _top + _entries.size()) ) {
        if ( _debug ) {
            System.out.println( "fetching a page " +
                                "starting at " +
                                index );
        }
        getPage( index );
    }
```

```
        int offset = index - _top;
        if ( (offset < 0) || (offset >= _entries.size()) ) {
            return new String( "No entry at " + index );
        } else {
            return _entries.elementAt( offset );
        }
    }
```

The typedown method is called to fetch a list item by string matching rather than by index:

```
    /**
     * Called by an application to scroll the list so that a
     * particular entry is visible.
     * Considers text to be an initial substring of an entry.
     *
     * @param text text to match
     * @return true if entries could be provided
     */
    public boolean typedown( String text ) {
        _pageControls[1] = _vlc =
            new LDAPVirtualListControl( text,
                                        _beforeCount,
                                        _afterCount );
        if ( _debug ) {
            System.out.println( "Setting requested start to " +
                                text + ", -" + _beforeCount +
                                ", +" + _afterCount );
        }
        return getPage();
    }
```

There are accessors for the properties, including the page size, and the following methods to allow a client to determine what the current window of the model is:

```
    /**
     * Called by application to find out the virtual selected
     * index
     *
     * @return the index of the first entry in the selected
     * window
     */
    public int getSelectedIndex() {
        return _selectedIndex;
```

```
    }

    /**
     * Called by application to find out the top of the buffer
     *
     * @return the index of the first entry in the buffer
     */
    public int getFirstIndex() {
        return _top;
    }
```

Our sample application that uses VListPanel is VListDialog (Figure 16-3). It takes all the parameters from the command line—host, port, search parameters—and creates a VListPanel and a few text fields. It registers the VListPanel as a property change listener of itself, so it can notify the panel of typedown changes:

```
public class VListDialog extends JDialog
                         implements DocumentListener {
    /**
```

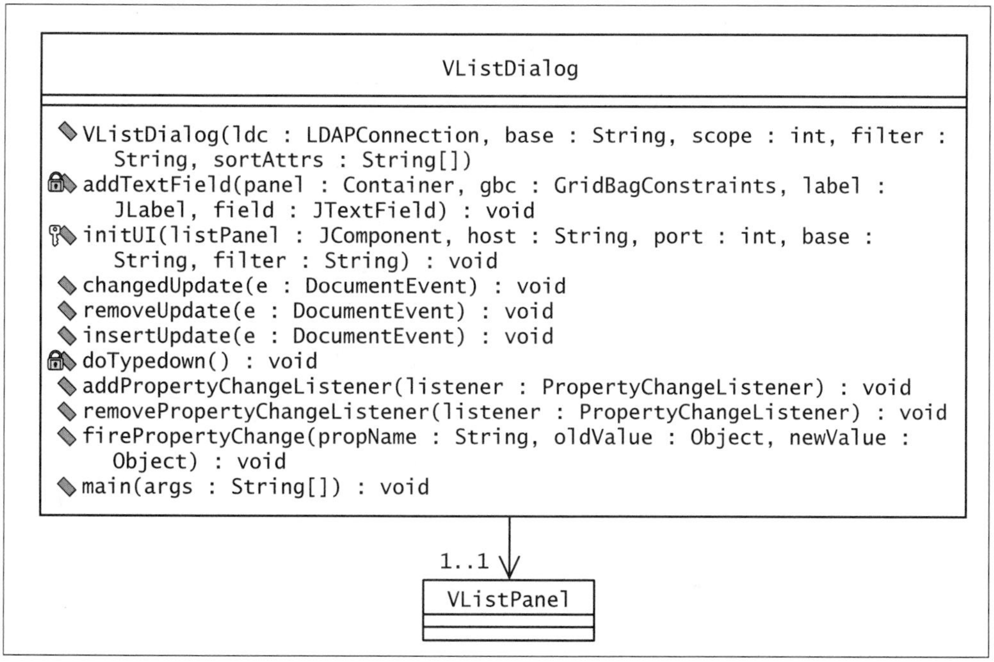

```
VListDialog
------------------------------------------------------------
VListDialog(ldc : LDAPConnection, base : String, scope : int, filter :
    String, sortAttrs : String[])
addTextField(panel : Container, gbc : GridBagConstraints, label :
    JLabel, field : JTextField) : void
initUI(listPanel : JComponent, host : String, port : int, base :
    String, filter : String) : void
changedUpdate(e : DocumentEvent) : void
removeUpdate(e : DocumentEvent) : void
insertUpdate(e : DocumentEvent) : void
doTypedown() : void
addPropertyChangeListener(listener : PropertyChangeListener) : void
removePropertyChangeListener(listener : PropertyChangeListener) : void
firePropertyChange(propName : String, oldValue : Object, newValue :
    Object) : void
main(args : String[]) : void

    1..1
VListPanel
```

FIGURE 16-3. VListDialog.

```
     * All configuration is done through parameters in the
     * constructor
     *
     * @param ldc a sufficiently authenticated connection to a
     * server
     * @param base the base DN for the search
     * @param scope the search scope
     * @param filter the search filter
     * @param sortAttrs one or more attributes to sort by
     */
    public VListDialog( LDAPConnection ldc, String base,
                        int scope, String filter,
                        String[] sortAttrs ) {
        super( new JFrame(), true );

        VListPanel listPanel =
            new VListPanel( ldc, base, scope, filter,
                            sortAttrs );

        // The panel is to be notified of changes in the
        // typedown field
        addPropertyChangeListener( listPanel );

        initUI( listPanel, ldc.getHost(), ldc.getPort(), base,
                filter );
        setTitle( base );
    }
```

The final interesting thing that VListDialog does is to register itself as a DocumentListener to the typedown text field. VListDialog will be notified whenever a user types or deletes a character in the field:

```
        // Add the field where the user can type in
        _typedown = new JTextField( "" );
        _typedown.getDocument().addDocumentListener( this );
```

Whenever the contents of the typedown text field change, VListPanel is notified:

```
    /**
     * Implement the DocumentListener interface.<BR>
     * Catch all changes in the typedown text field and update the
     * scrolling list.
     *
```

```
     * @param e the event from the typedown text field Document
     */
    public void changedUpdate(DocumentEvent e) {
        doTypedown();
    }
    public void removeUpdate(DocumentEvent e) {
        doTypedown();
    }
    public void insertUpdate(DocumentEvent e) {
        doTypedown();
    }

    /**
     * Tell the model to do typedown, and then scroll the list so the
     * selected index is visible
     */
    private void doTypedown() {
        firePropertyChange( "typedown", _oldText,
                            _typedown.getText() );
        _oldText = _typedown.getText();
    }
```

The application uses a PropertyChangeSupport object to facilitate the registration of listeners and dispatching of events:

```
    /**
     * Add a client to be notified when an authentication result
     * is in
     * @param listener a client to be notified of changes
     */
    public void addPropertyChangeListener(
                            PropertyChangeListener listener ) {
        _propSupport.addPropertyChangeListener( listener );
    }

    /**
     * Remove a client that had requested notification on
     * authentication
     * @param listener a client not to be notified of changes
     */
    public void removePropertyChangeListener(
                            PropertyChangeListener listener ) {
        _propSupport.removePropertyChangeListener( listener );
    }
```

```
    /**
     * Support for bound property notification
     * @param propName name of changed property
     * @param oldValue previous value of property
     * @param newValue new value of property
     */
    public void firePropertyChange( String propName,
                                    Object oldValue,
                                    Object newValue ) {
        _propSupport.firePropertyChange( propName, oldValue,
                                         newValue );
    }

private PropertyChangeSupport _propSupport =
              new PropertyChangeSupport( this );
```

Execute the application as follows. Note that some form of authentication is required (at least, with Netscape Directory Server) because VLV is by default not available to anonymous users.

```
java VListDialog localhost 389 "o=airius.com" "objectclass=person"
     "sn givenName" "uid=scarter, ou=People, o=airius.com" sprain
```

This query requests all person entries under o=Airius.com, sorted by last name, first name. When the application starts, the scrolling list is at the first entry in the search results (see Figure 16-4).

If you start typing something into the typedown field, the list scrolls so that the first matching entry becomes visible (see Figure 16-5), retrieving new entries from the directory if necessary.

Call Me When You're Ready: Persistent Search

Some applications need to know when certain entries or certain areas of a directory change. One example is a very directory-intensive server application that maintains a large cache of directory entries to reduce the number of searches it must do. Rather than polling the directory or refreshing the cache at regular intervals, the developer of the application would like the application to be notified when there are changes that make the cache invalid, so that the cache can be updated then.

The persistent search control is designed to address the need for notifications of changes in the directory. When a persistent search control is provided on a search, the search does not terminate, but stays active. When changes occur that would result in different search results from the time the search was requested, the results are returned to the client but the search remains active.

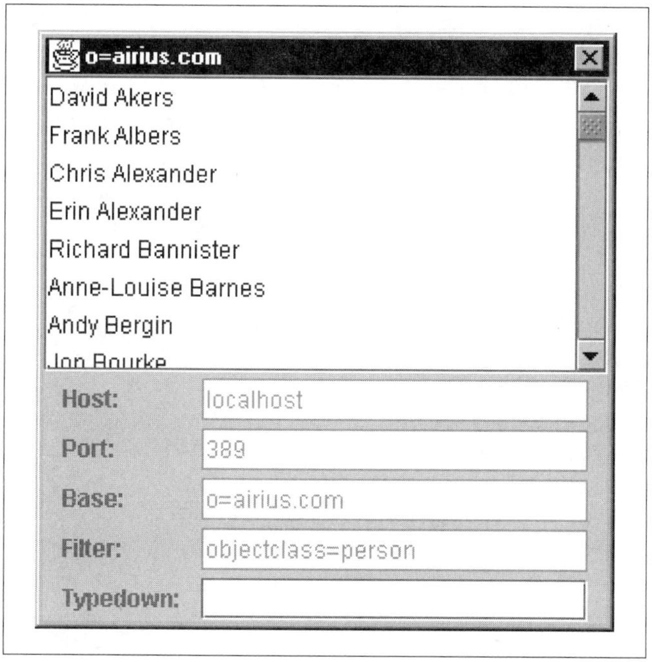

FIGURE 16-4. `VListDialog` *at start-up.*

FIGURE 16-5. `VListDialog` *after typing two characters.*

Most applications that use a persistent search dedicate a thread to it because the search blocks until there are changes.

The SDK contains a sample program that demonstrates a persistent search in one thread and a regular search simultaneously in another thread: `PersistSearch.java`. The class implements `Runnable` so that it can easily be executed in a thread. In the `run` method, the two threads do identical searches, except that one of them sets the batch size to 1 and adds a persistent search control to the operation:

```
LDAPSearchConstraints cons1 =
    (LDAPSearchConstraints)ld1.getSearchConstraints();
cons1.setBatchSize(1);
int op = LDAPPersistSearchControl.ADD;
boolean changesOnly = true;
boolean returnControls = false;
boolean isCritical = true;
LDAPPersistSearchControl control = new
    LDAPPersistSearchControl( op, changesOnly,
                              returnControls, isCritical );
cons1.setServerControls(control);
LDAPSearchResults res1 = ld1.search(searchbase, ld1.SCOPE_SUB,
                                    filter, attrs,
                                    false, cons1);
```

The program asks for notification only when entries are added to the directory. It doesn't want change controls returned with every entry, and it doesn't want the search to be executed if the server does not support persistent search. The constructor parameters for `LDAPPersistSearchControl` are as follows:

- `changeTypes`. The types of changes to be monitored. You can perform a bitwise OR on any of the following values and specify the result as the `changeTypes` parameter:
  - `LDAPPersistSearchControl.ADD` (to track new entries added to the directory)
  - `LDAPPersistSearchControl.DELETE` (to track entries removed from the directory)
  - `LDAPPersistSearchControl.MODIFY` (to track entries that have been modified)
  - `LDAPPersistSearchControl.MODDN` (to track entries that have been renamed)
- `changesOnly`. True if you do not want the server to return all existing entries in the directory that match the search criteria (you just want the changed entries to be returned).

- `returnControls`. True if you want the server to return entry change controls with each entry in the search results.
- `isCritical`. True if this control is critical to the search operation (if the server does not support this control, you may not want the server to perform the search at all).

Search results are received just as in any other search.

In the `LDAPPersistSearchControl` constructor, if the application specified true for `returnControls`, the server would return an `LDAPEntryChangeControl` with each search result. It could then determine the type of each change and the previous DN for an entry that has been deleted or that now has a new DN:

```
// Check if we have a control returned
LDAPControl[] c = _ldc.getResponseControls();
LDAPEntryChangeControl response = null;
if ( c != null ) {
    for( int i = 0; i < c.length; i++ ) {
        if ( c[i] instanceof LDAPEntryChangeControl) {
            response = (LDAPEntryChangeControl)c[i];
            break;
        }
    }
}
if ( response != null ) {
    switch( response.getChangeType() ) {
        case: response.ADD:
              break;
        case: response.DELETE:
              String oldDN = response.getPreviousDN();
              break;
        case: response.MODIFY:
              break;
        case: response.MODDN:
              String oldDN = response.getPreviousDN();
              break;
     }
}
```

Password Expiration Notification

If Netscape Directory Server has been configured to enable password expiration, it may send a password-expiring control to a client at the time the client authenticates. The control will be sent only if the client is authenticating with version 3 of the LDAP protocol and if the authenticating user's password is to expire within the expiration warning time configured for the server.

If the Directory Manager has reset a user's password, the user will receive a password-expired control if the client is authenticating with LDAP version 3.

You can identify these cases in your code and warn the user. The SDK contains a sample application—`PasswordPolicy.java`—that demonstrates the parsing of password expiration controls on authenticating.

A couple of local constants are declared for possible outcomes of checking for password expiration controls:

```
final static int NO_PASSWORD_CONTROLS = 0;
final static int PASSWORD_EXPIRED = -1;
```

First the possible exceptions on authenticating must be examined:

```
try {
    ld.authenticate( 3, DN, PW );
    System.out.println( "Authentication successful" );
} catch( LDAPException e ) {
    if ( e.getLDAPResultCode() ==
         LDAPException.INVALID_CREDENTIALS ) {
        System.out.println( "Invalid credentials" );
    } else if ( e.getLDAPResultCode() ==
                LDAPException.NO_SUCH_OBJECT ) {
        System.out.println( "No such user" );
    } else {
        System.out.println( "Error on authentication: " +
                            e.toString() );
    }
}
```

On success, a check is made to see if any password expiration controls were returned. If a password-expiring control was returned, the number of seconds until expiration is extracted:

```
/* Were any controls returned? */
int seconds = checkControls( ld );
switch( seconds ) {
    case NO_PASSWORD_CONTROLS:
            System.out.println( "No controls returned" );
            break;
    case PASSWORD_EXPIRED:
            System.out.println( "Password expired and must " +
```

```
                                    "be reset" );
                break;
        default:
                System.out.println( "Password expires in " +
                                    seconds + " seconds" );
    }

    private static int checkControls( LDAPConnection ld ) {
        LDAPControl[] controls = ld.getResponseControls();
        int status = NO_PASSWORD_CONTROLS;
        if ( controls != null ) {
            for( int i = 0; i < controls.length; i++ ) {
                if ( controls[i] instanceof
                     LDAPPasswordExpiredControl) {
                    status = PASSWORD_EXPIRED;
                    break;
                } else if ( controls[i] instanceof
                            LDAPPasswordExpiringControl) {
                    // Return the number of seconds until expiration
                    LDAPPasswordExpiringControl c =
                        (LDAPPasswordExpiringControl)controls[i];
                    status = c.getSecondsToExpiration();
                    break;
                }
            }
        }
        return status;
    }
```

Trust Me: The Proxied Authorization Control

Many server applications leverage the authentication and access control functionality of a directory server by taking a user's credentials and authenticating, and then doing a search using the user's identity; the results of the authentication indicate if the user is who she says she is, and the results of the search indicate if she is authorized to execute the particular task she has requested. Although authenticating is a quick operation for most directory servers, it is still an extra operation for each user, which could add up if the server receives frequent requests from different users.

An Internet Draft has been written for a control that can be provided along with any LDAP operation and that contains the DN of a directory entry. If the server deems the requester trustworthy enough, it will execute the operation using the identity specified in the control.

Netscape Directory Server 4.1 and later versions implement the control, and the control is supported in the SDK. If a request containing a proxied authorization control is received, the server checks if the requester has proxy access rights within the subtree specified for the operation (for example, the base DN for a search, or the DN for a modify operation). An ACI granting this right looks like this:

```
aci: (targetattr = "*")(version 3.0; acl "Proxy rights for admin";
    allow ( proxy) userdn = "ldap:///uid=admin, o=acme.com";)
```

Unless proxy rights have been granted to anonymous users (not a good idea!), the connection must have already been authenticated at that point. If the requester has proxy rights, the server evaluates access control for the operation as if it were requested by the DN in the control. For example:

```
LDAPConnection ld = new LDAPConnection();
 try {
     // Connect to server
     ld.connect( 3, hostname, portnumber,
                 "uid=admin,o=acme.com", "password" );

     // Create a "critical" proxied auth server control using
     // the DN "uid=charlie,ou=people,o=acme.com"
     LDAPProxiedAuthControl ctrl =
         new LDAPProxiedAuthControl(
                         "uid=charlie,ou=people,o=acme.com",
                         true );

     // Create search constraints to use that control
     LDAPSearchConstraints cons = ld.getSearchConstraints();
     cons.setServerControls( ctrl );

     // Send the search request
     LDAPSearchResults res =
         ld.search( "ou=people,o=acme.com",
                    ld.SCOPE_SUB, "(cn=Barbara*)",
                    null, false, cons );
```

The search will be executed as `uid=charlie` if the DN `uid=admin,o=acme.com` has proxy rights for the subtree `ou=people,o=acme.com`. If not, an `LDAPException` is thrown with the error code `INSUFFICIENT_ACCESS_RIGHTS`.

You might wonder, How does the application know that the user really is `uid=charlie` if it doesn't attempt to authenticate as `uid=charlie`? The authentication is assumed to have taken place earlier or outside of this code (for example, by a Web server), and does not need to be done here. One very important example in which this is the case is server applications that accept SSL client authentication. The server-side code (for example, a servlet running on a Web server that can do SSL authentication against a directory) is notified that the client has successfully completed SSL client authentication. The servlet then checks the DN for which the authentication was negotiated (available through the servlet API) and uses the DN in a proxied authorization control for all operations on behalf of the user.

Proxied authorization works very well in server-side programming also when certificates are not involved. Most server applications execute user requests as the identity of the user. A Web server may prompt the user for a user ID and password on attempting to enter a Web page, and authenticate the user against a directory. A servlet or other Web server–hosted service can find out the DN the user was authenticated as, but not the password, for security reasons. For the servlet to perform an operation with the identity of the user, it must reprompt for the password so that it can authenticate as the user to the directory. With proxied authorization, however, the servlet maintains its own authenticated connection but requests the operation to be performed on behalf of the user requesting it, using the DN it received from the Web server.

Your Very Own Controls: Using the BER Package

We mentioned earlier that most controls that are not proprietary to one company use Basic Encoding Rules to encode any data. The SDK includes a complete package for encoding and decoding data types that are used in LDAP: `netscape.ldap.stream.ber`. The BER package is not described in the general SDK documentation, and it is not covered by the Internet Drafts on the Java LDAP API.

Constructing a Control

Let's start by looking at how a VLV request control is constructed. All controls extend `LDAPControl`, which provides common methods and support, and define a unique `OID`. The `OID` is passed to the superclass constructor in any local constructors:

```
public class LDAPVirtualListControl extends LDAPControl {
    public final static String VIRTUALLIST =
                               "2.16.840.1.113730.3.4.9";
    public LDAPVirtualListControl( String jumpTo,
                                   int beforeCount,
                                   int afterCount  ) {
        super( VIRTUALLIST, true, null );
        setRange( jumpTo, beforeCount, afterCount );
    }
```

```
public LDAPVirtualListControl( int startIndex,
                               int beforeCount,
                               int afterCount,
                               int contentCount  ) {
    super( VIRTUALLIST, true, null );
    m_listSize = contentCount;
    setRange( startIndex, beforeCount, afterCount );
}
```

The parameters of the `LDAPControl` constructor used in this case are the `OID` of the control, a boolean `isCritical` (if it is `true`, a request containing the control will be rejected if the server does not support the control; if `false`, the server will ignore the control if it is not recognized), and a byte array containing an arbitrary value of the control. The value is passed as `null` in this case because the control creates a BER-encoded byte array from the constructor parameters in the `setRange` method.

The contents of the control are defined in ASN.1 notation as follows:

```
VirtualListViewRequest ::= SEQUENCE {
          beforeCount    INTEGER (0 .. maxInt),
          afterCount     INTEGER (0 .. maxInt),
          CHOICE {
              byIndex [0] SEQUENCE {
                  index             INTEGER,
                  contentCount      INTEGER
              }
              byFilter [1] jumpTo    Substring
          },
          contextID     OCTET STRING OPTIONAL
}
```

Note that there is an optional final `STRING` field. The control includes a `CHOICE` statement, so there are two possible data contents. The number in brackets after the name of each option is the tag that identifies which case is implemented in an instance of the control.

`LDAPVirtualListControl` constructs the first option as follows:

```
private final static int TAG_BYINDEX = 0;
private final static int TAG_BYFILTER = 1;

private byte[] createPageSpecification( int listIndex,
                                        int listSize,
                                        int beforeCount,
                                        int afterCount ) {
```

```
        /* A sequence */
        BERSequence seq = new BERSequence();
        seq.addElement( new BERInteger( beforeCount ) );
        seq.addElement( new BERInteger( afterCount ) );
        /* A sequence of list index and list size */
        BERSequence indexSeq = new BERSequence();
        indexSeq.addElement( new BERInteger(listIndex) );
        indexSeq.addElement( new BERInteger(listSize) );
        seq.addElement(
            new BERTag( BERTag.CONTEXT|BERTag.CONSTRUCTED|
                        TAG_BYINDEX,  indexSeq, true) );
        if ( _context != null ) {
            seq.addElement( new BEROctetString(_context) );
        }
        /* Suck out the data and return it */
        return flattenBER( seq );
    }
```

We create the required BER-encoded byte array by instantiating various basic BER objects (`BERInteger` in this case), adding them to sequence elements (`BERSequence`) as dictated by the ASN.1 for the particular control, and then streaming the outermost element to a byte array. Since the VLV request control contains a `CHOICE` field, it must also include a tag (`BERTag`) that indicates which of the options is present. The `flattenBER` method in `LDAPControl` (which is the superclass for all control classes) converts the results into a byte array appropriate for transmission in an LDAP request.

When a string rather than an index is used to identify the first result, the following code constructs the byte array.

```
    private byte[] createPageSpecification( String subFilter,
                                            int beforeCount,
                                            int afterCount ) {
        /* A sequence */
        BERSequence seq = new BERSequence();
        seq.addElement( new BERInteger( beforeCount ) );
        seq.addElement( new BERInteger( afterCount ) );
        seq.addElement( new BERTag(
                             BERTag.CONTEXT|TAG_BYFILTER,
                             new BEROctetString(subFilter),
                             true) );
        /* Optional context cookie */
        if ( _context != null ) {
            seq.addElement( new BEROctetString(_context) );
```

```
        }
        /* Suck out the data and return it */
        return flattenBER( seq );
    }
```

The string option uses a BEROctetString to encode the value and sets the tag for the CHOICE field to 1 (TAG_BY_FILTER). The BERTag.CONTEXT constant, which is OR'ed with the tag number, indicates that the tag number is specific to this control; it is not a global tag number shared with other BER elements.

The netscape.ldap.ber.stream package includes the classes listed in Table 16-1 for encoding basic data types. Of these classes, the ones you are most likely to use in writing new controls are BERInteger, BEROctetString, BERBoolean, and BEREnumerated.

The classes listed in Table 16-2 provide the constructs for grouping and tagging the data elements. The BERTag element always contains another element, which may be a basic type or another BERTag.

Decoding a BER-Encoded Byte Array

Now that we know how to construct the contents of a control using the BER package, how do we decode a byte array received from the server into something usable in an application? Let's look at LDAPVirtualListResponse.

TABLE 16-1. *BER classes for encoding basic data types.*

CLASS	CORRESPONDING ASN.1 ELEMENT
BERBitString	BitString
BERBoolean	Boolean
BEREnumerated	Enumerated
BERInteger	Integer
BERNull	NULL
BERNumericString	Numeric
BERObjectId	ObjectID
BEROctetString	OctetString
BERPrintableString	PrintableString
BERReal	Real
BERUTCTime	UTCTime
BERVisibleString	VisibleString

TABLE 16-2. *BER classes for grouping and tagging data elements.*

CLASS	CORRESPONDING ASN.1 ELEMENT
BERChoice	Choice
BERSequence	Sequence
BERSet	Set
BERTag	Tagged object

As with the request control, LDAPVirtualListResponse extends LDAPControl and passes its unique OID to the superclass constructor. The main local constructor takes a byte array as input and parses it into member variables:

```
public class LDAPVirtualListResponse extends LDAPControl {
    public final static String VIRTUALLISTRESPONSE =
                               "2.16.840.1.113730.3.4.10";
    /**
     * Constructs a new LDAPVirtualListResponse
     * object
     * @param value a BER-encoded byte array
     * @see netscape.ldap.LDAPControl
     */
    public LDAPVirtualListResponse( byte[] value ) {
        super( VIRTUALLISTRESPONSE, true, null );
        m_value = value;
        parseResponse();
    }
```

All response controls should have a constructor that takes an OID, a boolean (for criticality), and a byte array so that they can be instantiated by the SDK when received from the server:

```
    /**
     * Contructs an LDAPVirtualListResponse object
     * @param oid This parameter must be equal to
     * LDAPVirtualListResponse.VIRTUALLISTRESPONSE, or an
     * LDAPException is thrown
     * @param critical true if this control is critical
     * @param value the value associated with this control
     * @exception netscape.ldap.LDAPException If oid is not
     * LDAPVirtualListResponse.VIRTUALLISTRESPONSE
     * @see netscape.ldap.LDAPControl#register
```

```
 */
public LDAPVirtualListResponse( String oid, boolean critical,
                                byte[] value )
                                throws LDAPException {
    this( value );
    if ( !oid.equals( VIRTUALLISTRESPONSE ) ) {
         throw new LDAPException(
                            "oid must be " +
                            "LDAPVirtualListResponse." +
                            "VIRTUALLISTRESPONSE",
                            LDAPException.PARAM_ERROR );
    }
}
```

The ASN.1 notation for the VLV response control is as follows:

```
VirtualListViewResponse ::= SEQUENCE {
     targetPosition    INTEGER (0 .. maxInt),
     contentCount      INTEGER (0 .. maxInt),
     virtualListViewResult ENUMERATED {
         success                  (0),
         operationsError           (1),
         timeLimitExceeded        (3),
         adminLimitExceeded       (11),
         insufficientAccessRights (50),
         busy                     (51),
         unwillingToPerform       (53),
         sortControlMissing       (60),
         offsetRangeError         (61),
         other                    (80)
     },
     contextID     OCTET STRING OPTIONAL
}
```

The `LDAPVirtualListResponse` class decodes the byte array returned from the server by opening an input stream on it, creating a tag decoder, and then using `BERElement.getElement` to read the stream contents into a sequence object. `BERElement` is the superclass for all BER classes except `BERTagDecoder`. `BERTagDecoder` is an abstract class for interpreting tags specific to a particular "application."

The `netscape.ldap.clients.JDAPBERTagDecoder` class extends `BERTagDecoder` in providing a `getElement` method that is aware of all the tags used in BER encodings in LDAP version 3. `BerElement.getElement` extracts a byte array for one element from a stream and uses a `BERTagDecoder` to interpret any tags and construct an object (one of the classes in the BER package):

```
private void parseResponse() {
    /* Suck out the data and parse it */
    ByteArrayInputStream inStream =
        new ByteArrayInputStream( getValue() );
    BERSequence ber = new BERSequence();
    JDAPBERTagDecoder decoder = new JDAPBERTagDecoder();
    int[] nRead = new int[1];
    nRead[0] = 0;
    try  {
        /* A sequence */
        BERSequence seq =
            (BERSequence)BERElement.getElement( decoder,
                                                inStream,
                                                nRead );
        /* First is firstPosition */
        m_firstPosition =
            ((BERInteger)seq.elementAt( 0 )).getValue();
        m_contentCount =
            ((BERInteger)seq.elementAt( 1 )).getValue();
        m_resultCode =
            ((BEREnumerated)seq.elementAt( 2 )).getValue();
        /* Optional context cookie */
        if( seq.size() > 3 ) {
            BEROctetString str =
                (BEROctetString)seq.elementAt( 3 );
            m_context = new String(str.getValue(), "UTF8");
        }
    } catch(Exception x) {
        m_firstPosition = m_contentCount =
            m_resultCode = -1;
        m_context = null;
    }
}
```

A New Control

The following steps are required to implement a custom request control:

1. Extend `LDAPControl`.
2. Define a unique `OID`.

3. In the control constructor, call the superclass constructor with the `OID`.
4. Compose the contents of the control from parameters in the constructor and assign them to the `m_value` member as a byte array. Use the BER package if the contents are to be BER encoded.
5. Optionally, provide accessors for any control parameters.

The following steps are required to implement a custom response control:

1. Extend `LDAPControl`.
2. Define a unique `OID`.
3. In the control constructor, call the superclass constructor with the `OID`.
4. There should be a constructor that takes an `OID`, a criticality value, and a byte array; this constructor is called by the SDK to instantiate a control received from the server.
5. Parse a byte array in the constructor into member variables. Use the BER package if the contents are BER encoded.
6. Optionally, provide accessors for any member variables extracted from the byte array.
7. Register the control with the SDK, using `LDAPControl.register`.

Now let's put it all together and create our own request control and response control. The request control will be issued with a modify, add, or delete request. It contains an e-mail address and an arbitrary string message. If the server supports the control, it will send an e-mail message to the addressee in the control. The contents of the e-mail message will include the message from the control and a report on what directory modification was attempted and whether or not it succeeded. The response control contains an integer that indicates whether or not an e-mail message could be delivered, as well as the report that was delivered (or would have been delivered) in the e-mail message.

The ASN.1 notation for the request control is as follows:

```
ModificationEmailRequest ::= SEQUENCE {
            emailAddress   OCTET STRING,
            emailMessage   OCTET STRING
}
```

The `OID` is `5.5.5.5.5.1` (this is a fictitious `OID`; a valid `OID` can be requested by your organization from the IANA). The ASN.1 notation for the control and its `OID` are all we need to know to write the code for the control:

```
import netscape.ldap.LDAPControl;
import netscape.ldap.ber.stream.*;

public class EmailRequestControl extends LDAPControl {
    public final static String EMAILREQUEST  = "5.5.5.5.5.1";

    /**
     * Constructs an EmailRequestControl object
     * with an e-mail address and a message to send
     * @param address e-mail address to send a report to
     * @param message message to include in report
     * @param critical true if the LDAP operation
     * should be discarded for the case in which the server
     * does not support this control (in other words,
     * this control is critical to the LDAP operation)
     * @see netscape.ldap.LDAPControl
     */
    public EmailRequestControl( String address,
                                String message,
                                boolean critical) {
        super( EMAILREQUEST, critical, null );
        m_value = createSpecification( address, message );
    }

    /**
     * Create a "flattened" BER encoding of the requested
     * contents, and return it as a byte array
     * @param address e-mail address to send a report to
     * @param message message to include in report
     * @return the byte array of encoded data
     */
    private byte[] createSpecification( String address,
                                        String message ) {
        // A sequence
        BERSequence ber = new BERSequence();
        // Add the two parameters as string values
        ber.addElement( new BEROctetString( address ) );
        ber.addElement( new BEROctetString( message ) );
        // Suck out the data and return it
        return flattenBER( ber );
    }
}
```

The `OID` for the response control is `5.5.5.5.5.2`, and the ASN.1 notation is as follows:

```
ModificationEmailResponse ::= SEQUENCE {
            resultCode      INTEGER,
            emailMessage    OCTET STRING
}
```

Our response control class will then look like this:

```
import java.io.*;
import netscape.ldap.client.JDAPBERTagDecoder;
import netscape.ldap.LDAPControl;
import netscape.ldap.LDAPException;
import netscape.ldap.ber.stream.*;

public class EmailResponseControl extends LDAPControl {
    public final static String EMAILRESPONSE = "5.5.5.5.5.2";

    /**
     * Constructs a new EmailResponse object
     * @param oid Must be EmailResponseControl.EMAILRESPONSE
     * @param critical not used in the control
     * @param value a BER-encoded byte array
     * @exception netscape.ldap.LDAPException If oid is not
     * EmailResponseControl.EMAILRESPONSE
     * @see netscape.ldap.LDAPControl
     */
    public EmailResponseControl( String oid, boolean critical,
                                 byte[] value )
                                 throws LDAPException {
        super( EMAILRESPONSE, true, null );
        if ( !oid.equals( EMAILRESPONSE ) ) {
             throw new LDAPException(
                            "oid must be " +
                            "EmailResponseControl." +
                            "EMAILRESPONSE",
                            LDAPException.PARAM_ERROR);
        }
        m_value = value;
        parseResponse();
    }

    /**
     * Gets the result code from delivering an e-mail message
     * @return the result code from delivering an e-mail message
     */
```

```
    public int getCode() {
        return m_code;
    }

    /**
     * Gets the status report delivered with the e-mail message
     * @return the status report delivered with the e-mail message
     */
    public String getMessage() {
        return m_message;
    }

    /**
     * Parses the BER-encoded value of m_value
     */
    private void parseResponse() {
        // Suck out the data and parse it
        ByteArrayInputStream inStream =
            new ByteArrayInputStream( getValue() );
        BERSequence ber = new BERSequence();
        JDAPBERTagDecoder decoder = new JDAPBERTagDecoder();
        int[] nRead = new int[1];
        nRead[0] = 0;
        try  {
            // A sequence
            BERSequence seq =
                (BERSequence)BERElement.getElement( decoder,
                                                    inStream,
                                                    nRead );
            // First is the result code, then the message
            m_code =
                ((BERInteger)seq.elementAt( 0 )).getValue();
            BEROctetString str =
                (BEROctetString)seq.elementAt( 1 );
            m_message = new String(str.getValue(), "UTF8");
        } catch(Exception x) {
            m_code = -1;
            m_message = null;
        }
    }

    private int m_code = -1;
    private String m_message = null;
}
```

It is not likely you will find a server that accepts or returns our new e-mail controls anytime soon unless you write a server extension yourself, which is beyond the scope of this book.

When the Data Lives Elsewhere: Managing Referrals

We have touched on referrals throughout the book. Referrals are defined in the Internet Draft "draft-ietf-ldapext-namedref-00.txt" or a successor to it. An LDAP server may return one or more referrals in the form of LDAP URLs to a client in two cases: (1) one or more of the entries that would be referenced by an operation have the `referral` object class and a `ref` attribute that contains one or more LDAP URLs, or (2) the base DN of the operation falls outside of any naming context managed by the server. The former type of referral is called a **named reference**; the latter is a **superior reference**. The Java LDAP SDK generally treats the two types the same.

Catching and Processing Referral Exceptions

The default behavior of the SDK is to throw a referral exception if a referral is received from the server. For search requests, the exception is thrown while the client iterates through the search results; for all other operations the exception is delivered on the request itself. On enumerating the results of a search, you can choose to use the `nextElement` method or the `next` method. The former returns `Object`, which may be an entry, a referral exception object, or another exception object; it does not throw exceptions. The latter returns an entry but may throw a referral or other exception:

```
// Option 1. Use nextElement() and examine the object type
// returned
LDAPSearchResults res = ld.search( ENTRY,
                                   ld.SCOPE_ONE,
                                   "objectclass=*",
                                   attrs,
                                   false,
                                   cons );
while ( res.hasMoreElements() ) {
    Object o = res.nextElement();
    if ( o instanceof LDAPEntry ) {
        LDAPEntry entry = (LDAPEntry)o;
        // Do something with this entry...
    } else if ( o instanceof LDAPReferralException ) {
        LDAPReferralException e = (LDAPReferralException)o;
        LDAPUrl refUrls[] = e.getURLs();
        for (int i=0; i<refUrls.length; i++) {
            System.out.println(refUrls[i].getUrl() );
```

```
                // Do something with this referral...
            }
        } else {
            LDAPException e = (LDAPException)o;
            // Do something about this exception...
        }
    }

    // Option 2. Use next() and catch the exceptions.
    while ( res.hasMoreElements() ) {
        try {
            LDAPEntry theEntry = res.next();
            // Do something with this entry...
        } catch ( LDAPReferralException e ) {
            LDAPUrl refUrls[] = e.getURLs();
            for (int i=0; i<refUrls.length; i++) {
                System.out.println(refUrls[i].getUrl() );
                // Do something with this referral...
            }
        } catch ( LDAPException e ) {
            // Do something about this exception...
        }
    }
```

Using next, as in option 2 in the preceding example, is generally more convenient. All other requests must be handled in a way similar to option 2:

```
try {
    ld.delete( "uid=sam, ou=people, o=Airius.com" );
} catch ( LDAPReferralException e ) {
    LDAPUrl refUrls[] = e.getURLs();
    for (int i=0; i<refUrls.length; i++) {
        System.out.println(refUrls[i].getUrl() );
        // Do something with this referral...
    }
} catch ( LDAPException e ) {
    // Do something about this exception...
}
```

Automatic Referrals: Anonymous or under Client Control

Most LDAP client applications prefer to have referrals handled transparently by the SDK, outside of the main code body, rather than detecting and processing referrals everywhere an LDAP operation is executed. There are two ways to enable automatic referral handling:

- `LDAPConnection.setReferrals( ld.REFERRALS, new Boolean( true ) );`
- `LDAPConstraints.setReferrals( true );`

If the connection has the referral option set to true, or constraints are supplied with the referral option enabled, then the client code doing LDAP operations will never see a referral exception. The highlighted sections of the previous examples can be eliminated. If a referral is encountered during the execution of the operation, the SDK will make a new temporary connection to the referred-to server if necessary and continue the operation there. The `hopLimit` parameter of the constraints, or the `REFERRALS_HOP_LIMIT` option of the connection, determines how many links to follow on a referral before giving up. The default limit is 10.

The default behavior on automatic referral following is not to authenticate (that is, to use an anonymous connection) to the referred-to server. To supply credentials for the referred-to connection, you must implement the `LDAPRebind` interface and supply an instance of the implementation to `LDAPConstraints.setRebindProc` or to `LDAPConnection.setOption( LDAPConnection.REFERRALS_REBIND_PROC )`. The interface specifies a single method—`getRebindAuthentication`—to provide credentials, using a host name and port as input parameters.

It is common to supply the same credentials to the referred-to server as were used to authenticate to the original server, as in the following example:

```
protected void setDefaultReferralCredentials(
                            LDAPConnection conn ) {
    final LDAPConnection m_conn = conn;
    LDAPRebind rebind = new LDAPRebind() {
        public LDAPRebindAuth getRebindAuthentication(
            String host,
            int port ) {
                return new LDAPRebindAuth(
                    m_conn.getAuthenticationDN(),
                    m_conn.getAuthenticationPassword() );
            }
    };
    LDAPSearchConstraints cons = conn.getSearchConstraints();
    cons.setReferrals( true );
    cons.setRebindProc( rebind );
    conn.setSearchConstraints( cons );
}
```

The method extracts the credentials from an authenticated connection and stores them for use on referrals. When `LDAPRebindProc.getRebindAuthentication` is called by the SDK, an `LDAPRebindAuth` object is instantiated using the stored credentials.

You can add any additional logic required to your `LDAPRebindProc` implementation, including code to use different credentials based on the server host and port instead of using fixed credentials.

The `manageDsaIT` Control

Suppose you have a directory entry with the `referral` object class and a `ref` attribute containing an LDAP URL. The URL is incorrect or has changed, and you want to modify it. But whenever you try, you are referred to the server named in the `ref` attribute, which may not even exist or may not be responding to requests. To have the server treat the entry as a normal one with no referral, supply the `manageDsaIT` control along with your request.

The `manageDsaIT` control has no content beyond the basic control elements: an `OID` and an `isCritical` flag. No dedicated class is therefore required to encapsulate it. Use the control as follows; the example modifies the `ref` attribute of an entry containing a referral.

```
LDAPConstraints cons =
    ld.getConstraints();
cons.setServerControls(
    new LDAPControl( LDAPControl.MANAGEDSAIT, true, null ) );
LDAPModification mod =
    new LDAPModification( LDAPModification.REPLACE,
                          new LDAPAttribute( "ref",
                          "ldap://foo2.airius.com/" ) );
ld.modify( dn, mod, cons );
```

`LDAPBind` for Complete Client Control

`LDAPRebind` for referral credentials has a clear limitation: it can be used only to supply simple authentication (DN and password), and not SASL or other authentication methods.

The `LDAPBind` interface gives you more control—in fact, it forces you to take control—by letting you create the connection to the referred-to server yourself. It has a single method, `bind`, that takes an `LDAPConnection` as parameter. Your implementation may extract the host name, port, and credentials from the object and do whatever it takes to establish a connection. On failure, the method should throw an `LDAPException`.

The following trivial implementation does the same thing that the earlier `LDAPRebindProc` example did: it supplies the same credentials to the referred-to server as were used with the original server, and it uses simple authentication.

```
LDAPBind binder = new LDAPBind() {
    public void bind( LDAPConnection ld ) throws LDAPException {
        ld.connect( 3, ld.getHost(), ld.getPort(),
                    ld.getAuthenticationDN(),
                    ld.getAuthenticationPassword() );
    }
};
LDAPSearchConstraints cons = ld.getSearchConstraints();
cons.setBindProc( binder );
cons.setReferrals( true );
```

A hypothetical SASL implementation might look like this instead:

```
LDAPBind binder = new LDAPBind() {
    public void bind( LDAPConnection ld )
                      throws LDAPException {
        // Set up all SASL parameters
        Hashtable props = new Hashtable();
        props.add("javax.security.sasl.encryption.minimum",
                  "40");
        props.add("javax.security.sasl.encryption.maximum",
                  "128");
        props.add("javax.security.sasl.server.authentication",
                  "true");
        props.add("javax.security.sasl.maxbuffer", "4096");
        // What we want to authenticate as
        String dn = "uid=sam, ou=People, o=Airius.com";
        // Create a callback object for possible use by
        // the authentication process
        SimpleCallbackHandler cbh = new SimpleCallbackHandler();
        // Use GSSAPI as the authentication mechanism
        String[] mechNames = { "GSSAPI" };
        if( !ld.isConnected() ) {
            ld.connect( ld.getHost(), ld.getPort() );
        }
        ld.authenticate( dn, mechNames, props, cbh );
    }
};
```

And Now for Something Completely Different: Extended Operations

The section on controls earlier in this chapter showed how you can modify or extend the behavior of the standard LDAPv3 operations by including controls in the requests—provided that the server supports the particular controls. LDAPv3 goes one step further: it allows you to execute arbitrary requests as extended operations.

An extended operation is simply a request that contains arbitrary user-defined data and a response containing arbitrary data from the server. You could use it to turn your LDAP server into a controller for your household appliances and define commands for turning on the microwave and checking the temperature in the oven. But that's not really the intended use for LDAP extended operations. More likely uses for extended operations include requesting the server to perform a backup or to begin a synchronization session with another data source.

If you implement support for extended operations on the server, you will need to concern yourself with security and access control. You probably don't want just anyone to be able to trigger an extended operation (including starting a backup or synchronization). As discussed in Chapter 7, LDAP does not yet define a standard way to set or enforce access control. With Netscape Directory Server, access rights to use controls and extended operations are governed by entries under `cn=features,cn=config`. There is one entry for each control or extended operation that may have limited access rights defined. The RDN for the entry consists of the `OID`. The entry for the VLV request control looks like this by default (you can change the ACI to change the access rights):

```
dn: oid=2.16.840.1.113730.3.4.9,cn=features,cn=config
objectclass: top
objectclass: directoryServerFeature
oid: 2.16.840.1.113730.3.4.9
cn: VLV Request Control
aci: (targetattr != "aci")(version 3.0; acl "VLV Request
 Control"; allow( read, search, compare ) userdn = "ldap:///all";)
```

An example of a simple but still very useful extended operation would be to return the authentication DN of the current connection. You may question the usefulness of such an operation when the DN is available in the connection as `LDAPConnection.getAuthenticationDN()`. Although the authentication DN is available for simple authentication, it is not available for SSL client authentication. The client may have more than one certificate, and the SSL implementation decides which one to use by negotiating with the server. There may be no way for the client to find out which certificate was presented. Even if the client can access the certificate, most servers have a configurable system for mapping the subject DN in the certificate to an entry in the directory. It is often impossible for the client to know which entry that will be for each potential server.

The means of adding support for an extended operation to the server vary among LDAP server vendors. For Netscape Directory Server you would write a server plug-in, which is a shared library that is loaded when the server starts. Plug-ins can easily discover the DN that a connection is authenticated as and many other properties of the connection.

Execute an extended operation by constructing an `LDAPExtendedOperation` object and passing it to `LDAPConnection.extendedOperation`. The return value is another `LDAPExtendedOperation`. `LDAPExtendedOperation` takes an `OID` and a byte array as constructor arguments. The member variables can be accessed with `getID` and `getValue`. Our `getAuthDN` extended operation has no data to pass to the server, but a DN will be returned. The code to query for the authentication DN looks like this:

```
import java.util.Enumeration;
import java.io.UnsupportedEncodingException;
import netscape.ldap.*;
...
    // Define the OID of our extended operation
    public static final String GETIDEXTOP = "3.3.3.3.3.1";
...
    // Check if the server supports the GETIDEXTOP operation
    // by reading the root DSE and checking for supported
    // extensions
    String attrs[] = { "supportedExtension" };
    LDAPEntry entry = ld.read( "", attrs );
    LDAPAttribute attr = entry.getAttribute( attrs[0] );
    boolean doesSupport = false;
    if ( attr != null ) {
        Enumeration en = attr.getStringValues();
        while( (en != null) && en.hasMoreElements() ) {
            if ( GETIDEXTOP.equals(
                (String)en.nextElement() ) ) {
                doesSupport = true;
                break;
            }
        }
    }
    if ( doesSupport ) {
        // The server supports our op, so ask it for the auth DN
        LDAPExtendedOperation extOp =
            ld.extendedOperation(
                new LDAPExtendedOperation(
                                         GETIDEXTOP, null ) );
        String authDN = null;
        // The value must be converted from UTF8 to a Java
        // String
```

```
        try {
            authDN = new String( extOp.getValue(), "UTF8" );
        } catch ( UnsupportedEncodingException e ) {
        }
        System.out.println( "Authenticated as " + authDN );
    } else {
        System.out.println( "Server does not support the " +
                            "getAuthDN extended operation" );
    }
```

Aiming for 24×7: Failover and Reconnecting

The LDAPConnection.connect methods can take more than just a host name or IP address for the host name parameter. The parameter can be a space-delimited list of hosts, with an optional colon and port number for each—for example:

```
String hosts =
   "directory.knowledge.com:1050 people.catalog.com 199.254.1.2";
ld.connect( hosts, 20000 );
```

In this example, three alternative hosts are specified. The first one also has the port number identified; the second and third ones will use the port number passed as the second parameter to the method: 20000. The SDK will attempt to connect to the first host in the list. If that fails, it will try the second one, and so on.

You can tune the connection policy with LDAPConnection.setConnSetupDelay. The default policy is LDAPConnection.NODELAY_SERIAL—that is, to try each host in turn until one can be reached. In many cases, there will be an unacceptable delay if the first host or hosts are inaccessible because the server is down or because there is a network problem. The length of the delay may depend on your operating system and other factors, but it will typically be at least 45 seconds (the length of the TCP/IP socket time-out).

The other connection failover options—LDAPConnection.NODELAY_PARALLEL and parallel connection with a selectable delay—help manage this situation. With NODELAY_PARALLEL, the SDK will create threads that simultaneously attempt to connect to each of the specified hosts. The first one to successfully establish a connection "wins," and the other connections are discarded. Generally this means that if at least one LDAP server is up and running, your application won't be delayed by any others that are down. With the parallel option with a selectable delay, there is a delay (specified in seconds) between starting each thread; if the first thread can establish a connection within the delay interval, no attempt is made to contact other servers.

The following shows an example of each setting.

```
ld.setConnSetupDelay( LDAPConnection.NODELAY_SERIAL );
ld.setConnSetupDelay( LDAPConnection.NODELAY_PARALLEL );
ld.setConnSetupDelay( 10 ); // 10 seconds between threads
```

The setting is global to the physical connection, so it affects all clones.

Transparent Reconnection

Whether one or multiple hosts were specified, the SDK will transparently attempt to reconnect on any LDAP operation if both of the following are true:

- The connection was established earlier.
- The connection was lost because of a network error or an LDAP server error.

If multiple hosts were specified, any host with which a connection could not be established is transferred to an internal reserve list. If reconnection becomes necessary, hosts on the reserve list are probed only if there are no more hosts on the active list. If, then, a host on the reserve list becomes accessible, it is moved back to the active list, preventing a long delay for reconnecting each time if the first host in the originally specified list is unavailable.

Intelligent failover and transparent reconnection are nice features for a client-side application, but they are really significant for a server-side process that is to run for an extended period of time. For mission-critical environments, additional LDAP servers can be configured as replicas for hot switch-over. No special programming is required by a client of the SDK to take advantage of the features, other than specifying more than one host when connecting.

Controlling the Result Queue: The Connection Backlog

When an `LDAPConnection` object is connected to a server, it has a separate thread listening for incoming messages from the server. The messages are queued for delivery on the basis of the sequential operation number assigned at the time of a request. There may be multiple queues if more than one thread shares a physical connection or if multiple searches (with a batch size of 1) have been requested. The LDAP protocol is asynchronous, and in principle a message can be received at any time, even if no requests have been made. When a client issues a search request that results in a large number of entries being returned, the results may very well be delivered to the client faster than the client processes them (by enumerating `LDAPSearchResults`). Memory may be consumed to the point at which the Java Virtual Machine (JVM) crashes.

To limit the memory consumed in queueing incoming search results, the connection has a `BackLog` property that determines how many unread messages may accumulate before the listener thread stops accepting additional results. The default value is 100. The existence of the backlog mechanism is generally transparent to client operations. The client iterates through the search results, and never more than 100 results are waiting for it in the queue at any given time. As the client reads results from the queue, the listener thread resumes reading results from the socket and backfills the queue. No results are lost, memory consumption is limited, and no CPU cycles are spent on unnecessary busywork.

In some special cases a client may want to increase the backlog limit, or to decrease it to reduce the memory consumption of the SDK while receiving large result sets. The property is set with `LDAPSearchConstraints.setMaxBacklog( int maxBackLog )`. The property is global to all threads and clones sharing a physical connection.

The listener thread cannot know until after it has read a message from the incoming socket if the next message is intended for a thread doing a massive search or for a thread doing a modify operation that results in only a single response message from the server. So that threads doing operations other than searches are not blocked, the backlog limit is ignored if any concurrent operations are doing add, modify, delete, or rename.

It is possible to create a deadlock by starting a search that returns many results and then starting another search without enumerating the results of the first one. Such a deadlock is best handled by avoidance: use a separate `LDAPConnection` with its own physical connection for the second operation if the results of the first operation are not to be enumerated yet. In some cases the deadlock can instead be avoided by raising the backlog limit, but at the expense of increased memory usage.

Down to the Wire: Using the Asynchronous Interface

Underneath the synchronous operation interfaces we've used so far in this book is an asynchronous layer that is closer to the LDAP wire protocol. When you call `LDAPConnection.modify`, the request is immediately sent off to the server and the client then waits at a new dedicated message queue for a response. An internal listener thread receives messages from the server asynchronously. It examines the sequential operation number in each message and delivers the message to the corresponding queue. The waiting client then wakes up, reads the message, and returns from the `modify` call.

The synchronous interface is generally the preferred interface for operations that return a single result—that is, all operations except searches (of scope one-level or subtree). For searches, setting the batch size property to 1 keeps the client from being blocked while results are arriving. With these methods, all the low-level nitty-gritty is handled automatically.

In some cases, however, access to the low-level interfaces solves problems that are difficult to address using the synchronous methods. The main example is multiplexing the result stream from multiple simultaneous searches. If you start four searches with different connections (to the same or to different servers), you can interleave the enumerating of their search results by calling `next` on each one in turn until none have any more results to deliver. But if one of the searches blocks because its server is down or is not responding quickly, then the polling loop blocks (unless you have a separate thread or threads doing the enumeration on each result set). The asynchronous interface solves this problem by providing access to the internal message queues. A message queue can be created for one operation and assigned to another, so messages destined for either one are delivered to the same queue.

The asynchronous interface is defined by `LDAPAsynchronousConnection`, which is implemented by `LDAPConnection`. That means you can call any of its methods on an `LDAPConnection`.

`LDAPAsynchronousConnection` has methods for bind, add, delete, modify, rename, and search. The methods are the same as the synchronous ones, except that they take an additional argument—`LDAPSearchResponseListener` for search operations and `LDAPResponseListener` for all others—and they return an `LDAPSearchResponseListener` or `LDAPResponseListener` rather than `void`. If you pass in `null` for the listener argument, the connection will create a listener and return it. If you pass in a listener, the connection will use it for messages returned for the operation.

A listener is effectively a message queue. Calling its `getResponse` method blocks until there is a response available. You can call its `isResponseReceived` method to determine if there is a message available or if calling `getResponse` will block.

`LDAPSearchResponseListener` provides a `getSearchResults` method to return an `Enumeration` object. Enumerating the results object will either block until a single result is available (if the batch size is 1) or until all search results from all searches that the results object manages are available (if the batch size is 0).

The basic message class is `LDAPMessage`. Its `getType` method provides access to the type of the message, and its `getControls` method returns any controls returned by the server. The possible response message types are as follows:

```
BIND_RESPONSE

SEARCH_RESPONSE

SEARCH_RESULT

SEARCH_RESULT_REFERENCE

MODIFY_RESPONSE

ADD_RESPONSE
```

DEL_RESPONSE

MODIFY_RDN_RESPONSE

COMPARE_RESPONSE

EXTENDED_RESPONSE

LDAPResponseListener produces instances of LDAPResponse, which extends LDAPMessage in providing access to any error string, matched DN, referrals, and result code that are available in the message. The client of the asynchronous interface is responsible for checking the result code to see if the operation was successful or what went wrong if it failed; no LDAPException is thrown unless the operation could not even be started (for example, because the server was inaccessible).

Each object produced by an LDAPSearchResponseListener enumeration is either an LDAPSearchResult that contains a single LDAPEntry or an instance of LDAPSearchResultReference that contains one or more LDAP URLs. Both object types extend LDAPMessage, so they may include controls returned by the server.

Our first sample program demonstrates that operations do not block, and it illustrates the additional steps that must be taken to process messages when using the asynchronous interface:

```
public class AsynchSearch {
    public static void main( String[] args ) {
        String MY_FILTER = "objectclass=*";
        String MY_SEARCHBASE = "o=Airius.com";
        LDAPConnection ld = new LDAPConnection();
        try {
            ld.connect( "localhost", 389 );
            // Asynchronous authentication
            LDAPResponseListener r =
                ld.bind( "uid=jvedder, ou=People, o=airius.com",
                         "befitting",
                         (LDAPResponseListener)null );
            // Do something else, just to show that we're not
            // blocked yet
            System.out.println( "Started authenticating" );
            // Wait until it completes
            LDAPResponse response = r.getResponse();
            // Did the authentication succeed?
            int resultCode = response.getResultCode();
            if (resultCode != LDAPException.SUCCESS) {
                // Do what the synchronous interface does -
                // throw an exception
```

```
        String err =
              LDAPException.errorCodeToString(
                                           resultCode );
        throw new LDAPException (
                               err,
                               resultCode,
                               response.getErrorMessage(),
                               response.getMatchedDN());
    }

    // Start searching. Pass null for
    // LDAPSearchListener to obtain a new one.
    LDAPSearchListener l =
        ld.search( MY_SEARCHBASE,
                   ld.SCOPE_ONE,
                   MY_FILTER,
                   null,
                   false,
                   (LDAPSearchListener)null );
    // Loop on results until finished
    LDAPMessage msg;
    while( (msg = l.getResponse()) != null ) {
        // Next directory entry
        if ( msg instanceof
             LDAPSearchResultReference ) {
             LDAPSearchResultReference ref =
                (LDAPSearchResultReference)msg;
            String[] urls = ref.getUrls();
            // Do something with the referrals...
        } else if ( msg instanceof LDAPSearchResult ) {
            LDAPEntry entry =
                ((LDAPSearchResult)msg).getEntry();
            // The rest of the processing is the same
            // as for a synchronous search
            System.out.println( entry.getDN() );
        } else {
            // A search response
            LDAPResponse res = (LDAPResponse)msg;
            int status = res.getResultCode();
            if ( status == LDAPException.SUCCESS ) {
                // Nothing to do
            } else {
                String err =
                    LDAPException.errorCodeToString(
```

```
                                                  status );
                        throw new LDAPException(
                                             err,
                                             status,
                                             res.getErrorMessage(),
                                             res.getMatchedDN() );
                    }
                }
            }
        } catch( LDAPException e ) {
            System.out.println( "Error: " + e.toString() );
        }
...
```

The second example uses the asynchronous interface to multiplex the result streams from searches on three different servers:

```
public class MultiplexedSearch {
    public static void main( String[] args ) {
        String MY_FILTER = "objectclass=*";
        // Three hosts, three ports, three search bases
        String[] HOSTS =
            { "localhost", "ldap.acme.com", "ds.airius.com" };
        int[] PORTS = { 389, 24000, 32000 };
        String[] BASES =
            { "o=Airius.com", "o=acme.com",
              "dc=airius,dc=com" };
        LDAPConnection[] lds =
            new LDAPConnection[HOSTS.length];
        try {
            for( int i = 0; i < lds.length; i++ ) {
                lds[i] = new LDAPConnection();
                lds[i].connect( HOSTS[i], PORTS[i] );
                System.out.println( "Connected to " +
                                    HOSTS[i] + ':' +
                                    PORTS[i] );
            }
            // Get a response listener for one search
            LDAPSearchListener listener =
                lds[0].search( BASES[0],
                               lds[0].SCOPE_SUB,
                               MY_FILTER,
                               null,
                               false,
```

```
                         (LDAPSearchListener)null );
        // Share the listener
        for( int i = 1; i < lds.length; i++ ) {
            lds[i].search( BASES[i],
                           lds[i].SCOPE_SUB,
                           MY_FILTER,
                           null,
                           false,
                           listener );
        }

        // Loop on results until finished.
        // This is the same as in the previous example.
```

The third and final example does asynchronous multiplexed searches on different subtrees of the same server:

```
public class MultiSubtreeSearch {
    public static void main( String[] args ) {
        String MY_FILTER = "objectclass=*";
        String[] BASES =
            { "ou=People,o=Airius.com",
              "ou=Groups,o=Airius.com",
              "o=acme.com" };
        LDAPConnection ld = new LDAPConnection();
        try {
            ld.connect( "localhost", 389 );
            // Get a response listener for one search
            LDAPSearchListener listener =
                ld.search( BASES[0],
                           ld.SCOPE_SUB,
                           MY_FILTER,
                           null,
                           false,
                           (LDAPSearchListener)null );
            // Share the listener
            for( int i = 1; i < BASES.length; i++ ) {
                // Do the parallel searches on clones
                ld = (LDAPConnection)ld.clone();
                ld.search( BASES[i],
                           ld.SCOPE_SUB,
                           MY_FILTER,
                           null,
                           false,
```

```
                listener );
}

// Loop on results until finished.
// This is the same as in the previous example.
```

Conclusion

In this chapter we have seen how controls allow a client to access additional functionality that a directory may offer beyond what is specified by the various RFCs. We have looked at the controls that are predefined in the SDK, and at how to create new controls and extended operations. The chapter also has introduced the utility classes that make it easy to access and update the directory schema, and the options available for handling referrals. The options for failover and transparent reconnection have been discussed, and the asynchronous operations for handling results in a nonblocking manner have been presented.

We've now completed our tour of the Java LDAP API. We hope we're leaving you with some new ideas on what LDAP can do for you and how you can use the SDK to accomplish your directory goals.

P A R T V

APPENDICES

APPENDIX A

More to Learn about LDAP

Where do you go to learn more about using LDAP? Although it is not possible to keep a printed list current, we believe you will find the following information sources a valuable start.

Going to the Source: Internet Standards

Where to Get RFCs and Internet Drafts

RFC stands for "Request for Comments," but the acronym has assumed a life of its own. An RFC is no longer an invitation to discuss a standard, but rather a document adopted for publication by the Internet Engineering Task Force (IETF). Some RFCs define standards; others are categorized as Experimental or Informational. Most RFCs start off as Internet Drafts before being approved as RFCs.

RFCs and Internet Drafts are available at mirrored archives around the world. The following is a selection of sites for RFCs:

```
http://www.ietf.org/rfc/

http://info.internet.isi.edu:80/in-notes/rfc/files/

http://src.doc.ic.ac.uk/computing/internet/rfc/

ftp://ds.internic.net/rfc/

ftp://nisc.jvnc.net/rfc/

ftp://nis.nsf.net/internet/documents/rfc/

ftp://ftp.sesqui.net/pub/rfc/

ftp://src.doc.ic.ac.uk/computing/internet/rfc/

ftp://venera.isi.edu/in-notes/
```

You may access RFC 2251, for example, at the URL `http://www.ietf.org/rfc/rfc2251.txt` or at `http://info.internet.isi.edu:80/in-notes/rfc/files/rfc2251.txt`.

An Internet Draft name starts with "draft-." If it is issued in the context of an IETF working group, the next part of the name is "ietf-" and the name of the working group (see the list below for an example); otherwise the last name of one of the authors follows, and then some short descriptive text, a two-digit version number, and the ".txt" extension.

Internet Drafts are required to expire after six months at most, after which time they are withdrawn from the public mirror sites. At the time of expiration, one of three things typically happens:

- A new draft is issued with a higher sequential number. For example, "draft-ietf-ldapext-ldapv3-tls-04.txt" is replaced with "draft-ietf-ldapext-ldapv3-tls-05.txt." Often there are no changes from one version to the next. If you search for an Internet Draft and it is not available, try searching for the same draft with a higher number.
- The draft fades into oblivion.
- The draft is proposed to become an RFC.

The following is a selection of sites for Internet Drafts:

The IETF: `ftp://ftp.ietf.org/internet-drafts/`

Africa: `ftp://ftp.is.co.za/internet-drafts`

Canada: `ftp://ftp.normos.org/ietf/internet-drafts`

Italy: `ftp://ftp.nic.it/internet-drafts`

Pacific Rim: `ftp://munnari.oz.au/internet-drafts`

South America: `ftp://ftp.isi.edu/internet-drafts`

Sweden: `ftp://ftp.nordu.net/internet-drafts`

United States, West Coast: `ftp://ftp.isi.edu/internet-drafts`

LDAP RFCs

RFC 1823: "The C LDAP API"

RFC 1823, which defines the old LDAPv2 interface, will eventually be replaced by a document that is currently an Internet Draft: "The C LDAP Application Program Interface," which defines the LDAPv3 extensions to the C API for accessing LDAP.

RFC 2247: "Using Domains in LDAP/X.500 Distinguished Names"

This document defines an algorithm by which a name registered with the Internet Domain Name System (DNS) can be represented as an LDAP distinguished name.

RFC 2251: "Lightweight Directory Access Protocol (v3)"

This is the main RFC for LDAPv3, which defines the protocol operations, data representation, and data organization.

RFC 2252: "Lightweight Directory Access Protocol (v3): Attribute Syntax Definitions"

LDAP transmits most attribute values as strings, rather than as binary structures. For example, the number 4,000 is transmitted as "4000." This document defines the standard attribute type representations and specifies how attribute values are compared for each standard type during a search operation.

RFC 2253: "Lightweight Directory Access Protocol (v3): UTF-8 String Representation of Distinguished Names"

Each entry in an LDAP directory is uniquely identified by its distinguished name (DN), represented as a string. This document defines the syntax and structure of these names.

RFC 2254: "The String Representation of LDAP Search Filters"

The basic LDAPv3 RFC (RFC 2251) defines a binary format for search expressions passed from a client to a server. However, users of clients compose and submit search requests in an easily readable and printable string format, which is defined in RFC 2254.

RFC 2255: "The LDAP URL Format"

RFC 2255 defines the URL format for expressing an LDAP search. You can enter an LDAP URL in many browsers to perform an LDAP search.

RFC 2256: "A Summary of the X.500(96) User Schema for Use with LDAPv3"

Where possible, LDAP leverages the schema standardization work of X.500, rather than inventing new standards for schema information. This document defines standard attributes for representing a person in an LDAP entry. These attributes are based on the X.500 standard.

RFC 2259: "Internet X.509 Public Key Infrastructure Operational Protocols—LDAPv2"

This document addresses requirements to provide access to public-key infrastructure (PKI) repositories for the purposes of retrieving and managing PKI information based on LDAP.

RFC 2307: "An Approach for Using LDAP as a Network Information Service"

This document describes an experimental mechanism for mapping entities related to TCP/IP and the UNIX system into X.500 entries so that they may be resolved with the LDAP protocol.

RFC 2587: "Internet X.509 Public Key Infrastructure LDAPv2 Schema"

This document defines a minimal schema to support PKIX in an LDAPv2 environment, as defined in RFC 2559.

RFC 2589: "LDAPv3 Extensions for Dynamic Directory Services"

This document defines extended operations to support dynamic (short-lived) directory data storage.

RFC 2596: "Use of Language Codes in LDAP"

This document describes how language codes as defined in RFC 1766 are carried in LDAP and are to be interpreted by LDAP servers.

LDAP Internet Drafts

Internet Drafts are likely to disappear or acquire a new version number at least once every six months. There are almost a hundred drafts with some relationship to LDAP, although many simply define LDAP schema elements for use with a particular protocol and do not constitute an extension to LDAP itself. The following are documents within the charter of either the LDAPEXT (LDAP Extensions) or LDUP (LDAP Duplication and Update Protocol) working group, so they are more likely than others eventually to become a standard. The list was generated by a search at the IETF query site: `http://search.ietf.org/search/cgi-bin/BrokerQuery.pl.cgi?broker=internet-drafts&query=ietf-ldapext%20OR%20ietf-ldup&descflag=on`.

C API

"The C LDAP Application Program Interface" (draft-ietf-ldapext-ldap-c-api-04.txt)

This document defines a C language application program interface (API) to LDAP. The document replaces the previous definition of this API, defined in RFC 1823, updating it to include support for features found in version 3 of the LDAP protocol. New extended operation functions were added to support LDAPv3 features such as controls. In addition, other LDAP API changes were made to support information hiding and thread safety.

"LDAP C API Extensions for Persistent Search" (draft-ietf-ldapext-c-api-psearch-00.txt)

This document defines extensions to the LDAP C API to support the LDAP Persistent Search Simple Change Notification Mechanism. More specifically, this document defines functions to create Persistent Search controls and to parse Entry Change Notification controls.

"LDAP C API Extensions for Scrolling View Browsing of Search Results" (draft-smith-ldap-c-api-ext-vlv-00.txt)

This document defines extensions to the LDAP C API to support the LDAP extensions for scrolling-view browsing of search results. More specifically, this document defines functions to create Virtual List View request controls and to parse Virtual List View response controls.

Java API

"The Java LDAP Application Program Interface" (draft-ietf-ldapext-ldap-java-api-08.txt)

This document defines a Java language application program interface to LDAP, in the form of a class library.

"The Java LDAP Application Program Interface Asynchronous Extension" (draft-ietf-ldapext-ldap-java-api-asynch-ext-03.txt)

This document defines asynchronous extensions to the Java language application program interface to LDAP defined in "draft-ietf-ldapext-ldap-java-api-08.txt." Directory SDK for Java implements the API defined by this document and by "draft-ietf-ldapext-ldap-java-api-08.txt."

Access Control

"Access Control Requirements for LDAP" (draft-ietf-ldapext-acl-reqts-02.txt)

This document describes the fundamental requirements of an access control list model for the LDAP directory service. It is intended to be a gathering place for access control requirements needed to provide authorized access to and interoperability between directories. The RFC 2119 terminology is used in this document.

"Access Control Model for LDAP" (draft-ietf-ldapext-acl-model-04.txt)

This document describes the access control model for the LDAP directory service. It includes a description of the model, the LDAP controls, and the extended operations to the LDAP protocol. A separate document defines the corresponding APIs.

Replication

"LDAP Replication Architecture" (draft-ietf-ldup-model-02.txt)

This architectural document outlines a suite of schema and protocol extensions to LDAPv3 that enables the robust, reliable, server-to-server exchange of directory content and changes.

"LDAP V3 Replication Requirements" (draft-ietf-ldup-replica-req-01.txt)

This document discusses the fundamental requirements for replication of data that is accessible via the LDAPv3 protocol. It is intended to be a gathering place for general replication requirements needed to provide interoperability between informational directories.

"LDUP Replication Information Model" (draft-ietf-ldup-infomod-00.txt)

This document describes the information model and schema elements that support LDAP replication services that conform to "draft-ietf-ldup-model-01.txt."

"LDUP Update Reconciliation Procedures" (draft-ietf-ldup-urp-02.txt)

This document describes the procedures used by directory servers to reconcile updates performed by autonomously operating directory servers in a distributed, replicated directory service. These procedures are a joint development of the IETF and ITU-T for use in LDAP directory replication (LDUP), and the X.500 Directory Multi-master Replication Protocol.

Authentication and Security

"Authentication Methods for LDAP" (draft-ietf-ldapext-authmeth-04.txt)

This document specifies particular combinations of security mechanisms that are required and recommended in LDAP implementations.

"X.509 Authentication SASL Mechanism" (draft-ietf-ldapext-x509-sasl-02.txt)

This document defines a SASL authentication mechanism based on X.509 strong authentication, providing two-way authentication. This mechanism is only for authentication; it has no effect on the protocol encodings and is not designed to provide integrity or confidentiality services.

"Lightweight Directory Access Protocol (v3): Extension for Transport Layer Security" (draft-ietf-ldapext-ldapv3-tls-05.txt)

This document defines the Start Transport Layer Security (TLS) operation for LDAP. This operation provides for TLS establishment in an LDAP association and is defined in terms of an LDAP extended request.

"An LDAP Control and Schema for Holding Operation Signatures" (draft-ietf-ldapext-sigops-04.txt)

In many environments, clients require the ability to validate the source and integrity of information provided by the directory. This document describes an LDAP message control that allows for the retrieval of digitally signed information. The document defines an LDAPv3-based mechanism for signing directory operations in order to create a secure journal of changes that have been made to each directory entry. Both client- and server-based signatures are supported. An object class for subsequent retrieval of "journal entries" is also defined. This document specifies LDAPv3 controls that enable this functionality. It also defines an LDAPv3 schema that allows for subsequent browsing of the journal information.

Controls and Extended Operations

"LDAP Extensions for Scrolling View Browsing of Search Results" (draft-ietf-ldapext-ldapv3-vlv-03.txt)

This document describes a Virtual List View control extension for the LDAP search operation. The control allows a client to specify that the server return a contiguous subset of the search result set, rather than returning all results. This subset is specified in terms of offsets into the ordered list of results, or in terms of a greater-than-or-equal comparison value.

"LDAP Control for a Duplicate Entry Representation of Search Results" (draft-ietf-ldapext-ldapv3-dupent-02.txt)

This document describes a Duplicate Entry Representation control extension for the LDAP search operation. By using the control with an LDAP search, a client requests that the server return separate entries for each value held in the specified attributes. For instance, if a specified attribute of an entry holds multiple values, the search operation will return multiple instances of that entry, each instance holding a separate single value in that attribute.

"LDAPv3 Triggered Search Control" (draft-ietf-ldapext-trigger-01.txt)

This document defines an LDAPv3 control to be used on the search request to allow a client to retrieve information on changes that are made to the directory information tree held by that server.

"LDAP Control Extension for Server Side Sorting of Search Results" (draft-ietf-ldapext-sorting-02.txt)

This document describes two LDAPv3 control extensions for server-side sorting of search results. These controls allow a client to specify the attribute types and matching rules a server should use when returning the results to an LDAP search request. The controls may be useful when the LDAP client has limited functionality or for another reason cannot sort the results but still needs them sorted. Other permissible controls on search operations are not defined in this extension.

"Persistent Search: A Simple LDAP Change Notification Mechanism" (draft-ietf-ldapext-psearch-01.txt)

This document defines two controls that extend the LDAPv3 search operation to provide a simple mechanism by which an LDAP client can receive notification of changes that occur in an LDAP server. The mechanism is designed to be very flexible, yet easy for clients and servers to implement.

Other Extensions

"Families of Entries" (draft-ietf-ldapext-families-00.txt)

This document describes a model for grouping together collections of attributes into families of entries, for directory servers that follow the X.500 and LDAP information models. The document also describes protocol support, in the form of LDAP controls, that allows the user to treat a family of entries either as separate entries or as a combined entry when searching, retrieving, or deleting information from the DIT.

"Named Referrals in LDAP Directories" (draft-ietf-ldapext-namedref-00.txt)

This document defines a `ref` attribute and associated `referral` object class for representing generic knowledge information in LDAP directories. The attribute uses Uniform Resource Identifiers (URIs) to represent knowledge, enabling LDAP and non-LDAP services alike to be referenced. The object class can be used to construct entries in an LDAP directory containing references to other directories or services.

This document also defines procedures that directory servers should follow when supporting these schema elements and when responding to requests for which the directory server does not contain the requested object but may contain some knowledge of the location of the requested object. The referral feature has been supported by Netscape and other LDAP servers for a year or two already.

X.500 Documents

Many LDAP standards are based on the standards of X.500. You may find in reading an LDAP standards document that it references a matching rule or other protocol or syntax element that is not defined anywhere in the document. In most cases, the assumption is that the definitions of X.500 apply.

Unlike the LDAP standards documentation, the basic X.500 documents are not freely available on the Internet; they must be purchased from the ITU (International Telecommunication Union) or ISO (International Organization for Standardization). The following list of documents was extracted from the compilation by David Chadwick for the book *Understanding the X.500 Directory,* which is mentioned in the section on books later in this appendix.

The Directory (CCITT REC. X.500-X.521 | ISO/IEC Standard 9594:1993)

X.500: "Overview of Concepts, Models and Services"

X.501: "Models"

X.509: "Authentication Framework"

X.511: "Abstract Service Definition"

X.518: "Procedures for Distributed Operations"

X.519: "Protocol Specifications"

X.520: "Selected Attribute Types"

X.521: "Selected Object Classes"

X.525: "Replication"

The X.5xx documents may be purchased at `http://www.itu.int/itudoc/itu-t/rec/x/x500up/`.

The North American Directory Forum (NADF) Documents (April 1993)

SD-0: "NADF Standing Documents: A Brief Overview"

SD-1: "Terms of Reference"

SD-2: "Program Plan"

SD-3: "Service Description"

SD-4: "The Directory Schema"

SD-5: "An X.500 Naming Scheme for National DIT Subtrees and Its Application for C=CA and C=US"

SD-6: "Guidelines on Naming and Subtrees"

SD-7: "Mapping the North American DIT onto Directory Management Domains"

SD-8: "The Experimental Pilot Plan"

SD-9: "Charter, Procedure and Operations of the Central Administration for NADF"

SD-10: "Security and Privacy: Policy and Services"

SD-11: "Directory Security: Mechanisms and Practicality"

SD-12: "Registry of ADDMD Names"

EWOS Directory Functional Standards

A/711 (A/DI1): "Directory Access," published as ENV 41 210 (also published as ISP 10615 parts 1 and 2)

A/712 (A/DI2): "Directory System Protocol," published as ENV 41 212 (also published as ISP 10615 parts 3 and 4)

A/713 (A/DI32): "Dynamic Behaviour of DSAs for Distributed Operations," published as ENV 41 215 (also published as ISP 10615 part 6)

A/714 (A/DI31): "Directory User Agents Distributed Operation," published as ENV 41 217 (also published as ISP 10615 part 5)

Q/511 (F/DI11): "Common Directory Use," published as ENV 41 512 (also published as ISP 10616; see also ISO/IEC PDISP)

Q/512 (F/DI2): "Directory Data Definitions—Directory Use by MHS"

Q/513 (F/DI3): "Directory Data Definitions—FTAM Use of the Directory" (to be published as ISP 11190)

ETG XXX: "Introduction to Directory Profiles" (final draft)

ETG 017: "Error Handling in the OSI Directory" (final draft, May 1992)

ETG XXX: "Security Architecture for the Directory" (fifth draft in 1992)

Joint ISO Standards and CCITT Recommendations

ISO/IEC 8824:1988 | CCITT X.208: "Specification of Abstract Syntax Notation One (ASN.1)"

ISO/IEC 8824-2 DIS (1993) | CCITT X.208-2: "Abstract Syntax Notation One (ASN.1): Information Object Specification"

ISO/IEC 8825-1 | CCITT X.209-1: "Part 1: Basic Encoding Rules (BER)"

ISO/IEC 8825-3 DIS (1993) | CCITT X.209-3: "Part 3: Distinguished Encoding Rules"

ISO/IEC 9072-1 | CCITT X.219: "Remote Operations—Model, Notation and Service Definition"

ISO 8649:1988 | CCITT X.217: "Service Definition for the Association Control Service Element"

Other ISO Documents

ISO/IEC JTC 1/SC21 N6063: "Use of Object Identifiers to Access Directory Information" (May 1991)

ISO 3166:1988: "Codes for the Representation of Names of Countries"

ISO IS 10162/3: "Documentation Search and Retrieve Service Definition/Protocol Specification"

ISO 6523:1984: "Data Interchange—Structure for the Identification of Organisations"

ISO/IEC 10646-1:1993: "(E) Information Technology—Universal Multiple-Octet Coded Character Set (UCS)"

ISO/IEC PDISP 10616: "International Standardised Profile FDI11—Directory Data Definitions—Common Directory Use" (February 1993)

Books about LDAP

LDAP Concepts and Deployment

Understanding and Deploying LDAP Directory Services, by Timothy A. Howes, Mark C. Smith, and Gordon S. Good (MacMillan Network Architecture and Development Series, 1999)

This comprehensive tutorial provides the reader with a thorough treatment of LDAP directory services. Minimal knowledge of general networking and administration is assumed, making the material accessible to intermediate and advanced readers. It is the first book to explore the design and deployment of directory services, and it contains real-world examples of directory deployments illustrating effective design principles along with practical insight and advice from world-renowned experts.

LDAP Programming

LDAP: Programming Directory-Enabled Applications with Lightweight Directory Access Protocol, by Tim Howes and Mark Smith (MacMillan Technology Series, 1997)

This book provides a solid introduction to LDAP, including its history and architecture, and then covers LDAP API programming via C and C++ in clear, discrete examples that range from simple searching to filtering, reading, and updating LDAP directories. More advanced topics include asynchronous LDAP programming with threads, as well as building a command-line LDAP search utility. It does not cover LDAPv3.

Implementing LDAP, by Mark Wilcox (Wrox Press, 1999)

This book contains a brief overview of LDAP concepts and deployment issues, but it focuses on illustrating the options available for programming to LDAP. It devotes a chapter each to Netscape's C LDAP SDK, the PerLDAP SDK, Netscape Directory SDK for Java, Sun's JNDI (Java Naming and Directory Interface), and Microsoft's ADSI.

X.500

X.500 is not LDAP, but sometimes there are unexplained references to X.500 concepts in LDAP literature.

Understanding the X.500 Directory, by David Chadwick (Chapman & Hall, 1994)

This book is out of print, but some of it is available in an online version at `http://www.salford.ac.uk/its024/Version.Web/Contents.htm`.

The Directory Standard and Its Application, by Doug Steedman (Technology Appraisals, 1993)

LDAP Information on the Internet

LDAP FAQs and Presentations

`http://people.netscape.com/bjm/whyLDAP.html`

A System Administrator's View of LDAP. A system administrator's perspective on what you'll need to reap the benefits of using LDAP: a good understanding of what LDAP can and cannot accomplish, some familiarity with LDAP basics, and ideas on how to make the transition to LDAP.

`http://www.stanford.edu/%7Ehodges/talks/EMA98DirectoryServicesRollout/Steve_Kille/index.htm`

Steve Kille's (of Isode) talk "Why Do I Need a Directory When I Could Use a Relational Database?"

`http://www3.innosoft.com/ldapworld/ldapfaq.html`

Mark Wahl's (of Innosoft) LDAP FAQ.

`http://www.mjwilcox.com/ldap/ldapfaq.htm`

Mark Wilcox's LDAP FAQ.

LDAP Client SDKs

`http://www.mozilla.org/directory/`

Open Source for C, Java, and Perl programming, including the source for the SDK discussed in this book. Also some tools for LDAP administration.

`http://developer.netscape.com/tech/directory/downloads.html`

Precompiled SDKs for C, Java, and Perl. They are in principle the same as what is at `mozilla.org`, but generally the source code is available at `mozilla.org` before there is a release at Netscape.

`http://java.sun.com/products/jndi/`

Sun's JNDI.

LDAP Server Vendors

`http://www.software.ibm.com/enetwork/technology/directory/`

IBM SecureWay Directory.

`http://www.innosoft.com/`

Innosoft Directory Services.

`http://developer.netscape.com/docs/manuals/index.html?content=directory.html`

Netscape Directory Server Documentation.

`http://www.openldap.org/`

OpenLDAP. Open-source LDAP software, including servers, clients, and SDKs.

`http://www.rage.net/ldap/`

A project to integrate LDAP into Linux.

`http://www.oracle.com/html/oidds.html`

Oracle Internet Directory data sheet.

`http://www.novell.com/products/nds/ldap.html`

Novell LDAP Services for NDS.

Add-On Products for LDAP Directories

`http://www.oblix.com/solutions/csa/datasheets/data_corpdir.html`

Oblix Corporate Directory. Automates the Web-based provisioning of information and services that employees need, such as computers, phones, facilities, network services, help desk, e-mail, security privileges, and corporate directories.

`http://www.intracus.com/`

Intracus. Provides an application framework for White Pages and Yellow Pages applications called Directory Browser. Intracus Directory Wizard can be used to build or customize directory applications.

`http://www.padl.com/`

PADL Software. Flagship product is ypldapd, a gateway between LDAP and the Network Information System (NIS).

`http://www.pspl.co.in/PSEnList`

Persistent Systems. PS Enlist is a product that allows queries and updates to be made to an LDAP directory via an ODBC connection, providing access to the directory for applications that can communicate only through a relational interface.

Collections of LDAP Documents and Links

`http://www.ldapnews.org/`

LDAP news, reviews, tips, conference information, and links.

`http://www.kingsmountain.com/ldapRoadmap.shtml`

An LDAP Roadmap & FAQ.

`http://www.critical-angle.com/ldapworld/index.html`

Innosoft's LDAP World.

`http://dir.yahoo.com/Computers_and_Internet/Communications_and_Networking/Protocols/LDAP__Lightweight_Directory_Access_Protocol_/`

Yahoo's section for LDAP.

`http://www.ldapcentral.com/resources.html`

LDAP Central. Resource for directory services and LDAP; sponsored by Oblix.

`http://webopedia.internet.com/TERM/L/LDAP.html`

Webopedia. Online encyclopedia.

`http://www.hklc.com/ldapschema/`

A catalog of standard LDAP schema elements.

`http://www.alvestrand.no/objectid/`

Information on how `OIDs` are assigned and used, and a dictionary for looking up or browsing all known `OIDs`.

X.500

`http://www.nic.surfnet.nl/surfnet/projects/x500/introducing/`

An introduction to and overview of X.500.

`http://ds.internic.net/pub/src/x500/schema/`

X.500 schema definitions.

Miscellaneous

`ftp://ftp.rsa.com/pub/pkcs/ascii/layman.asc`

A layperson's guide to ASN.1 and BER.

Newsgroups Where LDAP Is Spoken

`snews://secnews.mcom.com:563/netscape.dev.directory`

This newsgroup is used mainly for discussions about programming for Netscape Directory Server, but other topics do come up.

`snews://secnews.mcom.com:563/netscape.server.directory`

This newsgroup is mostly for discussions about deploying and managing Netscape Directory Server.

`news://news.mozilla.org/netscape.public.mozilla.directory`

The `mozilla.org` site hosts the open-source LDAP SDKs for C, Java, and Perl. In reality, this newsgroup discusses mostly PerLDAP issues.

`news://devforums.novell.com/novell.devsup.njcl`

Novell LDAP newsgroup, mainly for JNDI.

`news://msnews.microsoft.com/`
`microsoft.public.win2000.beta.directory_srv`

Microsoft forum for Active Directory in Windows 2000, focusing mostly on configuration and deployment.

LDAP in Your Inbox

`ldap@umich.edu`

This mailing list originally was for discussion of the University of Michigan LDAP server project, but it has become a forum for general LDAP discussions. Subscribe by sending a message to `ldap-request@umich.edu` that reads "subscribe ldap."

`ietf-ldapext@netscape.com`

This is the forum for the LDAP Extensions working group of the IETF. Subscribe by sending a message to `ietf-ldapext-request@netscape.com` that reads "subscribe."

`ietf-ldup@imc.org`

The ietf-ldup mailing list is for discussions of the LDUP (LDAP Duplication and Update Protocol) on standards for replication between LDAP servers. Subscribe by sending a message to `ietf-ldup-request@imc.org` that reads "subscribe."

LDAP Servers at Your Disposal

The following are some of the LDAP servers that can be searched over the Internet with anonymous access. You can generally search them with an LDAP URL of the form `ldap://ldap.four11.com//???sn=apocalypse`. In other words, they generally have a suffix of `""`, and from there you can do a subtree search (the default in an LDAP URL) for all attributes (also the default). Some servers, such as Four11, seem to automatically append an asterisk to your search expression, so the search becomes a "begins with" search rather than an "equals" search.

In general, public servers have huge databases, and you will need to specify an extensive search filter to receive a reasonable number of search results. If the search would return more than the maximum allowed by the server (typically 50 or 100), the server may return the first 50 or so results or it may return no results at all. Some servers support searching by `cn` and others by `sn`, `givenName`, `uid`, or `mail`, or a combination of these attributes.

BigFoot: `ldap://ldap.bigfoot.com//`

Four11: `ldap://ldap.four11.com//`

Gottfried Hamm KommunikationsSysteme: `ldap://ldap.ghks.de//`

InfoSpace: `ldap://ldap.infospace.com//`

Netcenter membership directory: `ldap://memberdir.netscape.com//ou=member_directory,o=netcenter.com`

New York University: `ldap://ldap.nyu.edu/o=New%20York%20University,st=New%20York,c=US`

Stanford University: `ldap://directory.stanford.edu//dc=stanford,dc=edu`

SwitchBoard: `ldap://ldap.switchboard.com//c=us`

University of Georgia: `ldap://directory.uga.edu//o=uga,c=us`

University of Houston—Clearlake: `ldap://bigfoot.cl.uh.edu//`

University of Massachusetts: `ldap://home.oit.umass.edu//o=University%20of%20Massachusetts,c=U`

WhoWhere: `ldap://ldap.whowhere.com//`

APPENDIX B

Classes of the LDAP SDK

All the major public classes are presented here, with inheritance and referential relationships indicated. A few of the internal classes are included to illustrate how the SDK manages connections.

The `netscape.ldap` Package

`LDAPConnection` and Connection Management

`LDAPConnection` implements the `LDAPv3` interface (which extends `LDAPv2` and defines all the standard LDAP operations as synchronous methods) and the `LDAPAsynchronousConnection` interface (which defines asynchronous methods for the LDAP operations).

An `LDAPConnThread` manages a physical connection to an LDAP server on behalf of one or more `LDAPConnection` objects. All data to or from the server passes through the socket owned by the `LDAPConnnThread`.

An `LDAPConnSetupMgr` object is responsible for creating a socket for `LDAPConnThread` and for creating a new socket if the server goes down or if network problems cause the connection to be lost. The `LDAPConnSetupMgr` may have a list of servers for transparent failover.

By default, the `LDAPConnSetupMgr` uses `java.net.Socket` to create a connection. However, it can use an optional `LDAPSocketFactory` implementation to create a socket. The SDK does not contain classes for Secure Sockets Layer (SSL) communications, but it does include two implementations of `LDAPSocketFactory` to allow use of third-party SSL implementations. `LDAPSSLSocketFactory` supports the use of third-party packages that can supply an object that extends `java.net.Socket`, and `LDAPSSLSocketWrapFactory` supports packages that provide a `Socket` equivalent that does not extend `java.net.Socket`.

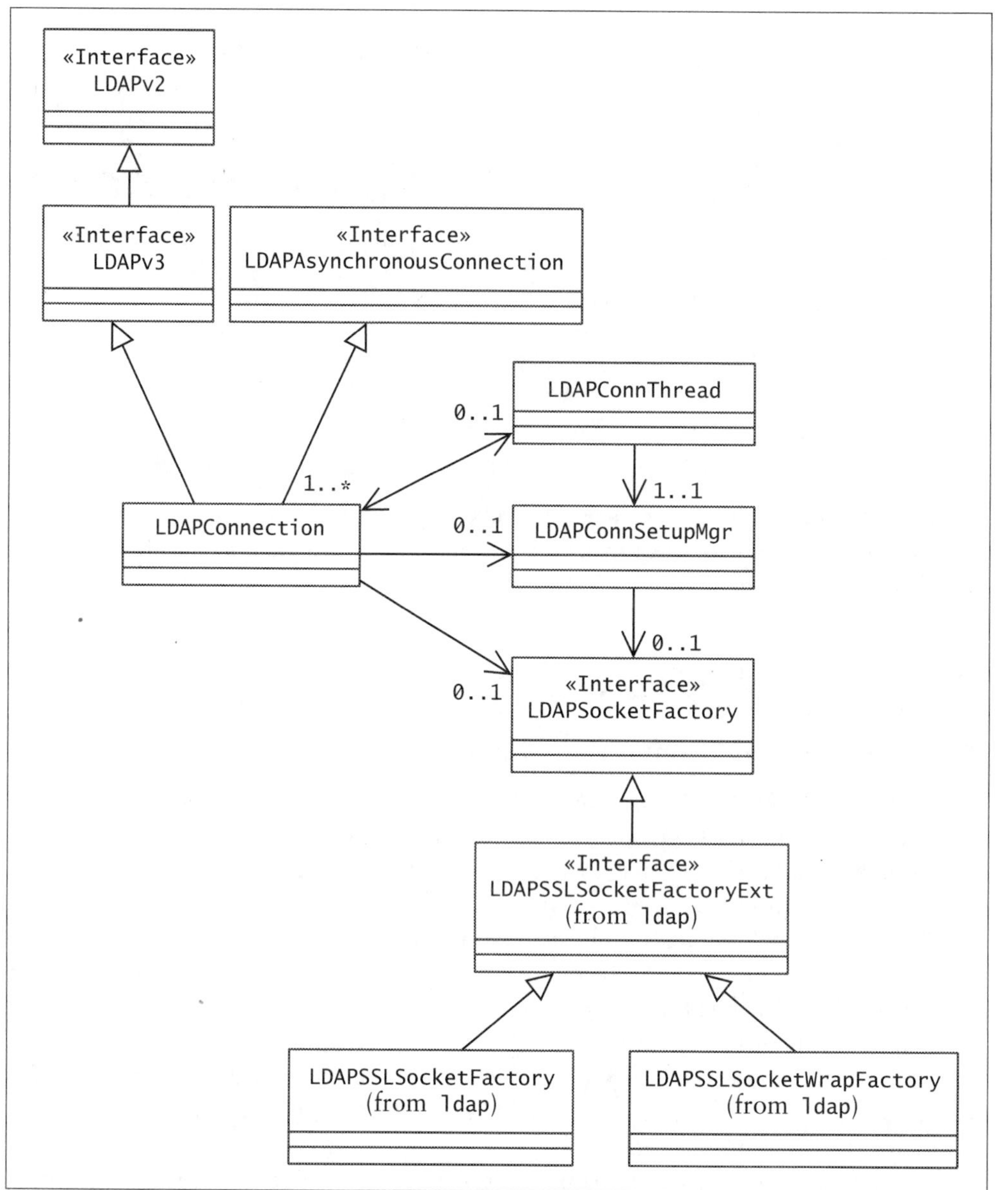

FIGURE B-1. `LDAPConnection` *and connection management.*

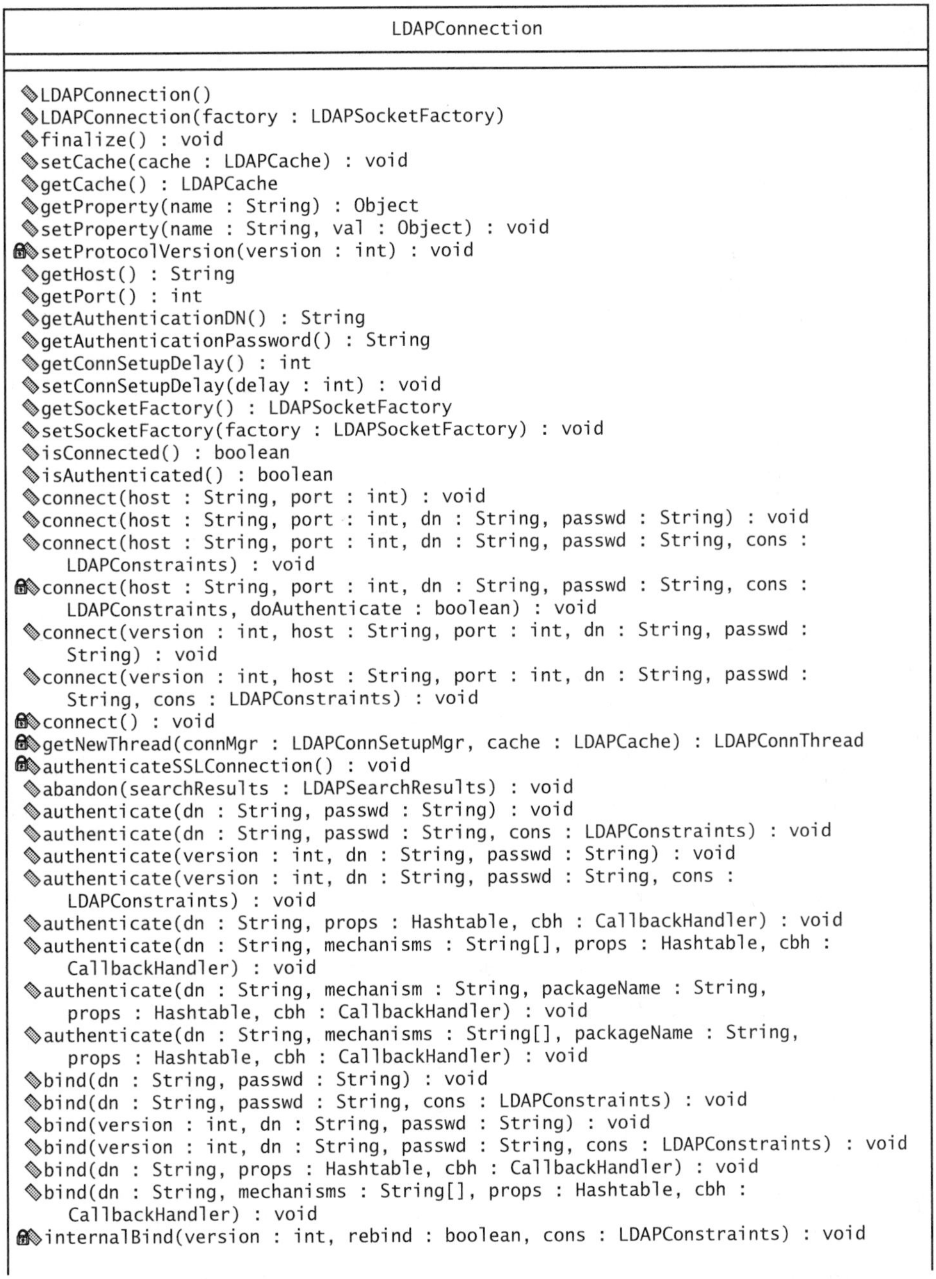

```
LDAPConnection

LDAPConnection()
LDAPConnection(factory : LDAPSocketFactory)
finalize() : void
setCache(cache : LDAPCache) : void
getCache() : LDAPCache
getProperty(name : String) : Object
setProperty(name : String, val : Object) : void
setProtocolVersion(version : int) : void
getHost() : String
getPort() : int
getAuthenticationDN() : String
getAuthenticationPassword() : String
getConnSetupDelay() : int
setConnSetupDelay(delay : int) : void
getSocketFactory() : LDAPSocketFactory
setSocketFactory(factory : LDAPSocketFactory) : void
isConnected() : boolean
isAuthenticated() : boolean
connect(host : String, port : int) : void
connect(host : String, port : int, dn : String, passwd : String) : void
connect(host : String, port : int, dn : String, passwd : String, cons :
   LDAPConstraints) : void
connect(host : String, port : int, dn : String, passwd : String, cons :
   LDAPConstraints, doAuthenticate : boolean) : void
connect(version : int, host : String, port : int, dn : String, passwd :
   String) : void
connect(version : int, host : String, port : int, dn : String, passwd :
   String, cons : LDAPConstraints) : void
connect() : void
getNewThread(connMgr : LDAPConnSetupMgr, cache : LDAPCache) : LDAPConnThread
authenticateSSLConnection() : void
abandon(searchResults : LDAPSearchResults) : void
authenticate(dn : String, passwd : String) : void
authenticate(dn : String, passwd : String, cons : LDAPConstraints) : void
authenticate(version : int, dn : String, passwd : String) : void
authenticate(version : int, dn : String, passwd : String, cons :
   LDAPConstraints) : void
authenticate(dn : String, props : Hashtable, cbh : CallbackHandler) : void
authenticate(dn : String, mechanisms : String[], props : Hashtable, cbh :
   CallbackHandler) : void
authenticate(dn : String, mechanism : String, packageName : String,
   props : Hashtable, cbh : CallbackHandler) : void
authenticate(dn : String, mechanisms : String[], packageName : String,
   props : Hashtable, cbh : CallbackHandler) : void
bind(dn : String, passwd : String) : void
bind(dn : String, passwd : String, cons : LDAPConstraints) : void
bind(version : int, dn : String, passwd : String) : void
bind(version : int, dn : String, passwd : String, cons : LDAPConstraints) : void
bind(dn : String, props : Hashtable, cbh : CallbackHandler) : void
bind(dn : String, mechanisms : String[], props : Hashtable, cbh :
   CallbackHandler) : void
internalBind(version : int, rebind : boolean, cons : LDAPConstraints) : void
```

FIGURE B-2. LDAPConnection.

```
updateThreadConnTable() : void
sendRequest(oper : JDAPProtocolOp, myListener : LDAPMessageQueue, cons :
    LDAPConstraints) : void
internalBind(cons : LDAPConstraints) : void
reconnect() : void
disconnect() : void
deleteThreadConnEntry() : void
deregisterConnection() : void
read(DN : String) : LDAPEntry
read(DN : String, cons : LDAPSearchConstraints) : LDAPEntry
read(DN : String, attrs[] : String) : LDAPEntry
read(DN : String, attrs[] : String, cons : LDAPSearchConstraints) : LDAPEntry
read(toGet : LDAPUrl) : LDAPEntry
search(toGet : LDAPUrl) : LDAPSearchResults
search(toGet : LDAPUrl, cons : LDAPSearchConstraints) : LDAPSearchResults
search(base : String, scope : int, filter : String, attrs : String[], attrsOnly :
    boolean) : LDAPSearchResults
search(base : String, scope : int, filter : String, attrs : String[], attrsOnly :
    boolean, cons : LDAPSearchConstraints) : LDAPSearchResults
checkSearchMsg(value : LDAPSearchResults, msg : LDAPMessage, cons :
    LDAPSearchConstraints, dn : String, scope : int, filter : String, attrs[] :
    String, attrsOnly : boolean) : void
compare(DN : String, attr : LDAPAttribute) : boolean
compare(DN : String, attr : LDAPAttribute, cons : LDAPConstraints) : boolean
add(entry : LDAPEntry) : void
add(entry : LDAPEntry, cons : LDAPConstraints) : void
extendedOperation(op : LDAPExtendedOperation) : LDAPExtendedOperation
extendedOperation(op : LDAPExtendedOperation, cons : LDAPConstraints) :
    LDAPExtendedOperation
modify(DN : String, mod : LDAPModification) : void
modify(DN : String, mod : LDAPModification, cons : LDAPConstraints) : void
modify(DN : String, mods : LDAPModificationSet) : void
modify(DN : String, mods : LDAPModificationSet, cons : LDAPConstraints) : void
modify(DN : String, mods : LDAPModification[]) : void
modify(DN : String, mods : LDAPModification[], cons : LDAPConstraints) : void
delete(DN : String) : void
delete(DN : String, cons : LDAPConstraints) : void
rename(DN : String, newRDN : String, deleteOldRDN : boolean) : void
rename(DN : String, newRDN : String, deleteOldRDN : boolean, cons :
    LDAPConstraints) : void
rename(dn : String, newRDN : String, newParentDN : String, deleteOldRDN :
    boolean) : void
rename(DN : String, newRDN : String, newParentDN : String, deleteOldRDN :
    boolean, cons : LDAPConstraints) : void
add(entry : LDAPEntry, listener : LDAPResponseListener) : LDAPResponseListener
add(entry : LDAPEntry, listener : LDAPResponseListener, cons : LDAPConstraints) :
    LDAPResponseListener
bind(dn : String, passwd : String, listener : LDAPResponseListener) :
    LDAPResponseListener
bind(dn : String, passwd : String, listener : LDAPResponseListener, cons :
    LDAPConstraints) : LDAPResponseListener
bind(dn : String, mechanisms : String[], packageName : String, props : Properties,
    cbh : CallbackHandler, listener : LDAPResponseListener) : LDAPResponseListener
bind(dn : String, mechanisms : String[], packageName : String, props :
    Properties, cbh : CallbackHandler, listener : LDAPResponseListener, cons :
    LDAPConstraints) : LDAPResponseListener
delete(dn : String, listener : LDAPResponseListener) : LDAPResponseListener
delete(dn : String, listener : LDAPResponseListener, cons : LDAPConstraints) :
    LDAPResponseListener
```

FIGURE B-2. LDAPConnection *(continued)*.

```
modify(dn : String, mod : LDAPModification, listener : LDAPResponseListener) :
    LDAPResponseListener
modify(dn : String, mod : LDAPModification, listener : LDAPResponseListener,
    cons : LDAPConstraints) : LDAPResponseListener
modify(dn : String, mods : LDAPModificationSet, listener : LDAPResponseListener) :
    LDAPResponseListener
modify(dn : String, mods : LDAPModificationSet, listener : LDAPResponseListener,
    cons : LDAPConstraints) : LDAPResponseListener
rename(dn : String, newRdn : String, deleteOldRdn : boolean, listener :
    LDAPResponseListener) : LDAPResponseListener
rename(dn : String, newRdn : String, deleteOldRdn : boolean, listener :
    LDAPResponseListener, cons : LDAPConstraints) : LDAPResponseListener
search(base : String, scope : int, filter : String, attrs[] : String, typesOnly :
    boolean, listener : LDAPSearchListener) : LDAPSearchListener
search(base : String, scope : int, filter : String, attrs[] : String, typesOnly :
    boolean, listener : LDAPSearchListener, cons : LDAPSearchConstraints) :
    LDAPSearchListener
compare(dn : String, attr : LDAPAttribute, listener : LDAPResponseListener) :
    LDAPResponseListener
compare(dn : String, attr : LDAPAttribute, listener : LDAPResponseListener, cons :
    LDAPConstraints) : LDAPResponseListener
abandon(id : int) : void
abandon(searchlistener : LDAPSearchListener) : void
getOption(option : int) : Object
getOption(option : int, cons : LDAPSearchConstraints) : Object
setOption(option : int, value : Object) : void
setOption(option : int, value : Object, cons : LDAPSearchConstraints) : void
getResponseControls() : LDAPControl[]
getConstraints() : LDAPConstraints
getSearchConstraints() : LDAPSearchConstraints
setConstraints(cons : LDAPConstraints) : void
setSearchConstraints(cons : LDAPSearchConstraints) : void
getInputStream() : InputStream
setInputStream(is : InputStream) : void
getOutputStream() : OutputStream
setOutputStream(os : OutputStream) : void
getResponseListener() : LDAPResponseListener
getSearchListener(cons : LDAPSearchConstraints) : LDAPSearchListener
releaseResponseListener(l : LDAPResponseListener) : void
releaseSearchListener(l : LDAPSearchListener) : void
checkMsg(m : LDAPMessage) : void
setResponseControls(current : LDAPConnThread, con : LDAPResponseControl) : void
prepareReferral(u : LDAPUrl, cons : LDAPConstraints) : LDAPConnection
createReferralConnection(e : LDAPReferralException, cons : LDAPConstraints) :
    LDAPConnection
performReferrals(e : LDAPReferralException, cons : LDAPConstraints, ops : int,
    dn : String, scope : int, filter : String, types[] : String, attrsOnly :
    boolean, mods[] : LDAPModification, entry : LDAPEntry, attr : LDAPAttribute,
    results : Vector) : void
performReferrals(connection : LDAPConnection, cons : LDAPConstraints, ops : int,
    dn : String, scope : int, filter : String, types[] : String, attrsOnly :
    boolean, mods[] : LDAPModification, entry : LDAPEntry, attr : LDAPAttribute,
    results : Vector) : void
performExtendedReferrals(e : LDAPReferralException, cons : LDAPConstraints, op :
    LDAPExtendedOperation) : LDAPExtendedOperation
clone() : Object
resultRetrieved() : void
checkCommunicator() : boolean
isNetscape() : boolean
printDebug(msg : String) : void
main(args : String[]) : void
```

FIGURE B-2. LDAPConnection *(continued)*.

```
performReferrals(e : LDAPReferralException, cons : LDAPConstraints, ops : int,
    dn : String, scope : int, filter : String, types[] : String, attrsOnly :
    boolean, mods[] : LDAPModification, entry : LDAPEntry, attr : LDAPAttribute,
    results : Vector) : void
performReferrals(connection : LDAPConnection, cons : LDAPConstraints, ops : int,
    dn : String, scope : int, filter : String, types[] : String, attrsOnly :
    boolean, mods[] : LDAPModification, entry : LDAPEntry, attr : LDAPAttribute,
    results : Vector) : void
performExtendedReferrals(e : LDAPReferralException, cons : LDAPConstraints, op :
    LDAPExtendedOperation) : LDAPExtendedOperation
clone() : Object
resultRetrieved() : void
checkCommunicator() : boolean
isNetscape() : boolean
printDebug(msg : String) : void
main(args : String[]) : void
```

FIGURE B-2. LDAPConnection *(continued).*

Basic LDAP Message and Data Encapsulation

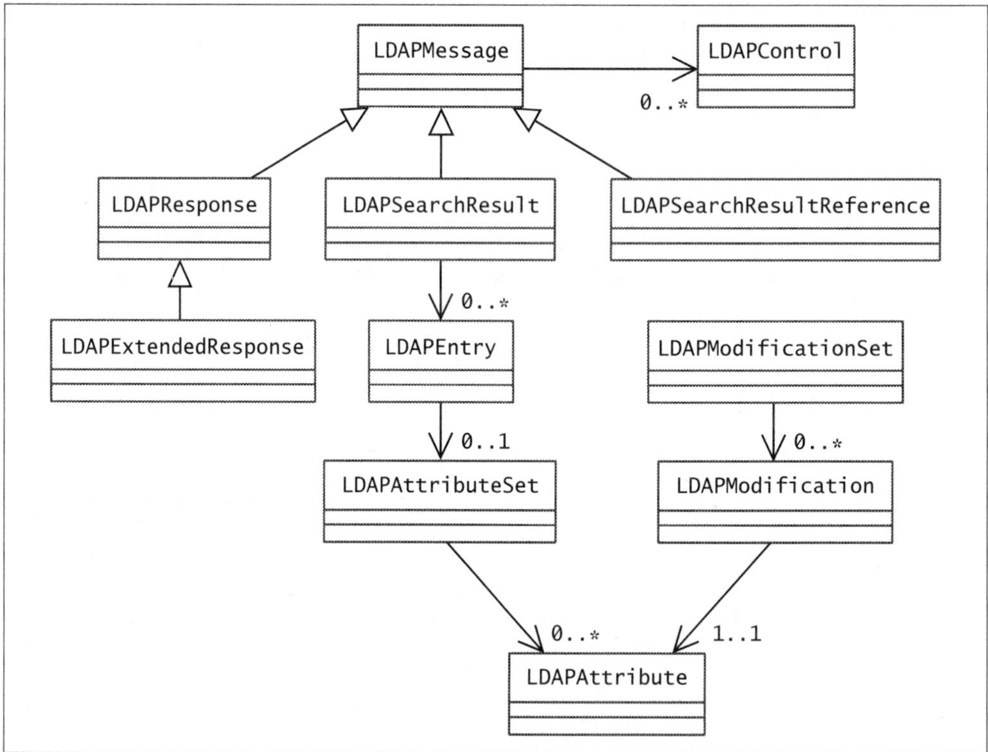

FIGURE B-3. LDAP *message and data types.*

An LDAPSearchResult contains a single LDAPEntry, which consists of a DN and a set of attributes. The LDAPAttributeSet may contain zero or more attributes, each of which contains zero or more values.

An LDAPModification consists of an LDAPAttribute and a specifier for the type of modification. An LDAPModificationSet contains zero or more LDAPModification objects.

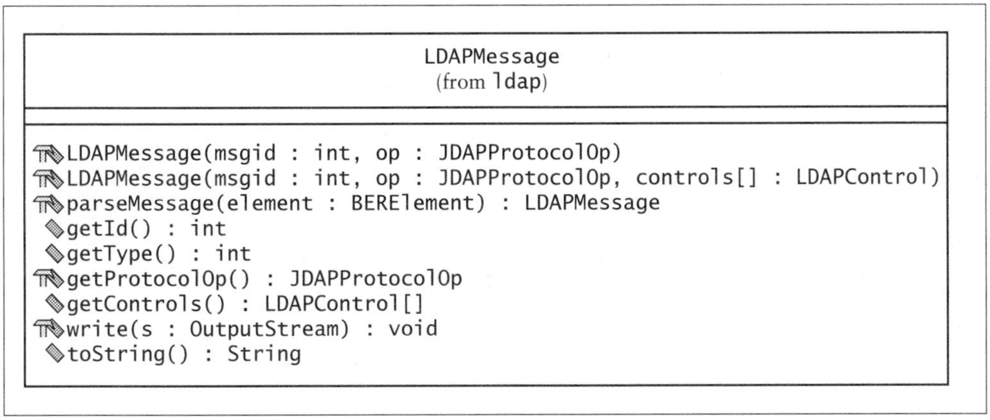

```
LDAPMessage
(from ldap)

LDAPMessage(msgid : int, op : JDAPProtocolOp)
LDAPMessage(msgid : int, op : JDAPProtocolOp, controls[] : LDAPControl)
parseMessage(element : BERElement) : LDAPMessage
getId() : int
getType() : int
getProtocolOp() : JDAPProtocolOp
getControls() : LDAPControl[]
write(s : OutputStream) : void
toString() : String
```

FIGURE B-4. LDAPMessage.

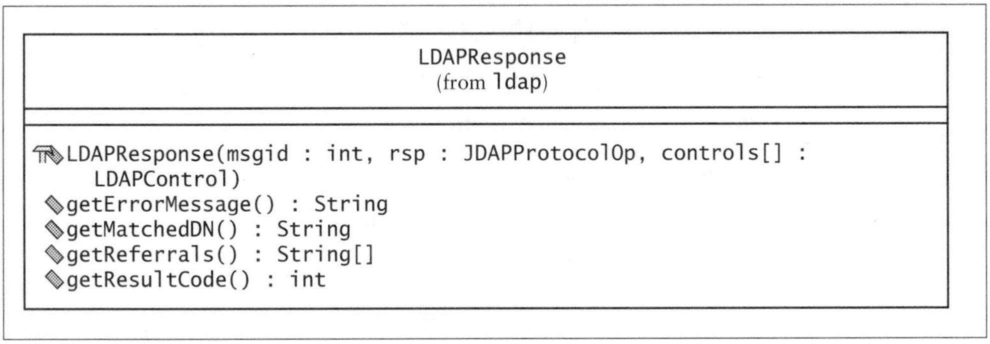

```
LDAPResponse
(from ldap)

LDAPResponse(msgid : int, rsp : JDAPProtocolOp, controls[] :
    LDAPControl)
getErrorMessage() : String
getMatchedDN() : String
getReferrals() : String[]
getResultCode() : int
```

FIGURE B-5. LDAPResponse.

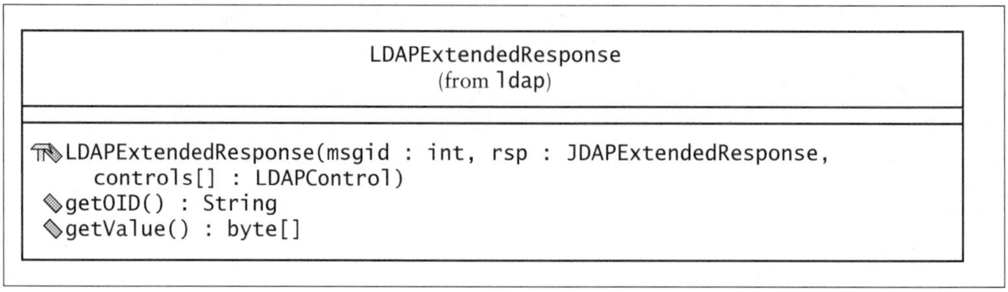

```
LDAPExtendedResponse
(from ldap)

LDAPExtendedResponse(msgid : int, rsp : JDAPExtendedResponse,
    controls[] : LDAPControl)
getOID() : String
getValue() : byte[]
```

FIGURE B-6. LDAPExtendedResponse.

```
LDAPSearchResult
(from ldap)

LDAPSearchResult(msgid : int, rsp : JDAPSearchResponse, controls :
    LDAPControl[])
getEntry() : LDAPEntry
```

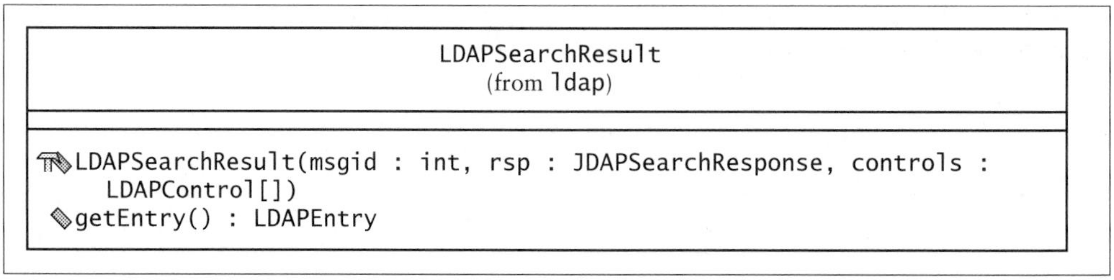

FIGURE B-7. LDAPSearchResult.

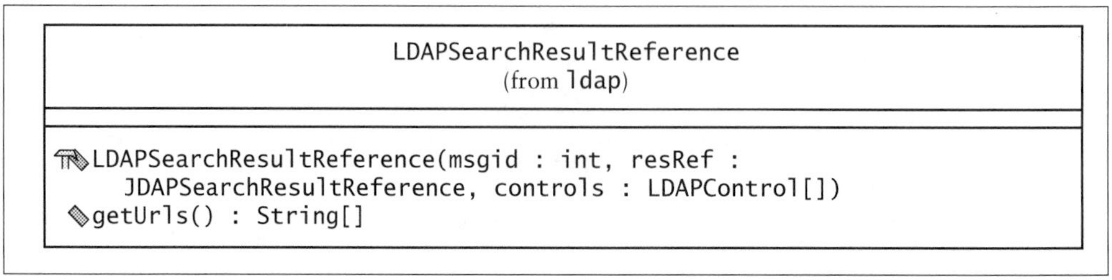

```
LDAPSearchResultReference
(from ldap)

LDAPSearchResultReference(msgid : int, resRef :
    JDAPSearchResultReference, controls : LDAPControl[])
getUrls() : String[]
```

FIGURE B-8. LDAPSearchResultReference.

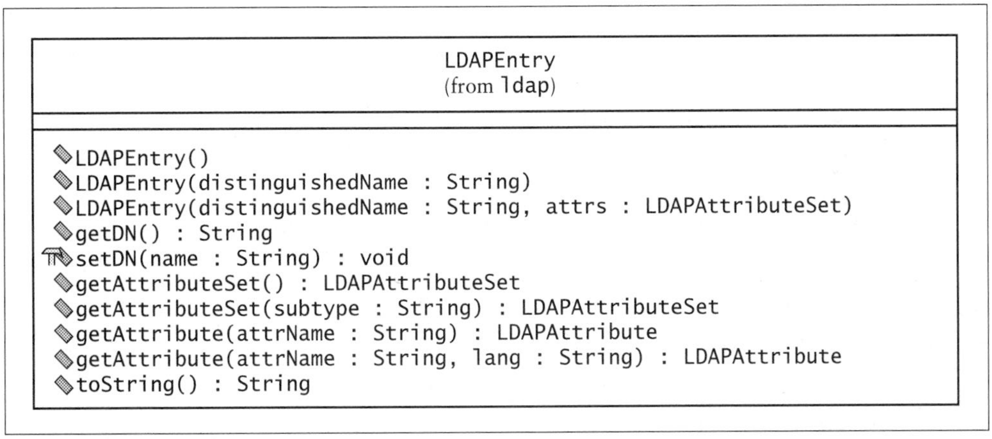

```
LDAPEntry
(from ldap)

LDAPEntry()
LDAPEntry(distinguishedName : String)
LDAPEntry(distinguishedName : String, attrs : LDAPAttributeSet)
getDN() : String
setDN(name : String) : void
getAttributeSet() : LDAPAttributeSet
getAttributeSet(subtype : String) : LDAPAttributeSet
getAttribute(attrName : String) : LDAPAttribute
getAttribute(attrName : String, lang : String) : LDAPAttribute
toString() : String
```

FIGURE B-9. LDAPEntry.

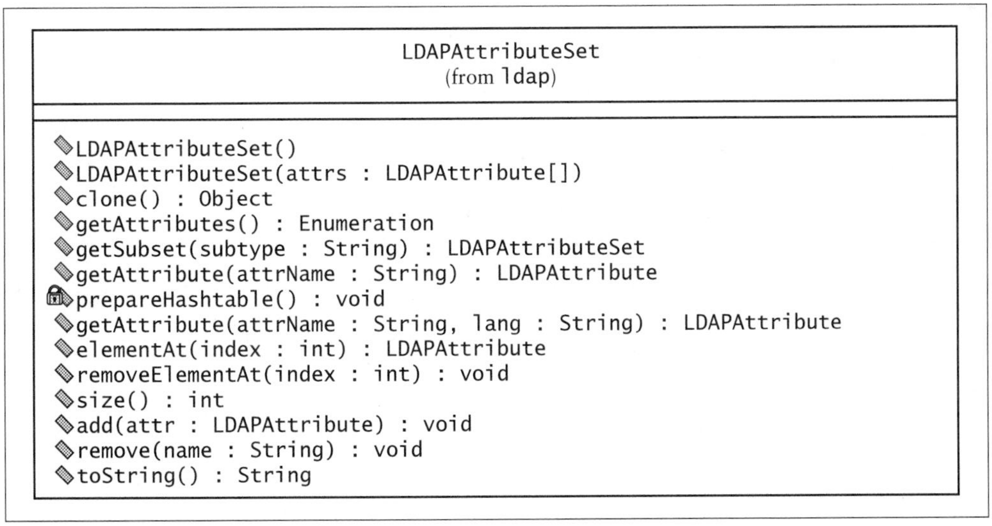

```
LDAPAttributeSet
(from ldap)

LDAPAttributeSet()
LDAPAttributeSet(attrs : LDAPAttribute[])
clone() : Object
getAttributes() : Enumeration
getSubset(subtype : String) : LDAPAttributeSet
getAttribute(attrName : String) : LDAPAttribute
prepareHashtable() : void
getAttribute(attrName : String, lang : String) : LDAPAttribute
elementAt(index : int) : LDAPAttribute
removeElementAt(index : int) : void
size() : int
add(attr : LDAPAttribute) : void
remove(name : String) : void
toString() : String
```

FIGURE B-10. LDAPAttributeSet.

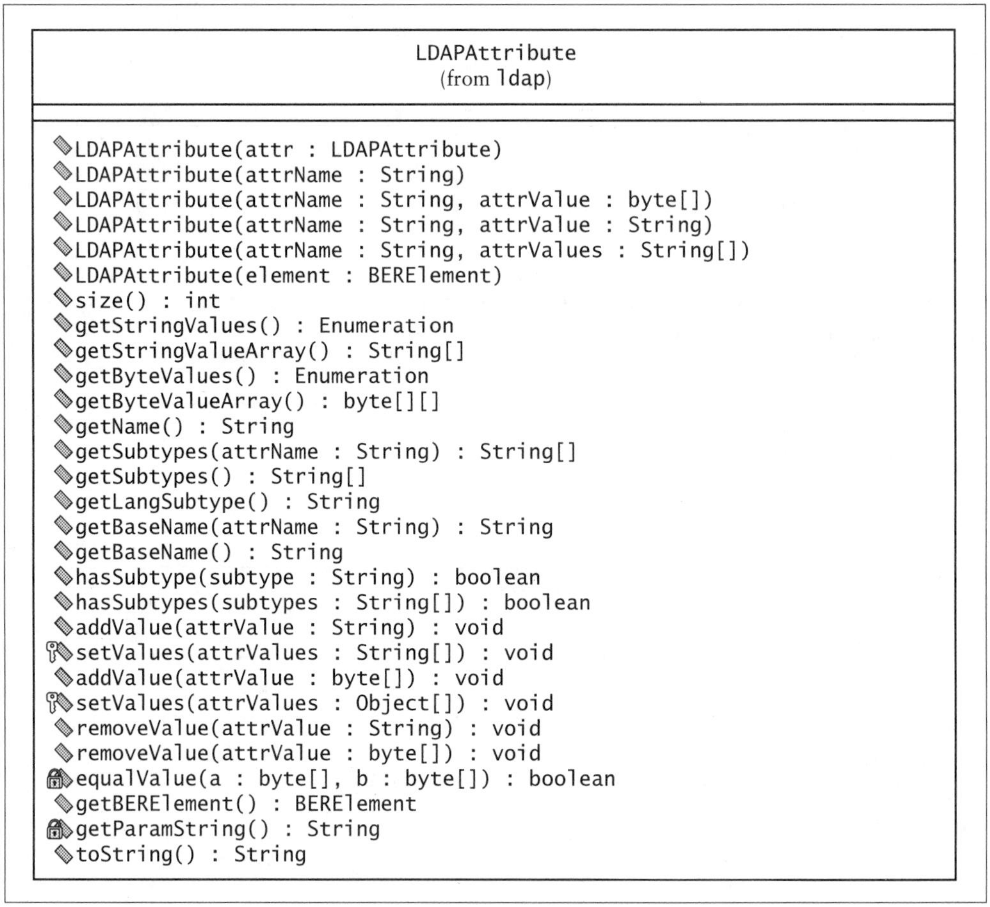

```
LDAPAttribute
(from ldap)

LDAPAttribute(attr : LDAPAttribute)
LDAPAttribute(attrName : String)
LDAPAttribute(attrName : String, attrValue : byte[])
LDAPAttribute(attrName : String, attrValue : String)
LDAPAttribute(attrName : String, attrValues : String[])
LDAPAttribute(element : BERElement)
size() : int
getStringValues() : Enumeration
getStringValueArray() : String[]
getByteValues() : Enumeration
getByteValueArray() : byte[][]
getName() : String
getSubtypes(attrName : String) : String[]
getSubtypes() : String[]
getLangSubtype() : String
getBaseName(attrName : String) : String
getBaseName() : String
hasSubtype(subtype : String) : boolean
hasSubtypes(subtypes : String[]) : boolean
addValue(attrValue : String) : void
setValues(attrValues : String[]) : void
addValue(attrValue : byte[]) : void
setValues(attrValues : Object[]) : void
removeValue(attrValue : String) : void
removeValue(attrValue : byte[]) : void
equalValue(a : byte[], b : byte[]) : boolean
getBERElement() : BERElement
getParamString() : String
toString() : String
```

FIGURE B-11. LDAPAttribute.

```
LDAPModificationSet
(from ldap)

LDAPModificationSet()
size() : int
elementAt(index : int) : LDAPModification
removeElementAt(index : int) : void
add(op : int, attr : LDAPAttribute) : void
remove(name : String) : void
toString() : String
```

FIGURE B-12. LDAPModificationSet.

```
LDAPModification
(from ldap)

LDAPModification(op : int, attr : LDAPAttribute)
getOp() : int
getAttribute() : LDAPAttribute
getBERElement() : BERElement
toString() : String
```

FIGURE B-13. LDAPModification.

Handling Messages from the Server

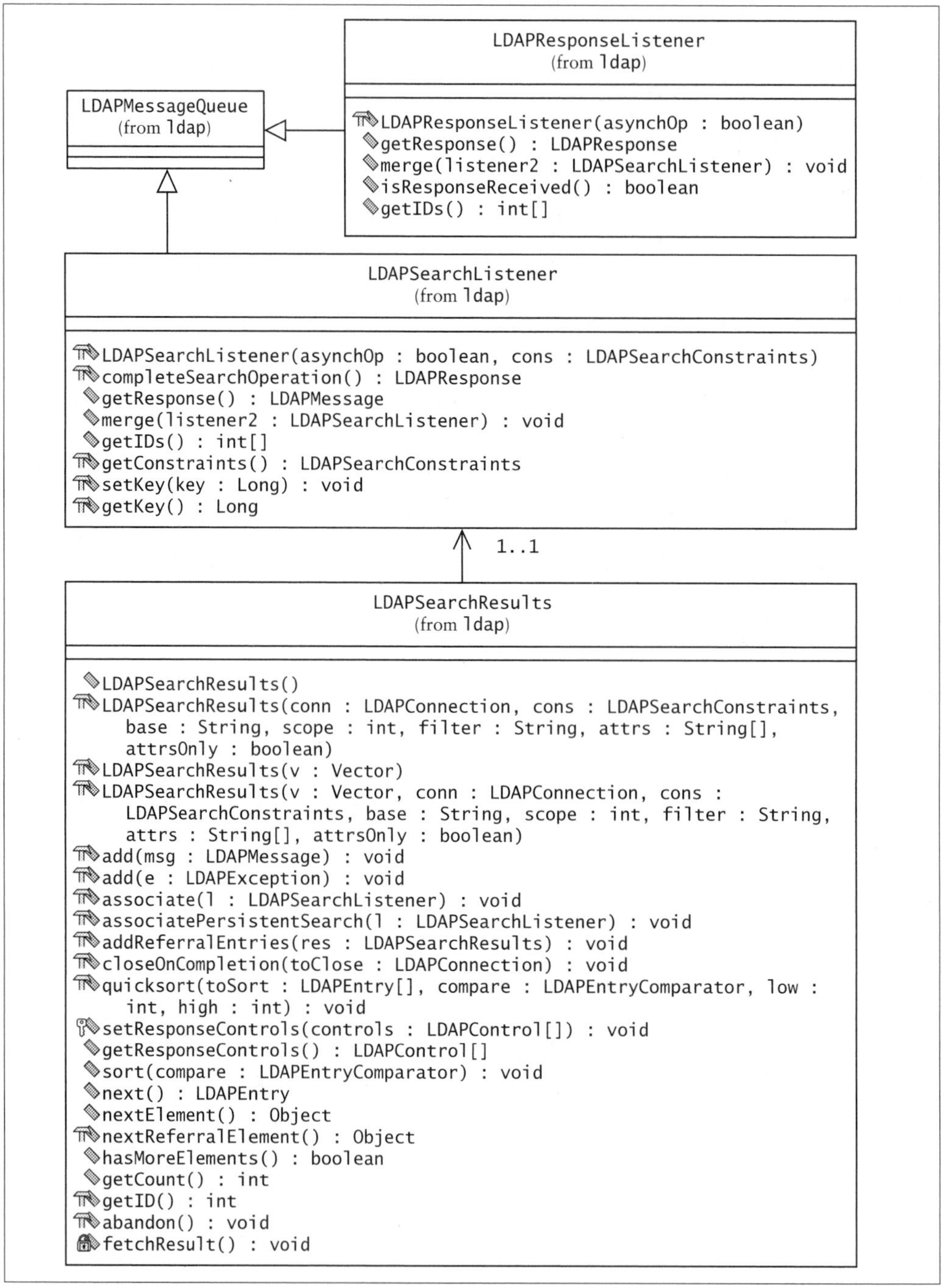

```
LDAPMessageQueue
(from ldap)

LDAPResponseListener
(from ldap)

LDAPResponseListener(asynchOp : boolean)
getResponse() : LDAPResponse
merge(listener2 : LDAPSearchListener) : void
isResponseReceived() : boolean
getIDs() : int[]

LDAPSearchListener
(from ldap)

LDAPSearchListener(asynchOp : boolean, cons : LDAPSearchConstraints)
completeSearchOperation() : LDAPResponse
getResponse() : LDAPMessage
merge(listener2 : LDAPSearchListener) : void
getIDs() : int[]
getConstraints() : LDAPSearchConstraints
setKey(key : Long) : void
getKey() : Long

1..1

LDAPSearchResults
(from ldap)

LDAPSearchResults()
LDAPSearchResults(conn : LDAPConnection, cons : LDAPSearchConstraints,
   base : String, scope : int, filter : String, attrs : String[],
   attrsOnly : boolean)
LDAPSearchResults(v : Vector)
LDAPSearchResults(v : Vector, conn : LDAPConnection, cons :
   LDAPSearchConstraints, base : String, scope : int, filter : String,
   attrs : String[], attrsOnly : boolean)
add(msg : LDAPMessage) : void
add(e : LDAPException) : void
associate(l : LDAPSearchListener) : void
associatePersistentSearch(l : LDAPSearchListener) : void
addReferralEntries(res : LDAPSearchResults) : void
closeOnCompletion(toClose : LDAPConnection) : void
quicksort(toSort : LDAPEntry[], compare : LDAPEntryComparator, low :
   int, high : int) : void
setResponseControls(controls : LDAPControl[]) : void
getResponseControls() : LDAPControl[]
sort(compare : LDAPEntryComparator) : void
next() : LDAPEntry
nextElement() : Object
nextReferralElement() : Object
hasMoreElements() : boolean
getCount() : int
getID() : int
abandon() : void
fetchResult() : void
```

FIGURE B-14. *Message queueing and delivery.*

Every operation (except for unbind) is associated with a message queue for responses from the server. For searches, the queue is implemented by LDAPSearchListener rather than LDAPResponseListener. For synchronous searches, the client of the SDK receives an LDAPSearchResults object as the return value of a search; the client does not interact directly with the listener object. However, when the client iterates through the results, the LDAPSearchResults object obtains results as needed from the listener.

Authentication and Reauthentication

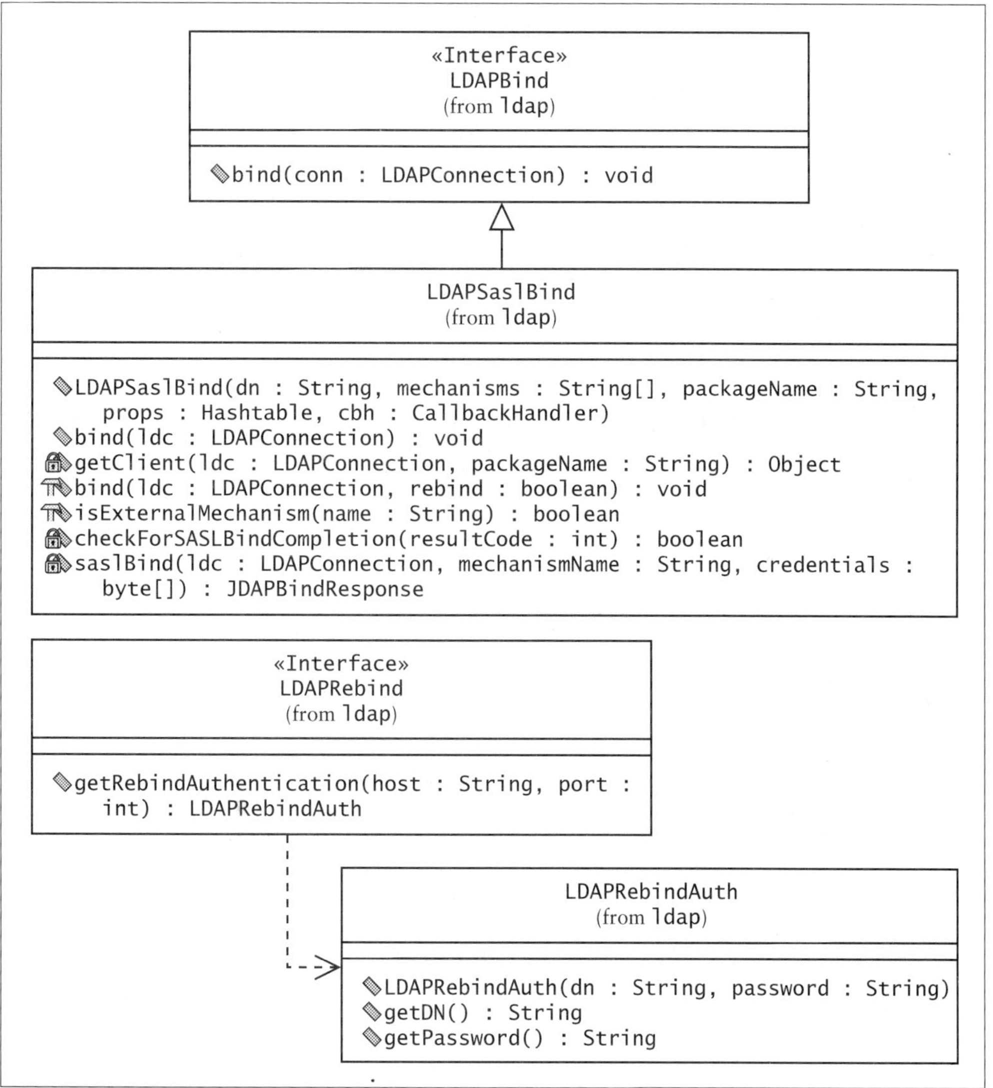

FIGURE B-15. *Classes for authentication and reauthentication.*

You can provide an implementation of either an LDAPRebind or an LDAPBind interface to provide credentials when the SDK is automatically following referrals. The LDAPRebind implementation must produce an LDAPRebindAuth object when a referral is to be followed. An LDAPBind implementation must perform whatever authentication is required for the referral itself. LDAPSaslBind is an internal implementation in the SDK for SASL authentication.

Exceptions

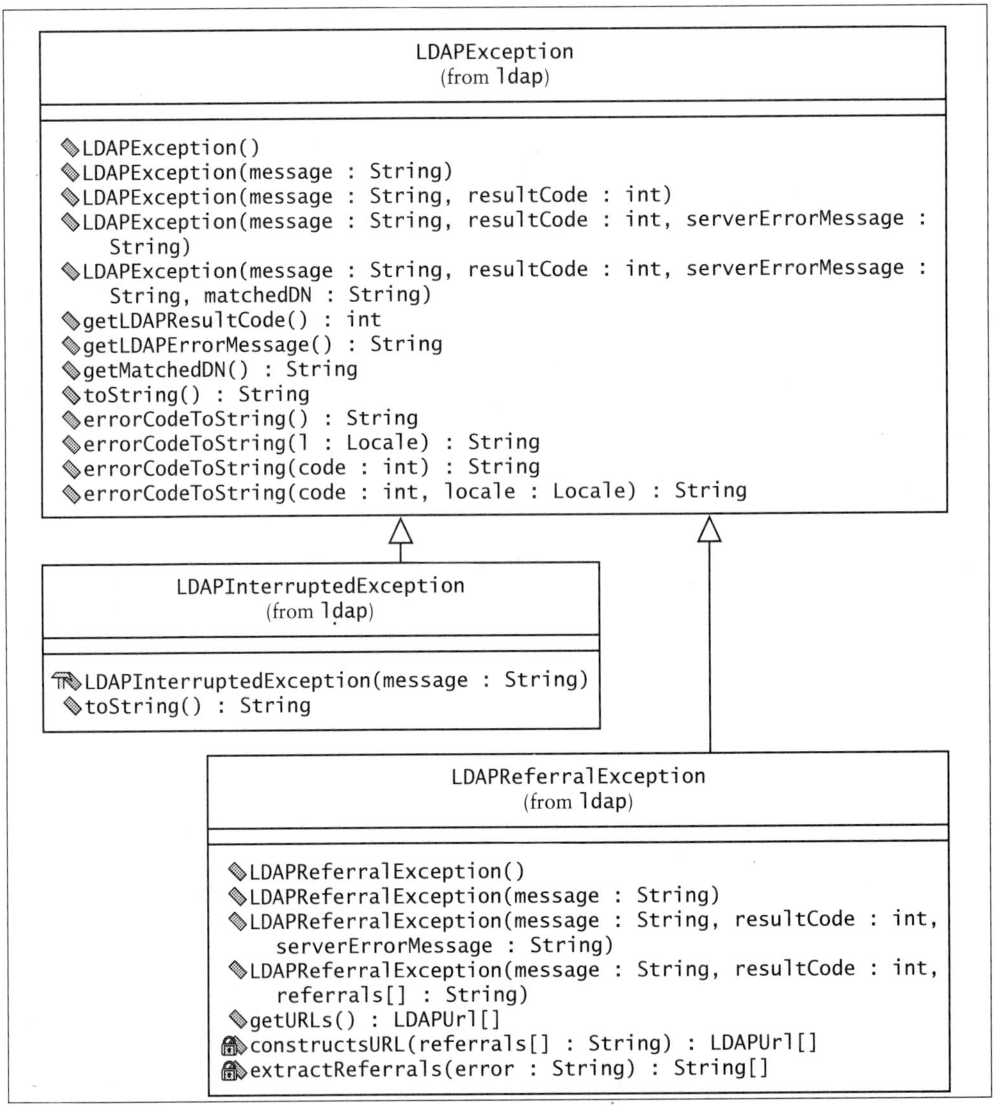

```
LDAPException
(from ldap)

LDAPException()
LDAPException(message : String)
LDAPException(message : String, resultCode : int)
LDAPException(message : String, resultCode : int, serverErrorMessage :
   String)
LDAPException(message : String, resultCode : int, serverErrorMessage :
   String, matchedDN : String)
getLDAPResultCode() : int
getLDAPErrorMessage() : String
getMatchedDN() : String
toString() : String
errorCodeToString() : String
errorCodeToString(l : Locale) : String
errorCodeToString(code : int) : String
errorCodeToString(code : int, locale : Locale) : String

LDAPInterruptedException
(from ldap)

LDAPInterruptedException(message : String)
toString() : String

LDAPReferralException
(from ldap)

LDAPReferralException()
LDAPReferralException(message : String)
LDAPReferralException(message : String, resultCode : int,
   serverErrorMessage : String)
LDAPReferralException(message : String, resultCode : int,
   referrals[] : String)
getURLs() : LDAPUrl[]
constructsURL(referrals[] : String) : LDAPUrl[]
extractReferrals(error : String) : String[]
```

FIGURE B-16. *Exceptions.*

LDAPReferralException is thrown when a referral is encountered during an LDAP operation if automatic referral following has not been enabled. LDAPInterruptedException is thrown if a thread is interrupted during execution of an operation. For all other errors, the base LDAPException is thrown.

Controls

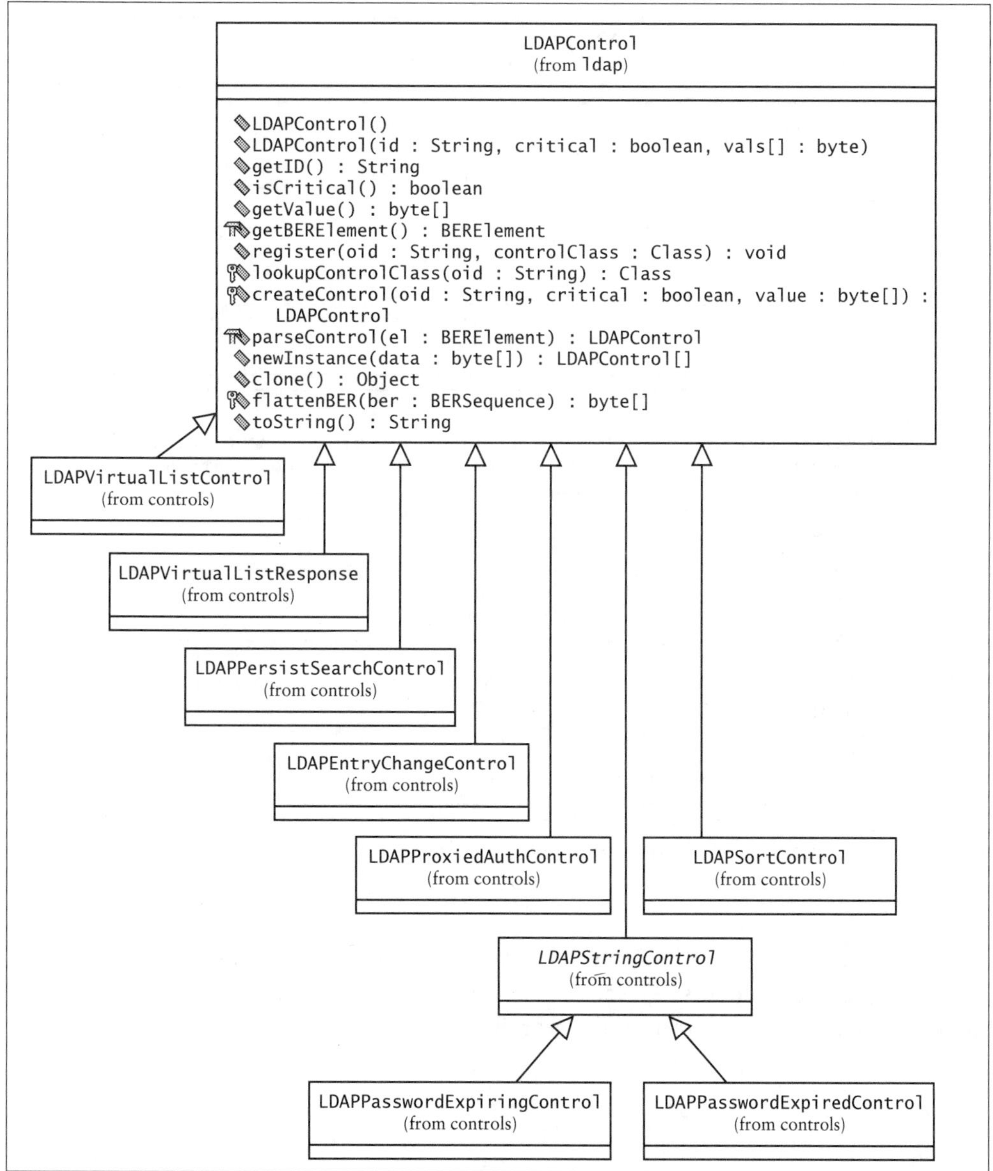

FIGURE B-17. *Controls.*

The base class LDAPControl can instantiate any control that has registered itself, including all the response controls in the SDK. The individual derived classes are responsible for encoding and decoding their individual contents, beyond the OID and criticality flag, which are common to all controls. Derived classes in the SDK belong to the netscape.ldap.controls package.

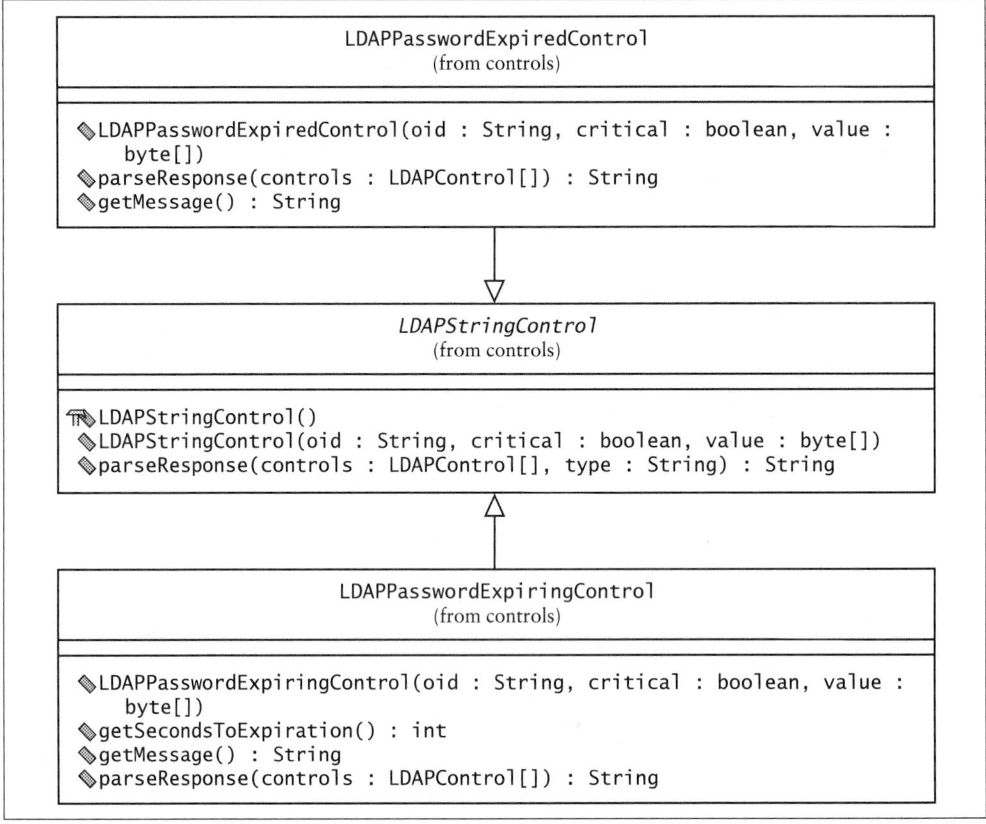

FIGURE B-18. *Password expiration controls.*

A base class LDAPStringControl provides support for managing a simple String as control contents. The two password expiration controls extend LDAPStringControl to interpret the stored value.

```
LDAPEntryChangeControl
(from controls)

LDAPEntryChangeControl()
LDAPEntryChangeControl(oid : String, critical : boolean, value :
   byte[])
setChangeNumber(num : int) : void
setChangeType(num : int) : void
setPreviousDN(dn : String) : void
getChangeNumber() : int
getChangeType() : int
getPreviousDN() : String
toString() : String
```

FIGURE B-19. LDAPEntryChangeControl.

```
LDAPPersistSearchControl
(from controls)

LDAPPersistSearchControl()
LDAPPersistSearchControl(changeTypes : int, changesOnly : boolean,
   returnControls : boolean, isCritical : boolean)
getChangeTypes() : int
getChangesOnly() : boolean
getReturnControls() : boolean
setChangeTypes(types : int) : void
setChangesOnly(changesOnly : boolean) : void
setReturnControls(returnControls : boolean) : void
parseResponse(c : byte[]) : LDAPEntryChangeControl
parseResponse(controls : LDAPControl[]) : LDAPEntryChangeControl
createPersistSearchSpecification(changeTypes : int, changesOnly :
   boolean, returnECs : boolean) : byte[]
toString() : String
typesToString(changeTypes : int) : String
```

FIGURE B-20. LDAPPersistSearchControl.

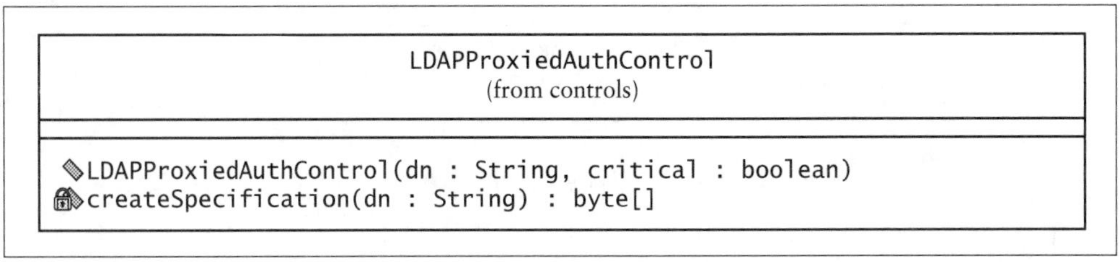

```
LDAPProxiedAuthControl
(from controls)

LDAPProxiedAuthControl(dn : String, critical : boolean)
createSpecification(dn : String) : byte[]
```

FIGURE B-21. LDAPProxiedAuthControl.

```
LDAPSortControl
(from controls)

LDAPSortControl(oid : String, critical : boolean, value : byte[])
getFailedAttribute() : String
getResultCode() : int
LDAPSortControl(key : LDAPSortKey, critical : boolean)
LDAPSortControl(keys : LDAPSortKey[], critical : boolean)
parseResponse(controls : LDAPControl[], results : int[]) : String
createSortSpecification(keys : LDAPSortKey[]) : byte[]
```

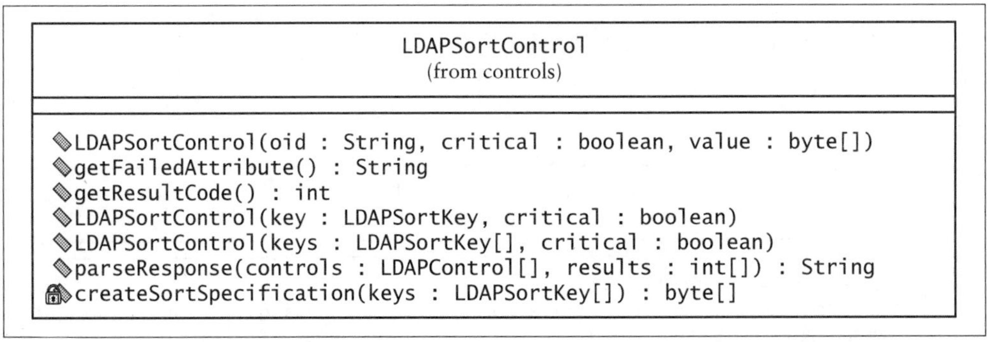

FIGURE B-22. LDAPSortControl.

```
LDAPVirtualListControl
(from controls)

LDAPVirtualListControl()
LDAPVirtualListControl(jumpTo : String, beforeCount : int, afterCount :
    int)
LDAPVirtualListControl(jumpTo : String, beforeCount : int, afterCount :
    int, context : String)
LDAPVirtualListControl(startIndex : int, beforeCount : int,
    afterCount : int, contentCount : int)
LDAPVirtualListControl(startIndex : int, beforeCount : int,
    afterCount : int, contentCount : int, context : String)
setRange(startIndex : int, beforeCount : int, afterCount : int) : void
setRange(jumpTo : String, beforeCount : int, afterCount : int) : void
getIndex() : int
getListSize() : int
setListSize(listSize : int) : void
getBeforeCount() : int
getAfterCount() : int
getContext() : String
setContext(context : String) : void
createPageSpecification(subFilter : String, beforeCount : int,
    afterCount : int) : byte[]
createPageSpecification(listIndex : int, listSize : int, beforeCount :
    int, afterCount : int) : byte[]
```

FIGURE B-23. LDAPVirtualListControl.

```
LDAPVirtualListResponse
(from controls)

LDAPVirtualListResponse()
LDAPVirtualListResponse(oid : String, critical : boolean, value :
    byte[])
LDAPVirtualListResponse(value : byte[])
getContentCount() : int
getFirstPosition() : int
getResultCode() : int
getContext() : String
parseResponse() : void
parseResponse(controls : LDAPControl[]) : LDAPVirtualListResponse
```

FIGURE B-24. LDAPVirtualListResponse.

Caching

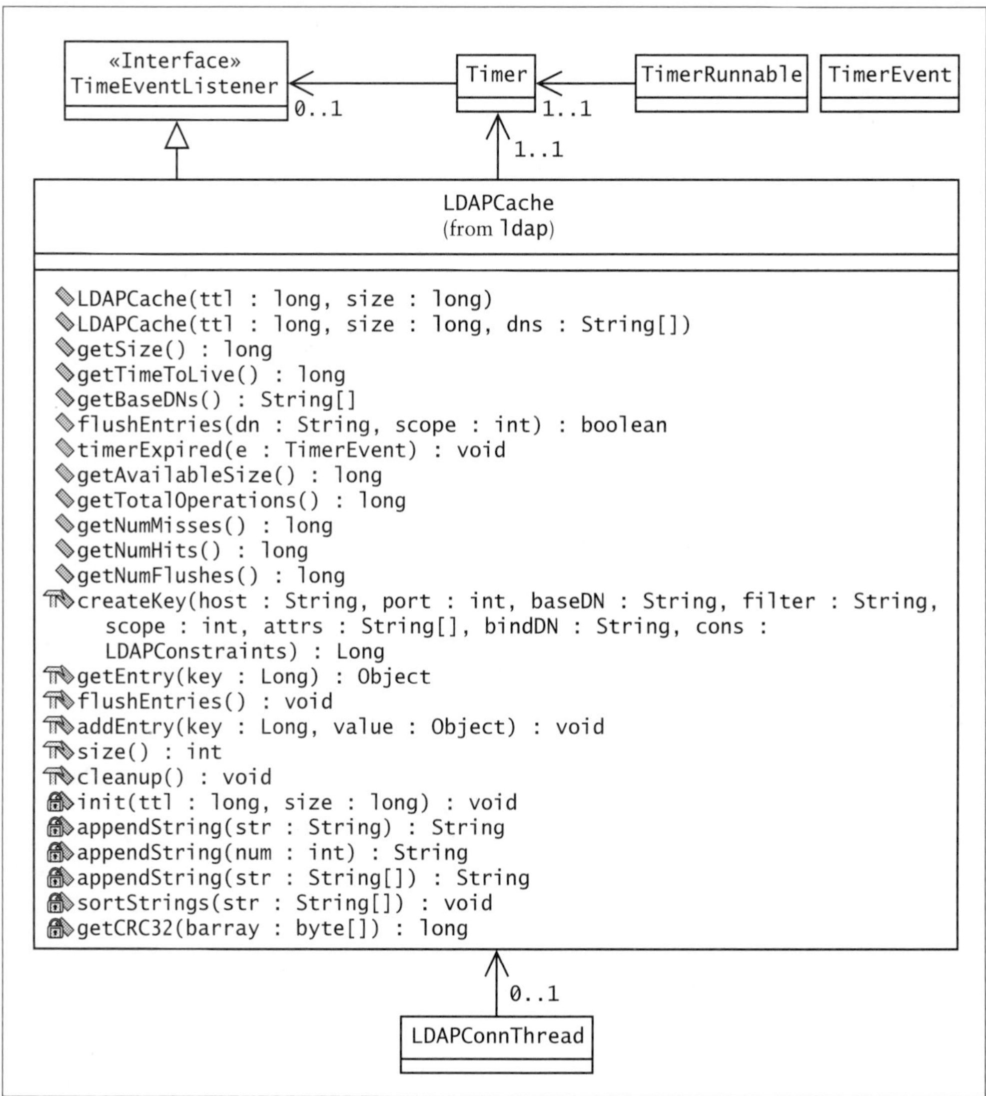

FIGURE B-25. *Caching.*

An LDAPConnThread object may have a cache, which uses a timer to expire any cached results.

Client-Side Sorting

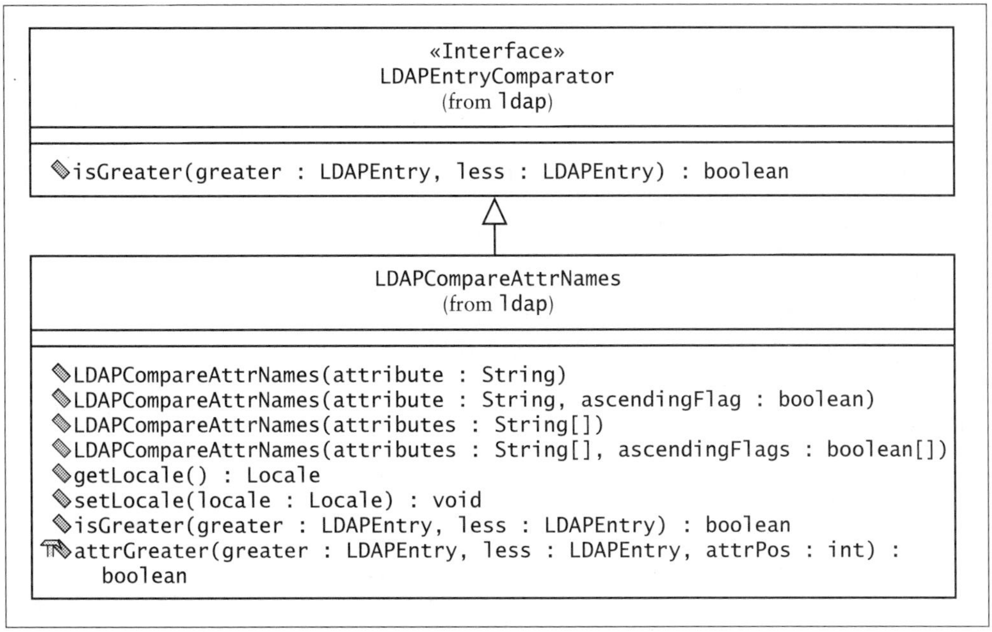

FIGURE B-26. *Entry comparison interface and implementation.*

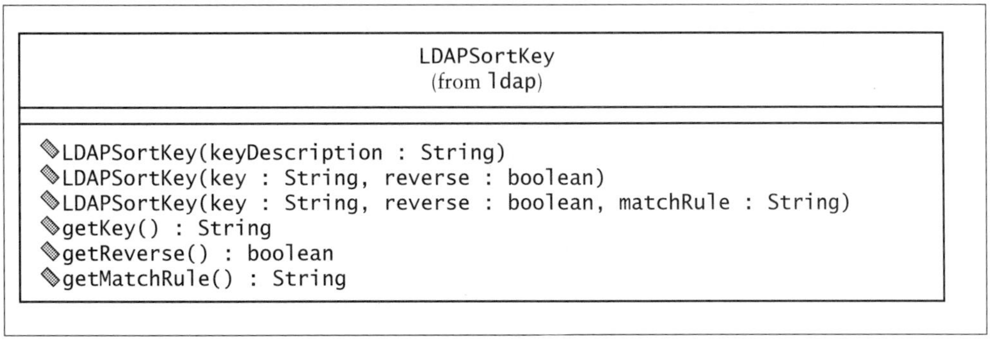

FIGURE B-27. LDAPSortKey.

Schema Representation

```
LDAPSchema
(from ldap)

LDAPSchema()
addObjectClass(objectSchema : LDAPObjectClassSchema) : void
addAttribute(attrSchema : LDAPAttributeSchema) : void
addMatchingRule(matchSchema : LDAPMatchingRuleSchema) : void
getObjectClasses() : Enumeration
getAttributes() : Enumeration
getMatchingRules() : Enumeration
getObjectClass(name : String) : LDAPObjectClassSchema
getAttribute(name : String) : LDAPAttributeSchema
getMatchingRule(name : String) : LDAPMatchingRuleSchema
getObjectClassNames() : Enumeration
getAttributeNames() : Enumeration
getMatchingRuleNames() : Enumeration
fetchSchema(ld : LDAPConnection, dn : String) : void
fetchSchema(ld : LDAPConnection) : void
isAttributeSyntaxStandardsCompliant(ld : LDAPConnection) : boolean
toString() : String
getSchemaDN(ld : LDAPConnection, dn : String) : String
readSchema(ld : LDAPConnection, dn : String, attrs : String[]) :
   LDAPEntry
readSchema(ld : LDAPConnection, dn : String) : LDAPEntry
printEnum(en : Enumeration) : void
main(args : String[]) : void
```

FIGURE B-28. LDAPSchema.

LDAPSchema fetches the schema from a server and then allows a client to access the various elements of the schema.

```
LDAPSchemaElement
(from ldap)

LDAPSchemaElement()
LDAPSchemaElement(name : String, oid : String, description : String)
getName() : String
getOID() : String
getDescription() : String
update(ld : LDAPConnection, op : int, attr : LDAPAttribute, dn :
    String) : void
update(ld : LDAPConnection, op : int, attrs : LDAPAttribute[], dn :
    String) : void
update(ld : LDAPConnection, op : int, name : String, dn :
    String) : void
add(ld : LDAPConnection, dn : String) : void
add(ld : LDAPConnection) : void
modify(ld : LDAPConnection, newValue : LDAPSchemaElement, dn :
    String) : void
modify(ld : LDAPConnection, newValue : LDAPSchemaElement) : void
remove(ld : LDAPConnection, dn : String) : void
remove(ld : LDAPConnection) : void
isObsolete() : boolean
parseValue(raw : String) : void
getValue() : String
getValue(quotingBug : boolean) : String
getValuePrefix() : String
getOptionalValues(names : String[]) : String
getCustomValues() : String
getValue(key : String, doQuote : boolean) : String
setQualifier(name : String, value : String) : void
setQualifier(name : String, values : String[]) : void
getQualifier(name : String) : String[]
getQualifierNames() : Enumeration
getQualifierString(ignore : String[]) : String
```

FIGURE B-29. LDAPSchemaElement.

Most schema element functionality is provided by the abstract base class LDAPSchemaElement.

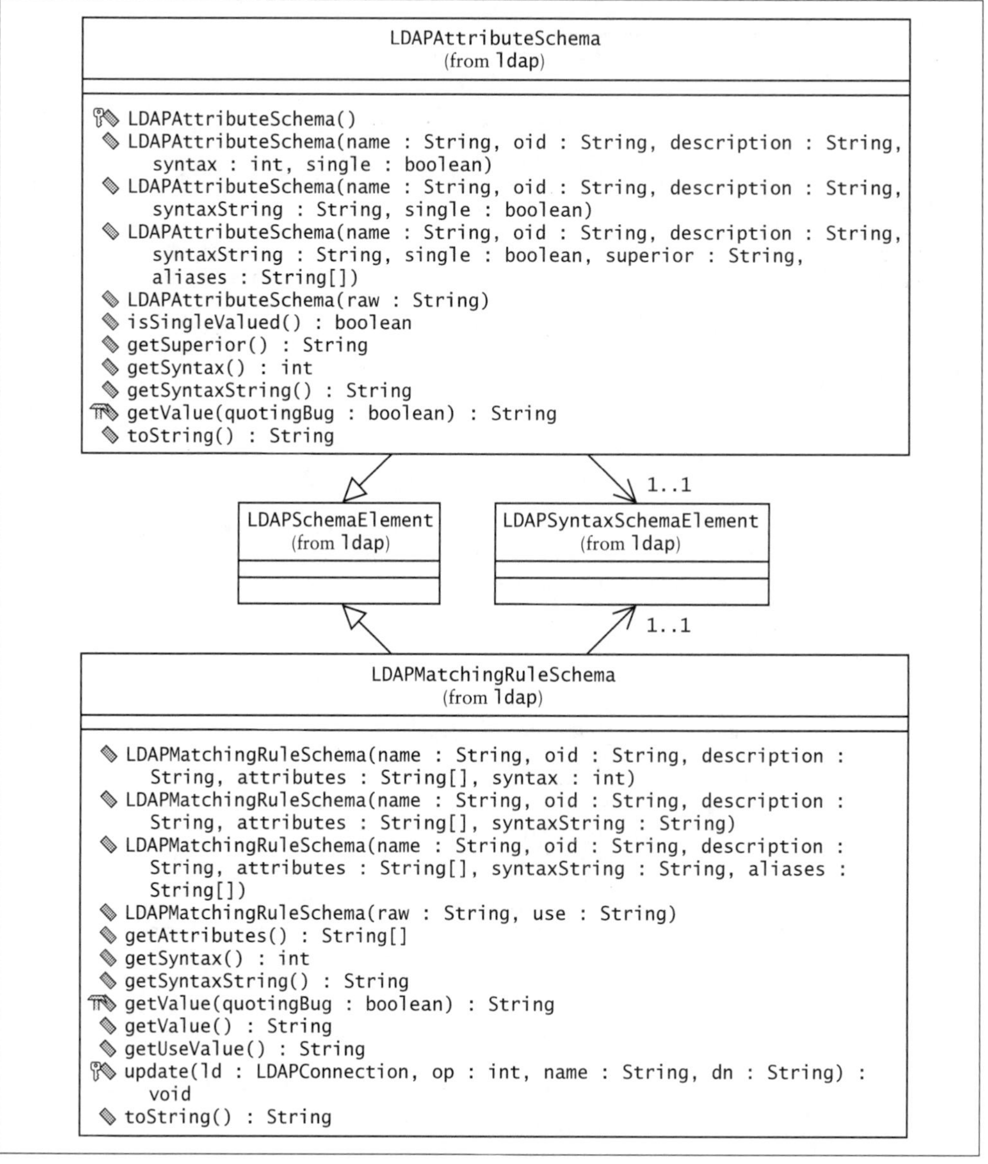

FIGURE B-30. *Attribute and matching-rule schema elements.*

Much of the common functionality of `LDAPAttributeSchema` and `LDAPMatchingRuleSchema` is encapsulated in the common base class `LDAPSchemaElement`. Both concrete classes delegate responsibility for syntax management, including conversions between `OID` and a string representation, to an `LDAPSyntaxElement` object.

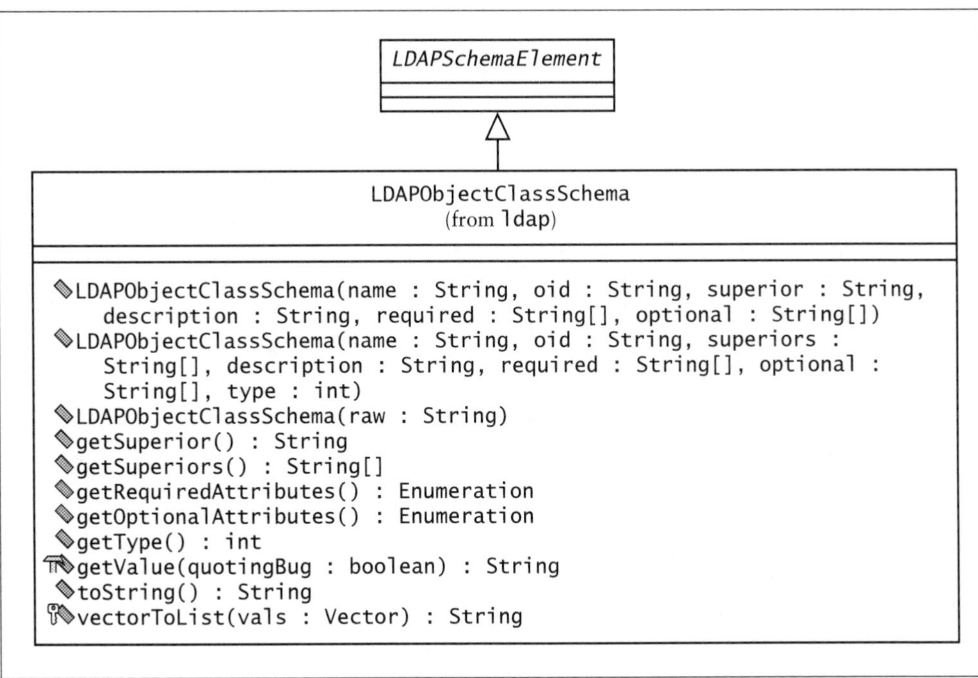

FIGURE B-31. LDAPObjectClassSchema.

Miscellaneous Utility Classes

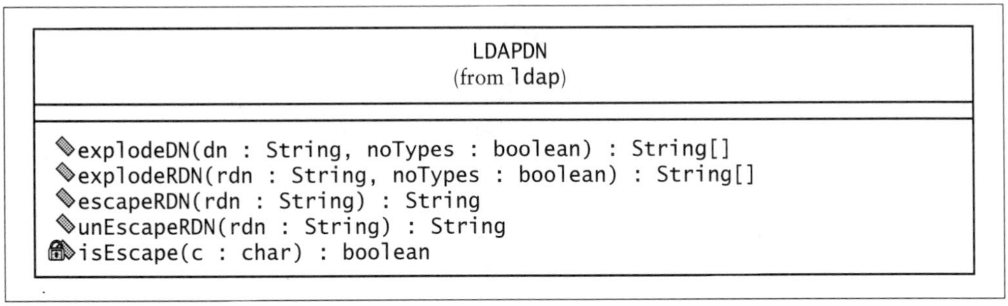

LDAPDN
(from ldap)

explodeDN(dn : String, noTypes : boolean) : String[]
explodeRDN(rdn : String, noTypes : boolean) : String[]
escapeRDN(rdn : String) : String
unEscapeRDN(rdn : String) : String
isEscape(c : char) : boolean

FIGURE B-32. LDAPDN.

LDAPDN provides a few helpful static methods for processing Strings that represent DNs. It uses the DN class of netscape.ldap.util internally.

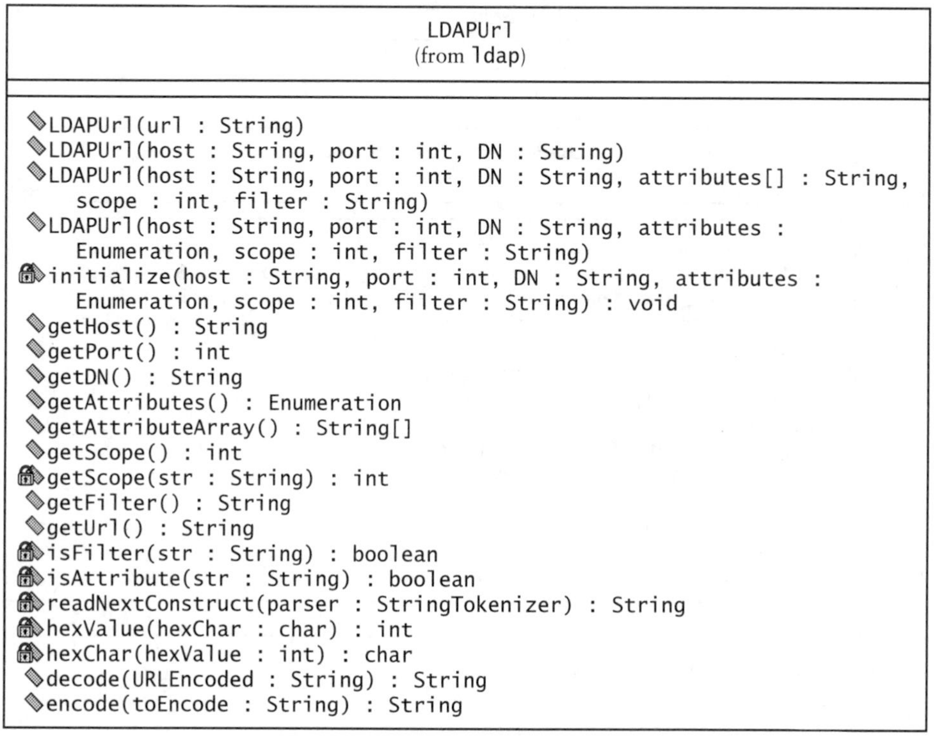

```
LDAPUrl
(from ldap)

LDAPUrl(url : String)
LDAPUrl(host : String, port : int, DN : String)
LDAPUrl(host : String, port : int, DN : String, attributes[] : String,
   scope : int, filter : String)
LDAPUrl(host : String, port : int, DN : String, attributes :
   Enumeration, scope : int, filter : String)
initialize(host : String, port : int, DN : String, attributes :
   Enumeration, scope : int, filter : String) : void
getHost() : String
getPort() : int
getDN() : String
getAttributes() : Enumeration
getAttributeArray() : String[]
getScope() : int
getScope(str : String) : int
getFilter() : String
getUrl() : String
isFilter(str : String) : boolean
isAttribute(str : String) : boolean
readNextConstruct(parser : StringTokenizer) : String
hexValue(hexChar : char) : int
hexChar(hexValue : int) : char
decode(URLEncoded : String) : String
encode(toEncode : String) : String
```

FIGURE B-33. LDAPUrl.

LDAPUrl can express search parameters. The LDAPConnection.search method can take an LDAPUrl as parameter.

The netscape.ldap.util Package

DNs and RDNs

```
DN
(from util)

DN()
DN(dn : String)
addRDNToFront(rdn : RDN) : void
addRDNToBack(rdn : RDN) : void
addRDN(rdn : RDN) : void
setDNType(type : int) : void
getDNType() : int
countRDNs() : int
getRDNs() : Vector
explodeDN(noTypes : boolean) : String[]
isRFC() : boolean
toRFCString() : String
toOSFString() : String
toString() : String
isDN(dn : String) : boolean
equals(dn : DN) : boolean
getParent() : DN
contains(dn : DN) : boolean
isDescendantOf(dn : DN) : boolean
isRFC(dn : String) : boolean
appendRDN(buffer : StringBuffer) : boolean
```

FIGURE B-34. DN.

```
RDN
(from util)

RDN(rdn : String)
explodeRDN(noType : boolean) : String[]
getType() : String
getValue() : String
toString() : String
isRDN(rdn : String) : boolean
equals(rdn : RDN) : boolean
```

FIGURE B-35. RDN.

LDIF Reader Classes

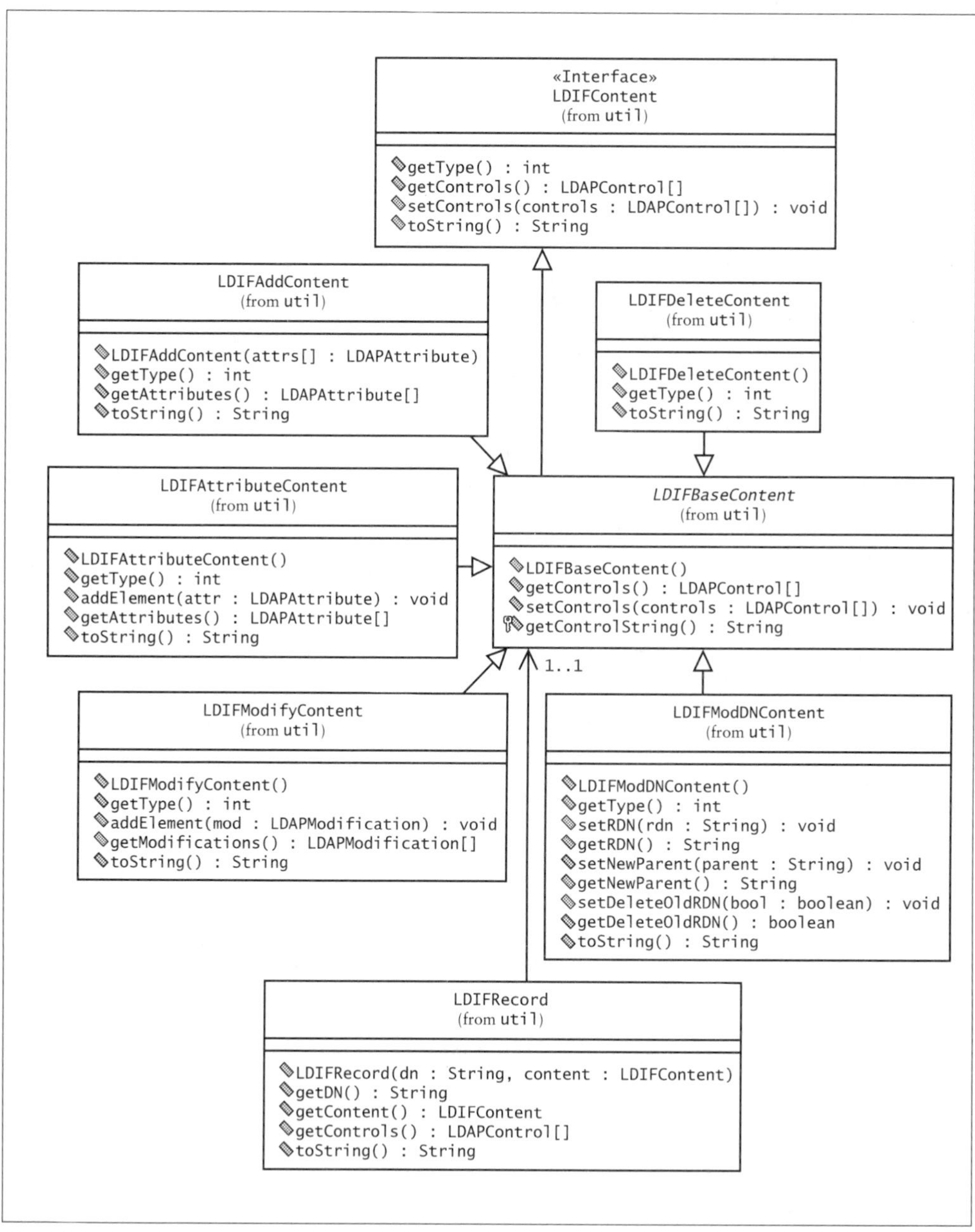

FIGURE B-36. *LDIF record classes.*

An LDIFRecord object contains a reference to an LDIFBaseContent object, which represents one of the types of LDAP operations that can be expressed in an LDIF record.

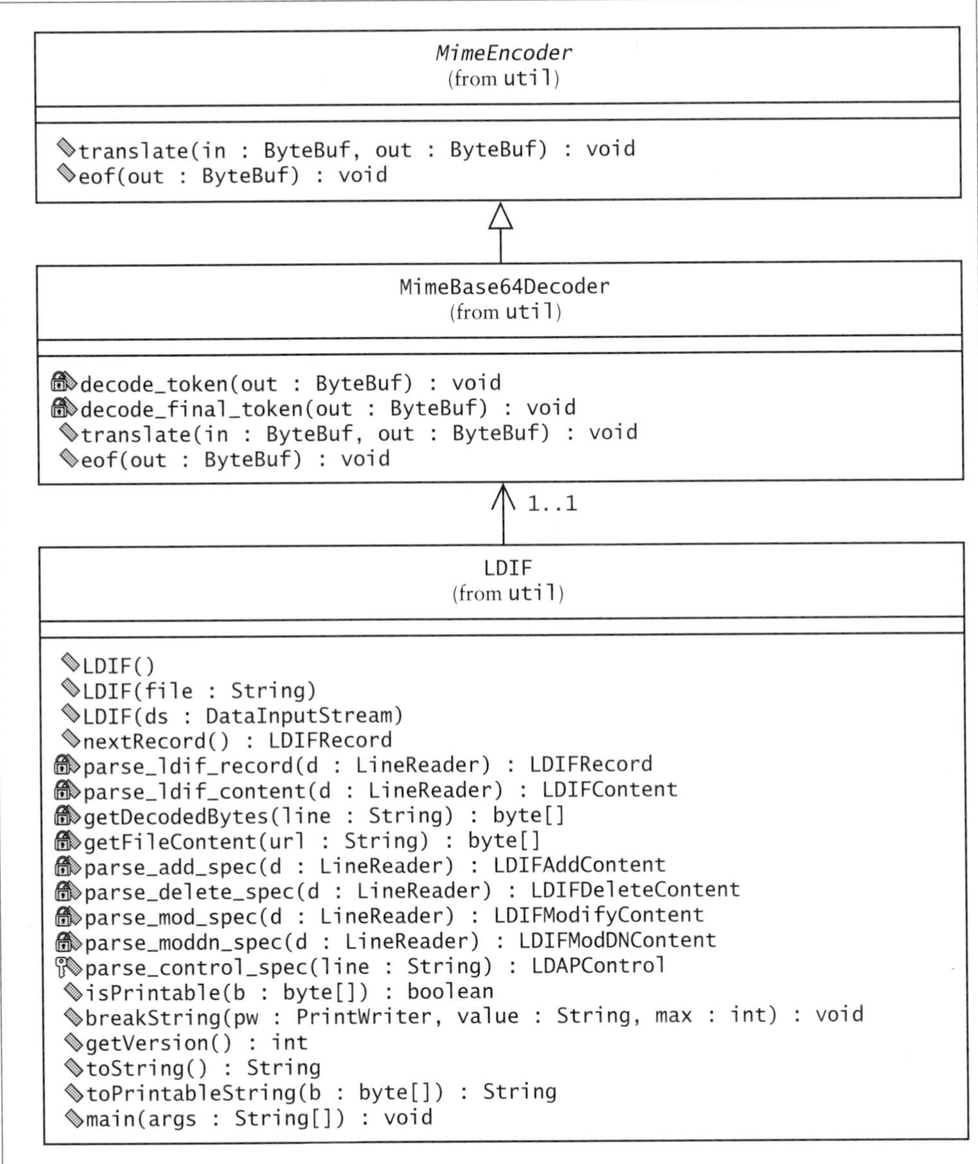

FIGURE B-37. *LDIF stream reader and base64 handlers.*

An `LDIF` object opens and manages a stream of input from an LDIF file. It instantiates an `LDIFRecord` object for each record found, and decodes values that are encoded in base 64 with a `MimeBase64Decoder` object.

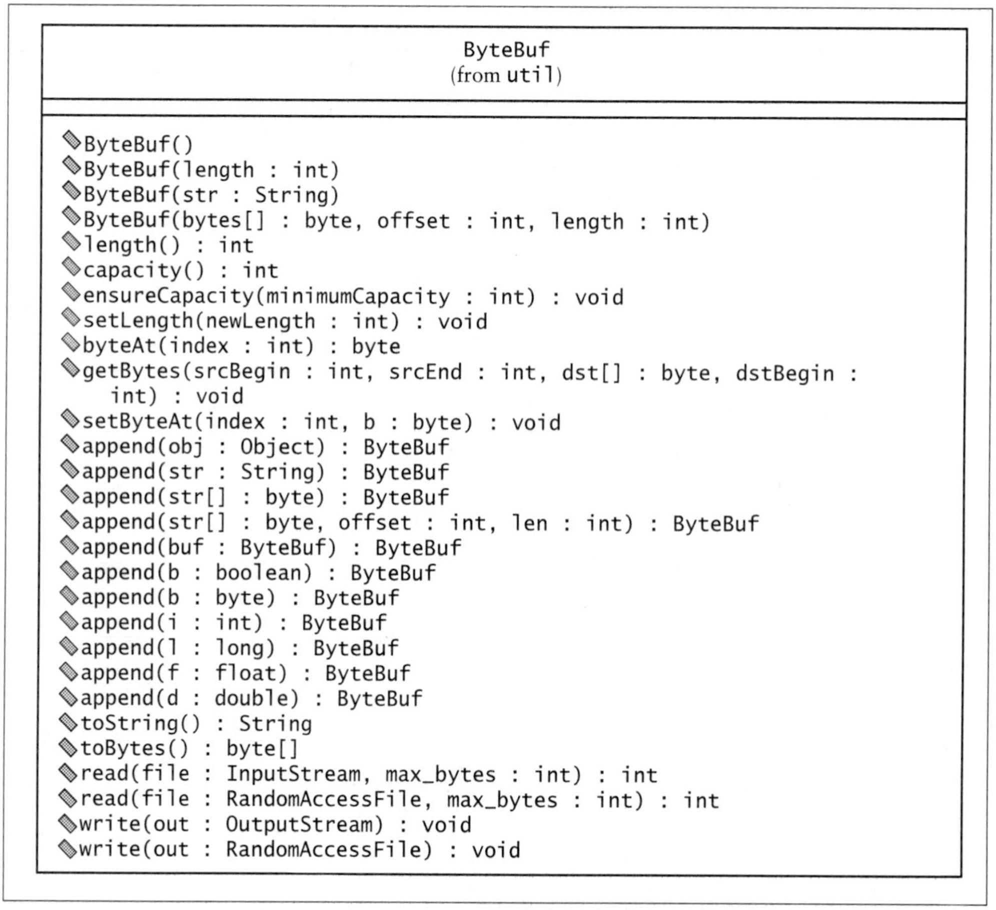

```
ByteBuf
(from util)

ByteBuf()
ByteBuf(length : int)
ByteBuf(str : String)
ByteBuf(bytes[] : byte, offset : int, length : int)
length() : int
capacity() : int
ensureCapacity(minimumCapacity : int) : void
setLength(newLength : int) : void
byteAt(index : int) : byte
getBytes(srcBegin : int, srcEnd : int, dst[] : byte, dstBegin :
   int) : void
setByteAt(index : int, b : byte) : void
append(obj : Object) : ByteBuf
append(str : String) : ByteBuf
append(str[] : byte) : ByteBuf
append(str[] : byte, offset : int, len : int) : ByteBuf
append(buf : ByteBuf) : ByteBuf
append(b : boolean) : ByteBuf
append(b : byte) : ByteBuf
append(i : int) : ByteBuf
append(l : long) : ByteBuf
append(f : float) : ByteBuf
append(d : double) : ByteBuf
toString() : String
toBytes() : byte[]
read(file : InputStream, max_bytes : int) : int
read(file : RandomAccessFile, max_bytes : int) : int
write(out : OutputStream) : void
write(out : RandomAccessFile) : void
```

FIGURE B-38. ByteBuf

Connection Pool

```
ConnectionPool
(from util)

ConnectionPool(min : int, max : int, host : String, port : int,
   authdn : String, authpw : String)
ConnectionPool(min : int, max : int, host : String, port : int)
ConnectionPool(host : String, port : int)
ConnectionPool(min : int, max : int, ldc : LDAPConnection)
ConnectionPool(min : int, max : int, host : String, port : int,
   authdn : String, authpw : String, ldc : LDAPConnection)
destroy() : void
getConnection() : LDAPConnection
getConnFromPool() : LDAPConnection
close(ld : LDAPConnection) : void
printPool() : void
disconnect(ldapconnObject : LDAPConnectionObject) : void
createPool() : void
addConnection() : int
setUpPool(size : int) : void
find(con : LDAPConnection) : int
setDebug(mode : boolean) : void
getDebug() : boolean
debug(s : String) : void
debug(s : String, severe : boolean) : void
```

FIGURE B-39. ConnectionPool.

A connection pool queues requests for a connection and distributes connections for a particular host and port from an internal set.

APPENDIX C

LDAP Utility Classes on the CD-ROM

Chapters 10 and 12 use a number of utility classes that are provided on the CD-ROM in the source code directories for those chapters. This appendix contains a brief summary of these classes and methods.

The `table` Package

public abstract interface **`ISortableTableModel`**
extends **`javax.swing.table.TableModel`**

Interface for table model that allows sorting.

`sortByColumn`

```
public void sortByColumn(int  column, boolean  isAscent)
```

Sorts the table by the given column, in ascending or descending order.

Parameters:

`column`: the index of the column on which to sort

`isAscent`: if true, sort in ascending order

`getIndexes`

```
public int[] getIndexes()
```

Gets the index values by which the table is sorted.

Returns:

the array of index values that translates between logical and physical row order

public class **SortableTableModel**
extends **javax.swing.table.DefaultTableModel**
implements **ISortableTableModel**

Table model for a table with sortable columns. It implements `TableModel` methods going through an index, for quick sorting without moving the data. The method signatures are the same as for `DefaultTableModel`.

SortableTableModel

```
public SortableTableModel()
```

getValueAt

```
public java.lang.Object getValueAt(int  row, int  col)
```

setValueAt

```
public void setValueAt(java.lang.Object  value, int  row, int  col)
```

sortByColumn

```
public void sortByColumn(int  column, boolean  isAscent)
```

getIndexes

```
public int[] getIndexes()
```

fireTableStructureChanged

```
public void fireTableStructureChanged()
```

public class ***SortHeaderListener***
extends
java.awt.event.MouseAdapter

Class to handle mouse clicks on table headers and cause sorting. The methods are those of MouseListener.

```
SortHeaderListener
```

```
public SortHeaderListener(javax.swing.table.JTableHeader  header,
                          SortButtonRenderer  _renderer)
```

mousePressed

```
public void mousePressed(java.awt.event.MouseEvent  e)
```

mouseReleased

```
public void mouseReleased(java.awt.event.MouseEvent  e)
```

public class ***SortButtonRenderer***
extends ***javax.swing.JButton***
implements ***javax.swing.table.TableCellRenderer***

Class to render a column header as a button with an up or down arrow icon.

NONE

```
public static final int NONE
```

DOWN

```
public static final int DOWN
```

UP

```
public static final int UP
```

SortButtonRenderer

```
public SortButtonRenderer()
```

getTableCellRendererComponent

```
public java.awt.Component
getTableCellRendererComponent(javax.swing.JTable  table,
                              java.lang.Object  value,
                              boolean  isSelected,
                              boolean  hasFocus,
                              int  row,
                              int  column)
```

Implements `TableCellRenderer.getTableCellRendererComponent`, returning a `JLabel` indicating if this is the primary sort column and if it is sorted in ascending or descending order.

setPressedColumn

```
public void setPressedColumn(int  col)
```

Sets the visual effect to be pressed or not.

setSelectedColumn

```
public void setSelectedColumn(int  col)
```

Sets the visual effect to be selected or not.

getState

```
public int getState(int  col)
```

Returns `NONE`, `DOWN`, or `UP`, depending on the state of the column.

public class **BlankIcon** *extends* **java.lang.Object**
implements **javax.swing.Icon**

Icon to use when no arrow is to be visible.

BlankIcon

```
public BlankIcon()
```

BlankIcon

```
public BlankIcon(java.awt.Color  color, int  size)
```

paintIcon

```
public void paintIcon(java.awt.Component  c, java.awt.Graphics  g,
                      int  x, int  y)
```

getIconWidth

```
public int getIconWidth()
```

getIconHeight

```
public int getIconHeight()
```

public class **BevelArrowIcon** *extends* **java.lang.Object**
implements **javax.swing.Icon**

Class to render a three-dimensional triangle or arrow pointing up or down.

UP

```
public static final int UP
```

DOWN

```
public static final int DOWN
```

BevelArrowIcon

```
public BevelArrowIcon(int  direction, boolean  isRaisedView,
                      boolean  isCODEssedView)
```

BevelArrowIcon

```
public BevelArrowIcon(java.awt.Color  edge1, java.awt.Color  edge2,
                      java.awt.Color  fill, int  size, int  direction)
```

paintIcon

```
public void paintIcon(java.awt.Component  c, java.awt.Graphics  g,
                      int  x, int  y)
```

getIconWidth

```
public int getIconWidth()
```

getIconHeight

```
public int getIconHeight()
```

public class ***TableSorter*** *extends* ***java.lang.Object***

Class to sort table data by one column, with a variety of data types.

TableSorter

```
public TableSorter(ISortableTableModel  model)
```

sort

```
public void sort(int  column, boolean  isAscent)
```

compare

```
public int compare(int  column, int  row1, int  row2)
```

compare

`public int compare(java.lang.Number o1, java.lang.Number o2)`

compare

`public int compare(java.util.Date o1, java.util.Date o2)`

compare

`public int compare(java.lang.Boolean o1, java.lang.Boolean o2)`

The util Package

public class ***DateUtil*** *extends* ***java.lang.Object***

Class to convert LDAP date format into a format more usable in a Java application.

DateUtil

`public DateUtil()`

getDateTime

`public static java.util.Date getDateTime(java.lang.String dbDate)`

Converts the date in LDAP format into a `java.util.Date` object.

formatDateTime

`public static java.lang.String formatDateTime(java.lang.String dbDate)`

Converts the date in LDAP format into a localized `String`.

public class ***Debug*** *extends* ***java.lang.Object***
implements ***java.io.Serializable***

Class to control the output of debugging statements. There are two levels of control for the output. First, the output can be prevented outright by disabling the trace flag. Second, the amount of output can be regulated by the trace level. By convention, we use ten levels, designated from 0 to 9, where 0 implies least output and 9 implies full output. By default, the trace level is set to 5, and the trace level designated to debugging statements without a specific level is also 5. These statements will be printed when the trace flag is enabled. To reduce the amount of output, debugging statements should be specified with this default level in mind. Note that all statements designated at the current trace level or below will be printed.

`setTrace`

```
public static void setTrace(boolean  fTrace)
```

Enables or disables debugging.

Parameters:

`fTrace`: boolean value

`getTrace`

```
public static boolean getTrace()
```

Determines whether debugging is enabled or disabled.

Returns:

boolean value

`isEnabled`

```
public static boolean isEnabled()
```

`setTraceLevel`

```
public static void setTraceLevel(int  iTraceLevel)
```

Sets the verbosity level of the debugging output.

Parameters:

`iTraceLevel`: integer value indicating which debugging statements to display

getTraceLevel

```
public static int getTraceLevel()
```

Retrieves the verbosity level of the debugging output.

Returns:

integer value indicating which debugging statements to display

println

```
public static void println(java.lang.String s)
```

Default debug statement that indicates a trace level of 5.

Parameters:

s: debug statement

print

```
public static void print(java.lang.String s)
```

Default debug statement that indicates a trace level of 5.

Parameters:

s: debug statement

println

```
public static void println(int level, java.lang.String s)
```

Debug statement specifying at which level to print.

Parameters:

level: trace level

s: debug statement

`print`

```
public static void print(int level, java.lang.String s)
```

Debug statement specifying at which level to print.

Parameters:

`level`: trace level

`s`: debug statement

`println`

```
public static void println(int s)
```

Default debug statement that indicates a trace level of 5.

Parameters:

`s`: debug statement

`print`

```
public static void print(int s)
```

Default debug statement that indicates a trace level of 5.

Parameters:

`s`: debug statement

`println`

```
public static void println(int level, int s)
```

Debug statement specifying at which level to print.

Parameters:

`level`: trace level

`s`: debug statement

print

```
public static void print(int  level, int  s)
```

Debug statement specifying at which level to print.

Parameters:

`level`: trace level

`s`: debug statement

public class **DirUtil** *extends* **java.lang.Object**

Utility class to prepare an LDAP connection, using a nonsecure or an SSL session (using SSLava from Phaos).

setDefaultReferralCredentials

```
public static void
setDefaultReferralCredentials(netscape.ldap.LDAPConnection  ldc)
```

Sets up the `LDAPConnection` to automatically follow referrals, using the same credentials as for the current connection.

Parameters:

`ldc`: an open connection to a directory server

makeLDAPConnection

```
public static netscape.ldap.LDAPConnection
makeLDAPConnection(boolean  useSSL)
```

Create an unconnected `LDAPConnection` object, with or without an SSL socket factory.

Parameters:

`useSSL`: if true, use an SSL socket factory

Returns:

an `LDAPConnection`

getLDAPConnection

```
public static netscape.ldap.LDAPConnection
getLDAPConnection(java.lang.String  host,
                  int  port,
                  java.lang.String  authDN,
                  java.lang.String  authPassword,
                  boolean  useSSL)
                  throws netscape.ldap.LDAPException
```

Establishes an `LDAPConnection` with default automatic referrals.

Parameters:

`host`: host to connect to

`port`: port on host to connect to

`authDN`: distinguished name for authentication

`authPassword`: password for authentication

`useSSL`: if true, establish an SSL connection

Returns:

an `LDAPConnection`

Throws:

`netscape.ldap.LDAPException` on any failure

getLDAPConnection

```
public static netscape.ldap.LDAPConnection
getLDAPConnection(java.lang.String  host,
                  int  port,
                  java.lang.String  authDN,
                  java.lang.String  authPassword)
                  throws netscape.ldap.LDAPException
```

Establishes an `LDAPConnection` with default automatic referrals.

Parameters:

`host`: host to connect to

`port`: port on host to connect to

`authDN`: distinguished name for authentication

`authPassword`: password for authentication

Returns:

an `LDAPConnection`

Throws:

`netscape.ldap.LDAPException` on any failure

public class **`ImageUtil`** *extends* **`java.lang.Object`**

Class to load an image file from a remote source or from the `CLASSPATH`.

getPackageImage

```
public static javax.swing.ImageIcon
getPackageImage(java.lang.String  name)
```

public class **`ResourceSet`** *extends* **`java.lang.Object`**
implements **`java.io.Serializable`**

Class to implement a simple API over the `java.util.PropertyResourceBundle` class, and the underlying `.properties` files.

ResourceSet

```
public ResourceSet(java.lang.String  bundle, java.util.Locale
locale)
```

Initializes a resource set.

Parameters:

`bundle`: a fully qualified property file name, within the current `CLASSPATH` and excluding the `.properties` suffix `locale`: the locale to be used to initialize the resource set

ResourceSet

```
public ResourceSet(java.lang.String  bundle)
```

A version of the `ResourceSet` constructor that uses the default locale.

Parameters:

`bundle`: a fully qualified property file, within the current `CLASSPATH` and excluding the `.properties` suffix

getString

```
public java.lang.String getString(java.lang.String  prefix,
                                  java.lang.String  name)
```

Returns the value of a named resource in the `ResourceSet`. The resource name is composed of `prefix`, followed by a hyphen, followed by `name`. This version assumes that no parameter substitution is necessary in the value.

Parameters:

`prefix`: the name prefix of the resource

`name`: the name suffix of the resource

getString

```
public java.lang.String getString(java.lang.String  prefix,
                                  java.lang.String  name,
                                  java.lang.String[]  args)
```

Returns the value of a named resource in the `ResourceSet`. The resource name is composed of `prefix`, followed by a hyphen, followed by `name`. If the value is found and it contains parameter substitution marks (`%num`, where `num` is an integer), these marks will be replaced by the corresponding member of the `args` array (`args[num]`). If `num` is invalid with respect to `args`, then the substitution will not take place.

Parameters:

`prefix`: the name prefix of the resource

`name`: the name suffix of the resource

`args`: values for parameter substitution

getString

```
public java.lang.String getString(java.lang.String  CODEfix,
                                  java.lang.String  name,
                                  java.lang.String  arg)
```

This version of `getString` differs only in that it takes a single `String` argument, rather than an array, as a convenience.

Parameters:

`prefix`: the name prefix of the resource

`name`: the name suffix of the resource

`arg`: a single value for parameter substitution

substitute

```
protected java.lang.String substitute(java.lang.String  s,
                                      java.lang.String[]  args)
```

getBundle

```
protected java.util.PropertyResourceBundle
getBundle(java.lang.String  bundle, java.util.Locale  locale)
```

Implements the `PropertyResourceBundle` loader.

Parameters:

`bundle`: the bundle identifier

`locale`: the locale

public class **SimpleReferral** *extends* **java.lang.Object**
implements **netscape.ldap.LDAPrebind, java.io.Serializable**

Class for having an LDAPConnection follow referrals by reusing the same authentication DN and password.

SimpleReferral

```
public SimpleReferral(java.lang.String  dn, java.lang.String  password)
```

Just saves the credentials on construction.
Parameters:

dn: the authentication DN

getRebindAuthentication

password: the authentication password

```
public netscape.ldap.LDACODEbindAuth
getRebindAuthentication(java.lang.String  host, int  port)
```

Always returns the same credentials for referrals.

Parameters:

host: the referred-to host (ignored)

port: the referred-to port (ignored)

Returns:

credentials for referral following

public class **SortUtil** *extends* **java.lang.Object**

Class to sort an array of Strings in place, using simple ASCII comparison, or true Unicode collation.

bubbleSort

```
public static void bubbleSort(java.lang.String[]  str, boolean
isAscii)
```

Sorts the array of `Strings` using bubble sort.

Parameters:

`str`: the array of `Strings` being sorted; contains the sorted result

`isAscii`: if false, true Unicode collation will be used

bubbleSort

```
public static void bubbleSort(java.lang.String[]  str)
```

Sorts the array of `Strings` using bubble sort.

Parameters:

`str`: the array of `Strings` being sorted; contains the sorted result. Comparison will be done using true Unicode collation.

APPENDIX D

Common LDAP Schema Elements

One of the benefits of LDAP compared to relational databases is that there is a substantial body of predefined schema elements, especially for managing user information. You can start adding data immediately to an LDAP server.

The standard LDAP schema elements are defined in RFC 2256, "A Summary of the X.500(96) User Schema for Use with LDAPv3"; RFC 2307, "An Approach for Using LDAP as a Network Information Service"; RFC 2247, "Using Domains in LDAP/X.500 Distinguished Names"; RFC 2377, "Naming Plan for Internet Directory-Enabled Applications"; and the Internet Draft "Definition of the inetOrgPerson LDAP Object Class." The lists that follow are not comprehensive; they contain only the most commonly used schema elements.

There is an online catalog for browsing standard LDAP schema elements at `http://www.hklc.com/ldapschema/`. Netscape publishes a comprehensive list of all schema elements it supports, including add-ons by various Netscape server products, at `http://home.netscape.com/eng/server/directory/schema/`.

Object Classes

As defined in RFC 2252, an object class may be **abstract, structural,** or **auxiliary.** An *abstract* object class may not be used by itself in an entry; a derived *structural* class is required. Each directory entry must include one *structural* object class. An entry may also include zero or more *auxiliary* (mix-in) classes.

Abstract Object Classes

NAME	OID	REQUIRED ATTRIBUTES	OPTIONAL ATTRIBUTES
top	2.5.6.0	objectClass	aci (only Netscape)
alias	2.5.6.1	aliasedObjectName	

Structural Object Classes

NAME	OID	SUPERIOR	REQUIRED ATTRIBUTES	OPTIONAL ATTRIBUTES
country	2.5.6.2	top	c	description searchGuide
locality	2.5.6.3	top		description l searchGuide seeAlso st street
organization	2.5.6.4	top	o	businessCategory description destinationIndicator facsimileTelephone Number internationalISDN Number l physicalDelivery OfficeName postOfficeBox postalAddress postalCode preferredDelivery Method registeredAddress searchGuide seeAlso st

NAME	OID	SUPERIOR	REQUIRED ATTRIBUTES	OPTIONAL ATTRIBUTES
				street telephoneNumber teletexTerminal Identifier telexNumber userPassword x121Address

organizationalUnit	2.5.6.5	top	ou	businessCategory
				description
				destinationIndicator
				facsimileTelephone
				  Number
				internationaliSDN
				  Number
				l
				physicalDelivery
				  OfficeName
				postOfficeBox
				postalAddress
				postalCode
				preferredDelivery
				  Method
				registeredAddress
				searchGuide
				seeAlso
				st
				street
				telephoneNumber
				teletexTerminal
				  Identifier
				telexNumber
				userPassword
				x121Address

person	2.5.6.6	top	cn sn	description seeAlso telephoneNumber userPassword

organizationalPerson	2.5.6.7	person		destinationIndicator
				facsimileTelephone
				  Number
				internationaliSDN
				  Number
				l
				ou

NAME	OID	SUPERIOR	REQUIRED ATTRIBUTES	OPTIONAL ATTRIBUTES
				physicalDeliveryOfficeName postOfficeBox postalAddress postalCode preferredDeliveryMethod registeredAddress st street teletexTerminalIdentifier telexNumber title x121Address
inetOrgPerson	2.16.840.1.1.13730.3.2.2.13730.3.2.2	organizationalPerson		audio businessCategory carLicense departmentNumber displayName employeeNumber employeeType givenName homePhone homePostalAddress initials jpegPhoto labeledURI mail manager mobile o pager photo preferredLanguage roomNumber secretary uid x500uniqueIdentifier userCertificate userPKCS12user userSMimeCertificate
groupOfNames	2.5.6.9	top	cn	businessCategory description member o

NAME	OID	SUPERIOR	REQUIRED ATTRIBUTES	OPTIONAL ATTRIBUTES
				ou owner seeAlso
groupOfUniqueNames	2.5.6.17	top	cn	businessCategory description o ou owner seeAlso uniqueMember
groupOfUrls	2.16.840.1.113730.3.2.33	top	cn	businessCategory description o ou owner seeAlso memberUrl
labeledURIObject	1.3.6.1.4.1.2	top		labeledURI
referral	2.16.840.1.113730.3.2.6	top		ref
dcObject	1.3.6.1.4.1.1466.344	top	dc	
subschema	2.5.20.1	top		attributeTypes cn dITContentRules dITStructureRules nameForms objectClasses matchingRuleUse matchingRules

Auxiliary Object Classes

NAME	OID	REQUIRED ATTRIBUTES	OPTIONAL ATTRIBUTES
posixAccount	1.3.6.1.1.1.2.0	cn gidNumber homeDirectory objectClass	description gecos loginShell userPassword

NAME	OID	REQUIRED ATTRIBUTES	OPTIONAL ATTRIBUTES
		uid uidNumber	
posixGroup	1.3.6.1.1.1.2.2	cn gidNumber objectClass	description memberUid userPassword

Attributes

An attribute may also be referenced by an alias, if one is defined. The table of attribute types that will be given shortly lists the standard aliases.

Attribute Syntaxes

Syntaxes define how attribute values are compared during a search or compare operation. LDAP allows specifying unique rules for each type of search and sort: equality, substring, and ordering. These rules are defined as additional qualifiers in the attribute definition, besides the syntax qualifier. However, Netscape Directory Server and many other LDAP servers ignore the additional qualifiers and just use the syntax qualifier.

RFC 2252 names a number of attribute syntaxes (inherited from X.500), but only a small subset is commonly used in LDAP. In the table of attribute types, the following shorthand is used for syntax types:

SHORTHAND	OID	DESCRIPTION
bin	1.3.6.1.4.1.1466.115.121.1.5	A binary value
ces	1.3.6.1.4.1.1466.115.121.1.26	IA5 String—case-sensitive string (on Netscape servers it is UTF8)
cis	1.3.6.1.4.1.1466.115.121.1.15	Directory String—UTF-8, case-insensitive string
dn	1.3.6.1.4.1.1466.115.121.1.12	A distinguished name
int	1.3.6.1.4.1.1466.115.121.1.27	Integer
tel	1.3.6.1.4.1.1466.115.121.1.50	Telephone number

Attribute Types

NAME	ALIASES	OID	SYNTAX	SINGLE-VALUED
aci		2.16.840.1.113730.3.1.55	bin	
aliasedObjectName		2.5.4.1	dn	
altServer		1.3.6.1.4.1.1466.101.120.6	ces	
attributeTypes		2.5.21.5	cis	
audio		0.9.2342.19200300.100.1.55	bin	
businessCategory		2.5.4.15	cis	
c	countryName	2.5.4.6	cis	
carLicense		2.16.840.1.113730.3.1.1	cis	
cn	commonName	2.5.4.3	cis	
createTimestamp		2.5.18.1	cis	
creatorsName		2.5.18.3	dn	
dc	domainComponent	0.9.2342.19200300.100.1.25	cis	
department Number		2.16.840.1.113730.3.1.2	cis	
description		2.5.4.13	cis	
destination Indicator		2.5.4.27	cis	
displayName		2.16.840.1.113730.3.1.241	cis	X
dITContentRules		2.5.21.2	cis	
dITStructure Rules		2.5.21.1	cis	
dn	distinguishedName	2.5.4.49	dn	
employeeNumber		2.16.840.1.113730.3.1.3	cis	X

NAME	ALIASES	OID	SYNTAX	SINGLE-VALUED
employeeType		2.16.840.1.113730.3.1.4	cis	
facsimileTelephoneNumber	fax	2.5.4.23	tel	
gecos		1.3.6.1.1.1.1.2	cis	X
gidNumber		1.3.6.1.1.1.1.1	cis	X
givenName		2.5.4.42	cis	
homeDirectory		1.3.6.1.1.1.1.3	ces	X
homePhone		0.9.2342.19200300.100.1.20	tel	
homePostal Address		0.9.2342.19200300.100.1.39	cis	
host		0.9.2342.19200300.100.1.9	cis	
info		0.9.2342.19200300.100.1.4	cis	
initials		2.5.4.43	cis	
international IsdnNumber		2.5.4.25	ces	
jpegPhoto		0.9.2342.19200300.100.1.60	bin	
l	locality localityName	2.5.4.7	cis	
labeledUri	labeledUrl	1.3.6.1.4.1.250.1.57	ces	
loginShell		1.3.6.1.1.1.1.4	ces	X
mail	rfc822Mailbox	0.9.2342.19200300.100.1.3	cis	
manager		0.9.2342.19200300.100.1.10	dn	
matchingRuleUse		2.5.21.8	cis	
matchingRules		2.5.21.4	cis	
member		2.5.4.31	dn	
memberUid		1.3.6.1.1.1.1.12	cis	

NAME	ALIASES	OID	SYNTAX	SINGLE-VALUED
memberUrl		2.16.840.1.113730.3.1.198	ces	
mobile	mobileTelephoneNumber	0.9.2342.19200300.100.1.41	tel	
modifiersName		2.5.18.4	dn	
modifyTimestamp		2.5.18.2	cis	
nameForms		2.5.21.7	cis	
namingContexts		1.3.6.1.4.1.1466.101.120.5	dn	
o	organizationName	2.5.4.10	cis	
objectClass		2.5.4.0	cis	
objectClasses		2.5.21.6	cis	
otherMailbox		0.9.2342.19200300.100.1.22	cis	
ou	organizationalUnitName	2.5.4.11	cis	
owner		2.5.4.32	dn	
pager	pagerTelephoneNumber	0.9.2342.19200300.100.1.42	tel	
physical Delivery OfficeName		2.5.4.19	cis	
postOfficeBox		2.5.4.18	cis	
postalAddress		2.5.4.16	cis	
postalCode		2.5.4.17	cis	
preferred Delivery Method		2.5.4.28	cis	X
preferred Language		2.16.840.1.113730.3.1.39	cis	X
presentation Address		2.5.4.29	ces	
ref		2.16.840.1.113730.3.1.34	ces	

NAME	ALIASES	OID	SYNTAX	SINGLE-VALUED
registered Address		2.5.4.26	cis	
roleOccupant		2.5.4.33	dn	
roomNumber		0.9.2342.19200300.100.1.6	cis	
searchGuide		2.5.4.14	ces	
secretary		0.9.2342.19200300.100.1.21	dn	
seeAlso		2.5.4.34	dn	
serialNumber		2.5.4.5	cis	
sn	surName	2.5.4.4	cis	
st	stateOrProvinceName	2.5.4.8	cis	
street	streetAddress	2.5.4.9	cis	
subschema Subentry		2.5.18.10	dn	
supported Application Context		2.5.4.30	cis	
supported Control		1.3.6.1.4.1.1466.101.120.13	cis	
supported Extension		1.3.6.1.4.1.1466.101.120.7	cis	
supported LDAPVersion		1.3.6.1.4.1.1466.101.120.15	int	
supported SASLMechanisms		1.3.6.1.4.1.1466.101.120.14	cis	
telephoneNumber		2.5.4.20	tel	
teletexTerminal Identifier		2.5.4.22	cis	
telexNumber		2.5.4.21	cis	

NAME	ALIASES	OID	SYNTAX	SINGLE-VALUED
title		2.5.4.12	cis	
uid		0.9.2342.19200300.100.1.1	cis	
uidNumber		1.3.6.1.1.1.1.0	cis	X
uniqueIdentifier		0.9.2342.19200300.100.1.44	cis	
uniqueMember		2.5.4.50	dn	
userCertificate		2.5.4.36	bin	
userPassword		2.5.4.35	bin	
userSMIME Certificate		2.16.840.1.113730.3.1.40	bin	
x121Address		2.5.4.24	ces	

APPENDIX E

LDAP Error Codes

The error codes that an LDAP server may return are defined in RFC 2251. In addition, a few error codes may be returned by the LDAP client (the SDK)—for example, to indicate that the server could not be reached. However, no document exactly defines the circumstances in which a server will return each possible error code in LDAP.

The following error codes apply to Netscape Directory Server, and probably to many other LDAP servers, but not to all. The list is not comprehensive. Codes without comments in the third column are not currently returned to clients by Netscape Directory Server or generated by the SDK.

ERROR CODE	LDAPEXCEPTION CONSTANT	POSSIBLE CAUSE(S)
0	SUCCESS	The operation completed successfully
1	OPERATION_ERROR	Invalid syntax for ACI or schema, or inappropriate control for the operation
2	PROTOCOL_ERROR	Invalid filter expression on search, or DN on add, modify, or delete
3	TIME_LIMIT_EXCEEDED	Either the server's or the client's specified search time limit was exceeded
4	SIZE_LIMIT_EXCEEDED	Either the server's or the client's specified limit on number of search results was exceeded
5	COMPARE_FALSE	A compare operation returns mismatch

6	COMPARE_TRUE	A compare operation returns match
7	AUTH_METHOD_NOT_SUPPORTED	The server does not support the requested authentication method
8	STRONG_AUTH_REQUIRED	The server requires an authentication method stronger than unencrypted user name and password
9	LDAP_PARTIAL_RESULTS	The client has bound with LDAPv2, or the server supports only LDAPv2, and the base DN specified by the client is not among the naming contexts of the server
10	REFERRAL	The server is configured to return a referral or search reference when an operation is directed toward this DN
11	ADMIN_LIMIT_EXCEEDED	To satisfy the search request, the server would need to process too many entries; the search may need to be narrowed, or the server's look-through limit raised
12	UNAVAILABLE_CRITICAL_EXTENSION	A control was provided with the request; the control was tagged as critical, but the server doesn't support it
13	CONFIDENTIALITY_REQUIRED	
14	SASL_BIND_IN_PROGRESS	SASL authentication is being negotiated between the client and the server
16	NO_SUCH_ATTRIBUTE	An attribute to be modified or deleted was not present in the entry
17	UNDEFINED_ATTRIBUTE_TYPE	
18	INAPPROPRIATE_MATCHING	
19	CONSTRAINT_VIOLATION	Invalid attribute for this entry, or new password does not meet password policy requirements
20	ATTRIBUTE_OR_VALUE_EXISTS	Attempt to add an identical attribute value to an existing one
21	INVALID_ATTRIBUTE_SYNTAX	

32	NO_SUCH_OBJECT	Attempt to bind with a nonexistent DN, to search with a nonexistent base DN, or to modify or delete a nonexistent DN
33	ALIAS_PROBLEM	
34	INVALID_DN_SYNTAX	Invalid DN or RDN specified on adding an entry or modifying an RDN
35	IS_LEAF	
36	ALIAS_DEREFERENCING_PROBLEM	
48	INAPPROPRIATE_AUTHENTICATION	
49	INVALID_CREDENTIALS	Invalid password or other credentials supplied on bind
50	INSUFFICIENT_ACCESS_RIGHTS	
51	BUSY	
52	UNAVAILABLE	Returned by SDK if server is not accessible
53	UNWILLING_TO_PERFORM	User not allowed to change password, password expired, operation not implemented (moddn), attempt to modify read-only attribute, attempt to delete all schema elements, attempt to delete an object class that has derived object classes, attempt to delete a read-only schema element, the database is read-only, no back end (database) is available for the operation, or other uncategorized error
54	LOOP_DETECT	
64	NAMING_VIOLATION	
65	OBJECT_CLASS_VIOLATION	Invalid attribute specified for modify operation on an entry
66	NOT_ALLOWED_ON_NONLEAF	Attempt to delete an entry that has child nodes
67	NOT_ALLOWED_ON_RDN	
68	ENTRY_ALREADY_EXISTS	

69	OBJECT_CLASS_MODS_PROHIBITED	
71	AFFECTS_MULTIPLE_DSAS	
80	OTHER	
81	SERVER_DOWN	SDK could not connect to server
89	PARAM_ERROR	No modifications on a modify operation, no attributes on an add operation, invalid scope or empty search filter on search, or other invalid argument to an SDK method
91	CONNECT_ERROR	SDK reports unexpected error connecting to server
92	LDAP_NOT_SUPPORTED	
93	CONTROL_NOT_FOUND	
94	NO_RESULTS_RETURNED	
95	MORE_RESULTS_TO_RETURN	
96	CLIENT_LOOP	
97	REFERRAL_LIMIT_EXCEEDED	SDK reports hop limit exceeded on referral processing

Index